Lecture Notes in Computer Science 760

Edited by G. Goos and J. Hartmanis

Advisory Board: W. Brauer   D. Gries   J. Stoer

Stefano Ceri   Katsumi Tanaka
Shalom Tsur (Eds.)

Deductive and Object-Oriented Databases

Third International Conference, DOOD '93
Phoenix, Arizona, USA, December 6-8, 1993
Proceedings

Springer-Verlag
Berlin Heidelberg New York
London Paris Tokyo
Hong Kong Barcelona
Budapest

Series Editors

Gerhard Goos
Universität Karlsruhe
Postfach 69 80
Vincenz-Priessnitz-Straße 1
D-76131 Karlsruhe, Germany

Juris Hartmanis
Cornell University
Department of Computer Science
4130 Upson Hall
Ithaca, NY 14853, USA

Volume Editors

Stefano Ceri
Politecnico di Milano, Dipartimento di Elettronica
Piazza Leonardo da Vinci, 32, I-20133 Milano, Italy

Katsumi Tanaka
Kobe University, Department of Computer and Systems Engineering
Rokkodai, Nada, Kobe 657, Japan

Shalom Tsur
The University of Texas, System Ctr. for High Performance Computing
Balcones Research Center
10100 N. Burnett Road, Austin, TX 78758-4497, USA

CR Subject Classification (1991): H.2.3, D.1.5-6, I.2.4, F.4.1

ISBN 3-540-57530-8 Springer-Verlag Berlin Heidelberg New York
ISBN 0-387-57530-8 Springer-Verlag New York Berlin Heidelberg

© Springer-Verlag Berlin Heidelberg 1993
Printed in Germany

Typesetting: Camera-ready by author
Printing and binding: Druckhaus Beltz, Hemsbach/Bergstr.
45/3140-543210 - Printed on acid-free paper

Preface

The Third International Conference on Deductive and Object-Oriented Databases is a continuation of the two previous conferences in this area. Its central tenet is the continuing belief that the object-oriented and deductive paradigms for the modeling, organization, and processing of data complement each other rather than competing, and that the solution of problems involving massive volumes of complex data can best be attempted by utilizing the best of both approaches in an integrated fashion.

Central questions in this area are therefore: "How do we design a tool that presents the best of the object-oriented and declarative ideas, blended into one seamless form? How can the users of this tool express their problems in a combination of declarative and procedural features as their needs dictate it?" The search for answers to these issues forms a continuing quest and we have attempted to include papers in this volume that contribute towards this goal.

This volume contains twenty-nine papers. Three invited papers (David Maier, Kotagiri Ramamohanarao, Rainer Manthey) well represent the current efforts towards establishing the technology of deductive and object-oriented databases though concrete prototyping and product-oriented project experiences: Proxies, Aditi, and IDEA.

Twenty-six regular papers were selected out of a total of seventy submissions. Eleven of them were selected by the European Program Committee after a Program Committee meeting held in Milan on June 30; ten were selected by the American Program Committee; and five were selected by the Far East Program Committee. The outcome of the Far East and American Committee was solely based on the referee reports received for each paper and the discussions among the members of the committees. As a noteworthy feature it should be mentioned that the global evolution of electronic mail made it possible to conclude the discussions among the different chairs without ever having to physically gather at one place.

The editors wish to thank all of those who committed their time and efforts towards the success of this conference, either by submitting papers and/or by reviewing them.

December 1993

Stefano Ceri
Katsumi Tanaka
Shalom Tsur

Message of the General Conference Chairperson

It gives me great pleasure to welcome the Third International Conference on Deductive and Object-Oriented Databases (DOOD93) to the Valley of the Sun in Scottsdale, Arizona. This is the first time the DOOD conference has been held in the Americas. The notable success of the first two conferences in Kyoto, Japan, and Munich, Germany, established a challenging benchmark for us to meet. Judging from the quality of the papers that were accepted, I feel confident that this tradition of success is being continued. The original goal of the DOOD conference was to bring together researchers and practitioners who are dealing with two of the most promising areas of database research, deductive logic and object-orientation. This goal is still valid, especially as it appears that there will be industrial DOOD systems emerging in the near future.

The high quality of the papers presented at the conference is a direct result of the hard work and diligence of the three program committees and external reviewers under the supervision and guidance of the Program Chairs: Prof. Stefano Ceri, Prof. Katsumi Tanaka and Dr. Shalom Tsur. I would like to express my sincere thanks for their efforts in selecting twenty-six high quality papers and to the authors. I also want to express my thanks to the three invited speakers, Prof. David Maier, Prof. Kotagiri Ramamohanarao and Prof. Rainer Manthey. In recognition of the movement of DOOD out of the research laboratory and into industrial environments, the conference is also featuring two panels, one devoted to DOOD research directions and the other exploring potential application domains for DOOD.

An interesting innovation for this conference is that several papers have been nominated for inclusion in a special issue of the *Journal of Intelligent Information Systems*, dedicated to DOOD topics, that is to appear in 1994.

The conference also includes several special activities for spouses and attendees that are intended to allow participants to gain a deeper appreciation of the Arizona locale. This includes an all-day tour to the Grand Canyon, immediately following the conference.

An undertaking of this magnitude cannot succeed without the assistance of numerous dedicated people who give unselfishly of their time and efforts. I would especially like to thank the chair of the organizing committee, Dr. Forouzan Golshani, for his extensive contributions. Thanks also are due to Prof. Robert Meitz, the treasurer, Ms. Robin Fulford, chair of publications and publicity and to Mr. Ted Karren, chair of registration.

I would like to express my gratitude to the chair of the DOOD Steering Committee, Dr. Jean-Marie Nicolas, and to each of the Steering Committee members. Finally, I would like to thank Prof. Jack Minker, Steering Committee Chair Emeritus, who remains one of the most important driving forces behind the success of this conference.

December 1993 Oris Friesen

General Chairperson
Oris Friesen (Bull HN)

Steering Committee Chairperson
Jean-Marie Nicolas (Bull SA)

Steering Committee Chairperson Emeritus
Jack Minker (University of Maryland)

Program Committee Chairpersons
America

Shalom Tsur (University of Texas)

Europe

Stefano Ceri (Politecnico di Milano)

Far East

Katsumi Tanaka (Kobe University)

Far East Coordinator
Shojiro Nishio (Osaka University)

Organizing Committee Chairperson
Forouzan Golshani (Arizona State University)

Treasurer
Robert Meitz (Arizona State University)

Publicity and Publications Chairperson
Robin Fulford (Bull HN)

Registration Chairperson
Ted Karren (Bull HN)

Sponsors:
- Arizona State University/Intelligent Information Systems Laboratory
- Bull Worldwide Information Systems
- American Express

Supporting Organizations:
- European Computer-Industry Research Centre (ECRC)
- Advanced Software Technology and Mechatronics Research Institute of Kyoto (ASTEM RI/Kyoto)

Cooperating Organizations:
- American Association for Artificial Intelligence (AAAI)
- Commission of the European Communities, DGXIII

Program Committee Members

America

Anthony Bonner
(Univ. of Toronto)
Suzanne Dietrich
(Arizona State Univ.)
Sumit Ganguly
(Rutgers Univ.)
Narain Gehani
(ATT Bell Laboratories)
Michael Kifer
(SUNY Stony Brook)
Jean-Louis Lassez
(IBM TJWatson Res.Ctr.)
Jack Orenstein
(Object Design Inc.)
Raghu Ramakrishnan
(Univ. of Wisconsin)
Ken Ross
(Columbia Univ.)
Jehoshua Sagiv
(Hebrew Univ.)
Olivia Sheng
(Univ. of Arizona)
Oded Shmueli
(Technion, Haifa)
Ouri Wolfson
(Univ. of Illinios, Chicago)
Clement Yu
(Univ. of Illinios, Chicago)
Carlo Zaniolo
(UCLA)

Europe

Serge Abiteboul
(INRIA, Paris)
Peter Apers
(Univ. of Twente)
Elisa Bertino
(Univ. of Genova)
Francois Bry
(ECRC, Munich)
Georg Gottlob
(Tech. Univ. Wien)
Peter Gray
(Univ. of Aberdeen)
Klaus Dittrich
(Univ. of Zurich)
Giorgio Ghelli
(Univ. of Pisa)
Rainer Manthey
(Univ. of Bonn)
Jan Paredaens
(Univ. of Antwerp/UIA)
Joachim Schmidt
(Hamburg Univ.)
Marc Scholl
(Univ. of Ulm)
Letizia Tanca
(Politecnico di Milano)
Patrick Valduriez
(INRIA, Paris)
Fernando Velez
(O2 Technology)
Laurent Vieille
(Bull SA)
Roberto Zicari
(J.-W. Goethe Univ.)

Far East

Qiming Chen
(Tsing-Hua Univ.)
Kazuhiko Kato
(Univ. of Tokyo)
Tok-Wang Ling
(Natl. Univ. of Singapore)
Hongjun Lu
(Natl. Univ. of Singapore)
Akifumi Makinouchi
(Kyushu Univ.)
Nobuyoshi Miyazaki
(Oki)
Shojiro Nishio
(Osaka Univ.)
Atsushi Ohori
(Oki)
Maria Orlowska
(The Univ. of Queensland)
Ron Sacks-Davis
(RMIT, Univ. Melbourne)
Toshihisa Takagi
(Univ. of Tokyo)
Kyu-Young Whang
(KAIST)
Kazumasa Yokota
(ICOT)
Masatoshi Yoshikawa
(Kyoto Sangyo Univ.)

Contents

Object-Oriented Database Technology

Language Semantics I

Applications and Usage of Logic

Query Optimization

Panel 2

Deductive and Object-Oriented Database Technology

Extensions to Object-Orientation

Object-Oriented Concepts

Data and Knowledge Modelling Concepts

Treating Programs as Objects: The Computational Proxy Experience

David Maier and Judith B. Cushing

Department of Computer Science and Engineering
Oregon Graduate Institute of Science & Technology
20000 N.W. Walker Road P.O. Box 91000
Portland, OR 97291-1000

Abstract. Migrating data to a new database model presents problems if there are existing application programs that must continue to access the data, for they cannot be converted immediately. If the target database is object-oriented, such a legacy program can be encapsulated as an object or a message. We argue that some applications will benefit from further "reification" of execution instances as database objects. We introduce a "computational proxy" mechanism and our prototype implementation of it for computational chemistry codes. We conclude with a discussion of where declarative capabilities would have been a useful adjunct to object-oriented database features.

1   Introduction

Object-oriented databases provide type definition facilities that cope well with complex structures that arise in advanced applications, such as scientific computing. While transitioning datasets to an object-oriented environment can be non-trivial, providing for existing application programs to access the data in its new form can be a greater challenge. It is not always possible or feasible to convert these programs immediately to interface to the database directly, for several reasons:

1. Programming resources are not available to make the modifications.
2. There is not an appropriate application programming interface for the language in which the application is coded.
3. The source code of the program is not maintained or is licensed locally.
4. There are users of the program who will need to access similar datasets in the old format.

Thus, there is often a need to continue running an application program in its existing form, while providing a bridge to the data in its new form. We note that object-oriented databases are usually introduced to supplant file-based data management, rather than replace an existing database management system. Hence, we direct our attention to existing applications with file-based data access. One approach is simply to write a database application that generates the appropriate data objects and writes an input file for the legacy program, then

Treating Programs as Objects: The Computational Proxy Experience

David Maier and Judith B. Cushing

Department of Computer Science and Engineering
Oregon Graduate Institute of Science & Technology
20000 N.W. Walker Road P.O. Box 91000
Portland, OR 97291-1000

Abstract. Migrating data to a new database model presents problems if there are existing application programs that must continue to access the data, bu that cannot be converted immediately. If the target database is object-oriented, such a legacy program can be encapsulated as an object or a message. We argue that some applications will benefit from further "reification" of execution instances as database objects. We introduce a "computational proxy" mechanism and our prototype implementation of it for computational chemistry codes. We conclude with a discussion of where declarative capabilities would have been a useful adjunct to object-oriented database features.

1 Introduction

Object-oriented databases provide type definition facilities that cope well with complex structures that arise in advanced applications, such as scientific computing. While transitioning datasets to an object-oriented environment can be non-trivial, providing for existing application programs to access the data in its new form can be a greater challenge. It is not always possible or feasible to convert those programs immediately to interface to the database directly, for several reasons:

1. Programming resources are not available to make the modifications.
2. There is not an appropriate application programming interface for the language in which the application is coded.
3. The source code of the program is not maintained or understood locally.
4. There are users of the program who still need to access existing datasets in the old format.

Thus, there is often a need to continue running an application program in its existing form, while providing a bridge to the data in its new form. We note that object-oriented databases are mostly introduced to supplant file-based data management, rather than replace an existing database management system. Hence, we direct our attention to existing applications with file-based data access.

One approach is simply to write a database application that accesses the appropriate data objects and creates an input file for the legacy program, then captures the output file and makes updates to the database. While this loose coupling of the program and the data may often be appropriate, for the domain of computational science where we are working, we desire a tighter binding. Runs of the program are tantamount to "experiments", and we want to record that the run took place, the results, and information about the run—rate of convergence, resource usage, exceptional conditions. Thus, we want the database to have ready access to information about program executions. Other application areas also exhibit this need to record program execution, such as the run of a design-rule checker against a circuit layout or a compilation in a CASE tool.

A more integrated approach—proposed more than once in the literature—is to leave the application program as is, and encapsulate it as a database object or a message of a database class. In the former case, the application is invoked when a message with the input data as an argument is sent to its wrapper object. In the latter, it runs when its corresponding message is sent to the object representing its input. Either approach assumes some way of calling out to the application or linking it in to the database executable, as well as constructing conversion routines between data objects and files. While "wrapping" a legacy application may work in some cases, we believe it will often be too limited an approach.

Capturing an external application program as a single object or message assumes a very input-output model, one where all the inputs are passed in as a unit, the program executes and the outputs are received as a unit. We believe this simple model can be inconvenient or inappropriate for many applications. We may want to separate supplying inputs from scheduling the execution of the program. In particular, when a computation is long, we might not want to wait while it executes. We would rather that the program run asynchronously from the database session, so we are free to do other things while it executes. Instead of treating the program execution as an atomic action, we may want to monitor its progress, in order to stop it, checkpoint it or observe intermediate results. Further, a single object or messages gives little help for organizing and gathering inputs or for structuring the translation process.

In this paper we offer a refinement of the naive wrapper approach that deals better with existing programs having complex inputs and long execution times. In addition to modeling the legacy program in the database, we also represent an individual invocation of the program as an object. Having such computation objects, or *Computational Proxies* as we term them, provides greater control over input assembly, scheduling invocation, execution monitoring and output processing. Furthermore, computational proxies offer a means to provide uniform interfaces to collections of programs whose inputs are semantically similar but syntactically diverse. The proxy mechanism is also a basis for constructing and managing suites and sequences of runs.

We are not alone in applying object-oriented databases to supporting scientific computing. A recent NSF report [CCT93] shows object-oriented approaches used for protein-structure data, medical research, macromolecules, global change data and scientific visualization. In particular, the MOOSE system [IL92] has dealt with modeling the complex inputs to a scientific simulation program.

Our main motivation was masking syntactic complexity, but proxies also serve to mask some details of processor heterogeneity and distribution, in the case where the underlying application runs in several dissimilar environments. From this vantage point, our work resembles other efforts in software systems to promote program interoperability, such as software "packaging" [CP91], middleware (see for example Bernstein [Be93]) and distributed object management systems [NWM93].

We report here on our use of computational proxies in the domain of computational chemistry, and then try to abstract lessons that can be applied in other domains, as well as indicating where more declarative formalisms would be a useful adjunct to object databases in support of our work.

2 Experience with Computational Proxies

The Computational Chemistry Database Project (CCDB), a joint effort of the Scientific Database Group at the Oregon Graduate Institute and the Molecular Science Research Center at Battelle's Pacific Northwest Laboratory, began as an exploration of the hypothesis that object-oriented databases could simplify the complex computing environment in which computational chemists find themselves. The resulting database infrastructure is predicated on providing not only relatively well understood data services but also extending object-oriented database functionality to provide computation services.

Ab initio molecular orbital methods apply quantum-mechanical techniques to molecular structure and energetics, solving the Schödinger equation to various levels of approximation. The solutions produce a wave function and associated electron density from which can be computed any observable molecular, property such as vibrational frequencies or electrostatic moments (dipoles, quadrupoles, etc.). Important inputs to these applications include an initial guess of molecular structure and a basis set of functions which together provide a starting point for iterating the Schrödinger equation. Other input parameters can be specified, depending on the particular application; these include the level of approximation to which to take the calculation, some maximum number of iterations, and the choice of a particular algorithm. The major outputs of the application include an optimized molecular structure, an energy value corresponding to that structure, and the corresponding wave function (also called electron density function or molecular orbitals). From the wave function are calculated the outputs of primary interest to non-theorists, for example, chemical properties such as electrostatic moments or hydrophobicity. In summary, these applications compute chemical properties directly from first principles using equations from quantum chemistry. Figure 1 gives an overview of inputs and outputs for computational chemistry codes.

A typical computing environment for a computational chemist consists of one or more of the application packages in fairly common use, such as Gaussian, GAMESS, MELDFX and HONDO. The application programs are very (100,000 to 300,00 lines of code), maintained remotely, computationally intensive, and

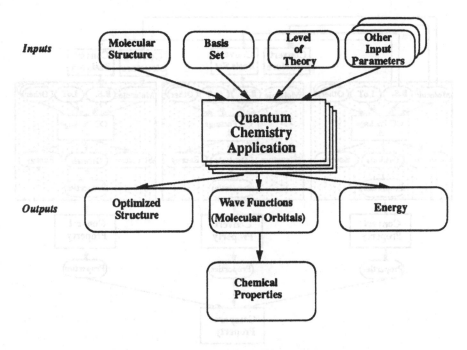

Fig. 1. Inputs and outputs for computational chemistry codes.

semantically similar but syntactically idiosyncratic. They require complex input files, create intermediate files of a gigabyte or more, and run on a variety of platforms from workstations to supercomputers. Output files are typically no larger than a few megabytes, but can be difficult to interpret. In the course of a single investigation, a chemist may generate hundreds of input and output files.

The considerable semantic complexity of the applications lies primarily in selecting input parameters appropriate for the subject molecule and desired results. A poor choice of input parameters will, at best, result in days or weeks of lost CPU hours. At worst, it can yield a plausible but incorrect result. The syntactic complexity lies in the relatively arcane formats of input and output files. Indeed, inputs or outputs of one application cannot easily be used as the input to another; considerable data transformation is required. Reformatting outputs of one program to use as inputs to another is a major problem for many chemists using these applications.

While much of the *semantics* of one application are transferable to another, the *syntax* is not. These applications were developed independently, over a long period of time; with few exceptions,[1] they are syntactically quite different. This *syntactic complexity* makes sharing of data between applications difficult. Figure 2 illustrates some of the conversions needed to run the same molecule through different application packages and compare outputs.

---

[1] GAMESS and HONDO are similar.

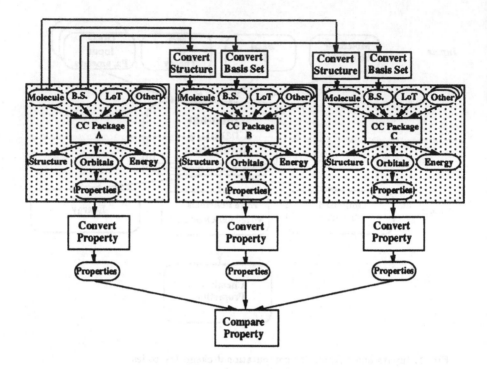

Fig. 2. Syntactical Complexity of Computational Chemistry Applications.

Our initial objective was to create a database of inputs and outputs of previous experiments to aid in selecting input parameters. In addition, the naming and managing hundreds of input and output files spread over multiple machines during the course of an investigation is too great a data management burden on the scientist. Continuing to use flat files is not a viable option for effectively sharing experimental results.

As a first step towards constructing the database, we designed a conceptual model covering the programs' major inputs and outputs. We chose and object-oriented database to implement that model, finding its language and modeling features (particularly encapsulation and direct representation of complex structures) to fit our requirements. An obvious additional advantage was that we could map conceptual-level classes, operations and hierarchies directly into counterparts in the database's data definition language (DDL) with little encoding. Figure 5 is a top-level view of the logical database design. This model was implemented in the ObjectStore object-oriented database management system [CMR+92b].

Experience using standalone programs to load the prototype database with experimental inputs and outputs, however, impelled us to seriously consider how to integrate the applications with the database and make the database the focal point for running computational experiments. Leaving the loading as a task separate separate from running an application would add to the chemist's overhead in running computational experiments and would inevitably prove error prone. We also wanted a more uniform interface to a diverse computational environment, and having the database separate from the applications did little to simplify the computing environment.

An obvious way to interface the applications to the database would have been to modify the programs to access and write to the database directly. The computational chemistry programs in question are simply too large, complex, and too often revised by others to make this approach feasible. A second alternative was to provide a "wrapper" for the computational applications, sending inputs to the wrapper and having it invoke application. However, this alternative is too simplistic; for example, it does not easily allow for automatically placing results of the computation back into the database, nor does it simplify monitoring of ongoing experiments.

Because the textual interface to these programs is easier to read and more stable than the application programs themselves, we decided to use the textual inputs and outputs as a basis for the interface, and to define an intermediate structure that would represent the computation in the database and help automate the control of ongoing experiments. We dubbed this mechanism a *computational proxy*. Computational proxies "stand-in", within the database, for computational experiments in preparation, currently in process, or recently completed.

Messages associated with the proxy class provide an interface to the computational programs used to run those experiments. The proxy encapsulates syntactic differences among semantically related applications, providing transformations of database items to application inputs and of application output into the database. Figure 3 shows this conceptual encapsulation of computational chemistry applications. When the user schedules a run, a proxy automatically transforms experimental attributes held in the database into textual inputs appropriate for a given application program. The inputs are shipped to the processor where the application is to run, and the application is invoked remotely on them. During the run, the user can interact with the proxy to halt and restart computation, view intermediate results (such as error terms) and monitor resource usages. Once the run has terminated, the proxy parses the outputs and places experimental results into the database in a form comparable to that of data for other applications. Thus, a database of experiment inputs and outputs is an immediate byproduct of launching experiments via the proxy mechanism.

Our first realization of the proxy mechanism consists of hand-coded programs that generated input files and parsed output files specifically for a given application. However, we feel that the user community should be able to register an application with the database descriptively by creating new objects, rather than by writing code specific to each application. We have thus focused our recent efforts on the ability to specify proxies declaratively. We call these specifications *templates*. The application descriptor, or *template*, defines the mapping between the domain-specific database and program-specific inputs and outputs.

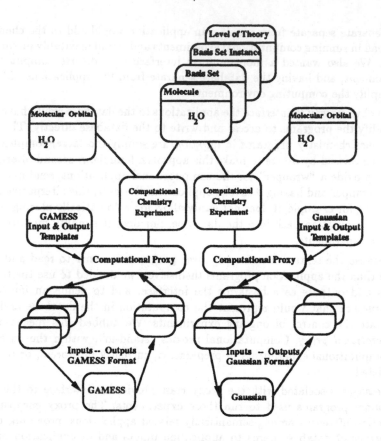

Fig. 3. Hiding syntactic complexity of computational codes.

We extended our logical data model to incorporate computational proxies. A computational proxy *represents* a process that is about to run, is running, or has run an experiment. A proxy *runs on* a *particular computer*, i.e., processor, that is connected to the same network services to which the proxy itself is connected. Any particular computer *is an instance of* some generic *computer platform*, e.g., the processor **coho** is a **Sun4** computer platform. If a proxy object *runs on* a particular processor, we say that the *experiment represented by that proxy runs on that processor.* In order for an experiment to run on a processor of a particular type of computer platform, the application it *uses* must be both *available for* the corresponding platform and *installed on* the particular processor. Figure 4 illustrates these conceptual relationships.

To date, we have implemented a computational proxy mechanism that interfaces directly to the GAMESS package. This prototype currently runs under C++ and ObjectStore on distributed Sun SparcStation2 platforms. We are currently working on the database structures that will allow the non-programmatic specifications of proxies for new applications [C93].

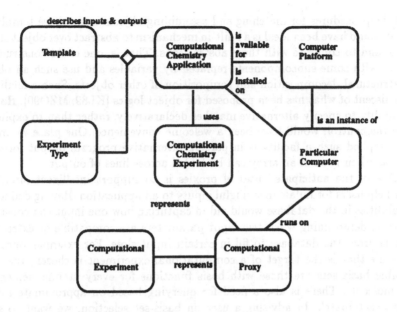

Fig. 4. Conceptual model for computational proxy.

3 Lessons and Desiderata

While we readily admit that computational proxies are not the solution to integrating all applications with object databases, we think they are applicable in other scientific domains and likely far beyond that. The approach seems appropriate where legacy programs have complex input and output structures, where computations are lengthy, where there are a variety of possible execution platforms and where it is desired to support intelligent interfaces for non-expert users. We believe modeling computations as well as data and programs as objects gives a natural basis on which to manage collections of computations. In the computational chemistry domain, one often wants to perform a collection of related runs where one or more parameters are varied over some range. For example, one might vary the distance between two molecular fragments in order to generate an energy surface. It seem a direct extension to construct "meta-proxies" that represent collections of executions. Another common pattern of activity is stringing together computations by different programs, with the output of one being the input to the next. Modeling such chains of computations as sequences of proxies seems a natural enhancement.

In examining our efforts to provide a higher-level definition system for specifying new proxy types, we feel that pattern-matching and rule-based reasoning capabilities as found in logic programming languages would have been a useful addition to the mainly procedural data manipulation language we were using. Much of our effort went into designing object structures for building templates and the procedures for matching and assembling objects using those templates. What would have been ideal is a built-in mechanism to abstract over object structures, and to compute with those abstractions. That is, one could construct an object with some subcomponents replaced by variables and use such an object for structural decomposition and composition of other objects. Such a facility is reminiscent of what has been proposed for object logics [KL89, MZO90]. Having the ability to specify alternative matches declaratively, rather than to explicitly code the control, would have been a welcome convenience. One place we might have applied such a facility is in parsing alternative program output formats, such as when rows of an array can be folded across lines of output.

One of the anticipated uses of proxies is to support intelligent interfaces that help users formulate meaningful inputs to an application. Having deductive capabilities in the database would aid in capturing how one input can constrain another, determining when two input parameters are compatible or extracting options from the database to fill in certain input slots. For example, once the molecule that is the target of a computational experiment is chosen, the only sensible basis sets are those with basis functions for every atomic element in the molecule. There is also a need for querying based on approximate rather than exact match. In advising a user on basis-set selection, we want to scan the database for like experiments. However, the measure of similarity is type dependent, varying for molecule, chemical property, and so forth. Here, the type extensibility features of object-oriented databases would complement a deductive query mechanism.

We also note that reification of computations, programs and resources as objects in the database expands the context in which deductive capabilities could be applied. One can now reason over events and resources on the computational side as well as data.

Our immediate plans are to evaluate the proxy approach in another scientific domain. We also want to improve support for registering new proxy types. Proxies are currently aimed at programs with a "batch" interface: all input available at the start of a run, output files available at completion. Long term, we would like to deal with legacy applications with more interactive interfaces.

4 Conclusions

Integrating existing application programs with an object database via proxy objects that represent individual executions of the programs has worked well for us. Proxy objects provide a framework for assembling and validating inputs, and for structuring the translation to and from file formats. They separate the selection of inputs from the scheduling of execution, and present a natural target within the database for inquiry about the status of a protracted run and accessing its intermediate results. Proxies also provide an environment for analyzing program outputs, which often cannot be interpreted correctly without knowledge of the associated inputs. In our domain of interest, they also serve to mask syntactic differences among semantically similar programs, to hide some aspects of processor distribution and heterogeneity, and to record experimental parameters to provide for replicability. While we have used proxies only with existing applications, the approach may be appropriate for newly written programs, if they are complex inputs or need monitoring during execution.

5 Acknowledgements

The authors would like to acknowledge the important collaboration between Computational Chemist Dr. David Feller of the Molecular Science Research Center, Battelle Pacific Northwest Laboratory, Richland, Washington. Without his understanding of ab initio computational chemistry applications and the needs of computational chemists, our project would not have been possible. We would also like to acknowledge the work of Meenakshi Rao and Don Abel, master's students at Oregon Graduate Institute and Portland State University, who ably programmed the Compute Monitor and Output File Parsing components of the Computational Proxy.

This work is supported by NSF grant IRI-9117008, additional grants from the Oregon Advanced Computing Institute (OACIS) and PNL, and software grants from Object Design, Inc. Gaussian is a registered trademark of Gaussian, Inc. and ObjectStore of Object Design, Inc. GAMESS is distributed by North Dakota State University and the USDOE Ames Laboratory.

References

[Abel94]   D. Abel. Loading an Object-Database from the Textual Output of Computational Programs. Master's thesis, Portland State University, Portland, OR, expected: June 1994.

[Be93]   P. A. Bernstein. Middleware: An Architecture for Distributed Systems Services. DEC Cambridge Research Lab report CRL 93/6, March 1993.

[CP91]   J. R. Callahan and J. M. Purtilo. A Packaging System for Heterogeneous Execution Environments. *IEEE Trans. on Software Engineering* 17(6), June 1991.

[CCT93]   W. W. Chu, A. F. Cardenas, and R. K. Taira, editors. *Proceedings of the AAAS Workshop on Advances in Data Management for the Scientist and Engineer*. NSF, Boston, Massachusetts, February 1993.

[CMR92a]   J. B. Cushing, D. Maier, and M. Rao. Computational chemistry database prototype: ObjectStore. Technical Report CS/E-92-002, OGI, Beaverton, OR, January 1992.

[CMR+92b]   J. B. Cushing, D. Maier, M. Rao, D. M. DeVaney, and D. Feller. Object-oriented database support for computational chemistry. *Sixth International Working Conference on Statistical and Scientific Database Management (SSDBM)*, June 1992.

[CMR93]   J. B. Cushing, D. Maier, and M. Rao. Computational proxies: Modeling scientific applications in object databases. Technical Report CS/E-92-020, OGI, Beaverton, OR, 1993.

[C93]   J. B. Cushing. Computational proxies: Modeling scientific applications in object databases. Ph.D. thesis, OGI, Beaverton, OR, expected: December 1993.

[IL92]   Y. Ioannides and M. Livny. MOOSE: Modeling Objects in a Simulation Environment. *Information Processing 89*, North Holland, August 1989.

[KL89]   M. Kifer amd G. Lausen. F-Logic: A Higher-Order Language for Reasoning about Objects, Inherhitance, and Scheme. *Proc. ACM SIGMOD International Conference on Management of Data*, Portland, OR, May-June 1989.

[MZO90]   D. Maier, J. Zhu, and H. Ohkawa. Features of the TEDM Object Model. *Proc. of the First International Conference on Deductive and Object-Oriented Databases*, Elsevier Science, 1990.

[NWM93]   J. R. Nicol, C. T. Wilkes, and F. A. Manola. Object Orientation in Heterogeneous Distributed Computing Systems. *IEEE Computer* 26(6), June 1993.

[Rao93]   M. Rao. Computational proxies for computational chemistry: A proof of concept. Master's thesis, OGI, Beaverton, OR, expected: December 1993.

12

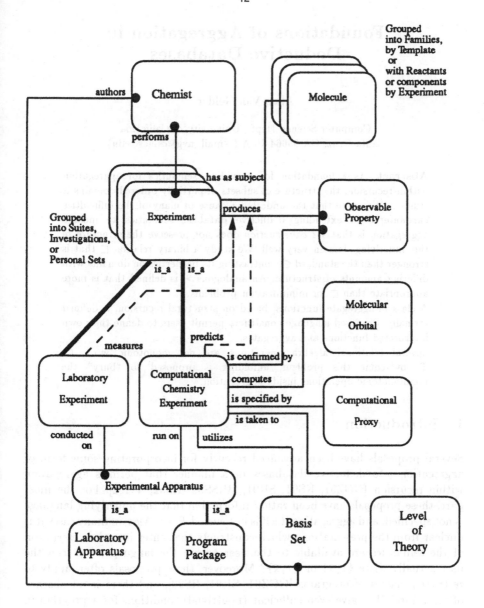

Fig. 5. Computational Chemistry Data Model.

Foundations of Aggregation in Deductive Databases

Allen Van Gelder

Computer Science Dept., University of California
Santa Cruz, CA 95064 USA (e-mail: avg@cs.ucsc.edu)

Abstract. As a foundation for providing semantics for aggregation within recursion, the structure of subsets of partially ordered domains is studied. We argue that the underlying cause of many of the difficulties encountered in extending deductive database semantics to include aggregation is that *set construction* does not preserve the structure of the underlying domain very well. We study a binary relation $\sqsubseteq$ that is stronger than the standard $\subseteq$, contrasting its properties on domains with differing amounts of structure. An analogous $\succ$ is defined that is more appropriate than $\sqsubseteq$ for minimization problems.

A class of aggregate functions, based on structural recursion, is defined formally. Proposed language constructs permit users to define their own interpreted functions and aggregates.

Several relational algebra operations are not monotonic w.r.t. $\sqsubseteq$. To overcome this problem, unfolding is proposed to "bury" the nonmonotonic operations inside aggregation.

1 Introduction

Several proposals have been advanced recently for incorporating some form of aggregation into deductive databases in a manner that permits aggregation within recursion [GGZ91, KS91, SR91, BRSS92, RS92, VG92]. For the most part, these proposals have been rather informal in that the underlying language is not specified, and aggregation itself is not even defined. Also, in many cases it is unclear from the presentations which constructs that enter into the description of the semantics are available to the user within the language; e.g., can the user actually write {1,2} or {1,X}? Moreover, these proposals often apply to restricted classes of programs [GGZ91, SR91, RS92], and there is an absence of procedures that give even sufficient (nontrivial) conditions for a program to fall into the class covered by the semantics. (Other proposals [KS91, BRSS92, VG92] apply to all programs, but may leave too much undefined, or may lead to outcomes that are difficult to predict, casting doubts on their usefulness.)

We argue here that the underlying cause of many of the difficulties encountered in extending deductive database semantics to include aggregation is that *set construction* does not preserve the structure of the underlying domain very well.

Given a domain D with at least a partial order, we shall study various attempts to define a "suitable" partial order on (a) the set of subsets (power set) of D, and (b) the set of finite subsets of D. We shall be interested in classifying induced binary relations as partial orders, lattices, total orders, or complete lattices.

1.1 Motivating Examples

The following motivating example illustrates the problems involved. It is adapted from two examples of Ross and Sagiv [RS92].

Example 1.1: The program wants to express the fact that corporation X votes fraction F of the stock of corporation Y if it directly owns some stock and "controls" intermediate corporations I that vote some stock of Y, such that all the parts sum to F. Without worrying about actual syntax, let us use the pseudo-code

$$votes(X, Y, F) \leftarrow F \text{ is } \sum_I \{F_I \mid \\ (I = Y \ \& \ owns(X, I, F_I) \ \& \ F_I = F_X) \vee \\ (votes(X, I, F_X) \ \& \ 0.5 < F_X \ \& \ votes(I, Y, F_I)))\}$$

to express the above rule.

First, consider an EDB $owns = \{(c, d, 0.4), (d, d, 0.2)\}$; that is, the $owns$ relation has the two tuples indicated. Clearly, c "should not" vote a controlling (> 0.5) interest of d, so the intended model is $votes = \{(c, d, 0.4), (d, d, 0.2)\}$. However, the rule has another model, $votes = \{(c, d, 0.6), (d, d, 0.2)\}$, which would make the directors of corporation d very unhappy. However, both models are minimal under $\subseteq$, so this does appear to be a satisfactory partial order for identifying preferred models.

Second, consider an EDB $owns = \{(a, b, 0.6), (b, b, 0.2)\}$. Applying the usual immediate consequence operator (call it $\mathbf{T}$), at stage 1 we derive $votes_1 = \mathbf{T}(\emptyset) = \{(a, b, 0.6), (b, b, 0.2)\}$, and at stage 1 we derive $votes_2 = \mathbf{T}(votes_1) = \{(a, b, 0.8), (b, b, 0.2)\}$. Therefore $\mathbf{T}$ is not monotonic under $\subseteq$, as $\emptyset \subseteq votes_1$, but $\{(a, b, 0.6), (b, b, 0.2)\} \not\subseteq \{(a, b, 0.8), (b, b, 0.2)\}$.

Therefore, $\subseteq$ does not seem to be a "strong enough" partial order for semantics of aggregation. This is the motivation to look for a definition of $<$ that makes $\{(a, b, 0.6), (b, b, 0.2)\} < \{(a, b, 0.8), (b, b, 0.2)\}$ (restoring monotonicity to $\mathbf{T}$) and makes $\{(c, d, 0.4), (d, d, 0.2)\} < \{(c, d, 0.6), (d, d, 0.2)\}$ (causing the unintended model to be nonminimal). $\Box$

1.2 Summary of Results

Under $\subseteq$, any two distinct sets of equal cardinality are incomparable. It is natural to try to strengthen this ordering by specifying (when $|A| = |B|$) that $A < B$ if the elements of $A - B$ are "generally smaller" than those of $B - A$, in some sense. Why shouldn't we have $\{0.6\} < \{0.8\}$? We shall study the properties of one such relation, which seems intuitive and conservative, which we denote by $\ll$, and its extensions to sets of unequal cardinality, $\sqsubset$ and $\succ$. (The latter is more appropriate than $\sqsubset$ for minimization problems.)

We show that $\ll$, $\sqsubset$, and $\succ$ lose some of the structure of the underlying domain of the elements. In particular, for $\ll$, $\sqsubset$, and $\succ$ to be lattices, they must be applied only to finite subsets, and the underlying domain must be a total order, not just a lattice (Theorems 4.3, 4.6, and 4.9). In this case, the lattice operations can be computed efficiently. In contrast, $\sqsubset$ may not be even a partial order when applied an infinite power set (Examples 4.2 and 4.3).

We shall give a formal definition for an aggregate function, based on structural recursion over an interpreted binary function that is associative and commutative (Section 3). We shall specify how interpreted functions and predicates enter the language, and how users can declare intended orders upon which to base $\sqsubset$ or $\succ$.

It is shown that several relational algebra operations are not monotonic w.r.t. $\sqsubset$ (Section 5). To overcome this problem, unfolding is proposed to "bury" the nonmonotonic operations inside aggregation. In many cases the result of the aggregation remains monotonic despite the presence of nonmonotonic operations in its formula, and a stratified semantics can be assigned to the program.

2 Notation

We stay close to the syntax of Prolog for rules. Symbols beginning with a capital letter are variables. Symbols beginning with lowercase letters and those comprised of special symbols are predicates or function symbols (including constants), depending on context. A typical rule:

$$lacks(X, S) \leftarrow p(X, Y) \ \& \ \neg member(X, S)$$

is read as "$lacks(X, S)$ holds (or can be solved) *if* for some Y, $p(X, Y)$ holds (or can be solved) and $member(X, S)$ does not hold". The *body* of the rule (the part to the right of the $\leftarrow$) may be a formula built with *and* ($\&$), *or* ($\vee$), *not* ($\neg$), and equality ($=$, $\neq$). To have a consistent syntax with aggregate expressions defined later, all operands of an "*or*" must contain exactly the same variables. A variable that appears in the body but not in the head is considered to be existentially quantified at the *smallest scope that includes all occurrences of that variable*.

2.1 Interpreted Functions

We retain the flexibility for a function symbol to be interpreted or uninterpreted, depending on context, as in Prolog and other logic-based languages. Functions are generally uninterpreted, and can be thought of as record names. However, certain predicates may evaluate (or interpret) some or all of their arguments.

1. Binary "$=$" does *not* evaluate either of its arguments. It succeeds by syntactically unifying them.
2. Binary "is" evaluates its second argument; this is the principal method of forcing evaluation of expressions; It is a run-time error for the second argument of is to be a free variable. However, is merely fails if it does not "know" how to evaluate the second argument.

3. Order relations $<, \leq, >, \geq$ evaluate both arguments.
4. Copying Prolog, "$=:=$" and "$=/=$" evaluate both arguments; the first succeeds if the results are equal, and the second succeeds if the results are unequal.

Note that the semantics of the above built-in predicates with regard to interpreted functions can be referred to the semantics of "is". For example, "$s < t$" for any terms s and t has the same meaning as "S is s & T is t & S $<$ T".

Normally, expressions must be variable-free when they are evaluated. These examples illustrate the conventions just described. When X appears, it is a free variable. We assume the user has not defined additional rules for is .

1+2 = 2+1	fails	X = 2+1	succeeds
1+2 is 2+1	fails	X =:= 2+1	is an error
3 is 2+1	succeeds	1+a =:= a+1	fails
1+2 =:= 2+1	succeeds	X is a+1	fails

As the last three examples illustrate, it is an error to try to evaluate an insufficiently instantiated term, but attempting to evaluate a term with an operand of the wrong type is just a failure. Thus interpreted "functions" are really partial functions, and may return "undefined". Some functions may be able to tolerate some undefined arguments, but predicates cannot. If the second argument of "is" evaluates to "undefined", the goal fails.

In a context where they will be interpreted, the usual arithmetic operators $+, -, *, /$, etc., are built-in. Certain standard functions, like *sqrt* and *log*, may be supplied. The user can define more interpreted functions and overload existing interpreted functions by giving additional rules for "is".

Example 2.1: Greatest common divisor can be added as a new binary function, gcd:

$$X \text{ is } \gcd(X, X).$$
$$G \text{ is } \gcd(X, Y) \leftarrow X < Y \ \& \ G \text{ is } \gcd(X, Y - X).$$
$$G \text{ is } \gcd(X, Y) \leftarrow X > Y \ \& \ G \text{ is } \gcd(X - Y, Y).$$

Notice that these rules employ the built-in function "$-$", and the built-in predicates $<$ and $>$. $\square$

Example 2.2: The interpreted function "$+$" can be extended (overloaded) for pairs:

$$(X, Y) \text{ is } (A, B) + (C, D) \leftarrow X \text{ is } A + C \ \& \ Y \text{ is } B + D.$$

Interpreted predicates $<$ and $=:=$ can be extended for pairs:

$$(A, B) < (C, D) \leftarrow A < C \ \& \ B \leq D.$$
$$(A, B) < (C, D) \leftarrow A \leq C \ \& \ B < D.$$
$$(A, B) =:= (C, D) \leftarrow A =:= C \ \& \ B =:= D.$$

These capabilities are not difficult to implement in a logical language, and are already available in some Prolog versions. $\square$

3 What is an Aggregate?

In this section we formalize the definition of aggregate functions. Aggregate functions will be defined with respect to interpreted types.

Definition 3.1: An *interpreted type* is a set of values, the *interpreted domain*, and a collection of interpreted functions on that domain. An *interpreted expression* is a term whose functions are interpreted. $\square$

Definition 3.2: A *relational template* (also called a *most general goal*) is an atomic formula of the form $p(X_1, \ldots, X_n)$, where $X_1, \ldots, X_n$ are distinct variables. It corresponds to the "full relation for p". That is, in any universe U the relational template is interpreted by $\{p(a_1, \ldots, a_n) \mid a_i \in U\}$. $\square$

Although some researchers seem to consider any mapping from sets to a single value as an aggregate, we shall consider only those mappings that can be defined with structural induction on a binary operator [SS84, SS91, BTBW92].

Definition 3.3: Let S be a domain corresponding to the relational template $p(X_1, \ldots, X_n)$. Let D be a domain. A *simple aggregate function* $\mathbf{f}$ is a pair (π, f), where $\pi : S \to D$ is called the *projection function* and $f : D \times D \to D$ is called the *set-reduction function*. Function f must be associative and commutative. Function π projects onto certain components of a tuple of S; its result is defined if and only if the retained components (possibly as a vector) comprise an element in D. Thus π may be a partial function. As a special case, the 0th component of any tuple equals 1.

The aggregate $\mathbf{f}$ is a function from certain finite subsets of S (possibly excluding $\emptyset$) into D, defined as follows:

1. If operator f has an identity element ϵ, then $\emptyset$ is in the domain of $\mathbf{f}$ and $\mathbf{f}(\emptyset) = \epsilon$; otherwise $\emptyset$ is not in the domain of $\mathbf{f}$. (Often a domain can be extended to give f an identity, as suggested in Example 3.2.)
2. For any single-tuple relation $r = \{t_1\}$, $t_1 \in S$, define $\mathbf{f}(\{t_1\}) = \pi(t_1)$; note that the result is undefined if $t_1 \notin D$.
3. For a finite relation $r \in S$ of cardinality $k > 1$, let t_1 be any tuple in r. Then

$$\mathbf{f}(r) = f\left(\pi(t_1), \mathbf{f}(r - \{t_1\})\right)$$

where the result is undefined if either argument of f is undefined. This value is well-defined (or well-undefined!) because f is associative and commutative, and r is finite.

We employ the standard notation for common binary operators and their associated simple aggregates, such as "+" and $\sum$, "$*$" and $\prod$, $\vee$ and $\bigvee$, $\cup$ and $\bigcup$, etc. $\square$

Example 3.1: To sum the second component of $p(X, Y, Z)$, define $\pi(p(X, Y, Z)) = Y$, and define f as +.

To sum the second and third components of $p(X, Y, Z)$, define $\pi(p(X, Y, Z)) = (Y, Z)$, define f as +, and overload the definition of +, by adding the rule for pairs, as described in Section 2.2. $\square$

Fig. 1. Extension of a domain D to provide identities for min and max.

With some additional structure on domain D it may be possible to extend the definition of $\mathbf{f}$ to infinite relations. However, computations on infinite relations are practical only in isolated, special cases, so this direction is not pursued.

Example 3.2: Let D be a domain with interpreted binary operators min and max, among others, but assume D has no minimum or maximum element. This example shows a typical method to extend a domain to include identities for those operators.

The binary operators min and max have no identity, First, add new elements ϵ_{min} and ϵ_{max} as identities for min and max, respectively. Thus, $min(a, \epsilon_{min}) = a$, while $max(a, \epsilon_{min}) = \epsilon_{min}$, etc. Essentially ϵ_{min} is the maximum element and ϵ_{max} is the minimum element in the extended domain. This may give a complete lattice (Definition 4.1) in some cases, but our motivation here is simply to provide identity elements for min and max.

But usually we are not done. Suppose "+" is also an interpreted operator on D. We might be able to define $\epsilon_{max} + a = \epsilon_{max}$ and $\epsilon_{min} + a = \epsilon_{min}$. However, there is probably no sensible definition of $\epsilon_{min} + \epsilon_{max}$. Therefore, add yet another element $'\mathtt{NaN}'$, and define

$$min('\mathtt{NaN}', a) = \epsilon_{max} \quad a \in D$$
$$min('\mathtt{NaN}', \epsilon_{max}) = \epsilon_{max}$$
$$min('\mathtt{NaN}', \epsilon_{min}) = '\mathtt{NaN}'$$

and so forth (see Figure 1) Thus $'\mathtt{NaN}'$ is incomparable with elements of D and serves as an absorptive value for meaningless results of operations other than min and max. This kind of extension already exists in the IEEE floating point standard, where "NaN" stands for "not a number". $\square$

Simple aggregates provide the building blocks for more complex aggregates. Thus *average* and *weighted average* are easily defined with a vector sum aggregate to produce (S, W), followed by the goal A **is** S/W.

An abstract data type *finite set* might be produced by an aggregate operation **setof**, with **union** as the underlying binary operator. This raises substantial semantic issues, which are the subject of much research [SS91, BRSS92, BTBW92, Won93].

There are many proposals for the syntax with which to incorporate aggregates into a logical language; the important practical point is to provide a "group by" capability. We shall use the following syntax (similar to Kemp and Stuckey [KS91]).

Definition 3.4: An *aggregate expression* is:

$$\mathbf{agg}(f, \mathtt{groupby}([group]),\ t \mid p(group, vars, t))$$

where:

1. f is a binary operator on some domain D;
2. $p(group, vars, t)$ is an atomic formula or an and-or[1] formula, with (tuples of) variables *group*, *vars*, and t.
3. $t \in D$ is a usually a variable (or comma-separated list of distinct variables if D is a vector domain) that appears only in this aggregate expression. For greater generality, the t before the "|" may be any nonaggregate expression that can be evaluated into D by interpreted functions. In this case, the t after the "|" consists of the variables appearing in the first t. In particular, the first t may be 1 to implement **count**.
4. [*group*] is a list of zero or more variables upon which the formula $p(group, vars, t)$ is to be partitioned for group-by purposes. If the list is empty, the **groupby** argument can be omitted. In normal usage, all variables in *group* appear outside the aggregate expression, although this is not an absolute requirement for the semantics.
5. Variables not appearing in *group* or t comprise *vars*, a set of variables that occur only in formula $p(group, vars, t)$, to be treated existentially.

Common aggregates may be built-in by combining "**agg**" and its binary operator into an aggregate name. □

Of course, an aggregate expression, just like any other expression, is *evaluated* only when it appears in a context requiring evaluation (e.g., within the second argument of "**is**").

Neither the "group-by" nor the ability to have and-or formulas in the expression nor the ability to make t a functional expression should add to the expressive power of the aggregation construct under any reasonable semantics. A new predicate name p_1 can be introduced with a single rule whose body is the and-or formula p, plus possibly an "**is**" goal to evaluate t. A second new predicate p_2 can have a single rule that projects p_1 onto the desired group-by variables; a p_2 goal is conjoined to the goal in which the aggregate appears (see next example).

Example 3.3: The sum expression of Example 1.1 can be written in the generic form, or with the built-in $\sum$:

---

[1] As in rule bodies, "or"s must have exactly the same variables in all operands.

```
agg(+, groupby([X,Y]), F_I |
    (I = Y & owns(X,I,F_X) & F_I = F_X) ∨
    (votes(X,I,F_X) & 0.5 < F_X & votes(I,Y,F_I))))
```

$$\sum(\text{groupby}([X,Y]), F_I \mid$$
$$(I = Y\ \&\ \text{owns}(X,I,F_X)\ \&\ F_I = F_X)\ \vee$$
$$(\text{votes}(X,I,F_X)\ \&\ 0.5 < F_X\ \&\ \text{votes}(I,Y,F_I))))$$

In both expressions X and Y are constant for any sum, being the "group-by" variables. Often they are bound elsewhere in the rule body, but this is not the case in Example 1.1. The two variables I and F_X may vary from tuple to tuple during one aggregation; by keeping them in the aggregate expression we avoid the need to treat multisets, and can always insist that aggregates operate on relations.

The above aggregate can be expressed in a simpler language by defining:

$$p_1(X,Y,I,F_X,F_I) \leftarrow (I = Y\ \&\ owns(X,I,F_X)\ \&\ F_I = F_X)$$
$$\vee\ (votes(X,I,F_X)\ \&\ 0.5 < F_X\ \&\ votes(I,Y,F_I)).$$

$$p_2(X,Y) \leftarrow p_1(X,Y,I,F_X,F_I).$$

The rule of Example 1.1 becomes:

$$votes(X,Y,F) \leftarrow p_2(X,Y)\ \&$$
$$F\ \text{is}\ \sum(F_I \mid p_1(X,Y,I,F_X,F_I))$$

There is now mutual recursion among p_1, p_2 and $votes$. $\square$

4 Induced Orders on Subsets and Multisets

As mentioned in the introduction, it seems desirable to be able to (partially) order sets by something stronger than the inclusion relation. We shall investigate a conservative (i.e., few edges) partial order denoted by $\ll$. Notice that a partial order has a nice structure when the number of edges is "just right"; adding more edges to a lattice can destroy the lattice property, and can even destroy the partial order property. Thus our first goal is to check the structure of $\ll$ under various conditions of the underlying domain over which the sets are formed.

Definition 4.1: Recall [BS81] that a *lattice* is a domain D with two binary operators, *meet* ($\sqcap$) and *join* ($\sqcup$), such that each is associative, commutative, idempotent ($x \cdot x = x$), and such that the pair satisfies the *absorption axioms*:

$$(x \sqcap (x \sqcup y)) = x \qquad \text{and} \qquad (x \sqcup (x \sqcap y)) = x$$

Effectively, *join* is a binary least upper bound operator, and *meet* is a binary greatest lower bound operator. Interchanging meet and join gives the *dual lattice*.

Recall that join (or meet) induces a partial order on D, and that a lattice is *complete* if every subset of D has a least upper bound and a greatest lower bound in D with respect to this partial order. $\square$

Finite lattices are always complete. The rationals with the usual order are not complete, even when restricted to a bounded closed interval. The set of all finite subsets of an infinite domain S, with inclusion order, is not a complete lattice, but can be made complete by adding S as a top element (if $|\cup_i (A_i)| = \infty$, then $\sqcup_i(A_i) = S$).

Observe that any pair of binary operators that satisfy the meet/join axioms can define a lattice. For example, the pair: (greatest common denominator, least common multiple) on the domain of natural numbers does so.

Definition 4.2: Let D be a domain with partial order "$<$", possibly corresponding to operators *join* ($\sqcup$) and *meet* ($\sqcap$). Let S be a domain corresponding to a relational template, and let $\pi : S \to D$ be a *projection function*, as described in Definitions 3.2 and 3.3. Let $\mathcal{S}$ be the collection of subsets of S that is of interest (usually all finite subsets or all subsets). Define the binary relation $\ll$ on *distinct* subsets, $A \in \mathcal{S}$, $B \in \mathcal{S}$, as follows:

$$A \ll B$$

if and only if there is a bijection (1-1 onto mapping) $\mu : A \to B$ such that $\pi(a) \leq \pi(\mu(a))$ for all $a \in A$. (Such a μ is called *extensive* [BS81], or sometimes *inflationary*.) When necessary for clarity, the notation μ_{AB} is used.

Alternatively, let $\mathcal{M}$ be a collection of multisets of D, with $\alpha, \beta \in \mathcal{M}$. The definition of $\ll$ can be extended as follows. Choose any index set I of sufficiently great cardinality, and create sets (not multisets) $A, B \subseteq D \times I$ such that the multiset projection (retaining duplicates) of A and B onto their first columns are respectively α and β. Now say $\alpha \ll \beta$ if and only if $A \ll B$ with projection function $\pi : D \times I \to D$.

Note that $A \ll A$ never holds, and $A \ll B$ never holds for A and B of different cardinalities. $\square$

Example 4.1: Let $A = \{p(a,1), p(b,1)\}$ and $B = \{p(a,1), p(b,2)\}$, and let π project onto the second argument. Clearly, $A \ll B$, with μ mapping the elements in the order given. Now abstract this to multisets: $A = \{1,1\}$, $B = \{1,2\}$. We permit μ to map the "first" 1 of A to 1 and map the "second" 1 of A to 2. Again, $A \ll B$. $\square$

Lemma 4.1: $A \ll B$ if and only if $(A - B) \ll (B - A)$.

Proof: μ can be made the identity on the common elements. $\blacksquare$

4.1 Finite Subsets

First, consider the case where $\mathcal{S}$ consists of finite subsets of S. Applying π to each element of some $A \in \mathcal{S}$ yields a finite multiset of D elements; for simplicity of notation we also call this multiset A. When D is totally ordered, such multisets have the following useful *ordered presentation*:

$$A = (a_1 \leq a_2 \leq \cdots \leq a_n)$$

where the a_i are not necessarily distinct. If D is only partially ordered, the presentation is any topological order, and may not be unique. We shall see that $\ll$ has less structure than $<$ in most cases.

Lemma 4.2: Let E and F be any two finite nonempty subsets of totally ordered domain D. Let E^- and F^- be those subsets with their respective maximum elements removed. If $E \ll F$, then (a) $\max(E) < \max(F)$ and $E^- = F^-$, or (b) $\max(E) \le \max(F)$ and $E^- \ll F^-$.

Proof: By definition of $\ll$, there is an extensive bijection $\mu_{EF} : E \to F$. If $\mu_{EF}(\max(E)) \ne \max(F)$, then another extensive bijection $\mu : E \to F$ can be defined for which $\mu(\max(E)) = \max(F)$, as follows: Let $\mu_{EF}(x) = \max(F)$, where $x \ne \max(E)$. Define $\mu(x) = \mu_{EF}(\max(E))$ and $\mu(\max(E)) = \max(F)$, and let $\mu = \mu_{EF}$ elsewhere. The lemma follows. ∎

Theorem 4.3: With the definitions above, assume $\mathcal{S}$ consists of finite subsets of S. Then

(a) Relation $\ll$ is a partial order.

(b) If in addition, $<$ is a total order (hence defines a lattice), then $\ll$ defines a lattice with

$$A \sqcup B \stackrel{\text{def}}{=} ((a_1 \sqcup b_1) \le \cdots \le (a_n \sqcup b_n))$$
$$A \sqcap B \stackrel{\text{def}}{=} ((a_1 \sqcap b_1) \le \cdots \le (a_n \sqcap b_n))$$

where a_i and b_i are based upon the ordered presentations of A and B.

(c) If $<$ is not a total order, then $\ll$ is not a lattice.

Proof: (a) By Lemma 4.1 we can assume A and B are disjoint. Consider the bipartite graph with nodes consisting of the elements of A and B, and with directed edges from $a_i \in A$ to $b_j \in B$ whenever $a_i \le b_j$. A complete matching exists (defining μ_{AB}) iff $A \ll B$. In this case, a reverse complete matching μ_{BA} cannot exist or else there would be $2n$ edges among the $2n$ nodes, making a cycle in the $<$ relation.

(b) Axioms for the new lattice can be verified by induction, using Lemma 4.2.

(c) Domain D must have two incomparable elements, say a and b. If either $a \sqcup b$ or $a \sqcap b$ (w.r.t $<$) fails to exist in D, then the singleton sets $\{a\}$ and $\{b\}$ lack either a lub or glb w.r.t. $\ll$, so assume both exist. Let A and B be the following subsets of D:

$$A \stackrel{\text{def}}{=} \{a, b\}$$
$$B \stackrel{\text{def}}{=} \{a \sqcap b, a \sqcup b\}$$

There are two distinct minimal upper bounds for A and B w.r.t. $\ll$: $\{a, a \sqcup b\}$ and $\{b, a \sqcup b\}$. ∎

Even if the domain of D is finite and totally ordered, $(\mathcal{M}, \ll)$ is not a *complete* lattice, where $\mathcal{M}$ consists of the finite multisets. (Upper bounds of arbitrary sets of finite multisets may need to be infinite.) The case where $\mathcal{M}$ includes infinite multisets is considered in Section 4.2.

4.2 Infinite Subsets

Now consider the case where $\mathcal{S}$ is the power set of S. Applying π to each element of some $A \in \mathcal{S}$ yields a possibly infinite multiset of D elements; for simplicity of notation we also call this multiset A. Here we find it is even more difficult to transfer the structure of D to $\mathcal{S}$.

First, suppose D is totally ordered *and finite*. Unfortunately, even in this restricted case, the next example shows that $\ll$ is not necessarily even a partial order.

Example 4.2: Let D be the ordered set $\{f, u, t\}$, which might be truth values in a simulation of some three-valued logic. Let A and B be countably infinite relations of the form $p(X, Y)$ where X is a list and $Y \in D$. Define $A_i = \{p(X, i) \in A\}$ for i ranging over D, with a similar definition for B_i. Assume the following cardinalities:

$$|A_f| = \infty, \ |A_u| = 0, \ |A_t| = \infty; \qquad |B_f| = \infty, \ |B_u| = 1, \ |B_t| = \infty;$$

Then $A \ll B$ (μ_{AB} maps one f-tuple to the u-tuple), and $B \ll A$ (μ_{BA} maps the u-tuple to one t-tuple). $\square$

The problem above was that an infinite number of elements had the same value in the ordered domain D that $\ll$ was based upon. We can try requiring relations of $\mathcal{S}$ to satisfy a functional dependency on D; that is, each element of D appears at most once in any relation. In this case, infinite relations can arise only if D itself is infinite. The following example shows that $\ll$ is not necessarily a partial order, even if D is totally ordered and compact, and the functional dependency is satisfied.

Example 4.3: Let D be the reals in the closed interval $[0, 3]$. Define unary relations A and B to be countable subsets of D as follows:

$$A = \{x \mid (0 < x < 1 + \sqrt{2}) \ \& \ x \text{ is rational}\}$$
$$B = \{y \mid (0 < y < 1 + \sqrt{2}) \ \& \ \sqrt{2}\, y \text{ is rational}\}$$

Then $A \ll B$ based on this μ_{AB}:

$$\mu_{AB}(x) = \left\{ \begin{array}{ll} \sqrt{2}\, x & (0 < x < 1) \\ \sqrt{2}(x + 1)/2 & (1 \le x < 1 + \sqrt{2}) \end{array} \right\}$$

Clearly, $\sqrt{2}\mu_{AB}(x)$ is rational whenever x is, and all elements of B are mapped into. Finally, $x < \mu_{AB}(x)$.

Construction of μ_{BA} to demonstrate $B \ll A$ is more involved, and will only be sketched (see Figure 2). The function is piecewise linear, with an infinite number of pieces, and monotonically increases from 0 to $(1 + \sqrt{2})$. Segment 0 begins at $(0,0)$ and has slope $\sqrt{2}$. Let $L_i(x)$ denote the linear function that defines segment i, for $i \ge 1$. L_i has slope $\sqrt{2}/2^i$. The y-intercept $(L_i(0))$ is chosen to be rational and to satisfy:

$$(1 + \sqrt{2}) < L_i(1 + \sqrt{2}) < L_{i-1}(1 + \sqrt{2})$$

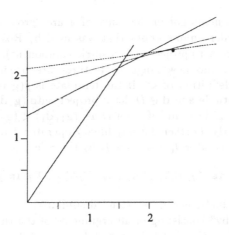

Fig. 2. Segments 0 through 3 in construction of μ_{BA} for Example 4.3.

Further, the sequence is chosen so that the intersection points of L_i and L_{i+1} converge monotonically to $((1 + \sqrt{2}), (1 + \sqrt{2}))$. All these constraints can be satisfied due to the density of the rationals. The lower envelope of $\{L_i\}$ is μ_{BA}. It is easy to show that each element of A (being rational) has an inverse image in each L_i that is of the form $\sqrt{2}\,r$, where r is rational. The maximum of these inverse images occurs at some finite i, and is in B. Therefore μ_{BA} is surjective (onto). The other requirements (injective and extensive) are obvious from construction. $\square$

4.3 More Structured Infinite Subsets

Although, $\ll$ behaves badly on general cases of infinite subsets, there is a more promising version that is based on restricting the mapping μ. Here we have the relational template S and the projection function π, per Definitions 3.2 and 3.3. Let us require that $\mu(t)$ cannot change the values of certain components of tuple t that are disjoint from the range of π (i.e., "projected out"); we shall call these the *group-by components*. Tuples related by $\ll$ must both be in a single partition based upon the group-by components.

The idea is that the group-by components may partition the infinite subset into infinitely many partitions, each of which is finite. Some techniques for reasoning about when this occurs have been developed [RBS87, EMHJ93].

Example 4.4: If π projects onto the third component and the first component is specified as "group-by", then $\mu(p(a, c, 1)) = p(a, d, 2)$ is permitted but $\mu(p(a, c, 1)) = p(b, c, 2)$ is not. This essentially partitions the $<$ relation into independent relations according to the group-by components. Effectively, "$1 <$ 2" is refined into "$p(a, \_, 1) < p(a, \_, 2)$, but $p(a, \_, 1) \not< p(b, \_, 2)$", where "$\_$" denotes anonymous variables. $\square$

When *all* components not in the range of π are "group-by", this approach gives the partial order among *atoms* that was used by Ross and Sagiv [RS92] (they further require π to project onto a single component).

We observe that no new language features are needed to express this refinement in the definition of $\ll$. If the template is $p(\mathbf{g}, \mathbf{e}, \mathbf{d})$, where $\mathbf{g} \in G$ is the group-by subtuple and $\mathbf{d} \in D$, let π project onto $(\mathbf{g}, \mathbf{d})$. We can define $<$ on the domain $G \times D$ in terms of $<$ on D as: $(\mathbf{g}_1, \mathbf{d}_1) < (\mathbf{g}_2, \mathbf{d}_2)$, if and only if $\mathbf{g}_1 = \mathbf{g}_2$ and $\mathbf{d}_1 < \mathbf{d}_2$. Further, for any binary operator f on D, we can define the corresponding operator f_{GD} on $G \times D$ by the rule

$$(X_G, X_D) \text{ is } f_{GD}((X_G, Y_D), (X_G, Z_D)) \leftarrow X_d \text{ is } f(Y_D, Z_D)$$

Other interpreted functions can be extended similarly.

With a "group-by" consisting of all arguments of the tuple except those in D, where D is finite, the bad behavior of Example 4.2 cannot occur, as the projection of a single partition must be a finite subset of D, not a multiset. However, when D is infinite the behavior of Example 4.3 can still occur.

Now let us consider S to consist of subsets of S that are possibly infinite, but such that each partition (having tuples that agree on the group-by components) is finite. (Continuing Example 4.4, a finite number of tuples in any one subset have a in component 1, a finite number have b, etc.) Then, Theorem 4.3 applies to each partition (and so do the negative connotations of the remarks and examples following that theorem).

Ross and Sagiv defined *interpretations* to be relations in which each partition had a *single* tuple. Domain D was required to be a complete lattice and they were able to conclude that the set of all interpretations was also a complete lattice. We are studying weaker assumptions.

4.4 Unequal Cardinalities

Another well-known concept of order among sets and multisets is inclusion ($\subseteq$). To obtain a more informative partial order we can combine $\subseteq$ with $\ll$.

Definition 4.3: We say that subset (or multiset) $A \sqsubset B$ if $A \subset B$ or there exists a C such that $A \ll C \subseteq B$. $\square$

Lemma 4.4: There exists C such that $A \ll C \subseteq B$ if and only if there exists E such that $A \subseteq E \ll B$.

Proof: (If) Let $C = \mu_{EB}(A)$.

(Only if) Assume w.l.o.g. that A and C are disjoint (or use identity throughout on common elements, see Lemma 4.1). Let $E = (A - B) \oplus \mu_{AC}(A \cap B) \oplus (B - C)$, where $\oplus$ denotes disjoint union. Let μ_{EB} be μ_{AC} on $(A - B)$ and the identity elsewhere. ∎

It is easy to see that $\sqsubset$ is transitive, so it defines a partial order whenever $\ll$ does.

Now suppose $\ll$ defines a lattice with $\sqcup$ and $\sqcap$ as join and meet, respectively, where S consists of the finite subsets (or finite multisets) of S. By Theorem 4.3, part (c), $<$ must be a total order. We can construct a least upper bound (binary) operator $lub_\sqsubseteq$ and a greatest lower bound (binary) operator $glb_\sqsubseteq$ for $\sqsubseteq$ as follows.

Definition 4.4: For two finite subsets A and B of totally ordered domain D, assume w.l.o.g. $|A| = m \leq |B|$. Let C_m consist of the m largest elements of B. Set

$$lub_\sqsubseteq(A, B) \stackrel{\text{def}}{=} (A \sqcup C_m) \cup (B - C_m)$$
$$glb_\sqsubseteq(A, B) \stackrel{\text{def}}{=} (A \sqcap C_m)$$

What might be nonintuitive here is that both $lub_\sqsubseteq$ and $glb_\sqsubseteq$ use the m largest elements of B. $\square$

Lemma 4.5: Let E and G be any two finite nonempty subsets of totally ordered domain D. Let E^- and G^- be those subsets with their respective maximum elements removed. If $E \sqsubseteq G$, then (a) $\max(E) < \max(G)$ and $E^- = G^-$, or (b) $\max(E) \leq \max(G)$ and $E^- \sqsubseteq G^-$.

Proof: Observe that $E \sqsubseteq G$ if and only if there is an F such that $\max(F) = \max(G)$ and $E \ll F \subseteq G$, by an argument similar to that in Lemma 4.2. By the same lemma, we can assume that $\mu_{EF}(\max(E)) = \max(F)$. The lemma follows. $\blacksquare$

Theorem 4.6: Operators $lub_\sqsubseteq$ and $glb_\sqsubseteq$ of Definition 4.4 are, respectively, the least upper bound and greatest lower bound for $\sqsubseteq$.

Proof: First, observe that $(A \sqcup C_m)$ and $(B - C_m)$ are disjoint, so their union is a disjoint union. This holds because, if $x \in (B - C_m)$ and $x \in (A \sqcup C_m)$, then $x \in A$ and there is some $y \in C_m$ such that $y \leq x$, which would contradict the definition of C_m.

The theorem now follows by induction on m. The inductive case is immediate from Lemma 4.5. The base case is $m = 1$, where $A = \{a\}$ and $C_1 = \{\max(B)\}$. If D is any upper bound of A and B, then $a \sqcup \max(B) \leq \max(D)$ and $B^- \sqsubseteq D^-$, where superscript "$-$" indicates removal of the maximum element. But $lub_\sqsubseteq(A, B) = \{a \sqcup \max(B)\} \cup B^-$, so $lub_\sqsubseteq(A, B) \sqsubseteq D$. The argument for $glb_\sqsubseteq(A, B)$ is similar. $\blacksquare$

Example 4.5: Let $A = \{3, 4\}$ and $B = \{1, 2, 5\}$. Then C_2 of Definition 4.4 is $\{2, 5\}$. Therefore, $glb_\sqsubseteq(A, B) = \{2, 4\}$ (call this E) and $lub_\sqsubseteq(A, B) = \{1, 3, 5\}$ (call this D). Now $D_2 = \{3, 5\}$, so $glb_\sqsubseteq(A, D) = \{3, 4\}$. Also, $lub_\sqsubseteq(E, B) = (E \sqcup C_2) \cup 1 = \{1, 2, 5\}$. $\square$

In many optimization applications we want $<$ and $\sqsubseteq$ to express preference: the second argument is preferable to the first. In minimization problems, the *first* argument of $<$ is preferable. However, the *second* argument of $\sqsubseteq$ is still preferable, intuitively, because it is always better to have more items to choose among, no matter what your criterion of preference among items is. In this case, $\sqsubseteq$ is not the appropriate combination.

To avoid confusion, we stay with the convention that the second argument is preferable, and define a new relation between relations called $\succ$. We use $>$ and $\gg$ as the transposes of $<$ and $\ll$.

Definition 4.5: We say that subset (or multiset) $A \succ B$ if $A \subset B$ or there exists a C such that $A \gg C \subseteq B$. The relation $\prec$ is the transpose of $\succ$.

For two finite subsets A and B of totally ordered domain D, assume w.l.o.g. $|A| = m \leq |B|$. Let C_m consist of the m smallest elements of B. Set

$$lub_\succ (A, B) \overset{\text{def}}{=} (A \sqcup C_m)$$
$$glb_\succ (A, B) \overset{\text{def}}{=} (A \sqcap C_m) \cup (B - C_m)$$

Note that both $lub_\succ$ and $glb_\succ$ use the m smallest elements of B.

An *upper bound* of A and B w.r.t. $\succ$ is a set C such that $C \succ A$ and $C \succ B$. If in addition, $D \succeq C$ holds for every upper bound D, then C is the *least upper bound*. The definitions of *lower bound* and *greatest lower bound* are analogous. □

It is important to remember that $A superset B$ implies $B \succ A$, and B is the least upper bound of A and B w.r.t. $\succ$. That is, the dual lattice of $\subset$ is used in connection with $\succ$. Properties of $\succ$ are analogous to $\sqsubset$, and are summarized below.

Lemma 4.7: There exists C such that $A \gg C \subseteq B$ if and only if there exists E such that $A \subseteq E \gg B$.

Proof: Same as Lemma 4.4. ∎

Lemma 4.8: Let E and G be any two finite nonempty subsets of totally ordered domain D. Let E^- and G^- be those subsets with their respective minimum elements removed. If $E \succ G$, then (a) $\min(E) > \min(G)$ and $E^- = G^-$, or (b) $\min(E) \geq \min(G)$ and $E^- \succ G^-$.

Proof: Similar to Lemma 4.5. ∎

Theorem 4.9: Operators $lub_\succ$ and $glb_\succ$ of Definition 4.5 are, respectively, the least upper bound and greatest lower bound for $\succ$.

Proof: Similar to Theorem 4.6; the argument for $glb_\succ$ is analogous to that for $lub_\sqsubset$. ∎

To summarize, if the underlying domain D has a partial order $<$, then we can use that to define partial orders $\sqsubset$ and $\succ$ on finite multisets that are stronger than $\subset$. If $<$ is a total order, then $\ll$ defines a lattice, and $\sqsubset$ and $\succ$ also define lattices. In this case, the ordered presentation of finite subsets (or multisets) makes the computation of the lattice operators straightforward and efficient.

4.5 Completion of Finite-Set Lattices

To ensure that a monotonic operator on a domain S has a least fixpoint, known methods require that all chains (totally ordered subsets) of S have a least upper bound (among other requirements). The general conditions under which $\sqsubseteq$ defines a lattice do not ensure this stronger property.

To begin with, infinite chains of singleton sets may exist. If the underlying domain is the rationals, the sequence may converge to an irrational. Therefore, in the underlying domain D over which sets are formed chains must be closed under upper bounds.

The other problem is that there may be no bound on the cardinality of elements in a chain of finite sets. To solve that problem, we may add one "infinite" element to each group-by partition of S. This infinite element is essentially the cross product of all domains not part of the group-by arguments. Least upper bounds of arbitrary partitions are defined by disjoint union. This ensures that monotonic operators on the extended S have least upper bounds.

5 Monotonicity

This section examines the monotonicity properties of $\sqsubseteq$, the partial order on relations (or multisets) developed in the previous section.

5.1 Monotonicity of Aggregation

Let f be the binary (associative, commutative) operator underlying the simple aggregate $\mathbf{f}$. Recall that f is *monotonic* (w.r.t. $<$) if $a \le b$ implies that $f(a, c) \le f(b, c)$, that is, f is monotonic in each argument. Now, a trivial induction shows:

Lemma 5.1: If f is monotonic w.r.t. $<$, then $\mathbf{f}$ on the domain of finite subsets of S is monotonic w.r.t. $\ll$. ∎

Ross and Sagiv called an aggregate *k-monotonic* when it is monotonic with respect to $\ll$ [RS92]. Here we see that the property is simply inherited from the underlying operator.

While $\sqsubseteq$ permits more subsets to be compared than does $\ll$, Lemma 5.1 does not extend to $\sqsubseteq$. For example, $+$ is monotonic, and $\{1\} \sqsubseteq \{-1, 1\}$, so $\sum$ is not monotonic w.r.t. $\sqsubseteq$ on domains with negative numbers.

A stronger condition on the underlying operator allows us to conclude that the aggregate is monotonic w.r.t. $\sqsubseteq$.

Lemma 5.2: Let f be monotonic w.r.t. $<$.
  (a) If $a \le f(a, b)$ for all a and b, then $\mathbf{f}$ on the domain of finite subsets of S is monotonic w.r.t. $\sqsubseteq$.
  (b) If $a \ge f(a, b)$ for all a and b, then $\mathbf{f}$ on the domain of finite subsets of S is monotonic w.r.t. $\succ$. ∎

Ross and Sagiv give a table of common aggregate functions that are monotonic by the above test on a variety of domains; their table considers only domains that are complete lattices, and permits aggregates to be applied to infinite sets [RS92]. Our goal is to establish a framework for establishing properties of user-defined aggregates that are not built into the language.

Corollary 5.3: Let domain D be a lattice and let **max** and **min** be the aggregates corresponding to $\sqcup$ and $\sqcap$.
(a) **max** and **min** are monotonic w.r.t $\ll$;
(b) **max** is monotonic w.r.t $\sqsubseteq$;
(c) **min** is monotonic w.r.t $\succ$. ∎

Recall that **max** is defined for $\emptyset$ if and only if the lattice D has a bottom element; **min**($\emptyset$) is defined if and only if there is a top element. It is not necessary that D be a complete lattice. For example, D could be the rationals in $[0, 1]$. However, as mentioned earlier, the rationals are not closed under upper bounds, so monotonic operators on finite sets of rationals may not have a least upper bound. Therefore, rationals will be a useful domain only in restricted situations.

5.2 Monotonicity of Immediate Consequences

For purposes of having a natural semantics, we would like the program's immediate consequence operator to be monotonic with respect to some appropriate structure over relations. For Horn programs, $\subset$ suffices, but as shown by Example 1.1, this appears to be too weak for programs with aggregates. We shall see that there are severe difficulties with making the immediate consequence operator monotonic w.r.t. $\sqsubseteq$.

Evaluation of the immediate consequence operator involves evaluating rule bodies, given relations for there subgoals. The evaluation uses relation algebra operators product, selection, projection and union (join is expressed by product and selection). These are all monotonic w.r.t $\sqsubseteq$. Of course, negation would not be monotonic, but let us consider just rules without negation.

Lemma 5.4: Product ($\times$) and and *disjoint* union ($\oplus$) are monotonic w.r.t. $\sqsubseteq$ and $\succ$.

Proof: The mapping for the first operand does not interfere with the mapping for the second. That is, if $A \sqsubseteq B$, define μ as the sum of μ_{AB} and μ_{CC} to show that $A \times C \sqsubseteq B \times C$, and $A \oplus C \sqsubseteq B \oplus C$, etc. ∎

The next example shows that projection, selection and union operations are not (necessarily) monotonic w.r.t. $\sqsubseteq$. Similar examples apply to $\succ$.

Example 5.1: Let several relations be denoted by

$$A_q = \left\{ \begin{array}{c} (a, 0) \\ (d, 3) \end{array} \right\} \qquad A_r = \left\{ \begin{array}{c} (a, 1) \\ (b, 3) \end{array} \right\}$$

$$B_q = \left\{ \begin{array}{c} (a, 2) \\ (d, 5) \end{array} \right\} \qquad B_r = \left\{ \begin{array}{c} (a, 2) \\ (b, 4) \end{array} \right\}$$

Here we note that the relations satisfy a functional dependency from the first to the second column, the latter being ordered by $<$. We see that $A_q \sqsubseteq B_q$ and $A_r \sqsubseteq B_r$.

However, $(A_q \cup A_r) \not\sqsubseteq (B_q \cup B_r)$ because the latter has only 3 tuples. Merging of duplicates also can make projection nonmonotonic: Let $C_q = \{(a,3),(d,3)\}$. Then $A_q \sqsubseteq C_q$, but $\pi_2(A_q) \not\sqsubseteq \pi_2(C_q)$.

Representing equi-join on second columns by a product and selection, we get:

$$\sigma_{2=2}(A_q \times A_r) = \{(d,3,b,3)\}$$
$$\sigma_{2=2}(B_q \times B_r) = \{(a,2,a,2)\}$$

and $\{(d,3,b,3)\} \not\sqsubseteq \{(a,2,a,2)\}$.

The built-in relations $=$, $\neq$, as well as order relations $<$, $>$, can be viewed as filters, or as unary operators on (at least) binary relations, whose output is a subset of the input relation. Let us call the unary operators eq, ne, lt, gt. They are monotonic w.r.t. $\subseteq$. However, they are not necessarily monotonic w.r.t $\sqsubseteq$: $eq(\{(1,1)\}) = \{(1,1)\}$ and $\{(1,1)\} \sqsubseteq \{(1,2)\}$, but $eq(\{(1,2)\}) = \emptyset$. Similar examples exist for the other filters. $\square$

From these examples we see that the immediate consequences operator will be monotonic w.r.t. $\sqsubseteq$ only in special cases. From the fact that nonmonotonicity can arise even though a functional dependency holds on the column with the ordered domain, we see that this FD restriction, assumed by Ross and Sagiv [RS92], does not ensure monotonicity. We would like to develop some tools for detecting when monotonicity is present.

There is considerable flexibility in defining $\sqsubseteq$ for each relation of a program, in that $<$ can be applied on various subsets of arguments, and defined in various ways on the same domain. As mentioned earlier, gcd and lcm can play the roles of *meet* and *join* for a lattice. Also, the dual of the lattice associated with $\sqsubseteq$ can be used leading to $\succ$.

For monotonicity of immediate consequences to be checked, the user will have to specify how partial or total orders are defined on each relation. Quite possibly one notion of order will lead to a monotonic immediate consequences operator while another will not. To incorporate this declaration into the programming language, we propose a construct similar to the aggregate expression:

$$\mathtt{order}(\mathtt{join}(f), \mathtt{meet}(g), \mathit{less}, \mathtt{groupby}([\mathit{group}]), t \mid p(\mathit{group}, \mathit{vars}, t))$$

This specifies that $\sqsubseteq$ for relation p is to be based on the domain of t with operators f, g and (total) order predicate *less*. Tuples are grouped by *group*, and only tuples in the same partition may be comparable. The remaining *vars* are immaterial: tuples in the same partition that differ on *vars* are still be comparable. If *less* defines only a partial order, the declaration begins with "partialorder". If *less* does not define a lattice, join(f) and meet(g) are omitted. If the intended partial order is $\succ$, the declaration begins with "minorder".

For monotonicity checking, we shall examine one strongly connected component (or maximal mutually recursive set) of predicates at a time. Following

Ross and Sagiv, we shall be quite happy if the immediate consequences operator is monotonic in the predicates of the current SCC with the relations of lower SCCs regarded as constants [RS92]. Then possibly a stratified model can be defined by iterated least fixpoints.

Even this limited ambition is doomed to failure in most cases. The problem is the nonmonotonicity of union and projection, which occur in most nontrivial programs. Union is required to combine conclusions from two rules for the same predicate. Ross and Sagiv point out that union can be forced to be disjoint union by tagging tuples according to the rule that derived them. This may or may not be an acceptable modification to the program. In any event, these tags are extra arguments that will usually need to be projected out in other rules. Projection remains as the nonmonotonic bugaboo.

We shall lower our expectations still further. If no aggregation occurs within the current SCC, we shall give it the normal Horn-clause semantics, regarding predicates in lower SCCs as fixed, or "EDB". If aggregation does occur, we shall attempt to rewrite the rules of the current SCC through unfolding, so that projection and union are "buried" within aggregation. The goal is to split the SCC so that some predicates are no longer interdependent. The hope is that aggregation "blurs" enough details so that monotonicity is restored in the new SCC that is "lowest", and that predicates that were eliminated from this SCC by unfolding are either nonrecursive, or are amenable to similar rewriting. An example makes this process clear.

Example 5.2: Let us consider a shortest paths program that cannot be handled by Ross and Sagiv because it fails their functional dependency requirement.

$$cp(X, Y, D) \leftarrow e(X, Y, D).$$
$$cp(X, Y, D) \leftarrow sp(X, I, E) \ \& \ sp(I, Y, F) \ \& \ D \ \text{is} \ E + F.$$
$$sp(X, Y, G) \leftarrow G \ \text{is} \ \min(D \mid cp(X, Y, D)).$$

Read cp as "candidate path" and sp as "shortest path". Relation e specifies a finite set of directed edges with lengths. The intended order is $\succ$ with the first two arguments as "group-by".

Even if we tag cp tuples to show which rule derived them, this program will fail the Ross-Sagiv FD test in view of the possible graph $e(a, a, 1), e(a, b, 1)$. We will inevitably derive $cp(a, b, 1)$ and $cp(a, b, 2)$.

To split the SCC of cp and sp, we "or" the rule bodies for cp and substitute this formula into the aggregate:

$$sp(X, Y, G) \leftarrow G \ \text{is} \ \min\{D \mid (e(X, Y, D) \ \& \ I = Y \ \& \ E = 0 \ \& \ F = 0)$$
$$\vee(sp(X, I, E) \ \& \ sp(I, Y, F) \ \& \ D \ \text{is} \ E + F)\}.$$

It can be shown that, if $sp(X, I, E)$ "gets smaller" w.r.t. $\succ$, then $sp(X, Y, G)$ either remains unchanged or "gets smaller" in the same sense. The same holds for $sp(I, Y, F)$. Thus the immediate consequence operator is monotonic on the new SCC consisting of sp only.

After computing a relation for sp, it will be held constant while the now nonrecursive cp is evaluated. (Very likely cp is not referenced elsewhere in the program, and this evaluation can be optimized away.) □

6 Conclusion and Future Work

We have established the basic properties for a stronger partial order than $\subseteq$ on finite subsets. However, this relation has several negative properties that need to be overcome before it provides a clear semantics. We showed that it can be used to give a stratified least fixpoint semantics to at least one program that is not handled by Ross and Sagiv [RS92]. Our principal motivation was to remove the restriction that the immediate consequence operator must satisfy a functional dependency (their cost consistency assumption). Whether this assumption is satisfied by a program is undecidable, and many sensible programs are known not to satisfy it; in fact, ad hoc "jury-rigging" was necessary in several of their examples to ensure the cost consistency assumption was met. In future work we plan to study the class of programs that have a stratified semantics in this scheme, and to develop tools for testing or verifying whether a program is in this class. The appendix gives some starting observations along these lines.

Acknowledgements

Discussions with Phokion Kolaitis were helpful. This research was partially supported by NSF grants CCR-89-58590 and IRI-9102513.

References

[BRSS92] C. Beeri, R. Ramakrishnan, D. Srivastava, and S. Sudarshan. The valid model semantics for logic programs. In *ACM Symposium on Principles of Database Systems*, 1992.

[BS81] S. Burris and H. P. Sankappanavar. *A Course in Universal Algebra*. Springer-Verlag, New York, 1981.

[BTBW92] V. Breazu-Tannen, P. Buneman, and L. Wong. Naturally embedded query languages. In *Int'l Conf. on Database Theory*, 1992.

[EMHJ93] M. Escobar-Molano, R. Hull, and D. Jacobs. Safety and translation of calculus queries with scalar functions. In *ACM Symposium on Principles of Database Systems*, 1993.

[GGZ91] G. Ganguly, S. Greco, and C. Zaniolo. Minimum and maximum predicates in logic programs. In *ACM Symposium on Principles of Database Systems*, pages 154–163, 1991.

[KS91] D. B. Kemp and P. J. Stuckey. Semantics of logic programs with aggregates. In *International Logic Programming Symposium*, pages 387–401, 1991.

[RBS87] R. Ramakrishnan, F. Bancilhon, and A. Silberschatz. Safety of recursive horn clauses with infinite relations. In *ACM Symposium on Principles of Database Systems*, 1987.

[RS92]   K. A. Ross and Y. Sagiv. Monotonic aggregation in deductive databases. In *ACM Symposium on Principles of Database Systems*, 1992.

[SR91]   S. Sudarshan and R. Ramakrishnan. Aggregation and relevance in deductive databases. In *Seventeenth International Conference on Very Large Data Bases*, pages 501–511, 1991.

[SS84]   D. Stemple and T. Sheard. Specification and verification of abstract database types. In *ACM Symposium on Principles of Database Systems*, pages 248–257, 1984.

[SS91]   T. Sheard and D. Stemple. Automatic verification of database transaction safety. *ACM Transactions on Database Systems*, 14(3):322–368, 1991.

[VG92]   A. Van Gelder. The well-founded semantics of aggregation. In *ACM Symposium on Principles of Database Systems*, 1992.

[Won93]   L. Wong. Normal forms and conservative prpoperties for query languages over collection types. In *ACM Symposium on Principles of Database Systems*, 1993.

Appendix A   Tools for Monotonicity Inference

The main idea is view relations as "graphs" of functions. Certain arguments are designated as the output; the remaining arguments are input. Because tuples may agree on input and disagree on output, we make a nested relation of all output arguments, and call that the output value for a particular input tuple. The output of a *set* of input tuples is the union of their individual outputs.

Example A.1: If the second argument of $<$ is regarded as "input" to a function, $lt(Y)$, then the output would be

$$lt(Y) = \{X \in D \mid X < Y\}$$

and for finite set $A \subseteq D$,

$$lt(A) = \cup_{Y \in A}\{X \in D \mid X < Y\} = \{X \in D \mid X < \sqcup(A)\}$$

Clearly, lt is monotonic w.r.t. $\sqsubseteq$ as well as $\subseteq$.

If the first argument of $<$ is regarded as "input", the resulting function, say $gt(X)$, is antimonotonic, or monotonically decreasing. The property of antimonotonicity can be useful, as the composition of two antimonotonic functions is monotonic.

Predicate $=$ can be regarded as the identity function with either its first or second argument as input. Clearly, it is monotonic w.r.t. $\sqsubseteq$. $\square$

The technique now is to rewrite rule bodies with each subgoal having distinct variables in its arguments (so their conjunction represents a product, rather than a join), and to add the necessary equalities to restore the original constraints of the rule body. Then design an input/output scheme that obeys these constraints:

1. Multiple rule bodies for the same predicate, or parts of one rule body connected by "or" ($\vee$) are combined with union. We assume all rules for a predicate are combined into one in this way.

2. Variables in the group-by positions of the head of the rule, and variables equal to them, are regarded as constants, neither input nor output.
3. Other arguments of subgoals of the current SCC are outputs of those subgoals, but they comprise the input to the immediate consequences operator acting on this rule.
4. Relations that evaluate their arguments with interpreted functions must have input variables in such functional expressions; that is, the argument of an interpreted function cannot be an output.
5. Each output variable is produced exactly once, but may be used in several input arguments; the subgoals can be ordered so that all input are consumed later than they are produced. Explicit projections must be shown when a subgoal outputs tuples and a consumer does not use the full tuple; some projections are not monotonic w.r.t. $\sqsubseteq$, so they need to be verified.
6. All non-group-by arguments of the head of the rule are produced as output by some subgoal, and these comprise the output of the immediate consequences operator acting on this rule. $\square$

Thus the input/output scheme essentially defines the immediate consequences operator as the composition of functions. If these functions are all monotonic (or certain pairs are antimonotonic, and their composition is monotonic), then so is the immediate consequences operator.

The Differential Fixpoint Operator with Subsumption

Gerhard Köstler[1],   Werner Kießling[1],   Helmut Thöne[2],   Ulrich Güntzer[2]

[1] Lehrstuhl für Informatik II, Universität Augsburg,
Universitätsstr.2, D-86135 Augsburg, Germany,
{ koestler | wk }@informatik.tu-muenchen.de
[2] Wilhelm-Schickard-Institut, Universität Tübingen,
Sand 13, D-72076 Tübingen, Germany
{ thoene | guentzer }@informatik.uni-tuebingen.de

Abstract. Declarative languages for deductive and object-oriented databases require some high-level mechanism for specifying semantic control knowledge. This paper proposes user-supplied subsumption information as a paradigm to specify desired, prefered or useful deductions at the meta level. For this purpose we augment logic programming by subsumption relations and succeed to extend the classical theorems for least models, fixpoints and bottom-up evaluation accordingly. Moreover, we provide a differential fixpoint operator for efficient query evaluation. This operator discards subsumed tuples on the fly. We also exemplify the ease of use of this programming methodology. In particular, we demonstrate how heuristic AI search procedures can be integrated into logic programming in this way.

1   Introduction

Declarative query languages have achieved a significant increase in programmer productivity by shifting the burden of finding efficient query execution plans to the query optimizer. In restricted cases like SQL for relational systems this approach has been quite successful. However, one easily can imagine applications where additional user-supplied control hints might expedite query evaluation even further. For computationally complete query languages in deductive or object-oriented databases such meta-information is even mandatory. For example, NP-complete programs specified in DATALOG^{func} + ^{neg} need extra semantic heuristic control knowledge to achieve tractability. In the spirit of Kowalski's celebrated equation "algorithm = logic + control" this paper proposes a mechanism for entering such semantic control knowledge into the query optimization process. In a first step here we concentrate on semantic knowledge in the form of *subsumption information*, which seems to be ubiquitous in applications. To mention just a few areas where subsumption has played an important role we refer to applications in theorem proving ([11]), in taxonomic reasoning ([2]), in semantic query optimization ([3]), in terminological logic ([18]), or in type subsumption ([1]). Subsumption also appears in probabilistic reasoning. E.g., given two conditional probability statements $0.70 \leq p(B|A) \leq 0.90$ and

$0.75 \leq p(B|A) \leq 0.85$, the second one clearly subsumes the first one. This is used in the DUCK-calculus for probabilistic uncertainty ([6], [9], [7]).

In this paper we propose a declarative mechanism for augmenting deductive and object-oriented query languages by *meta-programming with subsumption*. Our approach will maintain the strict separation of logic and control. To this purpose we have to extend logic programming theory accordingly. However, to emphasize, this paper is not targeted only for the theoretically inclined, but instead aims at practical realizability. The rest of this paper is organized as follows. Section 2 is concerned with the necessary extensions to fixpoint theory and model theory with a subsumption ordering $\sqsubseteq$. Based on a powerful fixpoint result for least $\sqsubseteq$-models, section 3 provides an efficient differential fixpoint operator. After these technical foundations we give several sample applications of our meta-programming methodology in section 4. We reconsider some aspects of aggregate queries in deductive databases and discuss one problem which may arise from object identity in object-oriented query languages. As a separate area of interest we show how intelligent heuristic search algorithms from AI can be incorporated into deductive databases using our approach. The paper ends with a conclusion and perspective of this contribution. Proofs omitted in this version can be found in the full version [12].

2 Fixpoints, Models and Subsumption

2.1 Fixpoints with Subsumption

Fixpoint theory applied in logic programming is based on the notion of equality. It uses the powerset lattice of the Herbrand base that is partially ordered by set inclusion. In this section we introduce a fixpoint iteration not based on equality but on any partial ordering of a basic set (e.g. the Herbrand base). This ordering can capture the application semantics that one element is prefered over another one, rendering the latter superfluous because of subsumption. Our new fixpoint iteration will solve the task of computing only the relevant part of the conventional fixpoint of a function, i.e. only those elements that are maximal under the given ordering.

Definition and Lemma 1 Basic Notions. *Let $\langle M, \sqsubseteq \rangle$ be a partial ordering, i.e. $\sqsubseteq$ is a binary, reflexive, antisymmetrical and transitive relation called* subsumption ordering. *Let $X, Y \in 2^M$.*

a) The binary relation $\sqsubseteq$ on 2^M is defined as
$X \sqsubseteq Y : \iff (\forall x \in X)(\exists y \in Y) x \sqsubseteq y$. *It is a pre-order, i.e. reflexive and transitive.*[3]

b) The binary relation $\sim$ on 2^M is defined as
$X \sim Y : \iff X \sqsubseteq Y \wedge Y \sqsubseteq X$. *It is an equivalence relation.*

---

[3] $\sqsubseteq$ on 2^M is sometimes called Hoare's ordering.

c) Let $[X], [Y] \in 2^M/\sim$ *denote equivalence classes. The relation* $\sqsubseteq$ *on* 2^M *is extended to* $2^M/\sim$ *by* $[X] \sqsubseteq [Y] : \iff X \sqsubseteq Y$. *It is a partial ordering and well-defined due to 1 b).* □

By the definition above the subsumption ordering given on a not necessarily finite set M is extended to a partial ordering on the equivalence classes of the powerset of M induced by $\sim$.

$X \sqsubseteq Y$ captures application semantics that X *is subsumed by* Y in the sense that Y is preferable over X, or Y is more useful than X, or Y is more intended than X, or Y is better than X, etc.

Example 1. Consider the following directed, cyclic graph:

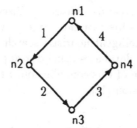

The edges are labeled by non-negative integers. The transitive closure including the costs of all paths are computed by the following logic program.

$$p(X, Y, C) \leftarrow e(X, Y, C).$$
$$p(X, Y, C) \leftarrow p(X, Z, C1), e(Z, Y, C2), C = C1 + C2.$$

Note that this program has an infinite fixpoint.
The basic set M in our example is the Herbrand base

$$B_P = \{p(X, Y, C) \mid X, Y \in \{n1, n2, n3, n4\}, C \in \mathbb{N}\} \ .$$

It is partially ordered by

$$p(X1, Y1, C1) \sqsubseteq p(X2, Y2, C2) : \iff X1 = X2 \wedge Y1 = Y2 \wedge C1 \geq C2 \ .$$

For this ordering extended to 2^{B_P} we have e.g.

$$\{p(n1, n3, 13), p(n1, n3, 23)\} \sqsubseteq \{p(n1, n3, 3)\} \ .$$

Moreover, e.g. we have $\{p(n1, n3, 13), p(n1, n3, 3)\} \sim \{p(n1, n3, 3)\}$.

We concentrate on special subsets of M called *reduced* sets and introduce an operation doing this reduction. For technical reasons we also introduce the notion of *expanded* sets. Important for defining reduced sets is the notion of chains maximal w.r.t. set inclusion. Let e.g. $M := \{a, b, c, d\}$ be partially ordered by

$a \sqsubseteq b \sqsubseteq c$ and $a \sqsubseteq d$. Then the maximal chains are $\{a, b, c\}$ and $\{a, d\}$.[4]

Definition 2 Reduced and expanded sets. Let $X \in 2^M$ and let C be the set of maximal chains of X w.r.t. set inclusion.

a) The *reduced version* of X, denoted by $\mathcal{R}(X)$, is defined as

$$\mathcal{R}(X) := \bigcup_{C \in \mathcal{C}} R_C \quad \text{where} \quad R_C := \begin{cases} \{m\} & \text{if } m = \max(C) \text{ exists} \\ C & \text{otherwise} \end{cases}$$

b) The *expanded version* of X, denoted by $\mathcal{E}(X)$, is defined as

$$\mathcal{E}(X) := \{y \in M \mid (\exists x \in X)\, y \sqsubseteq x\} \ .$$

c) $2^M_{\mathcal{R}} := \{\mathcal{R}(X) \mid X \in 2^M\}$ denotes the set of reduced sets. $\square$

Given $X \in 2^M$ the reduction $\mathcal{R}(X)$ has the following effect: maximal chains in X without maximum, as e.g. $C := \{1 - 1/n \mid n \in \mathbb{N}^+\}$ on $\langle \mathbb{R}, \leq \rangle$, are left unchanged. However, maximal chains with maximum are reduced to this maximum. Thus, for a finite set X, the reduced version $\mathcal{R}(X)$ consists of the maximal elements of X.
In our running example, we get e.g.

$$\mathcal{R}(\{p(n1, n3, 3), p(n1, n3, 13), p(n1, n3, 23), \ldots\}) = \{p(n1, n3, 3)\} \text{ and}$$

$$\mathcal{E}(\{p(n1, n3, 13)\}) = \{p(n1, n3, C) \mid C \geq 13\} \ .$$

Let now F be a mapping on 2^M, e.g. the immediate consequence operator $T_P(I) := \{A \in B_P \mid A \leftarrow B_1, \ldots, B_n$ is a ground instance of a rule in P, $\{B_1, \ldots, B_n\} \subseteq I\}$ of our sample logic program.

Definition 3 $\sqsubseteq$-monotonic functions. F is called $\sqsubseteq$-*monotonic* iff $X \sqsubseteq Y \Rightarrow F(X) \sqsubseteq F(Y)$. $\square$

It is easy to see that the T_P-operator of our sample program is $\sqsubseteq$-monotonic. Some elementary properties of reduced and expanded sets are stated in the following lemma.

Lemma 4. *Let $X, Y \in 2^M$, I be an index set, $\{X_i\}_{i \in I} \subseteq 2^M$ be a system of sets and $F: 2^M \rightarrow 2^M$ be a $\sqsubseteq$-monotonic mapping.*

a) $[X] = [\mathcal{R}(X)] = [\mathcal{E}(X)]$.
b) $X \sqsubseteq Y \Rightarrow \mathcal{R}(X) \sqsubseteq \mathcal{R}(Y)$ and $\mathcal{E}(X) \subseteq \mathcal{E}(Y)$.
c) $[\mathcal{R}(\bigcup_{i \in I} \mathcal{R}(X_i))] = [\mathcal{R}(\bigcup_{i \in I} X_i)]$.
d) $[\mathcal{R}(F(\mathcal{R}(X)))] = [\mathcal{R}(F(X))]$. $\square$

---

[4] More formally the maximal chains of a partially ordered set are the total ordered subsets that are maximal w.r.t. set inclusion. The fact that each element of M is contained in such a chain is guaranteed by maximal chain theorems of Hausdorf and Birkhoff.

As usual, fixpoint theory with subsumption is based on a complete lattice. The set of equivalence classes of reduced sets forms this lattice.

Lemma 5. $\langle 2_{\mathcal{R}}^M / \sim, \sqsubseteq \rangle$ *is a complete lattice with* $\mathrm{lub}\{[X_i]\}_{i \in I} = [\mathcal{R}(\bigcup_{i \in I} X_i)]$. *The top element is* $[\mathcal{R}(M)]$, *the bottom element is* $[\emptyset]$. $\square$

For each mapping $F : 2^M \to 2^M$ we introduce two associated new mappings.

Definition and Lemma 6. *Let* $F : 2^M \to 2^M$ *be a* $\sqsubseteq$*-monotonic mapping. Then the mappings* $F_{\mathcal{R}}$ *and* $F^\sim$ *defined as*
$$F_{\mathcal{R}} : 2^M \to 2^M, \qquad X \mapsto \mathcal{R}(F(X))$$
$$F^\sim : 2_{\mathcal{R}}^M / \sim \to 2_{\mathcal{R}}^M / \sim, \ [X] \mapsto [\mathcal{R}(F(X))] \ \ \text{are} \ \sqsubseteq\text{-monotonic, too.} \ \square$$

The $\sqsubseteq$-monotonicity of $F^\sim$ guarantees the existence of a least fixpoint.

Theorem 7 Existence of least fixpoint. *Let* $F : 2^M \to 2^M$ *be a* $\sqsubseteq$*-monotonic mapping. Then* $F^\sim$ *has a least fixpoint.* $\square$

Proof. Immediately by Lemma 5, Lemma 6 and the well-known fixpoint theorem of [23]. $\square$

For the rest of the paper let $F : 2^M \to 2^M$ be a $\sqsubseteq$-monotonic and $\subseteq$-continuous mapping. Then $F^\sim$ is $\sqsubseteq$-continuous, too, as defined by [14, p.27].

Lemma 8. $F^\sim$ *is* $\sqsubseteq$*-continuous.* $\square$

Since our sample program is definite (see [14]) the T_P-operator is $\subseteq$-continuous. Additionally T_P is $\sqsubseteq$-monotonic and therefore $\sqsubseteq$-continuous.
The following theorem relates fixpoint iteration of the functions F and $F^\sim$.

Theorem 9 Commutativity of LFP and $\mathcal{R}$. *Let* LFP$(F^\sim)$ *be the least fixpoint of* $F^\sim$ *and* LFP(F) *be the least fixpoint of* F^5. *Then*

a) LFP$(F^\sim) = F^\sim \uparrow \omega$.
b) $[\mathcal{R}(F \uparrow n)] = F^\sim \uparrow n = [F_{\mathcal{R}} \uparrow n]$ *for all* $n \in \omega$.
c) $[\mathcal{R}(\mathrm{LFP}(F))] = \mathrm{LFP}(F^\sim) = \mathrm{lub}\{[F_{\mathcal{R}} \uparrow n]\}_{n \in \omega}$. $\square$

Reducing the fixpoint of our sample program yields exactly the shortest paths. According to theorem 9 the same result can be achieved by reducing *on the fly*. An efficient method for this fixpoint iteration with subsumption is described in section 3.

Remark. For equality as subsumption ordering each set $X \in 2^M$ is already its reduced version and the equivalence classes consist of one element only. The functions F, $F_{\mathcal{R}}$ and $F^\sim$ coincide and the entire fixpoint of F is computed. Thus fixpoint iteration with set inclusion as partial ordering is just a special case of fixpoint iteration with subsumption. $\square$

---

[5] In this theorem we use the terminology of [14, §5].

2.2   Model Theory with Subsumption

Our next task is the adaptation of the model-theoretic interpretation of definite logic programs to programs with subsumption. To this purpose we introduce so-called $\sqsubseteq$-models which are closed under application of the T_P-operator w.r.t. the subsumption ordering $\sqsubseteq$. We will show the existence of a least $\sqsubseteq$-model and establish a connection to the fixpoint iteration with subsumption.

Let P be a definite program, let $\sqsubseteq$ be a subsumption ordering on the Herbrand base B_P of P, and assume that T_P is $\sqsubseteq$-monotonic.

Definition 10 $\sqsubseteq$-interpretation, $\sqsubseteq$-model. Let $[M] \in 2_{\mathcal{R}}^{B_P}/_{\sim}$.

a) $[M]$ is called a $\sqsubseteq$-*interpretation*.
b) $[M]$ is called $\sqsubseteq$-*model* iff $T_P(M) \sqsubseteq M$. $\square$

Note that the definition of $\sqsubseteq$-models is well-defined due to the $\sqsubseteq$-monotonicity of the T_P-operator. The intersection of all Herbrand models is known to be a Herbrand model. We can show a similar result for $\sqsubseteq$-models.

Definition and Lemma 11 Least $\sqsubseteq$-model. *Let $\mathcal{M}$ be the set of all $\sqsubseteq$-models. Then $M_{P,\sqsubseteq} := \mathrm{glb}(\mathcal{M})$ is a $\sqsubseteq$-model, called* least $\sqsubseteq$-*model.* $\square$

The p-atoms of the least $\sqsubseteq$-model of our sample program are

$$\begin{aligned}
\{&\mathsf{p}(n1, n2, 1), \mathsf{p}(n1, n3, 3), \mathsf{p}(n1, n4, 6), \mathsf{p}(n1, n1, 10), \\
&\mathsf{p}(n2, n3, 2), \mathsf{p}(n2, n4, 5), \mathsf{p}(n2, n1, 9), \mathsf{p}(n2, n2, 10), \\
&\mathsf{p}(n3, n4, 3), \mathsf{p}(n3, n1, 7), \mathsf{p}(n3, n2, 8), \mathsf{p}(n3, n3, 10), \\
&\mathsf{p}(n4, n1, 4), \mathsf{p}(n4, n2, 5), \mathsf{p}(n4, n3, 7), \mathsf{p}(n4, n4, 10)\} \ .
\end{aligned}$$

It is essential to link the least Herbrand model M_P of a program with the least fixpoint of the T_P-operator. We characterize the least $\sqsubseteq$-model as the least fixpoint of an iteration with subsumption and relate it with M_P.

Theorem 12 Fixpoint characterization of the least $\sqsubseteq$-model. *Let $\widetilde{T_P}$ be the mapping according to Def. 6. Then*

$$M_{P,\sqsubseteq} = \mathrm{LFP}(\widetilde{T_P}) = [\mathcal{R}(\mathrm{LFP}(T_P))] = [\mathcal{R}(M_P)] \ . \square$$

3   Differential Fixpoint Iteration with Subsumption

Now we introduce a new differential iteration scheme for bottom-up fixpoint evaluation called *delta-iteration with subsumption*. We restrict our attention to *finite* reduced sets and to functions $F: 2^M \to 2^M$ mapping *finite sets to finite sets*. According to the following lemma we can omit the equivalence class notation and use function $F_{\mathcal{R}}$ instead of $F^{\sim}$.

Lemma 13. *Let $X, Y \in 2_{\mathcal{R}}^M$ with $X \sim Y$ and X finite. Then $X = Y$.* $\square$

Due to the finiteness of all involved sets Theorem 9 b) can be simplified to:

Corollary 14. $\mathcal{R}(F \uparrow n) = F_{\mathcal{R}} \uparrow n$ for all $n \in \omega$. $\square$

The meaning of this corollary is that if the iteration with subsumption of function $F_{\mathcal{R}}$ terminates, then each maximal chain of the (not necessarily finite) fixpoint of the original mapping F has a maximum and exactly these maximal elements are computed by $F_{\mathcal{R}}$.

Delta-iteration with subsumption is based on two operations $\oplus$ and $\ominus$ on $2_{\mathcal{R}}^M$.

Definition 15. Let $X, Y \in 2_{\mathcal{R}}^M$ be finite, reduced subsets of M.

a) $X \oplus Y := \mathcal{R}(X \cup Y)$.
b) $X \ominus Y := X \setminus \mathcal{E}(Y) = \{x \in X \mid (\not\exists y \in Y)\, x \sqsubseteq y\}$. $\square$

The fixpoint iteration of $LFP(F^{\sim})$, as described in Theorem 9, can be implemented by a naive iteration scheme in a straightforward way. More efficient, however, is a differential iteration scheme, which we call *delta-iteration with subsumption*.[6]

Definition 16 Fixpoint-Iteration with subsumption. Let $F_{\mathcal{R}}$ be a mapping as defined above and let $\delta(S, \Delta) := F_{\mathcal{R}}(S \oplus \Delta) \ominus F_{\mathcal{R}}(S)$.

a) The *naive iteration scheme with subsumption* is defined as
initialization: $S_0 := \emptyset$;

iteration: $\qquad S_t \longrightarrow S_{t+1} := F_{\mathcal{R}}(S_t)$;
b) The *(semi-naive) delta-iteration scheme with subsumption* is defined as
initialization: $(T_0, \Delta_1) := (\emptyset, F_{\mathcal{R}}(\emptyset))$;

iteration: $\qquad (T_{t-1}, \Delta_t) \longrightarrow (T_t, \Delta_{t+1}) := (T_{t-1} \oplus \Delta_t, \delta(T_{t-1}, \Delta_t))$; $\square$

Theorem 17 Equivalence of naive and delta-iteration. *Let S_t, $t \geq 0$, be the sequence generated by naive iteration with subsumption and T_t, $t \geq 0$, be the sequence generated by delta-iteration with subsumption. Then*

a) $T_0 = S_0$ and $F_{\mathcal{R}}(T_{t-1}) = T_t = S_t$, $t \geq 1$.
b) $\Delta_t = S_t \ominus S_{t-1}$, $t \geq 1$. $\square$

Computing $\delta(S, \Delta)$ in the straightforward way is an extremely expensive operation and should be replaced by a more efficient differential expression. This is achieved by a so called *auxiliary function* $\mathrm{Aux}_{F_{\mathcal{R}}}(S, \Delta)$ with $\mathrm{Aux}_{F_{\mathcal{R}}}(S, \Delta) \ominus F_{\mathcal{R}}(S) = \delta(S, \Delta)$. The following lemma establishes a strong connection between auxiliary functions for F and $F_{\mathcal{R}}$.

Lemma 18 Auxiliary function for subsumption. *Let a mapping Aux_F on 2^M be an auxiliary function for F and $S, \Delta \in 2_{\mathcal{R}}^M$ finite sets such that $S \cap \Delta = \emptyset$. Then $\delta(S, \Delta) = \mathcal{R}(\mathrm{Aux}_F(S, \Delta)) \ominus F_{\mathcal{R}}(S)$.* $\square$

---

[6] For purpose of proof we adopt the formalism of [5].

In other words, any auxiliary function $\text{Aux}_F(S, \Delta)$ gained from formal differentiation by a standard semi-naive LFP-operator can be used directly for our subsumption filtering.

We result in a procedural formulation of the differential fixpoint operator with subsumption:

Delta_iterate_with_subsumption(F, $\sqsubseteq$):

$S := \emptyset;\ \Delta := \mathcal{R}(F(\emptyset));$

while $\Delta \neq \emptyset$ **do**

$\quad$ AUX $:= \mathcal{R}(\text{Aux}_F(S, \Delta));$

$\quad\quad S := S \oplus \Delta;\ \Delta := \text{AUX} \ominus S;$

end

---

4 Sample Applications

In this section we demonstrate how semantic information given as subsumption orderings can be used at the meta-level to control the computation of the desired part of the conventional fixpoint only.

4.1 Graph Traversal and Subsumption

We apply subsumption to graph traversal problems to demonstrate the usefulness of semantic subsumption information in this field.

Example 2. Reconsider the program of example 1 and assume that we are interested exactly in the shortest paths and that the graph would be acyclic.

The usual way of computing the shortest paths in an acyclic graph is through set grouping followed by minimum selection. In CORAL [19] or DECLARE [8] this could be achieved by adding the following rule to our sample program.

shortest_path(X, Y, min(<C>)) $\leftarrow$ p(X, Y, C).

Fixpoint iteration with subsumption achieves to obtain the same result in an efficient way. We only need to supply a subsumption ordering $\sqsubseteq$ on the p-atoms by specifying $\sqsubseteq$ as a *meta-rule*:

subsumed_by(p(X1, Y1, C1), p(X2, Y2, C2)) $\leftarrow$
$\quad$ X1 = X2, Y1 = Y2, C1 $\geq$ C2.

This meta-rule expresses that path p_1 between two given nodes is subsumed by a path p_2 iff the costs of p_1 are greater or equal than those of p_2. It defines a partial ordering $\sqsubseteq$ on the p-atoms. The T_P-operator of the given program is $\sqsubseteq$-monotonic. Delta-iteration with subsumption now yields only those paths in each iteration step that are still potential candidates for being shortest ones.

Severe safety problems may occur if the fixpoint of a program is infinite although the desired part is finite. In this case the naive method is not applicable at all. However, fixpoint iteration with subsumption can cope with this safety issue and derives the desired result.

Example 3. Consider a directed graph given by a relation
edge: E[start → node:X, end → node:Y] in O-Logic syntax and regard an O-Logic program proposed by Kifer and Wu [10] to compute the set of paths between nodes in the graph.[7]

    path: add(E, nil)[start ← X, end ← Y] ⇐
        edge: E[start → node:X, end → node:Y]
    path: add(E, P)[start ← X, end ← Y] ⇐
        edge: E[start → node:X, end → node:Z],
        path: P[start → node:Z, end → node:Y]

The object identifiers E and P represent an edge and a path object, respectively, and the object constructor add creates a new path object from a given one and an edge object. A query of the form **path**: P[start → a, end → b] ? would be answered by a set of atoms of the form

    path: add(e_1, add(e_2, ... add(e_k, nil) ...))[start → a, end → b] .

Assume that the graph is cyclic. Then object identity produces an infinite set of answers although we might only be interested in the set of paths without cycles. This set is obtained by fixpoint iteration with subsumption specifying the following subsumption ordering on the meta-level:

    subsumed_by(**path**: P1[start → A1, end → B1],
                path: P2[start → A2, end → B2]) ←
      A1 = A2, B1 = B2, subsequence (P2, P1).

The subsumption ordering $\sqsubseteq$ defined by this meta-rule is a partial ordering and the O-Logic program is $\sqsubseteq$-monotonic. Thus the result of fixpoint iteration with subsumption is the set of all paths without cycles.

---

[7] Note that the basic set M in this example is the set of O-Logic terms.

4.2 Heuristic Search and Subsumption

In this section we investigate how to incorporate bidirectional heuristic search into logic programming. This will be achieved by combining fixpoint iteration with subsumption and *sloppy delta-iteration* as introduced by [5], [21].

Example 4. Let edge(m, n, c) be the edges of a graph labeled by non-negative costs $c(m, n)$ with two distinguished nodes s and t. The task is to find the optimal path between s and t.
We perform bidirectional search on this graph by running two A*-algorithms [17], one starting at s and heading forward for t and another one starting at t and heading backward for s as shown by Fig. 1. Those nodes of the search

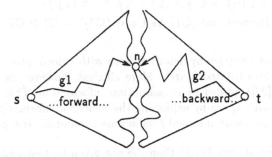

Fig. 1. Forward and backward search tree

trees already covered by the opposite direction — like n in Fig. 1 — are pruned yielding an algorithm similar to BS* [13]. The heuristic functions h_f and h_b used by the A*-algorithms to estimate the costs h_f^* and h_b^* of the optimal path from a node to the corresponding goal node should underestimate these costs, i.e. $h \leq h^*$ and satisfy the monotone restriction (see [17]), i.e. $h(m) \leq h(n) + c(m, n)$ for each node m and its successor nodes n.
We introduce two relations f_reached(n, g1, f1) for the forward and b_reached(n, g2, f2) for the backward search tree where n is a node, g_i are the costs of the currently optimal path from the corresponding start node to n and f_i are the heuristic estimates $h_i(n)$ plus g_i. A relation best_costs represents the costs of the currently best path between s and t. The search is described by the following logic program with interpreted functions h_f and h_b:

> f_reached(s, 0, h_f(s)).
> f_reached(M, G, F)   ← f_reached(N, G1, _), edge(N, M, C),
>   G = G1 + C, F = G + h_f(M).
> b_reached(t, 0, h_b(t)).
> b_reached(N, G, F)   ← b_reached(M, G2, _), edge(N, M, C),
>   G = G2 + C, F = G + h_b(N).

```
best_costs(∞).
best_costs(Q)              ← f_reached(N, G1, _), b_reached(N, G2, _),
                             Q = G1 + G2.
```

The following meta-rules specify tuples with non-optimal g-values and q-values, which can be discarded.

subsumed_by(f_reached(M1, G1, F1), f_reached(M2, G2, F2)) ←
   M1 = M2, ((G1 > G2) or (G1 = G2, F1 = F2)).
subsumed_by(b_reached(N1, G1, F1), b_reached(N2, G2, F2)) ←
   N1 = N2, ((G1 > G2) or (G1 = G2, F1 = F2)).
subsumed_by(best_costs(Q1), best_costs(Q2)) ← Q1 ≥ Q2.

Evaluation of this program by delta-iteration with subsumption corresponds to an uninformed breadth-first search. More efficient, however, is a *sloppy delta-iteration* ([21], [22]) guided by subsumption information. This scheme is able to reduce the search space by exploiting the heuristic information given by the f-value. Only tuples with minimal f-values are expanded. New generated tuples

a) whose f-values are not better than the one given by best_costs or
b) whose parent node is already reached by the opposite search direction

can be pruned.[8] E.g. all successors of node n of Fig. 1 can be pruned in the forward search tree because n is already reached in the backward direction. The (simplified) *sloppy delta-iteration with subsumption* for the immediate consequence operators $T_{P/f}$ and $T_{P/b}$ of the predicates f_reached and b_reached is shown in Fig. 2: S represents the tuples already expanded, Σ represents the sets of tuples yet unexpanded. AUX is the set of new tuples generated by an iteration step. The mapping Nice selects the tuples to be expanded in the next iteration step. Rest removes these tuples from Σ. Prune performs the pruning of the search tree as described above. Nice, Rest and Prune themselves can be specified by the following meta-logic program with a subsumption meta-meta-rule to select tuples with minimal f-values. We demonstrate this for the forward search only.[9] Relation f_sigma represents Σ_f, relation f_aux represents AUX_f. b_reached and best_costs correspond to the currently accumulated relations and can be treated as base relations at this meta-level.

---

[8] According to [17], if the monotone restriction is satisfied, a node selected for expansion by an A*-algorithm has already achieved its smallest g-value. Therefore its successors can be ignored if the node is already reached by the opposite search direction.

[9] Note that subsumption can be extended to negated non-recursive programs as the following one.

$$S_f := \emptyset; \ \Sigma_f := \mathcal{R}(T_{P/_f}(\emptyset)); \qquad\qquad S_b := \emptyset; \ \Sigma_b := \mathcal{R}(T_{P/_b}(\emptyset));$$

while $\Sigma_f \neq \emptyset$ **and** $\Sigma_b \neq \emptyset$ **do**

$\quad \Delta_f := \mathrm{Nice}_f(\Sigma_f); \ \Sigma_f := \mathrm{Rest}_f(\Sigma_f); \quad \Delta_b := \mathrm{Nice}_b(\Sigma_b); \ \Sigma_b := \mathrm{Rest}_b(\Sigma_b);$

$\quad \mathrm{AUX}_f := \mathcal{R}(\mathrm{Aux}_{T_{P/_f}}(S_f, \Delta_f)); \quad \mathrm{AUX}_b := \mathcal{R}(\mathrm{Aux}_{T_{P/_b}}(S_b, \Delta_b));$

$\quad S_f := S_f \oplus \Delta_f; \qquad\qquad\qquad\quad S_b := S_b \oplus \Delta_b;$

$\quad \mathrm{AUX}_f := \mathrm{AUX}_f \ominus (S_f \oplus \Sigma_f); \quad \mathrm{AUX}_b := \mathrm{AUX}_b \ominus (S_b \oplus \Sigma_b);$

$\quad \Sigma_f := \Sigma_f \oplus \mathrm{Prune}_f(\mathrm{AUX}_f); \quad \Sigma_b := \Sigma_b \oplus \mathrm{Prune}_b(\mathrm{AUX}_b);$

end

Fig. 2. Simplified sloppy delta-iteration with subsumption

f_nice(M, G, F) ← f_sigma(M, G, F).

f_rest(M, G, F) ← f_sigma(M, G, F), not f_nice(M, G, F).

f_prune(M, G, F) ← f_aux(M, G, F), not f_ignored(M, G, F).

f_ignored(M, G, F) ← f_aux(M, G, F), (edge(N, M, _), b_reached(N, _, _) or

$\qquad\qquad\qquad\qquad\qquad\qquad$ best_costs(Q), F ≥ Q).

subsumed_by(f_nice(M1, G1, F1), f_nice(M2, G2, F2)) ←

$\quad$ M1 = M2, ((F1 > F2) or (F1 = F2, G1 = G2)).

Note that the definition of f_ignored exactly corresponds to the pruning methods described above. Additional pruning methods as proposed by [13] could be integrated the same way by high-level meta-programming.

5 Related Work

As mentioned in the beginning subsumption plays an important role in various fields of computer science. However, we are not aware that subsumption has been investigated in deductive databases or logic programming to this extent. We can do a comparison for the special field of semantics of aggregates in logic programming, where quite a lot of work has been done to integrate such second-order constructs into logic progams (see e.g. [16], [4], [24], [20]). [20] introduce partial orderings on the Herbrand base by distinguishing a cost attribute in the atoms where the partially ordered domain of this cost attribute is required to form a complete lattice. Interpretations are forbidden to include two atoms differing only on the cost attribute. While there are some technical similarities, our objectives are different. Our general goal is to integrate user-supplied semantic knowledge into programs not in a syntactical way but by specifying meta-rules with clean semantics. CORAL [19] offers semantic annotations for predicates to control the evaluation of the program. Special subsumption orderings can be modeled by the @aggregate_selection annotation. A similar iteration scheme as delta-iteration with subsumption was proposed by [15] for a special subsumption ordering on non-ground facts: a non-ground fact a is subsumed by a non-ground fact b if $a = b\sigma$ for a substitution σ.

6 Conclusion

In this paper we described how user-supplied semantics in the form of subsumption information can be integrated into declarative query languages at a high level as meta-rules. By extending classical fixpoint and model theory we defined a formal semantics for these meta-rules and introduced an efficient differential fixpoint operator to evaluate logic programs with subsumption by discarding subsumed tuples on the fly. The feasibility of this approach was demonstrated by several sample applications. Especially we described a heuristic bidirectional search procedure known from AI using fixpoint iteration with subsumption. We plan to provide a library of other well-known AI search procedures, like e.g. AO*, using this methodology. This would enable the construction of more intelligent query optimizers for DOOD-systems. Moreover, developing a full syntactic framework for meta-programming by subsumption is a useful task to be done.

Acknowledgment: We thank Heribert Schütz for many fruitful discussions.

References

1. Hassan Ait-Kaci. Type subsumption as a model of computation. In *Proc. Int'l. Workshop on Expert Database Systems.* Benjamin Cummings Company, 1985.
2. A. Artale, F. Cesarini, and G. Soda. Introducing knowledge representation techniques in database models. In *Trends in Artificial Intelligence, Proc. 2nd Congr. of the Italian Association for Art. Int.*, pages 375–384, Palermo, Italy, Oct. 1991. Springer-Verlag.
3. U. S. Chakravarthy, J. Grant, and J. Minker. Logic-based approach to semantic query optimization. *ACM Trans. on Database Systems*, 15(2):162–207, 1990.
4. Sumit Ganguly, Sergio Greco, and Carlo Zaniolo. Minimum and maximum predicates in logic programming. In *Proc. ACM SIGACT-SIGMOD Symp. on Principles of Database Systems*, pages 154–163, Denver, CO, May 1991. ACM Press.
5. Ulrich Güntzer, Werner Kießling, and Rudolf Bayer. On the evaluation of recursion in (deductive) database systems by efficient differential fixpoint iteration. In *Proc. IEEE Conf. on Data Eng.*, pages 120–129, Los Angeles, CA, Feb. 1987.
6. Ulrich Güntzer, Werner Kießling, and Helmut Thöne. New directions for uncertainty reasoning in deductive databases. In *Proc. ACM SIGMOD Conf.*, pages 178–187, Denver, CO, May 1991.
7. Werner Kießling, Gerhard Köstler, and Ulrich Güntzer. Fixpoint evaluation with subsumption for probabilistic uncertainty. In *GI-Conference on Datenbanksysteme in Büro, Technik und Wissenschaft*, pages 316–333, Braunschweig, Germany, Mar. 1993. Springer-Verlag.

8. Werner Kießling, Helmut Schmidt, Werner Strauß, and Gerhard Dünzinger. DE-CLARE and SDS: Early efforts to commercialize deductive database technology. *VLDB Journal*, 1993. submitted.

9. Werner Kießling, Helmut Thöne, and Ulrich Güntzer. Database support for problematic knowledge. In *Proc. Int'l. Conf. on Extending Database Technology*, pages 421–436, Vienna, Austria, 1992.

10. Michael Kifer and James Wu. A logic for object-oriented logic programming. In *Proc. ACM SIGACT-SIGMOD Symp. on Principles of Database Systems*, pages 379–393, Philadelphia, PA, Mar. 1989.

11. Byeong Man Kim and Jung Wan Cho. A new subsumption method in the connection graph proof procedure. *Theoretical Computer Science*, 2:283–309, 1992.

12. Gerhard Köstler, Werner Kießling, Helmut Thöne, and Ulrich Güntzer. The differential fixpoint operator with subsumption. Technical Report TUM-I9315, Fakultät für Informatik, Technische Universität München, Apr. 1993.

13. James B. H. Kwa. BS*: An admissible bidirectional staged heuristic search algorithm. *Artificial Intelligence*, 38:95–109, 1989.

14. J.W. Lloyd. *Foundations of Logic Programming*. Springer-Verlag, Berlin, second edition, 1987.

15. Michael J. Maher and Raghu Ramakrishnan. Déjà vu in fixpoints of logic programs. In *North American Conference on Logic Programming*, pages 963–980, Cleveland, OH, 1989.

16. Inderpal Singh Mumick, Hamid Pirahesh, and Raghu Ramakrishnan. The magic of duplicates and aggregates. In *Proc. Int'l. Conf. on Very Large Data Bases*, pages 264–277, Brisbane, Australia, Aug. 1990.

17. Nils J. Nilson. *Principles of Artificial Intelligence*. Tioga Publishing Company, Palo Alto, CA, 1980.

18. Peter F. Patel-Schneider. A four-valued semantics for terminological logics. *Artificial Intelligence*, 38(3):318–352, 1989.

19. Raghu Ramakrishnan, Divesh Srivastava, and S. Sudarshan. CORAL—Control, Relations and Logic. In *Proc. Int'l. Conf. on Very Large Data Bases*, pages 238–250, Vancouver, BC, Canada, 1992.

20. Kenneth Ross and Yehoshua Sagiv. Monotonic aggregation in deductive databases. In *Proc. ACM SIGACT-SIGMOD Symp. on Principles of Database Systems*, pages 114–126, San Diego, CA, Jun. 1992. ACM Press.

21. Helmut Schmidt, Werner Kießling, Ulrich Güntzer, and Rudolf Bayer. Compiling exploratory and goal-directed deduction into sloppy delta-iteration. In *Proceedings of the Symposium on Logic Programming*, pages 233–243, San Francisco, CA, Sep. 1987.

22. Helmut Schmidt, Werner Kießling, Ulrich Güntzer, and Rudolf Bayer. DBA*: Solving combinatorial problems with deductive databases. In *Proc. GI/SI-Conference on Datenbanksysteme in Büro, Technik und Wissenschaft*, pages 196–215, Zürich, Switzerland, 1989.

23. A. Tarski. A lattice-theoretical fixpoint theorem and its applications. *Pacific J. Math.*, 5:285–309, 1955.

24. L. Vieille, P. Bayer, and V. Küchenhoff. An overview of the EKS-V1 system. Technical report, ECRC, Munich, Germany, Aug. 1991.

Datalog with non-deterministic choice computes *NDB-PTIME*

Luca Corciulo[2], Fosca Giannotti[1], and Dino Pedreschi[2]

[1] CNUCE–CNR, Via S. Maria 36, 56125 Pisa, Italy
e_mail: fosca@cnuce.cnr.it
[2] Dipartimento di Informatica, Univ. Pisa, Corso Italia 40, 56125 Pisa, Italy
e_mail: pedre@di.unipi.it

Abstract. This paper addresses the issue of non deterministic extensions of logic database languages. After providing a quick overview of the main proposals in the literature, we concentrate on the analysis of the *dynamic choice* construct from the point of view of the expressive power. We show how such construct is capable of expressing several interesting deterministic and non deterministic problems, such as forms of negation, and ordering. We then prove that Datalog augmented with the dynamic choice expresses exactly the non deterministic time-polynomial queries. We thus obtain a complete characterization of the expressiveness of the dynamic choice, and conversely achieve a characterization of the class of queries *NDB-PTIME* by means of a simple, declarative and efficiently implementable language.

1 Introduction

Two main classes of logic database languages have been proposed in the literature. One is the class of *FO* database languages, based on the relational calculus, i.e. on the first-order logic interpretation of the relational data model. The other one is the class of Datalog languages, a subset of the logic programming paradigm which supports and extends the basic mechanisms of the relational data model.

Indeed, both classes served as the basis of several extensions, aimed at enhancing the expressive power of the relational data model. For instance, the set of queries expressed by the relational algebra is strictly included in that of the *fixpoint queries* (the transitive closure is a fixpoint query which is inexpressible in the relational algebra), whereas it is well known that every fixpoint query can be expressed in *FO* extended with an inflationary fixpoint operator, or equivalently in Datalog extended with inflationary negation.

Unfortunately, the expressiveness achieved by this kind of deterministic extensions of logic database languages is not satisfactory. Surprisingly enough, no known deterministic logic language can express all deterministic queries computable in polynomial time (e.g., no known deterministic language expresses the *parity* query [7]).

From a pragmatical viewpoint, a clear need for non-determinism is also emerging from applications. The *all-answers* paradigm for query execution exacerbates the need for special constructs to deal with situations where the user is not interested in all the possible answers. This problem is exemplified by the following situation: a new student must be given one (and only one) advisor. If the application of various qualification criteria fails to narrow the search to a single qualified professor, then an arbitrary choice from the eligible faculty will have to be made and recorded.

Moreover, it has been pointed out in the literature that non deterministic operators provide an explicit means for controlling the computation. Several examples illustrating this point are given in this paper. Explicit control mechanisms are often essential in real applications, in order to achieve efficient implementations—a natural parallel arises here with the technique of meta-interpreters in other programming paradigms. From this perspective, a tight connection exists between non-determinism and ordered databases [16, 6]. It is worth observing that languages over ordered domains are more expressive than those over unordered domains [16].

These are the motivations underlying the introduction of non deterministic mechanisms in logic database languages. A first batch of proposals is due to Abiteboul and Vianu [3, 4, 5, 6], based on a non-deterministic *witness* construct for the fixpoint extensions of FO, and a non-deterministic operational semantics for Datalog¬ (*à la production systems*), giving rise to the class of $N\_Datalog$ languages. The expressive power of these classes of proposals has been thoroughly studied by the same authors, who show how certain non deterministic languages compute exactly the non deterministic time-polynomial queries (NDB-$PTIME$) and the non deterministic space-polynomial queries (NDB-$PSPACE$). On the other hand, these languages are described only in operational terms, without any declarative semantics, thus spoiling the logic nature of the original languages. Moreover, the proposals based on the witness construct are hardly amenable to efficient implementations, and therefore they do not suggest any construct which may be adopted in real database languages.

An alternative stream of proposals was started by Krishnamurthy and Naqvi [18], and later refined by Saccà and Zaniolo [20] and Giannotti, Pedreschi, Saccà and Zaniolo [13]. These proposals are based on a non deterministic *choice* construct for Datalog, which, in all cases, was designed on the basis of a declarative semantics—*choice models* in [18], and *stable models* in [20, 13]. Moreover, the choice construct can be efficiently implemented, and it is actually adopted in the logic database language $\mathcal{LDL}$ [19, 8]. On the other hand, an expressiveness characterization for these proposals is lacking, which allows to compare the choice construct with the other proposals.

The figure highlights the taxonomy of non deterministic logic languages. The dashed boxes indicate the mentioned two classes of proposals.

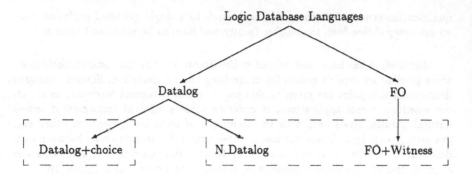

This work is aimed at bridging the existing gap between the two classes of proposals, by presenting an expressiveness characterization of Datalog augmented with one of the choice mechanisms, namely the *dynamic choice* construct introduced in [13]. This study is conducted both pragmatically, on the basis of examples, and formally, on the basis of known expressiveness results. In particular, we show how the dynamic choice construct is a powerful means for controlling the fixpoint computation, in order to express relevant problems such as computing the complement of a relation, or computing an arbitrary ordering of a relation.

Finally, in the main result of this paper, we show that Datalog with dynamic choice expresses exactly the non deterministic time-polynomial queries, a complexity class known as *NDB-PTIME*. The result is achieved by showing how the dynamic choice allows us to express the control needed to execute N_Datalog¬ programs over ordered domains—a language which is known to capture *NDB-PTIME*. The relevance of this result is clear: Datalog with the dynamic choice has the same (high) expressiveness of languages which:

- are considerably more complex—Datalog with dynamic choice is negation-less,
- are lacking a declarative semantics—Datalog with dynamic choice is sound (although not complete) w.r.t. stable model semantics,
- are hard to be efficiently implemented—Datalog with dynamic choice is the kernel of $\mathcal{LDL}$.

As a conclusion, a simple, declarative characterization of *NDB-PTIME* is achieved by means of the dynamic choice extension of pure Datalog: such a language, although remarkably simple, is then capable of expressing all non deterministic time-polynomial queries and, therefore, all *deterministic* ones.

The plan of the paper follows. In Section 2 a short survey of the main proposals of non deterministic extensions of logic database languages is provided. Particular emphasis is placed on Datalog extended with the dynamic choice construct. Section 3 and 4 show how to compute negation and ordering using the dynamic choice. Section 5 is devoted to illustrating the emulation of N_Datalog¬ , a language which embodies a form of nondeterminism typical of rule-based systems. Section 6 presents the main result, namely that Datalog with dynamic choice captures the complexity class *NDB-PTIME*; we then draw some conclusions, and briefly illustrate future research directions.

1.1 Preliminaries

We assume that the reader is familiar with the relational data model and associated algebra, the relational calculus (i.e. the *first-order queries*, denoted *FO*), and Datalog [17, 21, 9, 11]. In the extended language Datalog¬ the use of negation in the bodies of clauses (or *rules*) is also allowed; in another extension of Datalog, N_Datalog(¬), we shall also admit the presence of multiple atoms in the heads of clauses. Datalog(¬) (and N_Datalog(¬)) rules obey the *safety* constraint, i.e. each variable occurring in the head of a clause also occurs in a positive literal in the body. The operational semantics of Datalog, in the usual deterministic case, consists of evaluating "in parallel" all applicable instantiations of the rules. This is formalized using the consequences operator T_P associated to a Datalog program P, which is a map over (Herbrand) interpretations defined as follows:

$$T_P(I) = \{ A \mid A \leftarrow B_1, \ldots, B_n \in ground(P) \text{ and } I \models B_1 \wedge \ldots \wedge B_n \}$$

The least model M_P of program P can then be computed as the limit (union) of the finite powers of T_P starting from the empty interpretation, denoted $T_P \uparrow \omega$ [1]:

$$T_P \uparrow 0 = \emptyset$$
$$T_P \uparrow (i+1) = T_P(T_P \uparrow i), \quad \text{for } i > 0$$
$$T_P \uparrow \omega = \bigcup_{i \geq 0} T_P \uparrow i.$$

In the case of Datalog¬, this simple operational semantics can be slightly modified to realize to the so-called *inflationary negation*: the required change is to accumulate the powers of T_P as follows:

$$T_P \uparrow (i+1) = T_P \uparrow i \cup T_P(T_P \uparrow i), \quad \text{for } i > 0.$$

This fixpoint procedure is therefore monotonic only w.r.t. the positive knowledge, and computes, in general, non-minimal models.

The fixpoint (iterative) extensions of *FO* consist of augmenting the relational calculus with fixpoint operators, which provide recursion. The *inflationary fixpoint* operator IFP is defined as follows. Let Φ be a *FO* formula where the n-ary relation symbol S occurs. Then $IFP(\Phi, S)$ denotes an n-ary relation, whose extension is the limit of the sequence $J_0, \ldots, J_k, \ldots$, defined as follows (given a database extension, or instance, I):

- $J_0 = I(S)$, where $I(S)$ denotes the extension of S in I, and
- $J_{k+1} = J_k \cup \Phi(I[J_k/S])$, for $k > 0$, where $\Phi(I[J_k/S])$ denotes the evaluation of the query Φ on I where S is assigned to J_k.

Notice that IFP converges in polynomial time on all input databases. A *partial* fixpoint operator PFP can also be defined, which gives raise to possibly infinite computations: PFP is not considered in this paper. The first-order logic augmented with IFP is called *inflationary fixpoint logic* and is denoted by $FO+IFP$. The queries computed by $FO+IFP$ are the so-called *fixpoint queries*, for which various equivalent definitions exist in the literature [7, 15].

Close connections exist between the fixpoint FO extensions and the Datalog extensions [6]: Datalog¬ expresses exactly the fixpoint queries, i.e. it is equivalent to $FO+IFP$. This implies that Datalog¬ is strictly more expressive than Datalog with stratified negation, as the latter is known to be strictly included in $FO+IFP$.

Finally, the complexity measures are functions of the size of the input database. For Turing Machine complexity class C there is a corresponding complexity class of (non-deterministic) queries *(N)DB-C*. In particular, the class of (non-deterministic) database queries that can be computed by a (non-deterministic) Turing Machine in polynomial time is denoted by *(N)DB-PTIME*. It is conjectured that no deterministic language exists, capable of expressing all queries in *DB-PTIME*.

2 Non-deterministic extensions of logic database languages

In this section, several mechanisms for dealing with non-determinism in logic database languages are briefly surveyed. In particular, we present a non-deterministic construct for the fixpoint extensions of FO, a non-deterministic operational semantics for Datalog¬ (*à la production systems*), and a non-deterministic mechanism for pure Datalog. The first two classes of proposals are due to Abiteboul and Vianu [3, 5, 6], whereas the third class of proposals is due to Krishnamurthy and Naqvi [18] and Giannotti, Pedreschi, Saccà and Zaniolo [20, 13].

2.1 The witness operator

A non-deterministic extension of FO is achieved by introducing the so-called *witness* operator [3, 5, 6]. Informally, given a formula (query) $\Phi(X)$, the witness operator W_X applied to $\Phi(X)$ chooses an arbitrary X that makes Φ true. The extension of the inflationary fixpoint logic $FO+IFP$ with the witness operator is denoted by $FO+IFP+W$.

Let us define more precisely the semantics of W. Notice that, in presence of non-determinism, we have a *set* of possible interpretations for a given formula in $FO+IFP+W$, or equivalently, a set of possible sets of answers to a given query. Consider a formula $W_X(\Phi(X,Y))$, where Y is the vector of variables other than X that occur free in Φ. Then I is an interpretation of $W_X(\Phi(X,Y))$ iff, for some interpretation J of $\Phi(X,Y)$ such that $I \subseteq J$:

  – for each Y such that $\langle X, Y \rangle \in J$ for some X, there is a *unique* X_Y such that $\langle X_Y, Y \rangle \in I$.

Intuitively, one "witness" X_Y is arbitrarily chosen for each Y satisfying $\exists X.\Phi(X,Y)$. Alternatively, the meaning of W can be also described in terms of functional dependencies: the interpretation I is a maximal subset of J satisfying the functional dependency $Y \rightarrow X$.

Example 1. Consider a binary relation E such that $E(P, S)$ represents the fact that professor P is an eligible advisor of student S. Then the formula $W_P(E(P, S))$ realizes the non-deterministic query of assigning exactly one advisor to each student.

It should be noted that the witness operator is added to FO independently from the fixpoint operator. Accordingly, the fixpoint computation and the non-deterministic choices do not interfere, in the sense the non-deterministic choices of the witnesses are performed w.r.t. the current fixpoint approximation, without memory of the choices that were previously operated. In other words, the witness operator performs choices *locally* to a given step of the fixpoint computation.

From the viewpoint of the expressive power, the relevance of $FO+IFP+W$ is due to the following result of Abiteboul and Vianu [5]:

Theorem 1. *A query is in NDB-PTIME iff it is expressed in $FO+IFP+W$.* □

An analogous result of the same authors shows that $FO+PFP+W$, i.e. FO augmented with the partial fixpoint and the witness operators, expresses exactly the queries in *NDB-PSPACE*.

2.2 N_Datalog

A natural form of non-determinism for Datalog programs is obtained by relaxing the constraint that, at each step of the fixpoint computation, all applicable rules are executed. Thus, a non-deterministic operational semantics is obtained by firing, at each step, one (instance of an) applicable rule, based on a non-deterministic choice. This policy directly mirrors the behavior of rule-based (or production) systems, such as OPS5 or KEE. Notice that such an execution policy yields the same results as the usual Datalog fixpoint computation in absence of negation, as, in pure Datalog, an applicable rule remains applicable as new facts are inferred.

Abiteboul and Vianu [5] proposed to adopt the mentioned non-deterministic operational semantics for *N_Datalog¬*, an extension of pure Datalog which allows the use of negation in clause bodies, and multiple atoms in clause heads. Thus, an N_Datalog program is a finite set of rules of the form

$$A_1, \ldots, A_k \leftarrow L_1, \ldots, L_m$$

$(k \geq 1, m \geq 0)$, where each A_j is an atom and each L_i is a literal, i.e. an atom or its negation.

To define the non-deterministic operational semantics, the notion of *immediate successor* of an interpretation (i.e. a set of facts) I w.r.t. a rule r is introduced. Let $r' = A_1, \ldots, A_k \leftarrow L_1, \ldots, L_m$ be a ground instance of an N_Datalog¬ rule r such that all literals $L_1, \ldots, L_m$ in the body of r' are true in I. Then the interpretation $J = I \cup \{A_1, \ldots, A_k\}$ is called an *immediate successor of I using r*. We then define a computation of an N_Datalog¬ program P starting from an initial interpretation I_0 as a maximal sequence $I_0, \ldots, I_n, \ldots$ of interpretations such that, for $k \geq 0$, I_{k+1} is an immediate successor of I_k using some rule from P.

It is worth observing that such an operational semantics is inflationary, and thus computations are always finite (and, again, convergent in polynomial time).

Example 2. The following Datalog¬ program takes as input a binary relation G representing an undirected graph g, and computes (into the relation DG) an arbitrary orientation of g:

$$DG(X, Y) \leftarrow G(X, Y), G(Y, X), \neg DG(Y, X).$$

From the viewpoint of the expressive power, N_Datalog¬ is strictly included in *NDB-PTIME*. In fact, it is possible to show that such a language cannot express the query $P - \pi_1(Q)$, where P is a unary relation and Q a binary one. Thus, it is needed to extend N_Datalog¬ in order to capture all the queries in *NDB-PTIME*. Two possible approaches of remedying this problem are the following. One is allowing universal quantification in clause bodies: the resulting language is denoted N_Datalog¬∀. The second is violating the *data independence* principle, and allowing the use of *ordered* databases. In both cases we obtain languages that capture *NDB-PTIME*, and that are therefore equivalent to *FO+IFP+W*. This result is due to Abiteboul and Vianu [6].

Theorem 2. *A query is in NDB-PTIME iff it is expressed in N_Datalog¬∀ or, equivalently, in N_Datalog¬ over ordered databases.* □

An analogous result of the same authors shows that N_Datalog¬*, i.e. N_Datalog¬ augmented with negation in rule heads (interpreted as deletion of facts), expresses exactly the queries in *NDB-PSPACE*.

2.3 The family of choice operators

The proposals discussed in the previous sections 2.1 and 2.2 suffer from the lack of a declarative, model-theoretic semantics, which seriously compromises their logic connotation. Another approach was started by Krishnamurthy and Naqvi [18], and later refined by Saccà and Zaniolo [20] and Giannotti, Pedreschi, Saccà and Zaniolo [13]. The proposals described in this section are based on a non deterministic *choice* construct for Datalog, which, in all cases, was designed on the basis of a declarative semantics—*choice models* in [18], and *stable models* in [20, 13]. Moreover, the choice construct can be efficiently implemented, and it is actually adopted in the logic database language $\mathcal{LDL}$[19, 8]. On the other hand, an expressiveness characterization for these proposals is lacking, which allows to compare the choice construct with the previously discussed proposals. The rest of this section surveys the original proposal and two refinements, which improve from several viewpoints.

Static choice The choice construct was first proposed by Krishnamurthy and Naqvi in [18]. According to their proposal, special goals, of the form $choice((X), (Y))$, are allowed in Datalog rules to denote the functional dependency (FD) $X \rightarrow Y$. The meaning of such programs is defined by its *choice models*, as discussed next.

Example 3. Consider the following Datalog program with choice.

$a\_st(St, Crs) \leftarrow takes(St, Crs), choice((Crs), (St))$.
$takes(andy, engl)$.
$takes(ann, math)$.
$takes(mark, engl)$.
$takes(mark, math)$.

The choice goal in the first rule specifies that the a_st predicate symbol must associate exactly one student to each course. Thus the functional dependency $Crs \rightarrow St$ holds in the (choice model defining the) answer. Thus the above program has the following four choice models:

$M_1 = \{ a\_st(andy, engl), a\_st(ann, math)\} \cup X$,
$M_2 = \{ a\_st(mark, engl), a\_st(mark, math)\} \cup X$,
$M_3 = \{ a\_st(mark, engl), a\_st(ann, math)\} \cup X$,
$M_4 = \{ a\_st(andy, engl), a\_st(mark, math)\} \cup X$,

where X is the set of $takes$ facts.

A $choice$ $predicate$ is an atom of the form $choice((X), (Y))$, where X and Y are lists of variables (note that X can be empty). A rule having one or more choice predicates as goals is a $choice$ $rule$, while a rule without choice predicates is called a positive rule. Finally, a $choice$ $program$ is a program consisting of positive rules and choice rules.

The set of the choice models of a choice program formally defines its meaning. The main operation involved in the definition of a choice model is illustrated by the previous example. Basically, any choice model $M_1, ..., M_4$ can be constructed by first removing the choice goal from the rule and computing the resulting a_st facts. Then the basic operation of enforcing the FD constraints is performed, by selecting a maximal subset of the previous a_st facts that satisfies the FD $Crs \rightarrow St$ (there are four such subsets).

For the sake of simplicity, assume that P contain only one choice rule r, as follows:

$$r : A \leftarrow B(Z), choice((X), (Y)).$$

where $B(Z)$ denotes the conjunction of all the non-choice goals of r, and Z is the vector of variables occurring in the body of r (hence $Z \supseteq X \cup Y$.) The positive version of P, denoted by $PV(P)$, is the positive program obtained from P by eliminating all $choice$ goals. Let M_P be the least model of the positive program $PV(P)$, and consider the set C_P defined as follows:

$$C_P = \{ choice((x), (y)) \mid M_P \models B(z)\}$$

Consider next a maximal subset C'_P of C_P satisfying the FD $X \rightarrow Y$. With this preparation, a choice model of P is defined as the least model of the program $P \cup C'_P$.

Thus, computing with the static choice entails three stages of a bottom-up procedure. In the first stage, the saturation of $PV(P)$ is computed, ignoring choice goals. In the second stage, an extension of the choice predicates is computed by non-deterministically selecting a maximal subset of the corresponding query which satisfies the given FD. Finally, a new saturation is performed using the original program P together with the selected choice atoms, in order to propagate the effects of the operated choice.

The qualification *static* for this choice operator stems from the observation that the choice is operated once and forall, after a preliminary fixpoint computation. Because of its static nature, this form of choice cannot be safely used within recursive rules. As observed in [13], the choice models semantics fails when mixed with recursion, in the sense that the delivered results do not comply with any declarative reading. Moreover, the procedure for computing choice models is extremely inefficient, as operating the choices only after a general saturation phase is wasteful—a more efficient procedure should instead operate choices as soon as possible, in order to reduce the amount of work for future saturations. Finally, due to the impossibility of being adopted within recursion, the static choice has a limited expressive power. To remedy these drawbacks, some refinements of the static choice have been proposed, which are discussed next.

Model-theoretical choice An alternative approach to define a declarative semantics for the choice construct was proposed by Saccà and Zaniolo [20]. According to this proposal, programs with choice are transformed into programs with negation which exhibit a multiplicity of stable models. [3] Each stable model corresponds to an alternative set of answers for the original program. Following [20], therefore, given a choice program P, we introduce the *stable version* of P, denoted by $SV(P)$, defined as the program with negation obtained from P by the following two transformation steps:

1. Consider a choice rule of P, say

$$r : A \leftarrow B(Z), choice((X),(Y)).$$

where $B(Z)$ denotes the conjunction of all the non-choice goals of r, and Z is the vector of variables occurring in the body of r, and replace the body of r with the atom $chosen(Z)$:

$$r' : A \leftarrow chosen(Z).$$

2. add the new rule:

$$chosen(Z) \leftarrow B(Z), \neg diffChoice(Z).$$

3. add the new rule:

$$diffChoice(Z) \leftarrow chosen(Z'), Y \neq Y'.$$

where Z' is a list of variables obtained from Z by replacing variable Y by the fresh variable Y'.

---

[3] Stable models semantics is a concept originating from autoepistemic logic, which was applied to the study of negation in Horn clause languages by Gelfond and Lifschitz [12].

The transformation directly generalizes to FD involving vectors of variables, and to multiple choice goals. When the given program P is such that none of its choice rules is recursive, then P and its stable version are semantically equivalent in the sense that the set of choice models of P coincides with the set of stable models of $SV(P)$ on common predicate symbols [20].

Example 4. The following is the stable version of Example 3.

$a\_st(St, Crs) \leftarrow chosen(Crs, St).$
$chosen(Crs, St) \leftarrow takes(St, Crs), \neg diffChoice(Crs, St).$
$diffChoice(Crs, St) \leftarrow chosen(Crs, \overline{St}), St \neq \overline{St}.$
$takes(andy, engl).$
$takes(ann, math).$
$takes(mark, engl).$
$takes(mark, math).$

This programs admits four distinct stable models, corresponding to the four choice models of Example 3.

It should be remarked that, in choice programs, negation is only used to assign a declarative semantics to the choice construct. In other words, choice programs are *positive* Datalog programs augmented with choice goals.

This new characterization of choice overcomes the cited deficiencies of static choice of Krishnamurthy and Naqvi [18]. Indeed, the new formulation correctly supports the use of choice within recursive rules, avoiding the semantical anomalies of the static choice [13]. Moreover, it can be efficiently implemented by a straightforward fixpoint procedure which allows to interleave non-deterministic choices and ordinary rule applications in the bottom-up computation (the so-called *stable backtracking fixpoint* [20]). Nevertheless, the expressiveness of this form of choice can be considerably enhanced by adopting a particular instance of the cited fixpoint procedure.

Dynamic choice We now introduce a particular operational semantics for the choice construct, following the presentation of Giannotti, Pedreschi, Saccà and Zaniolo [13]. This operational semantics is an instance of the general bottom-up procedure of Saccà and Zaniolo [20] for computing stable models, and is obtained by adopting a particular policy of interleaving non-deterministic choices and the ordinary fixpoint computation. The resulting procedure is referred to as DCF for *dynamic choice fixpoint*, and the associated form of choice construct is referred to as *dynamic choice*.

The DCF procedure, and thus the dynamic choice construct, reflects the intuition that choices should be operated as soon as possible during the fixpoint computation. This design principle has two relevant consequences. First, a higher degree of efficiency is achieved, as early choices have the effect of reducing the number of inferred facts at the intermediate stages of the fixpoint computation, and possibly of anticipating its termination. Second, a higher degree of expressiveness is achieved: the next sections of this paper are devoted to this point. For instance, we will show

how the dynamic choice construct is expressive enough to capture various forms of negation for Datalog.

Informally, the DCF procedure behaves as follows. Given a choice program P and its stable version $SV(P)$, call $\mathbf{C}$ the set of *chosen* rules in $SV(P)$, $\mathbf{D}$ the set of *diffChoice* rules in $SV(P)$, and $\mathbf{O}$ the set of the remaining (original) rules in $SV(P)$.

Then, the DCF procedure is as follows:

1. find the fixpoint of the $\mathbf{O}$ part;
2. while there exists an enabled ground instance r of a *chosen* rule in $\mathbf{C}$, repeat:
   (a) execute r;
   (b) execute all rules in $\mathbf{D}$ enabled by r;
3. repeat steps 1 and 2 until no rule is enabled.

Notice that we used the term "execute" to mean the ordinary bottom-up computation mechanism of asserting the head of a rule whenever its body is true. The idea underlying the DCF procedure can be explained as follows. There are two modes of operation: a saturation mode and a choice mode. In the saturation mode, the consequences of the original rules are computed by an ordinary fixpoint mechanism. When nothing more can be deduced, the procedure switches to the choice mode. In the choice mode, a *chosen* rule together with the associate *diffChoice* rules are executed, until no more choices can be made. Then the procedure switches to the saturation mode again, and the process continues until a fixpoint is reached. Notice that the execution the *diffchoice* rules shrinks the set of enabled *choice* rules.

In other words, when DCF is in the choice mode, all the choices that are compatible with the functional dependency are operated, before DCF switches to the saturation mode again.

The following code formalizes the DCF procedure.

```
begin
M := ∅;  M̃ := ∅;
repeat
        OldM := M;
        M := S_O(M);
        while not C_M = ∅ do
            M̃ := M̃∪ {¬diffChoice_i(z)|
                        r : chosen(z) ← B, ¬diffChoice_i(z) ∈ C_M};
            M := M ∪ {chosen(z)|
                        r : chosen(z) ← B, ¬diffChoice_i(z) ∈ C_M};
            M := S_D(M);
            od;
until M ≠ OldM;
output M "is a choice model"
end.
```

The DCF procedure is correct with respect to the stable choice model semantics of the program, in the sense that the result of DCF is a stable choice model of the program. This claim can be easily established by observing that an *early choice* is clearly correct with respect to the functional dependencies, although it may inhibit possible later choices. This implies that DCF cannot compute any stable choice model of a program, but only some *preferred* ones. Therefore, dynamic choice is sound, although not complete, w.r.t. stable model semantics. The main interest for the dynamic choice construct lies in the fact that it is highly expressive—it allows to compute efficiently some relevant *deterministic* problems which cannot be expresses by deterministic, such as negation and ordering. These and other issues are addressed in the rest of this paper.

3 Computing negation with the choice operator

A remarkable example taken from [13] is the realization of a form of negation, which can be used to model stratified and inflationary negation for Datalog. The following choice program defines relation NOT_P as the complement of a relation P with respect to a universal relation U. We assume here that both P and U are extensional relations, although this constraint will be soon relaxed.

Definition 3. The choice program $NOT[P,U]$ consists of the following rules:

$$NOT\_P(X) \leftarrow COMP\_P(X,1).$$

$$COMP\_P(X,I) \leftarrow TAG\_P(X,I), choice((X),(I)).$$

$$TAG\_P(nil,0).$$
$$TAG\_P(X,0) \leftarrow P(X).$$
$$TAG\_P(X,1) \leftarrow U(X), COMP\_P(\_,0).$$

where nil is a new constant, which does not occur in the EDB. $\qquad\square$

According to the specified operational semantics of the dynamic choice, we obtain a set of answers where $COMP\_P(x,1)$ holds if and only if x is not in the extension of P. This behavior is due to the fact that the extension of $COMP\_P$ is taken as a subset of the relation TAG_P which obeys the FD $(X \rightarrow I)$, and that the dynamic choice operates early choices which binds to 0 all the elements in the extension of P. This implies that all the elements which do not belong to P will be chosen in the next saturation step, and hence bound to 1. The fact rule $TAG\_P(nil,0)$ is needed to cope with the case that relation P is empty.

More precisely, in the first saturation phase the facts and $TAG\_P(x,0)$ are inferred, for x in the extension of relation P. In the following choice phase the facts $chosen(x,0)$ are chosen, again for x in the extension of P, as all possible choices are operated. In the second saturation phase the facts $COMP\_P(x,0)$ are inferred for x in the extension of P, and the facts $TAG\_P(x,1)$ for all x in U. In the following choice phase the facts $chosen(x,1)$ are chosen in a maximal way to satisfy the FD, i.e. for x *not* in the extension of P, as all x in P have been chosen with tag 0 already. In the third saturation step the extension of NOT_P becomes the complement of P with respect to U.

The above argument is actually a sketch of the proof of the following result, which states the correctness of the program of Def. 3.

Proposition 4. *Let P and U be n-ary EDB relations. Then program $NOT[P,U]$ has a unique stable choice model M_{NOT}, and $M_{NOT} \models NOT\_P(x)$ iff $x \in U \setminus P$.* $\square$

Essentially, this example shows how the dynamic choice offers a flexible mechanism for handling the control needed to emulate the difference between two relations. It is shown in [10] that the above program can be refined in order to realize more powerful forms of negation, such as stratified and inflationary negation. This goal is achieved by suitably emulating the extra control needed to handle program strata and fixpoint approximations, respectively.

4 Ordering with the choice operator

It has been pointed out in the literature that a tight connection exists between non-determinism and ordered databases [16, 6]. On one hand, consider the case that a query Q relies on the ordering in which elements are stored in the database: when abstracted at the conceptual level, where physical details are unrelevant, Q exhibits a non-deterministic behavior. On the other hand, it is often possible to emulate ordering using non-deterministic mechanisms.

The following choice program $ORD[U]$ exploits the dynamic choice to compute an arbitrary ordering of the elements of an EDB relation U.

Definition 5. The choice program $ORD[U]$ consists of the following rules:

$$SUCC(min, Y) \leftarrow U(Y), choice((), (Y)).$$

$$SUCC(X, Y) \leftarrow \quad SUCC(\_, X), U(Y), SUCC(min, Z),$$
$$X \neq Y, \ Y \neq Z, \ choice((X), (Y)), choice((Y), (X)).$$

where min is a new constant, which does not occur in the EDB. $\square$

According to the specified operational semantics of the dynamic choice, we obtain a set of answers where the extension of relation $SUCC$ is a total, strict ordering over the input relation U. The first clause of program $ORD[U]$ starts the computation, by selecting an arbitrary element from U as the successor of min, i.e., as the actual minimum element of U. The second clause selects from U the successor y of an element x which has been already placed in order. The constraints in the body of the second clause enforce irreflexivity. In particular:

- $x \neq y$ prevents immediate cycles (e.g., $SUCC(a, a)$),
- $y \neq z$ prevents cycles with the minimum element z,
- the choice goals establish the bijection $x \leftrightarrow y$ which prevents the other possible cycles; also, y is uniquely determined by x.

The above argument is actually a sketch of the proof of the following result, which states the correctness of the program of Def. 5.

Proposition 6. *Let U be an EDB relation. Then, in any stable choice model M_{ORD} of program $ORD[U]$, the (transitive closure of the) relation $SUCC$ is an irreflexive total ordering over U.* $\square$

This application brings further evidence to the effectiveness of the dynamic choice as a control mechanism. It also suggests that the dynamic choice is highly expressive, as languages over ordered domains are known to be strictly more expressive than languages over unordered domains [16]. Indeed, the fact that dynamic choice can express ordering is essential in the proof of the main result of this paper.

5 Emulating N_Datalog with the choice operator

The aim of this section is to present a general transformation algorithm which allows to emulate the control needed to handle the non-deterministic semantics of N_Datalog¬. Ordering over a relation of a suitable cardinality is exploited to emulate the level of the fixpoint iteration of the N_Datalog¬ computation.

Definition 7. (*Transformation*) Let *Prog* be a N_Datalog¬ program. Let δ be the finite set of distinct constants occurring in *Prog*, and L the cardinality of δ. Let l be the number of distinct relations of *Prog*, and l_1 be the maximal arity of the relations in *Prog*. As a consequence, L^{l*l_1} is an upper bound for number of instances which are derivable from *Prog*. Given a set of variables $\{V_1, \ldots, V_{l*l_1}\}$, all variables occurring in the heads of a rule in *Prog* can be renamed using variables from this set.

Prog' is a choice program obtained from *Prog* according to the following steps:

1. Add the following facts:

$$LEVEL(min).$$

$$UNIV(a_1, \ldots, a_{l*l_1}).$$

for $a_j \in \delta, j = 1, \ldots, l*l_1$, together with the rules of the program $ORD[UNIV]$ as in Def. 5 as in Here, min is an array (of proper arity) of new constants.

2. Add the following rules defining the complement of a relation P respect another relation U. Such rules extend the program of Def. 3 to deal with the level of the fixpoint iteration. The notation $NOT[P, U](x, n)$ is used in the following to refer to the following program.

$$NOT\_P(X, N) \leftarrow COMP\_P(X, 1, N).$$

$$COMP\_P(X, I, N) \leftarrow TAG\_P(X, I, N), choice((X), (I)).$$

$$TAG\_P(nil, 0, N) \leftarrow LEVEL(N).$$
$$TAG\_P(X, 0, N) \leftarrow P(X), LEVEL(N).$$
$$TAG\_P(X, 1, N) \leftarrow U(X), COMP\_P(\_, 0, N).$$

where nil is a new constant.

3. For each rule R_i of *Prog*:

$$A_0(X_0), \ldots, A_m(X_m) \leftarrow P_1(Y_1), \ldots, P_k(Y_k), \neg Q_1(Z_1), \ldots, \neg Q_h(Z_h).$$

with $h, k, m \geq 0$, add the following rules:

$$NEW(U, N, i) \leftarrow P_1(Y_1), \ldots, P_k(Y_k),$$
$$NOT[Q_1, UNIV](Z_1, N), \ldots, NOT[Q_h, UNIV](Z_h, N),$$
$$NOT[A_0, UNIV](X_0, N).$$

$$\vdots$$

$$NEW(U, N, i) \leftarrow P_1(Y_1), \ldots, P_k(Y_k),$$
$$NOT[Q_1, UNIV](Z_1, N), \ldots, NOT[Q_h, UNIV](Z_h, N),$$
$$NOT[A_m, UNIV](X_m, N).$$

Here, i is a constant identifying the rule R_i, and U is an array of terms of arity $l * l_1$, which contains all variables in the head of the original rule; all the extra arguments of U are filled in with a new constant ∂.

4. Add the rule:

$$INSTANCE(Z, N, I) \leftarrow NEW(U, N, I), choice((N), (U, I)).$$

$$LEVEL(N_1) \leftarrow INSTANCE(\_, N, \_), SUCC(N, N_1).$$

where I is a variable denoting a generic rule from $Prog$, and Z is the set of variables $\{V_1, \ldots, V_{l*l_1}\}$.

5. Replace rule R_i with the following rules:

$$A_0(X_0) \leftarrow INSTANCE(Z, N, i).$$

$$\vdots$$

$$A_m(X_m) \leftarrow INSTANCE(Z, N, i).$$

$$\square$$

Before analyzing the transformation, let us recall the behavior of the non-deterministic semantics: at each fixpoint iteration a new instance is computed by choosing only one instantiation among the possible ones of the single rule chosen among the firable ones. At step 3 of the transformation the predicate $NEW(\_, i)$ collects *only* all the new instances derived using the rule R_i. In fact the meta-predicate $NOT[A_j, UNIV])$ ensures that instances for the predicate A_i occurring in the head of the rule have not been computed yet. At step 4 only one rule and only one instance of the selected rule are selected. At step 5 the predicates of the head of the selected rule are inferred. At this stage, a new value for $LEVEL$ can be inferred which will possibly fire rules of the meta-predicate $NOT[\_, UNIV]$.

It is worth remarking that in the non-deterministic semantics also the EDB facts are derived one at a time, so the transformation considers them as IDB rules with an equality between variables and constants the body.

The above argument is a rough sketch of the proof of the correctness of the transformation. To formalize this statement we need the following definition.

Definition 8. Let P be a N_Datalog¬ and P' a choice program. P and P' are *semantically equivalent* with respect to common predicate symbols if

- for each model M of P there exists a stable choice model M' of P' which coincides with M over common predicates, and $M \models \neg R(x)$ iff $M' \models NOT\_R(x)$ for each relation R occurring in P.
- for each stable choice model M' of P' there exists a model M of P which coincides with M' over common predicates, and $M \models \neg R(x)$ iff $M' \models NOT\_R(x)$ for each relation R occurring in P.

□

The above definition takes into account the fact that negative information is represented in choice programs with the NOT_R predicates.

Theorem 9. *Let P be a N_Datalog¬ and let P' a choice program obtained from P applying the transformation of Def. 7. Then P and P' are semantically equivalent.* □

Example 5. We show the transformation on a simple N_Datalog¬ program:

$$R_1: \quad P(x), Q(y) \leftarrow \neg R(a), S(x), T(y).$$
$$R_2: \quad S(x) \leftarrow T(x).$$
$$R_3: \quad T(a).$$

The following are the relevant rules of the corresponding choice program:

$LEVEL(min).$

$UNIV(a).$

$NEW(X,Y,N,1) \quad \leftarrow NOT[R,UNIV](a,N), S(X), T(Y),$
$\qquad\qquad\qquad\qquad NOT[P,UNIV](X,N)$

$NEW(X,Y,N,1) \quad \leftarrow NOT[R,UNIV](a,N), S(X), T(Y),$
$\qquad\qquad\qquad\qquad NOT[Q,UNIV](Y,N)$

$NEW(X,\partial,N,2) \quad \leftarrow T(X), NOT[S,UNIV](X,N)$

$NEW(a,\partial,N,3) \quad \leftarrow NOT[T,UNIV](a,N)$

$INSTANCE(X,N,I) \leftarrow NEW(X,Y,N,I), choice((N),(X,Y,I)).$

$P(X) \qquad\qquad \leftarrow INSTANCE(X,Y,N,1).$
$Q(Y) \qquad\qquad \leftarrow INSTANCE(X,Y,N,1).$

$S(X) \qquad\qquad \leftarrow INSTANCE(X,Y,N,2).$

$T(X) \qquad\qquad \leftarrow INSTANCE(X,Y,N,3).$

$LEVEL(N_1) \qquad \leftarrow INSTANCE(\_,\_,N,\_), SUCC(N,N_1).$

6 Datalog with dynamic choice computes NDB_PTIME

We are now in the position of summing up the results of the previous sections in the main result of this paper. It is stated by the following

Theorem 10. *A query is in NDB-PTIME iff it is expressed in Datalog with dynamic choice.*

Proof. The *only if* part follows from the following facts:

- Datalog with dynamic choice emulates N_Datalog¬ (Theorem 9),
- Datalog with dynamic choice expresses ordering (Proposition 6), and
- N_Datalog¬ over ordered domains expresses *NDB-PTIME* (Theorem 2).

The *if* part follows from the observation that Datalog with dynamic choice is an inflationary language, as operated choices are never retracted. □

Theorem 10 defines precisely the expressive power of Datalog augmented with the dynamic choice construct. As a consequence, we obtain that such a language embodies a simple, declarative and efficiently implementable characterization of *NDB-PTIME*, thus improving over previous results.

From a more pragmatical viewpoint, these results indicate that dynamic choice is a flexible mechanism for explicitly handling the control in the fixpoint computation. A natural parallel here is with the *cut* control mechanism of Prolog, which is however much more difficult to be explained in declarative terms [14]. Also, it is natural to ask ourselves whether the dynamic choice provides us with the basis for constructing *bottom-up meta-interpreters*, capable of turning logic database programs into efficient systems by exploiting a customized computation strategy. Another open problem is whether it is realistic to implement negation and ordering by choice in a real language.

Finally, we mention another direction for future work. Abiteboul and Vianu showed that certain non deterministic languages augmented with the extra possibility of performing *updates* are capable of expressing *NDB-PSPACE*, i.e., the non deterministic space-polynomial queries [6]. We conjecture that a similar result holds when augmenting Datalog with dynamic choice and an update construct, such as that of $\mathcal{LDL}$.

Acknowledgments

Thanks are owing to Victor Vianu, Luigi Palopoli, Carlo Zaniolo and Mimmo Saccà for their useful suggestions on the subject of this paper. In particular, we owe the ordering example to L. Palopoli.

References

1. K. R. Apt. *Introduction to Logic Programming.* In: Handbook of Theoretical Computer Science, vol B. (Ed. J. van Leeuwen) (1990). pp. 493-574.
2. S. Abiteboul, E. Simon, V. Vianu. *Non-Deterministic Language to Express Deterministic Transformation.* Proceedings of ACM Symposium on Principles of Database Systems, 1990. pp. 218-229.
3. S. Abiteboul, V. Vianu. *Transaction Languages for Databases Update and Specification.* INRIA Technical Report n. 715 (1987).

4. S. Abiteboul, V. Vianu. *Procedural Languages for Database Queries and Updates.* Journal of Computer and System Science 41 (2) (1990).

5. S. Abiteboul, V. Vianu. *Fixpoint Extension of First Order Logic and Datalog-Like Languages.* Proc. 4th Symp on Logic in Computer Science (LICS). IEEE Computer Press (1989). pp. 71-89.

6. S. Abiteboul, V. Vianu. *Non-Determinism in Logic Based Languages.* Annals of Mathematics and Artificial Intelligence 3 (1991). pp. 151-186.

7. A. Chandra, D. Harel. *Structures and Complexity of Relational Queries.* Journal of Computer and System Science 25 (1982). pp. 99-128.

8. D. Chimenti, et al., *The $\mathcal{LDL}$ System Prototype.* IEEE Journal on Data and Knowledge Engineering, Vol. 2, No. 1, (1990). pp. 76-90.

9. E.F. Codd. *Relational Completeness of Database Sublanguages.* Data Base Systems, (Ed. R. Rustin), Prentice-Hall, Englewood Cliffs, NJ (1972) pp. 33-64.

10. L. Corciulo. *Non determinism in deductive databases.* Laurea Thesis. Dipartimento di Informatica, Università di Pisa. 1993 (in Italian)

11. H. Gallaire, J. Minker, J.M. Nicolas. *Logic and Databases, a Deductive Approach.* ACM Computing Surveys 16(2) (1984). pp. 153-185.

12. M. Gelfond, V. Lifschitz. *The stable model semantics for logic programming.* Proc. 5th Int. Conf. and Symp. on Logic Programming, MIT Press, pp. 1080-1070, 1988.

13. F. Giannotti, D. Pedreschi, D. Saccà, C. Zaniolo. *Non-Determinism in Deductive Databases.* Proc. Deductive and Object-oriented Databases, Second International Conference, DOOD'93, (Eds. C. Delobel, M. Kifer, Y. Masunaga), Springer-Verlag, LNCS 566, pp. 129-146, 1991.

14. F. Giannotti, D. Pedreschi, C. Zaniolo. *Declarative Semantics for Pruning Operators in Logic Programming.* Methods of Logic in Computer Science (1993) To appear.

15. Y. Gurevich, S. Shelah. *Fixed-Point Extensions of First-Order Logic.* Annals of Pure and Applicate Logic 32 (1986). pp. 265-280.

16. N. Immerman, *Languages which Capture Complexity Classes.* SIAM J. Computing, 16,4, (1987). pp. 760-778.

17. P.C. Kanellakis. *Elements of Relational Databases Theory.* In: Handbook of Theoretical Computer Science, (Ed. J. van Leeuwen) (1990). pp. 1075-1155.

18. R. Krishnamurthy, S. Naqvi. *Non-Deterministic Choice in Datalog.* Proc. 3nd Int. Conf. on Data and Knowledge Bases, Morgan Kaufmann Pub., Los Altos (1988). pp. 416-424.

19. S. Naqvi, S. Tsur. *A Logical Language for Data and Knowledge Bases.* Computer Science Press, New York (1989).

20. D. Saccà, C. Zaniolo. *Stable Models and Non-Determinism in Logic Programs with Negation.* Proc. Symp. on Principles of Database System PODS'89 (1989).

21. J.D. Ullman. *Principles of Databases and Knowledge Base System.* Volume I and II. Computer Science Press, Rockville, Md (1988).

A Deductive and Object-Oriented Approach to a Complex Scheduling Problem

Yves Caseau

Bellcore,
445 South Street,
Morristown NJ 07960, USA.
caseau@bellcore.com

Pierre-Yves Guillo

Nynex Science and Technology
500, Westchester Avenue
White Plains, NY 10604, USA
guillo@nynexst.com

Eric Levenez

Ecole Centrale de Lyon
36, Avenue Guy de Collongue
69130 Ecully, FRANCE

Abstract. This paper presents the application of combined deductive and object-oriented technologies to a complex scheduling (timetable) problem. This approach emphasizes local propagation of constraints, which we perform with deductive rules, and combines it with global pruning heuristics, which we represent with methods (in a procedural manner) attached to objects. Because both components are essential to ensure success, we see this scheduling application as an interesting demonstration of the synergy between object-oriented and deductive technology. We provide a precise description of the problem, discuss what makes it difficult, and present detailed techniques that we used for its resolution.

1. Introduction

Timetable scheduling problems (e.g., course scheduling for universities [Car86]) are common problems that are usually solved by ad-hoc algorithms packaged as dedicated software. Such problems are not only difficult from a theoretical perspective (most of them are NP-hard problems) but also from a practical one as well. As we shall see later, they involve global constraints that require global analysis; thus, they cannot be solved by local constraint propagation. As a consequence, resolution algorithms (approximations) are written with traditional programming techniques instead of rules or constraints and are hard to modify or extend. In this paper we consider a timetable problem that occurs in the telecommunication industry, but is more general and representative of most crew-scheduling problems [NR92]. Because the constraints that define this problem are subject to many changes (dayly, such as a sick operator, or every three month, such as new business rules), an ad-hoc embedded algorithm was not judged a satisfactory solution (lack of flexibility).

The solution that we propose is interesting from two different viewpoints. On one hand, it is an original solution for a difficult problem, and it yields excellent results (as a result, a patent was filed). The software that implements the algorithms presented here was able to solve real staff scheduling problems (that were previously solved manually). On the other hand, this solution uses a combination of deductive and object-oriented technologies, and it can be clearly shown that both are needed. The deductive technology (mostly rules and a constraint resolution engine) adds flexibility to our approach, which can be easily customized or modified. Object-oriented technology allows both for a natural representation of data (which also simplifies customization [Me88]) and a simple integration with the procedural heuristics needed to supplement the generic resolution techniques.

Our goal is to the show the value of combining object-oriented and deductive techniques through the careful description and analysis of an application that is a "success story". We have found that, together with other applications such as time-constrained travel optimization [CK92], it constitutes a group of problems for which traditional algorithm techniques (even object-oriented) fail to deliver enough flexibility and traditional deductive techniques (even constraint logic programming) fail to deliver enough performance. Therefore, we concentrate on the synergy between these two families of techniques for solving our scheduling problem. We used the LAURE object-oriented deductive language [Ca89] [Ca91] to implement the prototype described in this paper, but other systems with a similar combination of paradigms could have been used (for instance, LIFE[AKP90]).

The paper is organized as follows: Section 2 describes a real-world, staff-scheduling problem that can be easily mapped into a constraint-satisfaction problem. We show why the resulting problem is hard to solve and why complex resolution strategies are needed. Section 3 presents the various techniques that we used to solve the problem, starting with classical constraint-propagation technique up to more advanced matrix analysis. For instance, we introduced the notion of *entropy* as a guide for the search. We give simple examples to justify the introduction of more complex techniques. Section 4 deals with the application of object-oriented and deductive paradigms to this problem. We show how the previously mentioned techniques have natural representation either with objects and methods, rules or constraints. Section 5 gives preliminary results and a comparison with related work.

2. A Complex Scheduling Problem

2.1 Staff Scheduling

The problem that we consider in this paper is the scheduling of a staff of operators for a couple of weeks. Each day a person can perform an activity from a set A, which contains work shifts (the day is divided into three) and several other activities (such as rest or backup). The goal is to produce an assignment matrix (see Figure 1), given a set of persons P and a set of week days W. The real problem that we used was to schedule managers for a directory-assistance center, with nine activities, 5 to 10 persons over a two weeks interval. However, we found that 7 persons, 7 days and 5 activities is enough to exhibit all the complexity of the problem, so we will take it as an example.

	Mo	Tu	We	Th	...
peter	D	N	O	M	
paul	D	B	M	N	
mary	N	O	D	D	
...					

A = {M,D,N,B,O}
P = {Peter, Paul, Mary, ...}
W = {Mo,Tu,We,Th,....}
M = morning
D = day
N = night
B = backup
O = day-Off

Figure 1: An Assignment Timetable

Assignments are restricted by global constraints. First, for each day we must have a minimum number of each activity. For instance, we may ask to have at least one manager on duty 24 hours a day and at least two during the day. Similarly, we may have a maximum number due, for instance, to office capacity. We also have similar constraints for each person. A person may have a maximum number for each activity; e.g., no more than two night assignments each week. A person may also have a minimum number for each activity; e.g., at least one day of rest each week. Thus, global constraints can be seen as min/max constraints on rows and columns of the assignment matrix.

There are also local constraints. The first one is derived from an incompatibility relation, which forbids certain activities to occur two days in a row. For instance, we will not assign a morning schedule after a night schedule. More precisely, if a person is assigned the activity *a* on a given day, s/he cannot be assigned an activity in *incompatible(a)* on the next day. The other local constraint is that week-ends are treated as a whole, i.e., the assignments for Saturday and Sunday must be the same.

The goal of the scheduling algorithm is to produce an assignment that satisfies global and local constraints as shown in Figure 2.

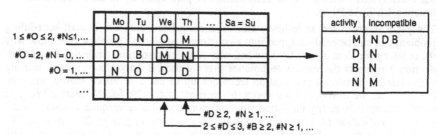

Figure 2: Constraints (and an incompatible assignment)

2.2 Complexity

This problem is a timetable problem [Car86] [MM92] but has many specific aspects of its own, as is always the case with timetable problems. It is an NP-hard problem for which there is no well-known good heuristic (although a vast a set of techniques have been proposed [Car86][MM92]). Assuming that the set of constraints can be divided into a set of hard constraints (that need to be satisfied) and a set of soft constraints, most timetable algorithms build a solution to the set of hard constraint with a heuristic and maximize the number of soft constraints that are satisfied using local search techniques. This works only if the set of hard constraints is not too hard, but is the only solution as soon as the problem gets large. In our case, the problem is not too large, but the set of hard constraints can be difficult to solve or can simply have no solutions.

Timetable problems are hard to solve with constraint logic programming. After reporting impressive successes for job-shop scheduling, CLP users have tried to address timetable problems whith far less success. The key is that local propagation is the right tool for job-shop scheduling, whereas timetable scheduling is dominated by the combination of global constraints that cannot be solved efficiently by local propagation. Recently, most CLP languages have been extended with *atmost/atleast* operators to efficiently represent min/max constraints (e.g., [VHD91]). Such operators are still implemented using local propagation, as we shall see in Section 3, and can be added easily to a CLP solver. The problem is that efficient resolution of a timetable problem requires a global computation on the set of min/max constraints, and not the efficient implementation of each of them separately. Thus, although it is very easy to represent a timetable problem with a language like CHIP, performance for real-size problems are totally inadequate.

However, the existence of last-minute constraints and the evolvability of business rules argue for a constraint-based approach. This is even more true for soft preference constraints that can be added to give "nicer" assignment to senior staff. This is a very strong incentive for writing these rules in some declarative manner, as constraints or deductive rules, so that the set of rules can be maintained easily. An ad hoc solution implemented as a C algorithm is likely to become obsolete rapidly and require large maintainance costs. As we shall see in Section 3, the difficulty resides in the interaction between the global and the local constraints. It is not possible simply to write an ad hoc solver for the global constraints and to couple it with a set of deductive rules representing the business rules. Local rules such as incompatibility do make the problem much more difficult (cf. Section 3.3) and new business rules may require a totally different resolution strategy.

3. Resolution Methods

3.1 Constraints

We use the following notations :

- A to represent the set of activities (with a variable *a* ranging over A),
- P to represent the set of persons (variable *p*),
- W to represent the set of week days (variable *w*), with *next(w)* and *previous(w)* defined with their obvious meanings.
- the matrix $r[p,w]$ to represent the resulting assignment (i.e., the person *p* takes the activity $a = r[p,w]$ on day *w*). We also use r to represent a partially instantiated assignment and write $r[p,w] = \perp$ when no activity has been assigned yet to *p,w*.
- the relation I to represent *incompatibility*, (i.e., I(a) is the set of activities that are incompatible with a and cannot be performed the next day).

Global constraints are represented by two matrices that give minimum and the maximum number of occurrences for a given activity. To avoid overloading notation, we will define *Max* and *Min* on the domain $(P \cup W) \times A$. For each person *p* and activity *a*, $Min[p,a]$ will be the minimum number of times the activity *a* has to be assigned to *p* during the time period (e.g., the week in our case) and $Max[p,a]$ will be the maximum number of times *a* may be assigned to *p* during the same period. Similarly, $Min[w,a]$ is the minimum number of persons to whom the activity *a* was assigned on day *w*. The constraints on r can be summarized as:

$$\forall a \in A, \quad \{ \forall p \in P, \quad Min[p,a] \leq |\{w \in W \mid r[p,w] = a\}| \leq Max[p,a] \ \} \wedge$$
$$\{ \forall w \in W, \quad Min[w,a] \leq |\{p \in P \mid r[p,w] = a\}| \leq Max[w,a] \ \}$$

where |S| denotes the cardinality of the set S.

In addition, we represent the local constraints as follows:

$$\forall p \in P, \ r[p, \text{saturday}] = r[p,\text{sunday}]$$
$$\forall a \in A, a' \in A, p \in P, \ (a' \in I(a) \wedge r[p,w] = a \ \wedge next(w) = w') \Rightarrow r[p,w'] \neq a'$$

Last, we need to represent information about the problem; thus, to represent states in the search. We use a set-valued matrix $S[p \in P, w \in W]$, where $S[p,w]$ is the set of activities that we consider to be possible at a given point in the search. The initial state of the problem is usually $S_1[p,w] = A$, but it could be reduced arbitrarily to reflect "last-minute" impossibilities. The previous constraints apply to a search state in a straightforward manner (thus, search states can be pruned).

Figure 3 represents such a problem and its mathematical representation.

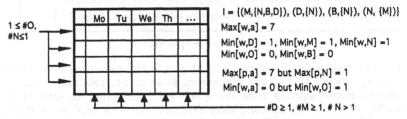

Figure 3: A Sample Problem

3.2 Counters

Rows and columns clearly play a very important role in this problem. For each activity and for each row/column (i.e., person/week day) we create two counters, *Num* and *Pos*, that represent the number of occurrences of the activity *a*, and the number of possible occurrences for an activity other than a. That is to say, using U to represent the union P $\cup$ W (because of the symmetry between rows and columns, it is easier to treat them in a unified manner) :

- Num[p,a] is $|\{w \in W \mid r[p,w] = a\}|$ and Num[w,a] is $|\{p \in P \mid S[p,w] = \{a\}\}|$. This will be used to represent the Max counter as $\forall u \in U$, Num[u,a] $\leq$ Max[u,a]. This constraint can be used at any time during the search (for pruning), whereas Min $\leq$ Num could not be used (this is what makes *atleast* constraints interesting).

- Pos[p,a] is $|\{w \in W \mid a \in S[p,w]\}|$ and Pos[w,a] is $|\{p \in W \mid a \in S[p,w]\}|$. Pos[$u,a$] is simply the number of possible occurrence of the activity a for p (whereas Num[u,a] is the number of actual occurrence). We use Pos to express minimum constraint and perform pruning on the search. As a matter of fact, the constraint is now $\forall u \in U$, Min[u,a] $\leq$ Pos[u,a].

Another way to consider this representation is to use a set of counters (cf. Section 4) with four attributes: *Min*, *Max*, *Num* and *Pos*. Both *Min* and *Max* are given for the problem and the other two can be maintained incrementally during the search:

- r[p,w] is set to a $\Rightarrow$ Num[p,a] and Num[w,a] are incremented by 1.
  (i.e. S[p,w] is set to $\{a\}$) $\forall$ a' $\neq$ a, Pos[p,a'] and Pos[w,a'] are decremented by 1.

- a is removed from S[p,w] $\Rightarrow$ Pos[p,a] and Pos[w,a] are decremented by 1.

We can now use the constraint to prune the search space.

- Num[u,a] = Max[u,a] $\Rightarrow$ if $u \in P$, a is removed from S[u,w] for all w such that $a \in S[u,w]$ and similarly if $u \in W$.

- Pos[p,a]= 0 $\Rightarrow$ r[p,w] is set to a for all w such that $a \in S[p,w]$

- Pos[w,a]= 0 $\Rightarrow$ r[p,w] is set to a for all p such that $a \in S[p,w]$

This is just another way of defining the management of *atmost/atleast* constraints [AB91][VHD91] by local propagation. We will now show why this is not enough. If we consider the problem represented in Figure 4, it is clear that it has no solution by considering the Day-Off activity. On the one hand, we do not allow more than one day-off by week day, but on the other hand we ask for two days off for each person. Therefore, there must be at most 7 day offs assigned and at least 14, which is clearly impossible.

$\forall w \in W$, Min[w,M] = 1, Min[w,D] = 2, Min[w,N] = 1, Min[w,B] = 2, Min[w,O] = 0

$\forall w \in W$, Max[w,M] = 2, Max[w,D] = 3, Max[w,N] = 2, Max[w,B] = 3, Max[w,O] = 0

$\forall p \in P$, Min[p,M] = 1, Min[p,D] = 2, Min[p,N] = 1, Min[p,B] = 2, Min[p,O] = 2

$\forall p \in P$, Max[p,M] = 2, Max[p,D] = 7, Max[p,N] = 1, Max[p,B] = 3, Max[p,O] = 7

Figure 4: An impossible problem

The interesting point is that it will take a lot of time to find that this problem has no solutions using only propagation rules. This is because we need to make many choices in order to obtain contradiction from the *minimum* constraints. As soon as the impossibility is not trivial, the complexity explodes. What we need to do is take advantage of the following rule (illustrated in Figure 5):

$$\forall a \in A, \sum_{p \in P} Min[p,a] \leq |\{(p,w) \mid r[p,w] = a\}| \leq \sum_{w \in W} Max[w,a]$$

$$\forall a \in A, \sum_{w \in W} Min[w,a] \leq |\{(p,w) \mid r[p,w] = a\}| \leq \sum_{p \in P} Max[p,a]$$

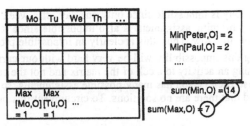

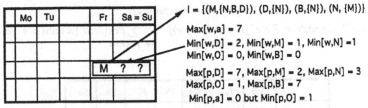

Figure 5: Matrix Consistency

This formula can be refined by using current estimates of minima and maxima instead of static ones.

$$\forall a \in A, \sum_{p \in P} \max(Num[p,a], Min[p,a]) \le |\{(p,w) \mid r[p,w] = a\}| \le \sum_{w \in W} \min(Pos[w,a], Max[p,a])$$

$$\forall a \in A, \sum_{w \in W} \max(Num[w,a], Min[p,a]) \le |\{(p,w) \mid r[p,w] = a\}| \le \sum_{p \in P} \min(Pos[p,a], Max[p,a])$$

This gives us a pruning heuristic that we can evaluate incrementally whenever the attributes *Num* or *Pos* are changed. This is a global resolution technique (as opposed to local propagation techniques), which work very well for tight problems (cf. Section 5). It will detect bottlenecks, created by wrong choices, much earlier than local propagation would do.

Let us also notice that there is a straightforward "tightening rule" that can be applied to the Min/Max attributes for each counter, the following are the rules for person counters, similar rules hold for week-day counters.

$$\forall a \in A, \forall p \in P, Max[p,a] \le |W| - \sum_{a' \ne a} Min[p,a']$$

$$\forall a \in A, \forall p \in P, Min[p,a] > |W| - \sum_{a' \ne a} Max[p,a']$$

For instance, Max[w,O] = 1 could be deduced automatically from the Min values in the example of Figure 4. This is a static rule that can be applied to each counter before starting the resolution.

3.3 Additional Global Heuristics to Capture Incompatibility

	Mo	Tu		Fr	Sa = Su
				M	? ?

I = {(M,{N,B,D}), (D,{N}), (B,{N}), (N, {M})}

Max[w,a] = 7

Min[w,D] = 2, Min[w,M] = 1, Min[w,N] =1
Min[w,O] = 0, Min[w,B] = 0

Max[p,D] = 7, Max[p,M] = 2, Max[p,N] = 3
Max[p,O] = 1, Max[p,B] = 7

Min[p,a] = 0 but Min[p,O] = 1

Figure 6: Incompatibility Bottleneck

The previous technique works well for detecting trouble caused by the min/max constraints. On the other hand, it does not take incompatibility into account. Let us now consider the example described in Figure 6. Since for each day w, Min[w,M] = 1, we know that someone must be assigned a morning on Friday. However, a morning assignment can only be followed by a day off or another morning assignment. A day-off assignment on Saturday is impossible since only one day off a week is allowed for each person. A Saturday morning assignment is also impossible since it would imply three morning assignments in a row. Thus, this is clearly an impossible problem.

However, detecting this impossibility will be very hard with our current approach since we focus on assigning an activity to a cell of the matrix and not the converse. Even if we focus on Friday first, each person has many possible assignments, so it will take a lot of time before we find that there are no solutions. To circumvent this problem, we use two techniques.

- Use a symmetrical representation. We have used a representation that assigns an activity to a cell of the matrix by building the matrix r[p,w]. We now introduce request objects to represent minimum constraints. A request R(p,a) represents one activity a that must be assigned to p (respectively, R(w,a) represents one activity a that must be assigned on day w). If Min[p,a] = m, we will create m requests R(p,a). Each request R(p,a) must be associated with a day w such that r[p,w] = a. This is a redundant symmetrical representation of the problem that will allow focusing on the problem from a different point of view. This is a classical technique (cf. the n-queens problem with symmetrical representation or the time-constrained traveling salesman problem [CK92]) that requires being able to link two problem representations (cf. Section 4).

- Use a heuristic to guide the search so that we pick difficult requests first. As for any constraint-satisfaction technique, the search is performed in the following manner. We pick a goal (either a cell or a request), we pick a possible assignment, and we propagate the consequence of this choice. We repeat this step recursively and backtrack on failure. The usual way to pick the goal is the first-fail principle [VH89] (choose the cell [p,w] with the smallest domain S[p,w]). Here, we need a domain-specific choice function that will detect "difficult" requests based on the incompatibility relation.

As a matter of fact, if we consider the request R(Friday,M), its starting domain is the full set of persons. This means that although this request is hard to assign (actually impossible), there is no distinction among persons that would make the first-fail principle work. A better solution is to associate a value called *entropy* to each request, which reflects how hard the request is to satisfy. The entropy is a rough estimate of how much assigning a request will reduce the choices for its neighbor. We define both left-to-right entropy (e+) and right-to-left entropy (e-) with the following definition (using a default entropy E as a seed).

$$\forall a \in A, e^+[a, monday] = E \wedge e^+[a, next(w)] = \sum_{a' \in A, a \in Next(a', w)} Pos[w, a'] \times \min(E, e^+[a', w])$$

$$Next(a, w) = \{a' \in A | \neg I(a, a') \wedge (a = a' \vee w \neq saturday)\}$$

$$\forall a \in A, e^-[a, sunday] = E \wedge e^-[a, previous(w)] = \sum_{a' \in Next(a, w)} Pos[w, a'] \times \min(E, e^-[a', w])$$

	Mo	Tu	We	Th	F	Sa	Su
Morning	14	14	12	9	4	7	12
Day	28	28	26	23	12	7	12
Night	28	28	28	28	12	7	12
Backup	28	28	26	23	12	7	12
day Off	35	35	33	30	16	0	12

Figure 7: Negative Entropy Matrix (E = 12)

For instance, Figure 7 shows the right-to-left entropy matrix for the previous problem (with E = 12). One can notice that the entropy of R(friday,M) is the lowest (among other requests) and that it is impossible to assign a day off on Saturday.

We now use the entropy to build our heuristic goal-choice function. Since the entropy is meant to represent the likelihood of a given choice being possible, we evaluate the difficulty of a choice as the product of its entropy and the cardinal of its domain.

```
entropy_choice():
    let v =10000,
        r = ⊥,
    for all cell [p,w] such that r[p,w] is not known (i.e., |S[p,w]| ≠ 1)
        let v1 = (|S[p,w]| × E),
            if (v₁ < v) then {v = v1, r = [p,w] }
    for all request R(a,w) such that R(a,w) is not assigned (i.e., r[a,w] = ⊥)
        let v1 = (|S[p,w]| × min(e⁺[a,w],e⁻[a,w]),
            if (v₁ < v) then {v = v1, r = R(a,w)}
    return r
```

Notice that this function chooses either a request or a cell as the node to be expanded during the search. The interest of using requests is that they allow the solver not to focus on a specific person when all persons are similar, but rather on a pair activity/day. On the other hand, focusing exclusively on requests first does not yield good results. In the previous algorithm, the default entropy E can be seen as a parameter. Our experience suggests that there is an empirical optimal value for E (a value too small will put too much emphasis on cells, and a value too large will put too much emphasis on requests, producing equally disappointing results). More detailed analysis work is needed to understand how the optimal value for E can be computed.

4. Application of Deductive and Object-Oriented Techniques

4.1 An Object-Oriented Representation

The first step towards the implementation of the previously described resolution algorithm is to build an object-oriented representation of the data that we manipulate. As an example, we provide parts of the LAURE code that would be necessary. For lack of space, the following program is not complete,but it represents all aspects of the real software. We first define activities, persons and week-days as classes of objects (using the class Resource to represent the union P ∪ W).

```
[define Activity class                        ;; the class of activities (a)
  with multi_slot(counter_a -> Counter),      ;; set of counters  c[_,a]
       multi_slot(request_a -> Request)]       ;; set of requests  R(_,a)
  [define Morning Activity] …

[define Resource class
  with multi_slot(counter_r -> Counter)]       ;; set of counters  c[w/p,_]

[define Week-day class superclass (Resource),  ;; The class of week days (w)
  with slot(next_day -> Week-day), slot(prev_day -> Week-day),
       multi_slot(cell_w -> Cell),             ;; set of cells [w,_]
       multi_slot(request_w -> Request)]        ;; set of Requests R(w,_)
  [invert next_day,prev_day]                   ;; declare two relation as inverses
    [define Monday Week-day] …

[define Person class superclass (Resource),    ;; the class of persons (p)
  with multi_slot(cell_p -> Cell)]             ;; set of cells [p,_]
```

We represent counters with their associated attributes, corresponding to the matrices of the previous sections. Similarly, we introduce requests and the incompatibility relation. Lastly, we introduce objects to represent cells of the assignment matrix.

```
[define Counter class superclass {object},
  with slot(ca -> Activity),                    ;; ca([x,a]) = a
       slot(cr -> Resource),                    ;; cr([x,a]) = x
       slot(Min -> integer, default 0), slot(Max -> integer, default ND),
       slot(e+ -> integer, default E), slot(e- -> integer, default E)]
  [define Pos attribute domain Counter, -> integer]
  [define Num attribute domain Counter, -> integer]

[define Request class superclass {object},
  with slot(ra -> Activity),                    ;; ra(R(w,a)) = a
       slot(rw -> Week-day),                    ;; rw(R(a,w)) = w
       slot(entropy -> integer),...

[define incompatible multi_attribute domain Activity, -> Activity]

[define Cell class superclass {object},
  with slot(p -> Person), slot(w -> Week-day),
       slot(next_day -> Cell), slot(prev_day -> Cell)]
```

We also define the two attributes that we want to build: *assign* (on Cell) and *place* (on Request). These attributes represent respectively r[p,w] and request assignment.Lastly, we define some methods derived from the formulas of Section 3, such as the following.

```
[define tighten(c:Counter) method
 => [for c in Counter,
     [let  n as [if (cr(self) % Person) ND else NP],
           new_min as n,            ;; will be n - sum(other min)
           new_max as n,            ;; will be n - sum(other max)
      [for c1 in counter_r(cr(self)),
          [if (c1 != self) [do (new_max <- (new_max - Min(c1)))]],
                           (new_min <- (new_min - Max(c1)))]],
       (Max(c) is min(Max(c),new_max)),
       (Min(c) is max(Min(c),new_min))]]
```

Here are the methods that computes the sum of the minima and maxima that we shall use for the dynamic matrix analysis (cf. Section 3.2). We store those values with four attributes (*max_person, max_day, min_person, min_day*).

```
[define max_person attribute domain Activity, -> integer]...

[define min_person!(self:Activity) method
 => [let n as 0,                    ;; computes the sum of minima on a row
     [for c in counter_a(self),
        [if (cr(c) % Person) (n <- (n + max(Num(c),Min(c))))]],
        [if (n > min_person(self)) (min_person(self) is n)]]]

[define min_day!(self:Activity) ... ;; computes the sum of minima on a column

[define max_person!(self:Activity) ... ;; computes the sum of maxima on a row

[define max_day!(self:Activity)  ... ;; computes the sum of maxima on a column
```

4.2 Deductive Rules

We use deductive rules to express the propagation rules that we have given in Section 3. Here are some of the LAURE rules (called axioms) that govern the modifications of the counters.The following axiom keeps a good value for the Max counter of an activity and a person or a week day.

```
[define max_counting axiom mode reversible,
  for_all  c:Counter, d:Cell,
  if assign(d) = ca(c), [or (cr(c) = w(d)),(cr(c) = p(d))],
  then (Num(c) is (Num(c) + 1))]]
```

This axiom keeps a good value for the *Pos* counter when we make a choice for assign. Note that we decrease Pos(c) only if the activity was still a possible choice.

```
[define pos_counting axiom mode reversible,
  for_all  c:Counter, d:Cell,
  if assign(d) != ca(c), [or (cr(c) = w(d)),(cr(c) = p(d))],
  then [if (assign(d) possible? ca(c)) (Pos(c) is (Pos(c) - 1))]]]
```

This axiom says that we cannot use an activity when the *Num* counter is equal to *Max*, We also modify the *Pos* values of related counters accordingly.

```
[define max_forbide axiom mode reversible,
  for_all  c:Counter, d:Cell,
  if Max(c) = Num(c),[or (cr(c) = w(d)),(cr(c) = p(d))],
  then [if [and (assign(d) unknown?), possible?(assign,d,ca(c))]
         [do  (assign(d) is_not ca(c)),
              can_no_longer_do(d,ca(c))]]]
```

Another axiom says that we must use an activity when its *Pos* counter comes to *Min*, assuming it is still possible. Similarly, we must reduce the *Pos* values of related counters. These axioms use the following two methods to update the counters and the requests. The object-oriented representation and the easy access to the domains of the resolution goals (set of possible values for assign(c:Counter) or place(r:Request) are essential to ease the description of the algorithm).

```
[define can_no_longer_do(d:Day,a:Activity) method
  => [for c in counter_a(a),
        [if [or (cr(c) = w(d)),(cr(c) = p(d))] (Pos(c) is (Pos(c) - 1))]
        [for r in request_w(w(d)), [if (ra(r) = a) (place(r) is_not p(d))]]]

[define can_only_do(d:Day,a:Activity) method
  => [let l as delete(a,possible(assign,d)),
        (assign(d) is_only a),
        [for a1 in l, can_no_longer_do(d,a1)]]]
```

We use a pair of rules to ensure the consistency between the two different views of the problem represented by the two attributes *place* and *assign*. Each time a request R(w,a) is assigned to a person p, we assign the activity a to the cell [p,w]. Reciprocally, when we assign the activity a to a cell [p,w], we see if there is a free request R(w,a) that could be assigned to p.

Lastly, we use a set of rules to trigger the matrix analysis dynamically each time that a row/column current minimum/maximum has changed, such as the following.

```
[define min_compute axiom mode reversible,
  for_all  a:Activity, c:Counter,
  if ca(c) = a, Num(c) > Min(c),
  then [if (cr(c) % Person) min_person!(a) else min_day!(a)]]

[define max_compute ....]

[define matrix_analysis axiom mode reversible,
  for_all  a:Activity,
  if [or (max_person(a) < min_day(a)), (max_day(a) < min_day(a))],
  then contradiction()]
```

We also represent the propagation of incompatibility with a deductive rule, as well as the week-end consistency (same assignment for Sundays and Saturdays).

4.3 Using a Constraint Solver as a Search Engine

The only part missing in our implementation is the search algorithm. This part is straightforward in a language like LAURE, which holds a constraint solver that we can use as a search engine, even though we use no explicit constraints. The LAURE main program has two simple parts. First, we define the goals for the resolution algorithm, using the operator *to_solve*. This assigns a domain to each goal (a set of possible values) and build a list of goals. The second part calls the resolution operator *explore* with two parameters. The first one is the name of the heuristic that we want to use to dynamically order the goals during the search (the function described in Section 3.3). The second one only tells that we want the first solution found during the search.

A complete description of how the constraint solver performs the search can be found elsewhere [Ca91a][Ca91b]. Here we give a brief description to emphasize the role of the rules and the methods defined on objects, and to illustrate the synergy between constraint satisfaction techniques (e.g., exhaustive search with heuristics, local propagation) and more traditional operations research techniques (e.g., cutting based on matrix analysis). The constraint solver executes recursively the following steps until there are no more unresolved goals.

- Pick a goal (R,x) from the list of unresolved goals using the "entropy_choice" heuristics from Section 3.3. Here, either x is a cell and R = *assign* or x is a request and R = *place*. If the list is empty, the algorithm ends with success.

- For all values y in the domain of (R,x) (i.e.,the set of possible values associated with R(x)), perform the next step (if the domain is empty, backtrack to the next choice for the previous goal or end with failure) :

  → Assert R(x) = y, then propagate (execute all rules). This will cause the value of many attributes to be changed, and in turn trigger other rules. If a contradiction is raised (an exception), backtrack to the next choice. It is important to realize that the rules will modify the domains of the remaining goals; thus, dynamically modifying the search space.

From a user perspective, the advantage of using such a constraint solver is the management of backtracking. When a contradiction is detected, or when a goal receives an empty domain, the search algorithm needs not only to undo the choice (R(x) = y) that causes this contradiction , but all consequences that were drawn from this assertion.

If the deductive and object-oriented language chosen for implementation does not support finite domain search, we need to write explicit search procedures using deductive rules, which is straightforward but cumbersome because we need to explicitly take care of backtracking. In particular, it also means that additional data structures are needed to store historical data along the search.

5. Discussion

5.1 Results

Most of the development was made with a set of small problems (7 days, 7 persons, 5 activities) from which we extracted three time measurements. The "best" time is the average time for strongly under-constrained problems, the "average" time is the average time for most problems that are non-trivial but not too constrained or clearly impossible. These problems are representative of the real world problems that need to be solved. The "worst" time is the average time for problems that are either impossible to solve (but not in a too obvious manner) or very constrained. These problems are not likely to occur, unless the algorithm is used for optimization when the constraints are tightened gradually. We compared three versions of our program. The first one uses only local propagation, and is thus very similar to what we would get with any other CLP language with built-in support for atleast/atmost constraints. The second one uses the matrix analysis as a cutting heuristic, and the third one is the complete version using all the techniques described in this paper.

	best	average	worst
Local Propagation	80ms	5s	10s
LP+ matrix analysis	200ms	1s	15s
complete	150ms	150 ms	150ms

Figure 8: Some preliminary results (on a SUN SPARC-10)

The complete algorithm seems to scale well, since it has been used for larger "real" problems (14 days, 9 activities, 5 to 10 persons) with resolution times in the 1-second range. More complete testing is necessary to verify the stability of the result. From a user perspective, these results are a success since the algorithm performs a job that was done manually in approximately 30 minutes.

It is more difficult to measure the result according to the other goals that we had set previously, such as flexibility or ease of maintenance. The whole program takes only 600 lines of LAURE code, which is very small compared to similar software written in C. Because LAURE supports constraints, new additional constraints can be added very easily at the last minute. The use of rules also makes it easy to add new cutting heuristics.

5.2 Comparison with Similar Problems

It is interesting to compare the approach we have taken here with other approaches taken for similar problems. Timetable-scheduling problems come in many different flavors. Most of the work in this area was spent on course assignment problems, which are not completely similar to this problem. However, they also are problems dominated by global constraints for which local propagation does not work well. Most experiences applying finite domains constraint solvers to such (toy) problems have reported disappointing unstable results (where changing one constraint can yield performance changes of many orders of magnitude). As a consequence, the state of the art for solving such problems [We85] [Car86] consists of ad-hoc search algorithms with a lot of expertise about how to build good assignments buried into heuristics. We did not have any ad-hoc software for our scheduling problem that we could compare to, but in addition to getting good and stable performance results, our deductive and object-oriented approach has the following advantages:

- *Clear encapsulation and combination of the heuristics.* This allows to add or remove a heuristic very easily. The role played by deductive rules as a glue between the search algorithm and the heuristics is crucial because it support separate development.

- *Support for additional constraints and for enriched data.* The object-oriented description of the data makes it possible to customize the program for any type of activity/staff. The use of the constraint solver as a search engine allows us to add new constraints to reflect new business rules.

There is an interesting similarity with the method that we had previously used to build a solution to the time-constrained traveling salesman problem [Sav89] [CK92]. These two problems are have following characteristics in common.

- The problem is easy to express with constraints, and the flexibility offered by constraint programming is a welcomed feature.

79

- When we run our constraint solver the first time, performance is very disappointing (and this is not due to LAURE's constraint solvers).
- The problem has some characteristics which prevent the use of some well-known algorithms, and therefore has been left to (naive) heuristics.
- Once we have found how to reuse some operations research techniques for the problem, performance improves sufficiently to get a practical solution.

We call such problems mixed problems, because they are different problems mixed into one new problem, which calls for new techniques to be used. It is clear that we would not try to use LAURE to solve a pure TSP problem (we have better ad hoc tools [L&al85]). Similarly, many interesting allocation or scheduling problems have been solved with "pure" constraint programming and do not require what we call mixed solutions. However, our experience is that mixed problems are a large part of optimization problems in the real world, for which hybrid approaches are well suited.

5.3 Benefits of Object-Oriented and Deductive Technologies

If we had to make a C implementation of the algorithm presented in this paper, the result would be a long and complex program. It is clear to us that we would not have been able to come to this solution if we did not have a fast prototyping language. A C procedural implementation would have to take care of the following aspects: data and set representation, triggering of the propagation, and backtracking. Of all these tasks, the propagation is the hardest one to do right and to maintain later when new business rules are added. This is why an object-oriented language would not help a lot. A SMALLTALK (or C++) implementation would make the data and set manipulation part easier to write (or read), but would keep the propagation part a maintenance bottleneck.

On the other hand, we need more than standard deductive techniques because we need to introduce domain-dependant heuristics. Using a constraint satisfaction language, the difficulty is how to write the methods that will operate on the objects and the domains. In most CLP languages, this is impossible. In more recent implementations that provide back-doors to the search engine, it is possible to add heuristics written in procedural language, but the resulting code is very hard to maintain. Using an object-oriented representation, such as in LAURE or PECOS [PA91], makes this operation simpler because the key components of the search engine are accessible as objects. On the other hand, PECOS lacks the deductive rule component to bind the heuristics to the choices made by the constraint solver, which requires all the propagation code to be written in a procedural form, which is error-prone and hard to maintain.

To summarize our findings, we have found that the following features were most useful:

- object-oriented representation of the data for easy customization and encapsulation of methods,
- use of deductive rules as an interface between the search algorithm and the methods that represent the heuristics,
- transparent access to the structures (represented as objects) manipulated by the search algorithm. This is crucial since it allows the heuristics (triggered by the rules) to manipulate the representation of the search tree and to perform the necessary operations (pruning, cutting, ...).

6. Conclusion

We have presented a new approach to solve a complex staff-scheduling problem, which has proved to be both very efficient and flexible. This approach combines an emphasis on local propagation of constraints, performed with deductive rules, and global pruning heuristics, represented with methods (i.e., in a procedural manner). Because both components are essential to ensure success, we see this application as an interesting demonstration of the synergy between object-oriented and deductive technology.

We provided a detailed description of the constraints that are involved in this problem and of techniques that we have used as heuristics. We did this for two reasons. On the one hand, the scheduling problem that we have addressed is a significant problem and the solution that we built is a real improvement over previous approaches. On the other hand, we believe that one needed a precise understanding of the problem mechanics (the interaction of the various components of the problem) to appreciate why the combination of different technologies is necessary.

Acknowledgments

We want to thank Norman Ramsey for his comments on this paper. We are also very grateful to Clyde Monma for his help on the subject of timetabling problems.

References

[AKP90] H. Aït-Kaci, A. Podelski. *The Meaning of Life*. PRL Research Report, DEC, 1990.

[AB91] A. Agoun, N. Beldiceanu: *Overview of the CHIP Compiler*. Proc. of the 8th ICLP, Paris, 1991.

[Ca89] Y. Caseau. *A Formal System for Producing Demons from Rules*. Proc. of DOOD89, Kyoto 1989.

[Ca91a] Y. Caseau. *An Object-Oriented Deductive Language*. Annals of Mathematics and Artificial Intelligence, special issue on deductive databases, March 1991.

[Ca91b] Y. Caseau. *Constraints in an Object-Oriented Deductive Database*. Proc. of DOOD91, Munich, 1991.

[Car86] M. Carter. *A Survey of Practical Applications of Examination Timetabling Algorithms*. Operations Research 34, 1986.

[CK92] Y. Caseau, P. Koppstein. *A Rule-Based Approach to a Time-Constrained Traveling Salesman Problem*. Presented at the Second International Symposium on Artificial Intelligence and Mathematics, January 1992, to appear.

[L&al85] E. Lawler, J. Lenstra, A. Rinnooy, D. Shmoys (eds.). *The Traveling Salesman Problem: a Guided Tour of Combinatorial Optimization*. Wiley, Chichester, 1985.

[MM92] T. McClain, Mazzola. *Operations Management*. Prentice Hall, 1992.

[Me88] B. Meyer : *Object-oriented Software Construction*. Prentice Hall, 1988.

[NB92] R. Nanda, J. Browner. *Introduction to Employee Scheduling*. Van Nostrand Reinhold, 1992.

[PA91] J.F. Puget, P. Albert. *PECOS: programmation par contraintes orientée objets*. Génie Logiciel et Systèmes Experts, vol. 23, 1991.

[Sav89] M. Savelsbergh. *The vehicle routing problem with time windows: minimizing route duration*. Ann. Oper. Res. 4, 1986..

[VH89] P. Van Hentenryck. *Constraint Satisfaction in Logic Programming*. The MIT press, Cambridge, 1989.

[VHD91] P. Van Hentenryck, Y. Deville. *The Cardinality Operator: A New Logical Connective for Constraint Logic Programming*. Proc. of the 8th ICLP, Paris, 1991.

[We85] D. de Werra. *An introduction to timetabling*. European Journal of Operational Research, 19, 1985.

On the Logical Foundations of Schema Integration and Evolution in Heterogeneous Database Systems*

Laks V.S. Lakshmanan   Fereidoon Sadri   Iyer N. Subramanian

Department of Computer Science, Concordia University, Montreal, Quebec
e-mail: {laks, sadri, iyerns}@cs.concordia.ca

Abstract: *Developing a declarative approach to schema integration in the context of heterogeneous database systems is a major goal of this research. We take a first step toward this goal in this paper, by developing a simple logic called SchemaLog which is syntactically higher-order but has a first-order semantics. SchemaLog can provide for a logical integration of multiple relational databases in a federation of database systems. We develop a fixpoint theory as well as a sound and complete proof theory for the definite clause fragment of SchemaLog and show their equivalence to the model-theoretic semantics. We argue that a uniform framework for schema integration as well as schema evolution is both desirable and possible. We illustrate the simplicity and power of SchemaLog with a variety of applications involving database programming (with schema browsing), schema integration, schema evolution, and cooperative query answering.*

1 Introduction

The rapid progress in database systems research over the past couple of decades has resulted in the evolution of diverse database environments with data and application programs generated specifically to each of these environments, but typically incompatible with one another. This has resulted in an inability to share data and programs across the different platforms, the need for which has become compelling. There is also much redundancy and incompatibility of data. This necessitates redundancy management and rewriting of application programs, involving huge investments. This motivates the need for *Heterogeneous database systems* (HDBS), capable of operating over a distributed network and encompassing a heterogeneous mix of computers, operating systems, communication links, and local database systems. HDBS are also referred to as Multi Database Systems (MDBS) and Federated Database Systems (FDBS) by different authors. The reader is referred to [ACM90] (in particular, see Sheth and Larson [SL90], [LLR90]) and Hsiao [Hsi92] for recent surveys in the field.

One aspect of heterogeneity stems from the difference in the structure of (similar) data and query languages across the individual database systems. It is the issue of making the differences among the structure and semantics of the data, transparent to the users, that is of interest to us. We call the process of *unifying*

---

* This research was supported in part by grants from the Natural Sciences and Engineering Research Council of Canada and the Fonds Pour Formation De Chercheurs Et L'Aide À La Recherche of Quebec.

the representation of *semantically similar* information that is represented in a *heterogeneous* way across the individual databases, *schema integration*. Schema integration is a crucial requirement for a HDBS.

Most of the approaches attempted so far for the schema integration problem have been ad hoc. The survey paper of Batini et. al [Bat86] discusses and compares 12 methodologies for schema integration. We can broadly classify the schema integration approaches into two.

1) Approaches based on defining a common data model: Most of the existing approaches attempted for schema integration belong to this category. The databases participating in the federation are mapped to a common data model (CDM) (such as the OO model) which acts as an 'interpreter' among them. The similarities in the information contents of the individual databases and their semantical inter-relationships are captured in the mappings to the CDM. In such a setting, the user queries the CDM using a CDM language and usually has to be aware of the CDM schema. In a more sophisticated scenario, 'views' which correspond to the schema of the participating databases are defined on the CDM, thus providing the user with a convenient illusion that all the information she gets is from her own database. (This is called *integration transparency*).

A "canonical" example of the CDM based approach is the Pegasus project of Ahmed et.al. [Ahm91]. Pegasus defines a common object model for unifying the data models of the underlying systems. Landers and Rosenberg [LR82] uses the functional model of DAPLEX as the CDM in their *Multibase* project, while *Mermaid* (Templeton etal [Tem87]) uses a relational CDM, and allows only for relational schema integration (with extensions to include text). Thus federation users may formulate queries using SQL. The major problem associated with the approaches in this category is the amount of human participation required for obtaining the CDM mappings. Dynamic changes in semantics or the schemas of the individual databases can also lead to rehauls in the CDM (mappings) requiring major (and hence costly) human interventions.

2) Approaches based on higher-order logics: The second approach for schema integration involves defining a higher-order language that can express queries ranging over the meta-information corresponding to the individual databases and their schemas. Thus a CDM, as defined in the previous case is not required: the higher-order language in some sense plays the role of the CDM here. The major advantage associated with this approach is the declarativity it derives from its logical foundations.

Krishnamurthy and Naqvi [KN88] proposes a horn-clause like language that can "range over" both data and meta-data by allowing higher-order variables. This language has most if not all of the power of Prolog and unlike Prolog, is declarative. It is based on bottom-up semantics and the approach replaces higher-order unification with the term matching operation. Krishnamurthy, Litwin, and Kent [KLK91] extends this language and demonstrates its relational schema integration capabilities. However, they do not provide a formal model-theoretic semantics for their language.

An interesting approach that falls in between the above two classifications is the

M(DM) model of Barsalou and Gangopadhyay [BG92]. M(DM) deals with a set of metatypes each formalizing the data model construct in second-order logic. Although the combination of logic, object orientation and metaprogramming gives much power to M(DM), its second-order nature raises questions about the possibility of practical implementations based on this approach. Also, its semantics appears quite complex.

Thus, we find the problem of schema integration being tackled at a very specific and local level than in its true spirit at a general and global level. Part of the reasons for this could be attributed to the complexities associated with the problem. We believe that *declarativity* is a key requirement for integrating and querying component databases in a HDBS. A logic based approach for schema integration would bring the advantages of clear foundations, sound formalism, and proof procedures thus providing for a truly declarative environment. Conventional database query languages are based on predicate calculus and are useful for querying the data in a database. But schema integration necessitates a functionality to query not only the data in a database but also its schema or meta-data. This calls for a higher-order language which treats "components" of such meta-data as "first class" entities in its semantic structure. In such a framework, queries that manipulate data as well as their schema "in the same breath" could be naturally formulated.

In this paper, we develop the logical foundations of schema integration of HDBS based on a higher-order logic called *SchemaLog*. Our syntax was inspired in part by that of [KN88]. However while they provide no formal semantics, we develop model-theoretic, fixpoint and proof-theoretic semantics for SchemaLog. Besides, technically the framework developed by us is different from theirs. SchemaLog, like HiLog (Chen et. al. [CKW90]), is syntactically higher-order but semantically first-order. In this paper, we confine ourselves to the schema integration problem for relational databases. Our eventual objective is to extend SchemaLog into a logic capable of providing for the integration of different data models (notably the object oriented model).

We first introduce SchemaLog informally with a motivating example (Section 2). The formal syntax and model-theoretic semantics are then developed (Section 3). We then consider programming in SchemaLog, develop the fixpoint semantics of the Horn clause fragment of SchemaLog, and establish the equivalence to the model-theoretic semantics (Section 4.1). We also develop a proof procedure and show that it is sound and complete (Section 4.2). We give a variety of examples illustrating the power and applicability of SchemaLog for the following problems: database programming, schema integration, schema evolution, and cooperative query answering (Section 5). We also make a case for adopting a uniform framework for schema integration and evolution and illustrate via examples how SchemaLog could fulfill this need. We compare SchemaLog with existing higher-order logics such as HiLog (Chen et. al. [CKW90]), F-logic (Kifer et. al. [KLW90]), HOL (Manchanda [Man89]), and COL (Abiteboul and Grumbach [AG87]), and also comment on the "design decisions" we made in the development of SchemaLog (Section 6). Finally, we give our conclusions and discuss future research (Section 7). For lack of space, we suppress all the proofs. The complete details of the results in this paper can be found in [LSS93].

2 SchemaLog by Example

In this section, we will introduce the syntax and intuitive meaning of our proposed language informally via an example. We will follow it with a formal account of the syntax and semantics in the next section.

Example 2.1 *Consider a federation of university databases consisting of relational databases univ_A, univ_B, and univ_C corresponding to each of the three universities A, B, and C. Each database maintains information on the university's departments, staff, and their average salary[2]. Let the schema for the three databases be the following.*

Database univ_A:
relation: *pay_info* : $(dept, category, avg\_sal)$

Database univ_B:
relation: *pay_info* : $(category, dept_1, dept_2, \ldots)$
(Note: Domain of $dept_1, dept_2$, etc. is that of avg_sal in univ_A)

Database univ_C:
relation: $dept_1$: $(category, avg\_sal)$
relation: $dept_2$: $(category, avg\_sal)$
$\ldots$

The *univ_A* database has a single relation *pay_info* which has one tuple for each department and each category in that department. The database *univ_B* also has a single relation, (also *pay_info*), but in this case, department names appear as attribute names and the values corresponding to them are the average salaries. *univ_C* has as many relations as there are departments, and has tuples corresponding to each category and its average salary in each of the $dept_i$ relations.

The heterogeneity in these representations is evident from the example[3]: the atomic values of *univ_A* ($dept_i$s) appear as attribute names in *univ_B* and relation names in *univ_C*. The user of one of these databases may need to interact with the other databases in the context of the federation of universities. We would like (for the user) to be able to express queries such as the following.

---

[2] It might be thought unusual to store average salaries in the database. But if the databases store statistical information on the different universities, this would indeed be natural.

[3] We are taking a simplified version of the problem by assuming the 'names' to be the same across the databases. In reality this might not be so; for eg. $dept_i$ in one db/relation might correspond to $department_i$ in another. But this issue can be suppressed here without loss of generality as such "name mappings" can be easily realized in our framework.

Q1: *Which are the departments that have an average salary of above $25K in all the three universities for any given category?*

Q2: *List similar departments in univ_B and univ_C that have the same average salary for similar categories of staff.*

Following [KLK91], we can visualize the "universe of discourse"[4] as a tuple of databases where each database is a tuple of relations and each relation is a set of tuples of objects (which are simply values). Identification of the set of tuples which constitute a relation could be accomplished by associating tuple-ids with them. Now the query Q1 can be expressed in SchemaLog as[5]:

$$? - univ\_A \, [\, pay\_info(T_1 : \ dept \rightarrow D, \ category \rightarrow C, \ avg\_sal \rightarrow S_1)],$$
$$univ\_B \, [\, pay\_info(T_2 : \ category \rightarrow C, \ D \rightarrow S_2)], \ D \neq \text{`category'},$$
$$univ\_C \, [\, D(T_3 : \ category \rightarrow C, \ avg\_sal \rightarrow S_3)], \ S_1 > 25K,$$
$$S_2 > 25K, \ S_3 > 25K$$

and query Q2 can be expressed as:

$$? - univ\_B \, [\, pay\_info(T_1 : \ category \rightarrow C, \ D \rightarrow S)], \ D \neq \text{`category'},$$
$$univ\_C \, [\, D(T_2 : \ category \rightarrow C, \ avg\_sal \rightarrow S)]$$

Notice that in query Q1, variable D ranges over domain values as well as attribute and relation names. It is this flexibility which makes such a querying medium highly expressive and declarative. The variables T_i intuitively stand for the tuple-ids corresponding to the tuples in the relations.

In queries Q1 and Q2, the variable D is explicitly compared with the attribute *category* as D occurs in a position which ranges over attributes. Thus an explicit comparison is required, unless it is known, for e.g. that there is no relation called *category* in *univ_C*.

3 SchemaLog - Syntax and Semantics

In this section we formally present the syntax and semantics of our language.

3.1 Syntax

We use strings starting with a lower case letter for constants and those starting with an upper case letter for variables. As a special case, we use t_i to denote arbitrary terms of the language. $\mathcal{A}, \mathcal{B}, \dots$ denote arbitrary well-formed formulas and A, B, ... denote arbitrary (ground) atoms.

The language $\mathcal{L}$ of SchemaLog has two sorts: a *db-sort*, and a *non-db-sort*. The vocabulary of $\mathcal{L}$ consists of pairwise disjoint countable sets $\mathcal{D}$ (of database symbols),

---

[4] The term universe of discourse is used informally here. It is technically different from the domain of a semantic structure of our logic which is formalized in Section 3.

[5] Existential variables can be projected out by writing rules. Here, we mainly focus on the intuition behind the syntax of SchemaLog.

S (of non-db symbols), $\mathcal{G}$ (of function symbols of different sorts $s_1 \times \ldots \times s_n \rightarrow s_{n+1}$ where $s_i \in \{db, non\text{-}db\}$), $\mathcal{V}_d$ (of db variables), and $\mathcal{V}_n$ (of non-db variables), the usual logical connectives $\neg, \vee, \wedge, \exists$, and $\forall$.

The set of terms $\mathcal{T}$ of $\mathcal{L}$ consists of *db-terms* $\mathcal{T}_{db}$, and *non-db-terms* $\mathcal{T}_{non}$. Every symbol in $\mathcal{D} \cup \mathcal{V}_d$ is a db-term. Every symbol in $\mathcal{S} \cup \mathcal{V}_n$ is a non-db-term. Whenever f is a function symbol of sort $s_1 \times \ldots \times s_n \rightarrow s$ and $t_1, \ldots, t_n$ are terms of sort $s_1, \ldots, s_n$ respectively, $f(t_1, \ldots, t_n)$ is an s-term, where s is either the *db-sort* or the *non-db-sort*.

An *atomic formula* of $\mathcal{L}$ is an expression of one of the following forms:

```
<db>[<rel>(<tid>: <attr> → <val>)]
<db>[<rel>(<attr>)]
<db>[<rel>]
<db>
```

where `<db>` is a *db*-term, `<rel>`, `<attr>`, `<tid>`, and `<val>` are *non-db*-terms. In an atom of the form `<db>[<rel>(<tid>: <attr> → <val>)]`, we refer to the terms `<db>`, `<rel>`, `<attr>`, and `<val>` as the *non-id components* and `<tid>` as the *id component*. The id component intuitively stands for tuple-ids (tid's). The *depth* of an atomic formula A, denoted $depth(A)$, is the number of non-id components in A. The depths of the four categories of atoms introduced above are 4,3,2, and 1 respectively. By our definition of atoms, an id-component appears only in atoms of depth 4. The well-formed formulas (wff's) of $\mathcal{L}$ are defined as usual: $\neg \mathcal{A}, \mathcal{A} \vee \mathcal{B}, \mathcal{A} \wedge \mathcal{B}, (\exists X)\mathcal{A}$, and $(\forall X)\mathcal{A}$ are wff's of $\mathcal{L}$ whenever $\mathcal{A}$ and $\mathcal{B}$ are wff's and X is a variable.

We also permit *molecular formulas* of the form $db[rel(tid : attr_1 \rightarrow val_1, \ldots, attr_n \rightarrow val_n)]$ as an abbreviation of the corresponding well-formed formula $db[rel(tid : attr_1 \rightarrow val_1)] \wedge \ldots \wedge db[rel(tid : attr_n \rightarrow val_n)]$.

A *literal* is an atom or the negation of an atom. A *clause* is a formula of the form $\forall X_1 \ldots \forall X_m (L_1 \vee \ldots \vee L_n)$ where each L_i is a literal and $X_1, \ldots, X_m$ are all the variables occurring in $L_1 \vee \ldots \vee L_n$. A *definite clause* is a clause of the form $A \leftarrow B_1, \ldots, B_n$ which contains precisely one atom called the *head* in its consequent. $B_1, \ldots, B_n$ is called the *body* of the definite clause. A *unit clause* is a clause of the form $A \leftarrow$, that is a definite clause with an empty body.

3.2   Semantics

Let U_{db} be a non-empty set of elements (called database *intensions* corresponding to the *db*-terms) and U be a non-empty set of elements (called non-database *intensions* corresponding to the *non-db*-terms). Consider a function $\mathcal{I}_{db}$ ($\mathcal{I}_{non}$) that maps each database (non-database) symbol to its corresponding intension in U_{db} (U) and a function $\mathcal{I}_{fun}$ which interprets the function symbols as functions of the appropriate sort. The true atoms of the model are captured using a function $\mathcal{F}$ which takes as arguments the name of the database, the relation name, attribute name, and tuple-id and maps to a corresponding individual value. Thus for a given atomic formula to be true, the function $\mathcal{F}$ corresponding to the formula (after mapping the symbols of the formula to their corresponding intensions) should be *defined* in the structure (and the values should match).

A *semantic structure* M for our language is a tuple $< U_{db}, U, \mathcal{I}_{db}, \mathcal{I}_{non}, \mathcal{I}_{fun}, \mathcal{F} >$ where

- U_{db} is a non-empty set of database intensions;
- U is a non-empty set of non-database intensions;
- $\mathcal{I}_{db}: \mathcal{D} \rightarrow U_{db}$ is a function that associates an element of U_{db} with each (database) symbol in $\mathcal{D}$;
- $\mathcal{I}_{non}: \mathcal{S} \rightarrow U$ is a function that associates an intension of U with each (non-database) symbol in $\mathcal{S}$.
- $\mathcal{I}_{fun}(f) : U_{s_1} \times \ldots \times U_{s_n} \rightarrow U_{s_{n+1}}$, where f is a function symbol of sort $s_1 \times \ldots \times s_n \rightarrow s_{n+1}$ in $\mathcal{G}$, and $s_i \in \{db, non\text{-}db\}$
- $\mathcal{F} : U_{db} \rightsquigarrow [U \rightsquigarrow [U \rightsquigarrow [U \rightsquigarrow U]]]$, where $[A \rightsquigarrow B]$ denotes the set of all partial functions from A to B.

A *vaf* (variable assignment function) is a function $\nu : V \longrightarrow U \cup U_{db}$ such that whenever $X \in V_d$, $\nu(X) \in U_{db}$ and whenever $X \in V_n$, $\nu(X) \in U$. We extend it to the set $\mathcal{T}$ of terms as follows.

- $\nu(s) = \mathcal{I}_{non}(s)$ for every $s \in \mathcal{S}$,
- $\nu(d) = \mathcal{I}_{db}(d)$ for every $d \in \mathcal{D}$, and
- $\nu(f(t_1, \ldots, t_k)) = \mathcal{I}_{fun}(f)(\nu(t_1), \ldots, \nu(t_k))$, where f is a function symbol of sort $s_1 \times \ldots \times s_k \rightarrow s_{k+1}$ in $\mathcal{G}$ and t_i are terms of sort s_i, where $s_i \in \{db, non\text{-}db\}$.

Let $t_1 \in \mathcal{T}_{db}$, $t_2, t_3, t_5 \in \mathcal{T}_{non}$, and $t_4 \in \mathcal{T}$ be any terms. The *satisfaction* of an atomic formula ϕ, in a structure M under a vaf ν is defined as follows.

- Let ϕ be of the form $t_1[t_2(t_4 : t_3 \rightarrow t_5)]$. Then $M \models_\nu \phi$ iff $\mathcal{F}(\nu(t_1))(\nu(t_2))(\nu(t_3))(\nu(t_4))$ is defined in M, and $\mathcal{F}(\nu(t_1))(\nu(t_2))(\nu(t_3))(\nu(t_4)) = \nu(t_5)$
- Let ϕ be of the form $t_1[t_2(t_3)]$. Then $M \models_\nu \phi$ iff $\mathcal{F}(\nu(t_1))(\nu(t_2))(\nu(t_3))$ is defined in M.
- Let ϕ be of the form $t_1[t_2]$. Then $M \models_\nu \phi$ iff $\mathcal{F}(\nu(t_1))(\nu(t_2))$ is defined in M.
- Let ϕ be of the form t_1. Then $M \models_\nu \phi$ iff $\mathcal{F}(\nu(t_1))$ is defined in M.

Satisfaction of compound formulas is defined in the usual way:

- $M \models_\nu (\phi \vee \psi)$ iff $M \models_\nu \phi$ or $M \models_\nu \psi$;
- $M \models_\nu (\neg\phi)$ iff $M \not\models_\nu \phi$;
- $M \models_\nu (\exists X)\phi$ iff for *some* vaf μ, that may possibly differ from ν only on X, $M \models_\mu \phi$;

For *closed* formulas, $M \models_\nu \phi$ does not depend on ν and we can simply write $M \models \phi$.

Before closing this section, we note that built-in predicates $(=, \neq, \leq, etc.)$ can be introduced and interpreted in SchemaLog in the usual manner. We shall freely make use of built-in predicates in our examples.

4 Programming in SchemaLog

4.1 Fixpoint Semantics

We will consider a program P to be a set of definite clauses. The notion of Herbrand base, Herbrand interpretation and Herbrand model follow that of the conventional ones with extensions induced by the nested structure of SchemaLog atoms.

Definition 4.1 *Let ϕ be an atomic formula of depth n, $1 \leq n \leq 4$. The restriction of ϕ to depth m, $m \leq n$, is the formula ϕ' obtained by retaining the first m non-id components of ϕ.*

E.g., The restriction of $t_1[t_2(t_4 : t_3 \rightarrow t_5)]$ to depth 3, 2, 1 are $t_1[t_2(t_3)]$, $t_1[t_2]$ and t_1 respectively. (The restriction to depth 4 is itself.)

Definition 4.2 *Let I be a set of ground atoms. Then the closure of I, denoted $cl(I)$, is defined as $cl(I) = \{A \mid \exists B \in I \text{ s.t. } A \text{ is the restriction of } B \text{ to depth } m, \text{ for some } m \leq depth(B) \}$*

A set of atoms I is closed if $cl(I) = I$.

We extend the notion of closure to a set $\mathcal{I}$ of sets of atoms by defining $cl(\mathcal{I}) =_{def} \{cl(I) \mid I \in \mathcal{I}\}$.

Let P be a definite program. Then the *Herbrand universe* of P is the set of all ground (i.e. variable-free) terms that can be constructed using the symbols in P. The *Herbrand base* B_P of P is the set of all ground atoms that can be formed using the logical symbols appearing in P. Note that by definition, the Herbrand base of a program is closed. A *Herbrand interpretation I* of P is any closed subset of B_P. It can be shown that a Herbrand interpretation obtained from first principles using the definition of a structure by interpreting all logical symbols as themselves and the function symbols in $\mathcal{G}$ in the usual "Herbrand" style is equivalent to this simpler notion of Herbrand interpretation. I is a *model* of P if it satisfies all the clauses in P. It is easy to show that the union (intersection) of closed subsets of B_P is closed. We then have,

Definition 4.3 *Let P be a definite program. Then $cl(2^{B_P})$, the set of all Herbrand interpretations of P, is a complete lattice under the partial order of set inclusion $\subseteq$. The top element of this lattice is B_P and the bottom element is Φ. Union and intersection correspond to the join and meet as usual.*

Definition 4.4 *Let P be a definite program. The mapping $T_P : cl(2^{B_P}) \rightarrow cl(2^{B_P})$ is defined as follows. let I be a Herbrand interpretation. Then $T_P(I) = cl(\{A \in B_P \mid A \leftarrow A_1, ..., A_n \text{ is a ground instance of a clause in } P \text{ and } \{A_1, ..., A_n\} \subseteq I\})$.*

We have the following results.

Lemma 4.1 *Let P be a definite program. The mapping T_P is monotonic and continuous.*

Lemma 4.2 *Let P be a definite program and I be a Herbrand Interpretation of P. Then I is a model for P iff $T_P(I) \subseteq I$.*

Theorem 4.1 *(Fixpoint characterization of Least Herbrand Model)*
Let P be a definite program. Let $\mathcal{M}(P)$ be the set of all Herbrand models of P and let $\cap \mathcal{M}(P)$ be their intersection. Then $\cap \mathcal{M}(P)$ is a model of P called the least Herbrand model of P. Further $\cap \mathcal{M}(P) = lfp(T_p) = T_p \uparrow \omega = \{A \mid A \in B_P \wedge P \models A\}$.

The proof of this theorem follows arguments very similar to those for classical logic programming (see [vEK76]). □

Allowing negation in SchemaLog programs is fairly straightforward. For example, stratified negation (see Apt et. al. [ABW88]) can be easily supported and the fixpoint semantics can be correspondingly extended.

4.2 Proof Theory of SchemaLog

In this section, we present a resolution based proof theory for SchemaLog. We consider the issues of Herbrand theorem, unification, and resolution. We consider the definite clause subset of $\mathcal{L}$ for the proof procedure[6].

Proposition 4.1 *Let S be a set of clauses and suppose S has a model. Then S has a Herbrand model.*

Lemma 4.3 *A set of clauses is unsatisfiable iff it is false with respect to all Herbrand structures.*

Theorem 4.2 *(Herbrand's Theorem) A set of wffs in clausal form is unsatisfiable iff there is a finite conjunction of ground instances of its clauses which is unsatisfiable.*

<u>Proof sketch</u>: It can be shown [LSS93] that there is a transformation from SchemaLog to first order logic such that a SchemaLog formula ϕ is true in a structure $\mathcal{M}$ under vaf ν iff the corresponding first order formula ϕ_f is true in the corresponding first order structure $\mathcal{M}_f$ under the vaf ν. Herbrand's theorem can now be proved from the above result using a technique similar to that used for predicate calculus [CL73]. □

---

[6] Actually, the proof theory is sound and complete for all clausal theories.

Unification: Unification in SchemaLog has to be treated differently from the way it is done conventionally. In our case, unlike in predicate calculus, there is a natural need for literals of unequal depth to be unified. To see this, consider the following example.

Consider the definite program $P = \{db[rel(attr)] \leftarrow \}$ asserting the existence of a database db, with a relation named rel, for which an attribute $attr$ is defined. Now, consider a query : $? - db[rel]$ which asks about the existence of a database db, with a relation named rel defined on it. Resolution, in the conventional sense would not result in a refutation (whereas it should!). Now let us "switch" the (head of the) rule and the goal, i.e. consider the program $P = \{db[rel] \leftarrow \}$ and the query $? - db[rel(attr)]$. Intuitively, we understand that the resolution should fail.

The above example illustrates two key issues: (1) Unification in SchemaLog involves 'unlike' literals and (2) unifiability is not commutative. Intuitively, the above issues are related to the definition of *closure* in the fixpoint theory. This in turn is associated with the nested structure of atoms allowed in our language. Thus, the conventional notion of unification needs to be extended. We discuss this next.

A *substitution* is a finite set of the form $\{t_1/X_1, \ldots, t_n/X_n\}$, where $X_1, \ldots, X_n$ are distinct variables, and every term t_i is different from X_i, where $1 \leq i \leq n$. A literal L_j is *reducible to* literal L_i, if L_i is L_j restricted to $depth(L_i)$. A *unifier* of literal L_i *with* literal L_j is a substitution θ such that $L_j\theta$ is reducible to $L_i\theta$. Literal L_i is *unifiable with* literal L_j if there is a unifier of L_i with L_j. A unifier σ of a literal L_i with literal L_j is a *most general unifier* (mgu) iff for each unifier θ for L_i with L_j, there exists a substitution λ such that $\theta = \sigma\lambda$.

We refer the reader to [LSS93] for complete details of the unification algorithm, which is essentially obtained by simple modifications to the corresponding algorithm for predicate logic. The modifications account for the differences in the syntax.

SLD-Resolution: Let C be a clause of the form $A \leftarrow B_1, \ldots, B_l$, G be a query $\leftarrow A_1, \ldots, A_k$, A_m be the selected atom in G, and let θ be the mgu of A_m with A. Then $G' \equiv \leftarrow (A_1, \ldots, A_{m-1}, B_1, \ldots, B_l, A_{m+1}, \ldots, A_k)\theta$ is called a *resolvent* of G and C using θ. Let P be a definite program and G a definite goal. An *SLD-derivation* of $P \cup \{G\}$ consists of a (possibly infinite) sequence $G_0 = G, G_1, \ldots$ of goals, a sequence $C_1, C_2, \ldots$ of variants of program clauses of P, and a sequence $\theta_1, \theta_2, \ldots$ of mgus such that each G_{i+1} is a resolvent of G_i and C_{i+1} using θ_{i+1}. An *SLD-refutation* of $P \cup \{G\}$ is a finite SLD-derivation of $P \cup \{G\}$ which has the empty clause $\square$ as the last goal in the derivation. The notions of correct and computed answers are defined in a manner identical to that for standard logic programming (e.g., see Lloyd [Llo87]). We can prove,

Theorem 4.3 *Soundness of SLD-Resolution:*
Let P be a definite program and G a definite goal. Then every computed answer for $P \cup \{G\}$ is a correct answer for $P \cup \{G\}$.

<u>Proof sketch</u>: This theorem can be proved by a simple induction on the length of the refutation. The details can be found in [LSS93]. □

Theorem 4.4 *Completeness of SLD-resolution:*
Let P be a definite program and G be a goal. For every correct answer θ for
$P \cup \{G\}$*, there exists a computed answer σ for* $P \cup \{G\}$ *and a substitution γ*
such that $\theta = \sigma\gamma$.

<u>Proof sketch</u>: The proof makes use of the *mgu lemma* and the *lifting lemma*. These lemmas can be proved in a way similar to that for predicate calculus. The details can be found in [LSS93]. □

Molecular programming vs Atomic programming

We mentioned in Section 3.1 that molecular formulas can be introduced in the syntax of SchemaLog as an abbreviation for a conjunction of atomic formulas. Molecular formulas can indeed provide a mechanism for direct, convenient programming. Let us illustrate this point with an example.

Consider the (good old!) example of grandfathers. The grandfather predicate can be defined (from the parent predicate) in SchemaLog using the rule $db[grandpa(f(X,Y) : pers \rightarrow X, \; fath \rightarrow Y)] \leftarrow db[par(T_1 : pers \rightarrow X, \; fath \rightarrow Z)], \; db[par(T_2 : pers \rightarrow Z, \; fath \rightarrow Y)]$[7]. Notice that this rule makes use of molecules. The precise model-theoretic semantics of molecular formulas in SchemaLog relies on their equivalence to a corresponding conjunction of atoms. However, as the reader can very well verify (!), expressing the same rule using only atoms[8] would be quite cumbersome. We remark that in a relational context, one could completely dispense with tid's (in an interface) as long as molecular programming is supported by the system. The system can always fill in the tid's. The point, however, is that tid's are needed in order to keep the model-theoretic semantics of SchemaLog simple. Besides, they are quite in keeping with our eventual objective of providing for the integration of disparate data models, including the object-oriented model. We remark that the fixpoint theory and proof theory of molecular programs are straightforward extensions of those for atomic programs. In the rest of this paper, we shall freely make use of molecules in our examples.

Programming Predicates

In the context of queries as well as view definitions, it will be convenient to have the (facility for) predicates (which are not part of any database) available. The difference between such predicates and those in a database is that they may be viewed as corresponding to views and hence one need not carry along the tid's with such predicates. We call such predicates *programming predicates* (for distinction from the database predicates). On the technical side, programming predicates can be easily incorporated in SchemaLog by introducing a separate

---

[7] The reason for the special manner in which the id-component of the head is constructed has to do with declarative programming of ad hoc recursive queries, as motivated by Ullman [Ull91]. The details are discussed at length in [LSS93].

[8] This will necessitate two rules – one for each argument of the predicate *grandpa*.

set of predicate symbols and then interpreting them "classically". We shall freely make use of programming predicates in the examples of Section 5.

5 Applications of SchemaLog

5.1 Database Programming and Schema Browsing

The main advantage of SchemaLog for database programming lies in its simplicity of syntax which buys it ease of programming. Yet its higher-order syntax gives it sufficient power to express complex queries in a natural way thus bringing programming closer to intuition. For instance let us take a look at the following example query adopted from [CKW90].

(Q3) *Find the names of all the binary relations in which the token 'john' appears.*

This query can be expressed in HiLog, the following way[9]:

$relations(Y)(X) \leftarrow X(Y, Z)$
$relations(Z)(X) \leftarrow X(Y, Z)$
$? - relations(john)(X)$

Now, consider a variant of Q3
(Q4) *Find the names of* all *the relations in which the token 'john' appears.*

It seems the only way such a query could be expressed in HiLog is by writing one set of rules for each arity of the various relations present in the database (this presupposes the user's knowledge of the schema of the database). By contrast, in SchemaLog this query can be expressed quite elegantly, as follows.

$relations(X, Rel) \leftarrow db[Rel(I: \quad A \rightarrow X)]$
$? - relations('john', Rel)$

Here, we have considered the query in the context of just one database. If all databases and relations where *'john'* occurs are of interest, we could write the rule

$whereabouts(X, DB, Rel) \leftarrow DB[Rel(I: \quad A \rightarrow X)]$

and ask the query $? - whereabouts('john', DB, Rel)$.

On the other hand, if we *specifically* want the binary relations in which *'john'* appears (query Q3), the expression of this query would be less direct (and concise) in SchemaLog than in HiLog. We can write the rules

$arity_{\geq 2}(Rel) \leftarrow db[Rel(A, B)], \quad A \neq B$
$arity_{> 2}(Rel) \leftarrow db[Rel(A, B, C)], \quad A \neq B, \quad B \neq C, \quad A \neq C.$
$arity_2(Rel) \leftarrow arity_{\geq 2}(Rel), \quad \neg arity_{> 2}(Rel).$
$binary\_where(X, Rel) \leftarrow db[Rel(I: \quad A \rightarrow X)], \quad arity_2(Rel).$

and ask the query $? - binary\_where('john', Rel)$. Here $\neg$ is stratified negation.

---

[9] Incidentally, the same browsing capability is available in F-logic too.

We leave it to the reader to judge which of the two types of queries Q3 and Q4 above is more "typical" and practically useful.

5.2 Schema Integration

The applicability of SchemaLog for schema integration was motivated with examples in Section 2. It might be argued that in order for a end user to use the language for querying databases belonging to a federation, she has to be aware of the schemas belonging to the individual databases she is interested in. The queries discussed in Section 2 are only for illustrating the power of the language. The idea is to use our language as a vehicle for formulating views over the databases so that the user could be provided *integration transparency*.

For instance, consider the following example[10] of "higher-order" view defined over the university federation of Example 2.1.

$db\text{-}view[\ p(f(D,C,S,univ\_A):\ department \to D,\ categ \to C,\ a\_sal \to S,$
$db \to univ\_A)] \leftarrow univ\_A[pay\_info(T:\ category \to C,\ dept \to D,\ avg\_sal \to S)].$

$db\text{-}view[\ p(f(D,C,S,univ\_B):\ department \to D,\ categ \to C,\ a\_sal \to S,$
$db \to univ\_B)] \leftarrow univ\_B[pay\_info(T:\ category \to C,\ D \to S)],\ D \neq category$

$db\text{-}view[\ p(f(D,C,S,univ\_C):\ department \to D,\ categ \to C,\ a\_sal \to S,$
$db \to univ\_C)] \leftarrow univ\_C[D(T:\ category \to C,\ avg\_sal \to S)]$

In this example, the (view) relation p is placed in a unified (derived) database called *db-view*. This illustrates the use of rules for defining views. The idea is that a logic program can define a unified view of different schemas in a HDBS, which can be conveniently queried by a federation user. The use of logic rules offers great flexibility in setting up such views.

Higher-order views are an interesting off-shoot of the capabilities of SchemaLog. Such view definition capabilities play an important role in schema integration, obviating the need for a CDM (see Section 1).

5.3 Schema Evolution

Evolution - The Conventional Outlook: *Schema Evolution* is the process of assisting and maintaining the changes to the schematic information and contents of a database. A main objective is to provide *evolution transparency* to the users whereby they would be able to pose queries to the database based on a (possibly old) version of the schema they are familiar with, even if the schema has evolved to a different state. The role of higher-order syntax for supporting schema evolution is an interesting research issue and is investigated further here.

Schema evolution is a somewhat abused term in the database field. There is no clear definition associated with this term and it has been interpreted to mean different things by different researchers. While Kim [Kim90] treats versioning of

---

[10] This example is an adaptation of a similar example in [KN88].

schema for object management as schema evolution, Nguyen and Rieu [NR89] considers the various schema change operations and the associated consequences as being its main issues. Osborn [Syl89] gives some interesting perspectives on the consequences of the polymorphic constructs in object-oriented databases and how this aids in avoiding 'code' evolution.

Our Perspective: Ullman [Ull87] argues for the need for allowing the user to be ignorant about the structure of the database and pose queries to the database with only the knowledge about the attributes (in all relations) of the database. This is an interesting aspect which will make the front-end to the user more declarative, as she is no longer bothered about the schema of the database. As pointed out by Ullman, all natural language interfaces essentially require a facility to handle such needs.

Consider an application which has schema changes happening in a dynamic way. Every time the schema gets modified, the previous application programs written for the database become invalid and the user will have to rewrite/modify them after 'updating' herself about the schema status. We maintain that a end user should not be bothered with the details about the schema of the database she is using, especially if it keeps changing often. A better approach would be to assume that the user has the knowledge of a particular schema and let her use this to formulate queries against the database, even after the schema has been modified. The idea is to shield the modifications to the schema of the database from the user as much as possible.

We argue that a uniform approach to schema integration and evolution is both desirable and possible. We view the schema evolution problem from the schema integration point of view in the following way. Each stage of the schema evolution may be conceptually considered a different (database) schema that we are dealing with. The mappings between different database schemas can be defined using logic programs in a suitable higher-order language such as SchemaLog. This framework affords the possibility of *schema-independent querying and programming*.

We consider an example to illustrate our approach. This example assumes there has been no loss of information in the meta-data, between different stages of the evolution.

Time t1:
$schema_1$: $rel_1(a_{11}, a_{12}, a_{13})$ $rel_2(a_{21}, a_{22})$.

Time t2 (current schema):
$schema_2$: $rel_1(a_{11}, a_{12})$ $rel'_1(a_{12}, a_{13})$ $rel_2(a_{21}, a_{22})$.

Relation rel_1 has been split into rel_1 and rel'_1 at time t2 (assuming the decomposition is loss-less join).

The following SchemaLog program defines a mapping between the two schemas.

$schema_1[rel_1(f(X,Y,Z) : a_{11} \rightarrow X, a_{12} \rightarrow Y, a_{13} \rightarrow Z)] \leftarrow$
$schema_2[rel_1(I' : a_{11} \rightarrow X, a_{12} \rightarrow Y)], schema_2[rel'_1(I'' : a_{12} \rightarrow Y, a_{13} \rightarrow Z)]$

$$schema_1[rel_2(f(X,Y): \quad a_{21} \to X, \quad a_{22} \to Y)]$$
$$\leftarrow \quad schema_2[rel_2(I': \quad a_{21} \to X, \quad a_{22} \to Y)]$$

Suppose the user has a view of $schema_1$; she can still pose queries with that view. The transformation program will take care of the relevant evolutionary relationship between the two schemas.

One complication that may arise in the context of schema evolution is that evolution might involve some loss of (meta-)information (say deletion of attributes). How can we produce meaningful answers to queries (based on an older version of the schema) which refer to such "lost" information? We suggest a *cooperative query answering* approach to this problem in the following section.

Cooperative Query Answering: Research in the area of cooperative query answering (CQA) for databases seeks to provide relevant responses to queries posed by users in cases where a direct answer is not very helpful or informative. An overview of the work done in this area can be found in Gaasterland et. al. [GGM92]. We also consider the aspect of CQA, concerned with answering queries in data/knowledge base systems by extending the scope of the query so that more information can be gathered in the answers, as discussed in Cuppens and Demolombe [CD88]. Responses can be generated by looking for answers that are related to the original answers, but are not necessarily literal answers of the original query.

Consider the application of schema evolution discussed in the previous section. We mentioned that in the case of evolution involving loss of meta-information, for a query that addresses the 'lost' (meta-)information, one should not just return a direct nil/false answer, but should provide more relevant information pertaining to the query. This cooperative functionality can be realized in SchemaLog as the following example illustrates.

Example 5.1 *Suppose attr is an attribute defined in a relation rel in schema s_{old}, and assume no concept in the new schema s_{new} corresponds to attr*[11].

The following program computes the "discontinued" parts of a schema.

$$items(Schema, R) \leftarrow Schema[R]$$
$$items(Schema, A) \leftarrow Schema[R(A)]$$
$$items(Schema, V) \leftarrow Schema[R(I : A \to V)]$$

$$discont(S_{new}, X) \leftarrow items(S_{old}, X), \neg items(S_{new}, X).$$

Here $\neg$ is just stratified negation. First, items pairs up schemas and the various items of information that exists in them: relation names, attribute names, and their values. Then discont simply says X is an item that is discontinued from the database. Embellishments can be easily made to this basic idea if information on

---

[11] Notice that the issue of having "correspondence tables" or mappings between old names and new ones as commonly arises in actual implementation and maintenance of federations can be suppressed without loss of generality, because such tables would simply add some edb relations to a logic program that maps S_{old} to S_{new}.

when certain item of (meta-)information was deleted or discontinued were to be kept. In such cases, in addition to telling the user "this item no longer exists in the current database" we can also tell them when it was dropped. A very similar approach can also be taken for identifying items which are newly introduced in S_{new} which never existed in S_{old}.

The second aspect of CQA of interest to us arises when we want to generalize responses to queries, but it is different from the earlier approach in many ways, as the following example illustrates. This example will also illustrate a very useful and powerful way of querying (also involving schema browsing).

Example 5.2 *Consider the query*
(Q5) Tell me all about 'john' that you can possibly find out from the database.

For simplicity, suppose john is a token (i.e. it is only a value) in the database we are considering. The following program expresses this query (T is the token of interest).

(1) $interest(R, I, A, T) \leftarrow db[R(I : A \rightarrow T)]$.
(2) $interest(R, I, A, T) \leftarrow interest(R, I, B, T), db[R(A)]$.
(3) $info(T, R, A, V) \leftarrow interest(R, I, A, T), db[R(I : A \rightarrow V)]$.

Rule (1) says if token T occurs as a value of attribute A for tuple I in relation R, then the 4-tuple $< R, I, A, T >$ is of interest. The second rule says if a certain 4-tuple is of interest with respect to a token T, then any other attribute of the same relation is also of interest. Finally rule (3) simply collects tuples T, R, A, V where T is a token, R is a relation name, A is an attribute name and V is a value (of the attribute A) which pertains to token T.

Now, (under the simple assumption that all about john is contained in a single database), the query Q5 can be expressed as

$? - info('john', R, A, V)$.

In a more complex situation where an item is not known to be a token (i.e. it could be an attribute, relation, or value), one can easily write appropriate rules in SchemaLog to browse/navigate through the schema and compile the relevant information. We close this section noting that CQA (together with schema browsing/navigation) does indeed find interesting applications in the context of a federation. E.g., 'john' could be an international criminal (!) on whom information may have to be tracked down from a (criminal) HDBS. The point is SchemaLog is well equipped to handle such situations. The (inevitably) numerous aliases of 'john' could be captured as an edb relation representing the correspondence mappings between names across the component databases of the federation.

6 Discussion

The notion of "higher-orderness" associated with a logic is ill-defined. Chen et. al. [CKW90] points this out and provides a clear classification of logics based on the order of their syntax and semantics. It is generally believed that higher-order syntax would be quite useful in the context of object-oriented databases, database programming, and schema integration. In this section, we compare SchemaLog with existing higher order logics. We also comment on the "design decisions" made in the development of SchemaLog.

HiLog (Chen et. al. [CKW90]) is a powerful logic based on higher-order syntax but with a first-order semantics. Parameters are arityless in this language and the distinction between predicate, function and constant symbols is eliminated. HiLog terms could be constructed from any logical symbol followed by any finite number of arguments. HiLog also blurs the distinction between the atoms and terms. Thus, the language has a powerful syntactic expressivity and finds natural applications in numerous contexts [see [CKW90] for details]. HiLog has a sound and complete proof theory. [CKW89] discusses the applicability of HiLog as a database programming language. The higher-order syntactic features of the language find interesting applications for schema browsing, set operations, and as an implementation vehicle for object-oriented languages. From the schema integration viewpoint, though HiLog has the concept of arityless-ness, the lack of a means in its syntax to refer to "places" corresponding to attributes or "method" names makes it cumbersome to express queries that range over multiple databases (or even multiple relations within the same database – see Section 5.1). Hence HiLog (without further extensions) seems to be unsuitable for schema integration purposes.

Kifer et. al. [KLW90] provides a logical foundation for object-oriented databases using a logic called *F-logic*. Like Hilog, F-logic is a logic with a higher-order syntax but a first-order semantics[12]. The logic is powerful enough to capture the object-oriented notions of complex objects, classes, types, methods, and inheritance. F-logic also has a schema browsing facility which hints at the possibility of its application as a schema integration language. However it does not have a means of referring to individual schemas (as first class citizens) which is vital in schema integration applications.

A higher-order language for computing with labeled sets is introduced in Manchanda [Man89]. The language supports structured data, object-identity, and sets. This also belongs to the above class of languages in that its semantics is first-order. This paper also illustrates a template mechanism to define the database schema. But it is not obvious how to extend this language to a framework which would support queries over higher-order objects across multiple databases.

Abiteboul and Grumbach [AG87] introduces a logic called COL for defining and manipulating complex objects. *COL* achieves the functionality for manipulating complex objects by introducing what are called (base and derived) "data functions". The syntax as well as the semantics of COL is higher-order. The syntax

---

[12] When non-monotonic method inheritance is not considered.

does not support the constructs necessary for schema integration applications.

In principle, one could augment HiLog or F-Logic with the facilities for naming individual schemas as well as naming attributes (in the case of HiLog). In our project, we have chosen to start from a "neutral zone" and try to build a logic that is as simple as possible while effectively solving the problem on hand. We also remark that making SchemaLog arityless (like HiLog) (also see discussions on molecular programs in Section 4) presents no problems for the semantics. In this paper, we have chosen to keep the logic no more complex than necessary for the problem studied here. We remark that even with this simplicity, SchemaLog appears to be quite powerful and easy to program in for several applications (see Section 5).

We close this section by noting that even though we have presented SchemaLog as a many-sorted logic in this paper, it is mainly for the sake of expositional clarity. The sorts are not really necessary and can be eliminated using techniques similar to those used in the reduction of many-sorted logic to standard first order logic.

7 Conclusions and Future Research

The objective of this work has been to study the logical foundations of the schema integration problem arising in heterogeneous database systems. With this in mind, we have developed a simple logic called SchemaLog. The simple yet flexible syntax of SchemaLog makes it possible to express powerful queries and programs in the context of schema integration. SchemaLog treats the data in a database, the schema of the individual databases in a federation, as well as the databases themselves as first class citizens. This makes SchemaLog (syntactically) higher-order. We have developed a simple first-order semantics for SchemaLog, based on the idea (*e.g.*, see [CKW90]) of making the intensions of higher-order objects explicit in the semantic structure and making the higher-order variables range over these intensions rather than the extensions they stand for. We have also developed a fixpoint theoretic and proof-theoretic semantics of SchemaLog (for definite clause programs). In fact, the framework can be easily extended to incorporate the various forms of negation extensively studied in the literature of deductive databases and logic programming (see [She88] for a survey), notably stratified negation, with minor modifications.

Even though SchemaLog is quite simple, our study (and our experience) indicates that it has a rich expressive power making it applicable to a variety of problems including database programming (with schema browsing), schema integration and evolution, and cooperative query answering.

In [LSS93], we give a reduction of SchemaLog to first-order logic. Several issues remain open. Our proof theory is complete only for clausal theories. Skolemization is an issue just as it is in HiLog and we are presently working on resolving it[13]. In this first step, we have confined ourselves to schema integration of mul-

---

[13] We cannot make use of the device used in HiLog to get around it, as SchemaLog (in its present form) is not arityless.

tiple relational databases. Once a complete proof theory is established for the whole logic, we propose to extend it in a direction which will provide a logical foundation for the schema integration of HDBS featuring disparate data models. We are also interested in an efficient implementation of SchemaLog (supporting molecular programming). Our ongoing work addresses these and related issues.

References

[ABW88] K. R. Apt, H. A. Blair, and A. Walker. Towards a theory of declarative knowledge. In J. Minker, editor, *Foundations of Deductive Databases and Logic Programming*. Morgan-Koffmann, 1988.

[ACM90] ACM. *ACM Computing Surveys*, volume 22, Sept 1990. Special issue on HDBS.

[AG87] S. Abiteboul and S. Grumbach. Col: A logic-based language for complex objects. In *Proc. of Workshop on Database Programming Languages*, pages 253–276, 1987.

[Ahm91] R. Ahmed et. al. The pegasus heterogeneous multidatabase system. *IEEE Computer*, Dec 1991.

[Bat86] C. Batini et. al. A comparitive analysis of methodologies for database schema integration. *ACM Comput. Surveys*, pages 323–364, Dec 1986.

[BG92] T. Barsalou and D. Gangopadhyay. An open framework for interoperation of multimodel multidatabase systems. In *IEEE Data Engg.*, 1992.

[CD88] F. Cuppens and R. Demolombe. Cooperative answering: a methodology to provide intelligent accesss to databases. In *Second Intl. conf. on Expert Database Systems*, 1988.

[CKW89] W. Chen, M. Kifer, and D. S. Warren. Hilog as a platform for database language. In *2nd Intl. workshop on Database Programming Languages*, June 1989.

[CKW90] W. Chen, M. Kifer, and D. S. Warren. A foundation for higher-order logic programming. Expanded paper, 1990.

[CL73] C.L. Chang and R. C. T. Lee. *Symbolic Logic and Mechanical Theorem Proving*. New York, Academic Press, 1973.

[GGM92] T. Gaasterland, P. Godfrey, and J. Minker. An overview of cooperative answering. *Journal of Intelligent Information Systems*, 1:123–157., 1992.

[Hsi92] D. K. Hsiao. Federated databases and systems: Part-one – a tutorial on their data sharing. *VLDB Journal*, 1:127–179, 1992.

[Kim90] Won Kim. *Introduction to Object Oriented Databases*. MIT Press, 1990.

[KLK91] R. Krishnamurthy, W. Litwin, and W. Kent. Language features for interoperability of databases with schematic discrepancies. In *ACM SIGMOD Conference on Management of Data*, pages 40–49, 1991.

[KLW90] M. Kifer, G. Lausen, and J. Wu. Logical foundations of frame-based languages. Technical Report 90/14, SUNY at Stony Brook, August 1990.

[KN88] R. Krishnamurthy and S. Naqvi. Towards a real horn clause language. In *Proceedings of the 14th VLDB Conf.*, pages 252–263, 1988.

[Llo87] J. W. Lloyd. *Foundations of Logic Programming*. Springer Verlag, second edition, 1987.

[LLR90] Witold Litwin, Mark Leo, and Nick Roussopoulos. Interoperability of multiple autonomous databases. *ACM computing surveys*, 22(3):267–293, Sept 1990.

[LR82]   T. Landers and R. Rosenberg.   An overview of multibase.   *Distributed Databases*, pages 153–184, 1982.

[LSS93] L.V.S. Lakshmanan, F. Sadri, and I. N. Subramanian. On the logical foundations of schema integration and evolution in heterogeneous database systems. Technical report, Concordia University, Montreal, July 1993.

[Man89] S. Manchanda. Higher-order logic as a data model. In *Proc. of the North American Conf. on Logic Programming*, pages 330–341, 1989.

[NR89]   G. T. Nguyen and D. Rieu. Schema evolution in object-oriented database systems. *Data and Knowledge Engg., North-Holland*, 4:43–67, 1989.

[She88] J. C. Shepherdson. Negation in logic programming. In J. Minker, editor, *Foundations of Deductive Databases and Logic Programming*. Morgan-Koffmann, 1988.

[SL90]   Amit P. Sheth and James A. Larson. Federated database system for managing distributed, heterogeneous and autonomous databases. *ACM computing surveys*, 22(3):183–236, Sept 1990.

[Syl89] Osborn Sylvia. The role of polymorphism in schema evolution in an object-oriented database. In *IEEE Trans. on Knowledge and Data Engg.*, pages 310–317, Sept 1989.

[Tem87] Templeton et. al. Mermaid: A front-end to distributed heterogeneous databases. In *Proc. IEEE 75, 5*, pages 695–708, May 1987.

[Ull87] J. D. Ullman. Database theory: Past and future. In *Proc. of the ACM PODS*, 1987.

[Ull91] J. D. Ullman. A comparison between deductive and object oriented database systems. In *Proc. Deductive and Object Oriented Databases Conf.*, pages 263–277, 1991.

[vEK76] M. H. van Emden and R. A. Kowalski. The semantics of predicate logic as a programming language. *JACM*, 23(4):733–742, October 1976.

Explaining Program Execution in Deductive Systems

Tarun Arora   Raghu Ramakrishnan
William G. Roth   Praveen Seshadri   Divesh Srivastava

Computer Sciences Department, University of Wisconsin–Madison, 1210 West Dayton Street, Madison, WI 53706, USA.

Abstract. Programs in deductive database and programming systems have a natural meaning that is based upon their mathematical reading as logical rules. High-level 'explanations' of a program evaluation/execution can be constructed to provide added functionality: (1) To debug a program by following a chain of deductions leading to an unexpected (and possibly incorrect) conclusion; (2) To follow the derivation of certain *correct* conclusions to determine why and how they are reached; (3) To identify consequences of a (typically, incorrect or unexpected) fact. This functionality can be utilized either to perform post-mortem analysis of a session, or to interactively develop programs by running queries and viewing their deductions simultaneously.

'Explanations' of programs are especially important in the context of deductive databases for three reasons: (1) These programs could involve recursion, and hence, the chain of inferences is often not evident. (2) When the input data set is large, it is very difficult for a user to inspect the data and determine which facts lead to which answers, and exactly how. (3) Such programs do not guarantee a fixed evaluation strategy, and this makes it difficult for a user to comprehend unexpected behavior of a program.

With this motivation, we have designed and implemented an explanation facility for the CORAL deductive database system. The design is based on the representation of a program evaluation as a set of derivation trees, and the facility provides a high-level explanation of the inferences carried out during program execution. A notable feature of the implementation is the boot-strapped use of CORAL in the implementation of the explanation tool. We believe that an explanation system can provide a novel approach to interactively *querying* data, and is useful even for standard relational databases.

1 Introduction

Rule-based systems offer a declarative programming paradigm and encourage a relatively high-level formulation of programs. If we consider systems based upon

The work of the authors was supported by a David and Lucile Packard Foundation Fellowship in Science and Engineering, a Presidential Young Investigator Award with matching grants from DEC, Tandem and Xerox, and NSF grant IRI-9011563.
The authors e-mail addresses are {arora,raghu,roth,praveen,divesh}@cs.wisc.edu.

extensions of Horn-clause rules, a *program* can be understood as a collection of statements of the form: 'If certain facts are true, additional facts can be inferred'. Such a reading of the program is natural and non-operational.

Based on this semantics, *explanations*, that visualize the results of program execution at a suitably high level, can be constructed. Such a capability is useful in a variety of situations. For example, it can be used to debug a program, by following a chain of deductions leading to an unexpected (and possibly incorrect) conclusion. Once an incorrect conclusion is pinpointed, the system can be used to identify other conclusions that arise from it. It can also be used to understand how certain *correct* conclusions are reached — for example, just as the parse tree for a sentence can be viewed as an explanation of why a certain string is accepted as a sentential form, so too, the facts deduced by a rule-based expert system can be 'explained' at the level of the rules and facts used in their derivations.

In this paper, we describe *Explain*, a menu-driven graphical tool for visualizing fact derivations in a logic programming/deductive database language. It is designed to operate in conjunction with the CORAL deductive database system [RSSS93b], and deals specifically with (extended) Horn-clause rules evaluated using bottom-up techniques. It differs significantly from debugging tools available for Prolog-style languages, which are designed for a top-down, backtracking evaluation strategy. A major difference between bottom-up and top-down strategies (used in Prolog-like systems) is that no guarantees are offered with respect to execution order in bottom-up evaluation, and thus, some non-operational abstraction of the computation must be used in explanations. The abstraction used in the *Explain* system is the 'derivation tree'.

The contribution of our work lies in the design and implementation of a clean and powerful explanation facility. The features for navigating derivation trees surpass what is available in other proposed systems, and we provide performance figures that show the system to be capable of handling large data sets with interactive response times. The *Explain* system is now available along with the CORAL system.[1]

2 Motivation

There are many features of deductive databases that do not lend themselves to using traditional debuggers:

- Programs are more sophisticated than non-recursive programs in languages such as SQL, and thus, the chain of inferences is often not obvious.
- The user of a program may be familiar with the rules of the program, but typically views a large set of facts as the *input*. For example, a program analyzing stocks accepts a set of market quotations as input. The derivation of an unexpected conclusion (e.g. 'buy IBM') might depend critically upon some of the input facts. Since the input set can be large, identifying precisely which facts led to the conclusion, and how they did so, is a non-trivial task.

---

[1] Source code in C++ is available via anonymous ftp from ftp.cs.wisc.edu.

Visual inspection of the input data is impossible because of its size, and it is difficult to query a database system to return such information.
- Bottom-up evaluation of logic programs does not guarantee a fixed evaluation strategy, and this makes it difficult for a user to understand the behavior of a program in operational terms.

We believe that an explanation system can provide a novel approach to interactively *querying* data, and is useful even for standard relational databases.

Example 1 : Stock Market Analysis A stock is considered to be *volatile*, if its price falls by more than half in a one-week period:

$$volatile(Stock) : - \ close(Day1, Stock, P1), close(Day2, Stock, P2),$$
$$Day2 > Day1, Day2 - Day1 <= 7, P1/P2 > 2.$$

A common trading heuristic is to use the moving average of the stock price to estimate whether a stock is moving upward or downward. The following rule states that a stock should be sold if its moving average falls by 10% in one week:

$$should\_sell(Stock) : - \ movavg(Day1, Stock, A1), movavg(Day2, Stock, A2),$$
$$Day2 > Day1, Day2 - Day1 <= 7, A1/A2 > 1.1.$$

The database relation *close* contains the daily closing prices for each stock, and can be quite large. The *movavg* predicate is also computed using the *close* relation; we omit the definition for brevity. If a user types in the query $?volatile(S)$, and receives an unexpected response $S =$'*Walmart*' indicating that Walmart is a volatile stock, it is likely that (s)he will want to follow up by asking why the stock was classified as volatile.

The price graph for WalMart may involve a sudden sharp spike on a single day, which the user may decide is an aberration. The next step is to determine if there are any other reasons why Walmart should be considered *volatile*. Assuming that the above rule is the only rule defining *volatile*, this reduces to checking if there is another instantiation of this rule such that Walmart is in *volatile*. Let us suppose that there is no other such instantiation. Then, the user may very well decide that the data for that day should be ignored. However, this poses a new problem: what other inferences have been made using the closing price of Walmart on that day? For example, the moving average of Walmart may well have dropped by over 10% over the week due to the (aberrant) sharp drop on that day, leading to a decision that Walmart stock should be sold!

Explain gives a user a menu-driven graphical tool to explore the derivation steps associated with the evaluation of the original query, and to thereby investigate each of the related follow-up questions mentioned above. In contrast, we invite the reader to consider how such questions could be posed in a standard SQL system. Note that the issue is not recursion, which is the feature traditionally recognized as missing from SQL. What is missing is a way of asking, given an SQL query and a fact, 'What answers to the query depend upon this fact?' While this example illustrated the difficulty of following query execution when the volume of data is large, a similar argument holds for programs like the bill-of-materials computation, where the difficulty is due to the complexity of the computation, not the size of the data.

Example 2 : Bill of Materials Our next example illustrates the importance of having explanations for programs that are more sophisticated than typical SQL queries. It shows that even when the data set is modest in size, explanations can be useful in tracing complex derivation steps. The following program computes the bill-of-materials for a complex mechanical part by recursively computing the bill-of-materials for each of its component parts:

$$b\_o\_m(Part, sum(<C>)) \qquad : - \; subpart\_cost(Part, SubPart, C).$$
$$subpart\_cost(Part, Part, Cost) \quad : - \; basic\_part(Part, Cost).$$
$$subpart\_cost(Part, Subpart, Cost) : - \; assembly(Part, Subpart, Quantity),$$
$$b\_o\_m(Subpart, TotalSubcost),$$
$$Cost = Quantity * TotalSubcost.$$

This kind of query is common in practice. It involves a combination of recursion and aggregation, and depends for correctness upon the acyclicity of the *assembly* relationship. It is certainly not trivial to determine how a *b_o_m* fact is computed from the input relations (*basic_part* and *assembly*). For example, suppose that the cost of a toilet is computed to be $800 (as has been known to be the case!). It would be most interesting to find out precisely which components or subcomponents contributed significantly to this high cost. Again, $\mathcal{Explain}$ allows us to examine the derivation of the *b_o_m* tuple of interest, and to answer this question.

3 An Overview of $\mathcal{Explain}$

3.1 The Requirements

We wanted to develop a graphical tool that is able to visualize the evaluation of a CORAL [RSSS93a] query. Such a tool could be used either for post-mortem analysis of query execution, or for co-ordinated program development and debugging. In either mode, it should support two operations:

1. Trace how a fact is *generated*, in order to pinpoint 'interesting' premises, and
2. Trace how a fact — derived or base — is *used* to generate other facts (e.g. to identify consequences of incorrect premises).

Further, it should be possible to easily interleave the two operations. The ability to present information at this level of facts and rules is important for any reasonable understanding of how answers are computed. The tool should be able to handle the full generality allowed by CORAL, including features like non-ground facts and aggregation over multisets.

Another desirable operation is to trace why a fact is *not* generated. Typically, if a certain fact is missing and a negated goal is therefore satisfied, a user may want to know why the missing fact could not be generated. This can be done in *Explain*, but is not easy to do. (See Section 6.2 for details.)

To better understand the issues involved in the design and implementation of *Explain*, a brief summary of the CORAL database system is in order. CORAL is a deductive database system that has been developed at the University of Wisconsin at Madison. It encourages the construction of queries as *modular* programs expressed in the style of (possibly recursive) logic rules [RSS92]. The evaluation of such rules is performed primarily in a bottom-up fashion, though other evaluation strategies are also supported. The system provides support for advanced features like negation and aggregation in rule bodies, and the presence of variables inside database facts. CORAL provides the user with a command-prompt interface for interactive use, and an interface with C++ to support application development. Persistence is supported for Datalog-style data via an interface to the Exodus storage manager.

3.2 Design Issues

We began with a complete and working version of CORAL, and we needed to add an explanation facility to it. The goal was to provide explanation of programs evaluated bottom-up.[2]

The following decisions were reached with regard to the design:

- The most meaningful way to describe the deduction of answers from facts is by maintaining and displaying derivation trees, that describe the instantiations of rules that lead to the generation of facts. (Derivation trees are described in greater detail in Section 4.) The interface must be graphical and menu-driven as far as possible, and reflect the abstraction of derivation trees. There must be the ability to view multiple derivations side-by-side and switch smoothly between the *derivation* of facts and the *use* of facts.
- The explanation tool should be an independent process that is not compiled into the rest of the CORAL system. In fact, it should be as independent of CORAL as possible, since this approach to visualization could potentially be extended to other rule-based systems. Hence, all interaction should use a clearly defined interface that is as general as possible.
- Since CORAL provides a clean abstraction of program modules, it is natural to look for explanations at the granularity of modules. This would have to be explicitly turned on or off on a per-module basis from within CORAL. The *Explain* tool should be able to display derivation information about any module execution that the CORAL user has specified. If the explanation facility is not in use, there should be no deterioration in the performance of CORAL commands.
- In general, the implementation of the *Explain* tool should support as many CORAL features (like aggregation, non-ground facts, etc.) as possible. Since

---

[2] Our tool does not currently support explanation of CORAL programs evaluated top-down. In principle, this could be done using a Prolog-style debugger.

the explanation information is going to be queried by the user, what better way to answer queries than to use CORAL to process them? *Explain* should therefore be implemented as an independent CORAL application using the CORAL/C++ features extensively. Its basic input data interface should be files of database facts, which can be handled by the CORAL query processing engine with minimal impedance mismatch. This is also aesthetically pleasing, in that CORAL is being used to explain its own execution.

We shall describe some of these decisions in greater detail at the end of Section 7 after the implementation of the system has been presented. At that stage, we will also discuss some alternative design decisions that we could have taken, and the motivation for the choices that we made. The broad design decisions have been described here so that subsequent section on the usage and the implementation of *Explain* might be better understood.

4 Derivation Trees

The representation of *derivations* is central to the design of the system. We use the *derivation tree* as the conceptual structure representing the generation of a fact due to the evaluation of logic rules.

Consider a derivation step in which a rule r (with n body literals) is used to infer a fact f; let $f1 \ldots fn$ be the facts used to instantiate the body of the rule. This derivation step is represented as a *tree fragment*, with root f and children $f1$ through fn, in order. (A base fact in a database relation is the root of a tree fragment with no children, since base facts can be viewed as trivial rules with empty bodies.)

A *derivation tree* for a fact is defined recursively as follows. For all base facts in database relations, the associated tree fragments are derivation trees. For all other facts f, a derivation tree consists of a tree fragment with root f, in which each child fi of f is the root of a derivation tree for fi.

From the above definitions, it should be clear that a derivation tree reflects precisely how a fact is inferred, starting from facts in database relations. *We can thus think of a derivation tree as an explanation of why or how a given fact is derived*; if there are several trees for a given fact, it can be derived in many ways, and each tree represents an explanation of one of these derivations. If a given program execution involves the generation of a particular set of facts, the set of all derivation trees of all these facts provides an explanation of the entire program. Thus, program execution can be represented by a collection of derivation trees. Obviously, such a representation of a program retains no information about the order of execution of derivations. The effects of the computation (in terms of the facts generated) are represented, but not the order in which they occurred. This reflects the model-based semantics provided by CORAL, where the meaning of a program is a model of the world that satisfies the rules of the program.

Since many derivation trees may share common sub-trees, it is highly inefficient to store the entire derivation tree for every fact generated in the course of a program execution. Tree fragments (essentially, encodings of a single rule instantiation) are recorded during program execution, and all actual derivation trees can be constructed by composing stored tree fragments in the appropriate manner. This is much more practical than storing entire derivation trees. The user of $\mathcal{E}xplain$ can essentially view any portion of the entire collection of derivation trees that corresponds to the program execution. What the tool displays at any point of time is a selective window on this collection, and the displayed portions are built incrementally from tree fragments as directed by the user.

5 How $\mathcal{E}xplain$ Is Used

5.1 Enabling Explanation during CORAL Execution

Queries to the CORAL database system are usually submitted by typing them in at a command-prompt (just as in most Prolog systems). Various commands are also permitted at the prompt, one of which is a command to turn on the generation of information that will be used by the explanation tool. This command can be specified selectively for some program modules, or generally across all modules. Complementary commands exist to turn off the generation of such information. The actual information generation involves the writing of facts to a file that will be accessed by $\mathcal{E}xplain$. There is one such 'dump' file for every CORAL program module for which explanation generation is turned on.

5.2 Layout of the User Interface

$\mathcal{E}xplain$ works in a windowing environment with a point and click user interface that consists of two basic components: a Definition Window and a Uses Window.

```
module anc.
export anc(bf).

anc(X, Y) : − edge(X, Y).
anc(X, Y) : − edge(X, Z), anc(Z, Y).

end_module.
```

Fig. 1. The *anc* module

Figure 1 shows a CORAL program module that defines the recursive ancestor relation. Figure 2 shows how the *Definition window* displays the dump of an execution of the anc module, showing how facts are 'defined' using program rules. There are two scrollable browsers in the Definition window. The top browser labeled **Predicates** shows a list of all the unique predicate names

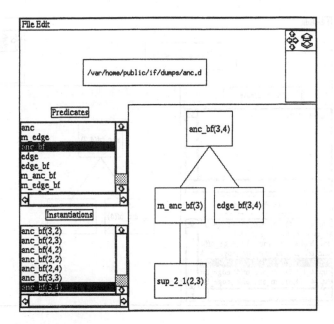

Fig. 2. The Definition Window

found in the dump file. When the user selects one of the predicates, all of the facts corresponding to that predicate are shown in the lower scrollable browser labeled **Instantiations**. When a particular fact is selected, its derivation tree is shown in the graphics window. The Definition window maintains a one level 'undo' operation for all derivation trees that are removed from the screen.

The *Uses window* shows the rule instances where a particular fact occurs in the body of the rule. An example of the Uses window is shown in Figure 3. The window has the same layout as the Definition window, though the browsers are different. The top browser shows the fact whose uses are being displayed. The lower browser shows the instantiated rules where the fact is used. To display a derivation (i.e. an instantiated rule), the user selects a rule in the lower browser, and the corresponding derivation tree is displayed. Once such a derivation tree is displayed, the Uses window provides functionality similar to that provided by the Definition window, in terms of selecting nodes and further exploring the derivation tree. For instance, by selecting $anc\_bf(4,2)$ in the example of Figure 3, rule instances in which this fact is used are shown; thus, the tree can 'grow upward'.

5.3 Typical Use of $\mathcal{E}xplain$

There are different kinds of insights that a user may wish to gain into the evaluation of a module.

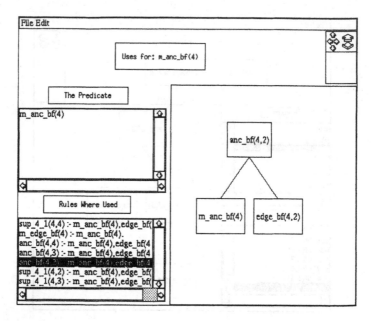

Fig. 3. The Uses Window

- The user might want to know: 'Which facts corresponding to a particular predicate have been generated?' In order to do this, the user selects a predicate name in the **Predicates** browser in the Definition window. As a result, all the facts corresponding to that predicate will appear in the **Instantiations** browser. These facts were derived as the result of successful instantiations of some rules in the module. To see a derivation of any particular fact, the user selects that fact from the **Instantiations** browser. This selection causes an appropriate instantiated rule to be displayed in the graphics window in the form of a derivation tree fragment. The root of this tree fragment is the fact derived using the rule, and the leaves are the facts that instantiate the body of the rule.

    - The leaves of the tree fragment can be expanded to show their derivations.
    - There are occasions when a fact can be derived in more than one way, and these can be scanned.
    - The derivation of a fact can also be 'un-expanded' by selecting the root fact of a derivation and pruning the derivation tree.

- The user might want to say: 'Show me all the rules where this fact is used?'. The desired fact is selected and the Uses Window is invoked to display all rules where the fact is used. Each particular use can be viewed as a portion of a derivation tree.

    (Note that the fact considered need not be a base fact — an incorrectly specified rule might lead to an unexpected derived fact even if all base facts are 'correct'.)

6   Advanced Features

So far, we discussed simple Datalog rules that are evaluated without optimizing transformations. However, CORAL supports complex terms and functor symbols, and it also allows the use of variables inside facts. CORAL also uses various optimization strategies that include the rewriting of the original rules using transformations like magic rewriting [BR87, Ram88]. We discuss some of these issues in this section.

6.1   Program Transformations

We note that since *Explain* records and displays actual derivations, these derivations are in terms of rules of the rewritten program, if the original program is optimized by applying some program transformation. Some program transformations are based upon special properties of the original program, and in general, it is not easy to map a derivation of the transformed program to a derivation of the original program, even when such a mapping exists. Clearly, a derivation tree in terms of the user's original program is likely to be more understandable, and it is important to try to present explanations in the context of the original program.

An important transformation which is usually applied by default is the Magic Sets transformation [BR87, Ram88]. This transformation is purely syntactic, and can be used on an arbitrary program. The objective is to constrain a forward-chaining fixpoint computation to generate only those facts that are relevant to answering a given user query. While a general discussion of this technique is beyond the scope of this paper, we make the following observations.

1. The Magic Sets transformation modifies the original program in a way that makes it easy to convert derivations over the rewritten program into derivations over the original program. The rewriting essentially adds 'magic' or 'filter' literals to each of the rules in the original program, and introduces new rules defining the filter predicates. To convert a derivation, we can simply discard any derivation (sub-)tree with a 'magic' fact as the root. Although the implemented version of *Explain* does not perform such a conversion, it is straightforward to implement, and results in the explanation of the execution at the level of the original user program.

2. In dealing with programs that contain negation or set-grouping, the rewriting introduces additional 'done' literals (which signal when the computation of a subgoal that must be fully evaluated is complete). Facts corresponding to these additional literals can also be discarded from derivation trees, if the explanation is desired in terms of the original program.

6.2   Handling Advanced CORAL Features

CORAL provides support for complex terms like functors (e.g. 'f(2,3)'), lists (e.g. [1,2,3]) and arbitrarily nested terms (e.g. 'f(2, g(4), [1,2,f(3)])'). Facts could also contain variables (e.g. *descend*(*adam*, *X*) means that everybody is a descendant of *adam*); such facts are called *non-ground*. CORAL allows multisets to be created using rules, and allows aggregate functions to be expressed over these sets. A restricted form of negation is also supported in CORAL rules. These advanced features need to be handled effectively by the explanation system, so that the meaning of programs using such features can be naturally represented.

Sets and Aggregation Consider the rule:

$$total(X, sum(< Y >)) : - value(X, Y).$$

This rule uses the aggregate function *sum* over the set of Y values that have a common X value. Set generation via grouping, and the use of aggregate operations in the head, need to be handled in a special manner since facts are produced incrementally. For example, if there are two facts $value(1, 2)$ and $value(1, 3)$ in the database, a query $?total(1, Answer)$ is evaluated by CORAL as follows: the first *value* fact retrieved might be $value(1, 3)$, and this creates an intermediate fact $total(1, 3)$. The next fact retrieved is $value(1, 2)$, and this results in the replacement of the intermediate fact by the new fact $total(1, 5)$.

The approach we take is to record the derivation of each of these intermediate *total* facts. In each derivation that uses the intermediate fact, the intermediate fact is actually included in the body of the recorded derivation (even though the fact really corresponds to the 'current value' of the head fact). Such intermediate facts are clearly marked in recorded derivations, and only appear in derivations leading upto the 'correct' fact; in the above example, the 'correct' fact is $total(1, 5)$. While this example dealt with grouping followed by the aggregate operation *sum*, the same mechanism is used when a set-value is generated. For instance, if the previous example is modified by omitting *sum* in the head literal, the intermediate fact would be $total(1, \{3\})$, and the 'correct' fact would be $total(1, \{2, 3\})$.

Negation Consider the rule:

$$p(X) : - value(X, Y), not \ q(Y).$$

At run-time, evaluation of the *q* goal checks to see that the (instantiated *q*-) fact is not derivable. If such a fact is derivable, this rule instantiation is unsuccessful. If such a *q*-fact is not derivable, this rule instantiation is successful, and is recorded. For example, if $q(5)$ cannot be derived, and there is a fact $value(1, 5)$, then the following derivation is recorded:

$$p(1) : - value(1, 5), not \ q(5).$$

$\mathcal{E}xplain$ treats '*not* $q(5)$' as a base fact, in that a tree containing this fact cannot be further expanded by expanding this fact. Thus, while it is clear that $q(5)$ could not be derived, the reasons for this must be pursued independently, by examining the execution of the goal $?q(5)$. The relevant set of derivations can be identified by looking for uses of the fact $magic\_q(5)$ if the computation uses one of the Magic Sets related rewriting algorithms. Essentially, the generation of the goal $?q(5)$ corresponds to the generation of the fact $magic\_q(5)$; this fact triggers all subsequent derivations in the solution of this goal. (For details, we refer the reader to [BR87, Ram88].)

In general, a weakness of $\mathcal{E}xplain$ is that it does not provide direct support for understanding why some facts are 'missing', i.e., why some facts that a user expects to be generated are not. As sketched in the previous paragraph, the 'relevant' portion of the computation can be examined if the user has some knowledge of the Magic Sets transformations, but this is not entirely satisfactory. Since the information dumped by $\mathcal{E}xplain$ completely describes the computation of negative goals, it should be possible to provide a more friendly interface to this information that enables a user to explore "why not" queries without knowledge of Magic Sets. This is an important direction for future work. Shmueli and Tsur [ST90] consider "why not" queries in a broader sense — "Why is a fact missing from the least model?", instead of "Why wasn't a fact generated (in the computation of a given query)?" — and suggest that the user's expectations must be captured in some 'intended model', and an explanation tool should provide ways for the user to test where the actual computation diverges from this model.

7 Overview of the Implementation

The $\mathcal{E}xplain$ system contains two components. The first component is a set of modifications to the CORAL run-time system that support dumping of instantiated rules into a file during program execution. The second component is a tool that allows the user to visualize the information in the dump file. In this section, we describe the modifications made to CORAL to facilitate dumping, as well as the implementation of the visualization tool.

7.1 Dumping Fact Derivations

Dumping of fact derivations is performed on a per-module basis and is done only when the user specifies the module for which the fact derivations need to be viewed.

The derivations for each fact corresponding to a predicate are stored in two relations that are unique to that particular predicate. The two relations are called def-predicate-name and use-predicate-name and have two fields each. The def relation has in its first field the result fact. The second field contains the derivation tree fragment, stored as a list. The def relation is used to retrieve the derivations of a given result fact. The use relation contains in its first field any fact that was part of the derivation of the result fact, i.e. any fact in the body of a rule used to derive the result fact. The second field contains the derivation list, of which the value in the first field is a part. The *use* relation is used to retrieve the derivations where a given fact is used. For example, consider a derivation of the form:

$$anc(2,3) : - anc(2,1), edge(1,3).$$

One tuple of the def_anc relation and two tuples of the use_anc relation are dumped:

$$def\_anc(anc(2,3), [anc(2,3), anc(2,1), edge(1,3)]).$$

$$use\_anc(anc(2,1), [anc(2,3), anc(2,1), edge(1,3)]).$$
$$use\_anc(edge(1,3), [anc(2,3), anc(2,1), edge(1,3)]).$$

Given these three tuples, we can easily determine how $anc(2,3)$ is derived or in which derivations $anc(2,1)$ and $edge(1,3)$ are used, by querying the two relations. This is exactly what $\mathcal{E}xplain$ does. Querying the data to retrieve derivation tree fragments involves relatively simple CORAL queries. The dump file is written at a point where a handle on an entire instantiated rule is available. This corresponds to the point at which the new fact is inserted into the relation at the head of the rule.

7.2   The Visualization Component

We now give a brief description of the implementation details of the visualization component. $\mathcal{E}xplain$ is implemented as an application of CORAL/C++. The data in the dump files is consulted and stored by $\mathcal{E}xplain$ in CORAL relations, and the CORAL/C++ interface routines are used to query, update and manipulate the data. The CORAL database system is used in three distinct ways in the implementation of the $\mathcal{E}xplain$ visualization component: embedded CORAL, consulted CORAL code, and imperative CORAL. These three components are all part of the CORAL language [RSS92]. *Embedded CORAL* is, as the name suggests, CORAL code that is embedded in C++ source. Any collection of CORAL commands can be embedded at any point within C++ code [RSSS93b]. CORAL rule programs stored in separate files are also 'consulted' from within the C++ code, and these rule programs can be executed from within the C++ code with the help of a library of interface routines designed to provide an 'imperative' interface to CORAL. The $\mathcal{E}xplain$ system is therefore an example of a significant application that is built *using* the features of CORAL.

Performance Considerations $\mathcal{E}xplain$ typically offers good interactive performance, in part because of the efficient index implementation of the underlying CORAL database system. We now provide some performance figures that show the system to be capable of handling substantial programs and data sets. There

Measure	Time
Execution time w/o recording derivations	11.57 sec.
Execution time with recording of derivations	52.43 sec.
Time to load dump file into graphical tool	235 sec.
Response time for graphical operations	< 1.0 sec.

Table 1. *Explain* Timings

are three timings of interest in considering a system like *Explain*: the slowdown
in program execution due to the 'dumping' of derivations, the time taken to
load the dumped information when the graphical interface tool is invoked, and
the response time for operations at the graphical interface (such as expanding or
pruning trees). We have run *Explain* on a number of programs, and typically, we
have noticed that execution is slowed down by a factor of about four due to the
dumping of derivations, and that the response time for operations at the graphical interface is never more than a fraction of a second. The time to load data is
not unduly large, but can be irksome when tens of thousands of derivations are
dumped. More concretely, Table 1 gives the numbers for the a bill-of-materials
program, running on a parts hierarchy of about 15,000 tuples and 100 basic
parts. The computation generated about 30,000 derivation tree 'fragments'. The
query and data set are from the Nail-Glue benchmark [DMP93].

Our conclusion is that a practical limit to the use of *Explain* is likely to
stem from the user's ability to comprehend large sets of derivations, rather than
the system's capacity. *Explain* can be made to record information on a per-
module basis, in order to avoid unnecessary explanations about computations in
well-understood (perhaps previously debugged) modules. It is also reasonable to
expect that users will try to graphically understand the execution of a program
by focusing on a relatively small computation (or a restricted portion of a large
computation), and that they will extrapolate the insight that they derive from
it to comprehend larger computations.

8 Discussion of Implementation Issues

8.1 Derivation of Complex Tuples

The use of CORAL in the *Explain* tool as the underlying database system is crucial in the context of handling complex terms. Since CORAL has the capability
to handle complex terms, no attempt to flatten them is required while dumping
explanation information. Similarly, non-ground facts present no problem, since
a variable can be dumped out as such, and will not cause any problems to the
Explain tool. We note that arithmetic and other built-in predicates are handled correctly in dumping rule instantiations. The treatment of negation and set
generation has already been discussed in detail 6.2.

8.2 Choice of Schema

Our main design choice in implementing the dump facility within CORAL was the choice of the schema for the dumped data. We decided on the current approach of *def* and *use* relations, since we intended using CORAL to process the dumped data. CORAL is well equipped to handle function symbols and complex terms like lists. Thus, we could store an entire derivation fragment (i.e. an instantiated rule) as a single fixed-arity tuple in the *def* relation. If CORAL did not have the ability to manipulate lists, we would have been forced to flatten our tuples, and break them up into smaller pieces.

When a derivation tree fragment is displayed using $\mathcal{E}xplain$, we expect that a very common action of the user will be to grow the tree an additional level by expanding one of the leaf facts into its derivation fragment. The representation of the instantiated rule body as a list of functors makes it easy to perform this operation, since one of the list elements can be directly used as the selection attribute for a CORAL lookup to retrieve the tuple for the new fragment. CORAL implements efficient index retrieval even when the indexed attributes are fields of complex terms.

It should be noted that this schema is space-inefficient in that instantiated rule bodies are stored multiple times (in both *def* and *use* relations). Storing multiple tuples for every fact produced is certainly an inefficient use of storage, and we are looking at new schemes to make this more efficient.

8.3 Separate Process Structure

Our decision to implement $\mathcal{E}xplain$ as a separate process from the CORAL system allowed the system development to proceed at a much faster rate than if we had attempted to build $\mathcal{E}xplain$ inside CORAL. It also involved minimal changes to the CORAL system itself.

9 Conclusion

$\mathcal{E}xplain$ is very useful in identifying the source of error when a program produces an unexpected result. The erroneous result could be caused by a poorly written set of rules, or bad data in the database. $\mathcal{E}xplain$ allows the user to examine all the rule instantiations, organized into derivation trees, that contributed to the creation of the result fact. To our knowledge, no other system with all of $\mathcal{E}xplain$'s capabilities has been implemented. In this section, a discussion of related research is presented, along with possible future extensions to this work.

9.1 Related Work

In [ST90], a debugging system for the LDL deductive database is presented. One of the operations supported by the LDL debugger is to take a generated fact which the user believes to be incorrect, and return an instantiated rule with this fact as the head. The user can then repeat this process, identifying one of the facts in the body of the instantiated rule as an incorrect fact. This operation corresponds in *Explain* parlance to selecting a fact in the Definition Window to expand the current derivation tree. However, the LDL debugger is more limited in the following respects: whereas *Explain* allows expansion and pruning of trees by choosing any 'fringe' node of a displayed portion of a tree, the LDL debugger only allows the expansion of a single path in the tree; the LDL debugger has a textual, non-graphical interface; and more importantly, the LDL debugger does not provide any support for the operations supported by the Uses Window abstraction in *Explain*. (Thus, it is not possible to identify the consequences of an incorrect, or unexpected, fact.)

Further, the outline of the LDL debugger implementation[3] indicates that the set of facts generated during a computation is dumped rather than the set of actual derivations. This means that the rules have to be used as indexes into the set of saved facts while constructing 'explanations' (using our terminology); thus, the explanation component is more closely tied to the underlying system than is the case with *Explain*. This design decision has some important implications — notably, the fact that the actual derivations are not recorded decreases the utility of the debugger in identifying errors in the run-time system. For example, if there is a program rule and a set of facts that can be used to instantiate the rule body, this represents a derivation that ought to be carried out (and is so identified by the explanation component of LDL). However, if this rule instantiation is in fact not carried out due to a system error, this error cannot be detected unless actual derivations are recorded! The separation of the dumping and the explanation components in *Explain* also has significant advantages with respect to extending the system to offer more functionality or to deal with other kinds of rule-based systems.

An interesting aspect of [ST90] is that the issue of 'missing facts', namely facts that the user expects to see generated, but that are not generated, is addressed. It is pointed out that given a missing fact, a partly instantiated rule can be returned to the user, and if the user instantiates this rule in accordance with his/her expectations of how the computation should have proceeded, the debugger can assist the user in searching 'down' a path in a derivation tree to identify a missing database fact. We have not addressed the issue of missing facts, since our focus has been on recording and presenting the derivations actually carried out during execution. However, we note that if the missing fact is associated with a negative goal, then the set of derivations relevant to (an attempt to generate) the missing fact can indeed be identified, as discussed in Section 6.2.

There has also been some interesting work with respect to the understanding of null answers to a query, and the identification of erroneous pre-suppositions contained in the query [Mot86, Mot90]. This is closely related to the issue of 'missing facts', and our research does not address this aspect of query explanation.

---

[3] This is described only briefly in [ST90], and the debugger is not available with the LDL system we have.

There is also a connection between $\mathcal{E}xplain$ and Prolog debuggers (see e.g., [Sha83, Sta, Duc92]), since both are used to debug logic programs, but there are many important differences. Deductive databases provide a model-based semantics, where the meaning of a program is a model of the world that satisfies the rules of the program. This semantics is independent of the particular execution strategy employed, and in fact, no assumptions can be made about the order in which facts are generated. Given this semantics, derivation trees are the best way to represent program computations, and in $\mathcal{E}xplain$, the focus is on recording the *set* of derivations, rather than the order in which these derivations occur. A Prolog-like system, on the other hand, provides explicit guarantees about the execution strategy, and this allows programmers to think and program in an imperative fashion. In such an environment, the order in which derivations occur is crucial to the understanding of the execution. [4]

Thus, the set of derivation trees (as defined here) is not an appropriate abstraction of a Prolog execution. In fact, given the Prolog strategy of backward chaining, it is difficult to efficiently generate explicit derivation trees. First, Prolog's depth-first search does not guarantee termination even if all derivation trees are finite (for example, programs without function symbols or arithmetic). (Iterative evaluation, on the other hand, ensures that all derivation trees are enumerated, and that evaluation terminates if all the trees are finite.) Second, the strategy of storing fragments and composing trees "on demand", which is essential for efficiently representing the set of derivation trees, is not easy to implement. While it is possible to write a simple Prolog meta-interpreter that constructs a derivation tree corresponding to a given execution path, this does not allow the kind of "browsing" of derivation trees that $\mathcal{E}xplain$ supports.

9.2 Future Work

As discussed in Section 6.2, it is desirable to provide a friendly interface for exploring why certain facts are not generated. At a broader level, it is our belief that derivation trees closely mirror the manner in which users think of rule-based programs. Extending our ideas to other rule-based systems offers an interesting challenge. Some other extensions are discussed below.

Extending the Implementation The current implementation of $\mathcal{E}xplain$ has acceptable performance, but can be improved upon. The storage of derivations should become more space efficient by retaining a single copy of each instantiated rule in a separate table. This will mean a noticeable saving of space since currently we are storing multiple copies of rule instantiations. This will however be at the cost of some increase in the response time.

A problem arises when a large number of derivations are dumped. A large number of facts may have to be displayed in the browser, and scrolling through them to find a desired fact may be difficult. The display of facts, which was

---

[4] The fixed execution strategy also itself to stack-based debuggers and tracing tools [Duc92, DE88, Sta].

intended to support cooperative querying, could in this case produce a most un-cooperative system! In the future, we expect to add a feature that will allow the user to filter out all 'uninteresting' facts and only view the ones of interest. Since all dumped data is stored as CORAL relations, such a filter can be implemented using CORAL's query processing facilities.

Modes of Operation The explanation facility will be be expected to satisfy different requirements in different contexts. It should be usable either for post-mortem analysis of program execution, or for coordinated program development and debugging. The first mode is useful when the user wishes to run programs, and when (s)he wants to see why the particular answer was generated. The dump files are created and can be analyzed at some later time. Such a post-mortem mode of operation is assumed for the example that we described in Section 5.

There are situations (e.g., when programs are being developed or when the CORAL system is being debugged) when it is useful to operate interactively, switching between CORAL and $\mathcal{E}xplain$. The user runs a query, sees how it is evaluated, performs some appropriate modification, and runs it again. This kind of alternation between query evaluation and answer explanation is easily possible in a windowing environment.

There is a third mode of operation which might be desirable, but is not currently implemented. Consider a CORAL program that for some reason results in *infinite looping* behavior. It would be very useful to be able to view the state of the computation at any given time, in terms of the derivation trees that have been generated upto that point.

Implementing this functionality would involve establishing a communication channel between CORAL and the $\mathcal{E}xplain$ tool (currently, the two communicate through the file system, which is ideal for a post-mortem mode of operation). It is quite easy to establish two-way communication between the two processes instead. Computation would proceed in lock-step, with every successful deriva-tion accompanied by the instantiation information being sent to the tool, and an acknowledgement being returned. The acknowledgement could be delayed while the user examines and comprehends the current information displayed by the tool. Here again, there is more than one possible design choice. Using two-way communication, the $\mathcal{E}xplain$ process could step through the execution of the program one derivation at a time. The other approach is to create fixed 'break-points' in CORAL at which the execution of a particular query will stop and wait for the explanation tool to send it a response.

This mode could be used by someone with reasonable knowledge of CORAL's execution algorithms to debug either a CORAL program or the CORAL system itself. It is essential for debugging programs that do not terminate. Adding this mode of operation should require little effort, since most of the functionality is already present in both systems.

Acknowledgements: We thank Mike Carey for discussions and suggestions about an early version of $\mathcal{E}xplain$. Mireille Ducassé of ECRC in Munich and François Staes of the University of Antwerp, Belgium responded generously to our literature request on logic and prolog debugging on the comp.lang.prolog USENET newsgroup. Eben Haber helped us understand the intricacies of Inter-Views.

References

[BR87] Catriel Beeri and Raghu Ramakrishnan. On the power of Magic. In *Proceedings of the ACM Symposium on Principles of Database Systems*, pages 269–283, San Diego, California, March 1987.

[DE88] M. Ducassé and A. M. Emde. A review of automated debugging systems. In *Proceedings of the 10th International Conference on Software Engineering*, pages 162–171, April 1988.

[DMP93] Marcia A. Derr, Shinichi Morishita, and Geoffrey Phipps. Design and implementation of the glue-nail database system. In *Proceedings of ACM SIGMOD International Conference on Management of Data*, 1993.

[Duc92] M. Ducassé. A general trace query mechanism based on prolog. In *Proceedings of the Fourth International Symposium on Programming Language Implementation and Logic Programming*, August 1992.

[Mot86] Amihai Motro. Seave: A mechanism for verifying user presuppositions in query systems. *ACM Transactions on Office Information Systems*, 4(4):312–330, October 1986.

[Mot90] Amihai Motro. Flex: A tolerant and cooperative user interface to databases. *IEEE Transactions on Knowledge and Data Engineering*, 2(2):231–246, June 1990.

[Ram88] Raghu Ramakrishnan. Magic templates: A spellbinding approach to logic programs. In *Proceedings of the International Conference on Logic Programming*, pages 140–159, Seattle, Washington, August 1988.

[RSS92] Raghu Ramakrishnan, Divesh Srivastava, and S. Sudarshan. Coral - control, relations and logic. In *Proceedings of the International Conference on Very Large Databases(VLDB)*, pages 238–249, 1992.

[RSSS93a] Raghu Ramakrishnan, Praveen Seshadri, Divesh Srivastava, and S. Sudarshan. *The CORAL User Manual*. University of Wisconsin,Madison, 1.0 edition, January 1993.

[RSSS93b] Raghu Ramakrishnan, Divesh Srivastava, S. Sudarshan, and Praveen Seshadri. Implementation of the CORAL deductive database system. In *Proceedings of ACM SIGMOD International Conference on Management of Data*, 1993.

[Sha83] Ehud Y. Shapiro. *Algorithmic Program Debugging*. MIT Press, Cambridge, Massachusetts, 1983.

[ST90] O. Shmueli and S. Tsur. Logical diagnosis of LDL programs. In *Proceedings of the Seventh International Conference on Logic Programming*, 1990.

[Sta] F. Staes. *The Interactive LOCO Debugger : User Manual*. University of Antwerp, UIA.

A Logic for Rule-Based Query Optimization in Graph-Based Data Models

Neil Coburn and Grant E. Weddell*

Department of Computer Science, University of Waterloo
email: ncoburn,gweddell@uwaterloo.ca

Abstract

We present a *wide-spectrum algebra* and *refinement calculus* designed to allow one to reason about query optimization in graph-based data models.

A query language is wide-spectrum if it can be used to express both user level queries as well as low-level evaluation strategies or access plans. This property enables rule-based query optimization to be viewed as the process of *refining* expressions in such a language: "non-procedural" sub-expressions are gradually replaced by more "procedural" sub-expressions until an unambiguous access plan results. We begin by presenting an algebra that is wide-spectrum in this sense. One subset of operations within the algebra can be used to define the formal semantics of a non-procedural query language for graph-based data models. Another subset can express common data access paradigms such as an index scan, the "cut" operator in Prolog or the nested-iteration join processing strategy.

We then present a refinement calculus over the algebra which defines when one algebraic expression subsumes another. The calculus makes it possible to formally prove the correctness of rewrite rules used in rule-based query optimizers, and is sufficiently expressive to admit rules encoding many forms of semantic query optimization.

1 Introduction

This paper addresses two trends in database applications and performance. It is well-known that recent applications of database systems, such as in computer-aided design (CAD) [13], in computer-aided software engineering (CASE) [7] and in advanced intelligent networks (AINs) [11] require an underlying data model that allows one to define and manipulate complex objects. Of equal importance is that such applications also require support for a *non-procedural* query language.

---

*This research was supported in part by the Natural Sciences and Engineering Research Council of Canada, by Bell-Northern Research Ltd., and by ITRC: Information Technology Research Centre of Ontario.

Our first contribution is a preliminary design for a *wide-spectrum* algebra for a simple graph-based data model.

The second issue that we address concerns query optimization. Effective query optimization has always been crucial to the efficient operation of database systems; the improved performance can be measured in orders of magnitude. This situation is becoming more pronounced as newer applications, such as CAD, CASE and AINs, create larger and more complex databases. Our second (and perhaps more important) contribution is the development of a *refinement calculus* based on the algebra that allows one to reason about rules in a rule-based query optimizer. As a special case, the calculus can be used to deduce that a specific access plan correctly implements a (user level) query.

Our initial requirements for the algebra derive from our view that any complex object model must have the relational model as a special case, and our desire that the algebra and refinement calculus can be used to reason about practical rewrite rules for, say, ANSI-standard SQL. This prompted us to set the initial requirements for the algebra as follows.

- It should be possible for the result of a query to contain duplicates.

- There must be a well-defined notion of ordering for the result of a query.

- The algebra should allow "parameterized" queries.

- The algebra should be wide-spectrum.

The last requirement relates to our understanding of the process of rule-based query optimization. An internal algebraic expression is first produced by parsing a user-defined query, usually expressed in SQL. This internal expression is then gradually rewritten, through a series of applications of rewrite-rules, into a detailed access plan for evaluating the query. Thus, query optimization may be viewed as the process of *refining* expressions: "non-procedural" sub-expressions are gradually replaced by more "procedural" sub-expressions until an unambiguous access plan results.

However, at present, most existing choices of languages for the internal algebra will only allow us to reason about this process over a very narrow spectrum, a circumstance illustrated by Figure 1. We consider an algebra to be *wide-spectrum* if it can be used to describe the query at any level of refinement during this process. That is, it is wide-spectrum if it can describe high-level non-procedural user queries, low-level procedural evaluation strategies, and any level of detail in between, a circumstance illustrated by Figure 2.

The algebra presented in this paper is wide-spectrum in this sense and also, it satisfies the other requirements listed above. Following a general trend [3, 4, 9, 12], we define the semantics in terms of a simple graph-based data model. Taking the view that a relational database is simply a bipartite directed graph, then one subset of operations in our algebra can be used to specify the formal semantics of a significant subset of ANSI-standard SQL (although the details are

Figure 1: QUERY OPTIMIZATION—PRESENT CASE.

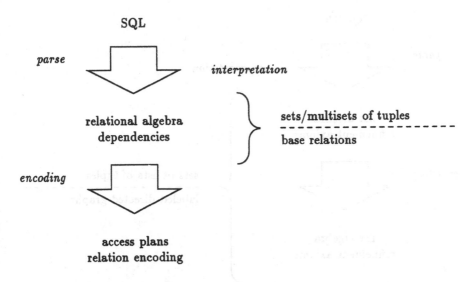

beyond the scope of this paper[1]). In fact, since arbitrary graphs can be queried, our algebra can capture the intention of queries expressed in object-oriented dialects of SQL, such as RELOOP [8]. Such dialects are referred to as SQL/CO (SQL/Complex Object) in Figure 2. A second subset of operations can be used to express common data access paradigms, such as the idea of an index scan, the "cut" operator in PROLOG, the nested iteration join strategy, and so on.

We then define a higher-order refinement calculus that can be used to define conditional subsumption relationships between sets of algebraic queries. At the lowest level, a sentence in this calculus can express that a particular access plan correctly implements a particular user-level query. At the next level of abstraction, sentences in the calculus can "encode" application integrity constraints and physical database design decisions, including a selection of indices, an object representation, and so on. Thus, the calculus can serve as the object language for both a *data definition language* (or DDL) compiler and a *storage definition language* (or SDL) compiler. Abstracting further, sentences in the calculus encode rewrite rules used in query optimization. This relates to our fundamental goal of developing a logic that can be used to prove the correctness of real-world rule-based query optimizers for graph-based data models. Finally, at the highest level of abstraction, the calculus can express axiom schema for deducing rewrite rules themselves. Examples of all these cases are given in the paper.

To date, several algebras for complex object models have been proposed [2, 5,

---

[1]Additional operators are needed to specify/implement aggregate operators and GROUP BY and HAVING clauses, as well as to properly account for the procedural interpretation of null values in SQL.[19]

123

Figure 2: QUERY OPTIMIZATION—OUR PROPOSAL.

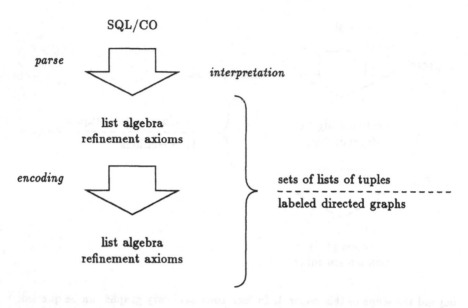

8, 9, 10, 17, 18]. Although the more recent algebras by Becker and Guting [2] and by Vandenberg and DeWitt [18] appear to satisfy all of the above requirements, they were unsuited to our particular circumstance because they incorporate a specific complex-object type system directly into the algebra. (Recall that part of our goal is to allow type declarations to be viewed as collections of sentences in our refinement calculus.) A number of authors have considered refinement constraints for query algebras [5, 20]. However, the constraint languages suffer from the selection of underlying algebra and are strictly first order—they do not appear capable of reasoning about more general rewrite rules.

Our interest in developing a logic for rule-based query optimization reflects a current trend to develop logics tailored for specific applications. For example, see [14] for a logic designed to reason about user-level object type definitions, and [6] for a logic designed to reason about state changes in logic programs and databases.

The remainder of the paper is organized as follows. We begin in the next section by specifying the syntax of sentences in our calculus (called *rules*). Our method of specifying this syntax is based on the concept of an *indexed non-terminal grammar* that introduces a notion of *substitution* in addition to the (language theoretic) notion of *derivation*. In Section 3, we define the semantics of our wide-spectrum algebra. Recall our comments above that this semantics is based on a notion of databases as directed labeled graphs. The semantics of our refinement calculus is then defined in Section 4. A motivating example to demonstrate the use of our calculus to deduce an access plan for a "complex object" query completes the section. Our summary comments follow in Section 5.

2 Syntax

We specify the syntax of our refinement calculus in terms of a context-free grammar. Recall that a grammar is described by a four-tuple $\langle N, T, R, Z \rangle$ where N and T are disjoint, finite sets of *non-terminal* and *terminal* symbols, respectively, R is a distinguished element of N called the *start symbol*, and Z is a finite set of *production rules* [16]. In a context-free grammar the left-hand-side of each production rule contains a single element of N. For a set of symbols V, let $W(V)$ denote the set of all sequences over symbols in V. In the following, we use p, q and r to refer to elements of $W(V)$. If pXq and prq are in $W(N \cup T)$ and $X \in N$, then (following convention) we write $pXq \rightarrow prq$ if $(X \rightarrow r) \in Z$. We use $\xrightarrow{*}$ to denote *derivation*; that is, the reflexive transitive closure of $\rightarrow$.

Relationships between specific queries are expressed as *ground rules* in our refinement calculus. The set of ground rules is generated by the grammar $\langle V_N, V_B, R, Z_B \rangle$, where V_N, V_B, and Z_B are defined by the productions in Table 1. We assume **S** (occurring in the second last production) denotes a countably infinite set of symbols isomorphic to the set of all finite strings over Roman letters, in which the first letter is in lower-case.

The ellipses ($\cdots$) should not be considered part of the grammar. Rather, each is intended to suggest locations where extensions to the grammar are desirable. In order of occurrence, the first ellipsis suggests where one might add additional sentential forms that directly express additional classes of semantic or syntactic constraints. The second ellipsis represents the possibility of adding algebraic operators which capture useful data access paradigms not currently expressible.

We write italicized non-terminal symbols of our grammar, possibly subscripted or primed, to refer to instances of these symbols. Thus, E and R, for example, refer to specific queries and rules respectively. Finally, we freely use commas in our examples to improve readability. Any occurrence of a comma should be interpreted as white space.

To illustrate a simple ground rule, consider the following RELOOP-like query [8] on a hypothetical employee object base.

> select a from e in emp, a in e.age
> order by a asc

The following expression E in our algebra can serve as the formal semantics of the query (as well as satisfying the sort condition, our semantics ensures that any result preserves duplicate age values):

$$\text{(Keep a (Sort a asc (Nest (Nest e, e : emp) a := e.age))).} \tag{1}$$

Table 1: A GRAMMAR FOR THE REFINEMENT CALCULUS

	productions	*description*
R	→ "(" Clause R R* ")"	Inference axiom.
	| "(" Ref E E ")"	Refinement constraint.
	| "(" Neq S S ")"	Syntactic constraint.
	| ...	
E	→ S	Object quantification.
	| S ":=" Pd	Navigation.
	| S ":=" S "{" S* "}"	Index scan.
	| S ":=" S "(" S* ")"	Method call.
	| S ":" S	Type checking predicate.
	| S "=" S	Equality predicate.
	| S "<" S	Ordering predicate.
	| "(" Keep S* E ")"	Keep.
	| "(" Filter S* E ")"	Filter.
	| "(" Not E ")"	Simple compliment.
	| "(" Cross E* ")"	Cross product.
	| "(" Nest E E ")"	Nested cross product.
	| "(" Inter E* ")"	Interleave.
	| "(" Cat E E ")"	Concatenation.
	| "(" Sort O* E ")"	Sort.
	| ...	
Pd	→ S | Pd "." S	Path description.
O	→ S D	Sort condition.
D	→ asc | desc	Sort direction.
S	→ (a symbol in **S**)	A class, attribute, function or variable name.
X*	→ ϵ | X | X* X*	(where X is one of {R, S, E, O})

To paraphrase in English, the expression requests that we

> ... sort a list of all combinations of employee objects and integer values, in which the latter is an age property value of the former, in ascending order of the integer components. For each result, retain only the integer component.

Now suppose that an index of all employees sorted by increasing value of their age exists, called "empIndex", and also that there exists a function called "accAge" which can be used to access the age of an employee object. An access plan in our algebra which *implements* (1) is as follows:

$$\text{(Keep a (Nest e := empIndex\{ \}, a := accAge(e))).} \tag{2}$$

Again, to paraphrase in English, the strategy is to

> ... scan the employee index, returning the age field value of each entry.

The ground rule R in our calculus expressing the correctness of this access plan is:

(Ref
(Keep a (Sort a asc (Nest (Nest e, e : emp) a := e.age))) (3)
(Keep a (Nest e := empIndex{ }, a := accAge(e)))).

To express more general rewrite rules that might be used, for example, in an object-oriented query optimizer, we introduce the concept of *indexed nonterminal grammars* as a means of abstracting (in our case) variable names, function names, subexpressions and so on. In particular, *arbitrary* rules are generated by the indexed non-terminal grammar $\langle V_N, V_T, R, Z \rangle$, where

$$V_T \stackrel{\text{def}}{=} V_B \cup \bigcup_{X \in V_N} \{X1, X2, X3, \ldots\}, \text{ and}$$

$$Z \stackrel{\text{def}}{=} Z_B \cup \bigcup_{X \in V_N} \{X \rightarrow X1, X \rightarrow X2, X \rightarrow X3, \ldots\}.$$

An example of a non-ground rule R in our calculus is:

(Ref
(Nest (Nest S1, S1 : emp) S2 := S1.age) (4)
(Nest (Nest S1, S1 : emp) S2 := accAge(S1))).

The rule is non-ground since it abstracts the choice of symbols used as variable names. The rule formally expresses how age property values are encoded for employee objects in the sense outlined above.

Another example of a non-ground rule R representing a more abstract inference axiom in our calculus is:

$$\text{(Clause (Ref (Nest E1 E3) (Nest E2 E4)) (Ref E1 E2) (Ref E3 E4)).} \tag{5}$$

The rule is non-ground in this case since it abstracts the choice of argument subqueries. The rule expresses that argument expressions of our *nested cross product* operator "Nest" can be independently optimized. We prove that this rule is an axiom in our logic in an appendix.

To summarize, the set of all queries, ground rules and rules in our logic are respectively defined by the following sets:

$$\{r \in W(V_B) \mid \mathbb{D} \xrightarrow{*} r\},$$

$$\{r \in W(V_B) \mid \mathrm{R} \xrightarrow{*} r\} \text{ and}$$

$$\{r \in W(V_T) \mid \mathrm{R} \xrightarrow{*} r\}.$$

As defined, the grammar $\langle V_N, V_T, \mathrm{R}, Z \rangle$ is infinite; observe V_T and Z. This suggests that there may be problems in parsing statements generated by this grammar. However, the infinite sets occur because of **S**, and because of our addition of indexed non-terminals to the alphabet. (We consider the latter as meta-variables.) The infinite grammar can be reduced to a finite grammar by: 1) replacing the production rule "S → (a symbol in **S**)" by a finite set of production rules of the form "S → a", "S → b", "S → aS", etc., and 2) replacing each Xi by $X1$ and removing the appropriate productions from Z. Let R' denote a rule obtained from R by substituting each Xi by $X1$. Then, clearly, the infinite grammar generates R if and only if the reduced finite grammar generates R'. Thus, questions of the form $\mathrm{R} \xrightarrow{*} X$ can still be answered efficiently.

A non-ground rule is a means of specifying an infinite set of ground rules having a particular pattern. We formally characterize this relationship by augmenting the language theoretic notion of *derivation* with the notion of *substitution*. A substitution has the form "Xi/q" where $Xi \in V_T$, and is *well-formed* if $q \in \{r \in W(V_T) \mid X \xrightarrow{*} r\}$. The substitution Xi/q applied to rule R, written $R(Xi/q)$, is the result of substituting each occurrence of Xi in R with q. Note that substitution is not recursive—any occurrence of Xi in q remains as is. For any rules R_1 and R_2, we write $R_1 \Rightarrow R_2$ if there exists a substitution, "Xi/q", such that $R_1(Xi/q) = R_2$. As expected, $\stackrel{*}{\Rightarrow}$ denotes the reflexive transitive closure of $\Rightarrow$. We write ψ, possibly primed, to denote a (possibly empty) sequence of substitutions.

For example, applying a sequence ψ of two (variable) substitutions "S1/e" and "S2/a" to rule (4) above yields the rule

(Ref
  (Nest (Nest e, e : emp) a := e.age)   (6)
  (Nest (Nest e, e : emp) a := accAge(e))).

Since $(4)\psi = (6)$, it follows by definition that $(4) \stackrel{*}{\Rightarrow} (6)$ is true.

Since ground rules have no occurrences of any terminal symbols of the form "Xi", we have the following.

LEMMA 2.1 *Let ψ be an arbitrary substitution sequence such that $R\psi$ is a ground rule, for some rule R. Then $R\psi = R\psi\psi'$, for any substitution sequence ψ'.*

Note that $\rightarrow$ applies a production rule to a single occurrence of a non-terminal symbol X, and that $\Rightarrow$ may be viewed as applying an *identical sequence* of production rules in parallel to each occurrence of some indexed copy of the non-terminal symbol Xi. Thus, if r is a string obtained from rule R by replacing each occurrence of an indexed non-terminal symbol Xi with its non-indexed counterpart X, then clearly $r \xrightarrow{*} R(Xi/q)$ if $X \xrightarrow{*} q$ (if the substitution is well-formed) and the following holds.

LEMMA 2.2 *If R is a rule and ψ is a sequence of well-formed substitutions, then $R\psi$ is a rule.*

In the remainder of this paper, we consider only well-formed substitutions.

3 Semantics of the Wide-Spectrum Algebra

Recall that queries in our calculus are generated from the "E" non-terminal by the grammar in Table 1. In this section, we define a *possible results* semantics for a query E by defining its interpretation as a *non-empty set of lists of tuples*. The interpretation function has two other arguments: 1) a database db containing a directed graph with vertices and arcs labeled by symbols in S, and 2) a tuple t that associates symbols in S with vertices in db. This third tuple parameter is needed to define the semantics of our mapping operator "Nest", and to satisfy the third requirement for our algebra: that it supports parameterized queries.

Our reason for starting with a "list of tuples" semantics instead of the more usual "set or multiset of tuples" semantics stems from the first and second requirements for our algebra: that it must be possible for the result of a query to contain duplicates, and that there should be a well-defined notion of ordering within the solution to a query. The latter relates to the need to be able to capture the semantics of the "ORDER BY" clause in SQL, and to be able to reason about the efficacy of ordered indices in access strategies for queries.

There are several reasons why a possible results semantics is needed instead of a simpler "list of tuples". Perhaps the most compelling relates to the fact that lists are *always* ordered, whereas some retrieval expressions accept the desired tuples in an arbitrary order. For example, consider when the result of a request for all employees must correspond to a single list l encoding a particular permutation of employees, and an access plan for the request which is based on a scan of some index of employees. If the index scan produces a list of employees which is in a different order from l, then it difficult to see how one justifies the use of this plan to implement the request. In our case, the interpretation of the request will correspond to the *set of all possible permutations* of employees. Thus, in our theory, refinement of the request to the index scan is justified on the grounds that one of these permutations (i.e. one of the lists) will correspond to the order of employees occurring in the (list produced by the) index scan.

One other point about our query semantics is worth mentioning. Since there is no presumed ordering on outgoing arcs in a database graph (and since our particular circumstance did not require this in any event), the result of applying our interpretation function is not something that occurs as a value in a database. However, this property of our query semantics does not require us to forego the possibility of supporting so-called "intentional knowledge." For example, it is straightforward to add operators with side-effects to our algebra that add vertices and arcs to a database according to the structure of a result tuple.

The remainder of this section is organized as follows. We begin by defining the remaining arguments to our interpretation function for queries: databases and tuples.[2] Since our semantics relies fundamentally on the notion of finite lists, we outline a finite list theory used by our interpretation function in the next subsection. In the final subsection, we specify the interpretation function itself by defining the possible results semantics for each of the fifteen operators comprising our algebra.

3.1 Databases

A database db is a eight-tuple: $\langle \mathbf{O}, \mathbf{D}, \mathbf{A}, Cl, P, \mathbf{M}, \mathbf{I}, \ll \rangle$. The first three components define a (possibly infinite) directed graph, $\mathbf{G} = \langle \mathbf{V}, \mathbf{A} \rangle$, consisting of a set of vertices $\mathbf{V} = \mathbf{O} \cup \mathbf{D}$ and a set of arcs $\mathbf{A}$. Vertices in $\mathbf{O}$ are called *objects* whereas those in $\mathbf{D}$ are called *values*. Although the number of values may be infinite, both the number of objects and arcs must be finite. Also, no arcs may originate from vertices in $\mathbf{D}$ (although they may be directed towards vertices in either $\mathbf{O}$ or $\mathbf{D}$).

Each vertex and arc is labeled by a symbol in $\mathbf{S}$ by the fourth and fifth components, Cl and P, respectively. We call a vertex label a *class* and an edge label a *property*. To simplify notation, we denote an arc $(u, v) \in \mathbf{A}$ for which $P((u, v)) = S$ (i.e. an arc from vertex u to vertex v labeled S) as $u \xrightarrow{S} v$.

Observe that the graph component of a database is regular in that we view all vertex labels as classes and all arc labels as properties. This is in contrast to the specification of complex object domains given by a number of authors [1, 4] in which some vertex labels correspond to a small fixed set of type constructors. Such vertex labels constrain the set of valid labels that may be placed on outgoing arcs. For example, a vertex labeled "set" may only have outgoing arcs labeled "contains". Since we assume no initial data definition or object typing, we are able to avoid the need for the factual database to consist of things labeled by type constructors such as "set", "union", "record" and so on.

The graph component is also simple, contrary to the suggestion in [9] that databases correspond to hypergraphs. The main argument in favor of hypergraphs in that they are a more natural model for n-ary functions. However, in

---

[2] As this order of presentation suggests, our data model does not have an explicit DDL. Recall that we have chosen instead to require any constraints on a database that might be implied by sentences in such a language to be given as explicit rules in our calculus. This achieves a level of uniformity and model extensibility. One may effectively evolve a model by admitting new families of rules as possible output from a DDL compiler.

Figure 3: AN EXAMPLE DATABASE.

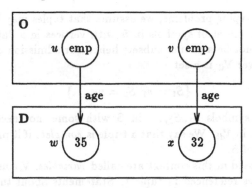

our case, an arbitrary collection of functions, called *methods*, is represented by the sixth component **M** of a database. We assume that **M** is a total function mapping each combination of a symbol in **S** (representing a method name) and finite list of vertices $(u_1, \ldots, u_m)$ to another vertex v.

Object indices are represented by the seventh component **I** of a database. In particular, **I** denotes a total function mapping each combination of a symbol in **S** (representing an index name) and finite list of vertices $(u_1, \ldots, u_m)$ to another finite list of vertices $(v_1, \ldots, v_n)$.

Finally, the eighth component represents a total ordering on **V**. We shall assume this ordering has the natural interpretation in cases where vertices are values representing integers or strings. For example, if $w, x \in$ **D** represent the integers 35 and 32 respectively, then $x \ll w$.

To summarize, signatures denoting the functionality of the various components of database

$$db = \langle \mathbf{O}, \mathbf{D}, \mathbf{A}, Cl, P, \mathbf{M}, \mathbf{I}, \ll \rangle$$

are as follows (where **V** = **O** ∪ **D**, and where **SET** and **LIST** denote type constructors for finite sets and finite lists).

$$\mathbf{A} : \to \mathbf{SET}(\mathbf{O} \times \mathbf{V}).$$
$$Cl : \mathbf{V} \to \mathbf{S}.$$
$$P : \mathbf{A} \to \mathbf{S}.$$
$$\mathbf{M} : (\mathbf{S} \times \mathbf{LIST}(\mathbf{V})) \to \mathbf{V}.$$
$$\mathbf{I} : (\mathbf{S} \times \mathbf{LIST}(\mathbf{V})) \to \mathbf{LIST}(\mathbf{V}).$$
$$\ll : (\mathbf{V} \times \mathbf{V}) \to \text{Boolean}.$$

The graph component of a small database for our hypothetical employee application appears in Figure 3. Note that there are two objects and two values in this database.

3.2 Tuples

In order to avoid typing problems, we assume that tuples may be infinite. Each tuple associates a subset of symbols in **S** with vertices in a database, $\mathbf{V}_{db}$. The subset of **S** need not be a proper subset; hence our admission of infinite tuples. Thus, a tuple t over $\mathbf{V}_{db}$ is a set

$$\{S_1 = v_1, S_2 = v_2, \ldots\}$$

which associates symbols $S_1, S_2, \ldots$ in **S** with some, not necessarily distinct, vertices, $v_1, v_2, \ldots$ in $\mathbf{V}_{db}$. We say that a tuple is *complete* if it provides a binding for each element of **S**.

The symbols used in this context are called *variables*. We use $\alpha(t)$ to denote the set of variables referenced in tuple t. Statements about tuple variables are made more readable by including parentheses in the statements; even though the parentheses do not appear in the tuple. Thus, if $t = \{\ldots, S_i = v_i, \ldots\}$ then we say that $(S_i = v_i) \in t$.

Let $\Omega \subseteq \mathbf{S}$. Then *tuple projection* and *tuple injection* are defined in turn as follows.

$$t[\Omega] \stackrel{\text{def}}{=} \{(S = v) \in t \mid S \in \Omega\}.$$

$$t_1 \prec t_2 \stackrel{\text{def}}{=} t_1 \cup (t_2[\alpha(t_2) - \alpha(t_1)]).$$

We write $t@S$ to denote the vertex v where $(S = v) \in t$. Tuples t_1 and t_2 are *equal* if and only if $\alpha(t_1) = \alpha(t_2)$ and for each $S \in \alpha(t_1)$, $t_1@S$ and $t_2@S$ denote the same vertex.

3.3 A finite list theory

Recall that we need a finite list theory to define our query semantics (in addition to set theory). Indeed, we presumed such a theory, above, when we defined the method and index components of a database.

A list l is a finite sequence $(e_1, \ldots, e_n)$ of elements. In our case, the elements of a list will correspond uniformly to vertices or to tuples. The syntax and (informal) semantics for a collection of functions over lists are given in Table 2.

Finally, we extend tuple projection and injection to operate on lists of tuples in the obvious manner.

$$l[\Omega] \stackrel{\text{def}}{=} \begin{cases} () & \text{if } len(l) = 0, \\ cons(hd(l)[\Omega], \ tl(l)[\Omega]) & \text{otherwise} \end{cases}$$

$$l \prec t \stackrel{\text{def}}{=} \begin{cases} () & \text{if } len(l) = 0, \\ cons(hd(l) \prec t, \ tl(l) \prec t) & \text{otherwise} \end{cases}$$

Table 2: LIST FUNCTIONS

syntax	description
$cons(e, l)$	List l with element e added to front.
$tcons(l, e)$	List l with element e added to back.
$app(l_1, l_2)$	l_2 appended to l_1.
$hd(l)$	First element of l.
$tl(l)$	The list l with $hd(l)$ removed.
$len(l)$	The number of elements in l.
$nth(l, i)$	ith element of a list.
$perm(l)$	Set of all permutations of list l.
$list(\{e_1, \ldots, e_n\})$	Forms the given elements into an arbitrary list.

3.4 The semantics of the query operators

We are now ready to define our possible results semantics for each of the operators comprising our query algebra listed in Table 1. Recall that our interpretation function requires a database db and tuple t as additional parameters. We assume t is also complete (i.e. that it provides a binding for each element of $\mathbf{S}$) in order to avoid a number of type compatibility problems with subexpressions. We use "double square" brackets, "[[" and "]]", to denote the interpretation of E with respect to database db and complete tuple t by writting

$$[\![E]\!]_{db}^t.$$

In addition to the finite list theory outlined in Table 2, several additional auxiliary functions, $\mathcal{F}$, $\mathcal{H}$ and $\mathcal{J}$, are also used in our specifications. The definition of these functions appears immediately following their first use. A brief informal discussion of the purpose and use of each operation accompanies its definition.

Before defining the semantics for object quantification, we first define satisfaction as it relates to arguments of our navigation and sorting operators.

DEFINITION 3.1 A database db and complete tuple t over $\mathbf{V}_{db}$ *reaches* vertex $v \in \mathbf{V}_{db}$ by path description Pd, written $(db, t, Pd) \rightsquigarrow v$, if and only if Pd is "S" and $t@S = v$, or Pd is "$Pd_1.S$" and there exists vertex $u \in \mathbf{V}_{db}$ such that $(db, t, Pd_1) \rightsquigarrow u$ and $u \xrightarrow{S} v \in \mathbf{A}_{db}$. □

DEFINITION 3.2 A database db and ordered pair of complete tuples t_1, t_2 over $\mathbf{V}_{db}$ is a *model* for sort condition list $(S_1\ D_1, S_2\ D_2, \ldots, S_n\ D_n)$, written

$$(db, t_1, t_2) \models (S_1\ D_1, S_2\ D_2, \ldots, S_n\ D_n),$$

if and only if $n = 0$ or one of the following conditions holds.

- If $t_1@S_1 \ll_{db} t_2@S_1$, then D_1 is "asc".

- If $t_2@S_1 \ll_{db} t_1@S_1$, then D_1 is "desc".

- If $t_1@S_1$ is the same vertex as $t_2@S_1$, then $(db, t_1, t_2) \models (S_2\ D_2, \ldots, S_n\ D_n)$.

A database db and list of complete tuples l is a *model* for sort condition list $(S_1\ D_1, \ldots, S_n\ D_n)$, written $(db, l) \models (S_1\ D_1, \ldots, S_n\ D_n)$ if and only if

$$(db, nth(l, i), nth(l, i+1)) \models (S_1\ D_1, \ldots, S_n\ D_n),$$

for all $1 \leq i < len(l)$. □

OBJECT QUANTIFICATION. "S" returns all permutations of a list of tuples that bind symbol S to all objects in the database.

$$[\![S]\!]_{db}^t \stackrel{\text{def}}{=} perm\left(\mathcal{F}\left(S, list(\mathbf{O}_{db})\right) \prec t\right),$$

where

$$\mathcal{F}(S, (u_1, \ldots, u_n)) \stackrel{\text{def}}{=} (\{S = u_1\}, \ldots, \{S = u_n\}).$$

NAVIGATION. "$S := Pd$" returns all permutations of a list of tuples that bind S to vertices reached from the argument tuple by path description Pd.

$$[\![S := Pd]\!]_{db}^t \stackrel{\text{def}}{=} perm\left(\mathcal{F}\left(S, list(\{v \in \mathbf{V}_{db} \mid (db, t, Pd) \rightsquigarrow v\})\right) \prec t\right).$$

INDEX SCAN. "$S := S'\{S_1, \ldots, S_n\}$" invokes $\mathbf{I}_{db}$ on arguments S' and $(t@S_1, \ldots, t@S_n)$, returning a singleton set consisting of a list of tuples binding S to corresponding vertices in the list of vertices returned by the call to $\mathbf{I}_{db}$.

$$[\![S := S'\{S_1, \ldots, S_n\}]\!]_{db}^t \stackrel{\text{def}}{=} \{\mathcal{F}(S, \mathbf{I}_{db}(S', (t@S_1, \ldots, t@S_n))) \prec t\}.$$

METHOD CALL. "$S := S'(S_1, \ldots, S_n)$" invokes $\mathbf{M}_{db}$ on arguments S' and $(t@S_1, \ldots, t@S_n)$, returning a singleton set consisting of a list of one tuple binding S to the vertex returned by the call to $\mathbf{M}_{db}$.

$$[\![S := S'(S_1, \ldots, S_n)]\!]_{db}^t \stackrel{\text{def}}{=} \{\mathcal{F}(S, \{\mathbf{M}_{db}(S', (t@S_1, \ldots, t@S_n))\}) \prec t\}.$$

TYPE CHECKING PREDICATE. "$S : S'$" returns a singleton set consisting of a list of its argument tuple t if the class label of the vertex bound to S in t is S', or a singleton set consisting of the empty list otherwise.

$$[\![S : S']\!]_{db}^t \stackrel{\text{def}}{=} \begin{cases} \{(t)\} & \text{if } Cl_{db}(t@S) = S', \\ \{(\,)\} & \text{otherwise.} \end{cases}$$

EQUALITY PREDICATE. "$S = S'$" returns a singleton set consisting of a list of its argument tuple t if the vertex bound to S in t is the same as the vertex bound to S' in t, or a singleton set consisting of the empty list otherwise.

$$[S = S']_{db}^{t} \stackrel{\text{def}}{=} \begin{cases} \{(t)\} & \text{if } t@S = t@S', \\ \{()\} & \text{otherwise.} \end{cases}$$

ORDERING PREDICATE. "$S < S'$" returns a singleton set consisting of a list of its argument tuple t if the vertex bound to S in t compares less than the vertex bound to S' in t; or a singleton set consisting of the empty list otherwise.

$$[S < S']_{db}^{t} \stackrel{\text{def}}{=} \begin{cases} \{(t)\} & \text{if } t@S \ll_{db} t@S', \\ \{()\} & \text{otherwise.} \end{cases}$$

We have replaced the relational project operator π with two operators: "Keep" and "Filter." Roughly, if one views a possible result of a query as a table, then the operators remove columns and rows respectively. Note that the filter operator introduces the possibility of nondeterminism in our semantics; possible results for some expressions can include both empty and non-empty lists.

KEEP. "(Keep $S_1, \ldots, S_n$ E)" removes, from tuples in its argument list, the variables not mentioned in $\{S_1, \ldots, S_n\}$.

$$[(\text{Keep } S_1, \ldots, S_n\ E)]_{db}^{t}$$
$$\stackrel{\text{def}}{=} \Big\{ l' \,\Big|\, \text{there exists } l \in [E]_{db}^{t} \text{ such that } l' = (l[S_1, \ldots, S_n] \prec t) \Big\}.$$

FILTER. "(Filter $S_1, \ldots, S_n$ E)" removes, from its argument list, each tuple which agrees on $\{S_1, \ldots, S_n\}$, with an earlier tuple in the list.

$$[(\text{Filter } S_1, \ldots, S_n\ E)]_{db}^{t} \stackrel{\text{def}}{=} \Big\{ \mathcal{H}\left(\{S_1, \ldots, S_n\}, (), l\right) \,\Big|\, l \in [E]_{db}^{t} \Big\}$$

where

$$\mathcal{H}\left(\{S_1, \ldots, S_n\}, l_1, l_2\right)$$
$$\stackrel{\text{def}}{=} \begin{cases} l_1 & \text{if } len\,(l_2) = 0, \\ \mathcal{H}\left(\{S_1, \ldots, S_n\}, tcons\,(l_1, hd(l_2))\,, tl(l_2)\right) \\ \quad \text{if } nth(l_1, i)[S_1, \ldots, S_n] \neq hd(l_2)[S_1, \ldots, S_n], \\ \quad \text{for all } 1 \leq i \leq len(l_1), \\ \mathcal{H}\left(\{S_1, \ldots, S_n\}, l_1, tl\,(l_2)\right) \\ \quad \text{otherwise.} \end{cases}$$

SIMPLE COMPLEMENT. "(Not E)" converts the null list into a list containing a single null tuple, and every other kind of list into one containing the null list.

$$[(\text{Not } E)]_{db}^{t} \stackrel{\text{def}}{=} \begin{cases} \{(t)\} & \text{if } [E]_{db}^{t} = \{()\}, \\ \{()\} & \text{if } () \notin [E]_{db}^{t}, \\ \{(), (t)\} & \text{otherwise.} \end{cases}$$

CROSS PRODUCT. "(Cross $E_1, \ldots, E_n$)" adds to its output the union of all permutations of lists of tuples. Each tuple in a given list consists of each possible combination of a tuple from the ith argument list with tuples from the remaining argument lists.

$$[\![(\text{Cross } E_1, \ldots, E_n)]\!]_{db}^t$$
$$\stackrel{\text{def}}{=} \begin{cases} \{(t)\} & \text{if } n = 0, \\ \bigcup_{i=1}^{n}\{l' \in perm(l) \mid \\ \qquad l \in [\![(\text{Nest } E_i \ (\text{Cross } E_1, \ldots, E_{i-1}, E_{i+1}, \ldots, E_n))]\!]_{db}^t\} \\ \text{otherwise.} \end{cases}$$

NESTED CROSS PRODUCT. "(Nest E_1, E_2)" is a mapping operator which appends to the output list the result obtained by evaluating its second operator on each tuple in the result of its first operator.

$$[\![(\text{Nest } E_1, E_2)]\!]_{db}^t \stackrel{\text{def}}{=} \bigcup_{l \in [\![E_1]\!]_{db}^t} \mathcal{J}(db, E_2, l)$$

where

$$\mathcal{J}(db, E, l_1) \stackrel{\text{def}}{=} \begin{cases} \{()\} & \text{if } len(l_1) = 0, \\ \left\{ app(l_2, l_3) \mid l_2 \in [\![E]\!]_{db}^{hd(l_1)} \text{ and } l_3 \in \mathcal{J}(db, E, tl(l_1)) \right\} \\ \text{otherwise.} \end{cases}$$

INTERLEAVE. "(Inter $E_1, \ldots, E_n$)" adds to its output the union of all permutations of the elements of its argument lists.

$$[\![(\text{Inter } E_1, \ldots, E_n)]\!]_{db}^t$$
$$\stackrel{\text{def}}{=} \begin{cases} \{()\} & \text{if } n = 0, \\ \bigcup_{i=1}^{n}\{l' \in perm(l) \mid \\ \qquad l \in [\![(\text{Cat } E_i \ (\text{Inter } E_1, \ldots, E_{i-1}, E_{i+1}, \ldots, E_n))]\!]_{db}^t\} \\ \text{otherwise.} \end{cases}$$

CONCATENATION. "(Cat E_1, E_2)" appends the result of its second argument to the result of its first argument.

$$[\![(\text{Cat } E_1, E_2)]\!]_{db}^t \stackrel{\text{def}}{=} \left\{ app(l_1, l_2) \mid l_1 \in [\![E_1]\!]_{db}^t \text{ and } l_2 \in [\![E_2]\!]_{db}^t \right\}.$$

SORT. "(Sort $S_1 \ D_1, \ldots, S_n \ D_n \ E$)" sorts its argument list according to the given sort condition list.

$$[\![(\text{Sort } S_1 \ D_1, \ldots, S_n \ D_n \ E)]\!]_{db}^t$$
$$\stackrel{\text{def}}{=} \left\{ l_1 \in \bigcup_{l_2 \in [\![E]\!]_{db}^t} perm(l_2) \ \middle| \ (db, l_1) \models (S_1 \ D_1, \ldots, S_n \ D_n) \right\}.$$

Finally, we demonstrate our interpretation function applied to various subexpressions of the example employee query (1). The results are based on the database illustrated in Figure 3.

$$[\![e]\!]_{db}^{t} \quad = \quad \{(\{e = u\} \prec t, \{e = v\} \prec t), (\{e = v\} \prec t, \{e = u\} \prec t)\}.$$

$$[\![a := e.age]\!]_{db}^{\{e=u\}\prec t}$$
$$= \quad \{(\{e = u, a = w\} \prec t)\}.$$

$$[\![(\text{Nest (Nest } e, e : emp) \ a := e.age)]\!]_{db}^{t}$$
$$= \quad \{(\{e = u, a = w\} \prec t, \{e = v, a = x\} \prec t),$$
$$(\{e = v, a = x\} \prec t, \{e = u, a = w\} \prec t)\}.$$

$$[\![(\text{Sort } a \ asc \ (\text{Nest (Nest } e, e : emp) \ a := e.age))]\!]_{db}^{t}$$
$$= \quad \{(\{e = v, a = x\} \prec t, \{e = u, a = w\} \prec t)\}.$$

$$[\![(1)]\!]_{db}^{t} \quad = \quad \{(\{a = x\} \prec t, \{a = w\} \prec t)\}.$$

4 Semantics of the Refinement Calculus

The next two definitions constitute the model and proof theory for rules in our refinement calculus.

DEFINITION 4.1 (*model theory*) A database db is a *model* for a ground rule R, written $db \models R$, if and only if any of the following three conditions hold.

1. If R is the syntactic constraint "(Neq S_1 S_2)", then S_1 and S_2 are distinct symbols.

2. If R is the refinement constraint "(Ref E_1 E_2)", then $[\![E_2]\!]_{db}^{t} \subseteq [\![E_1]\!]_{db}^{t}$ for any complete tuple t over $\mathbf{V}_{db}$.

3. If R is the inference axiom "(Clause R $R_1, \ldots, R_n$)", then $db \models R$ if $db \models R_i$ for each $1 \leq i \leq n$.

A database db is a model for a non-ground rule R, also written $db \models R$, if and only if $db \models R'$ for each ground rule R' where $R \stackrel{*}{\Rightarrow} R'$. R is a *logical consequence* of rules $R_1, \ldots, R_n$, written $\{R_1, \ldots, R_n\} \models R$, if and only if, for any database db, $db \models R$ if $db \models R_i$ for each $1 \leq i \leq n$. If $\{ \} \models R$, then we say that R is an *axiom*. □

DEFINITION 4.2 (*proof theory*) Let $\{R, R_1, \ldots, R_n\}$ denote an arbitrary collection of rules. There is a derivation of R from $\{R_1, \ldots, R_n\}$, written

$$\{R_1, \ldots, R_n\} \vdash R,$$

Table 3: INFERENCE AXIOMS FOR THE REFINEMENT CALCULUS.

name	definition
(substitution)	$\dfrac{R}{R\psi}$
(modus ponens)	$\dfrac{R_1,\ldots,R_n,(\text{Clause } R\ R_1,\ldots,R_n)}{R}$
(known axiom)	$\dfrac{\text{There exists a proof that } \{\ \} \models R}{R}$

if and only if $R = R_i$ for some $1 \le i \le n$, or can be derived from $\{R_1,\ldots,R_n\}$ using the inference axioms in Table 3. □

THEOREM 4.1 (soundness) *The inference axioms in Table 3 are sound; that is, if $\{R, R_1,\ldots,R_n\}$ is an arbitrary collection of rules, then $\{R_1,\ldots,R_n\} \vdash R$ implies $\{R_1,\ldots,R_n\} \models R$.*

PROOF: The soundness of the third axiom follows immediately from its definition. The soundness of the substitution axiom follows by transitivity of substitution and Lemma 2.2. (For any ground rule R', $R\psi \stackrel{*}{\Rightarrow} R'$ implies $R \stackrel{*}{\Rightarrow} R'$.)

We now prove that modus ponens is sound. In particular, we prove

$$\{R_1,\ldots,R_n,(\text{Clause } R\ R_1,\ldots,R_n)\} \models R.$$

If this is *not* true, then there exists a database db such that

1. $db \models R_i$, for each $1 \le i \le n$,

2. $db \models (\text{Clause } R\ R_1,\ldots,R_n)$ and

3. $db \not\models R$.

The latter implies that there exists a (possibly empty) substitution sequence ψ such that $R\psi$ is a ground rule where $db \not\models R\psi$. Also, by Lemma 2.1, there exists a (possibly empty) substitution sequence ψ' such that

$$(\text{Clause } R\psi\ R_1\psi\psi',\ldots,R_n\psi\psi')$$

is a ground rule where

$$(\text{Clause } R\ R_1,\ldots,R_n) \stackrel{*}{\Rightarrow} (\text{Clause } R\psi\ R_1\psi\psi',\ldots,R_n\psi\psi'),$$

and therefore the second condition implies

$$db \models (\text{Clause } R\psi \ R_1\psi\psi', \ldots, R_n\psi\psi').$$

But then, since $R_i \stackrel{*}{\Rightarrow} R_i\psi\psi'$ for each $1 \leq i \leq n$, the first condition implies $db \models R_i\psi\psi'$, for each $1 \leq i \leq n$, and therefore that $db \models R\psi$—a contradiction. $\square$

4.1 Data definition and incompleteness

Although our data model does not have a data definition language (DDL), most of the common forms of implicit constraints embodied by DDL languages for existing complex object model proposals can be explicitly represented by sets of rules in our refinement calculus. For example, consider the following schema graph concerning our employee database. The graph indicates, among other

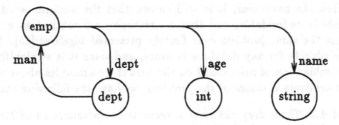

things, that each employee has a single-valued name attribute of type "string". In our terms, this suggests a need to distinguish databases which satisfy two conditions: 1) that any vertex labeled "emp" has a single outgoing arc labeled "name", and 2) that this arc leads to another vertex labeled "string". Any database which is a model for the rule

(Ref (Nest e, e : emp) (Keep e (Nest (Nest e, e : emp) n := e.name)))

or the rule

(Ref
  (Nest e, e : emp)
  (Nest (Nest e, e : emp) (Not (Nest n := e.name (Not n : String)))))

must satisfy the first or the second condition, respectively. Although the second rule is more elaborate than is necessary, it illustrates a pattern that can also be used to impose typing constraints on set-valued attributes.

Two rules exemplifying other important classes of constraints are the following. In contrast to the above, both are non-ground; we have chosen to abstract the selection of identifiers for the scanning and navigating operations.

- (*derived attributes*) A boss of an employee can be determined by finding the manager of the department of the employee.

    (Ref
      (Nest (Nest S1, S1 : emp) S2 := S1.boss)
      (Nest (Nest S1, S1 : emp) S2 := S1.dept.man))

- (*key constraints*) Employees have unique names.

(Clause
  (Ref
    (Nest (Nest S1, S1 : emp) (Nest S2 := S1.name, S2 = S3))
    (Filter (Nest (Nest S1, S1 : emp) (Nest S2 := S1.name, S2 = S3))))
  (Neq S3 S1) (Neq S3 S2))

The two preconditions in the second rule ensure our intention that S3 is a *query parameter*. Also, note the use of the filter operation with no argument symbols. According to our semantics, "filter on the empty set" will return only the first tuple produced by its argument subquery, if such a tuple exists. This operation is therefore an algebraic equivalent of the "cut" operation in Prolog.

These examples relate to the issue of finding a complete axiomatization for our calculus. In particular, it is well-known that the uniform word problem for monoids is undecidable, and that no recursive axiomatization is therefore possible for the same problem over finitely presented algebras [15]. Since the number of objects for any database is finite, and since it is straightforward to devise a combination of rules based on the first three examples above which can *encode* an arbitrary instance of the problem, we have the following theorem.

THEOREM 4.2 *There does not exist a recursive axiomatization of the calculus defined by the grammar in Table 1.*

Although this may seem unfortunate, the existence of a complete axiomatization is not an issue in view of the context of our investigations. Our desire is to provide a formal framework for reasoning about the process of optimization. Recall that one of our goals is that this framework is sufficiently expressive to allow one to reason simultaneously about SQL queries and "real world" access plans. Also, recall our earlier comments that the present language should be viewed as a kernel—that extensions to the language are desirable and likely.

4.2 Storage definition, axioms and query optimization

Storage design can also be expressed as rules in our refinement calculus. Some examples relating to the employee database are as follows.

- (*property encoding*) Function "accAge" can be used to access the age of an employee object.[3]

  (Ref
    (Nest (Nest S1, S1 : emp) S2 := S1.age)   (7)
    (Nest (Nest S1, S1 : emp) S2 := accAge(S1)))

---

[3] The rule was used earlier (4) as an example of a non-ground rule when we first presented the syntax of our logic.

- (*object indexing*) There is an index of all employees sorted by increasing value of their age, called "empIndex".

$$(\text{Ref (Nest S1, S1 : emp) S1} := \text{empIndex}\{ \}) \tag{8}$$

$$
\begin{aligned}
&(\text{Clause (Ref} \\
&\quad (\text{Nest} \\
&\quad\quad \text{S1} := \text{empIndex}\{ \} \\
&\quad\quad (\text{Nest S2} := \text{accAge(S1), S3} = \text{S2})) \\
&\quad (\text{Nest S1} := \text{empIndex}\{\text{S3}\}, \text{S2} := \text{accAge(S1)})) \\
&(\text{Neq S3 S1}) (\text{Neq S3 S2}))
\end{aligned}
\tag{9}
$$

$$
\begin{aligned}
&(\text{Ref} \\
&\quad (\text{Sort S2 asc (Nest S1} := \text{empIndex}\{ \}, \text{S2} := \text{accAge(S1)})) \\
&\quad (\text{Nest S1} := \text{empIndex}\{ \}, \text{S2} := \text{accAge(S1)}))
\end{aligned}
\tag{10}
$$

Recall the example SQL query on the employee database given in Section 2 and rule (3) in the same section which encoded the semantics of the query along with a choice of access plan based on functions "empIndex" and "accAge". We shall now prove that (3) is a logical consequence of rules (7), (8) and (10) above. Since our proof theory is sound by Theorem 4.1, we do this by exhibiting a derivation of (3) from $\{(7), (8), (10)\}$.

Our derivation requires that we prove five additional axioms, including rule (5) in Section 2. Recall that the rule asserts that argument expressions of operator "Nest" may be independently optimized. Two of the remaining four are analogous axioms for the "Keep" and "Sort" operators.

$$(\text{Clause (Ref (Keep S*1 E1) (Keep S*1 E2)) (Ref E1 E2))}. \tag{11}$$

$$(\text{Clause (Ref (Sort O*1 E1) (Sort O*1 E2)) (Ref E1 E2))}. \tag{12}$$

The final two axioms encode reflexivity and transitivity properties of expressions in our refinement calculus.

$$(\text{Ref E1 E1}). \tag{13}$$

$$(\text{Clause (Ref E1 E3) (Ref E1 E2) (Ref E2 E3))}. \tag{14}$$

Of course, a more thorough proof of correctness requires a formal demonstration that each of these rules is indeed axiomatic. Although space prevents us from doing this for each axiom, we include a proof for the case of transitivity (14) immediately following, and for rule (5) in an appendix, both due to Hui Zeng [21].

LEMMA 4.1 *Rule* (14) *above is an axiom.*

PROOF: We must show that $db \models$ (14), for any database db. If this is not true for some db, then there exists a ground rule R' such that (14) $\stackrel{*}{\Rightarrow} R'$ and $db \not\models R'$, where R' has the form

$$\text{(Clause (Ref } E_1 \; E_3) \text{ (Ref } E_1 \; E_2) \text{ (Ref } E_2 \; E_3)). \tag{15}$$

By definition, $db \not\models R'$ if and only if there exists a complete tuple t over $\mathbf{V}_{db}$ such that the following three conditions are satisfied:

1. $db \models (\text{Ref } E_1 \; E_2)$,

2. $db \models (\text{Ref } E_2 \; E_3)$,

3. $[\![E_3]\!]^t_{db} \not\subseteq [\![E_1]\!]^t_{db}$.

The first two conditions imply $[\![E_2]\!]^t_{db} \subseteq [\![E_1]\!]^t_{db}$ and $[\![E_3]\!]^t_{db} \subseteq [\![E_2]\!]^t_{db}$ respectively, but then $[\![E_3]\!]^t_{db} \subseteq [\![E_1]\!]^t_{db}$ holds by transitivity of set inclusion—a contradiction with the third condition. □

Our derivation starts with (8) above together with the reflexivity axiom (13). Applying substitutions "S1/e" and "E1/a := accAge(e)" on each respectively yields

$$\text{(Ref (Nest e, e : emp) e := empIndex\{ \})} \tag{16}$$

and

$$\text{(Ref a := accAge(e) a := accAge(e)).} \tag{17}$$

The substitution sequence

$$\text{(E1/(Nest e, e : emp), E4/E3, E3/a := accAge(e), E2/e := empIndex\{ \})}$$

on (5) yields

$$\begin{aligned}
&\text{(Clause} \\
&\quad \text{(Ref} \\
&\qquad \text{(Nest (Nest e, e : emp) a := accAge(e))} \\
&\qquad \text{(Nest e := empIndex\{ \}, a := accAge(e)))} \\
&\quad \text{(Ref (Nest e, e : emp) e := empIndex\{ \})} \\
&\quad \text{(Ref a := accAge(e) a := accAge(e)))}
\end{aligned} \tag{18}$$

and therefore by modus ponens on (16), (17) and (18) we have

$$\begin{aligned}
&\text{(Ref} \\
&\quad \text{(Nest (Nest e, e : emp) a := accAge(e))} \\
&\quad \text{(Nest e := empIndex\{ \}, a := accAge(e)))}
\end{aligned} \tag{19}$$

(We abbreviate this sort of argument in the following by saying, for example, that "(19) follows from (16) and (17) by independent optimization of nested cross product.")

A substitution sequence "(S1/e, S2/a)" applied to (7) yields

$$\begin{aligned}
&\text{(Ref} \\
&\quad \text{(Nest (Nest e, e : emp) a := e.age)} \\
&\quad \text{(Nest (Nest e, e : emp) a := accAge(e)))}
\end{aligned} \qquad (20)$$

and therefore

$$\begin{aligned}
&\text{(Ref} \\
&\quad \text{(Nest (Nest e, e : emp) a := e.age)} \\
&\quad \text{(Nest e := empIndex\{ \}, a := accAge(e)))}
\end{aligned} \qquad (21)$$

follows from (20) and (19) by transitivity. By independent optimization for "Sort" (12) and (21), we have:

$$\begin{aligned}
&\text{(Ref} \\
&\quad \text{(Sort a asc (Nest (Nest e, e : emp) a := e.age))} \\
&\quad \text{(Sort a asc (Nest e := empIndex\{ \}, a := accAge(e))))}
\end{aligned} \qquad (22)$$

The substitution sequence "(S1/e, S2/a)" applied to (10) then yields

$$\begin{aligned}
&\text{(Ref} \\
&\quad \text{(Sort a asc (Nest e := empIndex\{ \}, a := accAge(e)))} \\
&\quad \text{(Nest e := empIndex\{ \}, a := accAge(e)))}
\end{aligned} \qquad (23)$$

and therefore from (22) and (23) by transitivity:

$$\begin{aligned}
&\text{(Ref} \\
&\quad \text{(Sort a asc (Nest (Nest e, e : emp) a := e.age))} \\
&\quad \text{(Nest e := empIndex\{ \}, a := accAge(e)))}
\end{aligned} \qquad (24)$$

Finally, (3) follows by independent optimization of "Keep" (11) and (24).

5 Conclusions

We have presented a refinement calculus for a simple graph-oriented data model. The calculus can be used to assert refinement relationships between queries formulated in a wide-spectrum algebra. One subset of operations in the algebra can be used to express the formal semantics of a significant subset of ANSI-standard SQL queries, while another subset can express common data access paradigms. The calculus is higher-order in the sense that it can express more general rewrite rules and even inference axioms over rewrite rules, in addition to stating "implementation relationships" between specific queries and access plans.

The semantics of our algebra and calculus is based on a notion of databases as arbitrary directed labeled graphs. We say "arbitrary" to emphasize that we have not presumed the existence of any particular data definition or type language. Another property of the interpretation function for our query algebra is that it is based on a possible results semantics. We believe this property is crucial in a semantics flexible enough to allow both of the following sentences to be true.

Scanning index one can be used to implement a request for all employees.

Scanning index two can be used to implement a request for all employees.

Finally, we introduced the concept of *indexed non-terminal grammars*, and then used such a grammar to define the syntax of our logic. We believe such grammars have a potential for more widespread use in defining higher-order syntax often required by logics that reason about programs.

A Appendix

In this appendix, we prove that the argument expressions of the nested cross product operator "Nest" can be independently optimized. In particular, we prove that rule (5) in Section 2 is an axiom. We begin with the following lemma.

LEMMA A.1 *Let l denote a finite list of complete tuples over V_{db}, for some database db, and E_1, E_2 denote arbitrary queries. If $[\![E_1]\!]_{db}^t \subseteq [\![E_2]\!]_{db}^t$ for any complete tuple t over V_{db}, then $\mathcal{J}(db, E_1, l) \subseteq \mathcal{J}(db, E_2, l)$.*

PROOF: Proof is by induction on the length of l.
   Basis. If $len(l) = 0$, then $\mathcal{J}(db, E_1, l) = \mathcal{J}(db, E_2, l) = \{(\,)\}$, and the basis clearly holds.
   Induction. Now consider where $len(l) = n$, where $n > 0$. By definition:

$$\mathcal{J}(db, E_1, l) = \Big\{ app(l_1, l_2) \;\Big|\; l_1 \in [\![E_1]\!]_{db}^{hd(l)} \text{ and } l_2 \in \mathcal{J}(db, E_1, tl(l)) \Big\}.$$

Since $[\![E_1]\!]_{db}^t \subseteq [\![E_2]\!]_{db}^t$ for any complete tuple t over V_{db}, $l_1 \in [\![E_2]\!]_{db}^{hd(l)}$. Also, by the inductive assumption, $\mathcal{J}(db, E_1, tl(l)) \subseteq \mathcal{J}(db, E_2, tl(l))$, and therefore $l_2 \in \mathcal{J}(db, E_2, tl(l))$. Thus, $app(l_1, l_2) \in \mathcal{J}(db, E_2, l)$, and therefore $\mathcal{J}(db, E_1, l) \subseteq \mathcal{J}(db, E_2, l)$. $\qquad\square$

LEMMA A.2 *The rule*

   (Clause (Ref (Nest E1 E3) (Nest E2 E4)) (Ref E1 E2) (Ref E3 E4))   (25)

is axiomatic.

PROOF: Without loss of generality, consider an arbitrary database db and ground rule R'. If $(25) \overset{*}{\Rightarrow} R'$, then R' has the form

   (Clause (Ref (Nest E_1 E_3) (Nest E_2 E_4)) (Ref E_1 E_2) (Ref E_3 E_4)).

If $db \not\models R'$, then there exists a complete tuple t over V_{db} such that the following three conditions must hold:

   1. $db \models (\text{Ref } E_1 \ E_2)$,

2. $db \models (\text{Ref } E_3 \ E_4)$, and

3. $[\![(\text{Nest } E_2 \ E_4)]\!]_{db}^t \not\subseteq [\![(\text{Nest } E_1 \ E_3)]\!]_{db}^t$.

The first condition implies

$$[\![E_2]\!]_{db}^{t'} \subseteq [\![E_1]\!]_{db}^{t'}, \text{ for any complete tuple } t' \text{ over } \mathbf{V}_{db}, \qquad (26)$$

while the second condition implies

$$[\![E_4]\!]_{db}^{t''} \subseteq [\![E_3]\!]_{db}^{t''}, \text{ for any complete tuple } t'' \text{ over } \mathbf{V}_{db}. \qquad (27)$$

By definition

$$[\![(\text{Nest } E_1 \ E_3)]\!]_{db}^t = \bigcup_{l \in [\![E_1]\!]_{db}^t} \mathcal{J}(db, E_3, l)$$

and therefore (26) implies

$$[\![(\text{Nest } E_1 \ E_3)]\!]_{db}^t = \left(\bigcup_{l \in [\![E_2]\!]_{db}^t} \mathcal{J}(db, E_3, l) \right) \bigcup \left(\bigcup_{l \in [\![E_1]\!]_{db}^t - [\![E_2]\!]_{db}^t} \mathcal{J}(db, E_3, l) \right).$$

Also by definition

$$[\![(\text{Nest } E_2 \ E_4)]\!]_{db}^t = \bigcup_{l \in [\![E_2]\!]_{db}^t} \mathcal{J}(db, E_4, l).$$

But then (27) and Lemma A.1 above implies

$$\left(\bigcup_{l \in [\![E_2]\!]_{db}^t} \mathcal{J}(db, E_4, l) \right) \subseteq \left(\bigcup_{l \in [\![E_2]\!]_{db}^t} \mathcal{J}(db, E_3, l) \right)$$

and therefore that $[\![(\text{Nest } E_2 \ E_4)]\!]_{db}^t \subseteq [\![(\text{Nest } E_1 \ E_3)]\!]_{db}^t$ —a contradiction with the third condition above. $\square$

References

[1] S. Abiteboul and P. C. Kanellakis. Object identity as a query language primitive. In *Proc. ACM SIGMOD International Conference on Management of Data*, pages 159–173, June 1989.

[2] L. Becker and R. H. Guting. Rule-based optimization and query processing in an extensible geometric database system. *ACM Transactions on Database Systems*, 17(2):247–303, June 1992.

[3] C. Beeri. Formal models for object-oriented databases. In *Proc. 1st International Conference on Deductive and Object-Oriented Databases, Lecture Notes in Computer Science 566*, pages 370–395, December 1989.

[4] C. Beeri. A formal approach to object-oriented databases. *Data and Knowledge Engineering*, 5:353–382, 1990.

[5] C. Beeri and Y. Kornatzky. Algebraic optimization of object-oriented query languages. In *Proc. 3st International Conference on Database Theory*, pages 72–88, December 1990.

[6] A. J. Bonner and M. Kifer. Transaction logic programming. Preliminary Technical Report CSRI-270, Computer Systems Research Institute, University of Toronto, April 1992.

[7] A. W. Brown, A. N. Earl, and J. A. McDermid. *Software Engineering Environments: Automated Support for Software Engineering*. McGraw-Hill, 1992.

[8] S. Cluet, C. Delobel, C. Lécluse, and P. Richard. RELOOP, an algebra based query language for an object-oriented database system. In *Proc. 1st Inter. Conf. in Deductive and Object-Oriented Databases, Lecture Notes in Computer Science 566*, pages 294–313, December 1989.

[9] U. Dayal. Queries and views in an object-oriented data model. In *Proc. 2nd International Workshop on Database Programming Languages*, pages 80–102, June 1989.

[10] U. Dayal, N. Goodman, and R. H. Katz. An extended relational algebra with control over duplicate elimination. In *Proc. ACM Symposium on Principles of Database Systems*, pages 117–123, March 1982.

[11] J. M. Duran and J. Visser. International standards for intelligent networks. *IEEE Communications Magazine*, pages 34–42, February 1992.

[12] M. Gyssens, J. Paredaens, and D. Van Gucht. A graph-oriented object database model. In *Proc. 9rd ACM Symposium on Priciples of Database Systems*, pages 417–424, 1990.

[13] R. H. Katz. Toward a unified framework for version modeling in engineering databases. *ACM Computing Surveys*, 22(4):375–408, December 1990.

[14] M. Kifer and G. Lausen. F-Logic: a higher-order language for reasoning about objects, inheritance, and scheme. In *Proc. ACM SIGMOD International Conference on Management of Data*, pages 134–146, June 1989.

[15] M. Machtey and P. Young. *An Introduction to the General Theory of Algorithms*. North-Holland, 1978.

[16] A. Salomaa. *Formal Languages*. Academic Press, 1973.

[17] G. M. Shaw and S. B. Zdonik. An object-oriented query algebra. In *Proc. 2nd Int. Workshop on Database Programming Languages*, pages 103–112, June 1989.

[18] S. L. Vandenberg and D. J. DeWitt. Algebraic support for complex objects with arrays. In *Proc. ACM SIGMOD International Conference on Management of Data*, pages 158–167, June 1991.

[19] A.Y.Z. Xu. On the expressiveness of a complex-object algebra for parsing sql queries. Master's thesis, Department of Computer Science, University of Waterloo, 1993.

[20] M. Yannakakis and C. H. Papadimitriou. Algebraic dependencies. *Journal of Computer and System Sciences*, 25(1):2–41, August 1981.

[21] H. Zeng. An interactive design tool for complex object access. Master's thesis, Department of Computer Science, University of Waterloo, 1992.

Specifying Rule-based Query Optimizers in a Reflective Framework

Leonidas Fegaras, David Maier, Tim Sheard

Department of Computer Science and Engineering
Oregon Graduate Institute of Science & Technology
20000 N.W. Walker Road P.O. Box 91000
Portland, OR 97291-1000
{fegaras,maier,sheard}@cse.ogi.edu

Abstract. Numerous structures for database query optimizers have been proposed. Many of those proposals aimed at automating the construction of query optimizers from some kind of specification of optimizer behavior. These specification frameworks do a good job of partitioning and modularizing the kinds of information needed to generate a query optimizer. Most of them represent at least part of this information in a rule-like form. Nevertheless, large portions of these specifications still take a procedural form.

The contributions of this work are threefold. We present a language for specifying optimizers that captures a larger portion of the necessary information in a declarative manner. This language is in turn based on a model of query rewriting where query expressions carry annotations that are propagated during query transformation and planning. This framework is reminiscent of inherited and synthesized attributes for attribute grammars, and we believe it is expressive of a wide range of information: logical and physical properties, both desired and delivered, cost estimates, optimization contexts, and control strategies. Finally, we present a mechanism for processing optimizer specifications that is based on compile-time reflection. This mechanism proves to be succinct and flexible, allowing modifications of the specification syntax, incorporation of new capabilities into generated optimizers, and retargeting the translation to a variety of optimization frameworks.

We report on an implementation of our ideas using the CRML reflective functional language and on optimizer specifications we have written for several query algebras.

1 Introduction

There have been many recent efforts to develop extensible query optimizers. Modern query optimizers must keep pace with the increasing need for new data structures and algorithms, with increased functionality resulting from algebraic operations over new bulk data types, and with new optimization techniques. This need for change and experimentation is dramatic in the case of object-oriented database systems, partly because there are as yet no well-established query algebras and optimization techniques. This need suggests that optimizers should be specified declaratively and be composable from independent modules, to partition the optimizer specification task into chunks of independent knowledge.

The work reported here is a new language for specifying query optimizers as well as a methodology for constructing their implementations. Most current optimizer specification frameworks are concerned with knowledge engineering, that is, with organizing the optimizer specification into manageable pieces of independent knowledge. They are not so much concerned with succinct ways of representing this knowledge. Frequently large parts of the optimizer specifications are just chunks of procedural code that must be evaluated as is and are not suitable for further translation. (Note that optimizer specifications given as examples in many papers are actually just schematic forms of the real inputs.) Our intention is to develop a specification language in which optimizers can be expressed naturally in a concise and easily understandable syntax and a mechanism in which this syntax can be translated directly into executable code. Thus, in addition to the knowledge engineering aspect of specifying an optimizer (the partitioning of information), we are concerned with the knowledge representation aspect (how that information is expressed and processed). In contrast to most optimizer specification architectures, our specification framework is a complete tool that produces real code from declarative specifications that include a larger range of information. Our language can capture a wide range of optimization frameworks, in a declarative and easily extensible form. It is well-suited for experimentation and fast prototyping.

The query optimization task can be seen as a mapping from logical algebraic terms that represent database queries into physical plans that represent scripts for evaluating the queries, such that the produced plans are optimal with respect to some cost model. This mapping can be captured in the form of a *rule-based term-rewriting system* [4, 5, 1]. The optimization process involves searching the space of equivalent program forms, generated mainly by the syntactic transformations captured as rewrite rules, and by the alternative access paths for accessing the same database objects, such as by the indices for retrieving data from relational tables. When the search space is very large, considering all these alternatives exhaustively may result in an infeasible search. Consequently, search must be guided by a sophisticated control strategy that uses heuristic information and cost-estimation functions.

Rule-based term-rewriting systems are characterized by their declarative structure. They support a partial separation of control from the semantics of the rewrite rules. This separation and the independence between rules are properties that make the task of the optimizer specification more manageable. Rule-based systems are powerful tools for systematic description of query optimizers, supporting easy creation, extension, and maintenance of large systems. They facilitate error-free optimizer specifications as well as experimentation and fast prototyping.

For example, consider the following rule expressed in our language:

```
<< join('x,'y,'p1 and 'p2) >>
      = [ << intersect(join('x,'y,'p1),join('x,'y,'p2)) >> ]
```

The first line gives the rule head, which is a term pattern with pattern variables x, y, p1, and p2, while the second line gives the rule body, which is a term construction. The logical operation join(x,y,p) has three parameters: the outer relation x, the inner relation y, and the join predicate p. This rule indicates that a join whose predicate is a conjunction of two predicates p1 and p2 is transformed into an intersection of two joins: the first with predicate p1 and the second with p2. When a logical expression matches the head of the rule, all pattern variables are bound to the subterms of this logical expression. These subterms are then optimized by the same rewriting process. The rule body constructs a new term by replacing the variables with the new optimized terms associated with the variables.

A rule describes a pattern of a local syntactic transformation on an expression tree. Most rule-based term-rewriting systems in addition support a partial form of context sensitivity in the form of rule guards: that is, predicates that test semantic properties of the term being transformed. Experience with query optimizers and other term-rewriting systems suggests the need for more sophisticated context control. For example, query optimizers for relational databases that support sort-merge joins need to enforce sort order on some subplans [4, 8]. In addition, there are often groups of rules that should be applied in a strict or partial order. In general, there might exist a transformation script that describes a strategy for the successive application of atomic transformations. Incorporating such information into the search strategy could result in a system whose control is not completely isolated from its rewrite rules, thus lessening the benefits of rule-based systems. The alternative is to incorporate this knowledge about rule ordering as part of the rewrite context, switching context after each rule application. This approach implies that rules should not consist of pure syntactic transformations only, but include semantic transformations to the context as well.

Attribute grammars [7] suggest a method of solving this problem: they provide a declarative way of expressing both syntactic and semantic transformations. Attribute-grammars have been introduced as a method to describe context-sensitive semantics on top of a context-free syntactic base. They have been used as a tool for formally specifying programming languages as well as for automatic construction of their compilers. They introduce two types of attributes: *inherited* and *synthesized*. Semantic transformation at each grammar production is indicated by specifying how these attributes are propagated up and down a parse tree. Our optimizer specification language is based on attribute grammars, but there are some important differences. Even though a rewrite rule resembles a grammar production rule, terms in our language are not parse trees and attributes are propagated not only through rewrites but also inside of terms. By using term-rewriting systems with attributes we gain many advantages [13]. The attribute grammar framework is adequate to capture other optimizer specification frameworks, such as Volcano [5], in a more uniform and concise way. In fact, attributes are generalizations of logical and physical properties used in that and other optimizer frameworks. In addition, specifications are clearer because of the functional evaluation of attributes. Semantic and syntactic definitions are separated, yet they are both integrated into the same patterns of terms manipulated at each rule: each rule now specifies how terms are transformed and how attributes are propagated. The alternative is to maintain the rewrite context globally, performing destructive updates when a different context is needed between rewrites. This approach often leads to obscure specifications with potential for errors, especially when the rewriting system is specified by rules whose interleaving evaluation is unpredictable.

As an example of how attributes are propagated in our specification language consider the following rule taken from the domain of relational query optimization:

```
{order=exp_ord}
   << join( 'x <= { order=exp_ord },
            'y <= { order=[] },
            'p ) >>
= [ << nested_loop('x,'y,'p) >> ]
```

This rule basically says that join(x,y,p) is transformed into the physical algorithm nested_loop(x,y,p). The name order is an inherited attribute that represents the required (expected) sort order of the stream of tuples generated by a term. If a term is a join from which we expect any order exp_ord, then the expected sort order for the outer relation x is also exp_ord, while the expected order for the inner relation y is empty. That is, this rule propagates the expected order only to the outer relation of the join, because the order of the inner relation does not affect the sort order of the join result.

Our experience with the Volcano optimizer generator [5, 1] revealed that there are some routinely performed coding tasks during an optimizer specification that are highly stereotyped and therefore amenable to automation. If they are not abstracted to system-supported primitives, they consume a lot of energy during coding and they may result in obscure code, vulnerable to errors. These tasks involve effective manipulation of expression trees. Most tree transformations require decomposition of trees into their components, construction of trees from their constituent subtrees, and pattern matching. These tasks can be facilitated in a language that directly supports programming based on such operations. Examples of such languages include most pattern-based functional programming languages, such as SML [9].

For example, the following rewrite rule, in our specification language:

```
<< map(fn 'x => 'e) (map(fn 'y => 'u) 'z) >>
         = [ << map(fn 'y => '(subst(e,x,u))) 'z >> ]
```

implements the algebraic transformation:

$$\mathrm{map}(\lambda x.e(x))(\mathrm{map}(\lambda y.u(y))\,z) \;\rightarrow\; \mathrm{map}(\lambda y.e(u(y)))\,z$$

That is, the two map functions in the left side of the rewrite rule are decomposed into function parameters and function bodies, while the function of the derived map is constructed using the support function subst(e,x,u) that replaces all occurrences of x in the tree representation of e with u.

In addition, we need a language that is good for both optimizer specification and specification processing. The specification language should be close to the language we use when we write down the optimizer on paper. Specification processing must yield efficient optimizers and be flexible enough to incorporate changes in both processing and optimization strategy. We want the ability to adjust the behavior of optimizer implementations, by controlling how rewrite rules are compiled into procedures. This ability is very convenient when we need to retarget the optimizer specification as input to another optimizer generator, such as Volcano. Current optimizer specifications are not that easily manipulable themselves. For example, in Volcano only the transformation rules are translated automatically, the rest of the specification is more or less incorporated as is. These systems are called optimizer generators, but they are really optimizer frameworks, as they support a limited form of program generation. Much of what the user provides is bodies of certain optimizer routines. In our specification language, we have a large portion of the specification amenable to manipulation.

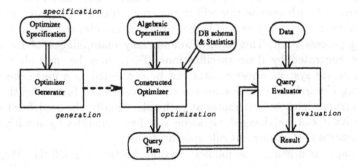

Fig. 1. The Architecture for Query Optimization and Evaluation

The ability to process the specification code during the specification process itself requires the aid of reflection. We are using CRML [12], a compile-time reflective version of SML, as the language for expressing both the specification of an optimizer and the processing of these specifications. CRML provides data structures that represent program fragments in SML. These data structures can be *reflected* into SML programs and compiled into machine code. Figure 1 shows our framework for query optimization and evaluation. The optimizer specification includes of a set of rewrite rules and a set of support functions. In our framework, rewrite rules are translated into recursive function representations that are further compiled into machine code by reflection. That way, reflection removes a layer of interpretation by generating customized programs, tailored individually to each different rule-base system. The constructed optimizer searches the space of alternative plans by recursively calling itself in some carefully selected prespecified points. No general pattern matching is necessary during rule evaluation as rule patterns are translated into efficient programs by using standard pattern decomposition techniques. Even though we can always use a standard compiler to produce customized programs, we have this "compiler" integrated as part of the specification language, because of our ability to reflect. Therefore, implementation changes of the optimizer specification can be easily incorporated as part of the specification process. In fact, our optimizer specification language consists of a fixed (but extensible) set of macros on top of CRML. Changing the behavior of the optimizer generator is achieved by changing the definition of these macros before optimizer specification. This scheme allows a flexibility and control beyond the capabilities of other optimizer specification systems. In addition, query plans generated by the constructed optimizers are CRML program representations that can be reflected into SML programs. Query evaluation is simply a matter of defining the physical operators as SML functions and evaluating the query plans as programs. This scheme results in rapid development of an evaluation-plan interpreter.

The control strategy currently provided to the constructed optimizers is a combination of bottom-up and top-down. The user is responsible for specifying which terms at each rewrite rule will follow each strategy. Programs generated from rule-base specifications are higher-order, parameterized by parts of the rewriting process itself. This form allows an easy manipulation of the control structure generated by these specifications. There may be multiple rule-base modules in our system whose control can be connected in a user-defined way, permitting hierarchical modules. Search can be controlled further by the use of special-purpose inherited attributes at each rule. Finally, the predefined control strategy itself can be changed for some rule-base modules by modifying the CRML macros that implement rule specifications.

The paper is organized as follows: Section 2 introduces CRML. We devote a large part of this paper to describing this language because we believe it is useful for many specification systems that require language extensions to be incorporated in the specification code itself. Section 3 describes the general framework on which our optimizer-specification language is based. Section 4 presents a complete query optimizer specification in the domain of relational databases. Section 5 gives the details of our specification language. Section 6 presents the optimizer specification for an object-oriented language. Section 7 presents the related work on extensible query optimizers. Finally, Section 8 concludes this paper.

2 Introduction to CRML

Compile-time reflection introduces program-generation capability into a language, thereby enabling automatic generation of many of the functions needed to build a solution for an application. CRML [12] is an implementation of compile-time reflection for a subset of SML, built on top of the Standard ML of New Jersey compiler [9].

Reflection is the "magic" that turns data into programs. Compile-time reflection allows user-written functions to access data calculated during compilation in order to construct program representations. These representations are then transformed, by reflection, into the programs they represent. Essentially, compile-time reflection allows program representations (as data) calculated at compile-time to be type-checked and submitted to the compiler itself. The compiler turns those representations into object code that is integrated with the rest of the compiler's output.

To this end, CRML contains features that allow the language SML to be its own meta-language. Language tools for meta-programming usually consist of an *object language* in which the programs being manipulated are sentences, and a *meta-language*, which is used to describe the manipulation. In CRML, SML serves both these roles. The object language is "encoded" (represented) as SML datatypes. There is a datatype for each syntactic feature of SML. Object language manipulations are described by computations on these "representation" datatypes.

Programs written in CRML are meta-programs because they can manipulate object programs. The key features that allows CRML to be its own meta-language are the features for turning representations into programs (*reflection*) and programs into representations (*reification*). In addition, CRML contains syntactic sugar (object brackets << >>, and escape ‘) for constructing and pattern matching program representations that reflect the structure of the corresponding actual programs. Thus, meta-programs that manipulate object programs may either use the explicit value constructors for the program-representation datatypes or use this "object-language" extension to SML's syntax. This syntax allows users to write in the meta-language programs without knowing the details of the encoding program-representation datatypes.

A CRML source program consists of a series of top-level declarations, some of which are meta-programs (meant to be evaluated at compile-time) and others of which are object programs (meant to be evaluated at run-time). Compile-time functions are meta-functions because they may manipulate the representations of the run-time functions. Object programs can actually be templates with varying degrees of completeness (varying from completely specified to almost completely blank). The meta-functions provide algorithms for "filling in" the incomplete portions of these program templates. This ability to calculate programs provides important abstraction mechanisms not available in traditional languages.

One way to think of CRML is as a preprocessor that the user can program, and out of which the user obtains a source-level program with no reflection, which is compiled in the normal way. In an incrementally compiled language, such as SML, the preprocessing and compilation phases can be intermixed.

Text within object-language brackets (<< >>) represents an SML program fragment. It is parsed but not immediately compiled. Instead, the associated program representation is returned as the value (of type **exp_rep**). Meta-language expressions may be included in the object-language text by "escaping" them with a backquote character (').

Inside object brackets, wherever a program fragment is expected, an *escape* operator may occur. The operand of the escape operator is expected to be an expression (in the meta-language) that provides the value to "fill in" the hole in the object code at that point. For example, if x, y, and z are variables in the meta-language of type **exp_rep**, then **<<if 'x then 'y else 'z>>** is the program representation of the **if** expression with meta-variable x as its premise, y as its then-clause, and z as its else-clause.

In the meta-language, object-bracketed expressions that appear in patterns are called *object patterns*. They match the representation of program fragments with similar shape. Escape operators applied to variables inside these object-patterns represent variables in the patterns, which "bind" to corresponding sub-expressions upon a successful match. This capability makes it particularly easy to write meta-functions that perform source-to-source transformations on the representations of program fragments. A function that performs the transformations $x + 0 \rightarrow x$, $x \times 1 \rightarrow x$, and $x * 0 \rightarrow 0$ on an object program can be expressed easily as:

```
fun simplify e = case e of
            << 'x+0 >> => x
          | << 'x*1 >> => x
          | << 'x*0 >> => << 0 >>
          | _          => e;
```

By using the escape operator in object programs it is possible to use reflection to construct arbitrarily complex program fragments, reminiscent of macro systems. CRML supports the definition of macros in the following manner. Let f be a function with type $exp\_rep^n \rightarrow exp\_rep$. The syntax of CRML permits the form **<f< x1, ..., xn >>** as a shorthand for '(f(<<x1>>,...,<<xn>>)). This syntax allows the expression-manipulating function f to be used as a macro. For example, a macro implementing an *if* expression in terms of the *case* construct could be implemented as:

```
fun If <<'x,'y,'z>> = <<case 'x of true => 'y | false => 'z>>
  | If _ = error;
```

Thus the expression **<If< k=3, 4, 5 >>** would expand to **case k=3 of true => 4 | false => 5**.

3 The Optimizer Specification Framework

Query optimizers in our framework are specified as term-rewriting systems expressed by a set of rewrite rules. Each rewrite rule describes a transformation from a logical algebra expression into either a logical algebra expression or a physical plan. Both logical expressions and physical plans are manipulated as program representations (of type **exp_rep**). In this way, program representations that represent logical expressions or physical plans take a form that reflects the meaning of these expressions. For example, it is more convenient to write << if 'x then 'y else 'z >> to represent an if-then-else expression than to use explicit value constructors to build the data structure that represents this expression. The advantage of using CRML program representations instead of user-tailored datatypes for representing expression trees is that CRML provides a rich library of functions to manipulate these trees and, more importantly, it provides a flexible and convenient reflective language to code their manipulations. Our optimizer specification language is very close to the language that one might use to specify an optimizer by writing it down on paper. This form facilitates error-free optimizer specifications as well as experimentation and fast prototyping.

Our rule-based term-rewriting system is based on attribute grammars [7]. An *attribute list* is a binding from a fixed set of attribute names to values. Each optimizer expressed in our specification language will have two attribute lists: *inherited* and *synthesized*.

The *inherited attributes* provide context during term-rewriting. Suppose that we are currently rewriting a term t. When a subterm s of t is chosen to be transformed, new inherited attribute values for s need to be computed. These new attributes values typically are derived from the inherited attribute values passed to term t before it was transformed. Therefore, inherited attribute values are propagated from one rewriting to the next. This scheme results in a purely functional term-rewriting system, because the rewriting context is passed only in the form of attributes, just as functions use parameters instead of global variables to pass information. By passing the rewriting context in a form of inherited attributes, rule-based optimizer specifications are easier to understand. Changes to context can be made locally to each rule, by specifying how the attribute values are propagated from their values before the application of the rule (that is, before this current rewriting) into the subterms chosen to be transformed next (that is, to the subsequent rewritings). In addition, memoization of the completed rewrites becomes possible, since each rewrite depends on the term to be transformed and on the inherited attribute values only.

Examples of inherited attributes include logical properties that need to be propagated and physical properties that need to be enforced. This scheme is consistent with other rule-based systems in the literature [4, 8]. One example of logical properties is schema information, such as relation names associated with their column names. Examples of physical properties include ordering of tuples in a relational expression, the site where objects reside in distributed databases, presence or absence of objects in memory, and the set of available access paths. Other use of inherited attributes is to control which rules can be considered during a rewrite. They can also be used for passing heuristic information to the main rewrite engine so that it can select more effectively which rules to apply next.

The *synthesized attributes* are attributes whose values are computed when a rewrite is complete. They form the physical properties of the produced plans. They are passed bottom-up from the leaves of a completely transformed term (that is, the leaves of a physical plan that evaluates a query) to the root of this term. Examples include the order of a stream of tuples produced by a physical plan, the selectivity estimation of join predicates, the cardinality of a stream of tuples, and the cost of a plan. In contrast to the inherited attributes, synthesized attributes are specified independently of the rules in the rule-base. This decision was made because different rules may yield similar physical plans, and thus they may require identical code to be expressed twice to calculate the properties of those plans. In addition, there may be rules that do not produce physical plans at all (such as rules that produce intermediate logical expressions that are meant to be transformed by other rules into physical plans), and hence will not have physical properties. In our system, synthesized attributes are associated with each physical operator type.

As an example of how inherited attributes are propagated and how synthesized attributes are accumulated consider the following rule taken from the domain of relational query optimization:

```
{ order=expected_order }
    << join( 'x <= { order=required_order(tables(x),p) },
             'y <= { order=required_order(tables(y),p) },
             'p ) >>
    = if subsumes(expected_order,#order(x))
         then [ << merge_join('x,'y,'p) >> ]
         else []
```

This rule translates a join into a merge_join. The identifier order is an inherited attribute that represents the required order of the stream of tuples generated by a term. The pattern variable expected_order is bound to the current value of the attribute order before the transformation. The expected order propagated to the inner and outer relations is computed by the support function required_order, which returns the columns of the outer and inner tables that participate in the join predicate. Function call tables(x) returns the names of all relations referred by the logical expression x. Note that when a logical expression matches the head of the rule, the pattern variables x, y, and p are bound to the subterms of this logical expression. These subterms are then optimized by the same rewriting process. The rule body constructs a new term by replacing the variables in the rule body with the new optimized terms associated with these variables. The notation #order(x) in the rule body returns the value of the synthesized attribute order computed after the completion of the transformation of x (that is, this is the real order of the physical plan assigned to x). If the expected order of join subsumes the real order of the outer relation, then the rule returns a merge_join. Otherwise it returns no plan (the rule is rejected).

Each optimizer specification in our language consists of a number of rule-bases, that is, a number of independent modules of knowledge, connected in a user-defined way. Each rule-base is compiled by the CRML compiler into a higher-order function, which is parameterized by parts of the rewriting process itself. This scheme allows easy manipulation of the control structure generated from a rule-base. The standard control strategy provided by our system is a combination of bottom-up and top-down. The user is responsible for specifying which term transformations will follow which strategy. Search can be further controlled by the use of inherited attributes. This compilation of rule-bases to programs is directed by a fixed number of small CRML macros that can be changed during the optimizer specification. This flexible scheme enables us to have rule-bases with different control strategy in a single optimizer. Note that changing the specification implementation does not require changing the specification itself. Even though the current implementation supports only one such set of macros, we are planning to support a wide range of them. There are other advantages to having the specification implementation expressed as macros: we can write these macros in such a way that the compilation of a rule-base is an input specification to another optimizer generator, such as Volcano, or a program that uses the search engine of another optimizer framework. As before, there is no need for changing the specification itself but only the macros.

4 Example: a Simple Optimizer for SQL

Before describing the complete syntax of our optimizer specification language, we present an example taken from the well-known domain of query optimization for relational databases [11], and inspired by the approach of the Volcano optimizer generator [5].

4.1 Attribute Specification

The following declaration in our specification language defines the inherited and synthesized attribute names used by the SQL optimizer:

```
<attributes< sql,
    inherited: { order: columns,
                 indices: (string * columns) list },
    synthesized: { order: columns, size: int,
                   cardinality: int, cost: real }
        = {order=[],size=1,cardinality=0,cost=max_real},
    iequal = fn (x,y) => (#order x)=(#order y),
    hash_table = lhash[997]
>>;
```

This macro defines an *attribute module* called sql. We may have multiple attribute modules in an optimizer specification and each module may be used by multiple rewrite rule modules. The inherited attribute order, which is of type columns (equal to the type exp_rep list), specifies the required order of the query output. It consists of a list of columns represented as a list of projections of the form table.attribute. Attribute value indices contains the set of available indices. Each index is represented as a list of columns (we may have multiple-column indices). We have four synthesized attributes: **order** gives the real order of a plan, **size** the size of tuples in bytes, **cardinality** the number of tuples, and **cost** the real cost. The part after the equal sign specifies the default values for the synthesized attributes. Function **iequal** is the equality function for inherited attributes. It is used during cycle detection and memoization. Variable **lhash** is a hash table of 997 entries which is used to memoize completed rewrites.

4.2 Query Representation

Our intention here is to write a function **optimize** that will accept any SQL query and return the evaluation plan with the lowest estimated cost. For example,

```
optimize( { order=[], indices=[("emp",[<<emp.status>>])] },
         << select( [ emp.name ],
                    [ emp, paper, conf ],
                    [ emp.eno=paper.eno, emp.eno=conf.eno,
                      paper.year=conf.year, emp.status="Professor",
                      paper.subject="DB", conf.name="VLDB" ] ) >> )
```

The first argument to **optimize** gives the initial values for the inherited attributes. Here relation **emp** is indexed by its column **status**. The second parameter to **optimize** represents the following SQL query:

```
select e.name
  from emp e, paper p, conf c
  where e.eno=p.eno and e.eno=c.eno and p.year=c.year
    and emp.status="Professor"
    and p.subject="DB" and c.name="VLDB"
```

This query is translated by a simple CRML function into the following algebraic form (this is the default translation derived directly from the query):

```
<< project( join(join(access(conf,[conf.name="VLDB"]),
                      access(paper,[paper.subject="DB"]),
                      [paper.year=conf.year]),
                 access(emp,[emp.status="Professor"]),
                 [emp.eno=paper.eno,emp.eno=conf.eno]),
           [emp.name] ) >>
```

Each join predicate is a conjunction of simple predicates and it is represented as a list of simple predicates. A simple predicate is a comparison between two table columns or between a table column and a value. These list forms can be processed by the functions **listify** and **unlistify**. Function **listify** transforms an **exp_rep** that represents a list construction into a list of **exp_reps**, while function **unlistify** performs the inverse operation. The **join** operator has three parameters: an outer relation, an inner relation, and a join predicate.

```
val rulefn = <rule< rules[sql]

(* 1 *) <<project('t,'p)>> = [<<Project('t,'p)>>],

(* 2 *) <<access('t,'p)>> = [<<table_scan('t,'p)>>],

(* 3 *) {order=ord,indices=idx}
   <<access('tbl,'p)>>
     = (map(fn (s,c) => <<index_scan('tbl,'(unlistify c),'p)>>)
         (filter(fn (s,c) => (s=tbl) andalso (subsumes(ord,c))))
                  idx),

(* 4 *) {order=exp_ord}
   <<join('x<={order=exp_ord},
          'y<={order=[]},
          'p)>>
     = [<<nested_loop('x,'y,'p)>>],

(* 5 *) {order=exp_ord}
   <<join('x<={order=required_order(tables(x),p)},
          'y<={order=required_order(tables(y),p)},
          'p)>>
     = if subsumes(exp_ord,#order x)
          then [<<merge_join('x,'y,'p)>>]
          else [],

(* 6 *) {order=(a::r)}
   <<'x<={order=[]}>>
     = if subsumes(a::r,#order x)
          then [<<sort('x,'(unlistify(a::r)))>>]
          else [],

(* 7 *) <<join('x,'y,'p)>> = [<<join('y,'x,'p)<={}>>],

(* 8 *)
<<join(join('x,'y,'p1),'z,'p2)>>
  = let val preds = append(listify p1,listify p2)
        val p3 = join_preds(tables(y),tables(z),preds)
        val p4 = join_preds(tables(x),union(tables(y),tables(z)),preds)
     in [<<join('x,join('y,'z,'(unlistify p3)),
              '(unlistify p4))<={}>>] end

)>>;
```

Fig. 2. Rewrite Rules for the SQL Query Optimizer

4.3 Rule Base Specification

Figure 2 specifies the rule set for the SQL query optimizer. This rule module is called **rules** and it uses the attribute module **sql**. Each rule can be seen as a mapping from a term (of type **exp_rep**) to a (possibly empty) list of terms. All these mappings are evaluated during a rewrite and all produced plans are accumulated into a list. If there is no match between the current term and the head of a rewrite rule, then the rule is viewed as returning an empty list of terms. The body of a rule can be any CRML expression that returns a list of terms. If it returns [], then essentially the rule rejects the expression.

Rule 1 translates the **project** algebraic operator into the **Project** physical plan. Both **t** and **p** are pattern variables that are bound to subterms when a term matches the head of the rule **project('t,'p)**. Their bindings, after they are recursively optimized, are used to construct the physical plan **Project('t,'p)** in the body of the rule. Rule 2 transforms an **access** to a relation into a sequential **table_scan**.

Rule 3 generates all possible **index_scans** for a table **t** whose order is subsumed by the expected order **ord**. The form {order=ord,indices=idx} before the head of the rule indicates that the inherited order attribute of the current term can be of any value **ord** and the list of available indices can be of any value **idx**. Variables **ord** and **idx** serve as free pattern variables, to be bound to attribute values before the transformation. In fact we may assign complex SML patterns to inherited attributes instead of simple variables, specifying the form of the expected attributes that are allowed to be passed to this rule. The body of Rule 3 is complex, because, in contrast to the other rules, it returns a list of terms whose length varies, depending on the number of applicable indices. (It may return an empty list). The **filter** function scans the index list **idx** to locate those that refer to the table **tbl** and have the appropriate order. Then **map** generates the **index_scan** terms for each such index. Function **subsumes** is a support function that tests if a list is a prefix of another list.

Rule 4 translates a **join** into a **nested_loop**. The form 'x<={order=exp_ord} indicates that the value of the inherited attribute **order** is set to **exp_ord** before term **x** is transformed by a subsequent rewriting. This form can also be expressed as 'x, meaning that the values of all inherited attributes are propagated to **x** as is. This abbreviation convention will not work for the second parameter 'y<={order=[]} because here order is changed to nil. Therefore, the head of the rule indicates that we can propagate the expected order only to the outer relation of the join, because the order of the inner relation does not affect the order of the join, as the inner relation needs to be scanned multiple times during the nested-loop join.

Rule 5 is the most interesting rule. It translates a **join** into a **merge_join**. The expected order required by the inner or outer relations is computed by the support function **required_order**, defined as follows:

```
fun required_order ( tbs, preds ) =
map(fn <<'t.'a='s.'b>>
    => if member(t,tbs) then <<'t.'a>> else <<'s.'b>>)
(filter(fn <<'t.'a='s.'b>> => true | _ => false) (listify preds));
```

The `filter` call selects the equality predicates from the predicate `preds` and the `map` call selects the part of an equality predicate that refers to a table in `tbs`. That is, `required_order` returns the columns of the outer or inner tables that participate in the join predicate. Function call `tables(x)` returns the names of all relations mentioned in the logical expression `x`. The notation (`#order x`) in the rule body returns the value of the synthesized attribute `order` computed after the completion of the transformation of `x` (that is, this is the real order of the physical plan assigned to `x`). If the expected order of join subsumes the real order of the outer relation, then the rule returns a `merge_join`. Otherwise it returns no plan.

Rule 6 is invoked only when the expected order is not empty (i.e., when it matches the pattern `a::r`). The inherited order of `x` is switched to empty before `x` is transformed again. Note that if we do not set the next expected order to nil, this rule will apply indefinitely, inserting a `sort` operator each time. The body of this rule checks if the real order of the transformed plan `x` (that is, the value of the synthesized attribute `order`) is what it was expected. If it is so, it enforces a sorting using the expected order.

Rule 7 expresses the commutativity of join. The produced join is tagged with `<={}`. This syntax indicates that this term needs to be passed to the rewriter again with the same inherited attributes. This form specifies a top-down transformation. Rule 8 gives the associativity of join. It is more expensive because it involves recomputing the predicates of the new joins (details are omitted here).

The synthesized attributes for the `sql` attribute module is computed by the following macro (only the portions for `sort` and `nested_loop` are shown):

```
<synthesized_attributes< sql,
    <<sort('x,'ord)>>
        = { order = ord,
            size = (#size x),
            cardinality = (#cardinality x),
            cost = (#cost x)+(#cardinality x)*(#size x)
                            *log((#cardinality x)*(#size x)) },
    <<nested_loop('x,'y,'p)>>
        = 'let val card = (#cardinality x)*(#cardinality y)
                            *(selectivity(p))
          in { order = (#order x),
               size = (#size x)+(#size y),
               cardinality = card,
               cost = (#cost x)+(#cost y)+((#size x)*card) } end,
    ... >>;
```

This macro call indicates that the cardinality of a stream of tuples produced by a nested loop is the product of the input cardinalities with the selectivity of the predicate.

5 The Syntax of the Optimizer Specification Language

Optimizer specifications consist of calls to three CRML macros: **attributes**, **synthesized_attributes**, and **rule**.

5.1 The rule Macro

The **rule** macro specifies the rewrite rules. It has the form:

<rule< module[attributes], rule1, rule2, ... >>

where **module** is the name of this rule module and **attributes** is the name of a previously defined attribute module that specifies the inherited and synthesized attributes for these rules. Each rule has one of the two following forms:

$$head = body$$
{ attr=pattern, ... } head = body

An attribute list **{ attr=pattern, ... }** before the head of a rule indicates that each inherited attribute **attr**, passed along with the term being transformed, must match the **pattern** in the attribute list. The names of these attributes must be inherited attribute names, but they can be in any order and some of them may even be left unspecified. In the latter case the inherited attribute can be of any value. (It is ignored and passed as is to the next rewriting). If these patterns are complex, they serve as guards to the rule. The children of the node matching the head of the rule are the subterms bound to the free variables of the head pattern. After we are provided the inherited attributes for the term being transformed (that matches the **head** of the rule), we may need to pass them to its children (to the subterms), possibly with modified values. For example, if the head is **f('x,'y)** then x and y will be bound to the left and right subterm of the matching term and they will be both transformed before the rule is applied. This recursive transformation of the subterms is a bottom-up rewriting, since subterms are transformed before the matching term. New inherited attributes are propagated to the subterm x by specifying **'x<={ attr=expr,... }**, where **attr** is an inherited attribute name and **expr** is an SML expression that depends on the variables in the **patterns** before the rule head. Again inherited attributes can be in any order and can be selectively omitted. In the latter case the inherited values passed to the children of a term are exactly the same as the values provided before the rewriting of this term.

The **body** of a rule is an SML expression that returns a list of terms. This list may be empty (no alternative expressions or plans are produced), or it may have one element (the typical case), or it may have more than one element (as when there are many alternative access paths for scanning a table). The rule body may have one of the following forms:

```
1     if expr then body else body
2     case expr of pattern => body | ...
3     let bindings in body end
4     [ << eterm >>, ... ]
```

where **expr** is any SML expression and **bindings** are SML let bindings. Term **<<eterm>>** is the construction of a plan to be returned from this rule. Any synthesized attribute returned by the subsequent rewrites, such as those associated with the pattern variables 'x or 'x<={...} in the head of the rule, can be accessed in any place in the rule body by using the form (#attr x), where **attr** is a synthesized attribute name.

If we want to specify a guard to a rule, such as a predicate p, we can write **if p then [<<eterm>>] else []** as the body of the rule. That is, if p is false we return no terms.

If there is a form **e<={ attr=val, ... }** in the text of **<<eterm>>** in **body**, then the term **e** is also transformed by the same rewriting process. In that case, the attributes are the new inherited attributes that are propagated to the new rewrite. This transformation is a top-down rewriting, since parts of the term are rewritten after the current rule is applied. These types of rules are used for specifying transformations from logical to logical operators (such as commutativity laws). The other types are used when we have logical to physical transformations (so that the produced plan does not need to be transformed again). The first rule type must be selected with caution, as it may yield an inefficient search. In addition, there is a danger of falling into an infinite loop, even though no rule is applied twice for the same term and the same inherited attributes. One example of such a case is the rule {a=n} <<'x>> = [<<'x<={a=n+1}>>].

There is also support for memoization. When a term x, associated with inherited attributes IA, is transformed into a list of expressions $[x_1, \ldots, x_n]$ (these are physical plans because the rewrite is complete) with their synthesized attributes $[SA_1, \ldots, SA_n]$, then the tuple $(x, IA, [(x_1, SA_1), \ldots, (x_n, SA_n)])$ can be stored in a system-provided memoization table. Therefore, rewriting a term x with IA involves searching this table to test if x and IA are already memoized. If they are, the resulting rewrite is retrieved from the table; if not, the result is calculated by applying the rewrite rules.

5.2 Search Strategy

The **rule** macro produces a function **fn (X,IA,REWRITE,CYCLES,ACC,BOT) => body**, where **X** is the term to be transformed, **IA** its inherited attributes, **REWRITE** is the recursive function that calls this produced function, **CYCLES** is used to prohibit partially completed rules being invoked twice on the same term with the same inherited attributes (such as, commutativity and associativity rules), which may lead to infinite recursion, **ACC** is the function that accumulates plans (usually **union**), and **BOT** is a list of plans in which the newly generated plans from one application are accumulated. Function **REWRITE** takes three parameters: the term to be transformed, its inherited attributes, and the **CYCLES** list. It returns a list of pairs of terms with their synthesized attributes. The **ACC** function can be very sophisticated. For example, instead of forming the union of all plans each time, it can select only a small number of them based on their cost. This scheme will make the search a beam search, which is a hill-climbing search where only the best plans are considered each time.

If we define the REWRITE function to be a call to the function `rulefn` which is produced by the `rule` macro (such as the `rule` macro in Figure 2):

```
fun REWRITE (x,IA,cycles) = rulefn(x,IA,REWRITE,cycles,union,[]);
```

then the REWRITE function has the following semantics:

```
REWRITE (x,IA,cycles) =
for each rule rule#: HEAD=BODY whose head matches x do:
  { if (x,IA,rule#) in cycles then return [];
    bind all free variables Xi in HEAD;
    calculate the new inherited attributes IAi for each Xi;
    Ri = REWRITE(Xi,IAi,[]);
    for each combination of (Ti,SAi) in Ri:
      { evaluate BODY with Xi=Ti;
        for each term e<={IAe} in BODY:
          replace e with REWRITE(e,IAe,(x,IA,rule#)::cycles);
        calculate the new synthesized attributes } };
accumulate all terms and synthesized-attributes found at each matching rule.
```

Note that no explicit term matching is required in the generated code because pattern matching in SML is achieved by standard pattern decomposition. Even though the control of the rewriting appears as a combination of bottom-up (the calls REWRITE(Xi,IAi,[]) for the subterms Xi of the head), and top-down (the calls REWRITE(e,IAe,...) for the subterms e of the body), it can be more general by using the inherited attributes to gain more complex search control.

A rewrite function for the sql optimizer that supports memoization is the following:

```
fun REWRITE (x,IA,cycles) =
case table_find(x,IA) sql of
  just(r) => r        (* already memoized *)
| _ => table_insert(x,IA,rulefn(x,IA,REWRITE,cycles,union,[])) sql;
```

There can be multiple `rule` macros in a rule-base system. One way of combining them is to use the following combinator:

```
fun vertical (f,g) =
fn (X,IA,REWRITE,CYCLES,ACC,BOT)
  => g(X,IA,REWRITE,CYCLES,ACC,f(X,IA,REWRITE,CYCLES,ACC,BOT));
```

where `f` and `g` are functions generated by `rule` macros. This vertical composition accumulates all plans produced either by `f` or `g`: it fuses the rules of `f` with the rules of `g`. There are other ways of combining rules. Another one is the horizontal composition:

```
fun horizontal (f,g) =
fn (X,IA,REWRITE,CYCLES,ACC,BOT)
  => fold(fn ((a,SA),r)
            => ACC(g(a,IA,REWRITE,[],ACC,[]),r))
        (f(X,IA,REWRITE,CYCLES,ACC,[])) BOT;
```

that is, after an intermediate plan a is produced by **f**, the rules in **g** are applied.

A **rule** macro can be used in the body of a rule defined in another **rule** macro (because any function that returns a list of terms can be called in a rule body). This ability is useful when we have a number of rule systems controlled by another rule system. In fact we may have a hierarchy of rule systems where a non-leaf rule system controls the evaluation of its children. This framework is similar to the one described by Mitchell, et al. [10].

6   An Optimizer for an Object-Oriented Language

In this section we specify an optimizer for object-oriented queries expressed in the ZQL[C++] language [1]. ZQL[C++] is an SQL-based object query language designed to be well-integrated with C++. Our approach to solving this optimization problem is influenced by the Volcano optimizer generator approach, as described by Blakeley, et al. [1].

One example of a ZQL[C++] query is the following:

```
select e.name, e.dept.name, e.job.name
  from Employee e in Employees
 where e.dept.plant.location="Dallas"
```

In [1] this query is translated directly into the following expression:

```
project(select(Mat(Mat(Mat(get(Employees):e,
                           e.job):j,
                       e.dept):d,
                   d.plant):p,
               p.location="Dallas"),
        (e.name,j.name,d.name))
```

where the form **e:x** assigns the name **x** (a range variable) to the output produced by expression **e**. That way the results of an expression can be accessed from various points. We express this query in our notation as:

```
project(select(Mat(Mat(Mat(get(Employees,e),
                           [e.job],j),
                       [e.dept],d),
                   [d.plant],p),
               [p.location="Dallas"]),
        [e.name,j.name,d.name])
```

Mat is the *materialize* operator that brings a set of inter-object references (i.e., object links) into a context. For example, in **Mat(x,[e.dept.plant],v)** the range variable **v** is bound to the result of materializing the path **e.dept.plant**. Variable **e** must be a range variable defined in expression **x**. Operator **Mat**, in contrast to algebraic operators, does not construct or consume values, but it extents the bindings of its input **x**.

```
val rulefn = <rule< rules[oodb],
(* 1 *)
<<Mat(Mat('e,'p,'y),'s,'x)>>
  = if refers(s,y)
    then []
    else [<<Mat(Mat('e,'s,'x),'p,'y)<={}>>],

(* 2 *)
<<Mat(Mat('e,'p,'y),'s,'x)>>
  = if refers(s,y)
    then [<<Mat('e,'(unlistify(append(listify(p),listify(s)))),'x)<={}>>]
    else [],

(* 3 *)
<<Mat('e,'p,'x)>>
  = case listify(p) of
      a::b::l
        => let val nv = <var<newname()>>
           in [<<Mat(Mat('e,['a],'nv),'(unlistify(b::1)),'x)<={}>>] end
    | _ => [],

(* 4 *) {extents=ext}
<<Mat('e,['path],'v)>>
  = case find(fn (_,pidx) => pidx=(last(path))) ext of
      just(index,_)
        => let val nv = <var<newname()>>
           in [<<join( 'e, get('index,'nv),
                          ['v.'(last(path))='nv.self] )<={}>>] end
    | _ => [],

(* 5 *) {path_indices=pi}
<<Mat('e,['path],'v)>>
  = case case find(fn (_,p) => p=path) pi of
      just(index,_)
        => let val nv = <var<newname()>>
           in [<<project(join('e,get('index,'nv),
                            ['v.'(last(path))='nv.from]),
                          [to])>>] end
    | _ => [],

(* 6 *) {extents=ext}
<<select(get('t,'x),['s='value])>>
  = if first(s)=x
    then case find(fn (_,pidx) => pidx=(last(s))) ext of
           just(index,_) => [<<index_scan('index,['(last(s))='value],'x)>>]
         | _ => []
    else [],
  ... >>;
```

Fig. 3. Rewrite Rules for the Object-Oriented Optimizer

We use two inherited attributes. Attribute `extents` is a list of all available class extents. For example, the extent of the class `department` may be kept as an explicit set named `Departments` that contains all objects from this class. Performing a projection such as `Employees.department` can then be achieved by the join `join(get(Employees,x),get(Departments,y),x.department=y.self)`. In addition, some chains of object links are stored explicitly as path indices (or access support relations [6]). Path indices are implemented as binary relations with columns `from` and `to`. They are indexed on `from` (our optimizer can be easily extended to support inverse path indices, that is, paths indexed on column `to`). This information is stored in the inherited attribute `path_indices`. The translation of `Mat` into `join` allows us to apply the standard relational optimization methods to the domain of object-oriented databases.

Figure 3 presents some of the rules for optimizing the object-oriented algebra expressed in our specification language. Rule 1 switches the positions of two adjacent materialize operations. This transformation is possible only when the path of the outer `Mat` does not depend on the range variable of the inner `Mat`. Rule 2 collapses two materialize operations into one. This operation can be done only if the range variable of the outer `Mat` is equal to the first path component of the inner `Mat`. Rule 3 is the inverse of rule 2: it splits a `Mat` into two `Mats`. Rule 4 translates a `Mat` into a `join`: if the `path` of `Mat` consists of only one path and there is an extent for this path in `extents` then materialize is translated into a join over this extent. The first and last operations applied to a path return the first and last component of the path, respectively. Rule 5 checks if there is a path index that implements a materialize operation. Rule 6 translates a selection over a table access into an indexed access, provided that there is an index for the selection predicate.

7 Related Work

Our work is influenced by the EXODUS and Volcano optimizer generators [1, 4]. EXODUS allows the database implementer to write a customized optimizer by providing explicit rules. The input to the EXODUS optimizer generator is a model description file, where the database implementer lists the set of operators of the data model, the set of "methods" to be considered when building and comparing access plans, the transformation rules that define legal transformations on the query trees, and the implementation rules that associate methods with operators. The EXODUS output is a customized optimizer that consists of query tree transformations derived from the model description file, support functions written in C code, and a search engine that evaluates the transformations. Volcano extends EXODUS in various ways. It provides more support for physical properties. It introduces a new family of operators, called enforcers, to be inserted in physical plans when these plans do not satisfy the expected properties. Volcano supports a flexible search engine and a flexible cost model. It also supports dynamic programming by memoizing the results of all rewrites. Our experience with the Volcano optimizer generator shows that it is the support functions, not the rewrite rules, that requires the bulk of the effort during optimizer specification. Even though term transformations are expressed declaratively, support functions, such as propagation of physical properties, are expressed procedurally. In addition, routinely performed operations, such as construction of query trees, are not supported directly in a more convenient language. Even though our work does not add more functionality to the the Volcano optimizer, we believe that our language is far clearer and more concise.

Another extensible query optimization framework based on attribute grammars is the one for Starburst, as described by Lohman [8]. This framework is not a rule-based term-rewriting system, even though their specifications define optimizers that perform term-rewriting. Each production rule (called a STAR) defines a transformation from a high-level non-terminal symbol into a low-level one. Query trees and plans (called LOLEPOPs) are passed as parameters to these symbols. Each rule may produce multiple plans or multiple non-terminal symbols, that is, a rule is viewed as a generator of plans. The plan generation and the hierarchical evaluation of rules provide a strict order to some parts of the search, yielding a more feasible search. As in our work, they introduce two types of attributes: required (inherited) and available (synthesized). The difference is that Starburst uses these attributes for representing properties only, not as a general mechanism for context control. In order to apply the same hierarchical transformations to all subnodes of a query tree and to enforce properties to plans, they have a Glue operation that glues operators together to achieve the required properties (in the same way Volcano uses enforcers).

There are other systems that use a declarative specification language to describe specific optimizers, but most of them, as far as we know, do not provide a specification implementation. One example is Freytag's work on rule-based query optimization for relational databases [2, 3].

8   Conclusion and Future Work

We believe our specification system for query optimizers is more comprehensive and more declarative than other systems to date. We intend to produce additional optimizer specifications to validate this hypothesis, particularly ones that use attributes to control optimization context, in the manner of Mitchell, et al. [10]. Our specification processor also appears quite flexible, and we plan to experiment with input syntax modifying and parametrizing the search strategy and retargeting the output to other search engines. CRML proved a powerful tool in constructing the specification processor. One extension we would like to see is easier extension of "object brackets" to deal with syntaxes other than that of SML. Such a capability would make it easier to experiment with the input syntax and the format for query expressions.

9 Acknowledgments

This work is supported in part by the Advanced Research Projects Agency, ARPA order number 18, monitored by the US Army Research Laboratory under contract DAAB-07-91-C-Q518.

References

1. J. Blakeley, W. McKenna, and G. Graefe. Experiences Building the Open OODB Query Optimizer. *Proceedings of the ACM-SIGMOD International Conference on Management of Data, Washington, D.C.*, pp 287–296, May 1993.
2. J. C. Freytag and N. Goodman. Translating Aggregate Queries into Iterative Programs. In *Proceedings of the Twelfth International Conference on Very Large Databases, Kyoto, Japan*, pp 138–146, August 1986.
3. J. C. Freytag. A Rule-Based View of Query Optimization. *Proceedings of the ACM-SIGMOD International Conference on Management of Data, San Francisco, California*, pp 173–180, December 1987.
4. G. Graefe and D. J. DeWitt. The EXODUS Optimizer Generator. In *Proceedings of the ACM-SIGMOD International Conference on Management of Data, San Francisco, California*, pp 160–171, December 1987.
5. G. Graefe and W. McKenna. The Volcano Optimizer Generator: Extensibility and Efficient Search. *IEEE Conference on Data Engineering, Vienna, Austria*, 1993.
6. A. Kemper and G. Moerskotte. Advanced Query Processing in Object Bases Using Access Support Relations. In *Proceedings of the Sixteenth International Conference on Very Large Databases, Brisbane, Australia*, pp 290–301. Morgan Kaufmann Publishers, Inc., August 1990.
7. D. Knuth. Semantics of Context-free Languages. *Mathematical Systems Theory*, 2(2):127–145, June 1968.
8. G. M. Lohman. Grammar-like Functional Rules for Representing Query Optimization Alternatives. *Proceedings of the ACM-SIGMOD International Conference on Management of Data, Chicago, Illinois*, 13(3):18–27, September 1988.
9. R. Milner, M. Tofte, and R. Harper. *The Definition of Standard ML*. The MIT Press, Cambridge, Massachusetts, 1990.
10. G. Mitchell, U. Dayal, and S. B. Zdonik. Control of an Extensible Query Optimizer: A Planning-Based Approach. In *Proceedings of the 19th VLDB Conference*, August 1993. To appear.
11. G. Selinger, M. Astrahan, D. Chamberlin, R. Lorie, and T. Price. Access Path Selection in a Relational Database Management System. *Proceedings of the ACM-SIGMOD International Conference on Management of Data, Boston, Massachusetts*, pp 23–34, May 1979.
12. T. Sheard. Guide to using CRML: Compile-Time Reflective ML. Unpublished manuscript, Oregon Graduate Institute, March 1993.
13. R. Wilhelm. Tree Transformations, Functional Languages, and Attribute Grammars. *Proceedings of the International Workshop on Attribute Grammars and their Applications, Paris, France*, pp 116–129, September 1990. LNCS 461.

Semantic Query Optimization
in Deductive Object-Oriented Databases

Jong P. Yoon † and *Larry Kerschberg* ‡

Department of Information and Software Systems Engineering
School of Information Technology and Engineering
George Mason University, Fairfax, VA 22030-4444
{†jyoon,‡kersch}@isse.gmu.edu

Abstract. This paper addresses the problem of semantic query reformulation in the context of object-oriented deductive databases. It extends the declarative object-oriented specifications of F-logic proposed by Kifer and Lausen using the semantic query optimization technique developed by Chakravarthy, Grant, and Minker. In general, query processing in object-oriented databases is expensive when a query incorporates declarative rules, methods and inherited properties. We introduce the technique of semantic query reformulation for F-logic queries which transforms the original query into an equivalent, semantically-rich query that is more efficiently processed. We also discuss the issues of conflict resolution strategies and query evaluation priorities for queries involving the upper bounds of objects in the F-logic "type" lattice.

1 Introduction

In traditional database systems, queries are typically optimized by either access method cost models or rule-based methods. Access methods constitute an index structure (or an efficient plan) for executing a user's declarative query. The rule-based methods generate an evaluation plan for a query. Some researchers [3, 4, 10, 13] have used heuristic rules to optimize queries. Rules are used to determine efficient search strategies.

It is difficult to associate rules to a query for efficient processing. To lessen this difficulty, a few researchers have developed so called semantic query reformulation [2, 3, 7]. Constraints are associated with a query which in turn becomes semantically optimized [2]. Integrity constraints may be added to queries as functional equations [3]. Type checking is performed at query compilation time [1]. We apply the query optimization concept [2] to queries expressed in F-logic [6]. We propose a query reformulation scheme by which a user-issued query is reformulated into an equivalent and semantically-rich query; the query incorporating rules and inheritances, and resolves conflicts between inherited and derived values. This paper is extended from the earlier work [5]. In particular, the query reformulation process exploits the partial ordering information for resolution between a query and other available information (e.g., rules) stated above. Using the partial ordering information makes it easier to deal with both single and multiple inheritances.

This paper is organized as follows: First, we review F-logic in Section 2. We examine research issues pertinent to semantic query optimization and develop the steps for query optimization in Section 3, including the aspects relevant

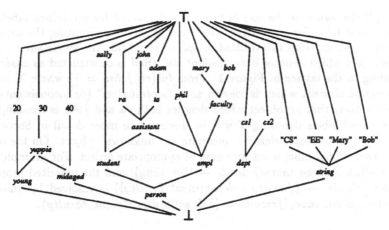

Figure 1: A Lattice of Database Example

to object-oriented databases. The query reformulation process is applied to four examples retaining various object-oriented features in Section 4. Due to several features of the object-oriented paradigm, multiple equivalent queries can be obtained from the original query. Evaluation priority for the reformulated queries is discussed in Section 5. Finally, Section 6 summarizes our work.

2   Preliminaries and Definitions

We introduce the background knowledge used in *F-Logic* in this section, leaving the syntactic and semantic details to the original paper [6]. The unique features of F-logic which are essential to our work will be described. Before describing the features of F-logic, the partial ordering theory [14] is introduced.

Lattice

A *lattice* is a formalism for an ordering of values based on their information content [14]. The lattice in Figure 1 shows part of the IS-A hierarchy. Notice that the IS-A relation in typical object-oriented databases (see Figure 4) is depicted reversely in a lattice. In Figure 1, the information content of *person* is contained in the information content of *student*. Similarly, *empl* contains more (or equal) information than *person*. Both *student* and *empl* are the upper bound of *person*. For example, a statement *student : john* (John is a student) is more informative than *person : john* because every student is a person, but not vice versa.

Lattices, therefore, determine the least upper bound (*lub*) of objects, which is the smallest upper bound of the objects. The *least upper bound* function, $lub(e_1, .., e_n)$, in short, returns the least upper bound type for a set of the arguments $e_1, ..e_n$. Our resolution of the type conflict is based on denotational semantics: (1) the *least upper bound* of types is constructed for a single-valued label; (2) the *union* of the sets of types is constructed for set-valued labels. A single-valued label for more than one object is set by computing the function *lub*. For example, from $lub(student, empl) = assistant$, the single-valued label of the object which denotes both *student* and *empl* is constructed as *assistant* according to the lattice in Figure 1. From $lub(ra, john) = \top$, where $\top$ means the greatest element which is viewed as a "meaningless" (or inconsistent) object, it is likely that an object which denotes both *ra* and *john* is meaningless. Single-valued labels denoting $\top$ will be discussed in more detail in Section 5. Similarly, $\perp$ is the least element, meaning an "unknown" object. On the other hand, a set-valued label is set by union of appropriate object. For example, the type conflict between $mary[friends \rightarrow \{bob, sally\}]$ and the inherited property $faculty[friends \rightarrow \{faculty : department\_faculty\}]$ is resolved by union of those two labels: $mary[friends \rightarrow \{bob, sally, department\_faculty\}$.

F-Logic

Now, we review the unique features of F-logic [6]. A class is viewed as an instance of a super-class. The object *student* can be viewed as representing the class of students and at the same time as an instance of its superclass represented by the object *person*. Each object has an *object identity* (*oid*).

F-Logic defines *terms*. The so called "F-term" $P : Q[label_i \rightarrow T_i]$ is a statement about an object Q asserting that it is an instance of the class P and has properties specified by the labels. Note P, Q and *label* denote "id-term," and T denotes "type constructor" which may be, in turn, an F-term. A term constructed by an F-term is called a *nested* term. The terms can be either constant symbols, variable symbols, or function symbols. T can be either single-valued, function-valued, or set-valued. $P : Q[label_i \rightarrow T_i]$ can be written as $P : Q$ if no labels are specified.

For example, consider the term $student : john[name \rightarrow$ "John"]. The object identity *john* is a student whose name is bound by "John." All terms are constant single-valued in this F-term. However, in

$$student : john[works\_for \rightarrow dept : cs[chair \rightarrow "Peter"]],$$

the type constructor *works_for* for *john* is a nested term $dept : cs[chair \rightarrow$ "Peter"]]. John works for the *cs* department where the chair is "Peter." In

$$faculty : peter[authorship \rightarrow \{publication: B\}],$$

the faculty *peter* has an authorship that is a set B which is in publication. The type constructor *authorship* for *peter* is set-valued.

Now, we discuss the decomposition and composition of terms. $X[label_1 \rightarrow a, label_2 \rightarrow Y]$ is equivalent to a conjunction of its atoms $X[label_1 \rightarrow a], X[label_2 \rightarrow Y]$. We call decomposition of the formula $X[label_1 \rightarrow a, label_2 \rightarrow Y]$ into the two atoms $X[label_1 \rightarrow a]$ and $X[label_2 \rightarrow Y]$ "*fission*," while the reverse process (composition of atoms) "*fusion*." For example, the two terms

<u>Facts</u>:

(1) $faculty : bob \; [name \rightarrow$ "Bob", $age \rightarrow 40, works \rightarrow dept :$
$\qquad cs_1[dname \rightarrow$ "CS", $mngr \rightarrow empl : phil]]$

(2) $faculty : mary \; [name \rightarrow$ "Mary", $age \rightarrow 30, friends \rightarrow \{bob, sally\},$
$\qquad works \rightarrow dept : cs_2[dname \rightarrow$ "CS"]]

(3) $assistant : john[name \rightarrow$ "John", $works \rightarrow cs_1[dname \rightarrow$ "CS"]]

(4) $student : sally[age \rightarrow middleaged]$

<u>General Class Description</u>:

(5) $faculty[supervisor \rightarrow faculty, age \rightarrow middleaged]$

(6) $student[age \rightarrow young]$

(7) $empl[supervisor \rightarrow empl]$

<u>Rules</u>:

(8) $E[supervisor \rightarrow M] \Longleftarrow empl : E[works \rightarrow dept : D[mngr \rightarrow empl : M]]$

Figure 2: F-Logic Example Specification

$student : john[name \rightarrow$ "John"], and
$student : john[works\_for \rightarrow dept : cs[chair \rightarrow$ "Peter"]]

are "fused" into a term

$student : john[name \rightarrow$ "John", $works\_for \rightarrow dept : cs[chair \rightarrow$ "Peter"]].

Inheritance

We assume *monotonic* inheritance. If $t_1 \preceq_O s_1, ..., $ and $t_n \preceq_O s_n$ then $f(t_1, ..., t_n)$
$\preceq_O f(s_1, ..., s_n)$, where $\preceq_O$ denotes the ordering in a lattice, where f is an n-ary
function and is used to construct objects. For example, if $person \preceq_O john$ then
$car(person) \preceq_O car(john)$.

eval Function

We also introduce an evaluation function, $eval(X, Y)$, a binary function with
arguments "object" and "attribute." The function $eval(X, Y)$ returns a set of
the values associated with the attribute Y of the object X.

$eval(X, Y) = \{y \mid y$ is a value of the attribute Y of class X such that
$X[Y \rightarrow y]$, or $X[Y \rightarrow \{y\}]\}$

In the above example, $eval(john, works\_for) = cs$ and $eval(cs, chair) =$ "Peter".

With this background of F-Logic, consider the facts and rules [6]. The objects
are depicted in a lattice as shown in Figure 1 and described in F-logic in Figure 2.
The object *mary*, named "Mary", is 30 years old, has the friends *bob* and *sally*,
and works at the department "CS" whose *oid* is cs_2 as in (2) below. The general
class descriptions play the role of *typing constraints*. The attribute *supervisor*,
not defined in *faculty*, is inherited by *faculty* as defined in (5). In the rule (8),
an employee E's supervisor is M if E works for a department managed by M.

3 Semantic Query Reformulation

This section discusses F-logic query reformulation. Before discussing the subject, we examine the research issues concerning object-oriented databases in F-Logic which we believe have not yet been taken into account.

- Unified Representation. Rule execution is by nature expensive, in contrast to database retrieval. How can rules be added to queries so that only the queries are evaluated?

- Multiple Reformulation Strategies. A query may be semantically reformulated by (1) rule evaluation and (2) property inheritance. Can a query specify both at the same time?

- Activeness. Rules are not actively executed as a query is posed. Conflicting values are not automatically resolved.

Example: Consider the query (12) [6]:

(12) $empl : X[supervisor \rightarrow Y, age \rightarrow middleaged : Z, works \rightarrow D[dname \rightarrow \text{``CS''}]]$

requesting information about all middle aged employees working for the "CS" departments. Suppose the database consists of the rule (8) and the general class description (5) in Figure 2. The issues are how to associate rules and general class descriptions with a query and what to do for conflicting results.   □

3.1 Query Reformulation Process

In a database S having rules and/or inherited properties (denoted as K for both) available, a query Q is posed. It is well known that the rules or inherited properties K are executed against the database S to prove that the query Q entails the answer A[1]. Logically speaking, $S, K \vdash A \supset Q$ holds. It can be rewritten as $S \vdash A \supset (\neg K \vee Q)$. Therefore, it is true that $S \vdash A \supset \neg(K \wedge \neg Q)$. That is, the query Q is equivalent to the reformulated query "$\neg(K \wedge \neg Q)$." Thus, the reformulated query is obtained by negating the resolvent of K and the negation of Q. Notice that the resolvent (or *residue* [2]) is the remaining atoms from resolution.

With the above rationale, we propose the process of query reformulation. Resolution of a rule with the negation of a query results in the negation of the reformulated query.

Query Reformulation Process:

1. **Negation.** A query is negated.
2. **Fission.** A rule and the negated query are decomposed into a set of atoms.
3. **Substitution.** To unify two atoms, (1) a class can be substituted with sub-classes since property inheritance is allowed; and then (2) a (query)

---

[1] That is, $S, K \vdash A \equiv Q$ holds. It is also held that $S, K \vdash (A \supset Q) \wedge (Q \supset A)$. Assuming that both A and Q are true, we can consider only $S, K \vdash A \supset Q$.

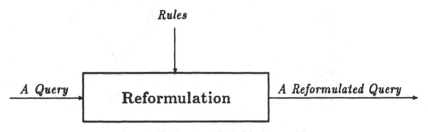

Figure 3: Update Reformulation

variable is substituted with another variable or (3) a variable is substituted with a query value. Note that this step will be discussed in detail in the following sub-section.

4. **Resolution.** Resolve the above two clauses. The resolvent is obtained.

5. **Fusion.** We compose the resolvents into a formula.

6. **Negation.** Finally, the negation of the fused formula is a reformulated query.

The above process is performed within the box in Figure 3. A given query is reformulated into a query with associated rules. The reformulated query is more semantically-rich than the original query. As seen, the resolution step requires substitution between atoms. We will discuss substitution in the following sub-section.

3.2 Object Type Unification

Unification is the process of determining whether two expressions can be made identical by appropriate substitutions for their variables. As we shall see, making this determination is an essential part of our semantic query optimization. A *substitution* is any finite set of bindings between atoms[2], the atoms in a query and the atoms in a rule.

Recall that to unify two atoms, (1) a class can be substituted with sub-classes since property inheritance is allowed; and then (2) a variable is substituted with another (query) variable or (3) a variable is substituted with a (query) value. In this section, we emphasize on how to obtain a substitution between classes. Since the information content of a super class is contained in the information content of a sub-class, variables of a super class are substituted with values (or variables) of a sub-class. More generally speaking, in the term $x : Q$, x are substituted with $lub(x, y)$ where $y : Q$ for an object Q. Of course, if x is a super class of y, x is substituted with y by means of inheritance. Consider the typical IS-A hierarchy example in Figure 4.

---

[2]Notice that resolution for semantic query processing does not require substitution of variables with expressions.

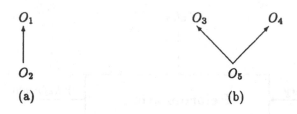

Figure 4: IS-A Hierarchy Example

In the figure, (a) depicts that O_1 is the super class of O_2. The object type O_2 is unified with O_1 because every object of O_2 is also in O_1 but not vice versa. The substitution is $\{O_1/lub(O_1, O_2)\} \equiv \{O_1/O_2\}$. Similarly, in the figure, (b) depicts that O_3 and O_4 are the super classes of O_5. Due to multiple inheritance, O_3 and O_4 can be unified through the their sub-class. The substitution is, then, $\{O_3/lub(O_3, O_4)\} \equiv \{O_3/O_5\}$, and $\{O_4/lub(O_3, O_4)\} \equiv \{O_4/O_5\}$. For example, the constitution $\{person : Q/student : Q\}$ is possible, but $\{student : Q/person : Q\}$ is not, because $lub(person, student) = student$. It is true that not all persons are students but all students are persons. Substitution of lattice information is very useful. Although x and y are not in a super or sub-class relation, both x and y can be substituted with $lub(x, y)$. For example, the substitution $\{student : Q/assistant : Q; empl : Q/assistant : Q\}$ are possible because $lub(student, empl) = assistant$. Using lattice information makes it easier to deal with unification under multiple inheritance.

Moreover, if an atom contains a nested term, in order to unify those two nested terms, an *eval* function is used so that the *lub* is obtained. For example, consider

(8) $E[supervisor \rightarrow M] \Longleftarrow empl : E[works \rightarrow dept : D[mngr \rightarrow empl : M]]$
(13) $E[supervisor \rightarrow N] \Longleftarrow student : E[grades \rightarrow course : C[instructor \rightarrow faculty : N]]$

The left-hand-side of two rules (8) and (13) can be unified by the substitution

$\{M/lub(eval(D, mngr), eval(C, instructor)); N/lub(eval(D, mngr), eval(C, instructor))\}$. As discussed in Section 2, $eval(D, mngr)$ returns an object which is an employee in this case. Clearly, the left-hand-side is bound by a least upper bound between a manager employee and a faculty as instructor.

4   Examples

We analyze the four possible cases of semantic query reformulation. (1) Query with rules, where deductive rules are associated with queries, (2) Query together with inheritance (single and multiple inheritance), where the structural properties such as relationships of super- and sub- objects are associated with queries, and (3) Query with methods (*Functions*), where methods which are functional operations are associated with queries (see [5]). Of course, these three cases can be mixed. In this paper, we demonstrate only two cases (1) and (2) above.

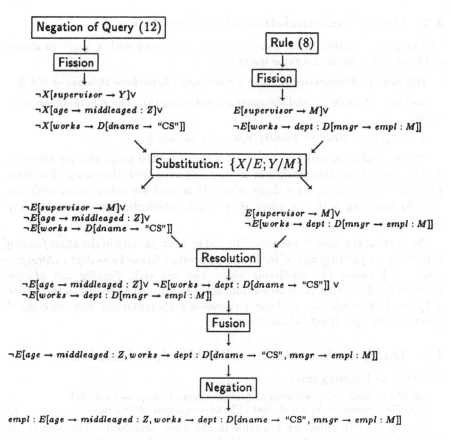

Figure 5: Query Reformulation with a Rule

4.1 Query Reformulation with a Rule

Consider the query (12) and the rule (8).

(12) $empl : X[supervisor \rightarrow Y, age \rightarrow middleaged : Z, works \rightarrow D[dname \rightarrow$ "CS"]]

(8) $E[supervisor \rightarrow M] \Longleftarrow empl : E[works \rightarrow dept : D[mngr \rightarrow empl : M]]$

The negations of (12) and (8) are arranged into two columns and the query reformulation process is applied as shown in Figure 5.

The atoms obtained from the negation of (12) and (8) are unified by substituting X with E and Y with M. Then, a pair of the two atoms, $E[supervisor \rightarrow M]$ and $\neg E[supervisor \rightarrow M]$, is removed. The reformulated query returns values for E, Z, D and M as requested by the original query. It turns out that this query specification incorporates the rule evaluation.

4.2 Query Reformulation with Inheritance

The property inherited from a super-class is associated with a query as shown in Figure 6. Consider the same query (12)

(12) $faculty : X[supervisor \rightarrow Y, age \rightarrow middleaged : Z, works \rightarrow D[dname \rightarrow$ "CS"]]

and both the rule (8) and the general description (5). The general description (5) is:

$faculty[supervisor \rightarrow faculty, age \rightarrow middleaged]$.

Before resolution with the query, rules and inherited properties are resolved. The resolvent from this resolution is, then, resolved with the query. The class $faculty$ of the general class description (5) is used for substitution with the rule (8) and then with the query (12). This substitution preserves property inheritance.

Notice that the label "$supervisor$" bound by both $faculty$ in the atom $faculty[$ $supervisor \rightarrow faculty]$ and M in the atom $faculty : E[works \rightarrow dept : D[mngr \rightarrow empl : M]]$ causes the conflicting $oids$. The two $oids$, $faculty$ and M, are bounded by the $\top$ that is returned from $lub(faculty, M)$ as shown in the lattice of Figure 1. This reformulated query expresses more semantics than the original query (12) by specifying lub functions.

4.3 Query Reformulation with Multiple Inheritance

Consider the following rules:

(8) $E[supervisor \rightarrow M] \Longleftarrow empl : E[works \rightarrow dept : D[mngr \rightarrow empl : M]]$
(13) $E[supervisor \rightarrow N] \Longleftarrow student : E[grades \rightarrow course : C[instructor \rightarrow faculty : N]]$

The above two rules are available in the class $assistant$. The rule (8) is inherited from $empl$, while the rule (13) is inherited from $student$. Suppose the following query is posed to list the supervisors for $assistant$:

(12) $assistant : X[supervisor \rightarrow Y, age \rightarrow middleaged : Z, works \rightarrow D[dname \rightarrow$ "CS"]]

Two inherited rules and the query are arranged into three columns and the query reformulation process is applied as shown in Figure 7. Notice that not all type constructors have to be unified. The type constructors are unified if they bind the same attribute. For example, $empl : M$ and $empl : N$ are not unified because their attributes are not the same but $mngr$ and $instructor$, respectively. However, in $E[supervisor \rightarrow M]$ and $E[supervisor \rightarrow N]$, M and N are unified because their attributes are binding the same $supervisor$.

5 Evaluation of Reformulated Queries

It is shown that upper bound objects contain more (specific) information than lower bound objects [14]. If more specific objects are considered in queries, more specific information can be obtained. We believe that *queries specified by the upper bound of objects should be evaluated first* similar to the "specificity"

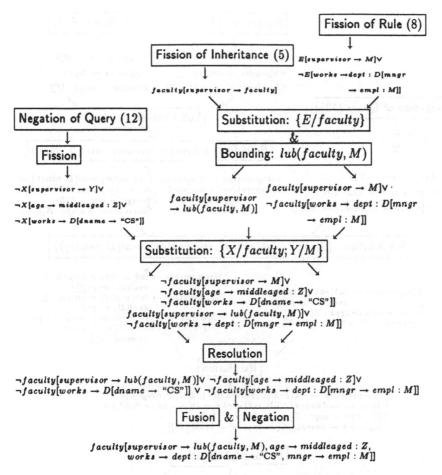

Figure 6: Query Reformulation with Inheritance

precedence in production systems. If two queries are posed at objects in two different levels of specificity (i.e., one object in a super class and the other in a sub-class), the query posed to objects at the more specific level is evaluated first. That is, a query posed to sub-objects is evaluated first.

Regarding the lattice information, if more than one object are denoted by a single-valued label, $[X \rightarrow lub(e_1, e_2, ..., e_n)]$, the label is, if not $\top$, set by computing the least upper bound of those objects. For example, consider $[instructor \rightarrow lub(student, empl)]$. The object $instructor$ which is both $student$ and $empl$ is $assistant$ due to $lub(student, empl) = assistant$. However, if $lub(e_1, .., e_n) = \top$, then the least upper bound may not be an acceptable solution. In this case, the lub function itself can be shown so that the single-valued label can denote either e_1, e_2, or e_n. Of course, interpretations of the lub can be leave to users. For example, in the case that $[good\_student \rightarrow lub(ra, john)] = [good\_student \rightarrow \top]$,

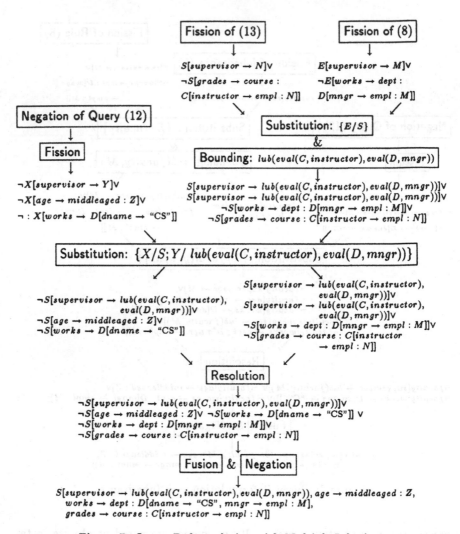

Figure 7: Query Reformulation with Multiple Inheritance

the label *good_student* may be either *ra* or *john* rather than concluding an "inconsistent" object.

Example 1. Consider the following two queries, Q1 and Q2, reformulated in Section 4.1 and 4.2, and the facts (1) and (2):

(Q1) $empl : E[age \to middleaged : Z, works \to D[dname \to$ "CS", $mngr \to empl : M]]$

(Q2) $faculty : E[supervisor \to lub(faculty, M), age \to middleaged : Z,$
$\qquad works \to dept : D[dname \to$ "CS", $mngr \to empl : M]]$

(1) $faculty : bob[name \to$ "Bob", $age \to 40, works \to dept : cs_1[dname \to$ "CS",
$\qquad\qquad mngr \to empl : phil]]$

(2) $faculty : mary[name \to$ "Mary", $age \to 30, friends \to \{bob, sally\},$
$\qquad\qquad works \to dept : cs_2[dname \to$ "CS"]]

Because Q2 is posed at *faculty* which is sub-class of *empl*, it is evaluated first. With the facts (1) binding M by *phil*, the answer (14) is obtained because $lub(faculty, phil) = \top$. With (2), the variable M is unknown or the least element, then, $lub(faculty, \bot) \equiv faculty$ and the answer is (15).

(14) $bob[supervisor \to lub(faculty, phil), age \to 40, works \to cs_1]$
(15) $mary[supervisor \to faculty, age \to 30, works \to cs_2]$

If (14) were used to evaluate Q1 first, the value for *supervisor* would be *phil* which causes a conflict with the value *faculty* inherited from the general description (5). These answers may resolve the conflict between *phil* and *faculty* by obtaining $\top$, "inconsistency," from $lub(faculty, phil)$ in Q2. However, if the value "inconsistency" is not acceptable to the attribute *supervisor*, the *lub* function may be shown for potential answers, say, either *faculty* or *phil*. □

If two queries are posed to objects in a same level of the specificity, the query specified by the upper bound of objects is evaluated first. That is, a query specified by objects at the more specific level is evaluated first.

Example 2. Section 4.4 illustrated how the query Q3 is reformulated into the query Q4. This example shows that the reformulated query Q4 has expressive power and is semantically richer than Q3.

(Q3) $assistant : X[supervisor \to Y, age \to middleaged : Z, works \to D[dname \to$ "CS"]]
(Q4) $assistant : E[supervisor \to lub(eval(C, instructor), eval(D, mngr)),$
$\qquad age \to middleaged : Z, works \to dept : D[dname \to$ "CS",
$\qquad mngr \to empl : M], grades \to course : C[instructor \to empl : N]]$

Consider the following facts:

(1) $faculty : bob [name \to$ "Bob", $age \to 40, works \to dept :$
$\qquad cs_1[dname \to$ "CS", $mngr \to empl : phil]]$
(3) $assistant : john[name \to$ "John", $works \to cs_1[dname \to$ "CS"]]
(4) $student : sally[age \to middleaged]$
(16) $ta : adam[age \to 30, works \to dept : cs_2[dname \to$ "CS"],
$\qquad grades \to course : os_1[instructor \to$ "Peter"]]

Consider the reformulated query Q4 first. The object in (1) is not applicable for this query. For the fact (3), the attribute *mngr* is bound by *phil* because he works for cs_1 whose manager is *phil*, and the attribute *instructor* is $\bot$ "unknown." That is,

$$lub(eval(cs_1, mngr), \bot) = lub(phil, \bot) = phil.$$

john's supervisor is *phil*. For *sally*, $lub(\bot, \bot) = \bot$, so her supervisor is unknown. However, in the same manner, *adam*'s supervisor is "Peter." Hence, the answer to the above reformulated query includes:

(17) $john[supervisor \rightarrow phil, age \rightarrow young]$
(18) $sally[supervisor \rightarrow \bot, age \rightarrow middleaged]$
(19) $adam[supervisor \rightarrow "Peter", age \rightarrow 30]$

Note that *john* is young because of the inherited property (6) $student[age \rightarrow young]$.

Without query reformulation, it is not possible to obtain sound answers from Q3. That is, although Q3 may produce answers by means rules and inherited properties, it does not deal with conflicting answers. The conflicting answers can be handled by Q4 efficiently as seen above. □

6 Conclusion

Simple F-logic queries can be reformulated into equivalent and semantically-richer queries that incorporate a rule, a more general description, or a method. We develop the query reformulation process. Reformulated queries may consist of the least upper bound *lub* of the conflicting values, thereby resolving conflicts. Queries with associated rules and inherited properties are semantically rich in that types can be checked by the associated rules specifying that type, query processing can be limited within a range if restricted by constraints, and answers may be intensional [8, 11]. Due to the several features of the object-oriented paradigm available and one or more rules considered, several queries can be generated for an original query. To resolve the conflicting answers, the evaluation precedence of the reformulated queries is also discussed. We believe that queries specified by upper bound objects should be evaluated first.

The unique contributions of this paper are:

- Semantic query optimization techniques have been extended to apply to object-oriented declarative databases, as those expressed in F-logic [6].

- Object-oriented query reformulation techniques extended the notions of semantic query optimization [2] to include active rules and inherited properties.

- Conflict resolution and query evaluation strategies are proposed to ensure the proper evaluation of multiple, semantically-equivalent queries derived from the initial F-logic expression.

Association of *recursive rules* [12] with a query is a topic for future research. Magic-set theory [9] may be also employed in our query reformulation process.

Acknowledgement

This research is supported in part by an ARPA grant, administered by the Office of Naval Research under grant number N0014-92-J-4038.

References

[1] A. Borgida. Type systems for query class hierarchies with non-strict inheritance. In *Proceedings of the ACM Symposium on Principles of Database Systems*, pages 394–400, 1989.

[2] Upen S. Chakravarthy, John Grant, and Jack Minker. Logic-based approach to semantic query optimization. *ACM Transactions on Database Systems*, 15(2):163–207, June 1990.

[3] Georges Gardarin and Rosana S. Lanzelotte. Optimizing object-oriented database queries using cost-controlled rewriting. In *Proc. of 3rd Int'l Conf. on Extending Database Technology*, pages 534–549, Vienna, Austria, 1992.

[4] Alfons Kemper and Guido Moerkotte. Advanced query processing in object bases using access support relations. In *Proc. Intl. Conf. on Very Large Data Bases*, pages 290–301, Brisbane, Australia, 1990.

[5] Larry Kerschberg and Jong P. Yoon. Semantic query reformulation in object-oriented databases. In *Proc. of the Workshop on Combining Declarative and Object-Oriented Databases*, pages 73–85, Washington, D.C., 1993.

[6] Michael Kifer and George Lausen. F-logic: A higher-order language for reasoning about objects, inheritance, and scheme. In *Proc. ACM SIGMOD Intl. Conf. on Management of Data*, pages 134–146, Portland, Oregon, 1989.

[7] Sanggoo Lee, Lawrence J. Henschen, and Ghassan Z. Qadah. Semantic query reformulation in deductive databases. In *Intl. Conf. on Data Engineering*, pages 232–239, 1991.

[8] A. Motro. Using integrity constraints to provide intensional answers to relational queries. In *Proc. Intl. Conf. on Very Large Data Bases*, pages 237–246, Amsterdam, 1989.

[9] Inderpal S. Mumick, Sheldon J. Finkelstein, Hamid Pirahesh, and Raghu Ramakrishnan. Magic is relevant. In *Proc. ACM SIGMOD Intl. Conf. on Management of Data*, pages 247–258. 1990.

[10] Hamid Pirahesh, Joseph M. Hellerstein, and Waqar Hasan. Extensible/rule based query rewrite optimization in Starburst. In *Proc. ACM SIGMOD Intl. Conf. on Management of Data*, pages 39–48, 1992.

[11] A. Pirotte and D. Roelants. Constraints for improving the generation of intensional answers in a deductive database. In *5th Int. Conf. on Data Engineering*, pages 652–659, LA, 1989.

[12] Kenneth A. Ross. Modular acyclicity and tail recursion in logic programs. In *Proceedings of the ACM Symposium on Principles of Database Systems*, pages 92–101. 1990.

[13] P. Griffiths Selinger and et al. Access path selection in a relational database management system. In *Proc. ACM SIGMOD Intl. Conf. on Management of Data*, pages 23–34, 1979.

[14] Joseph E. Stoy. *Denotational Semantics: The Scott-Strachey Approach to Programming Language Theory*. The MIT Press, Cambridge, MA, 1977.

Research in Deductive and Object-Oriented Databases

Moderator: Raghu Ramakrishnan

Computer Sciences Department
University of Wisconsin-Madison
Madison, Wisconsin 53706
USA

1 Introduction

The focus of this DOOD 93 panel will be on research directions in the area of deductive and object-oriented databases (DOODBs).

There has been a great deal of research in the area of deductive databases, as well as in the area of object-oriented databases, and it is reasonable to expect that much of this research will be relevant to systems that seek to combine deductive and object-oriented features. Indeed, much of the work that has gone into conventional relational databases should be applicable as well.

What are the important issues to address at this point in time? First, is the combination of deductive and OO technology a good direction for the next generation of databases? The answer to this must come mainly from a consideration of applications, but it is nonetheless an important question for researchers to bear in mind. Second, what are the problems in DOODBs for which existing solutions (in the areas of relational, deductive and OO databases) are likely to prove adequate? Can we tailor the design of DOODBs to avoid re-inventing the wheel? From a practical standpoint, to develop robust DOODBs quickly, a detailed look at this question is essential. Third, what are new problems created by combining deductive and OO features? Are there problems created by this mixture that did not exist previously? Are there problems that could be dealt with earlier using simple solutions, which no longer apply?

The above questions must be considered both at the level of *building* DOODBs, and at the level of *designing and using* DOODBs from a user perspective. It is hoped that the panel will provide a lively discussion of these issues.

An implementation overview of the Aditi deductive database system

Kotagiri Ramamohanarao

Department of Computer Science, University of Melbourne
Parkville, 3052 Victoria, Australia

Abstract

Deductive databases generalize relational databases by providing support for recursive views and non-atomic data. Aditi is a deductive database system based on the client-server model: it is inherently multi-user and capable of exploiting parallelism on shared-memory multiprocessors. The back-end uses relational technology for efficiency in the management of disk based data and uses optimization algorithms especially developed for the bottom-up evaluation of logical queries involving recursion. The front-end interacts with the user in a logical language that has more expressive power than relational query languages. We present the structure of Aditi, discuss its components in some detail, and present performance figures.

1 Introduction

Deductive databases are logic programming systems designed for applications with large quantities of data, the kinds of applications that are at present programmed in SQL embedded in a host language such as C. Deductive databases generalize relational databases by exploiting the expressive power of (potentially recursive) logical rules and of non-atomic data structures, greatly simplifying the task of application programmers.

The ultimate goal of the Aditi project at the University of Melbourne is to show that this generalization does not have to compromise performance. Applications that can run on relational systems should run on deductive systems with similar performance while being substantially easier to develop, debug and maintain. We keep performance for traditional applications competitive by using conventional relational technology whenever possible; we keep programming costs down by allowing developers to work at a level much higher than SQL and other traditional query languages. At this level, many problems can be solved without resorting to a host language. The higher level also allows the system to perform automatically better global optimization than is currently possible, because the humans who currently do global optimization cannot keep in mind all the relevant details at the same time. This is particularly important for the most sophisticated applications, such as expert systems that work on large amounts of data. Therefore deductive databases can make feasible complex applications that were not feasible before.

Aditi is named after the goddess who in Indian mythology is "the personification of the infinite" and "mother of the gods". The system has four main characteristics that together distinguish it from other deductive databases. First, it is disk-based to allow relations to exceed the size of main memory. Second, it supports concurrent access by multiple users. Third, it exploits parallelism at several levels. Fourth, it allows the storage of terms containing function symbols.

The work on Aditi started in the second quarter of 1988, and a beta-test version was released in January, 1993.

The structure of the paper is as follows. The rest of this section introduces the main components of Aditi. Section 2 shows the structure of databases and relations in Aditi. Section 3 describes the langauge used in Aditi to manipulate relations. Section 4 details the server processes and the low-level modules they use. Section 5 gives performance figures while section 6 concludes with some future directions.

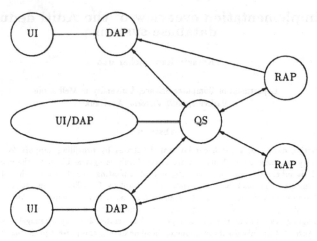

Figure 1: The structure of Aditi

1.1 The structure of Aditi

Aditi is based on the client/server model found in many commercial relational database systems. In this model, users interact with a user-interface process, and this client communicates with a back-end server process that performs the usual database operations, such as joining, merging, and subtracting relations, on behalf of the clients. Some systems have one server per client, while others have one server supporting multiple clients. In Aditi, each client has one server process dedicated to it, but it also shares some server processes with other clients. Figure 1 illustrates how the pieces fit together. The responsibilities of the three types of server processes are as follows:

DAP   Each Database Access Process or DAP is dedicated to a client process. DAPs are responsible for authenticating their clients to the rest of Aditi, and for controlling the evaluation of the queries of their clients.

RAP   Relational Algebra Processes or RAPs carry out relational algebra operations on behalf of the DAPs. RAPs are allocated to DAPs for the duration of one such operation.

QS   The Query Server or QS is responsible for managing the load placed by Aditi on the host machine by controlling the number of RAPs active at any time. In operational environments, there should be one QS per machine. However, in a development environment one can set up multiple QSs; each QS supervises an entirely separate instance of Aditi.

When a client wants service from Aditi, it sends a command to its DAP. The DAP executes some types of commands by itself and passes the other types (mostly relational algebra operations) to the QS. The QS queues the task until a RAP becomes available and then passes the task on to a free RAP for execution. At completion, the RAP sends the result to the requesting DAP and informs the QS that it is available for another task.

2   Databases and relations

Like other DBMSs, Aditi requires every relation to belong to a database, but it also allows a machine to accommodate several databases. We expect a typical arrangement to be a main production database containing detailed information about some enterprise mission, and several smaller databases in which individual users or groups record summary information, hypothetical data, test data and other information of interest only to them. The design of Aditi allows one query to gather together information from several databases, and allows users to put the result in yet another database if they wish.

2.1 Base relations

Aditi base relations have a fixed arity, but attributes currently do not have associated types; any term can appear in any attribute position of any relation. Each relation has a sequence of one or more attributes as its key. If requested, Aditi will ensure that a relation has at most one tuple with a given combination of values for the key attributes.

The creator of a base relation can currently choose between four storage structures.

The simplest storage structure does no indexing. The data is stored as an unsorted sequence of tuples. Although obviously not suited for large relations, this storage structure has very low overheads and is quite appropriate for small static or mostly-static relations, such as temporary relations created during query execution.

The second storage structure has B-tree indexing. The data is stored as a sequence of tuples, and a B-tree sorted on the key attributes of the relation serves as an index into this sequence; the sequence can be sorted if the user requests.

The third storage structure has a superimposed codeword index. The data is stored as a sequence of tuples where each tuple fits entirely into one *segment*. The index has a bit string for each segment. This bit string is the segment descriptor, and it is calculated by ORing together the tuple descriptors of all the tuples in the segment. Tuple descriptors in turn are derived by hashing the values of the attributes of the tuple and using each hash value to select a fixed number of bits to be set.

When one uses the same technique to generate a descriptor for a *partial-match* query on the relation, i.e. one that specifies values for some attributes but not others, one only sets the bits corresponding to the values of the specified attributes. Therefore the query descriptor will have fewer 1s than tuple descriptors. The key observations are that a tuple cannot match the query unless the tuple's descriptor has 1s in all positions where the query descriptor has 1s, and that a segment cannot contain a matching tuple unless the segment's descriptor has 1s in all positions where the query descriptor has 1s.

The first step in the retrieval process is therefore applying this test to all the segment descriptors. Since the test does not look at all the bits of segment descriptors, only the bits that are set in the query descriptor, the index stores the segment descriptors in a bit-slice fashion, with bit 0 of all descriptors first, then bit 1 of all descriptors next, and so on. This clusters together all the descriptor bits needed in the test and thus reduces both I/O and computation costs. However, the contiguous placement of the bit slices also places an upper bound on the number of segments of the relation; since in this storage method segments have no overflow pages, this implies a static maximum size for the relation. This is why we call this storage structure static superimposed codeword index, or *ssimc* for short.

The superimposed codeword index removes the need to retrieve pages that do not contain tuples matching the query, but these tuples themselves can be scattered throughout the data file. To improve clustering, and thus I/O performance and memory consumption, whenever Aditi inserts a tuple into an ssimc relation, it interleaves some bits from the hash values of the tuple's attributes (which it must compute anyway) to form a segment number, and inserts the tuple into the indicated segment whenever possible. If that segment is full, Aditi tries to find another segment with sufficient space. If none exists, the insertion fails.

The fourth storage structure, dsimc, is specifically designed for dynamic relations, in fact for relations whose size may fluctuate by several orders of magnitude. It is very similar to ssimc, but there are two key differences. First, dsimc stores all the bits of a descriptor together, removing the limit on the size of relations. Second, whereas ssimc relies mainly on superimposed codewords and uses multikey hashing as a tuple-placement heuristic, dsimc relies mainly on multikey linear hashing and uses superimposed codewords as a filtering heuristic. In fact, one can think of dsimc as multikey hashing, where before retrieving a data page, the system checks the page's descriptor to see whether the page contains any potentially matching tuples. Much of the time the answer will be "no", and in such cases we can avoid reading that data page and any associated overflow pages. The cost we pay is reading the descriptor, but this cost is small because the descriptor is small, and because it is clustered with other descriptors that the same query is likely to need.

Both ssimc and dsimc require relation creators to specify some information from which they compute the parameters of the superimposed coding and multikey hashing algorithms. There is a fair amount of research on techniques for deriving the optimal values of these parameters. The best place to look for a fuller explanation and details is in [21] for ssimc and [22] for dsimc; these papers have the full details of the two storage structures as well.

2.2   Derived relations

So far we have talked only about base relations. However, the power of deductive databases lies in derived relations, relations that can infer information at run-time. In Aditi, users define derived relations (also called derived *predicates*) by writing programs in Aditi-Prolog, a pure (declarative) variant of Prolog augmented with declarations. Some declarations tell the compiler about the properties of the predicate: e.g. which arguments will be known when the predicate is called; some others request specific rule transformations or evaluation strategies. The file "stops.al" is an example:

```
?- mode(stops(f,f,f)).
?- flag(stops, 3, diff).

stops(Origin, Destination, []) :-
      flight(Origin, Destination).
stops(Origin, Destination, [Stop|Stoplist]) :-
      flight(Origin, Stop),
      stops(Stop, Destination, Stoplist),
      not in_list(Stop, Stoplist).

?- mode(in_list(f,b)).
?- flag(in_list, 2, magic).
?- flag(in_list, 2, diff).

in_list(Head, [Head|_Tail]).
in_list(Item, [Head|Tail]) :-
      in_list(Item, Tail).
```

This code fragment defines two predicates (derived relations). stops gives all possible routes between all city-pairs: it represents routes as lists of intermediate stops. in_list checks whether its first argument is a member of the list that is its second argument.

The lines beginning with ?- are declarations to the compiler (declarations in Prolog-like languages traditionally look like queries because they also cause immediate action by the compiler). The first mode declaration states that stops supports queries such as ?- stops(From, To, Stoplist) in which all arguments are *free* variables. The second mode declaration states that in_list supports queries such as ?- in_list(City, [sydney, honolulu]) in which the first argument is a free variable but the second argument is *bound* to a completely specified (i.e. *ground*) term.

In general, every relation must have one or more mode declarations; base relations always have one mode consisting of all f's. A query matches a mode declaration if it has ground terms in all positions that the mode declares to be b (bound); the query may have any term in positions the mode declares to be f (free). Aditi allows a query on a relation only if it matches one of the modes of that relation. For example, since there is no "f,f" mode for in_list, Aditi will reject the query ?- in_list(City, Stoplist).

There are two reasons for requiring mode declarations:

- Some predicates have an infinite number of solutions unless certain arguments are specified in the call.

- Most optimization methods require that the optimizer know which arguments of each call are known when the call is processed.

It is the flag declarations that tell the compiler what optimizations and evaluation algorithms to use. With the flags shown above, Aditi will use differential (semi-naive) evaluation when answering queries on both relations; for in_list, it will use the magic set optimization as well. (Actually, the diff flags can be omitted, as differential evaluation is the default.)

The set of flags supported by the current version of Aditi allows users to request

- naive evaluation
- differential or semi-naive evaluation [2]
- predicate semi-naive evaluation [20]
- evaluation by magic set interpreter [19]
- the magic set transformation [3, 4]
- the supplementary magic set transformation [24]
- the context transformations for linear rules [12]
- parallel evaluation [15]
- top-down tuple-at-a-time evaluation (see section 4.3)

Users may specify several flags for one predicate. For example, one can request differential evaluation of a magic set transformed program, as in_list above does, or one can ask for a context-transformed program to be evaluated using a parallel implementation of the predicate semi-naive algorithm. However, not all combinations of flags make sense, e.g. the various magic set variants and the context transformation are all mutually exclusive.

The flexibility offered by the flag mechanism in selecting the set of optimizations to be applied to a predicate is essential to us as researchers when we investigate optimization methods and evaluation algorithms. Eventually, of course, we intend to distill the results of these investigations into code that *automatically* selects the best set of optimizations for each predicate in the program (like the strategy module of [17]).

Aditi-Prolog programs may include disjunction and negation. Unlike most deductive database systems, the use of negation need not be limited to stratified programs; we have developed a practical algorithm for computing answers to queries even in the presence of unstratified negation [10, 13]. This algorithm works on a magic-transformed program where each predicate has two slightly different versions. At each iteration, the algorithm uses one set of versions to compute a set of definitely true facts, the other set to compute a set of possibly true facts. The next iteration can then use the complement of the set of possibly true facts as the set of definitely false facts it needs to perform negation.

Aditi-Prolog supports the usual set of aggregate operations. Given an atomic query, one can ask for the minimum or maximum value of some attribute in the solution, the sum of the values of some attributes, the number of solutions, or a list of those solutions. In addition, one can ask for the solution to the query to be divided into groups based on the values of some attributes before the aggregate operation is carried out. For instance, the query

```
?- aggregate(Max = max(Dist), [], flightdist(_From, _To, Dist)),
        flightdist(From, To, Max).
```

will find the length of the longest flight in the database and print the origin, destination and length of the few flights (probably one) that have this distance. On the other hand, the query

```
?- aggregate(Max = max(Dist), [From], flightdist(From, _To, Dist)),
        flightdist(From, To, Max).
```

will print the details of at least one flight from each city, because the groupby list tells Aditi to divide the solutions of the flightdist relation into groups, one group per starting point, and then find the longest flight in each group.

When aggregation is part of an Aditi-Prolog program, it must respect stratification the same way as negation.

For further details of the language, see the Aditi-Prolog language manual [5].

The Aditi-Prolog compiler is called "apc". Its interface is intentionally similar to the interface of other compilers on Unix systems, e.g. cc. As arguments, one just names the files to be compiled:

```
1% apc stops.al
```

The resulting object file, "stops.ro" can be tested by loading it manually into the query shell. When the programmer is satisfied that the predicates in the file work correctly, he or she can make them a part of the database by executing the command

```
2% newderived stops.ro
```

3 The Aditi relational language

RL is a simple procedural language whose primitive operations are those needed for database implementation. These primitives include

- the standard relational algebra operations such as join, union, difference, select and project
- extended relational algebra operations such as union-diff and btmerge, which perform two or more standard relational algebra operations at the same time but with only one scan of the input relations
- data movement operations such as append (union without checking for duplicates), copy (which copies a relation) and assign (which copies a *pointer* to a relation)
- operations concerned with data structure optimization such as presort-relation
- aggregate operations such as count, max and min
- arithmetic and relational operations on integers and floating-point numbers and the usual operations on boolean values
- operations to retrieve information from the data dictionary

- operations to create, delete and clear relations
- operations to insert tuples into and delete tuples from relations
- operations to manage DAP threads (see section 4.1)
- operations to shut down the query server (and thus the DAP)

The control structures of RL are a similar mix of simplicity and sophistication: RL supports only gotos, conditional branches, and procedure calls.

The procedures are the key to RL. An RL program has a procedure for every mode of every derived predicate in the Aditi-Prolog program it was compiled from. As an example, consider the following Aditi-Prolog code:

```
?- flag(path, 2, context).
?- mode(path(b,f)).
path(X, Y) :- edge(X, Y).
path(X, Y) :- edge(X, Z), path(Z, Y).
```

This code declares a derived predicate called path that expects to be called with its first argument ground, and directs the compiler to apply the optimization method known as the context transformation [12]. The body of the predicate defines path to be the transitive closure of the edge relation, just as the trip predicate is a kind of transitive closure of the flight relation. We have chosen path as the example because the additional details in the code produced for trip would needlessly clutter the explanation.

The Aditi-Prolog compiler produces the following RL code for this definition:

```
procedure
path_2_1(init_path_2_1, output_path_2_1)
relation init_path_2_1, output_path_2_1;
{
        relation diff_mc_path_2_1_2_1, edge_4, final_mc_path_2_1_2_1;
        relation out_eq_1, out_eq_7, edge_9, output_mc_path_2_1_2_1;
        bool bool1;
        int size1;

        setbrel(final_mc_path_2_1_2_1, 2);
        settrel(diff_mc_path_2_1_2_1, 2);
        settrel(edge_4, 2);
        settrel(out_eq_1, 2);
        settrel(out_eq_7, 2);
        settrel(edge_9, 2);
        settrel(output_mc_path_2_1_2_1, 2);

        project(init_path_2_1,out_eq_1,"#(0,0),#(0,0)");
        btmerge(final_mc_path_2_1_2_1,out_eq_1,diff_mc_path_2_1_2_1,0);
        setprel(edge_4, "edge", 2);
label1:
        join(diff_mc_path_2_1_2_1,edge_4,"#(1,0)=#(0,1)","",
                out_eq_7,"#(0,0),#(1,1)");
        btmerge(final_mc_path_2_1_2_1,out_eq_7,diff_mc_path_2_1_2_1,0);
        cardinality(diff_mc_path_2_1_2_1, size1);
        gt(size1, 0, bool1);
        test(bool1, label1);
```

```
flatten(final_mc_path_2_1_2_1,output_mc_path_2_1_2_1);
setprel(edge_9, "edge", 2);
join(output_mc_path_2_1_2_1,edge_9,"#(1,0)=#(0,1)","",
     output_path_2_1,"#(0,0),#(1,1)");

clear(diff_mc_path_2_1_2_1);
clear(edge_4);
clear(final_mc_path_2_1_2_1);
clear(out_eq_1);
clear(out_eq_7);
clear(edge_9);
clear(output_mc_path_2_1_2_1);
}
```

Note the (intentional) similarity to the "look and feel" of a C program. The name of the RL procedure is derived from the name of the Aditi-Prolog predicate it implements (path), its arity (2), and the number of the mode it implements (1). The names of some of the local variables have two copies of this suffix; one comes from the arity and mode of path, the other from the arity and mode of the auxiliary predicate mc_path_2_1 created by the compiler as part of the context transformation on path_2_1 (the "mc" stands for "magic context"). The RL code above is in fact compiled from code that looks like this:

```
?- mode(mc_path_2_1(b,f)).
mc_path_2_1(C, C).
mc_path_2_1(C, A) :- mc_path_2_1(C, B), edge(B, A).

?- mode(path(b,f)).
path(X, Y) :- mc_path_2_1(X, A), edge(A, Y).
```

This code exists only inside the compiler. Since the auxiliary predicate cannot be called from anywhere else, its RL code has been inlined into the RL code of path itself.

4   The servers of Aditi

Sections 4.1 through 4.3 describe Database Access Processes, Query Servers and Relational Algebra Processes respectively.

4.1   Database Access Process

Users must go through DAPs to gain access to Aditi; the DAPs have the responsibility of enforcing the security restrictions (if any) on access to shared databases. DAPs are trusted processes; they always check whether the user on behalf of whom they are executing has the authority to carry out the operation he or she requests the DAP to perform. A front-end process (such as the query shell) can get access to Aditi in one of two ways. It can create a child DAP process for itself and set up a pipe to it, or it can have a copy of the DAP built into it. Though the latter method is faster, for obvious reasons it is confined to application programs that are themselves trusted. An example of a trusted application is the NU-Prolog interpreter. Since a NU-Prolog program cannot compromise the internal data structures of the NU-Prolog interpreter, all NU-Prolog programs are trusted as well (see figure 1).

After startup and the completion of the obligatory privilege check, DAPs go into a loop waiting for commands and executing them. These commands are not in Aditi-Prolog but in RL; DAPs contain an interpreter for RL. Each DAP has a table containing the names and the code of the RL procedures it knows about. At startup, this table will be empty, but by looking up the data dictionary the DAP can on demand retrieve the RL procedures of the database's derived relations.

To execute a query on a single predicate whose arguments are all distinct free variables, the front-end process tells the DAP to execute the corresponding RL procedure in its procedure table, if the predicate being accessed is a derived relation; otherwise it tells the DAP to execute the built-in setprel command with the name of the base relation as an argument. To execute any query more complex than this, the front-end process must compile the query into an RL procedure, load that RL procedure into the DAP, and tell the DAP to execute that procedure. The DAP will leave the results of queries in temporary relations; the front-end can then ask the DAP for the contents of these relations and may use them in later queries. If the result of the query is to be used as a set of tuples to be inserted into or deleted from a relation, the front-end will command the DAP to do that as well.

An RL procedure consists of a sequence of operations. The DAP interpreter executes some operations itself and sends others to the QS for assignment to some RAP. Operations that can require large amounts of computation, such as joins and unions, are performed by RAPs; operations with small time bounds, such as determining a relation's cardinality, creating a relation or inserting a tuple into a relation are performed directly by the DAP.

Normally, whenever the DAP sends a job to a RAP through the QS, it will wait for the RAP to report the completion of the job. However, the compiler can generate code in which sending a job to a RAP and waiting for a completion report are two separate actions, in between which the DAP can continue running. This allows a DAP to perform work in parallel with a RAP, and since the DAP can continue to issue other jobs to other RAPs, several RAPs can work for the same DAP at the same time.

There are two main sources of parallelism in Aditi-Prolog programs: parallelism between clauses and parallelism between atoms inside a clause. Parallelism between clauses is restricted by the nature of bottom-up evaluation, which must apply nonrecursive clauses before it goes into a loop applying the recursive clauses: therefore parallelism is possible only between two nonrecursive clauses and between two recursive clauses. Parallelism between atoms in a clause is possible only if neither atoms needs a value generated by the other.

The DAP executes every RL operation in the context of a thread. Sequential RL code only ever has one thread: parallel code creates and destroys threads as necessary. We have developed two compilation schemes for managing thread activity [15]: one is based on the fork-join approach and the other on dataflow methods. The fork-join approach is very simple: whenever the compiler knows that two or more operations or operation sequences are independent, it creates a thread for each operation sequence. The main thread launches all these threads simultaneously and then waits for all of them to complete before continuing.

In the general case, the compiler will generate one thread for each nonrecursive clause, with each of those threads launching separate threads for separate atoms, and it will generate a similar thread structure inside the loop. In practice the thread structure will be less complicated because independent atoms inside clauses are somewhat rare, and because many important predicates have only one non-recursive clause and/or only one recursive clause. However, as long as the predicate has *some* independent operations, the fork-join scheme will exploit it.

The weakness of the fork-join approach is its handling of loops. It cannot start the next iteration of a loop until the threads of all recursive clauses have completed even if the threads that have completed so far have produced the relations needed by some of the threads to start their part of the next iteration. This leads to a loss of concurrency. Our other compilation scheme therefore controls synchronization between threads by dataflow methods: a thread can execute its next operation if the operations that produce its input relations have completed.

Our experiments have proven that the dataflow method can yield greater concurrency and better performance than fork-join without increasing run-time overhead, but only if a set of mutually recursive predicates have some recursive rules independent of each other, which is quite rare. The cost is increased complexity in the RL interpreter and in the Aditi-Prolog compiler. In fact, while the RL interpreter in the DAP supports both schemes (it had to for us to run our experiments), the compiler currently generates only fork-join code.

Note that neither scheme requires the DAP itself to be parallel: all of the parallelism comes from the parallel operation of several RAPs. The DAP does maintain several thread contexts, but it executes in only one context at a time; it switches to another thread only when its current thread exits or blocks waiting for a reply from a RAP. Since the operations native to the DAP are all much shorter than a typical RAP operation, this is a very effective simulation of time-slicing.

4.2   Query Server

The Query Server (QS) is the central management process of Aditi; it must be running for Aditi to be available to users. At startup, it is responsible for initializing the entire database system according to a specified global configuration file and starting the appropriate number of RAPs. During normal operation, its main task is to keep track of the state of each RAP and to allocate tasks to free RAPs. The QS listens on its message queue waiting for various requests and either performs them immediately or queues them until they can be performed. Requests can come from DAPs and RAPs. A DAP can make requests to login to Aditi, to have a task executed, to get the status of the system, and to logout from Aditi. It can also send the QS a message to shut down the system if its user is authorised to do so. A RAP can tell the QS that it has finished an assigned task and is ready for another task, or it can inform the QS that it is aborting due to some fatal error.

By controlling the number of RAPs and DAPs running and keeping usage statistics for each user, the QS can perform load management for Aditi. Controlling the number of RAPs and DAPs allows the QS to prevent Aditi from overloading the host system. Recording usage statistics means that the QS can prevent individual users from overloading Aditi itself.

The QS can control the number of DAPs by refusing to login new DAPs when the load on the system is too high. Since DAPs place relatively small loads on the system, such action should be quite rare. Control over the number of RAPs is more critical: relational algebra operations are the most expensive operations performed in a database system and can easily overload the host machine. The QS prevents this by not passing DAP requests onto the RAPs when the load on the machine is dangerously high, and by not creating more RAPs than the machine can support. This way many DAPs can be running, providing service to many users, but the overall number of jobs being performed is strictly controlled.

4.3   Relational Algebra Process

Relational Algebra Processes (RAPs) are the workhorses of Aditi: they execute all of the most expensive operations in RL. Their name derives from the fact that these operations are all relational algebra operations, either standard ones (e.g. join, union, difference, select, project) or combinations such as union-diff and btmerge (see section 3). RAPs spend their life waiting for a job from the QS, executing the job, and sending the result to the requesting DAP while notifying the QS of their availability. A RAP exits only when the QS commands it to shut down or it encounters some fatal error.

The message that tells a RAP what to do specifies the name of the operation to be performed, the input relations, select conditions for these input relations, any data specific to the operation (e.g. join attributes), and a list of output relations along with projection information that specifies how each tuple in those relations is to be constructed from the result of the operation. All relational algebra operations can therefore be preceded by select operations and followed by project operations. The select conditions on the input relations often allow the RAP to confine its attention to the relevant parts of the input relations without incurring the overhead of creating temporary relations to hold those parts. In the same spirit, the projection information allows the RAP to allocate storage only for the part of the output that is actually required; the fact that more than one output relation can be specified (presumably each with a different projection) allows the RAP to avoid the overhead of scanning the result of the operation several times. A secondary benefit of pre-select and post-project is that they reduce the communication overhead between the DAP and the RAP (this is also true for combination operations like btmerge).

Depending on the size and structure of the argument relations, the RAP can choose from several algorithms for carrying out its various operations. The operation whose performance is most important is the join. Since no single join method works optimally in all situations, Aditi currently supports four join algorithms: sort/merge join, hash join, nested block join and indexed join.

Sort/merge join, like other sort-based Aditi operations, uses the external merge-sort algorithm described in [14]. To make sure that the overhead of extracting sort keys from a tuple is paid only once, not every time the tuple appears in a comparison, our implementation uses prepended sort keys [16]. Since the schema format supports relations with prepended keys, our sort routine can leave the sort keys in place, and will if the calling procedure indicates it wishes to use them. Thus relations can have their keys extracted and be sorted just once instead of once per operation; such presorting can substantially reduce query time.

Our sort routine can write its results to a temporary relation or pass them back on demand to the calling RAP operation. A RAP executing a sort/merge join will sort each input relation on the attributes being joined, and then scan the results looking for matching tuple pairs. The sort routine will help the join algorithm in two ways. First, it removes duplicate tuples as soon as it discovers them. This has proven essential for recursive queries because without duplicate elimination, the sizes of temporary files can grow exponentially: each iteration of a bottom-up computation can double the number of copies of a tuple in a relation (and more than double the time required to process the relation if the relation outgrows memory). Second, the merge-sort routine performs the final merge pass on demand just as the RAP requests the next tuple in its result, so that the final merge passes on the two input relations are interleaved with the scanning pass of the join algorithm itself. This arrangement reduces the number of passes over the data and the attendant I/O overhead. However, the sort/merge code still starts with a check to see whether either relation is already sorted on the join attributes; correctly sorted files are used as they are.

The purpose behind the sorting in sort/merge join is to bring tuples with the same join attributes together. The hash join algorithm does this clustering by splitting each input relation into partitions based on the hash value of the join attributes of each tuple. It then joins pairs of partitions with the same hash values in a nested loop fashion.

The hash join method is applicable in the same situations when the sort/merge join is. It will generally perform better than sort/merge join, the exceptions mostly being caused by its greater sensitivity to data skew and its inability to always remove duplicates from the input relations. This is because not all of a partition will be in memory when a tuple is inserted into that partition, and hence the tuple cannot be compared against all the tuples in that partition.

Although we are considering various heuristics that will allow us to choose dynamically between sort/merge join and hash join for joining large relations, currently the decision is made statically in the query server's configuration file. The configuration file also gives the size below which a relation is considered small: if at least one input relation to a join is small, then the RAP uses one of its other join methods.

The first of these methods, nested block join, requires that one of the relations be small enough to fit into memory. It loads the tuples from the small relation into a hash table in memory, and then scans the tuples in the large relation sequentially. As the scan reaches a tuple, the algorithm hashes its join attributes and looks in the hash table for tuples to join this tuple with. Because this algorithm examines the data in each relation only once, it is about four times faster than either sort/merge join or hash join. This speedup factor means that splitting up the small relation into memory-sized chunks and using nested block join on each chunk is worthwhile whenever the size of the small relation is less than four times the buffer size. It is the size of this memory buffer that is governed by the configuration file: we avoid computing this size automatically to allow us to switch easily between the various join methods for performance testing.

The last join method supported by Aditi is indexed join. This is the preferred method when one of the input relations only has a small number of tuples in it, and the other input relation has an index on the attributes required for the join. For each tuple in the small relation, the algorithm performs an indexed lookup on the other relation to retrieve all the tuples that have matching attribute values, and then joins them with the tuple from the small relation.

Currently only permanent relations can be indexed on attributes and so only joins with permanent relations will ever make use of this method. (The sort key of B-tree indexed temporary files is the hash value of the entire tuple, since this is what is needed for duplicate elimination.) Joins involving only temporary relations will only ever use the other join methods. This is not too much of a problem because temporary relations tend to be relatively small, and so joins involving large relations are very likely to have at least one input that is a permanent relation. Our tests show quite clearly the importance of indexing permanent relations so as to allow the use of this join method: appropriate indexing speeds up some of our tests by factors of up to 100. Section 5 gives an example of this, and also demonstrates that the appropriate indexing can depend strongly on the arguments specified in queries.

Currently, each relational algebra instruction is carried out on a single RAP, but there is no fundamental reason why multiple RAPs cannot cooperate on a single task. We are working on schemes that would enable multiple RAPs to co-operate in sorting a single relation in parallel, and on parallel hash based join algorithms [18].

At the opposite end of the spectrum, there are some tasks that are too small for RAPs. For example when Aditi evaluates predicates for list manipulation such as list reverse and append in a bottom-up set-at-a-time manner, each iteration of the RL code involves several relational algebra operations, several context switches, and several buffer cache accesses just to add or remove one element at the front of a list.

To avoid all this overhead, we have made tuple-at-a-time computation available to Aditi users by embedding a NU-Prolog interpreter in the DAP. Our preliminary experiments show that substantial gains in speed can be made by using this feature. For example, for reversing 700 lists of up to 40 elements each we observed a speedup of the order of 8,000. As we discussed in section 3, joins, and some other RL operations, can construct new values that can be included in result relations. Ordinarily this capability is used for arithmetic or to wrap some function symbols around an attribute, but it can also be used to invoke the NU-Prolog interpreter. Such use requires the predicate called to have been designated by the user as a top-down predicate in an Aditi-Prolog source file. When it sees such a flag, the Aditi-Prolog compiler puts the flagged predicate(s) into a separate file, invokes the NU-Prolog compiler on the file, and arranges for the storage of the output of the NU-Prolog compiler in the database. The DAP will load the code from there into the NU-Prolog interpreter on demand. Since the predicate will be processed by both the Aditi-Prolog and NU-Prolog compilers, it has to be acceptable to both; this is not difficult due to the close relationship between the two languages.

Small query						
size	8	10	12	14	16	18
orig	4.9: 1.0	28.9: 1.0	246.9: 1.0	3069.8: 1.0		
magic	0.3: 16.0	0.6: 50.1	1.7: 143.8	7.3: 423.0	38.0: NA	289.1: NA
context	0.2: 20.1	0.4: 80.4	0.8: 329.2	2.2: 1398.6	7.8: NA	30.4: NA

Large query						
size	8	10	12	14	16	18
orig	5.5: 1.0	30.6: 1.0	257.6: 1.0	3058.0: 1.0		
magic	5.6: 1.0	17.8: 1.7	56.8: 4.5	168.3: 18.2	453.0: NA	1160.0: NA
context	4.4: 1.3	8.6: 3.5	24.0: 10.7	52.1: 58.7	107.8: NA	209.2: NA

Table 1: Results for path queries.

5 Performance

In this section we report on three sets of experiments. All the tests were performed on a Silicon Graphics 4D/340S running IRIX 4.0.1 with four 33 MHz R3000 processors and 64 megabytes of memory. The tests were carried out in multiuser mode with other users present and active, but with the system load average below 2 most of the time. The test database was stored on a striped filesystem, track-interleaved across two SGI-supplied disk drives connected via two separate 4.0 Mb/s synchronous SCSI-1 interfaces. The drives have an average seek time of 11.9 ms, a single-track seek time of 2.5 ms, an average rotational latency of 6.25 ms (4800 rpm), and a maximum transfer rate of 2.3 Mb/s. All the times we report are elapsed real times in seconds computed as the average of four or more runs. We report elapsed times instead of CPU times because they show how the system would appear to a user, while CPU time measurements leave out context switches, disk I/O, and other similar effects.

The first set of experiments used the path predicate of section 3 to compare the context transformed and magic set transformed programs against the original program. Our test query was ?- t(X), path(X,Y) with the base relation t supplying input values for the call to path.

Our experiments varied the contents of the relations edge and t. The edge relation contained full binary trees of various sizes, i.e. tuples of the form edge(i, $2i$) and edge(i, $2i + 1$) for values of i ranging from 1 up to a maximum that depends on the size of the tree. Our six data sets used maximums of 255, 1023, 4095, 16383, 65535 and 262143, corresponding to tree depths of 8, 10, 12, 14, 16, and 18 respectively. Each version of the edge relation had a B-tree index on its first attribute.

We used two versions of the t relation. The first contained only the tuple "100"; we label the results achieved with this version "small query". The other version contained one hundred tuples randomly chosen from the middle three levels of the full binary tree of the relevant edge relation; we label the results achieved with this version "large query". The reason we only chose trees of even depths for edge is that the middle three levels move downward one level only when the total depth of the tree increases by two.

Table 1 reports our results. Rows correspond to optimization flags on the path relation, while columns correspond to the depths of the edge relation. Speedups are computed with respect to the untransformed program; they follow the times they refer to after a colon. One can make several observations based on the data in the table.

The number of tuples in the t relation makes virtually no difference for the untransformed program. It makes no difference because it computes the entire path relation and then joins it with the t relation.

The magic set transformed program always performs better than the untransformed program, and the context set transformed program always performs better than the magic transformed program. The magic / original performance ratio climbs very rapidly as the size of the edge relation increases. The context / magic performance ratio also climbs but not as rapidly, reaching a maximum of 9.5 to 1 at depth 18 for the small query and a maximum of 5.5 to 1 at depth 18 for the large query. This illustrates that the context transformation performs relatively better when the input to the transformed predicate is more specific.

Database designers can use the gain in efficiency that can be achieved by the use of the magic and context transformations in two ways. First, they can pass it on to users in the form of better response times: e.g. 2.2 seconds vs 51 minutes for the small query at depth 14, or subsecond responses at smaller depths. Second, they can maintain response times while increasing the size of relations. On the small query, the performance of the context transformed program at depth 18 is about the same as the performance of the untransformed program at a depth of about 10, or the performance of the magic transformed program at a depth of about 16.

The data in the table for depths 12 and 14, where the single tuple in the small query is in the middle three levels of the tree, shows that multiplying the number of tuples in the input by a 100 causes the time taken by the magic and context transformed program to go up only by a factor between 20 and 35. The reason for this is that part of the cost of query answering goes into the overheads of relational algebra operations (in the DAP, the RAP and interprocess communication). Since the large query causes the same number of relational algebra operations to be performed as a small query, the absolute cost of this overhead is the same in both cases. The cost of the overheads is a much higher proportion of the overall cost for the small query than for the large query.

The fact that figures grow faster in the small query table than in the large query table is at least partially due to the fact that the single tuple in the single query stays at one level in the tree while the hundred tuples in the large query move down in the tree.

Earlier papers on Aditi used a similar experiment but used different ways of picking tuples for the t relation; therefore those results are not strictly comparable with the results presented here. However, as a rough indicator our current results represent speedups of ten to fifty times over the results presented in previous papers on Aditi [25]. These speedups come from improvements in the Aditi back-end and in the Aditi compiler, the main improvements being the use of indexes in joins, the use of btmerge to eliminate duplicates, and keeping temporary relations in main memory whenever possible. We expect that the results will continue to improve in the future.

Our next test program is based on the first realistic application of Aditi, which is a database containing data about flights around the world [8]. Since we were unable to get real data in sufficient quantity, the information in this database, although derived from schedules published by airlines, is mainly the product of our imagination.

The four queries we are reporting results on all involve a hypothetical traveller called Phineas Fogg who wants to travel around the world as fast as possible. The four queries differ in the constraints imposed on the tour.

- Tour 1 must visit Asia, Europe, North America and the Pacific region.
- Tour 2 must visit Asia, Europe and North America.
- Tour 3 must visit Europe, North America and the Pacific region.
- Tour 4 must visit Europe and North America.

The tours must visit the named regions in the order in which they are given; all tours start and finish in Melbourne, Australia.

We have two implementations of the code that finds trips (sequences of flights) between cities. One uses a daily schedule that associates the availability of flights with an absolute date; the other uses a weekly schedule that associates this information with days of the week, subject to

Results for Phineas Fogg queries with daily schedule											
Query	Data				Dsimc				Btree			
	Magic		Context		Magic		Context		Magic		Context	
Tour1	381.1:	1.0	282.3:	1.3	20.5:	18.6	14.4:	26.5	17.5:	21.8	13.9:	27.4
Tour2	294.4:	1.0	232.3:	1.3	16.9:	17.4	11.7:	25.2	14.1:	20.9	11.0:	26.7
Tour3	360.2:	1.0	266.5:	1.3	18.0:	20.0	14.0:	25.7	15.4:	23.4	13.5:	26.6
Tour4	285.6:	1.0	211.1:	1.3	14.2:	20.0	11.7:	24.4	12.7:	22.5	10.5:	27.1

Results for Phineas Fogg queries with weekly schedule											
Query	Data				Dsimc				Btree			
	Magic		Context		Magic		Context		Magic		Context	
Tour1	30.3:	1.0	24.3:	1.2	28.6:	1.1	21.4:	1.4	27.9:	1.1	23.2:	1.3
Tour2	24.6:	1.0	19.4:	1.3	23.5:	1.0	16.6:	1.5	23.3:	1.1	18.1:	1.3
Tour3	28.2:	1.0	23.0:	1.2	25.3:	1.1	20.7:	1.4	26.1:	1.1	22.0:	1.3
Tour4	22.4:	1.0	17.8:	1.3	19.3:	1.2	15.1:	1.5	20.5:	1.1	16.8:	1.3

Table 2: Results for Phineas Fogg queries

seasonal restrictions. Airlines usually publish their schedules in the compact weekly format, but this format requires some processing before use.

We have tested all four queries with both daily and weekly schedules, with the predicate finding trips between cities compiled with the magic set optimization and with the context transformation, and with the schedule relation being stored without indexing, with dynamic superimposed codeword indexing and with B-tree indexing. The keys used for indexing are the origin and destination cities together with the desired date of travel. The reason why we did not include data for the case when the trip-finding predicate is compiled without optimization is that that predicate is allowed only with respect to queries that specify the starting-date argument, and therefore the predicate cannot be evaluated bottom-up without first being transformed by a magic-like optimization. The test results appear in table 2, whose speedups are computed with respect to the magic transformed program using no indexing.

The table tells us several things. First, the context transformation consistently yields results 20% to 40% better than the magic set optimization. Second, the type of indexing has a significant impact only for the daily schedule, in which case the schedule relation contains 54,058 tuples.

The four queries have 18, 12, 57 and 38 answers respectively. This is not apparent from the table due to two reasons. First, the tours with more answers are those that visit fewer regions and thus call `trip` a smaller number of times. Second, the cost of the joins invoked by `trip` depend mostly on the sizes of the input relations and very little on the size of the output relation.

As one expects, accessing such a large relation without an index has a large penalty, ranging from about 17-fold to about 24-fold. For these queries the trip predicate always specifies all three of the key arguments of the schedule relation, so B-tree indexing is as effective as it can be. Dsimc indexing yields slightly lower performance (by about 10% to 20%), mainly because dsimc uses the keys only to restrict its attention to a set of pages and cannot focus directly on the tuples of interest within those pages.

For the weekly schedule, in which the relation contains 1,044 tuples, most of the time is spent in computation, not retrieval, and so the type of indexing makes little difference: there is less than 10% variation among all the numbers. The main sources of this variation are probably the differences between the overheads of the various indexing methods.

Query	Btree	Dsimc	Data
From Melbourne	5.04	0.51	15.49
To Melbourne	16.19	0.37	14.90

Table 3: Results for retrievals with partially-specified keys

To show the effect of queries that specify values for only some of the attributes in the key, we tested two simple queries on the daily schedule relation. The first specified the origin and the date, the second the destination and the date. The results appear in table 3.

The table shows the limitations of B-tree indexing. If the query does not specify a key attribute, B-tree indexing cannot make use of any attributes following the unspecified one in the key list. In this case, the key list on the schedule relation was "origin, destination, date". The first query achieves moderate performance because it uses only the first key attribute; the second query results in very bad performance because it cannot use any of the key attributes (this performance is worse than unindexed due to overheads). On the other hand, the multi-attribute hashing scheme on which the dsimc method is built is not at all sensitive to the order of keys, so it can exploit two key attributes for both queries. The difference between the performance of the two dsimc queries can be explained by the different number of answers they have in our database (11 for the From Melbourne query and 7 for the To Melbourne query); the two queries take about the same time per answer.

The daily schedule relation contains 54,058 tuples of arity 8 and with an average size of 160 bytes. We used this as test data in measuring the rate at which tuples can be inserted into relations. The insertion rates into relations without indexing, with B-tree indexing and with dynamic superimposed codeword indexing were roughly 790 tuples per second, 420 tuples per second, and 60 tuples per second respectively. The lower speed of dsimc insertion is due to repeated copying of some tuples as the underlying linear hashed file doubles in size several times. This overhead can be avoided if the code knows in advance the number and average size of the tuples to be inserted.

Our final experiment concerns the use of tuple-at-a-time computation in bottom-up execution. Consider the program below, each of which computes a path between two given points in a graph.

```
?- mode(paths(b,b,f)).
?- flag(paths, 3, magic).

paths(From, To, [edge(From,To)]) :- parent(From, To).
paths(From, To, NewList) :-
        paths(From, Int, List),
        parent(Int, To),
append(List, [edge(Int, To)], NewList).
```

where append is the standard append predicate. Note that a call to append is required for each edge in order to maintain the list containing the path. Another version of this program is given below, in which the path is collected in reverse order, and the entire list is then reversed, thus requiring only one pass over the list.

```
?- mode(paths(b,b,f)).

paths(From, To, Path) :- paths_rev(From, To, Rev), reverse(Rev, [], List).

?- mode(paths_rev(b,b,f)).
```

Data	Right	Append		Reverse	
		BU	TD	BU	TD
Cylinder	16.1	576	12.4	1860	11.9
Tree	84.9	34.7	32.4	34.4	33.2

Table 4: Results for path queries

```
?- flag(paths_rev, 3, magic).

paths_rev(From, To, [edge(From,To)]) :- parent(From, To).
paths_rev(From, To, edge(Int,To).List) :-
        paths_rev(From, Int, List),
        parent(Int, To).
```

where **reverse** is the standard (non-naive) reverse predicate. Our experiments consisted of five versions of the paths program, being the two programs above with the append and reverse predicates evaluated in both a top-down and bottom-up manner, and for comparison purposes we also used the program below, which is very similar to the **stops** program of section 2.2. Note that this version of the program does not require any list processing.

```
?- mode(paths(b,b,f)).
?- flag(paths, 3, magic).

paths(From, To, [edge(From,To)]) :- parent(From, To).
paths(From, To, edge(From, Int).List) :-
        parent(From, Int),
        paths(Int, To, List).
```

We will refer to this program as the *right-linear* version of the program. Note that the other four versions of the program are all essentially *left-linear*, in that the recursive call comes before any others.

Two sets of data were used for each program. The first set was a cylinder containing 200 edges, and for which the input pair of nodes had a number of paths between them. The other set was a full binary tree containing 16,382 edges, in which case there is at most one path between any two nodes in the tree. The results are given in table 4, where we denote bottom up evaluation of list predicates by BU, and top down evaluation of list predicates by TD.

The results for the tree indicate that when there is only one list involved, the overheads of processing this list are fairly low, and that there is little difference between the top-down and bottom-up evaluations. However, there is a clear performance penalty to be paid for the right-linear program, despite the fact that there is no list processing involved. This is in accord with some other experiences of ours, in that it is usually more efficient to use a left-linear version of the program rather than a right-linear one.

For the cylinder, in which case there may be several paths between a given pair of nodes, it is clear that the bottom-up methods of list processing are significantly less efficient than their top-down counterparts. More surprisingly, the left-linear versions of the program with top-down list processing are both more efficient than the right-linear version. This shows the advantage of the judicious use of top-down evaluation, as in this case we can outperform a version of the program in which no explicit list manipulation is necessary.

Based on our experience with other tests, we can state that the effectiveness of many optimizations is strongly influenced by the number of iterations required to complete the bottom-up computation. Sometimes, a technique will introduce a one-off overhead that cannot be compensated for by the reduced cost per iteration because there are not enough iterations in the bottom-up computation. Presorting of relations is one such technique, although it can double performance on some queries. At other times, an optimization technique may speed up each iteration but require more iterations to answer a query. Unfortunately, one cannot always decide in advance whether a given optimization is worthwhile; the answer is often dependent on the query and the data. More experimentation is required to determine whether any useful heuristics exist. We envisage the compiler exploiting such heuristics by generating code that switches at run-time depending on the characteristics of the data between two or more ways of evaluating a query.

6 Conclusion

Aditi is a practical deductive database system. The lower layers are based on relational technology wherever possible but with necessary modifications such as support for tuples not in first normal form. The upper layers are derived mostly from research specific to deductive databases. Many aspects in both layers build on original research by members of the Aditi team [1, 2, 7, 9, 10, 11, 12, 13, 21, 23]. Much of this research in turn used Aditi as a testbed in which to try out and evaluate ideas.

Aditi is a true database system. It is disk based, it is multiuser, and it can exploit parallelism in the underlying machine. It has both textual and graphical user interfaces, including an interface that understands SQL. It also includes interfaces to the NU-Prolog language, to which Aditi-Prolog is closely related. NU-Prolog code can call Aditi-Prolog; this link allows Aditi applications to create their own user interface. Aditi-Prolog code also can call NU-Prolog to compute some predicates top-down and tuple-at-a-time when such evaluation speeds up query processing.

Our projects for the future include:

- Integrating our prototype compiler that generates code for non-stratified negation into the main Aditi system.

- Implementing high-level optimizations such as constraint propagation [11] and the new transformation for linear predicates [7].

- Implementing low-level optimizations such as redundant code elimination.

- Extending Aditi-Prolog by providing types and a sophisticated system of modes based on these types.

- Using the mode system to allow the handling of partially-instantiated data structures; we already know how to do this without subsumption tests.

- Adding object-oriented and higher-order features to Aditi-Prolog; we already have a draft language proposal.

- Finishing the implementation of the transaction system.

- Benchmarking Aditi against RDBMSs such as Oracle and Ingres on both relational and deductive type queries.

Those who would like to learn more about Aditi should refer to the Aditi users's guide [5], the Aditi-Prolog language manual [6], and the report describing the flights database from which the second set of tests in section 5 was drawn [8].

The Aditi system itself is available to interested researchers. It has already been distributed to about a dozen sites around the world.

Acknowledgements

Many people have contributed significantly to Aditi both by performing research and by developing software. In particular, the following people have actively contributed to the Aditi project: Jayen Vaghani, David B. Kemp, Zoltan Somogyi, Peter J. Stuckey, Tim S. Leask, and James Harland. We would like to acknowledge the contributions of Kim Marriott, John Shepherd, David Keegel, Warwick Harvey, Philip Dart and Jeff Schultz in this respect. We thank Gill Dobbie for her comments on a draft of this paper.

This research was supported by grants from the Australian Research Council through the Machine Intelligence Project, from the Victorian Department of Manufacturing and Industry Development, through the Collaborative Information Technology Research Institute, from the Australian Department of Industry, Technology and Commerce through the Key Centre for Knowledge-based Systems, and from the Australian Cooperative Research Center program through the Center for Intelligent Decision Systems.

References

[1] I. Balbin, G. Port, K. Ramamohanarao, and K. Meenakshi. Efficient bottom-up computation of queries on stratified databases. *Journal of Logic Programming*, 11:295–345, 1991.

[2] I. Balbin and K. Ramamohanarao. A generalization of the differential approach to recursive query evaluation. *Journal of Logic Programming*, 4(3):259–262, September 1987.

[3] F. Bancilhon, D. Maier, Y. Sagiv, and J. Ullman. Magic sets and other strange ways to implement logic programs. In *Proceedings of the Fifth Symposium on Principles of Database Systems*, pages 1–15, Washington DC., 1986.

[4] C. Beeri and R. Ramakrishnan. On the power of magic. In *Proceedings of the Sixth ACM Symposium on Principles of Database Systems*, pages 269–283, San Diego, California, March 1987.

[5] J. Harland, D. B. Kemp, T. S. Leask, K. Ramamohanarao, J. A. Shepherd, Z. Somogyi, P. J. Stuckey, and J. Vaghani. Aditi-Prolog language manual. Technical Report 92/27, Department of Computer Science, University of Melbourne, Melbourne, Australia, November 1992.

[6] J. Harland, D. B. Kemp, T. S. Leask, K. Ramamohanarao, J. A. Shepherd, Z. Somogyi, P. J. Stuckey, and J. Vaghani. Aditi users' guide. Technical Report 92/26, Department of Computer Science, University of Melbourne, Melbourne, Australia, November 1992.

[7] J. Harland and K. Ramamohanarao. Constraint propagation for linear recursive rules. In *Proceedings of the Tenth International Conference on Logic Programming*, Budapest, Hungary, June 1993.

[8] J. Harland and K. Ramamohanarao. Experiences with a flights database. Technical Report 92/28, Department of Computer Science, University of Melbourne, Melbourne, Australia, November 1992.

[9] D. Kemp and P. Stuckey. Analysis based constraint query optimization. In *Proceedings of the Tenth International Conference on Logic Programming*, Budapest, Hungary, June 1993.

[10] D. Kemp, P. Stuckey, and D. Srivastava. Query restricted bottom-up evaluation of normal logic programs. In *Proceedings of the Joint International Conference and Symposium on Logic Programming*, pages 288–302, Washington DC, November 1992.

[11] D. B. Kemp, K. Ramamohanarao, I. Balbin, and K. Meenakshi. Propagating constraints in recursive deductive databases. In *Proceedings of the First North American Conference on Logic Programming*, pages 981–998, Cleveland, Ohio, October 1989.

[12] D. B. Kemp, K. Ramamohanarao, and Z. Somogyi. Right-, left-, and multi-linear rule transformations that maintain context information. In *Proceedings of the Sixteenth International Conference on Very Large Data Bases*, pages 380–391, Brisbane, Australia, August 1990.

[13] D. B. Kemp, P. J. Stuckey, and D. Srivastava. Magic sets and bottom-up evaluation of well-founded models. In *Proceedings of the 1991 International Logic Programming Symposium*, pages 337–351, San Diego, California, October 1991.

[14] D. E. Knuth. *Sorting and searching*, volume 3 of *The Art of Computer Programming*, chapter 5.4.1. Addison-Wesley, Massachusetts, 1973.

[15] T. S. Leask, K. Ramamohanarao, and P. J. Stuckey. Exploiting parallelism in bottom-up computation in Aditi. In *Proceedings of the ILPS '91 Workshop on Deductive Databases*, pages 72–81, San Diego, California, October 1991.

[16] J. Linderman. Theory and practice in the construction of a working sort routine. *Bell Laboratories Technical Journal*, 63(8 (part 2)):1827–1843, October 1984.

[17] K. Morris, J. F. Naughton, Y. Saraiya, J. D. Ullman, and A. V. Gelder. YAWN! (yet another window on NAIL! *IEEE Data Engineering*, 10(4):28–43, December 1987.

[18] M. Nakayama, M. Kitsuregawa, and M. Takagi. Hash-partitioned join method using dynamic destaging strategy. In *Proceedings of the Fourteenth Conference on Very Large Data Bases*, pages 468–477, Los Angeles, 1988.

[19] G. Port, I. Balbin, and K. Ramamohanarao. A new approach to supplementary magic optimisation. In *Proceedings of the First Far-East Workshop on Future Database Systems*, pages 89–104, Melbourne, Australia, April 1990.

[20] R. Ramakrishnan, D. Srivastava, and S. Sudarshan. Rule ordering in bottom-up fixpoint evaluation of logic programs. In *Proceedings of the Sixteenth International Conference on Very Large Data Bases*, pages 359–371, Brisbane, Australia, August 1990.

[21] K. Ramamohanarao and J. Shepherd. A superimposed codeword indexing scheme for very large Prolog databases. In *Proceedings of the Third International Conference on Logic Programming*, pages 569–576, London, England, July 1986.

[22] K. Ramamohanarao and J. Shepherd. Partial match retrieval for dynamic files using superimposed codeword indexing. In E. Balagurusamy and B. Sushila, editors, *Computer systems and applications: recent trends*, pages 281–290. McGraw-Hill, New Delhi, India, November 1990.

[23] K. Ramamohanarao, J. Shepherd, I. Balbin, G. Port, L. Naish, J. Thom, J. Zobel, and P. Dart. The NU-Prolog deductive database system. In P. Gray and R. Lucas, editors, *Prolog and databases*, pages 212–250. Ellis Horwood, Chicester, England, 1988.

[24] D. Sacca and C. Zaniolo. Implementation of recursive queries for a data language based on pure horn logic. In *Proceedings of the Fourth International Conference on Logic Programming*, pages 104–135, Melbourne, Australia, May 1987.

[25] J. Vaghani, , K. Ramamohanarao, D. B. Kemp, Z. Somogyi, and P. J. Stuckey. Design overview of the Aditi deductive database system. In *Proceedings of the Seventh International Conference on Data Engineering*, pages 240–247, April 1991.

Negation and Aggregates in Recursive Rules: the $\mathcal{LDL}$++ Approach

Carlo Zaniolo

Computer Science Department, University of California

Los Angeles, California 90024

zaniolo@cs.ucla.edu

Natraj Arni and Kayliang Ong

Microelectronics and Computer Technology Corporation

Austin, Texas 78759

natraj@mcc.com and kayliang@mcc.com

Abstract

The problem of allowing non-monotonic constructs, such as negation and aggregates, in recursive programs represents a difficult challenge faced by current research in deductive databases. In this paper, we present a solution that combines generality with efficiency, as demonstrated by its implementation in the new $\mathcal{LDL}$++ system. A novel and general treatment of set aggregates, allowing for user-defined aggregates, is also presented.

1   Introduction

The area of non-monotonic reasoning has benefited significantly from research in deductive databases, as demonstrated by the introduction of the concept of stratified negation and stratified set aggregates [16]. This concept is significant since it removes several of the limitations and problems of Prolog's negation-by-failure, and it is conducive to efficient implementation, as demonstrated by systems such as *Glue-Nail*, $\mathcal{LDL}$ and *CORAL* [15, 22, 3]. However, as experience was gained with real-life applications [23], it became clear that stratification is too restrictive and there remain many important applications where negation and set aggregates are needed: such applications, range from processing Bill of Materials to finding the shortest path in a graph [5, 6].

Therefore, during the last five years, a substantial research effort has been devoted to solving the non-stratification issue. This endeavor has produced significant progress on the theoretical front, with the introduction of concepts such as locally stratified programs [16], well-founded models [12], and stable models [7], but it has not yet begotten a solution that is both general and efficient. Indeed our experience with deductive database applications [24], suggests that a practical solution must satisfy three difficult requirements, inasmuch as it must

- have a formal logic-based semantics

- have a simple and intuitive constructive semantics

- be amenable to efficient implementation.

Thus, in addition to requiring formal semantics and efficient implementation, any practical proposal must also stress the importance of having a simple concrete semantics: i.e., one that can be easily mastered by the application programmer, without a need for understanding demanding formalisms. For instance, a notion such as stratified programs can be mastered by a programmer, who can make full use of it without having to understand its formal perfect-model semantics. Furthermore, a compiler can verify efficiently that a given program satisfies the stratification condition, and then support such programs by a bottom-up computation. However, a familiarity with the abstract formalisms of logic and non-monotonic semantics is required to understand and make effective usage of notions such as well-founded models or stable models in writing programs. Furthermore, no simple syntactic check exists for deciding whether a program has a well-founded model or a stable model; when such models exist their computation can be very expensive. Notions such as modularly stratified programs, represent a first step toward efficient execution [20] but leave other issues unresolved—such as compile-time decidability, and uniform treatment of negation and set aggregates.

In this paper, we take a different approach— the synthesis of our experience with concrete $\mathcal{LDL}$ applications [23], and classical optimization problems [5, 6]. We focus on syntactically decidable subclasses of non-monotonic recursive programs which capture the expressive power of inflationary fixpoint semantics [14]. Therefore, we introduce a special class of locally stratified programs that is easy for a compiler to recognize and implement using the fixpoint-based computation of deductive DBs. This class, called XY-stratified programs is first introduced in Section 2, which focuses on programs with negated goals in recursive rules. In Section 3, we extend these notions to recursive rules with aggregates, as demanded by most of the critical applications. In Section 4, we concentrate on the implementation problem, and other practical issues, such as termination. In Section 5 we discuss the generality of the proposed approach by showing that classical problems requiring non-stratified negation and aggregates can be expressed naturally by programs in this class. We also show that the magic-set method and similar re-writing techniques used to propagate constraints in deductive databases, are applicable to XY-stratified programs as well.

We assume our reader to be familiar with the basic concepts pertaining to Datalog and logic rules, including the concept of locally stratified programs and the *iterated fixpoint procedure* to compute the perfect model of these programs [16, 18]. Given a program P, a set of rules of P defining a maximal set of mutually recursive predicates will be called a *recursive clique* of P.

2 XY-Programs

We begin with a simple example that computes the nodes Y of a graph g reachable from a given node a, along with least numbers of arcs needed to reach Y from a:

Example 1 *Reachable nodes:*

$r_0 : \mathtt{delta(nil, Y)} \leftarrow \mathtt{g(a, Y)}.$

r_1 : delta(s(I), Y) ← delta(I, X), g(X, Y),
                        ¬all(I, Y).

r_2 : all(s(I), Y) ← all(I, Y), delta(s(I), _).
r_3 : all(I, Y) ←   delta(I, Y).

This program presents several unusual traits. A most obvious one is the presence of terms such as nil, I, s(I) in the first arguments of the recursive predicates. These arguments will be called *stage arguments*, and their usage is for counting as in the recursive definition of integers: nil stands for zero and s(I) stands for I+1. [1]

The intuitive meaning of the program of Example 1 is quite obvious: it implements a fixpoint computation of a transitive closure, through the use of two predicates: delta contains the new values, and all is the union of all values computed so far. In rule r_1 all is used for checking that no previous (therefore shorter) path exists to this node.

The formal semantics of the program also supports its intuitive semantics. Because of its particular syntactic form, the program is locally stratified. Each stratum contains all atoms with the same number of **occurrences of the successor function symbol "s"** in their stage arguments. The strata are also ordered according to the number of occurrences of s in the stage argument.

For the program in Example 1, the bottom stratum has the form:

delta(nil, ...), all(nil, ...), delta(a, ...), all(a, ...)

the next stratum consists of all atoms of the form:

delta(s(nil), ...), all(s(nil), ...), delta(s(a), ...), all(s(a), ...)

and so on. As we shall see later, this particular syntactic form of the recursive rules, w.r.t. the stage arguments, makes it simple for a compiler to detect the occurrence of such a locally stratified program. Furthermore, this type of program can be implemented efficiently using a modified fixpoint computation. It is well-known that the perfect model of such a program is characterized by a transfinite computation called iterated fixpoint[16]. This proceeds as follows: the least fixpoint for the bottom stratum is first computed. Then, once the least fixpoint is computed for the n-th stratum, the least fixpoint is computed for the $n + 1$-th stratum. This transfinite computation of perfect models simplifies dramatically for the program at hand.

The computation of the bottom stratum simply copies all the g facts describing our graph. Then, the fixpoint at the lowest stratum of recursive atoms is reached after firing rule r_0 followed by r_3 thus obtaining all the perfect-model atoms with a stage value of nil. The fixpoint for the stratum s(nil) is reached by firing rule r_1 followed by r_2 and r_3. Then, the higher strata are inductively generated by firing these three rules in the same order. Therefore, the general transfinite procedure to compute perfect models here reduces to the customary

---

[1] In this paper we are using function symbols (interpreted and non-interpreted) to express more realistic applications. However, function symbols are not required for a formal treatment: an ordered domain of adequate size and a successor relationship is all it is needed. These can be expressed in pure Datalog (with the choice construct), thus allowing a formal analysis of the data complexity and expressive power of our programs.

fixpoint iteration. Moreover, various improvements can be made to this fixpoint computation to ensure that it executes efficiently. In fact, while rule r_2 seems to suggest that a complete copying of the old relation is needed at each step, no such operation is needed in reality. In fact, at each step of the computation, the only instances of rules that can produce new atoms are those instantiated with stage values from the current stratum: values from the old strata are not used and can be discarded. Thus, if we keep the values of the stage variable (denoting the stratum at which we are working) in a separate memory cell, all that is needed to perform the copying operation is to increase the value of this variable by one. Then, the only computation actually performed at each iteration is the firing of rules r_1 and r_3; thus the transfinite computation of this perfect model reduces to the usual seminaive fixpoint computation of a transitive closure.

As we formalize these ideas, we find that atoms with the same stage values for the general case can be partitioned into finer strata.

Given a recursive clique, Q, the first arguments of the recursive predicates of a rule r in Q will be called the *stage arguments* of r^2. We have the following definitions:

Definition 1 *Let Q be a recursive clique and r be a recursive rule of Q. Then r is called an*

- **X-rule** *if all the stage arguments of r are equal to a simple variable, say J, which does not appear anywhere else in r;*

- **Y-rule** *if (i) some positive goal of r has as stage argument a simple variable J, (ii) the head of r has stage argument $s(J)$, (iii) all the remaining stage arguments are either J or $s(J)$ and (iv) J does not appear anywhere else in r.*

In Example 1, r_3 is an X-rule, while r_1 and r_2 are Y-rules. A recursive clique Q will be said to be an *XY-clique when all its recursive rules are either X-rules or Y-rules.*

Priming: $p'(...)$ *will be called the primed version of an atom $p(...)$. Given an XY-clique, Q, its primed version Q', is constructed by priming certain occurrences of recursive predicates in recursive rules as follows:*

- *X-rules: all occurrences of recursive predicates are primed,*

- *Y-rules: the head predicate is primed, and so is every goal with stage argument equal to that of the head.*

The primed version of our example is as follows:

$$r_0 : \mathrm{delta}(\mathrm{nil}, Y) \leftarrow \ \mathrm{g}(\mathrm{a}, Y).$$
$$r_1 : \mathrm{delta}'(\mathrm{s}(I), Y) \leftarrow \ \mathrm{delta}(I, X), \mathrm{g}(X, Y),$$
$$\neg \mathrm{all}(I, Y).$$
$$r_2 : \mathrm{all}'(\mathrm{s}(I), Y) \leftarrow \ \mathrm{all}(I, Y), \mathrm{delta}'(\mathrm{s}(I), \_).$$
$$r_3 : \mathrm{all}'(I, Y) \leftarrow \ \mathrm{delta}'(I, Y).$$

---

^{2}This is only a matter of convention. Alternatively, we could let the last arguments of recursive predicates be our stage arguments.

Definition 2 *An XY-clique Q will be said to be* XY-stratified *when*

- *The primed version of Q is non-recursive*

- *All exit rules have as stage argument the same constant.*

A program will be said to be *XY-stratified* when every recursive rule that contains the set aggregation construct "< >" in its head or a negated recursive goal in its body belongs to an XY-stratified clique.

The dependency graph for a primed clique provides a very simple syntactic test on whether a program is *XY*-stratified. Furthermore, these programs are amenable to efficient implementation as proven in the following discussion.

The primed version Q' of an XY-stratified clique defines a non-recursive program: thus, the dependency graph of Q' contains no cycle. Thus there exists a topological sorting of the nodes of Q' which obeys stratification, and such that the unprimed predicate names precede the primed ones. For Example 1, for instance, the following is a topological sorting:

    all < delta < delta$'$ < all$'$.

The tail of such a sorting, restricted to the primed predicate names will be called a *primed sorting* of Q. For the previous example, we obtain the following primed sorting:

    delta$'$ < all$'$.

Now, we can partition the atoms in Herbrand Base B_Q of the *original Q* into classes according to their predicate name and their stage arguments as follows:

- there is a distinct class, say σ_0, containing all instances of non-recursive predicates in Q—i.e., those without a stage argument.

- all atoms with the same recursive predicate name and the same number of function symbols s in the stage argument belong to the same equivalence class $\sigma_{n,p}$, with n denoting the number of s function symbols in the stage argument of p. Thus, $all(s(nil), ...)$, and $all(s(a), ...$, belong to the same class (stratum) in our example.

The partition Σ of B_Q so constructed can be totally ordered, by letting σ_0 be the bottom stratum in Σ, and then letting $\sigma_{n,p} \prec \sigma_{m,q}$ if

- $n < m$, or

- if $n = m$ but p' precedes q' in the primed sorting of the clique.

The totally ordered Σ so constructed will be called the *stage layering* of B_Q. For Example 1, let Cs denote either nil, a or 1 and the Vs denote elements in Q's Herbrand Universe; then Σ has the following form:

    $\{g(V_1, V_2)\} \prec$
    $\{delta(C_1, V_3, V_4)\} \prec \{all(C_2, V_5, V_6\} \prec$
    $\{delta(s(C_3), V_7, V_8)\} \prec \{all(s(C_4), V_9, V_{10})\} \prec ...$

Then, we have the following theorem:

Theorem 1 *Each XY-stratified clique Q can be locally stratified according to a stage layering of B_Q. Then, for every instance r of each rule in Q, the head of r belongs to a layer strictly higher than the layers for the goals in r (strict stratification).*

Proof: If g is an unprimed goal g for r, then the stage argument of the head of r $h(r)$ contains one more s than g. If g is primed, then $h(r)$ is also primed and its name follows the name of g in the primed ordering. $\square$

Since the stratification is strict, in computing the iterated fixpoint, *the saturation for each stratum is reached in one step.* Therefore, the compiler can resequence the rules according to the primed sorting of their head names. Then, having derived all atoms with stage value J a *single pass through the rules of Q ordered according to the primed sorting* computes all the atoms with stage value $s(J)$.

Therefore, if p' is the k-th predicate name in the primed sorting, let T_k denote the *immediate consequence operator* [13, 18] for the recursive rules in Q defining p. The *composite consequence operator* Γ_Q, will be defined as follows:

$$\Gamma_Q(I) = T_n(T_{n-1}...(T_1(I))...)$$

where I denotes subset of Q's Herbrand Base B_Q, and $n \geq 1$. In Example 1, Γ_Q is the composition of the immediate consequence operator for rule r_1 with that for the two rules r_2 and r_3.

For Γ_Q to be applied correctly, all the atoms with lower values of stage variables must have been produced. Consider now the exit rules of Q, and let T_0 be the immediate consequence operator for these rules. By the second condition of XY-stratification, all ground atoms in $T_0(\emptyset)$ share the same stage argument. However, additional ground atoms with the same stage value might be obtained by firing the X-rules (only one pass through these rules is needed if we follow the topological stratification.) Therefore, with p_k the k-th predicate name in the primed sorting, let T_k^X denote the immediate consequence operator for X-rules with head name p_k, if any such rules exists, and the identity transformation otherwise. Thus, we can define the *composite consequence operator for the X-rules,* Γ_Q^X as follows:

$$\Gamma_Q^X(I) = T_n^X(T_{n-1}^X...(T_1^X(I))...)$$

Thus, the ground atoms with same stage arguments as the exit rules are: $\Gamma_Q^X(T_0(\emptyset))$.

Therefore, for Example 1, Γ_Q^X is the immediate consequence operator for rule r_3, thus, all atoms with a stage argument of *nil* can be computed by firing r_0 followed by r_3.

Now let us define, as customary, $T^0(I) = I$ and, by induction, $T^{n+1}(I) = T(T^n(I)) \cup T^n(I)$. Then $T^\omega(I)$ denotes the union of all $T^k(I)$, for $k \geq 0$, i.e., the result of applying the operator T up to the the first ordinal, beginning from I. Then, we can state our key result:

Theorem 2 *Let Q be a XY-stratified clique, with composite consequence operator Γ_Q and composite consequence operator for X-rules Γ_Q^X, then*

- *Q is locally stratified,*

- *Let M_Q be the perfect model of Q. Then $M_Q = \Gamma_Q^\omega(M_{nil})$, where $M_{nil} = \Gamma_Q^X(T_0(\emptyset))$ and T_0 is the immediate consequence operator for the exit rules of Q*

   Proof: It follows directly from the the previous discussion. □

Thus the perfect model of an XY-stratified clique can be constructed as in a positive program: by a fixpoint iteration to the first ordinal. Computation of XY-stratified programs proceeds as that for stratified programs: all the non-recursive predicates in the recursive XY-clique must be saturated before the recursive rules in the clique are computed.

3 Aggregates, Conditionals and Choice

Many important applications, such as BOM applications, and graph problems, require the use of set aggregates in non-stratified in programs. For instance, Floyd's least paths algorithm can be written as follows:

Example 2 *Floyd's Algorithm.*

```
delta(nil, X, X, 0).
delta(s(J), X, Z, min(< C >)) ←   delta(J, X, Y, C1),
                                  g(Y, Z, C2), C = C1 + C2,
                                  if(all(J, X, Z, C3) then C3 > C).
all(s(J), X, Z, C) ←   all(J, X, Z, C), ¬delta(s(J), X, Z, _).
all(J, X, Z, C) ←      delta(J, X, Z, C).
```

In $\mathcal{LDL}$, set aggregates are not built-in but defined by the user. All the user needs to do is to specify the rules defining (i) the aggregate for singleton set **single** and (ii) aggregate for $S = S_1 \cup S_2$ knowing the aggregates of the disjoint S_1 and S_2 **multi** . For instance, the definition of min is

```
single(min, X, X).
multi(min, Y1, Z1, Z) ←   if(Y1 < Z1 then Z = Y1 else Z = Z1).
```

Therefore, we now need to provide a formal semantics for such extensible aggregates: whereas previous approaches have focused on a fixed set of primitives [10, 19, 13]. Here we propose a semantics that is simple, general and conducive to efficient implementation, as demonstrated by the $\mathcal{LDL}++$ system [2]. Our approach builds on the choice construct, where formal logic-based semantics, usability in programming and computational efficiency have successfully converged— a second example of such a convergence after stratification.

The idea of **choice** was introduced in [11] to express non-determinism in a declarative fashion. Thus, a construct such as choice((X), (Y)) is used to denote that the functional dependency $X \to Y$ must hold in the models defining the meaning of this program, whereby the following program assigns to each student an advisor from the same area:

```
st_ad(St, Ad) ←   major(St, Area), faculty(Ad, Area),
                  choice((St), (Ad)).
```

Thus, while the result of joining major and faculty normally results in a many-to-many relation between students and professors (sharing the same area), the st_ad relation is restricted to be many-to-one, as a result of the presence of choice((St), (Ad)). In $\mathcal{LDL}$, this very powerful construct was disallowed in recursion, inasmuch as the functional-dependency based semantics proposed in [11] suffers from technical problems such as a lack of justifiability property and its unsuitability to efficient implementation due to its static nature [21]. These problems were solved by using, instead, a semantics based on the use of negation and stable models [8]. For instance, the meaning of the rule above is defined by its rewriting into the following non-stratified program:

Example 3 *An advisor for each student by non-stratified negation.*

```
st_ad(St, Ad) ←   major(St, Area), faculty(Ad, Area),
                  chosen(St, Ad).

chosen(St, Ad) ←   major(St, Area), faculty(Ad, Area),
                   ¬diffChoice(St, Ad).

diffChoice(St, Ad) ←   chosen(St, Ad), Ad ≠ Ad.
```

Programs so rewritten always have one or more stable model, and in each such a model the chosen atoms obey the *FD*: St → Ad [21]. The new semantics agrees with the original semantics for non-recursive programs, but solves the problems of the old semantics in programs where choice occurs in a recursive predicate. For instance, say that an undirected graph is stored as pairs of edges, g(Y,X), g(X,Y) then a spanning tree for this graph, starting from the source node a, can be computed as follows:

Example 4 *Finding the spanning tree of a graph.*

```
st(nil, a)
st(X, Y) ←   st(Z, X), g(X, Y), Z ≠ Y, choice((Y), (X)).
```

Now, while the declarative semantics of choice rests on the theoretical foundations of non-monotonic logic, a programmer need not be cognizant of the notion of stable models to make effective use of choice in his/her program; indeed, there is an equivalent operational semantics based on the notion of memorizing the old values of choice and checking each candidate new value for violations of the *FD* constraints. This operational semantics is also the basis for efficient implementations of the construct in $\mathcal{LDL}++$.

The semantics-by-rewriting approach used for choice can be generalized to set aggregates. Assume, for instance that there exists only one aggregate rule, as follows:

Example 5 *The sum of Y-values, after grouping by X-values.*

```
a₀ : p(X, sum(< Y >)) ←   body(X, Y).
```

The intuitive meaning of this rule, is that, for each X-value in body(X,Y), the sum of Y-values associated with this X must be computed and entered as second argument in P. This sum can be computed as follows:

Example 6 *Aggregates Defined Using Choice.*

a_1 : aggr(OP, 0, X, nil) ←   body(X, _).

a_2 : aggr(OP, s(J), X, Z) ←   aggr(OP, J, X, W), body(X, Y),
choice((X, s(J)), (Y)), choice((X, Y), (s(J))),
single(OP, Y, SY),
if(J = 0 then Z = SY
else multi(OP, SY, W, Z)).

a_3 : single(sum, X, X).

a_4 : multi(sum, Y1, Z1, Z) ←   Z = Z1 + Y1.

Now observe that the two choice goals in rule a_2 imply that a new value of Y is selected at each step (for each X), evaluated using **single**, and (except for the first step, J = 0) the result finally combined with previous partial results via **multi**. In our example **multi** simply executes the sum of the two operands.

Therefore, the two choice goals cause the recursive predicate to iterate through all tuples of **body** and performs the tallies specified by **single** and **multi**. Thus, **aggr** is a built-in function that remains the same for every set-aggregate, while **single** and **multi** are specified in the application program. (For instance, to count the elements of a set, **single** would have to return the value: 1. If we wanted to compute a max, **single** operates as in sum, but **multi** must select the larger of the two elements.)

The formal semantics of program of Example 5 can therefore be defined by rewriting a_0 into the following rule:

a_5 : p(X, S) ←   aggr(sum, J, X, S), ¬aggr(sum, s(J), X, _).

which simply states that, for each X, the proper aggregate value is obtained for the last value of Y—i.e., when the two choice goals in rule a_2 fail due to the fact that every element in body(X, Y) has already been considered.

These definitions can be extended to the general case, by reducing the situation of multiple variables and multiple goals to this basic template. When there are several rules with aggregate constructs in their heads, we assume that there exists a distinct $aggr_j$ for each such rule, r_j.

The criteria for restricting the usage of aggregates in recursion follow directly from these definitions. There is no restriction in using choice, since positive programs with choice goal always have a stable model [8]. Thus, to determine the semantic well-formedness of recursive programs, we only need to be concerned with the negation introduced by rule a_5 above: the original program is XY-stratified with respect to aggregates, iff the program obtained by re-writing the aggregates as described above is semantically well-formed.

The if-then-else construct is the final non-monotonic logic based construct of $\mathcal{LDL}$ and $\mathcal{LDL}$++ whose formal semantics is defined through negation. The second rule in the definition of the aggregate operator min is viewed as a short-hand notation for the following pair of rules:

```
multi(min, Y1, Z1, Z) ←   Y1 < Z1, Z = Y1.
multi(min, Y1, Z1, Z) ←   ¬(Y1 < Z1),  Z = Z1.
```

Thus, programs containing if-then-else constructs are stratified iff their expansion using negation is.

4 $\mathcal{LDL}$++ Implementation

XY-Stratified programs have the property that tuples generated at each iteration are only dependent on tuples generated at the last iteration. This property offers several opportunities for optimized implementation, insofar as tuples generated in iterations before the last one can be discarded, or, in some cases, they can be re-used with their old values. After considering several design tradeoffs for $\mathcal{LDL}$++, the approach described in this section was selected for the reason that it combines effective optimization with simplicity of implementation.

At compilation time, X-rules and Y-rules are reordered by the compiler and, thus, the programmer needs not write the rules in any particular order. Such reordering is always possible since the program satisfies the XY-stratification requirements.

At execution time, XY-stratified cliques are implemented by using two temporary relations for each recursive predicate. Each of these relations is used to store tuples at each alternate iteration of the saturation process. Thus for each recursive predicate p we keep two temporary relations $R_0(p)$ and $R_1(p)$.

At level 0, the exit rules and X-rules are executed once with tuples taken from and added to relations R_0. In levels above the 0-level, both X-rules and Y-rules are executed in their primed sorting order. The recursive goals in the Y-rules can either be primed (stage argument equal to $s(J)$) or not (stage argument equal to J). At level 1 (and other odd levels, 3, 5, ...) the unprimed recursive goals in Y-rules take their tuples from the relation R_0. Primed goals in the Y-rules and recursive goals in the X-rules consume tuples from the relation R_1. All new tuples generated by either kind of rule are stored into the R_1 relations. At the end of an odd-level iteration, the old values in the R_0 relation are no longer needed, and they are actually overwritten in the next step. At the even levels, 2, 4, ..., the roles of the two relations are switched: the unprimed values are taken from the R_1 copies and the new values are written into the R_0 copies.

In summary, the compilation of XY-Stratified programs proceeds as follows:

Compiling XY-stratified Cliques

C1. Detect the XY-cliques and recognize X-rules, Y-rules and exit rules

C2. Reorder the recursive X-rules and Y-rules based on the primed sorting

C3. Check that all exit rules share the same stage constant.

As mentioned earlier, the computation of the stage arguments is factored out from the computation of the rules. Thus the compiler simply projects out the stage argument from the recursive predicate in each rule. Then, the execution of these rules takes place as follows:

Executing XY-stratified Cliques

Step 1. The stage variable is assigned the stage constant from the exit rules.

Step 2. Fire the X-rules (without the stage argument) once

Step 3. Fire the recursive rules (without stage arguments) in the order arranged by the compiler

Step 4. If saturation is not reached, increase the value of the stage variable and resume from **Step 3.**

4.1 Copy and Deletion Rules

Toward making the implementation more efficient, we can recognize two classes of recursive rules in XY-Stratified program that lend themselves to optimization. These are the *copy* rules and the *deletion* rules—rules other than these will be referred to as regular rules.

The following rule, from of Example 1, is a *copy rule*:

$$r_2 : \mathtt{all}(\mathtt{s}(\mathtt{I}), \mathtt{Y}) \leftarrow \mathtt{all}(\mathtt{I}, \mathtt{Y}), \mathtt{delta}(\mathtt{s}(\mathtt{I}), \_).$$

The only computation required to implement such a rule, basically, is the evaluation of the **delta** goal. If this goal evaluates to false, no further computation is needed. If the **delta** goal evaluates to true, then we need to set $R_0^{\mathtt{all}}$ ($R_1^{\mathtt{all}}$) equal to $R_1^{\mathtt{all}}$ ($R_0^{\mathtt{all}}$) when we are operating in the *even (odd)* stratum. This can be achieved by simply letting the pointers for the two relations point at the same table. In general, the processing of predicate, say q defined by copy rules is similar to that required by the seminaive fixpoint as follows:

- the compiler reorders the rules to ensure that the copy rule defining say the predicate q precedes all the remaining rules defining q[3].

- As in the computation of seminaive fixpoint q consists of two parts: the old tuples q and the new ones δq. New tuples generated by the rules following the copy rule, are added to δq after checking they are not contained in $q \cup \delta q$ (duplicate check). A shared index structure gives access to both the tuples in q and those in δq.

- After all the rules for q have been executed q still contains all the values of $q(I, ...)$ while the values of $q(s(I), ...)$ must be retrieved from $q \cup \delta q$. At the end of the cycle, q is reset to $q \cup \delta q$ while δq is reset to empty.

In general, copy rules are Y-rules, where the first goal and the head are identical except for the stage argument, and all other goals are evaluated to either true or false for the given stage argument, independent of the variables in the first goal. Thus, copy rules have the following form:

---

[3] Observe that, in principle, at least, we could have several copy rules; but once a copy rule actually fires, the rest can be ignored.

$$p(s(I), X) \leftarrow \quad p(I, X),$$
$$q_1(I, Z_1), ..., q_n(I, Z_n), r_1(s(I), W_1), ..., r_m(s(I), W_m),$$
$$t_1(Y_1), ..., t_1(Y_1).$$

where $q_1, ..., q_n, r_1, ..., r_m, t_1, ..., t_1$, are predicates that always evaluate to either true or false for the given stage argument. (This is, for instance, the case when the variables X are disjoint from those in every $Z_1, ..., Z_n, W_1, ..., W_m$ and $Y_1, ..., Y_1$. A compile-time recognition of other cases is harder).

Consider now a rule having the following format:

Example 7 *A deletion rule.*

$$p(s(I), X) \leftarrow \quad p(I, X), \neg d(X).$$

This rule can be implemented by deleting from p the tuples that satisfy d: the cost of this operation is proportional to the cardinality of $d(X)$, which in many cases is much less than that of $p(I, X)$. This can be achieved with the same scheme as that employed in the execution of the copy rules; i.e. by placing the deletion rule before the regular rules, but after the copy rules [4] and then deleting the atoms specified by the negative goals in the rules. In general, a deletion rule has the following form:

$$p(s(I), X) \leftarrow \quad p(I, X), \neg d(A).$$
$$q_1(I, Z_1), ..., q_n(I, Z_n), r_1(s(I), W_1), ..., r_m(s(I), W_m)$$
$$t_1(Y_1), ..., t_1(Y_1).$$

where A is a subset of X, and $q_1, ..., q_n, r_1, ..., r_m \, t_1, ..., t_1$, are predicates that evaluate to either to true or false for the given stage argument, thus the set of variables X must be disjoint from those in every $Z_1, ..., Z_n, W_1, ..., W_m$ and $Y_1, ..., Y_1$.

Deletion rules are more problematic than the copy rules because the tuples they delete in the old relation may be needed in later rules. Consider the following example:

Example 8 *Problematic deletion rule.*

$$r_1 : p(s(I), X) \leftarrow \quad p(I, X), \neg g(X).$$
$$r_2 : q(s(I), X) \leftarrow \quad p(I, X), X > Y, p(s(I), X).$$

Based on the primed sorting, r_2 must follow r_1 because it uses both $p(s(I), X)$ and $p(I, X)$. Thus, if the deletion rule is implemented as suggested above, tuples in the old relation will be clobbered even when the recursive goal $p(I, X)$ is consuming from it ! In such a case, we have to execute r_1 like a normal Y-rule. For instance, multiple deletion rules for the same predicates must be treated as they were regular rules.

In general, the compilation of deletion rules should also be combined with the process of primed sorting of the predicate names. Let p be the predicate name of the head of a candidate deletion rule r: if there exists a primed sorting, such that $p(I)$ is not used in rules after r, then r is treated as a deletion rule. Otherwise r is implemented as a regular rule.

---

[4] As a special case, whenever any copy rule is fired, all the deletion rules must be ignored.

4.2 Choice and Termination in XY-stratified Programs

An important consideration in the practical deployment of XY-stratified programs is termination. Strictly speaking, saturation occurs only when all the recursive rules fail to deliver any new value. Thus for programs containing copy rules, such as the one above, the old values of p are copied into a set of new values and the fixpoint computation would never terminate. One solution to this problem is that of Example 1, where we have added a second goal to rule r_2 to ensure failure. However, the $\mathcal{LDL}++$ system is also capable of detecting two common situations when the computation is stopped before the computation of the perfect model has completed.

One such situation involves the use of choice constructs in the rules using the tuples produced by the XY-stratified clique. Take for instance Floyd's algorithm of Example 6. Assume that the recursive clique is called by the following rule:

$$\texttt{dist(X,Y,C)} \leftarrow \texttt{all(J,X,Y,C), } \neg\texttt{delta(J,\_,\_), choice((),(J)).}$$

The compiler recognizes that J is bound to a stage argument, and that the only J value of interest is the lowest value J' for which the rule is first satisfied. Once the system detects a second value $J \neq J'$ it immediately terminates the computation of the XY-stratified clique.

The previous example illustrates a useful application of choice outside the XY-stratified clique. Choice is also very useful inside an XY-clique, but it can be used only with major restrictions. These follow from the fact that choice requires the memorization of old values, while the implementation of XY-stratified clique is based on only one level of stage argument being needed at any time. Therefore, *only choice goals where the stage variable J appears in the first argument of choice (the left side of the FD) are allowed in recursive rules.*[5] Even so curtailed, choice can play an important role. For instance, Prim's minimum spanning tree algorithm can be expressed as follows:

Example 9 *Greedy Algorithms: Prim's Minimum Spanning Tree*

```
prim(0,nil,a).
leastf(s(J),least(< C >)) ←  fringe(J,X,Y,C).

prim(J,X,Y) ←  leastf(J,C),fringe(J,X,Y,C),choice((J),(X,Y)).

solved(s(I),Y) ←  solved(I,Y).
solved(J,Y) ←   prim(J,_,Y).

fringe(s(J),X,Y,C) ←  fringe(J,X,Y,C),¬prim(s(J),_,Y).
fringe(J,X,Z,C) ←    prim(J,X,Y),g(Y,Z,C),¬solved(J,Y).
```

The meaning of the recursive rules in this example is as follows: (1) find all the least-cost arcs in fringe, (2) choose one such arc and add it to prim (3) update the list of solved nodes (i.e., nodes with an incoming arc), (4) update the fringe, (5) remove from fringe arcs entering the new node, (6) add to fringe the arcs departing from the new node added to prim, provided that they do not lead back to solved nodes.

---

[5]Definition 1 will thus be modified to reflect this relaxation

The results produced by this program will used by a calling goal such as prim(_, X, Y) which ignores the values of the stage arguments. This enables the $\mathcal{LDL}++$ compiler to apply a second important criterion for termination. In fact if the content of recursive relations (without stage argument) at step $I + 1$ is identical to that at step I, then it will remain identical for every $J > I$; since the value of stage argument is not used by the calling goal, the computation can be stopped. Checking equality of contents is impractical, but the following sufficient condition can be tested efficiently: During the last iteration *(i) regular rules (i.e., those that neither copy rules nor deletion rules) have produced no atoms, and (ii) deletion rules, if any, have actually not deleted any tuple.* When both conditions occurred, the relations at the next step will be identical to those at this step; thus computation can be stopped for the XY-stratified clique. [6]

In summary, we have two powerful mechanisms for ensuring termination of XY-stratified cliques via external calls: an explicit one that uses choice on the stage variable, and an implicit one that is based on the existential usage of the stage variable in the calling goal.

5 XY-Stratified Programs

Let us begin with a Bill of Materials application where the given relation, $g(X, Y, Q)$, states that X uses subpart Y in quantity Q. Our application lists and counts the elementary components contained in each part. We solve the problem inductively. Our exit rule finds elementary parts (i.e., those that have no subcomponents), and aggregates them for their immediate super-parts. Then, at step $I + 1$, we propagate the partial tallys of elementary components, computed at step I. These partial tallys are finally summed up by the final_count rule, outside the clique.

Example 10 *BOM: for each part X counting its basic components Y.*

$$rgc(0, X, Y, sum(< Q >)) \leftarrow \quad g(X, Y, Q), \neg g(Y, \_, \_).$$
$$rgc(I + 1, X, Y, sum(< Q >)) \leftarrow \quad g(X, W, Q2), rgc(I, W, Y, Q1), Q = Q1 * Q2.$$

$$final\_count(X1, Y1, sum2(< (I, Q) >)) \leftarrow \quad rgc(I, X1, Y1, Q).$$

In this XY-stratified clique, we have used $I + 1$ instead of $s(I)$ in the stage arguments. The two notations are obviously equivalent and the $\mathcal{LDL}++$ compiler recognizes these programs as being XY-Stratified.

The sum2 predicate, in the non-recursive rule, adds up all the values of Q without eliminating duplicate values of I. Therefore it can be defined as follows:

$$single(sum2, (I, Q), Q).$$
$$multi(sum2, Y1, Z1, Z) \leftarrow \quad Z = Z1 + Y1.$$

This computation terminates after saturation is reached.

---

[6] In Example 9, relation prim becomes empty after all nodes have been solved and fringe is empty as well. Thus the computation stops independent on whether the compiler treats the first fringe rule as a deletion rule, or not. However, consider Floyd's algorithm of Example 2, assuming that the calling goal is delta(_, X, Y, C). Here, if the first all rule is recognized as a deletion rule, computation terminates as soon as delta becomes empty.

Example 11 *Dijkstra's single-source least-cost-path algorithm.*

$\text{cand}(\text{nil}, \text{a}, 0).$
$\text{cand}(\text{s}(J), Y, \min(< C >)) \leftarrow \quad \text{least}(J, C1), \text{cand}(J, X, C1), \text{g}(X, Y, C2),$
$\qquad\qquad\qquad\qquad\qquad\qquad \neg\text{alleast}(J, Y, \_),$
$\qquad\qquad\qquad\qquad\qquad\qquad \text{if}(\text{cand}(J, Y, C3) \text{ then } C3 > C).$
$\text{cand}(\text{s}(J), Y, C) \leftarrow \quad \text{cand}(J, Y, C), \neg\text{least}(J, Y).$
$\text{alleast}(\text{s}(J), Y, C) \leftarrow \quad \text{alleast}(J, Y, C).$
$\text{alleast}(\text{s}(J), Y, C) \leftarrow \quad \text{least}(J, Y, C).$
$\text{least}(J, \min(< C >)) \leftarrow \quad \text{cand}(J, \_, C).$

The termination behavior of this greedy program, w.r.t. an external calling goal, is similar to that of Prim's algorithm.

Corporations and Shares. Corporation A owns an SP percentage of the shares of corporation B; if it owns more than 50% of such shares then A controls B. When A controls B, then it (indirectly) owns all the shares owned by B. We need to compute all these indirect ownerships.

Example 12 *Transitive Control of Corporations*

$\text{delta}(0, C1, C2, SP) \leftarrow \quad \text{own}(C1, C2, SP).$
$\text{delta}(\text{s}(J), C1, C3, \text{sum2}(< (C2, SP) >)) \leftarrow \quad \text{control}(J, C1, C2),$
$\qquad\qquad\qquad\qquad\qquad\qquad\qquad\qquad \text{own}(C2, C3, SP).$
$\text{shares}(\text{s}(J), C1, C3, SP) \leftarrow \quad \text{shares}(J, C1, C3, SP), \neg\text{delta}(J, C1, C3, \_).$
$\text{shares}(J, C1, C3, SP) \leftarrow \quad \text{delta}(J, C1, C3, Q1),$
$\qquad\qquad\qquad\qquad\qquad\qquad \text{if}(\text{shares}(J, C1, C3, Q2)\text{then } SP = Q1 + Q2,$
$\qquad\qquad\qquad\qquad\qquad\qquad \text{else } SP = Q1).$
$\text{control}(J, C1, C2) \leftarrow \quad \text{shares}(J, C1, C2, SP), SP > 0.5.$

In this example as well, the value of the stage argument is of no consequence outside the clique, and the special termination test previously described is applicable.

5.1 Magic Set Method

The magic set method, and other compilation methods designed to propagate constraints into the recursive predicates, remain applicable to XY-stratified programs. Take for instance the BOM program, Example 10. If we are only interested in finding the elementary components used by a given part, say frame, we can ask the following query: ?final_count(frame, Y, Q). Thus, this binding is propagated through the non-recursive rule of Example 10, and the recursive predicate rgc is called with adornment rgc^{fbff}. This binding is propagated through the goal g(X, W, Q2) in the recursive rule, returning the same adornment: rgc^{fbff}. Thus the magic-set method is applied yielding:

Example 13 *BOM: after the magic set transformation.*

```
m.rgc($Y1).   % $Y1 denotes the bound value of Y1
m.rgc(W) ←   m.rgc(X), g(X, W, Q2).

rgc(0, X, Y, sum(< Q >)) ←        m.rgc(X), g(X, Y, Q), ¬g(Y, _, _).
rgc(I + 1, X, Y, sum(< Q >)) ←    m.rgc(W),
                                   g(X, W, Q2), rgc(I, W, Y, Q1), Q = Q1 * Q2.
```

Observe that the application of the magic-set method adds no semantic complication. The recursive clique remains XY-stratified. Alternatively one could be interested in finding the usage of a given elementary component by different parts, and, e.g., issue the query ?final_count(X, bolt, Q). This second query will be recognized, in the special class of left/right linear queries, and compiled by specializing the recursive clique with the instantiation of X with 'bolt'.

6 Conclusions

The problem of finding efficient solutions to logic-based languages and specifications is one of the most enduring challenges of computing. Researchers in deductive databases have experienced the difficulty of this problem in dealing with non-stratified negation and aggregates, where the many elegant solutions presented in the past have not yielded the level of efficiency and generality that is required by complex real-life applications. Different remedies have been proposed to overcome this problem. An obvious remedy is that of escaping to a procedural language for operations that cannot be performed efficiently in a logic-based language. In particular, Nail-Glue provides a procedural shell that minimizes the "impedance-mismatch" problem between the procedural language and the logic-based one [15].

A more radical suggestion proposed is to abandon the minimal-model and least-fixpoint semantics of programs in favor of an operational semantics based on the concept of *inflationary fixpoint* [14]. This idea has an obvious appeal for deductive database people, insofar as (i) it represents a natural abstraction of the bottom-up computation used to implement systems such as $\mathcal{LDL}$ or Nail! (ii) it is easy for a programmer to understand and powerful in terms of expressive power (iii) it actually coincides with the minimal model/least-fixpoint semantics for monotonic programs. On the downside however, this approach repeats the past mistakes made by Prolog designers. Having opted for a top-down depth-first approach to the implementation of Horn clauses, Prolog designers elected to adopt this as THE actual semantics for the language and the basis of non-monotonic and impure constructs, such as the cut, assert and negation. The result is that Prolog is completely inadequate in dealing with classical fixpoint-oriented problems such as those discussed in this paper. Of course, the adoption of an inflationary-fixpoint as the actual semantics of a deductive database language would lead to symmetric problems—such as a loss of data independence and the ability of optimizing programs that lend themselves to a top-down execution.

The approach proposed in this paper combines the advantages of inflationary fixpoint and those of declarative logic. In fact, XY-stratified Datalog programs always compute in polynomial time and every problem of polynomial data complexity can be expressed using XY-stratified programs (assuming ordered domains [14] or using choice). Also, equivalence-preserving compilation methods, such as the magic-set method, remain applicable. On the other hand, the formal logic-based semantics enhances the uses of the language as a formal methods tools—as demonstrated e.g., by its recent use in formalizing updates and rules in active databases [25].

In terms of technology evolution, it is interesting to underscore the similarities and differences between $\mathcal{LDL}$ and $\mathcal{LDL}++$. The basic non-monotonic constructs (i.e., negation, conditionals, aggregates and choice) have remained the same and there is upward compatibility from the older system to the new system. But the power of the language has been extended while its underlying formal semantics have been simplified and unified. In $\mathcal{LDL}$, set aggregates and choice were given a separate semantic definition (e.g., choice was defined in terms of Functional Dependencies). But in $\mathcal{LDL}++$ the semantics of these constructs, which are seemingly different in terms of syntax, and operational meaning, have been all reduced to the same semantic basis—i.e., negation. Choice is formally defined using negation in [8], and set aggregates were defined in this paper using choice and negation. This latter definition solves several problems left open by previous approaches [10, 19, 13].

References

[1] A.V. Aho, J.E. Hopcropt, and J.D. Ullmann. *The Design and analysis of Computer Algorithms*. Addison-Wesley, 1974.

[2] N. Arni, K. Ong, S. Tsur and C. Zaniolo. *The $\mathcal{LDL}++$ System: Rationale, Technology and Applications*. Submitted for publication.

[3] Chimenti, D. et al., "The $\mathcal{LDL}$ System Prototype," *IEEE Journal on Data and Knowledge Engineering*, vol. 2, no. 1, pp. 76-90, March 1990.

[4] M.P. Consens and A.O. Mendelzon. Low complexity aggregation in graphlog and datalog. In *Proceedings of the third International Conference on Database Theory*, 1990.

[5] S. Ganguly, S. Greco, and C. Zaniolo. *Minimum and Maximum Predicates in Logic Programming*. In *Proceedings of the Tenth ACM Symposium on Principles of Database Systems*, pages 154-113, 1991.

[6] S. Ganguly, S. Greco, and C. Zaniolo. *Propagation of Extrema Predicates into Recursive Logic Programs*. In *Unpublished Manuscript*, 1992.

[7] M. Gelfond and V. Lifschitz. The stable model semantics of logic programming. In *Proceedings of the Fifth Intern. Conference on Logic Programming*, pages 1070-1080, 1988.

[8] F. Giannotti, D. Pedreschi, D. Saccà, and C. Zaniolo. Nondeterminism in deductive databases. In *Proc. 2nd Int. Conf. on Deductive and Object-Oriented Databases*, 1991.

[9] S. Greco, C. Zaniolo, and S. Ganguly. *Greedy by Choice*. In *Proceedings of the Eleventh ACM Symposium on Principles of Database Systems*, pages 105-163, 1992.

[10] D.B. Kemp and P.J. Stackey. Semantics of Logic Programs with Aggregates. In *Proceedings 1991 Int. Logic Programming Symposium*, pages 338–401, 1991.

[11] R. Krishnamurthy and S. Naqvi. "Non-deterministic choice in Datalog," In *Proceedings 3rd Int.Conference on Data and Knowledge Bases*, 1988.

[12] A. Van Gelder, K.A. Ross, and J.S. Schlipf. The well-founded semantics for general logic programs. *Journal of ACM*, 38(3):620–650, 1991.

[13] A. Van Gelder. The Well-Founded Semantics of Aggregation. In *Proceedings of the Eleventh ACM Symposium on Principles of Database Systems*, pages 127–138, 1992.

[14] P.G. Kolaitis and C.H. Papadimitriou, Why not negation by fixpoint?, *JCSS*, 43(1), 125-144, 1991.

[15] Phipps, G., M.A., Derr and K. A. Ross, "Glue-Nail: a Deductive Database System," *Proc. 1991 ACM-SIGMOD Conference on Management of Data*, pp. 308-317 (1991).

[16] T. Przymusinski. On the declarative and procedural semantics of stratified deductive databases. In J. Minker, editor, *Foundations of Deductive Databases and Logic Programming*, pages 193–216. Morgan-Kaufman, Los Altos, CA, 1988.

[17] A. Przymusinska and T. Przymusinski. Weakly Perfect Model Semantics for Logic Programs. In *Proceedings of the Fifth Intern. Conference on Logic Programming*, pages 1106–1122, 1988.

[18] S. A. Naqvi, S. Tsur *"A Logical Language for Data and Knowledge Bases"*, W. H. Freeman, 1989.

[19] K.A. Ross, and Y. Sagiv. Monotonic Aggregation in Deductive Databases. In *Proceedings of the Eleventh ACM Symposium on Principles of Database Systems*, pages 127–138, 1992.

[20] K.A. Ross, Modular Stratification and Magic Sets for Datalog Programs, In *Proceedings of the Ninth ACM Symposium on Principles of Database Systems*, pages 160–171, 1990.

[21] D. Saccà and C. Zaniolo. Stable models and non-determinism in logic programs with negation. In *Proceedings of the Ninth ACM Symposium on Principles of Database Systems*, pages 205–217, 1990.

[22] Ramakrishan, R., Srivastava, D. and Sudarshan, S., *"CORAL*: A Deductive Database Programming Language," Proc. VLDB'92 Int. Conf, pp. 238-250, 1992.

[23] Tsur S., 'Deductive Databases in Action,' *Proc. 10th, ACM SIGACT-SIGMOD-SIGART Symposium on Principles of Database Systems*, pp. 205-218, 1990.

[24] Zaniolo, C., Intelligent Databases: Old Challenges and New Opportunities, *Journal of Intelligent Information Systems*, 1, 271-292 (1992).

[25] Zaniolo, C., A Unified Semantics for Deductive Databases and Active Databases, *Procs. Workshop on Rules in Database Systems*, Edinburgh, U.K., 1993.

IsaLog¬: A Deductive Language with Negation for Complex-object Databases with Hierarchies*

Paolo Atzeni, Luca Cabibbo, and Giansalvatore Mecca

Dipartimento di Informatica e Sistemistica, Università di Roma "La Sapienza"
Via Salaria 113, 00198 Roma, Italy
{atzeni,cabibbo,mecca}@infokit.ing.uniroma1.it

Abstract. The IsaLog¬ model and language are presented. The model has complex objects with classes, relations, and isa hierarchies. The language is strongly typed and declarative. The main issue is the definition of the semantics of the IsaLog¬ language. The novel features are mostly due to the interaction of hierarchies with negation in the body of rules. Two semantics are presented and shown to be equivalent: a stratified semantics based on an original notion of stratification, needed in order to correctly deal with hierarchies, and a reduction to logic programming with function symbols. The solutions are based on a new technique (explicit Skolem functors) that provides a powerful tool for manipulating object identifiers.

1 Introduction

Deductive languages for complex-object databases have received a great deal of attention recently. In this context, the data model includes *classes* of *objects*, that is, sets of real world objects with the same conceptual and structural properties, and *is-a relationships*, used to organize classes in *hierarchies*. Objects identifiers *(oid's)* are associated with objects, to permit duplicates and to allow for object sharing and inheritance.

One interesting research direction has been the extension of Datalog$^{(\neg)}$ for the management of such a data model. The most relevant proposals in this area are the languages IQL (Abiteboul and Kanellakis [2]) and ILOG (Hull and Yoshikawa [13]), which refer to data models in the traditional database sense. Other interesting ideas have also been proposed as extensions of logic programming languages (Maier [17], Aït-Kaci and Nasr [3], Chen and Warren [12], Kifer et al. [15,16]).

In this framework, we have recently proposed IsaLog [5], a logic programming language over a model with (flat) classes and (flat) relations, with isa relationships among classes. A distinctive feature of IsaLog is the use of *explicit*

---

* This work was partially supported by *MURST*, within the Project "Metodi formali e strumenti per basi di dati evolute", and by *Consiglio Nazionale delle Ricerche*, within "Progetto Finalizzato Sistemi Informatici e Calcolo Parallelo, Obiettivo LOGIDATA+". The second author is partially supported by Systems & Management S.p.A.

Skolem functors (an extension of the *implicit* Skolem functors of ILOG [13]) to deal with oid invention over hierachies of classes. A declarative semantics, a fixpoint semantics, and a reduction to ordinary logic programming with function symbols were defined and proven to be equivalent.

This paper shows how the technique of explicit Skolem functors allows for a clear definition of the semantics of oid invention, with respect to a model with hierarchies and a language with negation. The main contribution is the definition of a stratified semantics for IsaLog⁻ programs, with a notion of stratification based on a partition of clauses that cannot be reduced to a partition of predicate symbols. Then, a reduction to logic programming is shown, yielding an equivalent semantics. Interestingly, this reduction would not be possible without the use of explicit Skolem functors, thus confirming their importance.

The paper is organized as follows. In Section 2 we informally present the framework and the results of the paper; examples are used to illustrate the main issues. Section 3 is devoted to the definition of the model. The language syntax is defined in Section 4. Section 5 formally presents the main results of the paper, with the definition of the semantics of IsaLog⁻ programs. Conclusions and future research directions are sketched in Section 6. Proofs are omitted, due to lack of space; the reader is referred to the full paper [6].

2 Overview and Motivation

2.1 The Framework

The data model is based on a clear distinction between *scheme* and *instance*. Data is organized by means of three constructs: classes, relations, and functors. *Classes* are collections of objects; each object is identified by an *object identifier (oid)* and has an associated tuple value. *Relations* are just collections of tuples. *Functors* are mainly used to make oid invention fully declarative; for each functor the database instance contains a function from tuples to oid's. Tuples in relations, in object values, and in arguments of functions may contain domain values and oid's, used as references to objects.

Isa hierarchies are allowed among classes, with multiple inheritance and without any requirement of completeness or disjointness. Moreover, we do not require, as in other works [2], the presence of a *most specific class* for each object in the database, since this may lead to an unreasonable increase in the number of classes in the database.

The IsaLog⁻ language is strongly typed and declarative, a suitable extension of Datalog [11] capable of handling oid invention and hierarchies. Three different kinds of clauses are allowed in a program:

- *relation clauses*, that is, ordinary clauses defining relations;
- *oid-invention clauses*, used to create new objects;
- *specialization clauses*, used to "specialize" oid's from superclasses to subclasses; in fact, a specialization clause can be used to specify (on the basis of some conditions) that an object in a class C also belongs to a subclass C' of C.

A program is a set of clauses that specifies a transformation from an instance of the input scheme to an instance of the output scheme.

2.2 Oid Invention

The introduction of *object identifiers (oid's)* in a declarative context gives rise to interesting semantic problems, the main one being the need for *oid invention*, that is, creation of new objects to populate extensions of classes.

The literature proposes two leading approaches to object creation: the *pure object creating* and the *logic-programming* ones. The pure object creating approach — which is adopted by some proposals, including IQL [2], LOGRES [9], and LOGIDATA+ [7] — refers to a "fact for each instance" policy: an oid-invention clause generates a new oid for each satisfiable ground instance of its body. The main drawback of such a semantics consists in the lack of a means to explicitly control the generation of objects with the same value ("duplicates").

On the other side, the so-called logic-programming approach treats new oid's in the output as terms built by means of values and oid's in the input. The ILOG language [13] proposes a semantics of invention based on *Skolem functor terms*. Skolem functors are strongly related to logic-programming function symbols; in this framework, they provide a neat syntactic tool to specify the terms on which oid invention depends. ILOG comes with a transparent skolemization mechanism, in which such terms are chosen to be exactly those occurring in the clause head. This technique allows for a nice reduction to ordinary logic-programming semantics, thus making oid invention truly declarative, but has a major shortcoming: it does not permit the generation of duplicates (when needed). Therefore, in the ILOG framework, equality implies identity, against the main motivation for the use of oid's.

Let us give an example that outlines the importance of duplicates. Assume the joint catalogue of two libraries has to be produced. Each of the libraries has no duplicate volumes and its catalogue is described by a relation R_i, with the book title as a key. If we are interested in defining the class of books, we need to collapse volumes (in different libraries) corresponding to the same book. Instead, if we want the class of all volumes, we have to retain duplicates.

The technique we propose to manage such cases consists in making *Skolem functors* become *explicit*. An *explicit Skolem functor* for an IsALoG$^{(\neg)}$ scheme is a symbol, used to build typed terms in programs. Specifically, each functor is associated with a class, and:

- explicit functors generalize implicit ones: an explicit functor term for an oid of a class C has a set of "arguments" that include the attributes of C. This is necessary in order to avoid ill-definedness of object values (that is, the generation of objects with the same oid and different values). In addition, a functor for a class may contain other arguments;
- different functors may be associated with the same class.

In this way the generation of duplicates is allowed. Consider the previous example; in both cases the catalogue is generated by means of two clauses that create objects: in the first case we have the same functor (to collapse duplicates) and in the second, two functors.

$$book(\text{OID} : f_{book}(title : x), \ldots) \leftarrow R_1(title : x, \ldots).$$
$$book(\text{OID} : f_{book}(title : x), \ldots) \leftarrow R_2(title : x, \ldots).$$

$$volume(\text{OID} : f_{volume,1}(title : x), \ldots) \leftarrow R_1(title : x, \ldots).$$
$$volume(\text{OID} : f_{volume,2}(title : x), \ldots) \leftarrow R_2(title : x, \ldots).$$

We claim that explicit functors are a very powerful tool for the manipulation of objects. In fact, not only do they provide a neat way for handling oid invention, but they also carry information about oid creation. This permits to distinguish oid's in the same class on the basis of their origin (the class itself or a subclass, for example), and to access the values that "witnessed" the invention of the oid, even if they are transparent with respect to the class. This is very useful for manipulating *imaginary objects* [1], that is, new objects computed on demand, like a relational view concerning objects instead of tuples. It is apparent that these objects exist in some classes of the view, but not in the database. When we update the database and recompute the view, we can assign the same functor (witness of an invention) to the same imaginary object. If we have stored the assignment of oid's to functor terms of previous computations, we can ensure that an object receives the same identifier every time the query is computed, so that imaginary objects maintain their identity as the database evolves [14].

2.3 Isa Hierarchies and Negation

We argued above that functors represent a nice means to manipulate oid's in the general case. Here we claim that they become almost necessary when isa and negation are included in the model. As previously sketched, the treatment of hierarchies in our model has been chosen to be the most general one, allowing for multiple and incomplete inheritance without most specific classes. Such a context reasonably requires to drop the scheme disjointness assumption, to easily deal with programs in which a subclass is newly generated and inherits objects from a superclass defined in the input instance. Moreover, it is interesting to note how hierarchies and negation interact together, requiring an *ad hoc* treatment.

Example 1. Consider a graph represented by means of two classes: *node* and *arc*, with types *()* and *(from:node, to:node)* respectively. Suppose we want to trasform the graph into a strongly connected one, adding an arc for each pair of non-connected nodes, by means of the following program (where *new-arc* ISA *arc*):

$\gamma_1 : path(from{:}x, to{:}y) \leftarrow node(\text{OID}{:}x), node(\text{OID}{:}y), arc(\text{OID}{:}z, from{:}x, to{:}y).$
$\gamma_2 : path(from{:}x, to{:}y) \leftarrow path(from{:}x, to{:}w), arc(\text{OID}{:}z, from{:}w, to{:}y).$
$\gamma_3 : new\text{-}arc(\text{OID}{:}f_{new\text{-}arc}(from{:}x, to{:}y), from{:}x, to{:}y) \leftarrow$
$\qquad node(\text{OID}{:}x), node(\text{OID}{:}y), \neg\, path(from{:}x, to{:}y).$

The program appears to be stratified: its dependency graph contains no cycle with a negative edge. On the contrary, if we take into account hierarchies and their properties, we can argue that it is not stratified. In fact, since *new-arc* depends on (the negation of) *path* (clause γ_3), we can say that the same also holds for *arc*, since each new object in *new-arc* must also appear in *arc*. Then, since *path* depends on *arc* (clauses γ_1 and γ_2), we have a violation of the intuition behind stratification.

An intuitive proposal [9] for handling hierarchy semantics consists in the introduction of auxiliary clauses that enforce containment constraints associated with isa relationships. This means that for each pair of classes C_0 and C_1 in the scheme such that C_1 ISA C_0, we need to add a clause:

$$C_0(\text{OID}: x, A_1: x_1, \ldots, A_k: x_k) \leftarrow C_1(\text{OID}: x, A_1: x_1, \ldots, A_{k+m}: x_{k+m}).$$

(where $A_{k+1}, \ldots, A_{k+m}$ are the additional attributes in C_1) that forces objects in C_1 to belong to C_0 as well. These clauses, called the *isa clauses*, depend only on the scheme and not on the individual programs. The next example shows that this technique, well suited to a positive framework such as ISALOG [5], does not catch the complete meaning of negation.

Example 2. Consider the class *person* with type *(name:D, asset:D, father:person)* (where D is a *domain* of atomic values), and suppose *rich-person* ISA *person*, *self-made-man* ISA *rich-person*. Suppose we want to specialize people on the basis of their assets, with a special interest in rich people with a non-rich father:

$$\gamma_1 : rich\text{-}person(\text{OID}:x, name:n, asset:a, father:f) \leftarrow$$
$$person(\text{OID}:x, name:n, asset:a, father:f), a > 100K.$$

$$\gamma_2 : self\text{-}made\text{-}man(\text{OID}:x, name:n, asset:a, father:f) \leftarrow$$
$$rich\text{-}person(\text{OID}:x, name:n, asset:a, father:f),$$
$$\neg \ rich\text{-}person(\text{OID}:f, name:nf, asset:af, father:ff).$$

Clause γ_2 specifies the "specialization" of objects in *rich-person* to be objects in *self-made-man* as well, on the basis of some conditions that include a negation on *rich-person*. Intuitively, a natural semantics for this program is obtained by applying first (i) clause γ_1 and then (ii) clause γ_2. Essentially, step (i) computes *rich-person* and step (ii) computes *self-made-man*. Surprisingly, if the isa clauses associated with the scheme are added to the program, the resulting set of clauses is not stratified, that is, the dependency graph contains a cycle with a negative edge.

The shown examples suggest that:

- ordinary stratification [4], defined as a partition of clauses that essentially collapses to a partition of predicate symbols, fails when hierarchies are present;
- isa clauses do not represent a solution to the problem.

In the following sections we introduce an original semantics for ISALOG$^\neg$ programs, based on a notion of *isa-coherent stratification*, that is essentially a partition of clauses that cannot be reduced to a partition of predicate symbols. Then, a reduction to logic programming is shown, yielding an equivalent semantics. Interestingly, this reduction would not be possible without the use of explicit Skolem functors, thus confirming their importance.

3 The Data Model

We present only the essential aspects, omitting standard notions and details not needed in the sequel.

We fix a countable set D of *constants*, called the *domain*. An ISALOG scheme is a five-tuple $S = (C, R, F, \text{TYP}, \text{ISA})$, where

- C (the *class names*), R (the *relation names*), and F (the *functors*) are finite, pairwise disjoint sets;
- TYP is a total function on $C \cup R \cup F$ that associates
  - a flat *tuple type* $(A_1 : \tau_1, A_2 : \tau_2, \ldots, A_k : \tau_k)$ with each class in C and each relation in R; the A_i's are called the *attributes*, and each τ_i (the *type* of A_i) is either a class name in C or the domain D;
  - a pair (C, τ) with each functor $F \in F$, where: (i) C is a class name in C (the *class associated with* F) and (ii) τ is a tuple type whose attributes are disjoint from those of C and of its subclasses;
- ISA is a partial order over C, such that if $(C', C'') \in \text{ISA}$ (usually written in infix notation, C' ISA C'', and read C' is a *subclass* of C''), then $\text{TYP}(C')$ is a *subtype* of $\text{TYP}(C'')$ [10] (that is, for each attribute in $\text{TYP}(C'')$, the attribute also appears in $\text{TYP}(C')$, with the same type or (if the type is a class name) with a type that is a subclass). Multiple inheritance is allowed, with some technical restrictions, omitted for the sake of space.

It is convenient to define the *types of a scheme* S, where each type is a *simple type* (that is, either the domain D or a class name) or a *tuple type* (whose attributes have simple types associated).

As in every other data model, the scheme gives the structure of the possible *instances* of the database. The values that appear in instances are (i) constants from D; (ii) *object identifiers (oid's)* from a countable set $\mathcal{O}$, disjoint from D; (iii) *tuples* over tuple types, whose components are oid's or constants.

Following ILOG, we define instances as equivalence classes of pre-instances: pre-instances depend on actual oid's, whereas instances make oid's transparent.

A *pre-instance* s of an ISALOG scheme $S = (C, R, F, \text{TYP}, \text{ISA})$ is a four-tuple $s = (c, r, f, o)$, where:

- c is a function that associates with each class name $C \in C$ a finite set of oid's, preserving the containment constraints (associated with subclassing) and disjointness constraints (associated with distinct taxonomies).
- r is a function that associates with each relation name $R \in R$ a finite set of tuples over $\text{TYP}(R)$;
- o is a function that associates tuples with oid's in classes, with the appropriate type [1].

---

[1] The definition is not trivial — with respect to other models, such as IQL [2] — because we do not require for each object a *most specific class*.

- **f** is a function that associates with each functor $F \in \mathbf{F}$ (associated with a class C) a partial injective function $\mathbf{f}(F)$ from the set of tuples over the tuple type of the functor to a subset of the oid's in $\mathbf{c}(C)$ [2].
- if a tuple type has an attribute A whose type is a class $C \in \mathbf{C}$, then the value of the tuple over A is an oid in $\mathbf{c}(C)$ (this condition avoids "dangling references").

Two pre-instances s_1 and s_2 over a scheme $\mathbf{S}$ are said to be *oid-equivalent* if there is a permutation σ of the oid's in $\mathcal{O}$ such that (extending σ to objects, tuples, and pre-instances in the natural way) it is the case that $s_1 = \sigma(s_2)$. An *instance* is an equivalence class of pre-instances under oid-equivalence. When needed, $[s]$ will denote the instance whose representative is the pre-instance s.

4 ISALOG¬ Syntax

Let a scheme $\mathbf{S} = (\mathbf{C}, \mathbf{R}, \mathbf{F}, \text{TYP}, \text{ISA})$ be fixed. Also, consider two disjoint countable sets of *variables*: V_D (*value variables*, to denote constants) and $V_{\mathbf{C}}$ (*oid variables*, to denote oid's).

The *terms* of the language are:

- *value terms*, that are: (i) the constants in D and (ii) the variables in V_D;
- *oid terms*: (i) the oid's in $\mathcal{O}$, (ii) the variables in $V_{\mathbf{C}}$, and (iii) *functor terms* $F(A_1 : t_1, \ldots, A_k : t_k, A'_1 : t'_1, \ldots, A'_h : t'_h)$, where $F \in \mathbf{F}$ and $\text{TYP}(F) = (C, \tau)$, $\text{TYP}(C) = (A_1 : \tau_1, \ldots, A_k : \tau_k)$ and $\tau = (A'_1 : \tau'_1, \ldots, A'_h : \tau'_h)$.

The *atoms* of the language may have two forms (where terms in components are oid terms or value terms depending on the type associated with the attribute):

- *class atoms*: $C(\text{OID} : t_0, A_1 : t_1, \ldots, A_k : t_k)$, where C is a class name in $\mathbf{C}$, with $\text{TYP}(C) = (A_1 : \tau_1, \ldots, A_k : \tau_k)$ and t_0 is an oid term;
- *relation atoms*: $R(A_1 : t_1, \ldots, A_k : t_k)$, where R is a relation name in $\mathbf{R}$, with type $\text{TYP}(R) = (A_1 : \tau_1, \ldots, A_k : \tau_k)$.

The notions of *(positive* and *negative) literal, rule, fact,* and *clause* are as usual. The head and body of a clause γ are denoted with $\text{HEAD}(\gamma)$ and $\text{BODY}(\gamma)$, respectively. There are three relevant forms of clauses. A clause γ is:

- a *relation clause* if $\text{HEAD}(\gamma)$ is a relation atom;
- an *oid-invention clause* if $\text{HEAD}(\gamma)$ is a class atom $C(\text{OID} : t_0, A_1 : t_1, \ldots, A_k : t_k)$, where t_0 is a functor term $F(A_1 : t_1, \ldots, A_k : t_k, \ldots)$ not occurring in $\text{BODY}(\gamma)$ and C is the class associated with F;
- a *specialization clause* if $\text{HEAD}(\gamma)$ is a class atom $C(\text{OID} : t, \ldots)$, where t is an oid term and $\text{BODY}(\gamma)$ contains (at least) a class atom $C'(\text{OID} : t, \ldots)$ such that C and C' have a common ancestor (that is, a class C_0 such that C ISA C_0 and C' ISA C_0).

---

[2] In order to guarantee well-definedness in the generation of oid's, by avoiding circularity, a partial order is defined over oid's. Moreover, ranges of functors are required to be pairwise disjoint.

Hereinafter we consider only clauses of the above three forms. A *positive clause* is a clause whose body contains only positive literals.

An IsaLog⁻ *program* **P** over a scheme **S** is a set of clauses that satisfy some technical conditions: *well-typedness* (about typing of oid terms), *safety* (as usual), and *visibility* (no explicit oid's are allowed). An IsaLog *program* is an IsaLog⁻ program made of a set of positive clauses.

5   Semantics of IsaLog⁻ Programs

We have studied in a previous paper [5] the semantics of positive IsaLog programs, by means of three independent techniques (declarative, fixpoint, and reduction to logic programming), and shown their equivalence. The declarative semantics is based on a notion of *unique minimal model*. As opposed to what happens for the standard Datalog framework, it may be the case that the semantics for a program over an instance is undefined. There are two reasons for this: infinite generation of new objects and multiple inconsistent specialization of existing objects.

In this section we study the semantics of IsaLog⁻ programs. As usual, the introduction of negation may lead to the existence of multiple incomparable minimal models, thus requiring a criterion for the selection of one of the minimal models, as the "right" semantics of a program over an instance. We follow the approach based on the notion of stratification, which howerever requires a number of variations to be used in our framework, because of the presence of isa hierarchies.

5.1   Instances as Herbrand Interpretations

In this section we briefly explain how an IsaLog instance can be represented by means of a set of facts, a preliminary tool for the description of the semantics of IsaLog⁻ programs.

Given a scheme $\mathbf{S} = (\mathbf{C}, \mathbf{R}, \mathbf{F}, \mathrm{TYP}, \mathrm{ISA})$, the *Herbrand base* $\mathrm{H}_{\mathbf{S}}$ for **S** is the set of all ground facts with predicate symbols from **R** and **C** and terms with function symbols from **F** and values from $\mathcal{O}$ and D. A *Herbrand interpretation* is a finite subset of the Herbrand base. We define a function ϕ that associates a Herbrand interpretation with each pre-instance $\mathbf{s} = (\mathbf{c}, \mathbf{r}, \mathbf{f}, \mathbf{o})$ of **S**. We proceed in two steps:

1. $\phi^0(\mathbf{s})$ is the set of facts that contains one fact for each tuple in each relation and as many facts for an object o as the number of different classes to which the object belongs. Each of these facts involves only the attributes that are relevant for the corresponding class.

2. $\phi(\mathbf{s})$ is obtained from $\phi^0(\mathbf{s})$ by recursively replacing each oid o such that o equals $\mathbf{f}(F)$ applied to $(A_1 : v_1, \ldots, A_k : v_k)$, with the term $F(A_1 : v_1, \ldots, A_k : v_k)$. Note that this replacement is univocally defined (since the

functions are injective and have disjoint ranges) and terminates (because of the partial order among oid's) [3].

The function ϕ is defined for every pre-instance but it can be shown that is not surjective: there are Herbrand interpretations that are not in the image of ϕ. This happens if one of the following conditions (here informally defined) is violated:

WT (*well-typedness*): for each fact, all terms have the appropriate type.

CON (*containment*): for each fact $C_1(\text{OID} : t_0, \ldots)$, there is a fact $C_2(\text{OID} : t_0, \ldots)$ for each class C_2 such that $C_1 \text{ ISA } C_2$. This condition requires the satisfaction of the containment constraints corresponding to isa hierarchies.

DIS (*disjointness*): if two facts $C_1(\text{OID} : t_0, \ldots)$ and $C_2(\text{OID} : t_0, \ldots)$ appear, then classes C_1 and C_2 have a common ancestor in **S**.

COH (*oid-coherence*): if an oid term t_0 occurs as a value for an attribute whose type is a class C, then there is a fact $C(\text{OID} : t_0, \ldots)$. This condition rules out dangling references.

FUN (*functionality*): there cannot be two different facts for the same oid term with different values for some common attributes.

Conditions FUN, CON, and DIS guarantee that oid's object values are well defined throughout hierarchies.

It can be shown that a Herbrand interpretation over a scheme **S** satisfies conditions WT, CON, DIS, COH, and FUN with respect to **S** if and only if it belongs to the image of ϕ over the pre-instances of **S**.

Furthermore, ϕ preserves oid-equivalence, that is, $\phi(s_1)$ and $\phi(s_2)$ are oid-equivalent if and only if s_1 and s_2 are oid-equivalent. Therefore, we can define a function Φ that maps instances to equivalence classes of Herbrand interpretations: $\Phi : [s] \mapsto [\phi(s)]$. Since $\phi(s_1)$ is equivalent to $\phi(s_2)$ only if s_1 is equivalent to s_2, we have that Φ is injective. So, Φ is a bijection from the set of instances to the set of equivalence classes of Herbrand interpretations that satisfy the five conditions above. The inverse of Φ is therefore defined over equivalence classes of Herbrand interpretations that satisfy conditions WT, CON, DIS, COH, and FUN.

5.2 Isa-Coherent Stratification of IsaLog⁻ Programs

We need some preliminary definitions. Assume that a scheme **S** is fixed. We call *predicate symbol* of the scheme **S** every class and relation name. Given a clause γ, we say that γ *defines* a predicate symbol Q if one of the following conditions holds:

- γ is a relation clause with head $Q(\ldots)$;
- γ is an oid-invention clause with head $C(\ldots)$, with $C \in \mathbf{C}$ and $C \text{ ISA } Q$;
- γ is a specialization clause with head $C(\text{OID} : t, \ldots)$, with $C \in \mathbf{C}$, $C \text{ ISA } Q$, and there is no positive literal $C'(\text{OID} : t, \ldots)$ in $\text{BODY}(\gamma)$, with $C' \in \mathbf{C}$, such that $C' \text{ ISA } Q$.

---

[3] This procedure leaves some oid's in the facts — those that, as allowed by the definition of instance, do not appear in the range of any function.

Essentially, each clause defines a predicate symbol Q if it (possibly) generates new facts that involve Q: an oid-invention clause generates a new fact for each superclass of the predicate symbol in its head; a specialization clause generates a new fact only for some superclasses (because the corresponding facts for other superclasses already exist). Clearly, this distinction is relevant only for a language with class hierarchies: in languages without hierarchies, each clause defines exactly one predicate symbol.

Given an IsaLog¬ program $\mathbf{P}$ and a predicate symbol Q, the *definition of Q* (within $\mathbf{P}$) is the set of clauses in $\mathbf{P}$ whose set of defined symbols contains Q.

A partition $P_1 \cup \ldots \cup P_n$ of the clauses of $\mathbf{P}$ is an *isa-coherent stratification* of $\mathbf{P}$ (and each P_i is a *stratum*) if the following two conditions hold for $i = 1, \ldots, n$:

1. if a predicate symbol Q occurs in a positive literal in the body of a clause $\gamma \in P_i$, then the definition of Q is contained within $\cup_{j \leq i} P_j$;
2. if a predicate symbol Q occurs in a negative literal in the body of a clause $\gamma \in P_i$, then the definition of Q is contained within $\cup_{j < i} P_j$.

An IsaLog¬ program $\mathbf{P}$ is *isa-coherently stratified* if it has an isa-coherent stratification. It should be noted that this notion is apparently the same as the usual one: the difference is inside the notion of "definition" of a symbol [4].

Isa-coherently stratified programs can be characterized by means of properties of clauses (rather than predicate symbols, as it happens in the Datalog framework). We need a few definitions. We say that a clause γ_1 *refers to* a clause γ_2 if there is a predicate symbol Q that is defined by γ_2 and occurs in a literal in the body of γ_1; if such a literal is negative, then γ_1 *negatively refers to* γ_2. Given a program $\mathbf{P}$ we define its *clause dependency graph* $\mathrm{CDG}_{\mathbf{P}}$ as a directed graph representing the relation *refers to* between the clauses of $\mathbf{P}$. An edge (γ_1, γ_2) is *negative* if γ_1 negatively refers to γ_2.

Lemma 1. *A program $\mathbf{P}$ is isa-coherently stratified iff its clause dependency graph $\mathrm{CDG}_{\mathbf{P}}$ does not contain a cycle with a negative edge.*

5.3 Fixpoint Semantics of IsaLog¬ Isa-Coherently Stratified Programs

In this section we present the fixpoint semantics for IsaLog¬ programs. The presence of isa requires a modification of the traditional approach, as follows. Given a scheme $\mathbf{S} = (\mathbf{C}, \mathbf{R}, \mathbf{F}, \mathrm{TYP}, \mathrm{ISA})$ we define the *closure T_{ISA} with respect to* ISA as a mapping from the powerset $2^{H_{\mathbf{S}}}$ of $H_{\mathbf{S}}$ to itself, as follows:

$$
\begin{aligned}
T_{\mathrm{ISA}}(I_{\mathbf{S}}) = I_{\mathbf{S}} \cup \{ &C_2(\mathrm{OID} : t_0, A_1 : t_1, \ldots, A_k : t_k) \mid \\
&C_1(\mathrm{OID} : t_0, A_1 : t_1, \ldots, A_{k+h} : t_{k+h}) \in I_{\mathbf{S}}, \ C_1 \mathrm{ISA} C_2, \\
&\text{and } \mathrm{TYP}(C_2) = (A_1 : \tau_1, \ldots, A_k : \tau_k) \}
\end{aligned}
$$

---

[4] In ordinary theory of stratification [4], the *definition* of a predicate symbol Q (within a program $\mathbf{P}$) is the set of clauses in $\mathbf{P}$ whose head's predicate symbol is Q.

The closure with respect to isa enforces containment constraints on facts associated with hierarchies, as required by condition CON defined in Section 5.1.

Then, given a set of clauses Γ over a scheme $\mathbf{S}$, we define the trasformation $T_{\Gamma,0}$ associated with Γ as a mapping from $2^{H_{\mathbf{S}}}$ to itself, as follows (where the notions of substitution and satisfaction are standard):

$$T_{\Gamma,0}(I_{\mathbf{S}}) = \{\theta(\text{HEAD}(\gamma)) \mid \gamma \in \Gamma, I_{\mathbf{S}} \text{ satisfies } \theta(\text{BODY}(\gamma)), \text{ for a substitution } \theta\}$$

Then, the *immediate consequence operator* T_{Γ} associated with a set of clauses Γ over a scheme $\mathbf{S}$ is a mapping from $2^{H_{\mathbf{S}}}$ to itself:

$$T_{\Gamma}(I_{\mathbf{S}}) = T_{\text{ISA}}(T_{\Gamma,0}(I_{\mathbf{S}}))$$

Let us note that in Datalog frameworks, the immediate consequence operator essentially coincides with our operator $T_{\Gamma,0}$. The application of T_{ISA} is needed here to enforce condition CON, that is, isa relationships.

Let us note that transformation T_{Γ} preserves all the conditions satisfied by Herbrand interpretations that correspond to pre-instances, but condition FUN, which is not in general preserved [5].

Now, the semantics of an isa-coherently stratified program can be defined following the same steps as in the traditional framework [4]. However, most properties have a significantly different proof, because of the differences in the immediate consequence operator T_{Γ} due to hierarchies and in the definition of stratification.

Let us consider an isa-coherently stratified program $\mathbf{P}$ over a scheme $\mathbf{S}$. Let $P_1 \cup \ldots \cup P_n$ be an isa-coherent stratification of $\mathbf{P}$, and $I_{\mathbf{S}}$ be a Herbrand interpretation. Now we define a sequence of Herbrand interpretations by putting

$$M_{0,I_{\mathbf{S}}} = I_{\mathbf{S}}$$
$$M_{i,I_{\mathbf{S}}} = T_{P_i}\Uparrow\omega(M_{i-1,I_{\mathbf{S}}}), \text{ for } 1 \leq i \leq n$$

where each T_{P_i} is the operator T_{Γ}, for a set of clauses $\Gamma = P_i$, and $T\Uparrow\omega$ is the union of all the cumulative powers of an operator T: $T\Uparrow\omega(I) = \cup_{n\geq0}T\Uparrow n(I)$, with $T\Uparrow0(I) = I$ and $T\Uparrow(n+1)(I) = T(T\Uparrow n(I)) \cup T\Uparrow n(I)$. It can be shown that the last Herbrand interpretation $M_{n,I_{\mathbf{S}}}$ does not depend on the chosen stratification of $\mathbf{P}$, thus we can refer to it as $M_{\mathbf{P},I_{\mathbf{S}}}$.

We can now define the *isa-coherently stratified semantics* ST-SEM of ISALOG⁻ programs, as a partial function from instances to instances, as follows. Given an isa-coherently stratified program $\mathbf{P}$ over a scheme $\mathbf{S}$, and an instance [s]:

$$\text{ST-SEM}_{\mathbf{P}}([s]) = \begin{cases} \Phi^{-1}([M_{\mathbf{P},\phi(s)}]) & \text{if } M_{\mathbf{P},\phi(s)} \text{ is finite and} \\ & \text{satisfies condition FUN} \\ undefined & \text{otherwise} \end{cases}$$

5.4 Reduction to Logic Programming for IsaLog⁻ Programs

We have shown in a previous paper [5] that an elegant semantics for (positive) IsaLog programs can be defined as a reduction to logic programming. Given an IsaLog program **P** over a scheme **S** and an instance [s], this semantics is defined by means of three steps:

1. compute the Herbrand interpretation $\phi(s)$ associated with s;
2. compute the minimum model $\mathcal{M}$ of the logic program composed of: (i) (a syntactic variation of) the IsaLog program **P**, (ii) the set of facts $\phi(s)$, and (iii) the isa clauses associated with the scheme;
3. if $\mathcal{M}$ is in the image of ϕ, then let the LP-semantics of **P** over [s] be $\Phi^{-1}([\mathcal{M}])$ (or, equivalently, $[\phi^{-1}(\mathcal{M})]$), otherwise let it be undefined.

With respect to stratified programs, this approach is not satisfactory. Consider the program in Example 2: it has an isa-coherent stratification and thus it is isa-coherently stratified; on the other hand, the logic program obtained by adding the isa clause γ : *rich-person(OID:x,...)* ←*self-made-man(OID:x,...)* is not stratified in the ordinary sense. Essentially, the problem is caused by isa clauses that specify the propagation of objects from subclasses to superclasses more strongly than needed. In the example, the isa clause γ is actually needed only to support the creation of new objects, whereas it does nothing with respect to applications of clause γ_2, since γ_2 specializes in *self-made-man* objects that already belong to *rich-person*.

A solution to the problem is based on a finer specification of the propagation of objects: rather than adding isa clauses associated with a scheme, it uses additional clauses only with reference to the clauses of the program that require oid propagation. Specifically, for each clause γ that defines more than one predicate symbol, we add the following set of clauses (the *defined-symbol clauses*):

$$\{C_2(\text{OID} : t_0, A_1 : x_1, \ldots, A_k : x_k) \leftarrow \text{BODY}(\gamma) \mid$$
$$\text{HEAD}(\gamma) = C_1(\text{OID} : t_0, A_1 : x_1, \ldots, A_{k+m} : x_{k+m})$$
$$C_1 \text{ ISA } C_2, \ C_2(\neq C_1) \text{ is a defined symbol of } \gamma\}$$

Therefore, we have two different reductions to logic programming. We call them the *isa-clause (IC) reduction* and the *defined-symbol (DS) reduction*. We can therefore define two logic programming semantics for IsaLog⁻ programs (possibly with negation), the *IC-semantics* and the *DS-semantics*, respectively. It is convenient to define them in three steps again (where the first and third coincide with the analogous for positive programs):

1. compute $\phi(s)$;
2. compute the perfect model $\mathcal{M}$ (in the standard logic programming sense) of the logic program composed of: (i) the IsaLog⁻ program **P**, (ii) $\phi(s)$, and (iii) the isa clauses associated with the scheme (for the IC-semantics) or the defined-symbol clauses (for the DS-semantics);
3. if $\mathcal{M}$ is in the image of ϕ, then let the (IC- or DS-) semantics of **P** over [s] be $\Phi^{-1}([\mathcal{M}])$, otherwise let it be undefined.

We have the following results, which relate the two logic programming semantics with each other and with the fixpoint semantics. The first theorem shows that the DS-reduction can always be used instead of IC-reduction — the converse does not hold, as we argued with respect to the example above. As a consequence, the two semantics are equivalent with respect to positive programs. The second (and more important) theorem states the equivalence of the DS-semantics and the stratified semantics.

Theorem 2. *For every* IsaLog¬ *program, if the IC-reduction is stratified, then the DS-reduction is also stratified, and the IC-semantics and the DS-semantics coincide.*

Theorem 3. *For every* IsaLog¬ *program* **P**

- *the DS-reduction of* **P** *is stratified if and only if* **P** *is isa-coherently stratified;*
- *the isa-coherently stratified semantics* ST-SEM**p** *and the DS-semantics of* **P** *coincide.*

It is worth noting that the DS-reduction is heavily based on explicit Skolem functors. Let us argue by means of an example. Assume we have a scheme with the isa relationship between the classes *person* and *student*, whose respective type is *(name:D)* and *(name:D,id-no:D)*, and a program with an oid-invention clause:

$$\gamma : student(\text{OID} : f_{student} : (name:n,id\text{-}no:id), name:n,id\text{-}no:id) \leftarrow \text{BODY}(\gamma).$$

The DS-reduction introduces a clause

$$\gamma' : person(\text{OID} : f_{student} : (name:n,id\text{-}no:id), name:n) \leftarrow \text{BODY}(\gamma).$$

with the same body and the same functor term in the head. The use of the same functor guarantees that in each pair of facts generated by these clauses the oid is the same, and so they refer to the same object. This behavior could hardly be introduced without explicit functors. As a matter of fact, if implicit functors were to be used, the clause would produce two different functor terms for the two classes, thus generating different oid's.

6 Conclusions and Future Work

Several issues need to be further investigated, as follows.

- The characterization of the definedness of the semantics of programs over instances; more specifically, since functors possibly induce model infiniteness, we need to find (necessary and) sufficient conditions for a set of clauses to have a finite model.
- The management of integrity constraints, especially with regard to their preservation in derived data.
- The introduction of recursive methods attached to classes of the scheme.

References

1. S. Abiteboul and A. Bonner. Objects and views. In *ACM SIGMOD International Conf. on Management of Data*, pages 238–247, 1991.
2. S. Abiteboul and P. Kanellakis. Object identity as a query language primitive. In *ACM SIGMOD International Conf. on Management of Data*, pages 159–173, 1989.
3. H. Aït-Kaci and R. Nasr. LOGIN a logic programming language with built-in inheritance. *Journal of Logic Programming*, 3:185–215, 1986.
4. K. Apt, H. Blair, and A. Walker. Toward a theory of declarative knowledge. In J. Minker, editor, *Foundations of Deductive Databases and Logic Programming*, pages 89–148. Morgan Kauffman, Los Altos, 1988.
5. P. Atzeni, L. Cabibbo, and G. Mecca. IsALOG: A declarative language for complex objects with hierarchies. In *Ninth IEEE International Conference on Data Engineering, Vienna*, 1993.
6. P. Atzeni, L. Cabibbo, and G. Mecca. IsALOG¬: a deductive language with negation for complex-objects databases with hierarchies. Technical report, Dipartimento di Informatica e Sistemistica, Università di Roma "La Sapienza", 1993.
7. P. Atzeni and L. Tanca. The LOGIDATA+ model and language. In *Next Generation Information Systems Technology, Lecture Notes in Computer Science 504*. Springer-Verlag, 1991.
8. C. Beeri. A formal approach to object-oriented databases. *Data and Knowledge Engineering*, 5:353–382, 1990.
9. F. Cacace, S. Ceri, S. Crespi-Reghizzi, L. Tanca, and R. Zicari. Integrating object oriented data modelling with a rule-based programming paradigm. In *ACM SIGMOD International Conf. on Management of Data*, pages 225–236, 1990.
10. L. Cardelli. A semantics of multiple inheritance. *Information and Computation*, 76(2):138–164, 1988.
11. S. Ceri, G. Gottlob, and L. Tanca. *Logic Programming and Data Bases*. Springer-Verlag, 1989.
12. W. Chen and D.S. Warren. C-logic for complex objects. In *Eigth ACM SIGACT SIGMOD SIGART Symp. on Principles of Database Systems*, pages 369–378, 1989.
13. R. Hull and M. Yoshikawa. ILOG: Declarative creation and manipulation of object identifiers. In *Sixteenth International Conference on Very Large Data Bases, Brisbane*, pages 455–468, 1990.
14. M. Kifer, W. Kim, and Y. Sagiv. Querying object-oriented databases. In *ACM SIGMOD International Conf. on Management of Data*, pages 393–402, 1992.
15. M. Kifer and G. Lausen. F-logic: A higher order language for reasoning about objects, inheritance and scheme. In *ACM SIGMOD International Conf. on Management of Data*, pages 134–146, 1989.
16. M. Kifer and J. Wu. A logic for object-oriented logic programming (Maier's O-logic revisited). In *Eigth ACM SIGACT SIGMOD SIGART Symp. on Principles of Database Systems*, pages 379–393, 1989.
17. D. Maier. A logic for objects. In *Workshop on Foundations of Deductive Database and Logic Programming (Washington, D.C. 1986)*, pages 6–26, 1986.

On Efficient Reasoning with Implication Constraints

Xubo Zhang and Z. Meral Ozsoyoglu

Department of Computer Engineering and Science
Case Western Reserve University
Cleveland, OH 44106
{xzhang, ozsoy}@alpha.ces.cwru.edu

Abstract. In this paper, we address the complexity issue of reasoning with implication constraints. We consider the problem of deciding whether a conjunctive yes/no–query always produces the empty relation ("no" answer) on database instances satisfying a given set of implication constraints, which we refer to as the *IC-refuting problem*. We show that several other important problems, such as the query containment problem, are polynomially equivalent to the IC-refuting problem. More importantly, we give criteria for designing a set of implication constraints so that an efficient process, called "units-refutation" process can be used to solve the IC-refuting problem.

1 Introduction

Semantic constraints are logic rules specifying semantically meaningful database instances. In this paper we consider an important kind of semantic constraints called implication constraints that are expressible by empty headed Horn clauses having only positive database literals. Since early 1980's, there have been investigations on the utilization of such constraints to optimize relational queries [7, 9, 18, 2 etc.], i.e. semantic query optimization. The main tasks are to find inconsistent queries, eliminate joins, delete redundant θ-join predicates, and introduce selection conditions on indexed attributes. More recently, there are research studies investigating a much wider range of "constrained" problems in relational, deductive, and object-oriented databases; for example, the update problem [4], the redundancy problem in Datalog [12]; the recursive query optimization problem [11, 6, 16]; and the problem of providing intentional answers [17, 14]. The maintenance of non-redundant and consistent constraint bases is also studied [15].

All these works involve the reasoning with implication constraints, few studies have addressed the complexity issue. In this paper, we discuss one basic problem: the problem of deciding whether a conjunctive yes/no–query always produces the empty relation ("no" answer) on database instances satisfying a given set of implication constraints. We call this problem the IC-refuting problem. IC-refuting problem is important because, as we will show, it is closely related to the well known containment problem for conjunctive queries [1, 10, 19, 20 etc.], and many other problems. Before going into further discussions, let's consider an example.

Example 1. Suppose we have a database system for a small company. There is a relation scheme: **dept(dname, manager)**, and an implication constraint:

$$ic_1 : \textbf{dept}(D, M), D \neq sales, D \neq service \rightarrow,$$

which tells us that there are no other departments than "sales" or "service" department. Now, let us ask a query "are there three different departments?", i.e.,

$$Q = \{\langle\rangle : \textbf{dept}(D_1, M_1), \textbf{dept}(D_2, M_2), \textbf{dept}(D_3, M_3), D_1 \neq D_2, D_1 \neq D_3,$$
$$D_2 \neq D_3\}.$$

This is a what we call yes/no–query, where there is no free variable in the summary $\langle\rangle$, and the variables are existentially quantified. Assuming the constraint has been enforced, i.e., only relation instances satisfying ic_1 can be stored in the database, the answer for Q is always "no" (i.e., Q produces the empty set). This answer can be obtained without searching the actual database, but by *refuting* the query (formula) using the constraint. We can prove that, Q always answers "no" if and only if the following clauses are unsatisfiable:

$$(D_1 = sales \vee D_1 = service),$$
$$(D_2 = sales \vee D_2 = service),$$
$$(D_3 = sales \vee D_3 = service),$$
$$D_1 \neq D_2, \quad D_1 \neq D_3, \quad D_2 \neq D_3.$$

Indeed, exhaustively testing all the combinations of the (in)equality literals shows that the above clauses are unsatisfiable.

Now, let us look at the problem from another perspective: if we view Q as defining a constraint saying that there do not exist three different departments:

$$ic : \textbf{dept}(D_1, M_1), \textbf{dept}(D_2, M_2), \textbf{dept}(D_3, M_3), D_1 \neq D_2, \quad D_1 \neq D_3,$$
$$D_2 \neq D_3 \rightarrow,$$

we know ic is always true if ic_1 is enforced, because ic_1 logically implies ic. Thus ic is *redundant*.

More interestingly, we can view ic_1 as defining a yes/no–query Q_1 as follows, asking whether there is a department which is neither the "sales" department nor the "service" department:

$$Q_1 = \{\langle\rangle : \textbf{dept}(D, M), D \neq sales, D \neq service\}.$$

It is easy to see that $Q_1 \supseteq Q$ (the result of Q_1 always contains the result of Q on *any* database instance). Intuitively, if there exist three different departments, then one of them must be neither the "sales" department nor the "service" department. □

Later in the paper we prove that the IC-refuting problem is polynomially equivalent to the query containment problem [10, 8] and the constraint redundancy problem [15]. The query containment problem has recently been proved to be Π_2^p-complete [13], and so is the IC-refuting problem. Π_2^p is a class higher than NP in the polynomial structure [5].

More importantly, we give a characterization for a set of implication constraints, such that a much more efficient process, called *units-refutation*, can be used to solve the IC-refuting problem. For this type of constraint sets, the complexity of the IC-refuting problem can be reduced to NP-complete, and even to polynomial in a more practical case.

We give an example to show that for the constraint sets not satisfying our criterion, units-refutation process is not sufficient. But still we show that our results can be used to reduce the complexity. These issues will be addressed starting from section 3, while in section 2 we explain some preliminary concepts.

2   Preliminaries

We assume to have an underlying many sorted first order language. There is a finite set of domains (sorts) $\mathcal{D} = \{D_1, ..., D_d\}$. Any D_i is either *dense and totally ordered* with a transitive and irreflexive ordering predicate $>_{D_i}$, or is just equipped with the ordering predicates $=_{D_i}$ and $\neq_{D_i}$. By overloading notations, we omit the subscripts of these predicates.

An *(in)equality* is a formula in one of the two forms, $(X\ op\ Y)$ or $(X\ op\ b)$, where constant b and variables X and Y are from the same domain, $op \in \{<, \leq, >, \geq, =, \neq\}$. if the domain is dense and totally ordered, or $op \in \{=, \neq\}$ if otherwise.

A *database schema* consists of a number of *relation schemes*, each of which is denoted like $\mathbf{f}(\mathrm{att}_1, ..., \mathrm{att}_n)$, where $\mathbf{f}$ is the *relation name*, n is the *arity*, and att_i's are *attributes*. The domain of att_i is denoted as $Dom(\mathbf{f}[i])$.

A *conjunct* is an atomic formula of the form $\mathbf{f}(s_1, ..., s_n)$, where $\mathbf{f}$ is a relation name of arity n, and each s_i is either a variable or a constant of $Dom(\mathbf{f}[i])$. An *instance* of $\mathbf{f}$ is a subset of $Dom(\mathbf{f}[1]) \times ... \times Dom(\mathbf{f}[n])$. A *database instance* is a set of instances for its relation scheme.

A *query* is a first order formula of the form $\{\langle o_1, ..., o_k \rangle : \exists X_1, ..., \exists X_m[t_1, ..., t_p, c_1, ..., c_q]\}$, where $k \geq 0$, $p \geq 1$, and $q \geq 0$, and

1. $\langle o_1, ..., o_k \rangle$ is called *summary*, where each o_i is either a variable, called *distinguished variable* (dv), or a constant. We define the *type* of the query to be $\langle Dom(o_1), ..., Dom(o_k) \rangle$, where $Dom(o_i)$ is the domain of o_i.
2. X_i is called a *nondistinguished variable* (ndv) which is not a dv.
3. t_i is a conjunct; c_i is an (in)equality; commas between t_i's and c_j's denote logical "and".
4. Every variable (dv or ndv) must occur in some conjunct, or can be (transitively) equated either to a variable appearing in some conjunct or to a constant.

The result of applying a query Q to a database instance Db, denoted as $Q(Db)$, is the set of all the instantiations of the summary such that the query formula is satisfied. We will only consider queries whose (in)equality subformula (if any) is satisfiable. A *yes/no-query* is a query whose summary is $\langle\rangle$. The result of a yes/no-query is either a set containing an empty summary $\{\langle\rangle\}$, or an empty set $\{\}$, the former can be interpreted as answering "yes" while the letter as answering "no". We will also use *union queries*. A union query is of the form $union(Q_1, ..., Q_r)$, where $Q_1, ..., Q_r$ $(r \geq 1)$ are queries of the same type. The result of $union(Q_1, ..., Q_r)$ on a database instance Db is the set union of $Q_i(Db)$'s, for $i = 1, ..., r$. The *containment* between queries (of the same type), denoted as, e.g., $Q_1 \supseteq Q$, means $Q_1(Db) \supseteq Q(Db)$ for any database instances Db. Q is *equivalent* to Q_1, denoted $Q \equiv Q_1$, if $Q \supseteq Q_1$ and $Q_1 \supseteq Q$.

An *implication constraint* (IC) is a formula of the form $t_1, ..., t_p, c_1, ..., c_q \rightarrow$, where $t_1, ..., t_p, c_1, ..., c_q$ is in the same format as the body of a yes/no-query. Its variables are considered universally quantified. We also assume $c_1, ..., c_q$ is satisfiable. A database instance satisfies an IC, if all instantiations of the IC with tuples in the corresponding relation instances make the IC true. A database instance satisfies an IC-base, if it satisfies all the ICs in the base.

Notations. We denote variables by upper case letters, denote relation and attribute names by small case strings in bold face, and denote constants by lower case strings. Some times we write queries and ICs in a shortened form, like $\{\langle O \rangle : F, I\}$ and $F, I \rightarrow$ respectively, in which $\langle O \rangle$ is the summary, F is the conjunct subformula, and I is the (in)equality subformula. For ICs, (disjunctive) clausal forms are also used, for example, $\neg t_1 \vee ... \vee \neg t_p \vee \neg c_1 \vee ... \vee \neg c_q$, or more concisely, $\neg F \vee \neg I$. $\neg I$ is called the (disjunctive) (in)equality subclause.

3   The IC-refuting Problem

Definition 1 (IC-refuting Problem). Given an IC-base $\mathcal{I}_C$, and a yes/no-query Q, the IC-refuting problem is to decide whether Q always produces the empty relation on database instances satisfying $\mathcal{I}_C$, i.e., whether $\mathcal{I}_C \models Q \equiv \{\}$.

Before giving a necessary and sufficient condition for the IC-refuting problem, we need to define a few more notations. First, we call a query $Q = \{\langle O \rangle : F, I\}$ in *normal form*, if there are only distinct occurrences of variables in the subformula $\{\langle O \rangle : F\}$. Q is called in *compressed form* if there are no explicit or implied equalities in I. For example, $\{\langle M \rangle : \mathbf{dept}(sales, M)\}$ is a compressed form query, and it can be rewritten into normal form: $\{\langle M \rangle : \mathbf{dept}(D, M_1), D = sales, M = M_1\}$. The normal and compressed forms for ICs are defined similarly if we view ICs as yes/no-queries. Any query can be (polynomially) rewritten into normal or compressed forms.

Definition 2 (Symbol Mapping). Let Q and Q_1 be two queries of the same type. A symbol mapping [10, 20] $\rho : Q_1 \rightarrow Q$ is a *function* from the set of symbols (variables and constants) of Q_1 to that of Q that satisfies the following conditions:

1) it is an identity on constants;
2) it induces a mapping that maps the summary of Q_1 to that of Q;
3) it induces a mapping from the set of conjuncts of Q_1 to that of Q.

A symbol mapping also induces a mapping on (in)equalities and on queries. For a symbol mapping ρ and a conjunction of (in)equalities I, we write $\rho(I)$ to denote the formula obtained from I, under the mapping induced from ρ. We can similarly define symbol mappings from ICs to yes/no–queries if we view ICs as yes/no–queries. Notice that symbol mappings are purely syntactic, in that we do not take (in)equalities into consideration.

Example 2. Let $Q = \{\langle M \rangle : \mathrm{dept}(D_1, M), \mathrm{dept}(D_2, M), D_1 \neq D_2\}$, and

$$Q_1 = \{\langle M_1 \rangle : \mathrm{dept}(D, M_1), D \neq sales\}.$$

One of the symbol mappings from Q_1 to Q is as follows:

$$\{M_1 \mapsto M, \; D \mapsto D_1\}. \; \square$$

Theorem 3. *Let $\mathcal{I}_C$ be an IC-base, in which all constraints are in normal forms, and $Q = \{\langle \rangle : F, I\}$ be a yes/no–query in compressed form. $\mathcal{I}_C \models Q \equiv \{\}$ if and only if there are constraints $ic_1 : F_1, I_1 \to, \; ..., ic_r : F_r, I_r \to$ in $\mathcal{I}_C$, and symbol mappings:*

$$\rho_{1,1}, ..., \rho_{1,n_1}(n_1 > 0) : \; ic_1 \to Q,$$

$$\vdots$$

$$\rho_{r,1}, ..., \rho_{r,n_r}(n_r > 0) : \; ic_r \to Q$$

such that I implies $\rho_{1,1}(I_1) \vee ... \vee \rho_{1,n_1}(I_1) \vee ... \vee \rho_{r,1}(I_r) \vee ... \vee \rho_{r,n_r}(I_r)$.

Sketch of the proof. Let $\mathcal{I}_C = \{ic_1, ..., ic_r, ic_{r+1}, ..., ic_m\}$, where $ic_1, ..., ic_r$ are the ICs on which symbol mappings to Q can be defined. Let $ic_j = \neg F_j \vee \neg I_j$, for $j = 1, ..., m$, and let $\mathbf{V_Q}$ denote the ndv's of Q, $\mathbf{V_1}, ..., \mathbf{V_m}$ denote the ndv's of $ic_1, ..., ic_m$ respectively.

Logically, $\mathcal{I}_C \models Q \equiv \{\}$ is equivalent to saying that the following formulas are not satisfiable:

$$\exists \mathbf{V_Q}[F(\mathbf{V_Q}), I(\mathbf{V_Q})],$$

$$\forall \mathbf{V_1}[\neg F_1(\mathbf{V_1}) \vee \neg I_1(\mathbf{V_1})],$$

$$\vdots$$

$$\forall \mathbf{V_m}[\neg F_m(\mathbf{V_m}) \vee \neg I_m(\mathbf{V_m})],$$

Expressing the axioms of density and total-orderedness in clausal form, and with all the tautologies of constants, we can thus use the resolution with paramodulation process [3] to get an unsatisfiable set of *(in)equality* clauses. Since all the ICs are in normal form, every possible unification between conjunct literals can be performed and paramodulation is not needed. This leads to the conclusion of the theorem. □

Example 3. Continued from Example 1. There are only three symbol mappings from ic_1 to Q, where we recall that

$ic_1 = \mathbf{dept}(D, M), D \neq sales, D \neq service \to$, and

$Q = \{\langle\rangle : \mathbf{dept}(D_1, M_1), \mathbf{dept}(D_2, M_2), \mathbf{dept}(D_3, M_3), D_1 \neq D_2, D_1 \neq D_3,$
$\quad D_2 \neq D_3\}$.

They are:

$\rho_1 = \{D \mapsto D_1, \ M \mapsto M_1\}$,

$\rho_2 = \{D \mapsto D_2, \ M \mapsto M_2\}$, and

$\rho_3 = \{D \mapsto D_3, \ M \mapsto M_3\}$.

By the above theorem, $\{ic_1\} \models Q \equiv \{\}$ if and only if $(D_1 \neq D_2, \ D_1 \neq D_3, \ D_2 \neq D_3)$ implies $(D_1 \neq sales, D_1 \neq service) \vee (D_2 \neq sales, D_2 \neq service) \vee (D_3 \neq sales, D_3 \neq service)$. □

4 Polynomially Equivalent Problems

In this section, we are going to consider the relationship between the IC-refuting problem and the following problems, and show that they are polynomially equivalent to the IC-refuting problem:

1) the generalized IC-refuting problem,
2) the query containment problem,
3) the generalized query containment problem,
4) the IC redundancy problem.

We will also show that another related problem, namely the (in)equality redundancy problem is polynomially reducible to the IC-refuting problem. The basic observation here is that queries and implication constraints can be viewed as playing complementary roles, and they can be transformed to each other in a certain way.

First we consider the **generalized IC-refuting problem**, in which queries are not necessarily yes/no–queries but may have arbitrary summaries. Solving this problem allows us to find intrinsic inconsistency of the query with respect to the semantics of the database. This is one of the main issues in semantic query optimization and intentional query answering. Formally, the generalized IC-refuting problem is to decide whether $\mathcal{I}_C \models Q \equiv \{\}$, i.e., whether a query Q always produces an empty relation on database instances satisfying an IC-base $\mathcal{I}_C$ (here $\{\}$ should be understood as having the same *type* as Q). The following proposition tells us that this problem is polynomially equivalent to the IC-refuting problem.

Proposition 4. *The generalized IC-refuting problem is polynomially equivalent to the IC-refuting problem.*

Proof. The (polynomial) reduction of the IC-refuting problem to the general IC-refuting problem is obvious. Here we only show the reduction of the other direction. Let $\mathcal{I}_C = \{ic_1, ..., ic_n\}$, and $Q = \{\langle O \rangle : F, I\}$. We prove $\mathcal{I}_C \models Q \equiv \{\}$ if and only if $\mathcal{I}_C \models \{\langle \rangle : F, I\} \equiv \{\}$.

$\mathcal{I}_C \models Q \equiv \{\}$ logically means that the formulas $\exists \mathbf{V}_D \exists \mathbf{V}_N [F, I]$, ic_1, ..., and ic_n are unsatisfiable, where $\mathbf{V}_D$ and $\mathbf{V}_N$ are the dv's and ndv's of Q respectively. This is exactly $\mathcal{I}_C \models \{\langle \rangle : F, I\} \equiv \{\}$. $\square$

Example 4. Consider the query Q in Example 1, asking whether there are three different departments. Let us modify it into a query to list the triplets of different department names, i.e.,

$$Q' = \{\langle D_1, D_2, D_3 \rangle : \mathrm{dept}(D_1, M_1), \mathrm{dept}(D_2, M_2), \mathrm{dept}(D_3, M_3),$$
$$D_1 \neq D_2, D_1 \neq D_3, D_2 \neq D_3\}.$$

Given *any* IC-base $\mathcal{I}_C$, we can see that $\mathcal{I}_C \models Q \equiv \{\}$ if and only if $\mathcal{I}_C \models Q' \equiv \{\}$. Indeed, if there are no three different departments then we can not list any triplet of different departments; and the reverse is also true. $\square$

In the introduction we have seen the relationship between the IC-refuting problem and the query containment problem. We now define a more general notion of query containment problem. Let $Q, Q_1, ..., Q_r$ be queries of the same type. The *query containment problem* is to decide whether $union(Q_1, ..., Q_r) \supseteq Q$. To show the equivalence between this problem and the IC-refuting problem, we first give a theorem on the necessary and sufficient condition of the containment.

Theorem 5. *Let* $Q = \{\langle O \rangle : F, I\}$ *be in compressed from,* $Q_1 = \{\langle O_1 \rangle : F_1, I_1\}$, ..., $Q_r = \{\langle O_r \rangle : F_r, I_r\}$ *be normal form queries of the same type. then* $union(Q_1, ..., Q_r) \supseteq Q$ *if and only if there are* $n_1 + ... + n_r \geq 1$ *symbol mappings:* $\rho_{1,1}, ..., \rho_{1,n_1} : Q_1 \rightarrow Q$, ..., $\rho_{r,1}, ..., \rho_{r,n_r} : Q_r \rightarrow Q$, *such that* I *implies* $\rho_{1,1}(I_1) \vee ... \vee \rho_{1,n_1}(I_1) \vee ... \vee \rho_{r,1}(I_r) \vee ... \vee \rho_{r,n_r}(I_r)$.

The proof is similar to that of Theorem 3, and is omitted here. In [20], we proved a similar theorem where Q is in compressed form, and Q_1, ..., Q_r are reflexive queries that can be in any form.

Proposition 6. *The query containment problem is polynomially equivalent to the IC-refuting problem.*

Proof. First we show the reduction from the query containment problem to the IC-refuting problem. Since it is polynomial to transform a query into normal or compressed forms, we assume $Q = \{\langle O \rangle : F, I\}$ be in compressed from, $Q_1 = \{\langle O_1 \rangle : F_1, I_1\}$, ..., $Q_r = \{\langle O_r \rangle : F_r, I_r\}$ be normal form queries of the same type. From Theorem 3 and Theorem 5 it follows that $union(Q_1, ..., Q_r) \supseteq Q$ if and only if $\{ic_1, ..., ic_r\} \models Q' \equiv \{\}$, where $ic_i = out(O_i), F_i, I_i \rightarrow$ for $i = 1, ..., r)$, and $Q' = \{\langle \rangle : out(O), F, I\}$, where *"out"* is an unused predicate name whose domain specifications correspond to the type of Q.

By the same reasoning we can show the reduction of the IC-refuting problem to the query containment problem. In fact, given an IC-base $\mathcal{I}_C$ consisting of normal form ICs $ic_1 : F_1, I_1 \rightarrow, ..., ic_r : F_r, I_r \rightarrow$, and a compressed yes/no-query Q, $\mathcal{I}_C \models Q \equiv \{\}$ if and only if $union(\{\langle\rangle : F_1, I_1\}, ..., \{\langle\rangle : F_r, I_r\}) \supseteq Q$. □

We can further generalize the containment problem by considering constraints. More specifically, given an IC-base $\mathcal{I}_C$, a union query $union(Q_1, ..., Q_r)$, and a query Q, the **generalized query containment problem** is to decide whether $\mathcal{I}_C \models union(Q_1, ..., Q_r) \supseteq Q$, i.e., whether $union(Q_1, ..., Q_r)(Db) \supseteq Q(Db)$ on any database instance Db satisfying $\mathcal{I}_C$. This generalized problem, however, does not have higher complexity.

Proposition 7. *The generalized query containment problem is polynomially equivalent to the IC-refuting problem.*

Proof. The reduction of the IC-refuting problem to the generalized query containment problem has been shown in the previous proposition. Using a similar reasoning in the proof of the previous proposition, we can prove the reduction of the other direction: given an IC-base $\mathcal{I}_C$ in which all the ICs are in normal form, a compressed query $Q = \{\langle O \rangle : F, I\}$, and normal form queries $Q_1 = \{\langle O_1 \rangle : F_1, I_1\}, ..., Q_r = \{\langle O_r \rangle : F_r, I_r\}$ of the same type, then $\mathcal{I}_C \models union(Q_1, ..., Q_r) \supseteq Q$ if and only if $\mathcal{I}_C \cup \{ic_1, ..., ic_r\} \models Q' \equiv \{\}$, where $ic_i = out(O_i), F_i, I_i \rightarrow$ for $i = 1, ..., r$, and $Q' = \{\langle\rangle : out(O), F, I\}$. Here *"out"* is an unused predicate name whose domain specifications correspond to the type of Q. □

In maintaining an IC-base, when we are to add a new implication constraint to an IC-base, we need to decide whether the candidate constraint is implied by the IC-base. This is a recently investigated issue in [15]. The example in the introduction illustrated the relationship between this problem and the IC-refuting problem. Now we give a more formal statement. Given an IC-base $\mathcal{I}_C$ and an implication constraint ic, the **IC redundancy problem** is to decide whether $\mathcal{I}_C \models ic$, i.e., whether ic is logically implied by the constraints in $\mathcal{I}_C$.

Proposition 8. *The IC redundancy problem is polynomially equivalent to the IC-refuting problem.*

Proof. Here we only give the two reductions and omit the proofs, as they are similar to that of the previous propositions. The reduction of the IC-refuting problem to the IC redundancy problem is: given an IC-base $\mathcal{I}_C$ and a yes/no-query $Q = \{\langle\rangle : F, I\}$, $\mathcal{I}_C \models Q \equiv \{\}$ if and only if $\mathcal{I}_C \models (F, I \rightarrow)$.

The reduction of the IC redundancy problem to the IC-refuting problem is: given an IC-base $\mathcal{I}_C$ and an IC $ic : F, I \rightarrow$, $\mathcal{I}_C \models ic$ if and only if $\mathcal{I}_C \models \{\langle\rangle : F, I\} \equiv \{\}$. □

Another important issue in semantic query optimization is to determine redundant selection (in)equalities. We may want to introduce some redundant (in)equalities, e.g., ones on indexed attributes; we may also want to eliminate some other redundant predicates, e.g., ones across relations. Moreover, removing redundant (in)equalities is needed for deciding whether a join can be removed in the presence of implication and *referential* constraints [9, 2]. Precisely, let $Q = \{\langle O \rangle : F, I, c\}$ be a query in which c is an (in)equality, and $\mathcal{I}_C$

be an IC-base, the **(in)equality redundancy problem** is to decide whether $\mathcal{I}_C \models Q \equiv \{\langle O \rangle : F, I\}$, i.e., Q and $\{\langle O \rangle : F, I\}$ always produce the same answer on any database instances satisfying $\mathcal{I}_C$. Although this problem is not known to be polynomially equivalent to the IC-refuting problem, the proposition below shows that it can be reduced to the IC-refuting problem.

Proposition 9. *The (in)equality redundancy problem is (polynomially) reducible to the IC-refuting problem.*

Proof. Given an IC-base $\mathcal{I}_C$ and a query $Q = \{\langle O \rangle : F, I, c\}$, where c is an (in)equality, $\mathcal{I}_C \models Q \equiv \{\langle O \rangle : F, I\}$ if and only if $\mathcal{I}_C \models Q \supseteq \{\langle O \rangle : F, I\}$, since it is always true that $\mathcal{I}_C \models \{\langle O \rangle : F, I\} \supseteq Q$. Now, we have reduced the (in)equality redundancy problem to the generalized query containment problem, which in turn can be reduced to the IC-refuting problem by Proposition 7. $\square$

5 Units-Refuting IC-Bases

5.1 Units-Refutation

From Theorem 3 in the last section, it is not difficult to see that, if we can identify the situation where we can reduce the complexity of deciding whether I implies $\rho_{1,1}(I_1) \vee ... \vee \rho_{1,n_1}(I_1) \vee ... \vee \rho_{r,1}(I_r) \vee ... \vee \rho_{r,n_r}(I_r)$, then we can reduce the complexity of the IC-refuting problem. This is logically equivalent to deciding whether the set of (in)equality clauses $\{I, \neg\rho_{1,1}(I_1), ..., \neg\rho_{r,n_r}(I_r)\}$ is unsatisfiable.

Definition 10 (Units-Refutation). Given a set of (in)equality clauses $\mathcal{C}_\mathcal{L}$, the *units-refutation* is a process defined as follows: use several single-literal clauses to eliminate a contradictory literal in another clause cl, and replace the resulting clause for cl in $\mathcal{C}_\mathcal{L}$. Repeat the above steps, until an empty clause is obtained or no more literals can be eliminated.

Notice that units-refutation is similar to the "unit resolution" [3], where there are only two parent clauses involved in each resolution step. Here we may use more than one (in)equalities to refute another (in)equality.

Example 5. For $\{(E_1 \neq E_2 \vee T = manager), (T \neq manager \vee S > 50), (E_1 = E_2)\}$, the units-refutation process proceeds as follows:

$$\{(E_1 \neq E_2 \vee T = manager), (T \neq manager \vee S > 50), (E_1 = E_2)\} \Longrightarrow$$
$$\{(T = manager), (T \neq manager \vee S > 50), (E_1 = E_2)\} \Longrightarrow$$
$$\{T = manager, S > 50, E_1 = E_2\}. \square$$

When units-refutation process terminates with an empty clause, the set of clauses is unsatisfiable. Generally speaking, an exponential algorithm is needed to determine an unsatisfiable set of (in)equality clauses. Although units-refutation process is not sufficient for general IC-bases, it only takes polynomial time (with respect to the number of literals in the clause set), since to decide whether a conjunction of (in)equalities is satisfiable is polynomial with respect to the number of literals in the conjunction [15, 19].

Definition 11. An IC-base $\mathcal{I}_C$ is called a units-refuting base if for any yes/no-query $Q = \{\langle\rangle : F, I\}$, if $\mathcal{I}_C \models Q \equiv \{\}$, then there are constraints $ic_1 : F_1, I_1 \rightarrow$, ..., $ic_r : F_r, I_r \rightarrow$, and symbol mappings:

$$\rho_{1,1}, ..., \rho_{1,n_1}(n_1 > 0) : ic_1 \rightarrow Q,$$

$$\vdots$$

$$\rho_{r,1}, ..., \rho_{r,n_r}(n_r > 0) : ic_r \rightarrow Q$$

such that the units-refutation process can be used to obtain an empty clause from $I, \neg\rho_{1,1}(I_1), ..., \neg\rho_{1,n_1}(I_1), ..., \neg\rho_{r,1}(I_r), ..., \neg\rho_{r,n_r}(I_r)$.

Recall theorem 3: when $\mathcal{I}_C \models Q \equiv \{\}$, there always exists constraints $ic_1, ...,$ ic_r and corresponding symbol mappings $\rho_{1,1}, ..., \rho_{1,n_1}, ..., \rho_{r,1}, ..., \rho_{r,n_r}$, such that $I, \neg\rho_{1,1}(I_1), ..., \neg\rho_{1,n_1}(I_1), ..., \neg\rho_{r,1}(I_r), ..., \neg\rho_{r,n_r}(I_r)$ are unsatisfiable. The desired property here for units-refuting bases is that the units-refutation process is *sufficient* to decide whether $I, \neg\rho_{1,1}(I_1), ..., \neg\rho_{1,n_1}(I_1), ..., \neg\rho_{r,1}(I_r), ..., \neg\rho_{r,n_r}(I_r)$ are unsatisfiable or not for any I and any symbol mappings $\rho_{1,1}, ..., \rho_{1,n_1}, ...,$ $\rho_{r,1}, ..., \rho_{r,n_r}$.

Example 6. In Example 3, we used Theorem 3 to show that $\{ic_1\} \models Q \equiv \{\}$ if and only if the following clauses are unsatisfiable:

$(D_1 = sales \vee D_1 = service)$,
$(D_2 = sales \vee D_2 = service)$,
$(D_3 = sales \vee D_3 = service)$,
$D_1 \neq D_2, \quad D_1 \neq D_3, \quad D_2 \neq D_3$.

Theses clauses are indeed unsatisfiable, but the units-refutation process can not get us the empty clause. It is easily seen that we can eliminate no more literals using single-literal clauses $D_1 \neq D_2$, $D_1 \neq D_3$, and $D_2 \neq D_3$. So, $\{ic_1\}$ is not a units-refuting base. □

We will give examples of units-refuting bases after we give a criterion for it. First of all, we want to prove that the complexity of IC-refuting problem for units-refuting bases is NP-complete.

Theorem 12. *For any units-refuting IC-base, the IC-refuting problem is NP-complete.*

Proof. First we prove the problem is NP by showing that the number of symbol mappings needed in the units-refutation process is polynomially bounded. Actually this number is always $\leq 6\times(number\ of\ variables\ and\ constants\ in\ the\ query)^2$, which is the number of all possible (in)equalities that can be built using the symbols in the query. This is so because in the worst case the units-refutation process will produce a single-literal clause from every original (in)equality clause. Now, this number of symbol mappings can be *guessed* polynomially; and by units-refutation process, we can *check* whether they are unsatisfiable also in polynomial time.

The NP-hardness is obvious, since the NP-complete containment problem for *equality queries* [1] can be reduced to it (see the discussion following Theorem 17). □

5.2 Conflicting (In)equalities

In order to find conditions for an IC-base to be units-refuting, we first consider the relationships between a pair of (in)equalities.

Definition 13 (Potentially-Conflicting). Let c_1 and c_2 be two (in)equalities, and c_1' and c_2' be obtained from c_1 and c_2 respectively, by renaming the variables so that c_1' and c_2' have no common variables. Then c_1 and c_2 are called potentially-conflicting (or simply **conflicting**) if there exists a (finite) set of (in)equalities I, such that both $I \cup \{c_1'\}$ and $I \cup \{c_2'\}$ are satisfiable, but $I \cup \{c_1', c_2'\}$ is unsatisfiable.

For example, $X \geq 3$ and $Y = 1$ are conflicting, because $\{X \geq 3, Y = 1, X = Y\}$ is unsatisfiable; but $X \geq 3$ and $Y \neq 5$ are not conflicting. An (in)equality may also be (potentially) conflicting to itself, e.g., $D = sales$ and $D = sales$: after we rename D to D_1 in one of the above literals, we get a pair of conflicting literals, $D = sales$ and $D_1 = sales$.

One important property of a pair of non-conflicting (in)equalities c_1 and c_2 is that $\rho_1(c_1)$ and $\rho_2(c_2)$ is non-conflicting for any symbol mappings ρ_1 and ρ_2, since a symbol mapping can be expressed by a set of equalities. In refuting a query, different instances of ICs may be used, hence we need this property. Also notice that if c_1 and c_2 are not conflicting, then $\{c_1, c_2\}$ is always satisfiable.

It is easy to see that two (in)equalities over different domains are not conflicting. Using the graph-theoretic method and results in [15], we can prove the conflicting relations between any pair of (in)equalities, as listed in Table 1 and Table 2, where Table 1 is for dense and totally ordered domains, and Table 2 is for other domains. Entries marked with "*NC*" means the pair is not conflicting; other non-blank entries specify the conditions for the pair not to be conflicting; all the blank entries indicate the pair is conflicting.

	$X > a$	$X \geq a$	$X = a$	$X \neq a$	$X < a$	$X \leq a$	$X > Y$	$X \geq Y$	$X = Y$	$X \neq Y$
$U > b$	NC	NC	$a > b$	NC	$a > b$	$a > b$				NC
$U \geq b$	NC	NC	$a > b$	$a \neq b$	$a > b$	$a > b$				
$U = b$	$a < b$	$a < b$		$a \neq b$	$a > b$	$a > b$				
$U \neq b$	NC	$a \neq b$	$a \neq b$	NC	NC	$a \neq b$				NC
$U < b$	$a < b$	$a < b$	$a < b$	$a < b$	NC	NC	NC			NC
$U \leq b$	$a < b$	$a < b$	$a < b$	$a \neq b$	NC	NC				
$U > V$										NC
$U \geq V$										
$U = V$										
$U \neq V$	NC			NC	NC		NC			NC

Table 1. Conflict table for dense and totally ordered domains

	$X = a$	$X \neq a$	$X = Y$	$X \neq Y$
$U = b$		$a \neq b$		
$U \neq b$	$a \neq b$	NC		NC
$U = V$				
$U \neq V$			NC	NC

Table 2. Conflict table for other domains

Given an IC-base, we have the set of its (in)equality subclauses $\{\neg I_1, ..., \neg I_n\}$. In this set, a literal is called a *conflicting literal* if it is conflicting with itself or some other literals in the set. A clause which has at most one conflicting literal is called a *single-conflicting* clause. Notice that conflicting literals and single-conflicting clauses are always defined with respect to a specified set of clauses.

Example 7. In the set with one clause $\{(D = sales \vee D = service)\}$, both literals are conflicting literals, because each literal is conflicting with, say, itself and the other literal. Thus the clause is not a single-conflicting clause. $\square$

5.3 Units-Refuting Bases and Implementation

In this subsection we give a sufficient condition for an IC-base to be units-refuting. After that, we will discuss how to use our result to lower the complexity of solving the IC-refuting problem for units-refuting bases, and non-units-refuting bases as well.

First of all, we give some lemmas about properties of single conflicting clauses. Our first lemma tells us that single-conflictingness is preserved under symbol mappings.

Lemma 14. *Let* $\{ic_1 : \neg F_1 \vee \neg I_1, ..., ic_r : \neg F_r \vee \neg I_r\}$ *be a set of ICs. Let* $\rho_{i,1}, ..., \rho_{i,n_i}$ *be symbol mappings on* ic_i *(to some query* Q*), for* $i = 1, ..., r$. *Then* $\neg \rho_{i,j}(I_i)$ $(i = 1, ..., r, j = 1, ..., n_i)$ *is a single-conflicting clause of* $\{\neg \rho_{1,1}(I_1), ..., \neg \rho_{r,n_r}(I_r)\}$, *if* $\neg I_i$ *is a single-conflicting clause in* $\{\neg I_1, ..., \neg I_r\}$.

The following lemma tells us that single-conflictingness is preserved when subset of subclauses are considered.

Lemma 15. *Let $C_{\mathcal{L}} = \{cl_1, ..., cl_n\}$ and $C_{\mathcal{L}}' = \{cl'_{i_1}, ..., cl'_{i_m}\}$ be two sets of (in)equality clauses, such that $1 \leq i_1 < ... < i_m \leq n$, and every cl'_{i_j} is a subclause of cl_{i_j}. Then cl'_{i_j} $(j = 1, ..., m)$ is a single-conflicting clause of $C_{\mathcal{L}}'$, if cl_{i_j} is a single conflicting clause in $C_{\mathcal{L}}$.*

The proofs of the above lemmas are straightforward from the definitions of conflicting literals and single-conflicting clauses, so they are omitted. Our last lemma tells us that after the units-refutation process, if a clause having two or more literals is a single-conflicting clause, then it is always satisfiable together with other clauses.

Lemma 16. *Let $C_{\mathcal{L}1}$ be a set of (in)equalities, and $C_{\mathcal{L}2}$ be a set of multi-literal (in)equality clauses (ones having two or more literals), such that $C_{\mathcal{L}1} \cup \{c_0\}$ is satisfiable for every literal c_0 in $C_{\mathcal{L}2}$. Suppose $C_{\mathcal{L}1} \cup C_{\mathcal{L}2}$ is unsatisfiable. Then no minimal unsatisfiable subset of $C_{\mathcal{L}1} \cup C_{\mathcal{L}2}$ contains a single-conflicting clause of $C_{\mathcal{L}2}$.*

Proof. Let $C_{\mathcal{L}}$ be a minimal unsatisfiable subset of $C_{\mathcal{L}1} \cup C_{\mathcal{L}2}$ and cl be a single-conflicting clause in $C_{\mathcal{L}2}$. Suppose $cl \in C_{\mathcal{L}}$, we construct a contradiction.

Since $C_{\mathcal{L}} - \{cl\}$ is satisfiable, we can form a set C of literals each from a different clause in $C_{\mathcal{L}} - \{cl\}$, such that C is satisfiable. Let c be a non-conflicting literal of cl in $C_{\mathcal{L}2}$. We know $C \cup \{c\}$ is unsatisfiable. Let C_1 be a minimal unsatisfiable subset of $C \cup \{c\}$. C_1 must contain c, and at least one other literal c' from $C_{\mathcal{L}2}$, as $C_{\mathcal{L}1} \cup \{c_0\}$ is satisfiable for every literal c_0 in $C_{\mathcal{L}2}$. Because C_1 is a minimal unsatisfiable set, $C_1 - \{c\}$ and $C_1 - \{c'\}$ are both satisfiable. But since c and c' are not conflicting, we know C_1 is also satisfiable. A contradiction. $\square$

From the above three lemmas, we can easily prove the following theorem, which is one of our main results for units-refuting bases.

Theorem 17. *An IC-base $\mathcal{I}_C$ is units-refuting if, starting with its set of (in)equality subclauses, and by repeatedly determining a single-conflicting clause and deleting it from the set, we can get an empty set.*

As a very special case, if there are only *equalities* in the (in)equality subformulas of the ICs in $\mathcal{I}_C$, then $\mathcal{I}_C$ is units-refuting. The reason is that equalities become $\neq$-inequalities in the disjunctive clauses, and any pair of $\neq$-inequalities are not conflicting. We have a more interesting example as follows.

Example 8. We have already seen the relation scheme **dept** and IC ic_1 in Example 1. The whole database consists the following relational schemes:

dept(dname, manager) and **emp(ename, salary, title)**.

The domain specifications for the attributes are:

1. $Dom(\textbf{ename}) = Dom(\textbf{manager})$;

2. *Dom*(**ename**), *Dom*(**dname**), and *Dom*(**title**) are distinct domains of strings, equipped with $=$ and $\neq$;
3. *Dom*(**salary**) is the set of rational numbers.

The IC-base $\{ic_2, ic_3, ic_4\}$ is a units-refuting base, where ic_2, ic_3, and ic_4 are the following implication constraints:

$$ic_2 : \text{emp}(E_1, S, T), \text{dept}(D, E_2), E_1 = E_2, T \neq manager \to,$$
$$ic_3 : \text{emp}(E, S, T), T = technician, S \geq 30 \to,$$
$$ic_4 : \text{emp}(E, S, T), T = manager, S < 50 \to,$$

where ic_2 says that if an employee is a manager of some department, then his title is "manager". ic_3 says that a "technician" earns less than \$30k. ic_4 says a "manager" earns \$50k or more. The set of the (in)equality subclauses of $\{ic_2, ic_3, ic_4\}$ is as follows:

$$\{cl_2 : (E_1 \neq E_2 \vee T = manager), \ cl_3 : (T \neq technician \vee S < 30),$$
$$cl_4 : (T \neq manager \vee S \geq 50)\}.$$

cl_2 and cl_3 are both single-conflicting clauses, because in cl_2 only $T = manager$ is a conflicting literal, and in cl_3 only $S < 30$ is a conflicting literal. Deleting cl_2 and cl_3, we get $\{cl_4\}$, and cl_4 becomes single-conflicting, because the two (in)equalities of cl_4 are not conflicting literals in $\{cl_4\}$ now.

However, the IC-base $\{ic_1, ic_2, ic_3, ic_4\}$ is not units-refuting, where ic_1 is $\text{dept}(D, M), D \neq sales, D \neq service \to$ in Example 1, because ic_1 is not single-conflicting even without any other clauses. In fact, Example 6 shows that units-refutation is not sufficient to prove $\{ic_1\} \models Q \equiv \{\}$.

In the next section we will show that our IC-base is units-refuting for queries having distinct predicate names. □

Now that we have given a sufficient condition for units-refuting bases, we discuss the issue on implementing an efficient algorithm to solve the IC-refuting problem. In fact, the three lemmas above (Lemma 14, 15, 16) can help us to lower the complexity of the IC-refuting problem even for non-units-refuting bases.

Given an IC-base $\mathcal{I}_C$ and a query Q, first we find out all the symbol mappings from the ICs to Q. In worst case, there are exponentially many symbol mappings. But in practical cases, this number is usually very restricted due to the following factors: 1) only those ICs whose predicate names also appear in the query can be mapped to the query; 2) the number of mappings also depends on the number of times a predicate name appears in the query, and if the query only has distinct predicate names (more discussion in next section), there will be polynomial number of symbol mappings.

Suppose $\mathcal{C}_\mathcal{L} = \{I, cl_1, ..., cl_r\}$ is the set of (in)equalities of Q and the (in)equality subclauses of the ICs after the symbol mappings. We know that $\mathcal{I}_C \models Q \equiv \{\}$ if and only if $\mathcal{C}_\mathcal{L}$ is unsatisfiable. First we do units-refutation on $\mathcal{C}_\mathcal{L}$. Upon termination, we get the updated $\mathcal{C}_\mathcal{L}$.

If $\mathcal{I}_C$ is units-refuting, we can tell at once whether $\mathcal{I}_C \models Q \equiv \{\}$ by looking for the empty clause. If $\mathcal{I}_C$ is not units-refuting, we can repeatedly delete the multi-literal single-conflicting clauses from $C_{\mathcal{L}}$, and do exponential checking only on the remaining clauses.

6 Units-Refuting Bases for DPN-Queries

In practice, we often encounter queries which do not have multiple conjuncts with the same name. We will call such queries *distinct-predicate-name* (DPN) queries. In this section, we are going to discuss the criterion of the units-refuting bases for DPN-queries. In this case, the IC-refuting problem is polynomial, because there are only polynomial number of symbol mappings from the ICs to the query. In fact, given a DPN-query, there is at most one instance of each IC involved in the refutation. So, in searching for single-conflicting clauses, we don't need to consider conflicting literals within the same clause.

Given a set of (in)equality clauses, a literal is called a *extra-conflicting literal* if it is conflicting with a literal in some other clause. A clause which has at most one extra-conflicting literal is called a *single-extra-conflicting* clause. Single-extra-conflicting clauses play a similar role as single-conflicting clauses. In fact, if we replace the phrase "single-conflicting" by "single-extra-conflicting" in Lemma 15 and Lemma 16, the results are still true.

The following lemma and theorem tells us that we can allow some kind of clauses *other than* the single-extra-conflicting clauses and still have a units-refuting base for DPN-queries.

Lemma 18. *Let $C_{\mathcal{L}1}$ be a set of (in)equalities, and $C_{\mathcal{L}2}$ be a set of multi-literal (in)equality clauses, such that $C_{\mathcal{L}1} \cup \{c_0\}$ is satisfiable for every literal c_0 in $C_{\mathcal{L}2}$. Then $C_{\mathcal{L}1} \cup C_{\mathcal{L}2}$ is satisfiable if $C_{\mathcal{L}2}$ has the following property (*):*

Every literal c in $C_{\mathcal{L}2}$ is conflicting with at most one literal in some other clause in $C_{\mathcal{L}2}$.

Proof. We can build a satisfiable set, C, of (in)equalities each from a different clause in $C_{\mathcal{L}2}$. Initially, C contains a literal c from a clause cl of $C_{\mathcal{L}2}$, and we delete cl from $C_{\mathcal{L}2}$. While $C_{\mathcal{L}2}$ is not empty we repeat the following steps:

1. choose a clause from $C_{\mathcal{L}2}$ which has a conflicting literal c' with the last inserted literal of C (if there is no such clause then pick any clause);
2. pick a literal other than c' from the clause, put it into C, and delete the clause from $C_{\mathcal{L}2}$.

It is easy to see that C thus formed consists of literals pairwisely non-conflicting, so $C_{\mathcal{L}1} \cup C$ is satisfiable. Hence $C_{\mathcal{L}1} \cup C_{\mathcal{L}2}$ is satisfiable. $\square$

Theorem 19. *An IC-base $\mathcal{I}_C$ is DPN-units-refuting if, starting with the set of its (in)equality subclauses, and by iteratively determining a single-extra-conflicting clause and deleting it from the set, we can get a set of clauses satisfying the property (*) in Lemma 18.*

Proof. Straightforward from Lemma 18. $\square$

Example 9. Continued from the last example. We show $\{ic_1, ic_2, ic_3, ic_4\}$ is DPN-units-refuting base. Since a single-conflicting clause is also a single-extra-conflicting clause, so by Theorem 19, we get $\{(D = sales \lor D = service)\}$ after deleting cl_2, cl_3, and cl_4. Obviously this set satisfies the property (*) of Lemma 18, as it has only one clause.

In fact, $\{ic_1, ic_2, ic_3, ic_4, ic_5\}$ is still a DPN-units-refuting IC-base, in which we have another constraint ic_5 telling that no employee is the manager of both the "sales" department and the "service" department:

$$ic_5 : \text{dept}(D_1, M_1), \text{dept}(D_2, M_2), D_1 = sales, D_2 = service, M_1 = M_2 \rightarrow,$$

because in $\{(D = sales \lor D = service), (D_1 \neq sales \lor D_2 \neq service \lor M_1 \neq M_2)\}$ every literal is conflicting with at most one extra-literal. $\square$

If an IC-base is not a DPN-units-refuting base, the implementation principle discussed at the end of the previous section is still applicable: after the units-refutation process, a multi-literal single-extra-conflicting clause can not be in any minimal unsatisfiable set of clauses. Hence we can delete the multi-literal single-extra-conflicting clauses, and do the exponential checking only on the remaining clauses.

7 Conclusion and Future Work

In this paper we have identified the IC-refuting problem as a central problem in reasoning with implication constraints. Many other important problems are shown to be polynomially equivalent to it. We also gave criteria for designing IC-bases such that the units-refutation process can be used to solve the IC-refuting problem. For this type of IC-bases, the complexity of the IC-refuting problem can be reduced from Π_2^p-complete to NP-complete, and even to polynomial in a more practical case. For IC-bases not totally satisfying our characterization, we can use our lemmas to reduce the complexity. Here we suggest two future directions in continuing this research, one is to dynamically decide single-conflicting clauses, i.e., to decide single-conflicting clauses with respect to given queries, in this way we are expecting to be able to further reduce the number of multi-literal clauses we have to check exponentially; the other direction is to incorporate other types of semantic constraints, e.g., referential constraints, along with the implication constraints.

References

1. Chandra,A.K., and Merlin,P.M. Optimal implementation of conjunctive queries in relational databases. Proc. ACM STOC, 77-90, 1976.
2. Chakravarthy,U.S., Grant,J. and Minker, j., Logic-Based Approach To Semantic Query Optimization, ACM TODS, Vol.15, 1990, pp 162-207.
3. C-L Chang and R. C. Lee, Symbolic Logic and Mechanical Theorem Proving. Academic Press, 1973.

4. C. Elkan, Independence of Logic Database Queries and Updates, Proc. of 9th ACM Symp. on PODS, pp 154-160, 1990.

5. C. Garey M. and Johnson D.S., Computers and Intractability: A Guide to the theory of NP-completeness. W.Freeman and Co., San Francisco, 1979.

6. J. Han, Constraint-Based Reasoning in Deductive Databases. Proc. of 7th Data Engineering, 1991, pp 257-265.

7. M.M. Hammer and S.B. Zdonik. Knowlgy Based Query Processing. Proc. 6th VLDB, 1980, pp 137-147.

8. Kanellakis,P.C., Kuper,G.M., and Revesz,P.Z. Constraint Query Languages, Proc. of 9th ACM Symp. on PODS, pp 288-298, 1990.

9. J.J. King. QUIST: A System for Semantic Query Optimization in in Relational Databases. Proc. 7th VLDB, 1981, pp 510-517.

10. Klug,A.,On Conjunctive Queries Containing Inequalities, JACM vol 35:1,pp 147-160,1988.

11. S. Lee and J. Han, Semantic Query Optimization in Recursive Databases. Proc. of 4th Data Engineering, 1988, pp 444-451.

12. A. Levy and Y. Sagiv, Constraints and Redundancy in Datalog. Proc. of 11th ACM Symp. on PODS, pp 67-80, 1992.

13. R. van der Meyden, The Complexity of Querying Infinite Data about Linearly Ordered Domains, Proc. of the 11th ACM Symp. on PODS, pp331-345, 1992.

14. A. Motro, Using Integrity Constraints to Provide Intentional Answers to Relational Queries. Proc. 15th VLDB, 1989, pp 237-246.

15. Ozsoyoglu,Z.M., Shenoy S.T., Ishakbeyoglu N.S., On The Maintenance of Semantic Integrity Constraints, 1990.

16. H.H. Pang, H.J. Lu, and B.C. Ooi, An Efficient Query Optimization Algorithm. Proc. 7th Data Engineering, 1991, pp 326-335.

17. A. Pirotte and D. Roelants, Constraints for Improving the Generation of Intentional Answers in a Deductive Database. Proc. 5th Data Engineering, 1989, pp 652-659.

18. S.T. Shenoy and Z.M. Ozsoyoglu, A System for Semantic Query Optimization. Proc. SIGMOD, 1987.

19. J.Ullman. Principles of Database and Knowledge-Base systems, volume II., Computer Science Press, 1989.

20. Xubo Zhang and Z.M.Ozsoyoglu, The Containment and Minimization of Inequality Queries. Tec. Report, CES 92-18, CWRU, 1992

Bottom-Up Query Evaluation with Partially Ordered Defaults*

Stefan Brass and Udo W. Lipeck

Institut für Informatik, Universität Hannover
Lange Laube 22, D-30159 Hannover, Fed. Rep. Germany
E-mail: (sb|ul)@informatik.uni-hannover.de

Abstract. We propose a query-evaluation algorithm for database specifications consisting of overridable rules (defaults) and non-overridable
rules (axioms). Both kinds of rules may contain disjunctions. Preferences
among the defaults are given by a partial order which corresponds to a
subclass relationship allowing multiple inheritance. We use a bottom-
up theorem proving procedure. It is applied to the set of (disjunctively)
assumed default instances which essentially can again be computed by
bottom-up evaluation. Our approach has two main advantages: First, it
gives a simple foundation for bottom-up evaluation in the presence of
defaults; this can be taken as a basis for different optimizations. Second,
in contrast to other deduction algorithms, it is able to handle partially
ordered defaults with a skeptical / minimal model semantics.

1 Introduction

Our goal is to extend deductive databases [14, 10, 20] by overridable rules in
order to increase the reusability of such specifications. This closely corresponds
to inheritance in object-oriented approaches. Viewing the object classes as the
modules of the specification, it seems clear that it should be possible to define
rules inside the classes (and not on top of them as in some other approaches).
But then the rules become subject of inheritance and can be overridden by more
specific information in the subclasses.

So the overridable rules are nothing else than defaults which are assumed as
long as no contradicting information is known. The defaults of this type (called
supernormal defaults) were studied in [21, 5, 8, 3, 13].

Basically, the subclass relation corresponds to the priorities between the defaults (defaults in subclasses override defaults in superclasses). We allow multiple
inheritance, so the priority relation can be an arbitrary partial order. Partially
ordered defaults were investigated in [8, 6, 23, 3, 1].

This is also closely related to ordered logic programming [17] (which depends much more on the distinction between head and body of a rule than
our approach), F-logic [16] (which inherits values and not rules), terminological

---

* This work was partially supported by the CEC under the ESPRIT Working
Group 6071 IS-CORE (Information Systems — COrrectness and REusability).

reasoning [1] and inheritance networks in artificial intelligence [24] (which are concerned with the classification of objects).

Finally, we allow disjunctive information [18]. There are quite a lot of applications for this, e.g. legal rules, ambiguity in natural-language understanding, or non-unique explanations for observed symptoms. Furthermore, multiple inheritance is a source of incomplete information, if conflicting values are inherited.

Example 1. Suppose we have a database about persons related in some way to a university. So there should be an object class for persons with subclasses for employees and for students.

Now we want to store the addresses of the persons: Every person has a private address, employees have an office address in addition, and students have an address in the town of the university (semester address) besides their private (home) address. We treat these attributes as object-local predicates, and enforce the single-valuedness with additional constraints (see below).

So persons can have more than one address, but we need a unique mailing address. This is determined by a (query) method *mail_addr*. For general persons the mailing address is the private address, for employees the office address, and for students the semester address. We introduce also a method *age* to determine the approximate age of a person from his/her year of birth. There are three instances: the student *cathy*, the employee *alex*, and *bob*, who is a teaching assistent, i.e. an employee and a student.

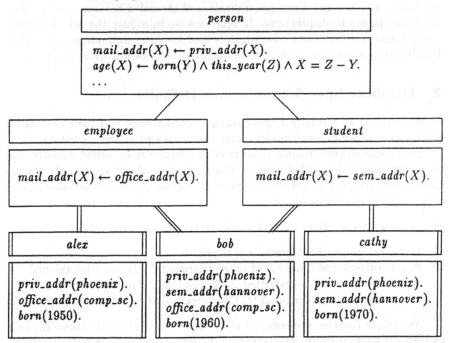

Given this specification, the query *alex.mail_addr(X)* should be answered with $X = comp\_sc$, and *cathy*'s mailing address is *hannover*. But *bob* who is employee and student, poses a problem. It depends on the organisation of the institute whether it is better to send his post to his office address or his semester address. To keep as much information as possible, we can give the disjunctive answer $X = comp\_sc \lor X = hannover$. □

The purpose of this paper is to lay the foundations of query evaluation for such specifications. We do this by generalizing the usual bottom-up approach, as we already did in [7] for specifications without priorities. In contrast to [7], we also make the set of assumed default instances explicit, this should make the approach much easier to understand. In [22], an algorithm was proposed for query evaluation in disjunctive databases with stratified negation. Our approach is much more general with respect to the defaults, but [22] is goal-directed.

With certain simplifications, our algorithm works as follows: First, we compute default instances or combinations thereof which cannot be assumed (conflicts). Second, we in effect add their complement to the original rules, i.e. we determine which default instances have to be assumed. The critical and most interesting point about this is of course the handling of disjunctive conflicts respecting the priorities. This may result in disjunctively assumed default instances. Third, we only have to draw conclusions from this enlarged set of formulas by usual bottom-up evaluation or appropriate optimizations.

Our paper is structured as follows: In section 2 we define database specifications and their declarative semantics. In section 3 we review positive hyperresolution, which is the direct generalization of the naive bottom-up evaluation for Horn clauses to disjunctions. In section 4 we introduce the set of disjunctively assumed default instances, which is used for query evaluation in section 5. Finally, we give a short summary and outline directions for future work.

2 Database Specifications with Defaults

In this section, we formally define database specifications and their declarative semantics in order to measure the correctness of the proposed algorithm.

Such a specification mainly consists of overridable rules, called defaults, and non-overridable rules, called axioms. The given facts about specific objects are usually non-overridable, but the designer can declare any rule as non-overridable (e.g. integrity constraints).

Definition 1 (Specification). A database specification consists of

1. Σ, a signature without function symbols,
2. Φ, a consistent and finite set of range-restricted Σ-clauses (the axioms),
3. Δ, a finite set of range-restricted Σ-clauses (the defaults),
4. $\sqsubseteq$, a strict partial order on Δ ($\delta_1 \sqsubseteq \delta_2$ means that δ_1 is more important).

We exclude function symbols and allow only range-restricted clauses in order to keep the answers finite. The signature, however, may contain infinitely many constants (strings, integers, etc.). The priority relation $\sqsubseteq$ directly corresponds to the subclass relation.

Example 2. To simplify the presentation, we make the implicit object arguments of example 1 explicit using the variable *Self* to denote the object of interest. So the rules in the *person*-class are transformed into:

$$mail\_addr(Self, X) \leftarrow priv\_addr(Self, X) \wedge person(Self). \tag{1}$$

$$age(Self, X) \leftarrow born(Self, Y) \wedge this\_year(Z) \wedge X = Z - Y$$
$$\wedge person(Self). \tag{2}$$

These rules are treated as overridable, and therefore become elements of Δ. The rules about employees and students result in the following defaults:

$$mail\_addr(Self, X) \leftarrow office\_addr(Self, X) \wedge employee(Self). \tag{3}$$

$$mail\_addr(Self, X) \leftarrow sem\_addr(Self, X) \wedge student(Self). \tag{4}$$

Since these rules were specified in subclasses of *person*, they take precedence over rules defined there. So we have (3) $\sqsubset$ (1), (4) $\sqsubset$ (1), (3) $\sqsubset$ (2), and (4) $\sqsubset$ (2). However, rule (2) does not conflict with rules (3) and (4), so it is not overridden. Note also that rules (3) and (4) are uncomparable with respect to $\sqsubset$.

Now let us consider the axioms. First, the facts about specific objects are directly translated, e.g. *priv_addr(alex, phoenix)*. Then we need a type theory derived from the subclass / instance relationships:

employee(alex).	*student(bob).*
employee(bob).	*student(cathy).*
person(Self) ← *employee(Self).*	*person(Self)* ← *student(Self).*

Since *mail_addr* should be a function, we need also a key constraint:

$$false \leftarrow mail\_addr(Self, X) \wedge mail\_addr(Self, Y) \wedge X \neq Y. \tag{5}$$

I.e. it is impossible that an object has two distinct mailing addresses (the same constraint is also needed for *age*).

As usual in databases, we adopt the closed world assumption, formalized by means of negation defaults for all predicates, e.g. $\neg priv\_addr(Self, X)$. We treat these implicit defaults as weaker than all of the above ones. □

Now we have to define the intended models of such a specification. Of course, they should be Σ-Herbrand models of Φ, and they should satisfy as many of the defaults Δ as possible (respecting their priorities $\sqsubset$). We formalize the satisfaction of defaults by means of a preference relation $\prec_{(\Delta, \sqsubset)}$ on the models ($I_0 \prec_{(\Delta, \sqsubset)} I$ means that I_0 is preferable to I, so the minimal models are the most preferable ones). But first note that the default rules themselves are not the units of satisfaction, but their instances are:

Definition 2 (Default Instances).

1. $\Delta^* := \{\delta\theta \mid \delta \in \Delta, \theta \text{ is a ground substitution for } \delta\}.$

2. The priority relation $\sqsubseteq$ is extended to Δ^* by: $\delta_1\theta_1 \sqsubseteq \delta_2\theta_2 :\Longleftrightarrow \delta_1 \sqsubseteq \delta_2$.
(This works only if no element of Δ^* is an instance of two defaults in Δ. Simply add $\lor false$ etc. to make them syntactically different.)
3. $\Delta^\lor := \{\delta_1 \lor \cdots \lor \delta_n \mid \delta_i \in \Delta^*, n \in \mathbb{N}\}$.

In the following, we refer to the elements of Δ^* also as "defaults". In fact, one can view Δ as a mere shorthand for denoting Δ^*.

Definition 3 (Satisfied Default Instances). Given a Herbrand interpretation I, we write $\Delta^*(I) := \{\delta \in \Delta^* \mid I \models \delta\}$ for the set of valid default instances.

Now suppose for a moment that there are no priorities specified, i.e. all defaults are of equal importance. Then obviously a model is the better, the more default instances it satisfies, so we would define

$$I_0 \prec_\Delta I :\Longleftrightarrow \Delta^*(I_0) \supset \Delta^*(I).$$

In the usual case of negation defaults, this condition is equivalent to $I_0 \subset I$, which was the historical reason for calling the most preferable models "minimal".

Next assume that the priority relation $\sqsubseteq$ is not an arbitrary partial order, but given by priority levels ℓ: $\delta_1 \sqsubseteq \delta_2 :\Longleftrightarrow \ell(\delta_1) < \ell(\delta_2)$. This corresponds to the stratification levels in stratified databases. Now a model I_0 is of course still better than I iff it satisfies uniformly more defaults than I ($I_0 \prec_\Delta I$), but it is also better if it satisfies a more important default in place of a less important one. So if we know a default δ_0 which is satisfied by I_0, but not by I, we need no further restriction on the (strictly) less important defaults.

If $\sqsubseteq$ is an arbitrary partial order, a single δ_0 is no longer sufficient to delimit the less important defaults. Instead, we need a set Δ_0. Then, $I_0 \prec_{(\Delta,\sqsubseteq)} I$ iff we can construct the following situation:

Δ^* :

no restriction	$\Big\}$ less important than Δ_0
$I_0 \models \delta,\ I \not\models \delta$	$\Big\}$ Δ_0
$I_0 \models \delta \iff I \models \delta$	

Definition 4 (Less Important Defaults). Given $\Delta_0 \subseteq \Delta^*$, we write $\Delta_0^\sqsupset := \{\delta \in \Delta^* \mid \delta_0 \sqsubset \delta$ for at least one $\delta_0 \in \Delta_0\}$ for the set of less important defaults.

Definition 5 (Preferred Model). $I_0 \prec_{(\Delta,\sqsubseteq)} I$ iff there is $\Delta_0 \subseteq \Delta^*$, $\Delta_0 \neq \emptyset$ s.t.

1. For every $\delta_0 \in \Delta_0$ holds $I_0 \models \delta_0$ and $I \not\models \delta_0$.
2. For every $\delta \in \Delta^* - (\Delta_0 \cup \Delta_0^\sqsupset)$ holds: $I_0 \models \delta \iff I \models \delta$.

It can be shown that $\prec_{(\Delta,\sqsubseteq)}$ is transitive and irreflexive, and "well-founded" in the sense that every model is minored by a minimal one [6].

Definition 6 (Correct Answer). Let a specification $\langle \Sigma, \Phi, \Delta, \sqsubset \rangle$ be given.

1. A Σ-Herbrand interpretation I is an intended model of this specification iff it is a model of Φ and there is no other model I_0 of Φ with $I_0 \prec_{(\Delta, \sqsubset)} I$.
2. A formula ψ is a consequence of this specification ($\Phi \mathrel{\vphantom{|}\vdash}_{(\Delta, \sqsubset)} \psi$) iff ψ is true in all intended models.
3. A set $\{\theta_1, \ldots, \theta_k\}$ of substitutions for the result variables of a query ψ, usually written as $\theta_1 \vee \cdots \vee \theta_k$, is a correct answer iff $\Phi \mathrel{\vphantom{|}\vdash}_{(\Delta, \sqsubset)} \psi\theta_1 \vee \cdots \vee \psi\theta_k$ and no proper subset of $\{\theta_1, \ldots, \theta_k\}$ has this property.

3 Bottom-Up Evaluation with General Clauses

Since we have to work with disjunctions, either because of disjunctive rules or because of conflicting defaults, we need a generalization of the usual bottom-up derivation procedure. This is known as positive hyperresolution [11] and is also used in disjunctive logic programming [18]. In [7] we have shown that it can be implemented in a set-oriented way by means of database techniques like operations on nested relations.

Horn-clauses are usually evaluated by inserting matching facts for the body literals and deriving the fact corresponding to the head literal, e.g.:

$$p(a)$$
$$\uparrow$$
$$\boxed{p(X) \leftarrow q_1(X) \wedge q_2(X, Y).}$$
$$\uparrow \qquad \uparrow$$
$$q_1(a) \qquad q_2(a, b)$$

Now the idea for the generalization is to work with "disjunctive facts" (positive ground clauses) instead of simple facts (positive ground literals). So each of the facts matching the body literals has a "disjunctive context". Then the result of applying the rule is the disjunction of the facts corresponding to the head literals and the facts contained in the disjunctive contexts:

$$p(a) \vee p(b) \vee r(c) \longleftarrow$$
$$\uparrow \qquad \uparrow$$
$$\boxed{p(X) \vee p(Y) \leftarrow q_1(X) \wedge q_2(X, Y).}$$
$$\uparrow \qquad \uparrow$$
$$q_1(a) \qquad q_2(a, b) \vee r(c) \longrightarrow$$

To formally define positive hyperresolution, we only have to modify the usual "direct consequence" operator T_Φ. To simplify the notation, we identify a disjunctive fact $d = \lambda_1 \vee \cdots \vee \lambda_n$ with the set $\{\lambda_1, \ldots, \lambda_n\}$ and assume that the rules are written with positive literals only (e.g. $p \vee q \leftarrow r$ instead of $p \leftarrow \neg q \wedge r$).

Definition 7 (Derivable Facts).

1. $T_\Phi(\mathcal{D}) := \mathcal{D} \cup \{d \mid$ there is $\hat\lambda_1 \vee \cdots \vee \hat\lambda_n \leftarrow \lambda_1 \wedge \cdots \wedge \lambda_m \in \Phi^*$
   and $d_1, \ldots, d_m \in \mathcal{D}$ with $\lambda_i \in d_i$ $(i = 1, \ldots, m)$
   such that $d = \{\hat\lambda_1, \ldots, \hat\lambda_n\} \cup \bigcup_{i=1}^m (d_i - \{\lambda_i\})\}$.
2. Let $H_0(\Phi)$ be the least fixpoint of T_Φ, i.e. $T_\Phi^n(\emptyset)$ s.t. $T_\Phi^{n+1}(\emptyset) = T_\Phi^n(\emptyset)$.
3. Then let $H(\Phi)$ denote the set of minimal disjunctions from $H_0(\Phi)$ (i.e. no subdisjunction is also contained in $H_0(\Phi)$).

Such a fixpoint is reached after a finite number of iterations since the derived disjunctive facts can contain only constants explicitly appearing in Φ. Then we have derived all minimal disjunctive facts which are implied by Φ. This is the soundness and completeness:

Lemma 8. $H(\Phi) = \{d \text{ positive ground clause} \mid \Phi \vdash d, \Phi \not\vdash d' \text{ for every } d' \subset d\}$.

In [11] an optimization is given to avoid the need to split a disjunctive fact with n literals in n possible ways into "active literal and context". In fact, for range-restricted clauses this splitting can be done in a unique way [4]. Goal-directed versions of positive hyperresolution are investigated in [12, 22].

4 The Database Completion

In this section, we define a set $comp_{(\Delta, \sqsubset)}(\Phi)$ such that

$$\Phi \vdash_{(\Delta, \sqsubset)} \psi \iff comp_{(\Delta, \sqsubset)}(\Phi) \vdash \psi.$$

For special cases (namely negation defaults for minimizing predicate extensions), such database completions are known from the literature, e.g. the ECWA [15]. But on the one hand, this was not intended to be directly used for query evaluation, therefore no emphasis was laid on the exclusion of unnecessary formulas — $comp_{(\Delta, \emptyset)}(\Phi)$ is a strict subset of the ECWA, and much smaller. On the other hand, our approach can be directly generalized to priorities and even partially ordered defaults.

Our database completion is defined in terms of conflicts. Conflicts formalize which defaults cannot be assumed. For instance, if $\Phi \vdash \neg\delta$, then $\{\delta\}$ is a conflict. But in general, we also have to consider sets of defaults which cannot be assumed together:

Definition 9 (Conflict). A conflict is a set $\Gamma \subseteq \Delta^*$ of default instances such that $\Phi \cup \Gamma$ is inconsistent and Γ is $\subseteq$-minimal with this property.

The minimality ensures that no default instances are contained in a conflict without need. So, if again $\Phi \vdash \neg\delta$, then $\{\delta, \delta'\}$ should be no conflict, because $\{\delta\}$ is sufficient. Note that the set of conflicts is finite because it can contain only constants explicitly appearing in $\Phi \cup \Delta$.

Example 3. If a rule is overridden, there is a conflict between the inherited and the new version. For instance, in example 2, the following instances of the defaults (1) and (3) form a conflict:

$$mail\_addr(alex, phoenix) \leftarrow priv\_addr(alex, phoenix) \wedge person(alex).$$
$$mail\_addr(alex, comp\_sc) \leftarrow office\_addr(alex, comp\_sc) \wedge employee(alex).$$

The axioms entail that the preconditions of the two rules are satisfied, but two mailing addresses would be inconsistent with the key constraint (5). Here we will use the priority between the defaults to resolve the conflict: the second default instance is assumed.

But there are also conflicts where both defaults are of equal importance, e.g. for the teaching assistant *bob*:

$$mail\_addr(bob, comp\_sc) \leftarrow office\_addr(bob, comp\_sc) \wedge employee(bob).$$
$$mail\_addr(bob, hannover) \leftarrow sem\_addr(bob, hannover) \wedge student(bob).$$

In this case we will conclude the disjunction of the two. □

Now we know the defaults or combinations of defaults which cannot be assumed. Of course, we need the defaults or disjunctions of defaults which can be assumed. Two cases are clear:

1. If $\delta \in \Delta^*$ does not appear in any conflict, we can of course assume it unconditionally. Every minimal model has to satisfy it since it is consistent with any set of already assumed defaults.
2. If, on the other hand, $\{\delta\}$ forms a conflict by itself, no model of Φ can satisfy it, so it is false in all minimal models and we cannot assume it.

Now let us consider the more difficult cases where defaults are mutually exclusive. We assume first that there are no priorities specified, i.e. $\sqsubset = \emptyset$.

So let $\delta_0 \in \Delta^*$ be a default. We call a conflict Γ relevant to δ_0 iff $\delta_0 \in \Gamma$. So let $\{\Gamma_1, \ldots, \Gamma_n\}$ be the set of conflicts relevant to δ_0 and let $\Gamma_i = \{\delta_0, \delta_{i,1}, \ldots, \delta_{i,m_i}\}$. Let I be any minimal model. If I does not satisfy δ_0, the minimality ensures that there cannot be any model satisfying this default in addition to those satisfied by I. But this means that δ_0 was just the missing part to complete a conflict:

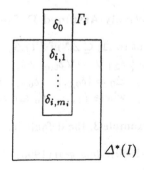

So all minimal models have to satisfy the following formula:

$$\delta_0 \vee (\delta_{1,1} \wedge \cdots \wedge \delta_{1,m_1}) \vee \cdots \vee (\delta_{n,1} \wedge \cdots \wedge \delta_{n,m_n}). \tag{6}$$

Conversely, if a model I of Φ satisfies (6), there can be no preferable model satisfying δ_0 in (proper) addition to the defaults valid in I (because it would complete a conflict). Therefore, if we now let δ_0 range over all default instances, and construct the formulas corresponding to (6), every model of this set must be a minimal model of Φ.

Now the set of disjunctively assumed defaults consists of (6) in clausal form:

$$comp_{(\Delta,\sqsubseteq)}(\Phi) := \Phi \cup \{ \delta_0 \vee \delta_1 \vee \cdots \vee \delta_n \mid \delta_0 \in \Delta^*, \; \delta_i \in \Gamma_i - \{\delta_0\} \; (1 \leq i \leq n)$$
$$\text{where } \Gamma_1, \ldots, \Gamma_n \text{ are all conflicts}$$
$$\text{relevant to } \delta_0 \}.$$

There are again the two important special cases: If δ_0 does not appear in any conflict, $\delta_0 \in comp_{(\Delta,\sqsubseteq)}(\Phi)$ holds (take $n = 0$). If $\Gamma_1 := \{\delta_0\}$ is a conflict, the condition cannot be satisfied (because there is no δ_1), so δ_0 is not assumed.

Let us now consider priorities, but first only the case where $\sqsubseteq$ is given by a level mapping ℓ, i.e. $\delta_1 \sqsubseteq \delta_2 \iff \ell(\delta_1) < \ell(\delta_2)$. As before, we can conclude that if δ_0 is not satisfied by a minimal model I, then $\Delta^*(I) \cup \{\delta_0\}$ contains a conflict. But in fact we know more, namely that already

$$(\Delta^*(I) - \{\delta_0\}^{\sqsupset}) \cup \{\delta_0\}$$

contains a conflict: If there were a model I_0 satisfying δ_0 in addition to the defaults satisfied by I and having the same or greater importance than δ_0, then I_0 would be preferable. But this is impossible since I is minimal. So we know that δ_0 has to complete a conflict which contains only defaults of the same or greater importance than δ_0. The other conflicts can simply be ignored when we construct the disjunctively assumed defaults. Intuitively we solve such conflicts in favour of the defaults of greater importance (including δ_0).

So all we have to do is to adapt our notion of "relevance": A conflict Γ is relevant to δ_0 iff $\delta_0 \in \Gamma$ and $\Gamma \subseteq \Delta^* - \{\delta_0\}^{\sqsupset}$.

Now we allow $\sqsubseteq$ to be an arbitrary partial order. As suggested by the definition of minimal model, it no longer suffices to look only at a single default δ_0 when constructing the disjunctions (but see subsection 5.3):

Definition 10 (Disjunctively Assumed Defaults).

1. A conflict Γ is relevant to $\Delta_0 \subseteq \Delta^*$ iff $\Gamma \cap \Delta_0 \neq \emptyset$ and $\Gamma \subseteq (\Delta^* - \Delta_0^{\sqsupset}) \cup \Delta_0$.
2. $comp_{(\Delta,\sqsubseteq)}(\Phi) := \Phi \cup \{ \delta_{0,1} \vee \cdots \vee \delta_{0,m} \vee \delta_1 \vee \cdots \vee \delta_n \in \Delta^{\vee} \mid$
$$\Delta_0 = \{\delta_{0,1}, \ldots, \delta_{0,m}\} \neq \emptyset, \; \delta_i \in \Gamma_i - \Delta_0 \; (1 \leq i \leq n)$$
$$\text{where } \Gamma_1, \ldots, \Gamma_n \text{ are all conflicts relevant to } \Delta_0 \}.$$

Example 4. Continuing example 3, the default instance

$$age(bob, 33) \leftarrow born(bob, 1960) \wedge this\_year(1993) \wedge 33 = 1993 - 1960 \wedge person(bob)$$

can be assumed unconditionally ($n = 0$), because it is not contained in any conflict. The default instance

$$mail\_addr(alex, comp\_sc) \leftarrow office\_addr(alex, comp\_sc) \wedge employee(alex)$$

can also be assumed directly because the only conflict in which it appears is one with a default of less importance, so it is ignored. A conflict of two uncomparable defaults was

$$mail\_addr(bob, comp\_sc) \leftarrow office\_addr(bob, comp\_sc) \wedge employee(bob).$$
$$mail\_addr(bob, hannover) \leftarrow sem\_addr(bob, hannover) \wedge student(bob).$$

Both defaults are also contained in a conflict with the *priv_addr*-default for general persons, but this is again ignored. So, no matter which default we choose as δ_0, the other one is disjunctively added as δ_1, and we assume the disjunction of the two. This is the reason for the disjunctive answer $X = comp\_sc \vee X = hannover$ if we ask for the mailing address of *bob*. □

Finally, we formally prove that the models of $comp_{(\Delta,\sqsubset)}(\Phi)$ are exactly the minimal models of Φ, i.e. the intended models of the specification:

Theorem 11. $I \models comp_{(\Delta,\sqsubset)}(\Phi) \iff I$ *is a minimal model of* Φ.

Proof. $\Longleftarrow$: Let I be a minimal model, but assume that there is $\delta_{0,1} \vee \cdots \vee \delta_{0,m} \vee \delta_1 \vee \cdots \vee \delta_n \in comp_{(\Delta,\sqsubset)}(\Phi)$ with $I \not\models \delta_{0,j}$ $(1 \leq j \leq m)$, and $I \not\models \delta_i$ $(1 \leq i \leq n)$. Let $\Delta_0 := \{\delta_{0,1}, \ldots, \delta_{0,m}\}$. Because of the minimality of I, there is no model of Φ satisfying $(\Delta^*(I) - \Delta_0^{\rightarrow}) \cup \Delta_0$ (any such model would be $\prec_{(\Delta,\sqsubset)}$-preferable to I). Let Γ be a $\subseteq$-minimal subset such that $\Phi \cup \Gamma$ is inconsistent (so Γ is a conflict). Since I satisfies the other defaults, we have $\Gamma \cap \Delta_0 \neq \emptyset$. So Γ is one of the Γ_i $(1 \leq i \leq n)$ used in constructing the disjunction in question. But now on the one hand, $\Gamma - \Delta_0$ is satisfied in I by construction, on the other hand, one of the δ_i must be contained in $\Gamma - \Delta_0$, and $I \not\models \delta_i$. This is a contradiction.

$\Longrightarrow$: Let $I \models comp_{(\Delta,\sqsubset)}(\Phi)$, but assume that there is $I_0 \models \Phi$ with $I_0 \prec_{(\Delta,\sqsubset)} I$, i.e. there is $\Delta_0 = \{\delta_{0,1}, \ldots, \delta_{0,m}\}$ with the properties of definition 5, in particular $I \not\models \delta_{0,j}$ for $j = 1, \ldots, m$. Let $\Gamma_1, \ldots, \Gamma_n$ be all conflicts relevant to Δ_0. Since $\Phi \cup (\Delta^*(I) - \Delta_0^{\rightarrow}) \cup \Delta_0$ is consistent (I_0 is a model), it follows that $\Gamma_i \not\subseteq (\Delta^*(I) - \Delta_0^{\rightarrow}) \cup \Delta_0$. So for $i = 1, \ldots, n$ there is $\delta_i \in \Gamma_i$ with $\delta_i \notin (\Delta^*(I) - \Delta_0^{\rightarrow})$ and $\delta_i \notin \Delta_0$. Because of $\delta_i \in \Gamma_i \subseteq (\Delta^* - \Delta_0^{\rightarrow}) \cup \Delta_0$ and $\delta_i \notin \Delta_0$ it follows that $\delta_i \notin \Delta_0^{\rightarrow}$. But then we can conclude $\delta_i \notin \Delta^*(I)$, i.e. $I \not\models \delta_i$. Therefore I does not satisfy $\delta_{0,1} \vee \cdots \vee \delta_{0,m} \vee \delta_1 \vee \cdots \vee \delta_n \in comp_{(\Delta,\sqsubset)}(\Phi)$, which is again a contradiction. □

5 Query Evaluation

In this section, we sketch a simple query evaluation algorithm based on our database completion.

5.1 First Step: Computation of Conflicts and Potential Answers

The first step of the query evaluation algorithm is to compute the conflicts (as defined in section 4) and potential answers:

Definition 12 (Potential Answer). A potential answer is a set $\{\theta_1, \ldots, \theta_k\}$ of answer substitutions and a set $\{\delta_1, \ldots, \delta_n\}$ of default instances such that

1. $\Phi \cup \{\delta_1, \ldots, \delta_n\}$ is consistent,
2. $\Phi \cup \{\delta_1, \ldots, \delta_n\} \vdash \psi\theta_1 \vee \cdots \vee \psi\theta_k$,
3. the pair $(\{\theta_1, \ldots, \theta_k\}, \{\delta_1, \ldots, \delta_n\})$ is minimal, i.e. it is not possible to remove a substitution or a default without violating 2.

The computation of conflicts and potential answers can be done by applying the deduction algorithm of section 3 to the following set of formulas:

Definition 13 (Extended Axiom Set). Let $\hat{\Phi}$ consist of

1. the axioms Φ,
2. a formula $notappl_\delta(X_1, \ldots, X_n) \leftarrow \neg(\delta)$ for every $\delta \in \Delta$, where $notappl_\delta$ is a new predicate and $X_1, \ldots, X_n$ are the variables appearing in δ,
3. the formula $answer(X_1, \ldots, X_n) \leftarrow \psi$, where $answer$ is a new predicate and $X_1, \ldots, X_n$ are the variables appearing in the query ψ.

Definition 14 (Facts Denoting Default Instances and Answers).

1. We write $notappl[\delta']$ for $notappl_\delta(c_1, \ldots, c_n)$ if δ' is the θ-instance of δ, where $\theta = \langle X_1/c_1, \ldots, X_n/c_n \rangle$.
2. We write $answer[\theta]$ for $answer(c_1, \ldots, c_n)$ if $\theta = \langle X_1/c_1, \ldots, X_n/c_n \rangle$.

The bottom-up evaluation procedure applied to $\hat{\Phi}$ computes all minimal disjunctive facts derivable from $\hat{\Phi}$. Now we only have to select the disjunctive facts corresponding to conflicts and potential answers:

Lemma 15.

1. $\{\delta_1, \ldots, \delta_n\}$ is a conflict iff $notappl[\delta_1] \vee \cdots \vee notappl[\delta_n] \in H(\hat{\Phi})$.
2. $(\{\theta_1, \ldots, \theta_k\}, \{\delta_1, \ldots, \delta_n\})$ is a potential answer iff

$$answer[\theta_1] \vee \cdots \vee answer[\theta_k] \vee notappl[\delta_1] \vee \cdots \vee notappl[\delta_n] \in H(\hat{\Phi}).$$

5.2 Second Step: Computing only a Subset of the Completion

The naive algorithm for query answering is to compute the set $comp_{(\Delta, \sqsubseteq)}(\Phi)$, and to derive instances of the query ψ from these formulas by the bottom-up evaluation algorithm of section 3. But this is of course not practical, since $comp_{(\Delta, \sqsubseteq)}(\Phi)$ can be very large or even infinite (because default instances containing "unknown" constants are assumed). However, we are only interested in default instances on which potential answers or conflicts depend:

Definition 16 (Critical Default Instance). $\delta \in \Delta^*$ is critical if there is a potential answer $(\{\theta_1, \ldots, \theta_k\}, \{\delta_1, \ldots, \delta_n\})$ or a conflict $\{\delta_1, \ldots, \delta_n\}$ such that $\delta = \delta_i$ for some i.

Now, for these finitely many default instances, we can simply evaluate the definition of $comp_{(\Delta, \sqsubset)}(\Phi)$ (recall that we already know all conflicts). This subset of the database completion is in fact sufficient for query answering:

Definition 17 (Critical Subset of the Completion). Let Ψ consist of

1. $\hat{\Phi}$ (as above), and
2. for every $\delta_{0,1} \vee \cdots \vee \delta_{0,m} \vee \delta_1 \vee \cdots \vee \delta_n \in comp_{(\Delta, \sqsubset)}(\Phi)$, such that $\delta_{0,i}$ $(i = 1, \ldots, m)$ and δ_j $(j = 1, \ldots, n)$ are critical, the formula

$$false \leftarrow notappl[\delta_{0,1}] \wedge \cdots \wedge notappl[\delta_{0,m}] \wedge notappl[\delta_1] \wedge \cdots \wedge notappl[\delta_n]$$

(i.e. at least one of the defaults is applicable).

Theorem 18. $\theta_1 \vee \cdots \vee \theta_k$ *is correct iff* $answer[\theta_1] \vee \cdots \vee answer[\theta_k] \in H(\Psi)$.

Proof. (Sketch) Let Δ' be the set of critical default instances. It can be shown that every $\prec_{(\Delta, \sqsubset)}$-minimal model is also $\prec_{(\Delta', \sqsubset)}$-minimal, and for every $\prec_{(\Delta', \sqsubset)}$-minimal model there is a $\prec_{(\Delta, \sqsubset)}$-minimal model which does not differ in the truth values of Δ'. But correct answers depend only on defaults appearing in potential answers, and therefore in Δ'. □

5.3 Sufficiency of Simple Loops

Of course, when computing the relevant disjunctions in $comp_{(\Delta, \sqsubset)}(\Phi)$, we should avoid a loop over all subsets $\Delta_0 \subseteq \Delta^*$. But in fact only very few combinations of defaults have to be considered, and only in very special circumstances. Note that if $\Delta_0 \subset \Delta_1$ and $\Delta_1^{\sqsupset} \subseteq \Delta_0^{\sqsupset}$, then Δ_1 would produce only superdisjunctions of those generated by Δ_0 (because a conflict relevant to Δ_0 is relevant to Δ_1, too). So we do not need to consider Δ_1. This rule also explains why we have to consider only singleton sets if there are no priorities ($\Delta_1^{\sqsupset} = \emptyset$) or only priority levels (choose a $\delta_0 \in \Delta_1$ with minimal level). And in the general case, we have to look only at combinations of defaults in different and unrelated places of the inheritance hierarchy.

In fact, only the pattern in the following example with "crossing conflicts" requires non-singleton Δ_0. Since such cross-situations seem to be quite artificial, it might be possible to look only at single δ_0 in practice.

Example 5. Let $\Delta^* := \{p, q, r, s\}$, $p \sqsubset r, q \sqsubset s$ and $\Phi := \{\neg p \vee \neg s, \neg q \vee \neg r\}$:

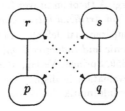

For $\delta_0 := p$, we would construct the disjunction $p \vee s$, the same for $\delta_0 := s$, and for the other two defaults we would construct $q \vee r$. These disjunctions do not exclude the non-minimal model $I := \{r, s\}$.

But for $\Delta_0 := \{p, q\}$ the disjunction $p \vee q$ would be constructed. Of course, we can consider also $\Delta_0 := \{r, s\}$. This would lead to $r \vee s \vee p \vee q$. $\qquad\qquad \square$

6 Conclusions

We have proposed a bottom-up query evaluation algorithm for specifications consisting of partially ordered overridable rules, and including disjunctive information. This is a solution to an important aspect of integrating object-oriented and deductive databases, namely the (multiple) inheritance of rules.

As far as we know, this is the first practical deduction algorithm for partially ordered supernormal defaults with this skeptical/"circumscription-like" semantics (ordered logic programming and F-logic have a different semantics). The top-down algorithm proposed in [2] can only handle priority levels. The algorithm from [1] explicitly computes single extensions (minimal models).

Of course, optimizations are needed in order to make our algorithm really useful for large database applications. But we believe that it is first important to distinguish between the basic algorithm and the optimizations.

The most important optimization would be to make our algorithm goal-directed, e.g. by meta-interpretation or magic sets [9]. First approaches to a goal directed hyperresolution are [12, 22]. It is also known that general theorem proving is not necessarily very much less efficient than Prolog programming [19].

It is interesting that we need no iteration over the priority levels as [2] or the usual evaluation of stratified databases (which are special cases).

Our work can also be applied to transform specifications consisting of axioms and defaults into specifications consisting only of axioms (with a finite set of exceptions). This is another interesting alternative for implementation.

Of course, the semantics of conflicts in multiple inheritance considered here is not the only possible one. In future work, we will try to generalize our approach in this direction.

References

1. F. Baader, B. Hollunder: How to prefer more specific defaults in terminological default logic. Research Report RR-92-58, DFKI, Kaiserslautern, 1992.
2. A. B. Baker, M. L. Ginsberg: A theorem prover for prioritized circumscription. In *Proc. 11th Int. Joint Conf. on Artificial Intelligence (IJCAI)*, 463–467, 1989.
3. S. Brass: Deduction with supernormal defaults. In G. Brewka, K. P. Jantke, P. H. Schmitt (eds.), *Nonmonotonic and Inductive Logics, 2nd International Workshop (NIL'91)*, 153–174, LNAI 659, Springer-Verlag, 1993.
4. S. Brass: Efficient query evaluation in disjunctive deductive databases. Internal Report 93Br02, Institut für Informatik, Universität Hannover, 1993.

5. S. Brass, U. W. Lipeck: Specifying closed world assumptions for logic databases. In J. Demetrovics, B. Thalheim (eds.), *2nd Symp. on Mathematical Fundamentals of Database Syst. (MFDBS'89)*, 68–84, LNCS 364, Springer-Verlag, 1989.
6. S. Brass, U. W. Lipeck: Semantics of inheritance in logical object specifications. In C. Delobel, M. Kifer, Y. Masunaga (eds.), *Deductive and Object-Oriented Databases, 2nd Int. Conf. (DOOD'91)*, 411–430, LNCS 566, Springer, 1991.
7. S. Brass, U. W. Lipeck: Generalized bottom-up query evaluation. In A. Pirotte, C. Delobel, G. Gottlob (eds.), *Advances in Database Technology — EDBT'92, 3rd Int. Conf.*, 88–103, LNCS 580, Springer-Verlag, 1992.
8. G. Brewka: *Nonmonotonic Reasoning: Logical Foundations of Commonsense.* Cambridge University Press, 1991.
9. F. Bry: Query evaluation in recursive databases: bottom-up and top-down reconciled. *Data & Knowledge Engineering 5 (1990)*, 289–312.
10. S. Ceri, G. Gottlob, L. Tanca: *Logic Programming and Databases.* Surveys in Computer Science. Springer-Verlag, Berlin, 1990.
11. C.-L. Chang, R. C.-T. Lee: *Symbolic Logic and Mechanical Theorem Proving.* Academic Press, New York, 1973.
12. R. Demolombe: An efficient strategy for non-horn deductive databases. *Theoretical Computer Science 78 (1991)*, 245–259.
13. J. Dix: Default theories of Poole-type and a method for constructing cumulative versions of default logic. In B. Neumann (ed.), *Proc. of the 10th European Conf. on Artificial Intelligence (ECAI 92)*, 289–293, John Wiley & Sons, 1992.
14. H. Gallaire, J. Minker, J.-M. Nicolas: Logic and databases: A deductive approach. *Computing Surveys 16 (1984)*, 153–185.
15. M. Gelfond, H. Przymusinska, T. Przymusinski: The extended closed world assumption and its relationship to parallel circumscription. In *Proc. 5th ACM SIGACT-SIGMOD Symp. Princ. of Database Syst. (PODS'86)*, 133–139, 1986.
16. M. Kifer, G. Lausen, J. Wu: Logical foundations of object-oriented and frame-based languages. Technical report, SUNY at Stony Brook, 1990.
17. E. Laenens, D. Vermeir: A fixpoint semantics for ordered logic. *Journal of Logic and Computation 1:2 (1990)*, 159–185.
18. J. Lobo, J. Minker, A. Rajasekar: *Foundations of Disjunctive Logic Programming.* MIT Press, Cambridge, Massachusetts, 1992.
19. R. Manthey, F. Bry: SATCHMO: a theorem prover implemented in Prolog. In E. Lusk, R. Overbeek (eds.), *9th Conf. on Automated Deduction (CADE-9)*, 415–434, LNCS 310, Springer-Verlag, 1988.
20. S. Naqvi, S. Tsur: *A Logical Language for Data and Knowledge Bases.* Computer Science Press, New York, 1989.
21. D. Poole: A logical framework for default reasoning. *Artificial Intelligence 36 (1988)*, 27–47.
22. V. Royer: Backward chaining evaluation in stratified disjunctive theories. In *Proc. of the Ninth ACM SIGACT-SIGMOD-SIGART Symposium on Principles of Database Systems (PODS'90)*, 183–195, 1990.
23. M. Ryan: Defaults and revision in structured theories. In *Proceedings of the IEEE Symposium on Logic in Computer Science (LICS'91)*, 362–373, 1991.
24. K. Thirunarayan, M. Kifer: A theory of nonmonotonic inheritance based on annotated logic. *Artificial Intelligence 60 (1993)*, 23–50.

Our papers are available via ftp from wega.informatik.uni-hannover.de (130.75.26.1).

An Extension of Path Expressions to Simplify Navigation in Object-Oriented Queries

Jan Van den Bussche*   Gottfried Vossen†
University of Antwerp   University of Muenster

Abstract

Path expressions, a central ingredient of query languages for object-oriented databases, are currently used as a purely navigational vehicle. We argue that this does not fully exploit their potential expressive power as a tool to specify connections between objects. In particular, a user should not be required to specify a path to be followed in full, but rather should provide enough information so that the system can infer missing details automatically. We present and study an extended mechanism for path expressions which resembles the omission of joins in universal relation interfaces. The semantics of our mechanism is given in the general framework of a calculus-like query language. Techniques from semantic query optimization are employed to obtain efficient specifications. We also consider the possibility that links can be traversed backwards, which subsumes previous proposals to specify inverse relationships at the schema level and also fully exploits the meaning of inheritance links.

1 Introduction

Query languages for object-oriented databases (OODBs) have become an active field of research in recent years [3, 12], with a central topic being the design of languages that are at the same time easy to use and powerful. Since it is common in OODBs that objects directly reference each other, query languages for such databases require some form of navigation, which is usually provided by means of *path expressions (PEs)* [16]. When PEs are used, establishing a desired navigation path may be a complex task, for example due to the requirement that correct typing must be obeyed along the path.

The goal of this paper is to demonstrate that various simplifications are possible when navigating through an OODB. The idea of simplifying (logical) navigation goes back to work on universal relation (UR) interfaces [4, 5, 15, 20].

---

*Research Assistant of the NFWO. Address: Dept. Math. & Computer Sci., University of Antwerp (UIA), Universiteitsplein 1, B-2610 Antwerp, Belgium. E-mail: vdbuss@uia.ac.be

†Address: Institut für Wirtschaftsinformatik, University of Muenster, Grevenerstr. 91, D-48159 Muenster, Germany. E-mail: vossen@informatik.rwth-aachen.de

There, the issue was to free users from the need to write down complex join expressions when querying a database; instead, they pose queries in terms of attributes alone, and the query processor has to expand this into an ordinary query, say, in relational algebra. Moreover, in [1] it has been shown how the UR model can be extended such that inheritance and aggregation information can be used to exploit attribute "compatibility," and how a UR query language can be provided with path expressions correspondingly.

Since PEs in an OODB can be viewed as collections of *implicit* (pre-computed) joins, it is natural to investigate the problem of simplifying logical navigation in this context as well. A first approach in this direction has been reported in [8], where the UR query language PIQUE [15] was adapted to the context of a semantic data model. [12] suggests to allow "wildcards" as abbreviations in PEs, which may be replaced by a sequence of attributes.

In the present paper, we will present a general abbreviation mechanism for PEs (without wildcards) which allows them to be specified more concisely. In particular, attributes may be omitted from the specification of a PE, and links between classes may be traversed in their given or in their inverse direction. In addition, our PEs can contain not only attribute names, but also class names. This renders them powerful enough to serve not only as where-clause specifications, but also as for-clause specifications (using SQL terminology). Indeed, in our approach to path expressions the distinction between where- and from-clauses becomes obsolete.

Abbreviated PEs are evaluated by "completing" them into so-called full ones. Completions will be inferred using knowledge of the inheritance and aggregation links from the underlying database schema. To this end, we associate with a schema a directed graph whose edges represent those links and are assigned weights based on a notion of "conceptual distance." This renders it possible to infer and disambiguate what a user has in mind by assuming that he is aiming for the *shortest* connection between data objects that is implied by his expression.

If several shortest paths exist, we take the union of them, inspired by the credulous approach in AI. In this process, we can avoid combinatorial explosion— a typical drawback of the credulous approach—by employing techniques from semantic query optimization [7]. Our credulous approach will also turn out to have the *liberal typing* for PEs, introduced in [12], as a special case. Note also the similarity in spirit with the window function for UR interfaces proposed in [4].

The core of our abbreviation mechanism will be described in the general framework of an object-oriented calculus-like query language. The formal semantics of this language is specified by a translation to the conventional relational calculus (using an obvious relational representation of an OODB). In this way, all semantical properties known of the relational calculus become readily accessible (e.g., for evaluation and optimization purposes). In particular, the implicit joins expressed by a PE are made explicit by the translation. Because our object-oriented calculus is so simple and general, it will be straightforward to incorporate our ideas into other query languages.

The organization of this paper is as follows: In Section 2, we introduce our model of OODBs, and motivate our work by discussing various shortcomings in the usage of traditional PEs in object-oriented query languages. In Section 3, we define the weighted schema graph corresponding to an object-oriented schema, using a relational representation of OODBs. In Section 4, we introduce our extended notion of PEs and study ways of automatically expanding abbreviations into full specifications. In Section 5 we exhibit a general framework for calculus-like query languages in which our PE mechanism can be used. We give formal semantics by a translation to relational calculus. This translation is shown to be safety-preserving. Finally, in Section 6, we briefly discuss a number of further issues that follow from our work. We go deeper into the matter of traversing aggregation links backwards (which we omit from the main formal development for clarity of presentation), and show how our results can be carried over into this more general setting. We also comment on the complexity of our abbreviation mechanism.

2 Motivation

To motivate our investigation, we first review the traditional notion of path expression as underlying most query languages for OODBs [16]. We indicate several shortcomings of the common usage of PEs, and show how these can be overcome. To make the presentation easier to read, we first sketch our OODB model and present a running example.

Following ORION [13], we assume that an OODB schema consists of a set of *class names* which are organized in an *isa* hierarchy. The classes are connected via aggregation links by associating with each class name a number of attribute declarations which are "local" to that class. Since we do not consider attribute overriding in this paper, we assume that if c isa c', then the sets of attributes specified for c and c' are disjoint. Of course, c will inherit all attributes from c'.

Each attribute has an arbitrary class name as type and an indication whether it is single- or set-valued. The type of an attribute is the class to which values of the attribute belong. Classes can be system-defined (e.g., *Integer*, *String*) or user-defined. We will focus on user-defined classes in this paper. Objects have a unique identifier and a possibly complex value consisting of all attribute values. For simplicity, we do not distinguish between attributes and (side-effect free) methods. This implies that we only consider methods without parameters; the generalization to methods with parameters is well-known and straightforward (e.g., [12]). Throughout this paper, we will use an abbreviated version of an example from [12] as our running example. The sample schema is depicted in the usual graphical way in Figure 1. In this figure, single arrows denote aggregation links and double arrows is-a links, and a star indicates that the attribute in question is set-valued.

Traditionally (e.g., [2]), a *path expression (PE)* over a given OODB schema is an expression of the form $x.A_1.A_2.\ldots.A_n$, $n \geq 1$, where x is a variable standing for an object of class C_1, A_1 is an attribute of that class, and for $1 < i \leq n$, A_i

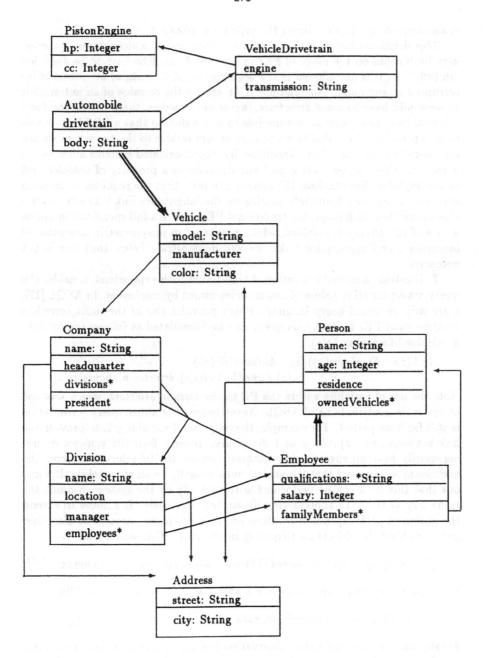

Figure 1: OODB schema of the running example.

is an attribute of class C_i, being the type of attribute A_{i-1} in class C_{i-1}.

This definition has several immediate consequences, which impose unnecessary limitations on the usage of PEs in queries. First, PEs have to be specified "in full," i.e., it is not allowed that a sequence $A_1.A_2.....A_n$ of attributes is interrupted at any point. For example, if we ask for the cc value of an automobile x, we would have to use $x.drivetrain.engine.cc$. However, there is just one (and minimal) way to connect an automobile to a cc value, so that a PE like $x.cc$ suffices in principle. Note that this situation is comparable to the one where we ask for the color of automobile x. Traditionally, object-oriented systems allow to use $x.color$ for this purpose, although formally, *color* is a property of vehicles, not of automobiles. Nevertheless, the system can infer that the required connection is correct using the schema information on the inheritance link between the two classes involved. It follows that traditional PEs require a full specification unless a case of inheritance is involved, which results in an unsymmetric treatment of inheritance and aggregation links; we will demonstrate below that this is not necessary.

To illustrate a second limitation of traditional path expressions, consider the query asking for all cc values of automobiles owned by employees. In XSQL [12], a recently proposed query language which provides one of the most complete treatments of PEs to date, this query can be formulated as follows (recast into a calculus-like syntax here):

$$\{z \mid (\exists x : Employee(x))(\exists y : Automobile(y)) :$$
$$[x].ownedVehicles[y].drivetrain.engine.cc[z]\}$$

Note the use of variables within the PE in the form of *selectors*, which was one of the main contributions of XSQL. Nevertheless, the above query formulation is still far from perfect. For example, the only use of variable y is to provide the link between (*owned*)*Vehicle* and *drivetrain*. Indeed, formally vehicles do not necessarily have an engine, while automobiles do; the $[y]$-selector enforces the additional requirement that the vehicle must actually be an automobile. It turns out that this trick can be performed automatically by the system in much the same way as the path abbreviation illustrated previously. It suffices to extend the notion of path expression to allow not only attribute names, but also class names to bind the objects participating in the path. This would lead to

$$\{z \mid (\exists x : Employee(x)) : [x].ownedVehicles.Automobile.drivetrain.engine.cc[z]\}.$$

But clearly, we can do away with the x variable in the same way, yielding

$$\{z \mid Employee.ownedVehicle.Automobile.drivetrain.engine.cc[z]\}.$$

Finally, basing ourselves on the observation (similar to an earlier one) that there is only one minimal way to connect employees to cc values, we can as well write:

$$\{z \mid Employee.cc[z]\}.$$

Our exposition below will demonstrate that this effect can formally be made precise. We also point out that a side-effect of the extension to allow class names inside path expressions is that the distinction between from- and where-clause specifications (using SQL terminology) becomes obsolete, in the sense that a qualification such as *Employee(x)* is equivalent to the PE *Employee[x]* (which could occur as a subexpression of a larger PE).

As a final remark, the reader may have noticed that in the above discussion, we have implicitly considered inheritance links to be bidirectional, e.g., going from *Automobile* to *Vehicle* in the first example, and conversely in the second. Again, there is no reason why this should not hold for aggregation links as well. Indeed, several proposals have recently been made regarding this point [10, 14, 18]. A general discussion on the impact of "inversion" in path èxpressions will be delayed to Section 6. Until then, it suffices to say that an inversion mechanism will be easily incorporable in our proposal as described in the sequel.

3 Schema Graphs and Schema Paths

Given a schema in the model introduced in the previous section, a weighted graph can be associated with it whose edges capture the various inheritance and aggregation links comprised. We next introduce a simple and straightforward representation of the OODB model by the relational model. Using this representation we will be able to use well-understood terminology to describe the semantics of PEs.

It is well-known [11] how an OODB schema S can be represented by a relational database schema $D(S)$, consisting of unary and binary relation schemas, and a number of constraints; this representation is only used for formal or conceptual purposes and is implementation-independent. Unary relations hold the oid's associated with each class, while binary relations consist of an oid column plus one of the attributes of the corresponding class. Hence, for each class name c, there is a relation named c with c as the only attribute; for each attribute A of c there is a binary relation named c-A with attributes c and A (a tuple in c-A will consist of an oid associated with c and a value for A). The relations corresponding to our running example will include, among others:

```
Person(Person); Person-name(Person, name);
Employee(Employee); Employee-familyMembers(Employee, familyMembers);
Company(Company); Company-president(Company, president).
```

The constraints are functional, inclusion and exclusion dependencies [6], used to model the obvious properties of single-valued attributes, inheritance, referential integrity, and disjointness of classes unrelated in the inheritance hierarchy; in our running example, these will include, among others:

```
Person → name, Employee[Employee] ⊆ Person[Person]
Company-president[president] ⊆ Employee[Employee]
Vehicle-manufacturer[manufacturer] ⊆ Company[Company]
Company[Company] ∩ Person[Person] = ∅
```

Each given OODB schema can uniquely be represented in relational terms in this way. Hence, instances over the OODB schema can simply be introduced as instances over the relational representation satisfying the constraints. Again, we stress that this relational representation of an OODB is for conceptual purposes only; it allows us to rely on well-known (i.e., relational) concepts for explaining our ideas, and certainly does not imply that we assume the OODB to be stored on top of a relational system.

We next associate a schema graph with a given OODB schema, which straightforwardly follows from the relational representation of the latter. Since it will be our goal to show how a user can specify connections between database objects using PEs, this graph will turn out to be useful for making this explicit.

If S is an OODB schema, the *schema graph* $G(S)$ is a directed, weighted graph defined as follows: For each relation R in the relational representation of S there is a node in $G(S)$. If R is unary, i.e., corresponds to a class c, that node has the form '(c, c)'; if R is binary, i.e., corresponds to a class c and one of its attributes A, that node has the form '(c, A)'. The edges of $G(S)$ either connect "class identifiers" with their "component attributes", attributes with the class identifier of their type, or the class identifiers of isa-related classes. More specifically, we distinguish the following types of edges in $G(S)$, where c is a class and A is an attribute of c:

(a) an edge $(c, c) \to (c, A)$,

(b) an edge $(c, A) \to (c', c')$ if A is of type c',

(c) an edge $(c', c') \to (c, c)$ and an edge $(c, c) \to (c', c')$ if c isa c' holds in S.

Finally, we assign weights to the edges of a schema graph. The intuition behind these weights is to have a notion of "conceptual distance" between objects in the database. The goal will then be to allow a user to specify the *shortest* path or subpath between two given points by specifying these points only. Intuitively, the weights distinguish the cases where a join would be necessary in the relational representation from those where no join is needed; in the latter case, we simply assign weight 0. However, in the former case, instead of just assigning weight 1, we assign weight i [a] if the edge represents an inheritance [aggregation] relationship, resp.; as will be seen, this allows us to capture precisely the semantics we have in mind for abbreviated PEs. In detail, weights are assigned as follows:

Edges of type (a) (using the above list) indicate the access of a class attribute. since attribute values are directly associated with oid's for each class, we assign these edges weight 0 (i.e., there is no conceptual distance). Edges of type (b) indicate how to go from one class to the next via an aggregation link; we assign these edges weight a. Edges of type (c) state how to go from a subclass to a superclass or vice versa. Subclass oids are a subset of their superclass oids, so we assign edges from sub- to superclass weight 0. Going from super- to subclass, e.g., to check whether a person object is in fact a student, is less trivial; these edges have weight i. Figure 2 shows an excerpt from the schema graph for our running example.

Now let S be schema and $G(S)$ the schema graph of S. A *schema path* is a sequence of nodes pairwise connected by an edge. If $p = (v_1, \ldots, v_n)$ is a schema

274

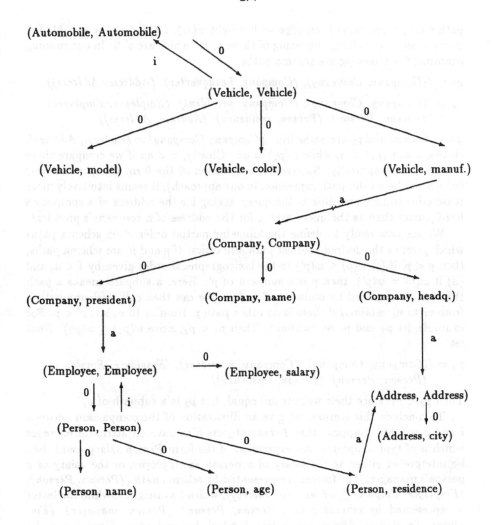

Figure 2: Part of the schema graph for our running example.

path s.t. $e_i = (v_i, v_{i+1})$ is an edge with weight $w(e_i)$, $1 \leq i < n$, the *weight* of p, denoted $w(p)$, is a string consisting of those $w(e_i)$ which are $\neq 0$. In our running example, the following are schema paths:

$p_1 = ((Company, Company), (Company, headquarter), (Address, Address))$

$p_2 = ((Company, Company), (Company, president), (Employee, Employee),$
$\quad (Person, Person), (Person, residence), (Address, Address))$

Thus, both p_1 and p_2 are paths from *(Company Company)* to *(Address, Address)*. Notice that $w(p_1) = a$, while $w(p_2) = aa$. Clearly, $a < aa$ if we compare these strings lexicographically. So given an expression of the form *Company.address* (which will be a valid path expression in our approach), it seems intuitively more reasonable to interpret this as the query asking for the address of a company's headquarter than as the query asking for the address of a company's president.

We are now ready to define the following partial order $<$ on schema paths which gives us the desired shortest path semantics: If p and p' are schema paths, then $p < p'$ if (i) $w(p) \leq w(p')$ in the lexicographical order given by $i < a$, and (ii) if $w(p) = w(p')$, then p is a subpath of p'. Here, a subpath means a path that can be obtained by omission of nodes. We can then call a schema path p from v_1 to v_n *minimal* if there is no other path p' from v_1 to v_n s.t. $p' < p$. For example, let p_1 and p_2 be as above. Then $p_1 < p_2$, since $w(p_1) \leq w(p_2)$. Next let

$p_3 = ((Company, Company), (Company, president), (Employee, Employee),$
$\quad (Person, Person), (Person, residence))$

Then $p_3 < p_2$, since their weights are equal, but p_3 is a subpath of p_2.

To conclude this section, we give an illustration of the comparison between i and a weights. Suppose that *Person* objects also have an attribute *manager* which is of type *Employee*. An expression of the form *Person.salary* could then be interpreted either as the salary of a person as employee, or the salary of a person's manager. The former is represented by schema path *((Person, Person), (Employee, Employee), (Employee, salary))*, which has weight i, while the latter is represented by schema path *((Person, Person), (Person, manager), (Employee, Employee), (Employee, salary))*, which has weight a. Since $i < a$ the first interpretation is the minimal one. This matches the intuition that the first is the most natural interpretation of *Person.salary*, since it remains in the same "is-a context" of Persons and Employees, in the sense of Neuhold and Schrefl [17].

4 A Generalization of Path Expressions

Formally, we define a *path expression (PE)* as a string of the form

$$\{s_0.\}A_1\{s_1\}.....A_n\{s_n\}, n \geq 1$$

where each A_i, $1 \leq i \leq n$, is an attribute or a class name, and each s_j, $0 \leq j \leq n$, is a *selector* of the form $[t]$, where t is a variable or a constant. The curly braces indicate that selectors are optional.

Selectors were first proposed in XSQL as a means to bind variables to objects participating in the path, or to restrict such objects to a constant. For technical simplicity, we will assume that no PE with a class name in its first position begins with a selector. This assumption is harmless since such esoteric cases will not occur in practice. For example, $[p].Person$ is not allowed, but $Person[p]$, which is equivalent, is.

Notice that PEs as defined here need not be fully specified; a major difference to traditional PEs is that we allow abbreviations. Recalling from Section 2, the PE $Employee.ownedVehicles.Automobile.drivetrain.engine.cc[z]$ can be alternatively stated as, e.g., $Employee.Automobile.cc[z]$. The basic idea for giving such incomplete expressions a semantics is to expand them into "full" expressions, using the weight of the corresponding schema paths as a selection criterion in case there are several expansions, i.e., to use the minimal expansion. For example, in our running example there exist several paths from class $Employee$ to class $Automobile$; in terms of the schema graph from Figure 2, these are:

$$p_1 = (Employee, Employee), (Person, Person), (Person, ownedVehicles),$$
$$(Vehicle, Vehicle), (Automobile, Automobile)$$

$$p_2 = (Employee, Employee), (Employee, familyMembers), (Person, Person),$$
$$(Person, ownedVehicles), (Vehicle, Vehicle), (Automobile, Automobile)$$

Notice that $w(p_1) = ai$, while $w(p_2) = aai$; thus, p_1 yields a "shorter" connection between employees and engines (a schema path with smaller weight), so p_1 would be used to expand the above PE. Minimal expansions are formally defined below.

A PE $A_1.....A_n$, $n \geq 1$, where selectors are ignored, is said to be *full* if A_1 is a class name, and there exist nodes $v_i = (c_i, A_i)$, $1 \leq i \leq n$, in the corresponding schema graph s.t. $(v_1 ... v_n)$ is a path in that graph. The following can be proved by induction:

Lemma 1 *For every full PE $A_1 ... A_n$ as above, the corresponding schema path $(v_1 ... v_n)$ is unique. Furthermore, $v_1 = (c_1, A_1)$ satisfies $A_1 = c_1$.*

As mentioned in Section 2, our full PEs are already more powerful than traditional ones, since they can contain class names (serving the same function as from-clause bindings in languages like XSQL); this generalization is necessary for our abbreviation mechanism to be flexible.

Now let p be a given PE. An *expansion* of p w.r.t. the underlying schema is any full PE p' which contains p as a subexpression, and contains not more selectors than p. Here, a subexpression means an expression that can be obtained by an omission of symbols. Finally, a *minimal* expansion is an expansion whose corresponding schema path is minimal.

Notice that the expansion of a given PE thus starts with a class name and has an associated schema path. Expansions of PEs are in general not unique. Continuing the previous example, the two expansions of PE $Employee.Automobile[x]$ are $Employee.Person.ownedVehicles.Vehicle.Automobile[x]$ and $Employee.familyMembers.Person.ownedVehicles.Vehicle.Automobile[x]$.

The first one is minimal and indeed corresponds to the intended meaning. Clearly, full PEs contain a lot of redundant class names, but these will be eliminated by the reduction procedure introduced in the next section.

We finally note again that the process of expanding a given PE will not always have a unique solution. For example, the expression *name[Johnson]* should yield all objects for which *name* is defined and equal to Johnson. Notice that these objects could be either companies or persons, since both corresponding classes have an attribute *name*. In other words, there are two minimal expansions *Company.name* and *Person.name*. Under a "credulous" approach, the evaluation procedure as defined in the next section will take their union. We point out that the *liberal typing* of PEs, introduced in [12], can be explained as a special case of this credulous approach.

5 Evaluating Generalized Path Expressions

In this section, we demonstrate that our extended mechanism for PEs can be adopted by various query languages for OODBs. To support this claim, we exhibit a general, calculus-like language called OOC ("object-oriented calculus"), whose syntax employs PEs as introduced in the previous section, and whose semantics will be stated in terms of the conventional relational calculus over the relational representation of OODB schemas given in Section 3.

Building up from PEs and comparisons as atoms, we define formulas and queries of OOC syntactically in the standard manner:

(i) An *atomic formula* is either a PE or of the form $t \ominus t'$, where t and t' are terms (i.e., variables or constants) and $\ominus$ is a comparison symbol;

(ii) if Φ, Φ_1, and Φ_2 are formulas and x is a variable, then $\Phi_1 \wedge \Phi_2$, $\Phi_1 \vee \Phi_2$, $\neg\Phi$, $(\exists x)\, \Phi$, and $(\forall x)\, \Phi$ are formulas.

Notice the simple and uniform format of our atomic formulas; path expressions (and comparisons) are all that is needed due to the possible presence of class names in PEs. In particular, an equivalent to from-clauses as in XSQL is not needed. We define *free* and *bound* variables in a formula in the standard way [19]. An *OOC query* is now an expression of the form

$$\{x_1 \ldots x_n \mid \Phi(x_1, \ldots, x_n)\},$$

where formula Φ has exactly $x_1, \ldots, x_n$ as free variables.

As a simple example, $\{c \mid manufacturer.city[c]\}$ is an OOC query. As will become clear, this query asks for all cities where a manufacturer (of vehicles) is located. As another example,

$$\{n \mid (\exists e)Employee[e].name[n] \wedge (\forall a)(\forall x)[e].Automobile[a] \wedge [a].cc[x] \Rightarrow x > 2000\}$$

asks for the names of those employees, all whose owned automobiles have an engine with cc larger than 2000.

We now indicate a precise way to define the semantics of an OOC query, mostly by way of examples. Since we assume that an OODB can conceptually be represented as a relational database, and since the semantics of relational calculus is well-known, it suffices to translate each PE occurring in the query into a relational calculus subformula that evaluates to the intended meaning of the PE. The relational calculus query resulting from the replacement of all PEs by their translations can then be evaluated over the relational database we associated to the OODB schema in Section 3. We emphasize again that this is only a conceptual approach.

In the previous section, we associated with each PE a number of *full* PEs, namely, its minimal expansions. Recall from Lemma 1 that full PEs have a unique corresponding schema path. This schema path is the key to evaluating the full PE. However, since full PEs are as explicit as possible, they contain a lot of redundant class names which would cause redundant steps in the evaluation procedure. We eliminate this redundancy as follows. Let p be a full PE. The *reduction* of p is obtained by eliminating each class name occurring in it, provided the elimination does not incur a loss of variables, and provided the class name does not occur either at the beginning or the end of the path.

Recall the query $\{c \mid manufacturer.city[c]\}$. Path expression $manufacturer.city[c]$ has several expansions. For example,

$$Vehicle.manufacturer.Company.divisions.Division.employees.Employee.$$
$$Person.residence.Address.city[c]$$

is an expansion (with weight $aaaa$). However, the intended meaning of the query is *not* the cities of the employees of manufacturers, but rather the cities of the headquarter of the manufacturer itself. This corresponds to

$$Vehicle.manufacturer.Company.headquarter.Address.city[c]$$

which is a *minimal* expansion (with weight aa), in this example the only one. Reduction yields $manufacturer.headquarter.city[c]$. The extent will now be a relational calculus subformula having as free variables precisely the variables occurring as selectors in p; in the example just considered, we thus obtain:

$(\exists t_{11}) \ldots (\exists t_{32})$ $(Vehicle\text{-}manufacturer(t_{11}:Vehicle, t_{12}:manufacturer) \wedge$
$\quad Company\text{-}headquarter(t_{21}:Company, t_{22}:headquarter) \wedge$
$\quad Address\text{-}city(t_{31}:Address, t_{32}:city) \wedge t_{12}=t_{21} \wedge t_{22}=t_{31} \wedge t_{32}=c)$

In general, the *extent* of a full path expression p whose reduction is of length m is defined as the relational calculus subformula

$$(\exists)(R_1 \wedge \cdots \wedge R_m \wedge equalities),$$

where each R_i is of the form $c_{j_i}\text{-}A_{j_i}(t_{i1}:c_{j_i}, t_{i2}:A_{j_i})$ or $c_{j_i}(t_{i1})$, t_{i1} and t_{i2} are domain variables for the attributes, and the equalities are a conjunction of atomic join or selection conditions (where the latter stem from the selectors in p), and where $(\exists)$ denotes the full existential closure of all t_{ij} variables.

Having defined extent(p) for full PEs, we now define the translation of an arbitrary PE p' as the disjunction $\bigvee_{m \in M} extent(m)$, where M is the set of minimal expansions of p'. This formalizes the credulous approach mentioned earlier.

For a different example, assume that the database schema also has a class *Professor* isa *Employee*, whose attribute *teaches* can take a set of *Courses* as value. The query $\{p \mid president[p].teaches[\text{math}]\}$ asks for presidents of companies who happen to be professors as well, and teach math. The PE again has only one minimal expansion, $president[p].Employee.Professor.teaches[\text{math}]$, which has as extent:

$$(\exists\, c)(\exists\, o)\ (Company\text{-}president(c, p) \land Professor\text{-}teaches(p, o) \land o = \text{math})$$

We now briefly comment on the notion of *safety* in our OOC context. There is a syntactical notion of safety for relational calculus queries [19] which guarantees that they can be evaluated in finite time. We can adapt the definition of [19] to the OOC calculus; the only difference is that atomic formulas may now be PEs. We then obtain the following desirable property (the proof is omitted):

Theorem 1 *If an OOC formula is safe in the adapted sense, then its relational calculus translation is safe in the ordinary sense.*

We now return to the query presented earlier, which brings up the issue of optimization:

$$\{n \mid (\exists e)Employee[e].name[n]\land(\forall a)(\forall x)[e].Automobile[a]\land[a].cc[x] \Rightarrow x > 2000\}.$$

This query contains three PEs. If we translate each of them separately into relational calculus, we loose their interconnections, resulting in a poor overall translation. For instance, consider the second PE $[e].Automobile[a]$. When looked upon in isolation, e can be interpreted as a Person or an Employee. Formally, the PE has two minimal expansions. However, from the first PE, in which e also participates, it is clear that only the Employee interpretation is relevant to the query. So, when writing out the overall translation in safe form, it will contain a conjunct of the form:

$$Employee(e) \land Person(e) \land \dots,$$

which can be simplified by removing the atom $Person(e)$, since we have the inclusion dependency $Employee \subseteq Person$. We are then left with two syntactically equal disjuncts, one of which can be eliminated.

There exist similar situations where exclusion dependencies can be used to eliminate disjuncts. For example, in the formula $president[p].age[60]\land[p].name[n]$, retrieving all names n of presidents aged 60, the second PE, in isolation, can interpret p as a Company or a Person; both classes have an attribute *name*. However, using the first PE, we know that p must be a person. Therefore, the absurd subformula of the form $Company\text{-}president(c, p) \land Company\text{-}name(p, n) \land$ ..., which will appear in the result of the naive translation, can be eliminated. Indeed, this subformula is unsatisfiable, because of the dependencies $Company\text{-}president[president] \subseteq Employee$, $Employee \subseteq Person$, $Company\text{-}name[Company] \subseteq Company$, and $Person \cap Company = \emptyset$.

It turns out that the query simplifications just illustrated can be automated, using techniques known from semantic query optimization. [7] describes a powerful optimization algorithm which takes as input a non-recursive Datalog query with stratified negation, and a set of integrity constraints written as Horn clauses. The algorithm simplifies the query using the information from the constraints, and it can be adopted in our context roughly as follows:

By Theorem 1, the relational calculus translation of a safe OOC query is safe, and hence can be translated into a non-recursive Datalog query with stratified negation. Furthermore, recall from Section 3 that our constraints are simple cases of functional, inclusion, and exclusion dependencies. These dependencies can easily be rewritten as Horn clauses. For our purposes, only the inclusion and exclusion dependencies are relevant. To give the query optimizer as much information as possible, we do not only provide it with the explicitly given dependencies, but also with their logical consequences. Because the dependencies are "unary", it is relatively straightforward to generate their logical closure by a transitive closure-like procedure. The algorithm from [7] will then simplify the relational calculus translation of a safe OOC query as desired.

6 Discussion

We have argued for a more general perspective on PEs, going beyond a purely navigational usage. Extending their capabilities to specify connections between objects, we showed how incompletely specified expressions can be evaluated in a transparent way. This generalizes previous work in the context of the relational model on UR interfaces. On the other hand, our approach is general enough to be incorporated into vastly any query language for OODBs, e.g., SQL extensions as described in [16].

Our view of PEs as a connection specification mechanism is based on a generalization of PEs which allows them to contain class names in the middle, not just in the beginning. Indeed, this can be seen as an elegant way to avoid the use of "from-clauses" by explicitly including class bindings into a path. As a result, the notion of PE has been extended in several ways: Links existing between the classes of an OODB schema can freely be used in PEs in either direction, and abbreviations may be applied wherever the user wants them.

For reasons of clarity, we above restricted the use of inversions to cases where a path goes from a superclass to one of its subclasses, i.e., to inheritance links. However, our general approach to database connections also works for aggregation links and hence allows for *bi-directional* paths, i.e., paths in which attribute links may be traversed in forward or backward direction, in general. We briefly describe an example next.

Consider the expression *Employee.location*. If we just consider uni-directional paths, this expression can only be interpreted as retrieving for each employee the locations of the divisions of those companies that are manufacturers of some vehicle owned by that employee. However, a much more natural interpretation of the above expression would be to retrieve for each employee the location of the division where he is employed. This connection traverses the *employees* link backwards, as the corresponding full expansion shows:

$$Employee.employees^{-1}.Division.location.$$

Inversions in PEs can also be used explicitly, allowing for the convenient formulation of certain queries. Suppose that we ask for the names of all companies of which Perot is president. Without inversions, this query requires an evaluation of two PEs: First, *Company[c].name[n]* is used to obtain company names. Second, *[c].president.name[Perot]* is used to select those companies of which Perot is president. By allowing to use links in both directions, the same could be obtained in one expression as follows:

$$[Perot].name^{-1}.president^{-1}.Company.name[n]$$

It can be shown that all technical results presented in the preceding sections can be carried over to the generalized setting of PEs containing inversions as well. Of course, since more connections can now be followed, a PE will have less chance of having only one minimal expansion. So, the user will not always be able to use abbreviations as dramatically as is possible in the uni-directional case. However, this will largely be compensated by the added ability to use inversions.

We mention that our PE mechanism could be extended further by explicitly adding a fixpoint operator for dealing with recursion due to cycles in an OODB schema. Suppose a class *Person* has an attribute *name* of type *String*, and an attribute *child* of type *Person*. If we ask for all grandchildren of John, our current proposal allows to express this using the PEs

$$Person[o].name[John] \text{ and } [o].child.child.name[x]$$

Asking for all descendants of John could be handled by a fixpoint construct of the form $[o].child^*.name[x]$, as in [9].

We conclude this paper with a comment on the complexity of our PE expansion mechanism. Finding minimal expansions of PEs can be accomplished using well-known efficient shortest-path algorithms. However, in case multiple minimal expansions exist, our credulous approach will take the union of all of them. This is a hidden source of complexity. Indeed, it is not difficult to construct a database schema where two classes are connected by an exponential number of paths of the same weight. However, in practice, the number of minimal expansions will usually be low, and their union can often be simplified using the query simplification techniques described at the end of the previous section.

Acknowledgement. The authors are grateful to Catriel Beeri and Michael Schrefl for helpful comments on an earlier version of this paper.

References

[1] C. Beeri, H.F. Korth: Compatible Attributes in a Universal Relation; Proc. 1st ACM PODS 1982, 55–62

[2] E. Bertino, W. Kim: Indexing Techniques for Queries on Nested Objects; IEEE TKDE 1, 1989, 196–214

[3] E. Bertino, M. Negri, G. Pelagatti, L. Sbattella: Object-Oriented Query Languages: The Notion and the Issues; IEEE TKDE 4, 1992, 223–237

[4] J. Biskup, H.H. Brüggemann: Universal Relation Views: A Pragmatic Approach; Proc. 9th VLDB 1983, 172–185

[5] V. Brosda, G. Vossen: Update and Retrieval in a Relational Database through a Universal Schema Interface: ACM TODS 13, 1988, 449–485

[6] M.A. Casanova, V.M.P. Vidal: Towards a Sound View Integration Methodology; Proc. 2nd ACM PODS 1983, 36–47

[7] U.S. Chakravarthy, J. Grant, J. Minker: Logic-Based Approach to Semantic Query Optimization; ACM TODS 15, 1990, 162–207

[8] T.H. Chang, E. Sciore: A Universal Relation Data Model with Semantic Abstractions; IEEE TKDE 4, 1992, 23–33

[9] M. Consens, A. Mendelzon: GraphLog: A Visual Formalism for Real Life Recursion; Proc. 9th ACM PODS 1990, 404–416

[10] A. Heuer, J. Fuchs, U. Wiebking: OSCAR: An Object-Oriented Database System with a Nested Relational Kernel; in: H. Kangassalo (ed.), *Entity-Relationship Approach: The Core of Conceptual Modeling*, North-Holland 1991, 103–118

[11] R. Hull, M. Yoshikawa: ILOG: Declarative Creation and Manipulation of Object Identifiers; Proc. 16th VLDB 1990, 455–468

[12] M. Kifer, W. Kim, Y. Sagiv: Querying Object-Oriented Databases; Proc. ACM SIGMOD 1992, 393–402

[13] W. Kim: *Introduction to Object-Oriented Databases*; The MIT Press, Cambridge, MA, 1990

[14] C. Lamb, G. Landis, J. Orenstein, D. Weinreb: The ObjectStore Database System; CACM 34 (10) 1991, 50–63

[15] D. Maier, D. Rozenshtein, S. Salveter, J. Stein, D.S. Warren: PIQUE: A relational query language without relations; Information Systems 12, 1987, 317–335

[16] F. Manola: Object Data Language Facilities for Multimedia Data Types; Techn. Report TR-0169-12-91-165, GTE Labs., Inc., 1991

[17] E.J. Neuhold, M. Schrefl: Dynamic Derivation of Personalized Views; Proc. 14th VLDB 1988, 183–194

[18] M.H. Scholl, C. Laasch, C. Rich, H.J. Schek, M. Tresch: The COCOON Object Model; Techn. Report 193, Departement Informatik, ETH Zürich 1992

[19] J.D. Ullman: *Principles of Database and Knowledge-Base Systems* Vol. I; Computer Science Press, Rockville, MD, 1988

[20] G. Vossen: *Data Models, Database Languages, and Database Management Systems*; Addison-Wesley 1991

Query Classes*

Martin Staudt, Matthias Jarke, Manfred A. Jeusfeld, Hans W. Nissen

Informatik V, RWTH Aachen, Ahornstr. 55, 52056 Aachen, Germany

Abstract. Deductive object-oriented databases advocate the advantage of combining object-oriented and deductive paradigms into a single data model. Certainly, the query language in such a data model has to reflect the amalgamation because it works as the interface to the user and/or application program. This paper proposes a language to formulate queries as classes related to the schema classes and constrained by an associative membership condition. Answers are then regarded as their instances. The interpretation is based on a deductive database view of queries. Generic query classes are introduced with a simple parameter substitution construct. The syntactic separation of structural and associative conditions opens the way to semantic query optimization: subsumption between the structural parts of queries can be decided efficiently.

1 Introduction

The query language of a database determines which and how information can be retrieved from the database. Users generally demand a query language to be declarative and efficient (i.e. easy to optimize). In the case of (deductive) object-oriented databases the query language must be closely related to the data model. Ideally, queries would be just class descriptions where instances are not inserted by the user but computed by the query evaluator.

For this purpose, we propose an amalgamation of paradigms from object-oriented databases (*query by class*), deductive databases (*query by rule*), and knowledge representation languages (*query by concept*). The next section reviews related work on each of the aspects. Section 3 contains the exposition of our query language, discusses the interaction between the paradigms and reports shortly on the influence of each of the three faces on the implementation of query classes in the deductive object base management system ConceptBase. Finally, section 4 briefly presents fields of applications where our approach has been successfully used.

---

* This work was supported in part by the Commission of the European Communities under ESPRIT Basic Research Action 6810 (Compulog 2) and by the Ministry of Science and Research of Nordrhein-Westfalen.

2 Three Views of Queries

The basic understanding of what constitutes a query strongly influences the design of a query language and a query processing concept, and thus which of the desirable features it can offer. In this section, we review query models followed in the areas of object-oriented databases, deductive databases, and AI concept languages which understand queries, respectively, as

- classes of answer objects manipulated by methods,
- deduction rules with parameterized answer attributes, or
- concepts with automatic classification through subsumption relationships.

It turns out that each of these approaches basically follows the idea to make queries the same kind of thing it also handles otherwise. Each is particularly suitable for certain application areas of query handling. Moreover, there are specific reasons for this suitability which lie in the very nature of the approaches. In the last subsection, we draw together these observations to come up with a list of requirements our query model has to satisfy.

Query by Class: The Object-Oriented Approach. Object-oriented databases (OODB) combine the paradigms of object identity, class membership, inheritance, and methods from object-oriented programming languages with the database functionalities of persistence, concurrency, security, and declarative querying.

Since classes are the mechanism for managing sets of objects it is natural to use them also for describing query results, seen as sets of answer objects. A general advantage of queries as classes is that answers can be managed the same way as the objects in the OODB. Methods for processing answer objects can be attached to query classes. The answer objects can be organized in generalization/aggregation hierarchies and reuse methods of OODB classes. Moreover, the integration of methods in OODB suggests an implementation approach to query evaluation/view maintenance based on triggers attached to specific object/query class subtypes.

Query by Rule: The Deductive Approach. A deductive database consists of a finite set of facts (extensional database), and a finite set of deductive rules (intensional database). We restrict ourselves to rules where negation in the conclusion literal is disallowed and negated literals in the rule body must obey the stratification condition (Datalog⁻). With these assumptions the preferred interpretation is a certain minimal Herbrand model, the so-called perfect model. It can be computed using a fixpoint operator [10]. Queries in deductive databases look rather simple compared to object-oriented databases but they have some advantages. The membership condition is defined by the rules which have a matching conclusion literal. Thus, it is very easy to formulate parameterized versions of a query just by replacing one or more variables by a constant.

Implementation techniques for query optimization have been thoroughly investigated yielding algorithms for recursion optimization (magic sets [3], query/subquery approach [27]), and deductive integrity enforcement (e.g. [8], [21]).

View maintenance algorithms (storing the result of a query and keeping it up-to-date with the database) have been less studied but are rather simple generalizations of integrity enforcement. Some work has been done on updating views in deductive databases, esp. by abductive reasoning [17].

Query by Concept: A Type Inferencing Approach. Starting with KL-One [7], concept languages in artificial intelligence have pursued the idea to define knowledge bases as type lattices of so-called concepts. Because of the restricted usage of logical connectives a dedicated syntax for concept expressions has been developed: the axioms (schema) are written as $C \sqsubseteq E$ (necessary condition) or $C = E$ (necessary and sufficient condition) where E is constructed from other defined concepts and binary predicates expressing relationships between concepts.

The main purpose is to relate concepts to each other, e.g. to derive the *subsumption* between two concepts C and D. One should note that concept languages make statements for all possible models of the theory whereas database languages usually only consider the current database state as their model.

Systems such as CANDIDE [2] and CLASSIC [5] use concept descriptions as a flexible query language for databases. Queries are just considered as a new concept which is positioned in the concept lattice by subsumption algorithms. Answers to the query are all instances of all subconcepts and some instances of the direct super concepts (satisfying the additional constraints of the new concept).

The benefit of concept lattices is that the search space of a query (i.e., a new concept) is greatly reduced. The exact placement of a query into the lattice opens the ability for intensional query answering: instead of enumerating all instances of the query the system answers with the names of the subconcepts of the query (slightly more complicated for the contribution of the direct super concepts). On the other hand, if the extension of a super concept is materialized then a query subsumed by such a concept may reuse the extensions as a fine range.

Summary of Requirements. Our short review has shown that each approach has advantages supporting certain functionalities of a desired query system. The question addressed in our approach is how to integrate the three approaches. The following basic observations underly our solution, the query class:

- Queries as classes and queries as concepts offer the same object-oriented structure for questions and answers; therefore, this will be our approach.
- To integrate objects and rules, we need an object model with a logic-based semantics that allows a two-way transition between both. Our model of choice, Telos (see section 3), goes even further by offering an object model with a standard deductive database semantics, it has a precise translation into facts, rules, and integrity constraints of a deductive database.
- Concept language subsumption algorithms can be expected to work safely and effectively only for a sublanguage of the query language offered, e.g., by a full deductive database. A way has therefore to be found to offer both aspects separately. Complete subsumption is only done on the sublanguage

(subsequently called type system). As in programming languages and in constraint logic programming, the communication between both formalisms is one-way, that is, the type system influences query processing but not vice versa.

3 Query Classes in O-Telos

The O-Telos data model [14] is a variant of the knowledge representation language Telos [20]. In the following subsections we introduce the basic properties of the data model and show how queries in each of their roles fit into this framework. With each role we explain briefly its influence on the implementation of query classes in ConceptBase [13], a deductive object base management system. A detailed description of the implementation is given in [25].

The syntax of query classes is a class definition with superclasses, attributes, and a membership condition. The interpretation is based on a deductive rule containing predicates for each of the clauses in the class definition. Integration with concept languages is viewed as the extraction of the structurel part of a query class, i.e., the portion of the query which is representable as a concept expression.

3.1 Representing Objects and Formulas

We define deductive object bases as deductive databases with builtin axioms formalizing the three object-oriented abstraction dimensions of classification, aggregation, and generalization. More specifically, a deductive object base is a triple $DOB = (OB, R, IC)$ where OB is the extensional object base, R and IC contain deduction rules and integrity constraints. The axioms are represented as predefined formulas in R and IC. Let ID and LAB be sets of identifiers, and labels resp. An **extensional O-Telos object base** is a finite set

$$OB \subseteq \{P(o, x, l, y) \mid o, x, y \in ID, l \in LAB\}.$$

The elements of OB are called **objects** with identifier o, source and destination components x and y and name l. Objects of the form $P(o, o, l, o)$ are called *individuals*, $P(o, x, in, c)$ describes an instantiation relationship whereas specializations are of the form $P(o, c, isa, d)$. All other objects $P(o, x, l, y)$ are called attributes. This arrangement of an extensional object base permits an intuitive representation as a semantic net: individuals as nodes, all other objects as links. A third view on deductive object bases results in a frame-based notation of objects which only relies on object labels. Around the name l of an object o we group the names of all other objects which have o as source component.

The running example in this paper is based on the following scenario from a medical database: *Patients are persons, suffer from diseases and take drugs which have an effect on diseases.* The frame notation of the objects Patient and Drug is e.g. the following:

```
Patient isA Person with        Drug with
  attribute                      attribute
    suffers:Disease;               against:Disease
    takes:Drug                   end
end
```

We use the following literals when defining the complete axiomatization but also when specifying deductive rules and integrity constraints: (x in y) denotes an instantiation relationship between x and y, (c isA d) an specialization relationship between c and d, and (x m y) indicates that there exists an attribute of category m with source x and destination y.

O-Telos requires a set of 35 axioms and axiom schemata implemented as builtin deductive rules or integrity constraints of the deductive object base [14]. Here, we refer to a few important ones. Like most OODB and semantic data models, O-Telos requires that instances of an object are also instances of its superclasses. Another important property of the language is realized by the attribute typing axiom: instantiation relationships between objects imply instantiation relationships between their source resp. destination components. A similar restriction holds for specialization links and allows a consistent way of refining attributes of classes by their subclasses. Thus, although attributes of an object are not explicitly inherited by subclasses they can nevertheless be instantiated by their instances.

Instantiation links between objects in OB constitute different layers within an object base. O-Telos does not restrict the number of layers; classes can be instances of other classes (metaclasses), these can be instances of metametaclasses, and so on. In addition to the O-Telos axioms the sets R and IC contain application specific deduction rules and integrity constraints which are specified in a many-sorted first order language. Variable quantifications range over classes and are interpreted as instantiation relationships.

As an example a deduction rule can be defined that deduces for a given patient doctors who are suited to give him medical treatment. The constant this refers to the instances of the class which carries the rule. Similarly one may impose an integrity constraint on Patient that all instances actually must have a filler for the suffers attribute. As a consequence of the attribute typing axiom, the variable ranges can be used to determine type errors inside a formula.

```
Patient isA Person with
  attribute
    suited_doc:Doctor
  rule
    suited_rule:$ forall p/Doctor,d/Disease
                  (this suffers d) and (p specialist d)
                  ==> (this suited_doc p) $
  constraint
    mustsuffer:$ exists d/Disease (this suffers d) $
end
```

3.2 Queries as Classes

The query language CBQL [24] represents queries as classes whose instances are the answer objects to the query. These query classes are themselves instances of the predefined object `QueryClass` and contain necessary and sufficient membership conditions for their instances (=answers). These conditions can be used to check whether a given object is an instance of a query class or not. On the other hand, they can be used to compute the set of answer objects. Query classes have superclasses to which they are connected by an isa-link. These superclasses restrict the set of possible answers to their common instances.

Two different kinds of query class attributes can be distinguished. *Retrieved attributes* are already defined for one of the superclasses of the query class. An explicit specification of such an attribute in a query class description means that answer instances are given back with values for this attribute, similar to relational projection. In addition a necessary condition for the instantiation by an admissible value is included. The attributes of superclasses can also be refined, i.e. the target class is substituted by a subclass which results in an additional value restriction. If we assume a subclass `Antibiotics` of `Drug` the query class

```
QueryClass MaleOldAntibioticsPatient isA MalePatient,OldPatient with
   attribute
      takes:Antibiotics
end
```

has those male and old patients as instances who take antibiotics. In addition the concrete drugs are included in the answer description.

Computed attributes have values derived in the query evaluation process. Neither the extensional object base contains this relationship between the answer instance and the attribute value, nor is it inferable by deduction rules. For prescribing how to deduce these new relationships by analogy to deduction rules and integrity constraints, many-sorted first order logic expressions are admissible as building elements for query classes.

```
QueryClass WrongDrugPatient isA Patient with
   attribute, parameter
      wrong:Drug
   constraint
      wrongconstr:$ (this takes wrong) and
                     not exists d/Disease ( (this suffers d) and
                                            (wrong against d) ) $
end
```

As in section 3.1 this refers to the answer instances of `WrongDrugPatient`, namely all patients who take a drug which is against a disease they don't suffer from. The computed attribute `wrong` is identified with the variable of the same name within the formula. All deduced wrong drugs are part of the answer.

The logical expression in query classes descriptions can also contain arbitrary other constraints for the answer instances which would then work like the selection operation in relational databases.

In order to avoid the frequent reformulation of similar more specialized queries, attributes of query classes can be declared as *parameters*. Substitution of a concrete value for such an attribute or specialization of its target class by a subclass leads to a subclass of the original query which implies a subset relationship of the answer sets. For the parameter `wrong` the expressions

```
WrongDrugPatient(Aspirin/wrong)
WrongDrugPatient(wrong:Antibiotics)
```

denote two derived query classes which restrict the answer instances of **Wrong-DrugPatient** to those patients who take **Aspirin** resp. a drug of the class **Antibiotics** as wrong drug. For example, **WrongDrugPatient(Aspirin/wrong)** is a shorthand for the (non-parameterized) query class

```
QueryClass WrongAspirinPatient isA Patient with
  constraint
    Aspiconstr:$ (this takes Aspirin) and
                 not exists d/Disease ( (this suffers d) and
                                        (Aspirin against d) ) $
end
```

Expressions denoting (derived) query classes are allowed to occur within the definitions of other query classes and objects and are managed as full-fledged objects, too. Most of the compilation steps applied to normal classes are also applied to them, e.g. type checking of attributes. ConceptBase stores queries as any other class. When methods are defined for schema classes then all subclasses including query classes inherit these methods.

3.3 Queries as Rules

In deductive databases queries are represented as intensional relations derived by a set of rules. We have shown above that O-Telos object bases are just special cases of deductive databases. Obviously it should be possible to extend this view to query classes.

The definition of a query class Q induces a so called *query literal* $Q(x, x_1, ..., x_n)$ whose arity depends on the number of attributes and parameters of Q. The first argument x of Q stands for the answer object identifiers. Query classes are transformed to rules[2] concluding their corresponding query literals. By convention the object identifier of an individual with name **i** is written as **#i**.

- For each superclass C of Q the body of this rule contains a literal $In(i, \#C)$ where $\#C$ is the object identifier of the class C and i is a new variable replacing **this** in the query class description.
- Attributes **a:C** of the first type (defined for a superclass or refined) result in a conjunction $In(v, \#C) \land A(i, a, v)$ where v is a new variable.
- Attributes **a:C** of the second type just require $In(v, \#C)$ where v is a new variable.
- The logical formula describing the derivation of attribute values and other additional restrictions is transformed straightforward by substituting the newly introduced variables v and i for their symbolic counterparts **a** and **this**, replacing all occuring object names by object identifiers and resolving typed quantifications.

---

[2] We use a predicate-like notation of the literals to formulate deduction rules: In(x,y) for (x in y) and A(x,m,y) for (x m y).

– As a last step all generated expressions have to be linked by conjunctions. The new variables become arguments of the query literal.

Following these steps the example query class `WrongDrugPatient` is transformed to the following rule:

$$\forall i, v \; In(i, \#Patient) \wedge In(v, \#Drug) \wedge$$
$$\wedge A(i, takes, v) \wedge \neg \exists d \; In(d, \#Disease)$$
$$\wedge A(i, suffers, d) \wedge A(v, against, d)$$
$$\Rightarrow WrongDrugPatient(i, v)$$

Each query class yields exactly one rule concluding its corresponding query literal. Hence with closed world assumption the rule body provides a necessary and sufficient characterization of class membership.

The deduction rule form of queries not only provides a clean semantics but also a whole array of algorithms for evaluation and optimization known from the deductive database area [10]. In ConceptBase, the deductive rules are rewritten with the magic set method [3]. The main advantage of our query language is that it completely falls into Datalog⁻. Thus, virtually any evaluation method from this area is applicable. Optimization of rules and integrity constraints benefits from the predefined axioms of the object model by elimination of redundant predicates [15]. This also enhances the maintenance of materialized views, i.e. stored answers to a query [16]. Recently, compilation of deductive rules into algebra expressions has been added to ConceptBase. It profits from the fact that the object model provides an access predicate for each class attribute.

3.4 Queries as Concepts

In programming languages objects (variables, functions, etc.) usually have types. Type constructors for tuples ([]), sets ({ }), lists etc. allow to handle objects of arbitrarily complex structure. In the same way most object-oriented databases distinguish between objects and values on the one hand and classes and types on the other hand. Objects have an unique identity and an assigned value of a certain type. Classes are object containers which collect objects of the same type (sometimes called member type).

O-Telos only provides the diction of classes where membership is constrained by the builtin axioms and by user-defined constraints. Nevertheless we can extract type information from classes. A class definition is divided into a 'clean' part, i.e. its type, and a 'dirty' part containing all aspects for which the type system is not powerful enough. The example class

```
Patient isA Person with
  attribute
    suffers:Disease;
    takes:Drug
end
```

carries the information that patients have attributes **takes** and **suffers**, each with certain value restrictions. In addition, patients have attributes (e.g. **name** and **address**) defined for the superclass **Person**. Under consideration that **takes** and **suffers** can have multiple fillers, a (member) type of **Patient** could be the following:

$$[suffers : \{DiseaseT\}, takes : \{DrugT\}, name : string, address : AddressT]$$

where AT is a shorthand for the type of a class **A**. The relationship between types in OODB's and concept languages are discussed in [4]. It turns out that the latter allow more restrictions on objects than the common plain type languages.

Following the syntax used in the concept language literature for our patient example, we get a member type $PatientT$ for **Patient**.

$$PatientT \sqsubseteq \forall suffers.DiseaseT \sqcap \forall takes.DrugT \sqcap PersonT$$

The type information can be regarded as being a layer orthogonal to the object base definition presented in 3.1.

The 'type view' of deductive object bases introduced so far only used the $\forall$- and $\sqcap$- constructor for types and represented necessary conditions in the sense that e.g. every patient is also a person and that all attribute fillers for the **takes** attribute are drugs. Both conditions are guaranteed by O-Telos axioms. The type expression above doesn't cover neither the constraint nor the deductive rule specified for **Patient** in 3.1. These parts of the class definiton are referred to as the dirty part of a class definition.

On the other hand type restrictions may also be interpreted as sufficient membership conditions for their instances which in concept languages leads to the distinction between (defined) *concepts* and *primitive concepts* (the latter with only necessary conditions) [6]. Thus we can say that ordinary classes in an O-Telos object base have primitive concepts as their types. Primitive concepts (as e.g. $PatientT$) are directly subordinated under their corresponding type expression in the lattice which exactly represents the interpretation as necessary conditions. Defined concepts are related to their defining expression by equality.

There is an obvious correspondence between query classes and defined concepts since both state sufficient membership conditions. As with ordinary classes query classes often have 'dirty' parts not expressible by the type language. It can be distinguished between query classes that actually use only type language conform constructs – with a defined concept as their type – and those who have additional parts and hence have just a primitive concept as their type.

The goal of a separation between a type layer and the usual object layer for a deductive object base is to shift several kinds of inferences to the type layer which promises more efficient computations due to the lower complexity of the underlying language. The concept language community has examined a broad palette of type languages and offers efficient algorithms for several of them [12]. If one of these languages is chosen as type language for a deductive object base with corresponding syntactic object counterparts for type language constructs (as e.g., **atleastn** and **atmostn** above) we can apply these well understood inference algorithms at the type level to infer new information at the object level. The more complete the type language is, the more conditions of classes and query classes can be expressed in concept expressions and used for these inferences. A simple example is to support a type language extension with cardinality restrictions $\geq n\,r$ and $\leq n\,r$ for fillers of an attribute r by additional new built-in attribute categories atmostn and atleastn.

One example how inferences at the type layer may affect operations on the object layer is the computation of subsumption relationships between queries in order to avoid superfluous recomputations and reuse queries with stored answers. The determination of such relationships between queries and views that are materialized promises increasing efficiency. An efficient calculus for deciding subsumption in this case is presented in [9]. The following simple query classes shall demonstrate this.

```
QueryClass DrugPatient isA Patient with
   attribute
      takes:Drug
end

QueryClass AntibioticsPatient isA Patient with
   attribute
      takes:Antibiotics
   constraint
      appconstr:$ (this suffers Appendicitis) $
end
```

DrugPatient contains all those patients that take atleast one drug, AntibioticsPatient requires a value restriction for takes to drugs of the class Antibiotics, at least one filler for takes and Appendicitis as filler for suffers. Note that the specified value filler[3] Appendicitis belongs to the 'dirty' part of AntibioticsPatient and hence this query class has only a primitive concept as its type. It can be deduced that

$$AntibioticsPatientT \sqsubseteq PatientT \sqcap \forall takes.AntibioticsT \sqcap \geq 1\,takes$$
$$\sqsubseteq PatientT \sqcap \geq 1\,takes = DrugPatientT$$

provided that $AntibioticsT \sqsubseteq DrugT$.

Whenever the query AntibioticsPatient has to be evaluated and the object base already contains the answers to DrugPatient since it is designed as materialized view, it is not necessary to scan all patients in the object base but only the precomputed answer set of drug taking patients.

4 Applications

The implementation of query classes in ConceptBase has turned out to be a useful basis for several application areas that can exploit the different facets of queries as classes, as rules, and as concepts. While some of these applications

---

[3] Several concept languages offer an enumeration construct which would allow to express such a condition in the type language.

used the query language concept as is, others base extensions such as access to external data stores on it.

Software databases and repositories. *Dynamic clusters* are introduced in [22] as collections of objects where the membership frequently changes. Instead of procedurally assigning objects to such classes, a membership condition expressed as a query class automatically classifies objects into the correct clusters. Due to the deductive nature of query classes, the dynamic aspect of re-assigning objects is completely covered by view maintenance. The application mainly profits from queries as classes: the dynamic cluster is a query class persistently stored on the object base. It also profits from the representation of classes as objects in O-Telos. In fact, there are many queries which actually have class objects as anwers. This feature of query classes is sometimes called *schema querying* or *meta querying*.

Security management. Security is becoming an increasing concern in many databases. The Group Security Model GSM [26] uses generalization and aggregation to define task-based access to parts of the object base (identified by classes). The question what information a certain task may access is encoded as a query class. Thus, the deductive view is applied for evaluation while the object-oriented view and the availability of parameterized query classes are exploited for the precise and concise characterization of access right patterns.

Integration of heterogeneous databases. In many applications, the information to be processed is distributed in more or less autonomous information bases. Data may be replicated or even contradictory, the languages may be heterogeneous. We have made a first attempt with query classes to schema integration of distributed relational databases [19]. The system represents the base relations and their abstractions to the integrated schema uniformly as query classes. The deductive interpretation is used for accessing the base relations from queries formulated at the level of the integrated schema. Object-oriented principles come into play when organizing the communication between the external databases: each database can be seen as a class with a small interface of methods offered to the integrated system.

5 Conclusions

This paper presented a way to integrate the view of queries as classes, rules, and concepts. In one sentence the idea is the following: queries are expressed as classes, evaluated as deductive rules, and semantically optimized as concepts. The first view offers easy formulation since relationship of queries to schema classes is expressed by subclass and attribute statements in a simple frame notation. The second view, queries as rules, provides the efficient evaluation algorithms like magic sets and mapping to algebra expressions. Finally, we proposed to extract the structural part from a query (queries as concepts) and make it subject to reasoning on subsumption relationship between the answer sets of two queries.

Previous integration efforts only concentrated on two of the three aspects of queries. Similar to our approach, CoCoon [23] integrates concepts with classes but with a fixed and very simple type system (only lattice of attribute names). [1] presents a query language combining deduction with object-orientation. An integration of deductive rules and concept languages is investigated in [11]. Views in the object-oriented query language XSQL [18] are quite similar to query classes by seperating the signature of the answer objects from the membership condition. However, XSQL is too expressive (wrt. object model and generation of OID's inside a query) for allowing the optimization techniques discussed here.

Several applications of query classes in ConceptBase have validated the usefulness of the idea but also pointed out the need for various extensions, both from the user side (imprecise and intelligent question answering) and from the system side (integration of multiple formalisms). Finally, the symmetric evaluation of updates on answers to queries (view update) is a major challenge: a declarative language for both updates and retrieve methods.

References

1. S. Abiteboul, "Towards a deductive object-oriented database language", *Data & Knowledge Engineering*, 5, 1990, pp. 263–287.
2. H.W. Beck, S.K. Gala, and S.B. Navathe, "Classification as a query processing technique in the CANDIDE semantic data model", in *Proc. 5th Int. Conf. on Data Engineering*, 1989, pp. 572–581.
3. C. Beeri and R. Ramakrishnan, "On the power of magic", in *Proc. 6th ACM SIGMOD-SIGACT Symp. on Principles of Database Systems*, 1987.
4. A. Borgida, "From type systems to knowledge representation: natural semantics specifications for description logics", *Int. Journal of Intelligent and Cooperative Information Systems* 1(1), pp. 93–126, 1992.
5. A. Borgida, R.J. Brachman, D. McGuiness, and L.A. Resnick, "CLASSIC: A structural data model for Objects", in *Proc. ACM-SIGMOD Int. Conf. on Management of Data*, 1989, pp. 58–67.
6. R.J. Brachman, D.L. McGuinness, P.F. Patel-Schneider, L.A. Resnick, and A. Borgida, "Living with CLASSIC: When and how to use a KL-ONE-like language", in *Principles of Semantic Networks*(Sowa J.,ed.), Morgan Kaufmann, 1991.
7. R.J. Brachman and J.G. Schmolze, "An overview of the KL-ONE knowledge representation system", *Cognitive Science* 9(2), pp. 171–216, 1985.
8. F. Bry, H. Decker, and R. Manthey, "A uniform approach to constraint satisfaction and constraint satisfiability in deductive databases", in *Int. Conf. on Extending Database Technology*, 1988, pp. 488–505.
9. M. Buchheit, M.A. Jeusfeld, W. Nutt, and M. Staudt, "Subsumption between queries to object-oriented databases", appears in *Proc. EDBT'94*, Cambridge, UK, March 1994.
10. S. Ceri, G. Gottlob, and L. Tanca, *Logic programming and databases*, Springer-Verlag, 1990.
11. F.M. Donini, M. Lenzerini, D. Nardi, and A. Schaerf, "A hybrid system with datalog and concept languages", in *Trends in Artificial Intelligence*, (Ardizzone E., Gaglio S., Sorbello F., eds.), LNAI 549, Springer Verlag, pp. 88-97, 1991.

12. B. Hollunder, W. Nutt, M. Schmidt-Schauss, "Subsumption algorithms for concept description languages", in *Proc. 9th European Conf. on Artificial Intelligence*, pp. 348–353, 1990.
13. M. Jarke (ed.), *ConceptBase V3.1 user manual*, Report Aachener Informatik-Berichte Nr. 92-17, RWTH Aachen, Germany, 1992.
14. M.A. Jeusfeld, *Update control in deductive object bases* (in German). Infix-Verlag, St.Augustin, Germany, 1992.
15. M.A. Jeusfeld and M. Jarke, "From relational to object-oriented integrity simplification", in *Proc. 2nd Int. Conf. on Deductive and Object-Oriented Databases*, *LNCS 566*, Springer-Verlag, pp. 460–477, 1991.
16. M.A. Jeusfeld and M. Staudt, "Query optimization in deductive object bases", in *Query Processing for Advanced Database Applications*, (Freytag et al., eds.), Morgan-Kaufmann, 1993.
17. A.C. Kakas and P. Mancarella, "Database updates through abduction", in *Proc. 16th Int. Conf. on Very Large Databases*, 1990, pp. 650–661.
18. M. Kifer, W. Kim, Y. Sagiv, "Querying object-oriented databases", in *Proc. ACM-SIGMOD Int. Conf. on Management of Data*, San Diego, Ca., 1992, pp. 393–402.
19. A. Klemann, *Schema integration of relational databases* (in German), Diploma thesis, Universität Passau, Germany, 1991.
20. J. Mylopoulos, A. Borgida, M. Jarke, and M. Koubarakis, "Telos: a language for representing knowledge about information systems", in *ACM Trans. Information Systems* 8(4), pp. 325–362, 1990.
21. A. Olivé, "Integrity constraints checking in deductive databases", in *Proc. 17th Int. Conf. on Very Large Databases*, 1991, pp. 513–524.
22. T. Rose, M. Jarke, J. Mylopoulos, "Organizing software repositories - modeling requirements and implementation experiences", in *Proc. 16th Int. Computer Software & Applications Conf.*, Chicago, Ill., 1992.
23. M.H. Scholl, C. Laasch, and M. Tresch, "Updatable views in object oriented databases", in *Proc. 2nd Int. Conf. on Deductive and Object-Oriented Databases*, Munich, Germany, 1991.
24. M. Staudt, *Query representation and evaluation in deductive object bases* (in German), Diploma thesis, Universität Passau, Germany, 1990.
25. M. Staudt, H.W. Nissen, M.A. Jeusfeld, "Query by class, rule, and concept", in *Applied Intelligence*, Special issue on Knowledge Base Management, (Mylopoulos L., ed.), 1993.
26. G. Steinke, "Design aspects of access control in a knowledge base system", in *Computers & Security*, 10, 7, 1991, pp. 612–625.
27. L. Vieille, "Recursive axioms in deductive databases: The query-subquery approach", In *Proc. 1st Int. Conf. on Expert Database Systems*, 1986.

Database Updating Revisited

D. Laurent[1,2], V. Phan Luong[2,3], N. Spyratos[2]

[1] Université d'Orléans, LIFO, F-45067 Orléans Cedex 2, France
[2] Université de Paris-Sud, LRI, U.R.A. 410 du CNRS, Bât. 490
F-91405 Orsay Cedex, France
[3] Université de Provence, Place V. Hugo, F-13331 Cedex 3, France

Abstract. We address the issue of updating derived data in universal relation interfaces and in deductive databases. The proposed approach consists in marking those facts whose deletions are desired, and in processing these marks so as to appropriately answer queries. The database semantics is given in a general framework by fixpoint construction of three derivation operators computing exceptions, positive and negative facts.

The presented approach is applied to two different database formalisms using derived facts, namely, universal relation and Datalog^{neg} databases.

1 Introduction

In traditional approaches to database updating, updates are considered as *low-level* operations in the sense that they concern only information explicitly stored in the database. Consider, for example, a relational database dealing with employees, departments and projects, and containing two relations r_1 and r_2 over schemes *EMP DEPT* and *EMP PROJ*, respectively. The presence in the database of a tuple such as *John CS* means that employee *John* works in the *CS* department, and the presence of a tuple such as *John A* means that employee *John* works for project *A*. By querying this database, we can obtain the following tuples:

(*i*) *John CS A* (by joining the relations r_1 and r_2), and

(*ii*) *CS A* (by projecting the above join over *DEPT PROJ*).

Assume now that a user wants to represent the fact that there is a new project *B* in the *CS* department. To do this, the user must insert the tuple *CS B* and such an insertion is not possible, unless:

1. the user provides an employee name, say *e*, and

2. the tuples *e CS* and *e B* are inserted in the relations r_1 and r_2, respectively.

That is, the insertion of *CS B* must be *translated* into the insertions of *e CS* and of *e B*, and this translation is not *unique*, since the employee *e* is not given in the user's update.

Similarly, assume that a user wants to delete the tuple *John CS A*. Here again, the deletion must be *translated* into one of the deletions of *John CS* or of *John A* from the database. (Since updates are usually required to modify the database as little as possible, we are not allowed to remove both of the above tuples.)

As a consequence, the translation is not *unique,* since the user does not specify whether *John CS* or *John A* is to be removed.

The above examples give an indication of the problems encountered when updating *derived* data. These problems, generally referred to as non-deterministic updating ([2], [3], [7], [10], [12], [13], [14], [16], [20], [21], [24]), are among the most important problems in database updating. In this paper, we address the issue of updating derived data in relational and deductive databases. Our approach consists in marking those facts whose deletions are desired, and in processing these additional marks so as to appropriately answer queries.

Our approach is given in a general framework in which database semantics is obtained by fixpoint construction of three derivation operators acting on an abstract set whose elements we call items (an item can be a tuple or a fact or an elementary piece of information in general). The motivation for the proposed approach comes from recent results on intensional updates in universal relation interfaces and in deductive databases [13], [14]. In the remaining of this introductory section, we outline these results briefly and we point out the prominent features that led us to the general approach proposed in this paper.

First, we outline the results of [13], concerning universal relation interfaces. We assume that the database scheme is not fixed and we regard the database just as a set of tuples in which we may insert or delete any tuple. We do *not* remove tuples (physically) from the database. That is, if a tuple is deleted then we simply mark it as being deleted. So, at any given moment the database consists of two parts, the set of all unmarked tuples, that we shall denote by INS, and the set of all marked tuples, that we shall denote by DEL.

Now, when a tuple such as *John CS A* is inserted in the database then we consider it (intuitively) as a true tuple. Similarly, when a tuple is deleted from the database then we consider it as a false tuple. However, this way of regarding tuples has two immediate consequences. First, if we regard a tuple such as *John CS A* as true, then we must regard all its subtuples as true too and, second, if we regard a tuple as false then we must regard all its supertuples as false too.

These considerations lead us to define the semantics of a database using the following two operators: the operator *POS* that derives true tuples from those *assumed* true (*i.e.* from those in INS) and the operator *NEG* that derives false tuples from those *assumed* false (*i.e.* from those in DEL).

We call the database *consistent* if the set of inserted tuples contains no false tuples, *i.e.* if $INS \cap NEG(DEL) = \emptyset$. However, the above way of regarding derivation of tuples in universal relation interfaces may lead to inconsistencies.

For example, assume that $POS(INS)$ is the set of all subtuples of tuples in INS and that $NEG(DEL)$ is the set of all supertuples of tuples in DEL. If we insert the tuple *John CS A* and then delete the tuple *John CS*, we end up regarding the tuple *John CS A* as *both* true and false. We can avoid such inconsistencies as follows: we accept every derivation of true tuples in a consistent database *except* if the derivation produces a tuple in $NEG(DEL)$. In other words, the tuples in $NEG(DEL)$ act as *exceptions* to the inference mechanism defined by *POS*. Thus, we call semantics of the database the pair

$$(POS(\text{INS}) \setminus NEG(\text{DEL}) , NEG(\text{DEL})).$$

We regard tuples that are not in the semantics (*i.e.* neither in $POS(\text{INS})$ nor in $NEG(\text{DEL})$) as unknown tuples. As a consequence, it is important to note that we obtain a "three-valued" semantics, in the sense that a tuple can be true, false or unknown (with respect to a given database). In other words, our approach does not rely on the so-called *closed world assumption* of [19].

Summarizing our discussion so far, in universal relation interfaces, we define the insertion or the deletion of a tuple as follows:

insert t : – if t is not in the database, then place t in the database,
     else unmark t;
   – remove from the database all marked strict subtuples of t.

delete t : – if t is not in the database, then place t in the database;
   – mark t as being deleted;
   – remove from the database all unmarked strict supertuples of t.

What is important to note with respect to the above definitions is that (a) insertions and deletions become deterministic operations, (b) if the database is consistent then it remains consistent after every insertion or deletion of a tuple t, and (c) the insertion or the deletion of a tuple "triggers" further changes as in the case of active databases.

Relating our approach to other works, we mention here [2], [21], and [6] that are based on the weak instance model. Their main drawbacks are that they fail to accept certain insertions (due to the *fixed* scheme assumption), and that non-deterministic cases of deletion cannot be avoided, even if functional dependencies are considered, as in [21]. On the other hand, the approaches of [12], [16], which are based on the partition model, assume a non-fixed database scheme. This assumption allows for deterministic insertions, but is not sufficient to obtain deterministic deletions (see [12]). However, we note that in [16] *all* updates are deterministic, but at the cost of "over-deletion."

We outline now the results of [14], concerning deductive databases. We assume that we can store facts over intensional predicates explicitly and we regard the database as a set of facts and a set of rules, in which we can insert or delete any fact. We do *not* remove facts (physically) from the database. That is, if a fact is deleted then we simply mark it as being deleted. So, at any given moment the database consists of two parts, the set of all unmarked facts, that we shall denote by INS, and the set of all marked facts, that we shall denote by DEL. As in the case of universal relation interfaces, when a fact such as $assign(John, CS, A)$ is inserted in the database then we consider it (intuitively) as a true fact. Similarly, when a fact is deleted from the database then we consider it as a false fact.

Additional true and false facts can be derived using the rules. For example, in the presence of the rule $assign(E, D, P) \leftarrow works\_in(E, D), works\_for(E, P)$, the inserted facts $works\_in(John, CS)$ and $works\_for(John, A)$ allow for the derivation of the true fact $assign(John, CS, A)$. In this respect, the well-known "immediate consequence" operator ([5], [8], [22]) achieves this derivation by means of a least fixpoint computation. If, moreover, we allow rules to contain negations in their bodies, then we must regard the derivation process as defined from two operators $POS(F)$ and $NEG(F)$ over sets of positive or negative facts F (as in the case of well-founded semantics [5], [23]).

We call a database *consistent* if it contains no fact which is both inserted and deleted, *i.e.* if $\text{INS} \cap \text{DEL} = \emptyset$. However, starting from a consistent database, we may obtain inconsistencies during the derivation process. For example, let us consider the rule $assign(E, D, P) \leftarrow works\_in(E, D), works\_for(E, P)$ together with the inserted facts $works\_in(John, CS)$, $works\_for(John, A)$ and the deleted fact $assign(John, CS, A)$. The given rule and the inserted facts derive the (true) fact $assign(John, CS, A)$ which is a deleted fact! One way to avoid such inconsistencies is to consider the deleted facts as exceptions to the derivation rules.

In order to correctly handle these exceptions, we define the semantics of a database as the limit of the following sequence:

- $SEM^0 = \text{INS} \cup \neg.\text{DEL}$, and
- $SEM^{i+1} = (POS(SEM^i) \setminus \text{DEL}) \cup \neg.(NEG(SEM^i) \cup \text{DEL})$, for $i > 0$.

This way of computing the database semantics reflects the intuition that deleted facts act as *exceptions* to the derivation rules. So, we have two distinct ways to obtain a negative fact f : either f is an exception (because f is a deleted fact), or the semantic operator NEG derives f from the inserted facts, the deleted facts and the rules.

Summarizing our discussion so far, in the case of deductive databases, we define the insertion or the deletion of a fact f as follows:

    insert f : – if f is not in the database, then place f in the database;
             – if f is marked, then unmark f.
    delete f : – if f is not in the database, then place f in the database;
             – mark f as being deleted.

We note that, contrary to universal relation interfaces, exceptions (*i.e.* deleted facts) explicitly contribute to the derivation of positive facts in the semantics of the database. For example, the deleted fact $works\_in(John, CS)$ can contribute to the derivation of the fact $works\_hard(John)$ in the presence of the rule $works\_hard(E) \leftarrow \neg works\_in(E, CS)$.

In this context, it is interesting to note that the work of [9] uses exceptions in order to generalize negation by failure. These exceptions contribute to the derivation of new facts, as in our approach. However in [9], exceptions are *computed* through "metalevel constraints," and cannot be explicitly *specified* in the program, as we do in the case of deletions in our approach.

Comparing our approach with other works, we first note that marking facts as being deleted is related to [24], where updates on deductive databases are defined by means of *history predicates*. In [24], however, deleted facts are only used in order to process updates whereas, in our approach marked facts play an essential role in *query answering*.

One approach that leads to a deterministic updating can be found in [10] where knowledge bases are updated in such a way that *all* resulting states satisfying minimal change are computed. On the other hand, a radically different approach to updating consists in giving a transaction language. In [1] this approach is summarized by the sentence: "update = logic + control." However, the specification of these transactions is left to the user who cannot be sure to have solved all potentially non-deterministic cases. The formalism proposed in [20] seems to be an interesting approach in this respect.

In the light of our discussions so far, we can say that non-determinism of updating can be avoided in both paradigms if (a) we allow all informations to be stored in the database explicitly, and (b) we keep track of deleted information through a marking technique. Thus, following the terminology of [7], we consider all updates as *extensional* updates. However, the way in which information is marked and the way in which marked information is processed during derivations are apparently different in the two paradigms. Indeed:

1. In universal relation interfaces, marking a tuple t entails that other tuples must be removed from the database as well whereas, in a deductive database, marking a fact f does not entail that other facts must be removed from the database.

2. In universal relation interfaces, marked tuples act only as exceptions to derivations whereas, in a deductive database, marked facts not only act as exceptions, but also contribute to the derivation of new facts.

In what follows, we show that both paradigms are instances of one and the same mathematical framework. More precisely, in Section 2, we present our formal model in which database semantics is given by fixpoint construction of three derivation operators computing exceptions, positive tuples (facts) and negative tuples (facts). We show that insertion and deletion of tuples (facts) may require further changes on the database, thus requiring the database to be "active" if consistency is to be maintained. In Section 3, we apply our formalism to universal relation interfaces and to Datalog^{neg} databases, showing that both paradigms are instances of the same mathematical framework. Finally, Section 4 offers some concluding remarks and suggestions for further research. Proofs are omitted, due to lack of space; the reader is referred to the full paper [15].

2 The Formal Model

In this section, we consider a model in which derivations are processed incrementally through two operators on tuples or facts: the one concerns true tuples or facts and the other concerns false tuples or facts. During the derivation of true tuples or facts, deleted tuples or facts are treated as exceptions, *i.e.* they are discarded from the derivation and are incorporated in the derivation of false tuples of facts.

2.1 Definitions and Notations

We start with a set T whose elements we call *items*. In the case of a relational database, T would be the set of all tuples that one can form using symbols from the attribute domains. In the case of a Datalog^{neg} database, T would be the set of all facts in the underlying Herbrand base.

We call *i_pair*, a pair $P = (I, J)$ where I and J are sets of items, and we define the *consistency* of an i_pair as follows.

Definition 1. Given an i_pair $P = (I, J)$, we call I the positive part of P and J the negative part of P, and we write $pos(P) = I$ and $neg(P) = J$. Moreover, we call P *consistent* if $pos(P) \cap neg(P) = \emptyset$.

We compare i_pairs as follows: we call i_pair $P = (I, J)$ *smaller* than i_pair $P' = (I', J')$, denoted by $P \sqsubseteq P'$, if $I \subseteq I'$ and $J \subseteq J'$.

We now define a database to be a *quintuple* $\Delta = (\text{INS}, \text{DEL}, \xi, \pi, \nu)$ where INS and DEL are sets of items and ξ, π, ν are functions operating on items and referred to as the *exception operator*, the *positive operator* and the *negative operator*, respectively. More precisely, we have the following definition.

Definition 2. A *database* Δ is a quintuple $(\text{INS}, \text{DEL}, \xi, \pi, \nu)$ where:

- INS is the set of inserted items.
- DEL is the set of deleted items.
- ξ takes as argument a set of items and returns a set of items. We assume that:
  - $I \subseteq \xi(I)$, for every set of items I, and
  - ξ is *union-compatible*, i.e. $\xi(I \cup I') = \xi(I) \cup \xi(I')$, for all sets of items I and I'.
- π and ν each takes an i_pair as argument and returns a set of items. We assume that:
  - INS $\subseteq \pi(\text{INS}, \text{DEL})$,
  - π and ν are monotonic, i.e. $P \sqsubseteq P' \Rightarrow \pi(P) \subseteq \pi(P')$ and $\nu(P) \subseteq \nu(P')$, for all i_pairs P and P', and
  - π and ν are *mutually consistent*, i.e. for every consistent i_pair P, the i_pair $(\pi(P), \nu(P))$ is consistent.

Roughly speaking, ξ computes the set of all items that will act as exceptions in the derivation process defined through the operators π and ν. Moreover, one step of the derivation process computes an i_pair P' from a given i_pair P as follows: the positive and negative parts of P' are obtained by applying respectively the positive and negative operators to the i_pair P. In other words, P' is defined by $pos(P') = \pi(P)$ and $neg(P') = \nu(P)$. We shall see shortly in which way exceptions act on this computation.

It is easy to see that, due to union-compatibility, ξ is monotonic. Thus, the sequence

$\xi^0(\text{DEL}) = \text{DEL}$,

$\xi^\alpha(\text{DEL}) = \xi(\xi^{\alpha-1}(\text{DEL}))$, for every ordinal α having a predecessor,

$\xi^\alpha(\text{DEL}) = \bigcup_{\beta < \alpha} \xi^\beta(\text{DEL})$, for every limit ordinal α

has a limit. This limit is the *least fixpoint of ξ with respect to* DEL, and it is denoted by $lfp(\xi(\text{DEL}))$, or ξ_Δ for short. We note that, because of the above assumptions on ξ, we have: DEL $\subseteq \xi_\Delta$ and $\xi_\Delta = \bigcup_{\tau \in \text{DEL}} (lfp(\xi(\{\tau\})))$.

2.2 Database Semantics

Let $\Delta = (\text{INS}, \text{DEL}, \xi, \pi, \nu)$ be a database. In order to define the semantics of Δ, we start with the sets INS and DEL, and we perform least fixpoint computations using the operators ξ, π and ν.

We define an operator σ that takes an i_pair P as argument and returns an i_pair $\sigma(P)$ defined by:

$$pos(\sigma(P)) = \pi(P) \setminus \xi_\Delta \quad \text{and} \quad neg(\sigma(P)) = \nu(P) \cup \xi_\Delta.$$

Following the above definition of σ, *after* the exceptions are computed, they are taken into account in the computation of the semantics of the database as follows: the exceptions are removed from the positive part of the computed i_pair and they are put into the negative part of the computed i_pair. So, our approach can be seen as a particular case of making use of default rules [18].

It is the least fixpoint of σ with respect to the i_pair (INS, DEL) that we shall call the *semantics* of Δ. To this end, we need the following theorem which states the basic properties of σ in terms of those of ξ_Δ, π and ν.

Theorem 3. *Let $\Delta = (\text{INS}, \text{DEL}, \xi, \pi, \nu)$ be a database. Then:*

1. *σ is monotonic, i.e. for all i_pairs P and P', if $P \sqsubseteq P'$ then $\sigma(P) \sqsubseteq \sigma(P')$.*
2. *If P is a consistent i_pair, then so is $\sigma(P)$.*
3. *$\text{DEL} \subseteq neg(\sigma(\text{INS}, \text{DEL}))$ and, if $\text{INS} \cap \xi_\Delta = \emptyset$ then $\text{INS} \subseteq pos(\sigma(\text{INS}, \text{DEL}))$.*

Now, let us note that the set of all i_pairs equipped with the preordering $\sqsubseteq$ becomes a complete lattice if for all i_pairs $P = (I, J)$ and $P' = (I', J')$, we define

$$lub(P, P') = (I \cup I', J \cup J') \quad \text{and} \quad glb(P, P') = (I \cap I', J \cap J').$$

Thus, as σ is monotonic, the sequence

$\sigma^0(\text{INS}, \text{DEL}) = (\text{INS}, \text{DEL})$,

$\sigma^\alpha(\text{INS}, \text{DEL}) = \sigma(\sigma^{\alpha-1}(\text{INS}, \text{DEL}))$, for every ordinal α having a predecessor,

$\sigma^\alpha(\text{INS}, \text{DEL}) = (\bigcup_{\beta < \alpha} pos(\sigma^\beta(\text{INS}, \text{DEL})), \bigcup_{\beta < \alpha} neg(\sigma^\beta(\text{INS}, \text{DEL})))$,

for every limit ordinal α

has a limit. This limit is the *least fixpoint of σ with respect to* (INS, DEL). It is precisely this fixpoint that we call the *semantics* of Δ, as stated in the following definition.

Definition 4. Given a database $\Delta = (\text{INS}, \text{DEL}, \xi, \pi, \nu)$, the least fixpoint of σ with respect to the i_pair (INS, DEL) is called the *semantics of Δ*, and is denoted by σ_Δ.

As an immediate consequence of Theorem 3, we have:

1. If (INS, DEL) is consistent, then so is σ_Δ.
2. If $\text{INS} \cap \xi_\Delta = \emptyset$, then $\text{INS} \subseteq pos(\sigma_\Delta)$ and $\text{DEL} \subseteq neg(\sigma_\Delta)$.

In the light of our discussion so far, we define a database Δ to be consistent if there are no items that are in both sets INS and ξ_Δ.

Definition 5. A database $\Delta = (\text{INS}, \text{DEL}, \xi, \pi, \nu)$ is *consistent* if $\text{INS} \cap \xi_\Delta = \emptyset$.

It follows that: if Δ is consistent, then so is σ_Δ. We refer to the items of $pos(\sigma_\Delta)$ (respectively of $neg(\sigma_\Delta)$) as *positive* items (respectively as *negative* items) with respect to Δ.

Remark 1 - In the case where the database contains no exceptions, *i.e.* when $\xi_\Delta = \emptyset$, we have $pos(\sigma(P)) = \pi(P)$ and $neg(\sigma(P)) = \nu(P)$. Intuitively, this means that our approach can be seen as an extension of traditional approaches which do not use exceptions.

Remark 2 - In the presence of constraints such as functional dependencies, the semantics σ_Δ of the database must be consistent with respect to these constraints as well. We shall come back to this remark in the following Section 3.

2.3 Update Semantics

Definition 6. Let $\Delta = (\text{INS}, \text{DEL}, \xi, \pi, \nu)$ be a consistent database and let τ be an item.
Insertion: In order to insert τ in Δ
  – add τ in INS, and
  – remove from DEL all items μ such that $\tau \in lfp(\xi(\{\mu\}))$.
We denote by $ins(\Delta, \tau)$ the database after the insertion of τ has been performed.
Deletion: In order to delete τ from Δ
  – remove from INS all items of $lfp(\xi(\{\tau\}))$, and
  – add τ in DEL.
We denote by $del(\Delta, \tau)$ the database after the deletion of τ has been performed.

The following proposition states that the insertion and the deletion of τ as defined above are performed correctly, *i.e.* (*i*) if Δ is consistent then so are the resulting databases $ins(\Delta, \tau)$ and $del(\Delta, \tau)$, and (*ii*) τ is a positive item with respect to $ins(\Delta, \tau)$ and τ is a negative item with respect to $del(\Delta, \tau)$.

Proposition 7. *Let Δ be a database Δ and let τ be an item.*

1. *If Δ is consistent then so is $ins(\Delta, \tau)$ and $\tau \in pos(\sigma_{ins(\Delta, \tau)})$.*
2. *If Δ is consistent then so is $del(\Delta, \tau)$ and $\tau \in neg(\sigma_{del(\Delta, \tau)})$.*

We note that the above definitions of insertion and deletion imply (in general) modifications of *both* INS and DEL. These modifications are indispensable in order to preserve the consistency of the database.

3 Applications

In this section we apply our formalism to universal relation interfaces and to Datalog^{neg} databases. Further applications on view updating and on active databases will be reported in a forthcoming paper.

3.1 Universal Relation Interfaces

In a universal relation interface one assumes that the database scheme is not fixed and one regards the database just as a set of tuples δ in which we may insert or delete any tuple we wish. The set of tuples δ is usually required to satisfy a set F of functional dependencies ([2], [12], [13], [17], [22]). These assumptions are convenient for user interaction with the database, but lead to non-deterministic updating and other related problems that we have seen in the introduction.

In order to apply our approach in this context, given a database δ, we define a "shadow" database $\Delta = (\text{INS}, \text{DEL}, \xi, \pi, \nu)$ as follows:

- $\text{INS} = \delta$.
- DEL is the set of tuples that have been deleted from the database.
- For every set of tuples I, $\xi(I)$ is the set of all supertuples of tuples in I. Clearly, ξ is monotonic, union-compatible and satisfies $I \subseteq \xi(I)$, for every set of tuples I.
- For every i_pair $P = (I, J)$, where I and J are sets of tuples, define:
$$\pi(P) = \{q \mid \exists \tau \in I : q \text{ is a subtuple of } \tau\} \cup \{xya \mid xy, xa \in I, X \to A \in F\}.$$
  Clearly, π is monotonic and satisfies $I \subseteq \pi(P)$, for every i_pair $P = (I, J)$.
- For every i_pair $P = (I, J)$, where I and J are sets of tuples, define: $\nu(P) = \emptyset$. Clearly, ν is monotonic and, moreover π and ν are mutually consistent.

It follows that the formalism introduced in the previous section applies here and we define the semantics of δ to be those of Δ. We note that the negative operator ν above always computes the empty set. This reflects the fact that the relational model is concerned *only* with true tuples.

If the tuples of δ satisfy the functional dependencies, following Definition 5, a database $\Delta = (\text{INS}, \text{DEL}, \xi, \pi, \nu)$ is consistent iff INS contains no supertuple of a tuple in DEL.

Example 1. Let $U = \{A, B, C, D\}$ be a relational universe, let $\delta = \{ac, cd, ac', c'd\}$ be a database over U and let $F = \{B \to D, C \to D, AD \to C\}$ be a set of functional dependencies. Moreover, assume that the tuples bd and $ac'd$ have been deleted from the database. We define the database $\Delta = (\text{INS}, \text{DEL}, \xi, \pi, \nu)$ by:

$$\text{INS} = \{ac, cd, ac', c'd\} \qquad \text{and} \qquad \text{DEL} = \{bd, ac'd\}.$$

(and ξ, π, ν as done earlier). Here, ξ_Δ contains all supertuples of bd and $ac'd$. Clearly, INS and ξ_Δ are disjoint, so Δ is consistent. The semantics σ_Δ of Δ is defined by:

$$pos(\sigma_\Delta) = \{a, c, c', d, ac, cd, ac', c'd, acd, ad\} \qquad \text{and} \qquad neg(\sigma_\Delta) = \xi_\Delta.$$

We note that, $pos(\sigma_\Delta)$ contains all tuples in INS as well as all subtuples of the tuples in INS. Moreover, $pos(\sigma_\Delta)$ contains acd and all its subtuples, because ac and cd are inserted and $C \to D$ is in F. However, $ac'd$ is *not* in $pos(\sigma_\Delta)$ because $ac'd$ is deleted. So, $ac'd$ can be seen as an *exception* to the join rule applied to the dependency $C \to D$ and to the tuples ac' and $c'd$ of INS. We note that the tuples of $pos(\sigma_\Delta)$ do not violate the dependency $AD \to C$. $\quad\square$

As stated in the following proposition, π correctly computes the tuples obtained by the extension chase procedure of [17] and their subtuples.

Proposition 8. *Let δ be a relational database satisfying a set F of functional dependencies. Let $echase_F(T_\delta)$ be the tableau obtained through the extension chase procedure applied to the tuples in δ and to the functional dependencies of F. If* $DEL = \emptyset$ *then:*

$$pos(\sigma_\Delta) = \bigcup_{X \subseteq U} \Pi\!\downarrow_X (echase_F(T_\delta)),$$

where $\Pi\!\downarrow_X$ means total projection over X (i.e. $\Pi\!\downarrow_X$ contains variable-free tuples over X, [17]).

It is important to note that, in this paradigm, the role of functional dependencies is twofold because:

1. functional dependencies act as *derivation rules* in the definition of π and,
2. as usual in the relational model, functional dependencies are constraints that must be satisfied by the tuples in $pos(\sigma_\Delta)$.

As a consequence of point 2 above, insertions are conditioned by a test performed on the semantics $\sigma_{\Delta'}$ of the updated database Δ'. On the other hand, as deletions cannot generate contradictions with functional dependencies, no test is required during their processing. Thus we have:

Insertion: In order to insert τ in δ
  - add τ in the set INS, and
  - remove from DEL all subtuples of τ.
  - If $pos(\sigma_{\Delta'})$ satisfies the dependencies in F then accept the insertion else reject the insertion.

Deletion: In order to delete τ from δ
  - remove from INS all supertuples of τ, and
  - add τ in the set DEL.

Example 1. (continued) Let us insert the tuple abd in the database δ defined above. Since bd is a deleted subtuple of abd, bd is removed from DEL. Thus, the resulting database $\Delta' = (\text{INS}', \text{DEL}', \xi, \pi, \nu)$ is defined by:

$$\text{INS}' = \{ac, cd, ac', c'd, abd\} \qquad \text{and} \qquad \text{DEL}' = \{ac'd\}.$$

The semantics $\sigma_{\Delta'}$ of Δ' is defined by:

$pos(\sigma_{\Delta'}) = pos(\sigma_\Delta) \cup \{abd, ab, bd, b\}$, and
$neg(\sigma_{\Delta'}) = \xi_{\Delta'} = \{q \mid q \text{ is a supertuple of } ac'd\}$.

It is easily seen that the functional dependencies of F are satisfied by $pos(\sigma_{\Delta'})$, entailing that the insertion is accepted.

Let us now delete the tuple a from the database δ defined above. Since ad and ac' are inserted supertuples of a, we must remove them from INS. Thus, the resulting database $\Delta' = (\text{INS}', \text{DEL}', \xi, \pi, \nu)$ is defined by:

$$\text{INS}' = \{cd, c'd\} \qquad \text{and} \qquad \text{DEL}' = \{bd, ac'd, a\}.$$

The semantics $\sigma_{\Delta'}$ of Δ' is defined by:

$pos(\sigma_{\Delta'}) = \text{INS}'$ and $neg(\sigma_{\Delta'}) = \xi_{\Delta'} = \{q \mid q \text{ is a supertuple of } bd \text{ or of } a\}$. $\square$

3.2 Datalog^{neg} Databases

In traditional approaches ([5], [8], [22]), a Datalog^{neg} database δ is a pair $\delta = (F, R)$ where F is a set of facts and R is a set of safe rules over a first order function-free alphabet. For such databases we consider the so-called well-founded semantics [23] that we recall here.

Given a first order alphabet $\mathbf{A}$, a *partial interpretation* of $\mathbf{A}$ is a consistent set of positive or negative literals. More formally, Int is a partial interpretation of $\mathbf{A}$ if there exist two sets of facts I and J such that $I \cap J = \emptyset$ and $Int = I \cup \neg.J$ (where $\neg.J$ denotes the set $\{\neg f \mid f \in J\}$). Then, given a Datalog^{neg} database δ we denote by $inst\_\delta$ the set of all instantiated rules obtained by fully instantiating the rules in δ. For every such instantiated rule r, $head(r)$ denotes the fact which constitutes the head of r and $body(r)$ denotes the set of the ground literals in the body of r.

The *well-founded model* of δ [23] is a partial interpretation of $\mathbf{A}$ which is defined to be the least fixpoint computed from two operators that we now recall:

1. The membership immediate consequence operator $T^{\in}$ is defined by:
$$T^{\in}(Int) = \{head(r) \mid r \in inst\_\delta, body(r) \subseteq Int\},$$
   for every partial interpretation Int.
2. Given a partial interpretation Int, the greatest unfounded set with respect to Int, denoted by $GUS(Int)$, is the union of all sets U such that:
$$(\forall r \in inst\_\delta)(head(r) = f \Rightarrow \exists L \in body(r) : \neg L \in Int \vee L \in U).$$

The well-founded semantics of δ is the limit of the following sequence of partial interpretations: $Int_1 = T^{\in}(\emptyset) \cup \neg.GUS(\emptyset)$, and for $i > 1$, $Int_i = T^{\in}(Int_{i-1}) \cup \neg.GUS(Int_{i-1})$.

Datalog^{neg} databases constitute a significant step forward from classical relational databases, as they offer a more declarative style and more expressive power [5], [8], [22]. However, as we have seen in the introduction, their updating presents difficult problems, especially when it comes to updating intensional predicates.

In order to apply our approach in this context, given a Datalog^{neg} database $\delta = (F, R)$, we define a "shadow" database $\Delta = (\text{INS}, \text{DEL}, \xi, \pi, \nu)$ as follows:

- INS $= F$.
- DEL is the set of facts that have been deleted.
- For every set of facts I, $\xi(I) = I$, *i.e.* ξ is the identity function.
  Clearly, ξ is union-compatible and satisfies $I \subseteq \xi(I)$, for every set of facts I.
- For every i-pair $P = (I, J)$, where I and J are sets of facts,
  $\pi(P) = T^{\in}(I \cup \neg.J)$.
  It can be seen from [23] that the operator $T^{\in}$ is monotonic and that every inserted fact τ belongs to every $T^{\in}(I \cup \neg.J)$. Thus, following our formalism, π is monotonic and satisfies INS $\subseteq \pi(\text{INS}, \text{DEL})$.
- For every i-pair $P = (I, J)$, where I and J are sets of facts,
  $\nu(P) = GUS(I \cup \neg.J)$.

It has been shown in [23] that the operator GUS is monotonic and that $T^{\in}(I \cup \neg .J) \cup \neg .GUS(I \cup \neg .J)$ is a partial interpretation. So, following our formalism, ν is monotonic and π and ν are mutually consistent.

It follows that the formalism introduced in Section 2 applies here and we define the semantics of δ to be those of Δ. We note that, seeing the definition of ξ, for every fact τ, we have $lfp(\xi(\{\tau\})) = \{\tau\}$. Therefore, following Definition 5, the database $\Delta = (\text{INS}, \text{DEL}, \xi, \pi, \nu)$ is consistent if $\text{INS} \cap \text{DEL} = \emptyset$.

Example 2. Consider a database $\delta = (F, R)$ where $F = \{r(a, b), s(b, c)\}$ and where R is the following set of rules:

$$R \; : \; q(x, y, z) \leftarrow r(x, y), s(y, z)$$
$$p(x, z) \leftarrow q(x, y, z)$$
$$t(x, z) \leftarrow q(x, y, z), \neg p(x, z)$$

Moreover, assume that the fact $p(a, c)$ has been deleted from the database. We define the database $\Delta = (\text{INS}, \text{DEL}, \xi, \pi, \nu)$ by:

$$\text{INS} = \{r(a, b), s(bc)\} \qquad \text{and} \qquad \text{DEL} = \{p(a, c)\}$$

(and ξ, π, ν as done earlier). Here, we have $\xi_\Delta = \{p(a, c)\}$ thus Δ is consistent and it can be seen that the semantics σ_Δ of Δ is defined by:

$$pos(\sigma_\Delta) = \{r(a, b), s(b, c), q(a, b, c), t(a, c)\} \quad \text{and} \quad neg(\sigma_\Delta) = HB \setminus pos(\sigma_\Delta)$$

where HB denotes the underlying Herbrand base. We note that, in addition to the facts of INS, $pos(\sigma_\Delta)$ contains the facts $q(a, b, c)$ and $t(a, c)$. Indeed, $q(a, b, c)$ has been obtained from the inserted facts, using the first rule, and $t(a, c)$ has been obtained from $q(a, b, c)$ and the negation of the deleted fact $p(a, c)$, using the last rule. On the other hand, $p(a, c)$ is not in $pos(\sigma_\Delta)$ because it is a deleted fact. So, $p(a, c)$ can be seen as an *exception* to the second rule above. □

In the case of a Datalog^{neg} database, since $lfp(\xi(\{\tau\})) = \{\tau\}$ for every fact τ, Definition 6 applies as follows:

Insertion: In order to insert τ in δ
- add τ in the set INS, and
- if τ is in DEL then remove τ from DEL.

Deletion: In order to delete τ from δ
- if τ is in INS then remove τ from INS, and
- add τ in the set DEL.

Example 2. (continued) Let us insert the fact $p(a, c)$ in the database δ defined above. Since $p(a, c)$ is in DEL, we must remove it from DEL. Thus, the resulting database $\Delta' = (\text{INS}', \text{DEL}', \xi, \pi, \nu)$ is defined by:

$$\text{INS}' = \{r(a, b), s(b, c), p(a, c)\} \qquad \text{and} \qquad \text{DEL}' = \emptyset.$$

The semantics $\sigma_{\Delta'}$ of Δ' is defined by:

$$pos(\sigma_{\Delta'}) = \{r(a, b), s(b, c), q(a, b, c), p(a, c)\}\cdot \text{ and } neg(\sigma_{\Delta'}) = HB \setminus pos(\sigma_{\Delta'}).$$

Let us delete the fact $r(a,b)$ from the database δ defined above. Since $r(a,b)$ is in INS, we must remove it from INS. Thus, the resulting database $\Delta' = (\text{INS}', \text{DEL}', \xi, \pi, \nu)$ is defined by:

$$\text{INS}' = \{s(b,c)\} \quad \text{and} \quad \text{DEL}' = \{p(a,c), r(a,b)\}.$$

The semantics $\sigma_{\Delta'}$ of Δ' is defined by:

$$pos(\sigma_{\Delta'}) = \text{INS}' \quad \text{and} \quad neg(\sigma_{\Delta'}) = HB \setminus pos(\sigma_{\Delta'}). \qquad \square$$

4 Concluding Remarks and Further Research

We have seen a new method for updating databases which allows the insertion or deletion of *any* item in a deterministic manner. The key idea is to mark deleted items and to use them as explicit exceptions to the derivation rules. We have defined the database semantics in terms of both inserted and deleted items and of three fixpoint operators which compute items that act as exceptions to the derivation rules, the true items, and the false items, respectively.

We have applied our method to two seemingly different database paradigms, namely, universal relation interfaces and Datalog^{neg} databases. In the context of Datalog^{neg} databases, in particular, it seems that by defining the exception operator ξ in a less trivial way than as identity, we can have a method which generalizes the approaches of [13] and [14]. We are currently investigating this research direction. Additionally, we are also investigating properties of updates in order to minimize the overhead incurred by the storage of marked items.

Finally, we would like to point out the importance of such a general approach to database updating because, in addition to the paradigms dealt with in this paper, our approach provides a general framework (*i*) for studying temporal aspects in databases (for example based on the general approach of [11]), (*ii*) for studying view updating, based on [4], and (*iii*) for adding production rules in the database in order to enforce consistency, thus rendering the database active.

References

1. S. Abiteboul: Updates, a New Frontier. ICDT, Intl. Conf., *LNCS*, Springer-Verlag, 1988.
2. P. Atzeni, R. Torlone: Updating Databases in the Weak Instance Model. ACM SIGACT-SIGMOD-SIGART, Symp. on Principles of Database Systems, 1989.
3. P. Atzeni, R. Torlone: Updating Intensional Predicates in Datalog. *Data & Knowledge Engineering*, 8, 1992.
4. F. Bancilhon, N. Spyratos "Update Semantics of Relational Views. ACM *Transactions On Database Systems*, 6(4), 1981.
5. N. Bidoit: Negation in Rule-Based Database Languages: a Survey. *Theoretical Computer Science*, 78, 1991.
6. V. Brosda, G. Vossen: Update and Retrieval in a Relational Database through a Universal Schema Interface. ACM *Transactions On Database Systems*, 13(4), 1988.
7. F. Bry: Intensional Updates: Aduction via Deduction. Intl. Symposium on Logic Programming, 1990.

8. S. Ceri, G. Gottlob, L. Tanca, *Logic Programming and Databases*. Surveys in Computer Science, Springer-Verlag, 1990.
9. K. Eshghi, R.A. Kowalski: Abduction Compared with Negation by Failure. Intl. Symposium on Logic Programming, 1989.
10. G. Grahne, A.O. Mendelzon, P.Z. Revesz: Knowledgebase Transformations. ACM SIGACT-SIGMOD-SIGART, Symp. on Principles of Database Systems, 1992.
11. C.S. Jensen, R.T. Snodgrass: Temporal Specialization. 8th *IEEE* ICDE, 1992.
12. D. Laurent, N. Spyratos: A Partition Approach to Updating Universal Scheme Interfaces. To appear in *IEEE Transactions on Knowledge and Data Engineering*, 1993.
13. D. Laurent, V. Phan Luong, N. Spyratos: Deleted Tuples are Useful when Updating through Universal Scheme Interfaces. 8th *IEEE* ICDE, 1992.
14. D. Laurent, V. Phan Luong, N. Spyratos: Updating Intensional Predicates in Deductive Databases. 9th *IEEE* ICDE, 1993.
15. D. Laurent, V. Phan Luong, N. Spyratos: Database Updating Revisited. Technical Report LIFO 93-4, 1993.
16. Ch. Lécluse, N. Spyratos: Implementing Queries and Updates on Universal Scheme Interfaces. VLDB Intl. Conf., 1988.
17. D. Maier, *The Theory of Relational Databases*. Computer Science Press, 1983.
18. R. Reiter: A Logic for Default Reasoning. *Artificial Intelligence*, 13, 1980.
19. R. Reiter: Towards a Logical Reconstruction of Relational Database Theory. in *On Conceptual Modelling* (M. L. Brodie, J. Mylopoulos, J. W. Schmidt), Springer-Verlag, 1984.
20. R. Reiter: On Formalizing Database Updates: Preliminary Report. EDBT Intl. Conf., 1992.
21. R. Torlone, P. Atzeni: Updating Deductive Databases with Functional Dependencies. DOOD Intl. Conf., *LNCS* 566, Springer-Verlag, 1991.
22. J.D. Ullman, *Principles of Databases and Knowledge Base Systems*. Vol. I-II, Computer Science Press, 1989.
23. A. Van Gelder, K.A. Ross, J.S. Schlipf: The Well-founded Semantics for General Logic Programs. *J. of the ACM*, 38(3), 1991.
24. M. Winslett: A Model-Based Approach to Updating Databases with Incomplete Information. ACM *Transactions On Database Systems*, 13(2), 1988.

Super-Key Classes for Updating Materialized Derived Classes in Object Bases

Shin'ichi KONOMI[1], Tetsuya FURUKAWA[1] and Yahiko KAMBAYASHI[2]

[1] Computer Center, Kyushu University, Higashi, Fukuoka 812, Japan
email: {konomi,furukawa}@cc.kyushu-u.ac.jp
[2] Integrated Media Environment Experimental Laboratory, Kyoto University,
Sakyo, Kyoto 606, Japan
email: yahiko@kuis.kyoto-u.ac.jp

Abstract. We describe data structures that allow efficient updates of materialized classes derived from relationship of classes in object bases. Materialization of derived classes reduces costs of retrievals and increases costs of updates. Costs of updates increase remarkably when several paths of objects derive the same object. If object bases satisfy the super-key condition proposed in this paper, consistencies of object bases are maintained by local navigations and the remarkable increase of the costs is avoided. Any object base can be transformed to satisfy the super-key condition by adding extra classes and their objects. In this manner, increasing redundancies allows efficient updates.

1 Introduction

In databases, redundant data structures introduced to reduce costs of retrievals often increase costs of updates. Database management systems should allow efficient retrievals with minimal increase of update costs.

Views in databases are proposed to provide flexibility without affecting underlying data. Views in object bases are also proposed introducing imaginary objects, virtual classes and virtual class hierarchies [1]. Costs of retrievals that are required to produce views depend on access paths of underlying data and complexity of view definitions.

Materialization of views allows fast retrievals of views regardless of access paths of underlying data and complexity of view definitions. However, when updates occur in object bases, extra costs are required to keep materialized views consistent.

Compared with replicated data in distributed databases, materialized views cause more expensive update overheads since they may require recomputation of views. The following example shows characteristics of updating materialized views.

Example 1. Let us consider a video database. The whole sequences of frames (images) are partitioned into scenes. In Fig.1(a), Mick and Paul appear at Airport in Scene1, Mick, Paul, and a dog at Airport in Scene2, and Mick and John at Hotel in Scene3. Figure 1 (b) shows objects and their connections in the video database.

Presence1 and Presence2 are derived objects where Presence1 is Mick's presence at Airport and Presence2 is Mick's presence at Hotel.

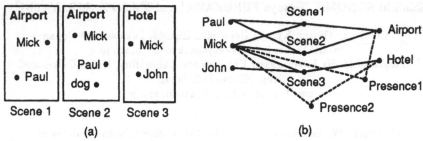

Fig. 1. Video database

Suppose the derived objects are materialized and Scene2 is deleted in editing the video. Since Mick is at Airport in Scene2, Mick may lose his presence at Airport. However, after retrieving connections of objects, we find that he is still at Airport in Scene1. Thus, Presence1 is not deleted. □

There are three different approaches for efficient maintenance of materialized views:

Optimal Refresh Frequency of Materialized Views: Analytical modeling and optimal refresh policies of materialized view maintenance are presented in [12].

Screening of Updates of Materialized Views: Blakeley et al.[2] present conditions for detecting when an update of a base relation cannot affect a derived relation and for detecting when a derived relation can be updated using only the data of the derived relation itself and the given update operation.

Incremental Updates of Materialized Views: The algorithm presented in [9] derives the minimal incremental relational expressions that need recomputation. Roussopoulos[10] discusses incremental updates of a stored collection of pointers pointing to records of underlying relations needed to materialize a view.

Here we focus on the third approach and discuss efficient methods of incremental updates of materialized classes derived from relational expressions including projections.

In this paper, data structures that permit efficient incremental updates of materialized derived classes are described. When classes are derived from a path of classes in a class schema, the key of the path is defined to be utilized for updates. Class schemas satisfy the super-key condition presented in this paper if derived classes and the keys of the paths from which the classes are derived are contained in the same subgraphs of class schemas. If class schemas satisfy the super-key condition, incremental updates are performed efficiently by detecting multiple paths of underlying objects utilizing objects of classes in keys. A procedure to transform class schemas so that they satisfy the super-key condition is presented. Though the procedure add extra classes and introduce more redundancies into object bases, it allows efficient deletions of objects.

Section 2 gives the definition of our model of object bases. Section 3 introduces materialized derived classes in object bases. Section 4 gives a procedure to maintain consistencies of materialized derived classes. Section 5 discusses data structures that allow efficient update propagations introducing the super-key condition and super-key classes. Section 6 describes design of object bases for efficient update propagations. Section 7 gives our conclusion.

2　A Model of Object Bases

The model described here focuses on connections of objects and relationships of classes from which classes are derived. Objects are values associated with their identifiers. Values of objects are assumed to be classified as follows:

basic values: The special symbol *nil* or values from domain D, the union of all the domains in a database.

set-values: A set $\{id_1, id_2, \ldots, id_n\}$ is a set-value where id_i $(1 \leq i \leq n)$ is an object identifier (OID).

tuple-values: Let id_i $(1 \leq i \leq m)$ be an OID and a_i $(1 \leq i \leq m)$ be an attribute. $< a_1 : id_1, a_2 : id_2, \ldots, a_m : id_m >$ is a tuple-value.

Objects belong to classes and classes are structured in class hierarchies with ISA relationships, denoted by $\dashrightarrow$. Classes are defined when object bases are designed. One of the above types of values is assumed to be specified in each class. If tuple-values are specified in a class, attributes are also specified in the class.

Relationships of classes and connections of objects are classified as follows:

Set relationships and set connections A set relationship from a class C to a class C' is denoted by $C \twoheadrightarrow C'$. Objects in class C are set-value objects $o = (id, \{id_1, id_2, \ldots, id_n\})$ and all the objects identified by $id_1, id_2, \ldots, id_n$ are in class C'. A set connection is a set of m links from object o to an object identified by id_i $(1 \leq i \leq m)$.

Reference relationships and reference connections A reference relationship from a class C to a class C' on attribute a_i is denoted by $C \overset{a_i}{\rightsquigarrow} C'$. $C \rightsquigarrow C'$ is used instead of $C \overset{a_i}{\rightsquigarrow} C'$ if the attribute is trivial. The set of all the attribute of class C is denoted by $Att(C)$. Objects in class C are tuple-value objects $o = (id, < a_1 : id_1, a_2 : id_2, \ldots, a_m : id_m >)$ and object o' identified by one of id_i $(1 \leq i \leq m)$ is in class C'. A reference connection is a link from o to o'.

ISA relationships ISA relationship from a class C to a class C' is denoted by $C \dashrightarrow C'$.

A class schema is a labeled directed graph $S(V, E)$ where set of vertices V represents the set of all the classes in the schema and set of edges E represents the set of all the relationships of classes in the schema.

Example 2. Figure 2 shows a part of the class schema for the video database in Fig.1. Each vertex in the figure represents a class. ISA relationships in the figure show that classes Person and Animal are subclasses of class Creature. Arrows with attribute names represent reference relationships. Objects in class Scene references objects in class Location as values of attribute Place, objects in class Animal or Persons as values of attribute Appearance. Arrows with doubled arrowheads represent set relationships. Objects in class Persons references objects in class Person as sets.

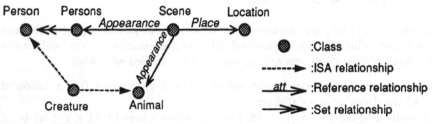

Fig. 2. Class schema for video database

□

An object graph is a labeled directed graph $O(v, e)$ where v is a set of vertices and e is a set of edges. Each vertex of v corresponds to one of a basic-value, a set-value or a tuple-value object. Each edge of e corresponds to a link in reference connections or in set connections.

Example 3. Figure 3 shows an object graph corresponding to the class schema in Fig.2. Objects in each class are encircled under the name of the class. □

Definition 1. Let $S'(V', E')$ be a connected subgraph of class schema $S(V, E)$ and $O(v, e)$ and $O'(v', e')$ be object graphs of $S(V, E)$ and $S'(V', E')$, respectively. $S'(V', E')$ and $O'(v', e')$ are an class subschema of $S(V, E)$ and an object subgraph of $O(v, e)$, respectively. Note that O' is a subgraph of object graph O if O' is an object subgraph of O. □

Objects in object graph $O(v, e)$ and classes in class schema $S(V, E)$ are related by function *inst*. $inst(C)$ represents all the object in class C. Paths of classes $P_S = (C_1, C_2, \ldots, C_n)$ is a path in the undirected graph that corresponds to class schema S. P is used instead of P_S if S is trivial. $inst(P_S)$ is a set of paths $p = (o_1, o_2, \ldots, o_n)$ where $o_i \in inst(C_i)$ $(1 \le i \le n)$. Paths can be represented with lists of vertices assuming that only one edge exists between two adjacent objects.

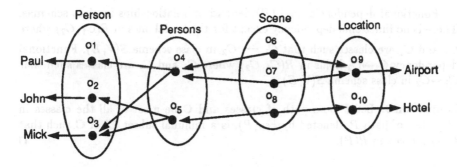

Fig. 3. Object graph

Definition 2. Let S be a class schema and $P_S = (C_1, C_2, \ldots, C_s)$ be a path of classes. A relation of P_S, denoted by $R(P_S)$, is relation $R(C_1, C_2, \ldots, C_s)$. Instances of $R(P_S)$ is a set of tuples $(o_1, o_2, \ldots, o_s)$ where $p = (o_1, o_2, \ldots, o_s)$ and $p \in inst(P_S)$. $R(C_1, C_2, \ldots, C_s)$ is a relation in the relational model whose attributes and tuples correspond classes and set of objects. □

Functional dependencies in relation $R(P)$ are functional dependencies in relation $R(C_1, C_2, \ldots, C_s)$ in the relational model. $R(P)[C_i = o]$ and $R(P)[C_{k_1}, C_{k_2}, \ldots, C_{k_t}]$ denote selection and projection as in the relation model. Let P' be a subgraph of P and $\{C_{k_1}, C_{k_2}, \ldots, C_{k_t}\}$ be the set of all the classes in P'. $R(P)[P']$ denotes projection $R(P)[C_{k_1}, C_{k_2}, \ldots, C_{k_t}]$. Note that $R[P][P'] = R[P']$.

Example 4. Let $P = (\text{Person}, \text{Persons}, \text{Scene}, \text{Location})$ be a path of classes and functional dependencies Scene → Persons and Scene → Location be asserted. Table 1 shows an instance of relational schema $R(P)$. Since functional dependencies Scene → Persons and Scene → Location hold in $R(P)$, a key of $R(P)$ is {Scene, Person}.

Table 1. Relation of path (Person, Persons, Scene, Location)

Person	Persons	Scene	Location
o_1	o_4	o_6	o_9
o_1	o_4	o_7	o_9
o_2	o_5	o_8	o_{10}
o_3	o_4	o_6	o_9
o_3	o_4	o_7	o_9
o_3	o_5	o_8	o_{10}

□

Functional dependencies in $R(P)$ depend on relationships in class schemas. There is no functional dependency except for the trivial ones in $R(C_1, C_2)$ where C_1 and C_2 are classes such that $C_1 \twoheadrightarrow C_2$ in class schema $S(V, E)$. Functional dependency $C_1 \rightarrow C_2$ holds in $R(C_1, C_2)$ where C_1 and C_2 are classes such that $C_1 \rightsquigarrow C_2$ in class schema $S(V, E)$.

Definition 3. Let P be a path of classes and **C** be a set of all the classes in P. A key of path P, denoted by $key(P)$, is a minimal subset **C'** of **C** such that **C'**$\rightarrow$**C** holds in $R(P)$. $\square$

3 Materialized Derived Classes in Object Bases

When derived classes are materialized to allow fast retrievals, redundancies increase in object bases and costs of updates increase.

Example 5. In the class schema of Fig.4, class **Presence** is added to the class schema in Fig.2. Correspondences of locations and persons are easily retrieved from objects in class **Presence**.

Suppose object o_7 of **Scene** is deleted. Since navigations from o_7 gives o_4, o_1 (Paul), and o_9 (Airport), the connection between o_1 (Paul) and o_9 (Airport) may be lost after the deletion of o_7. If no connection between o_1 (Paul) and o_9 (Airport) exists, object o_{12} of class **Presence** should be deleted to keep the class schema consistent. However, after navigating from all the objects in class **Scene**, i.e., o_6, o_7, and o_8, to class **Person** and to class **Location** we find o_1 (Paul) and o_9 (Airport) is still connected through o_6 after the deletion of o_7. In this case, object o_{12} is not deleted. $\square$

An object derived from an object graph O is assumed to have tuple value $< a_1 : id_1, a_2 : id_2, ..., a_s : id_m >$ where id_i ($1 \leq i \leq m$) identifies an object in O. A class derived from a class schema S is a class of objects derived from an object graph of S.

Definition 4. Let o be an object, C be the class of o, P be a path of classes, and $p \in inst(P)$. If every OID that appears as a value of object o is in p, o is an object derived from p, denoted by $o \triangleleft p$. If, for every object o that belongs to C, there exists $p \in inst(P)$ such that $o \triangleleft p$, C is a class derived from P, denoted by $C \triangleleft P$. $\square$

Derived class C can be materialized in the following manner for quick retrievals of objects in C.

Given class schema S, path of classes P_S and class $C^+ \triangleleft P_S$, C^+ can be added to S by merging $S(V, E)$ and class schema $S^+(V^+, E^+)$ that is constructed as follows:

(1) Let C^+ be the class of tuple-value objects $o = (id, < a_1 : id_1, a_2 : id_2, ..., a_n : id_m >)$. Add C^+ to V^+.

316

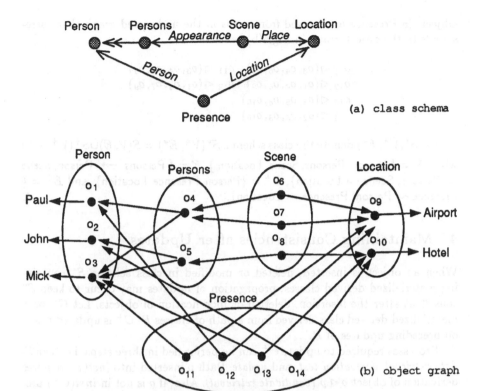

(a) class schema

(b) object graph

Fig. 4. Introduction of materialized derived class and objects

(2) Let C_i be such a class in S that includes the object identified by id_i for every object o in C^+. Add an edge $C^+ \rightsquigarrow C_i$ to E^+ for each C_i.

$S^*(V^*, E^*)$ denotes an class schema obtained by merging $S(V, E)$ and $S^+(V^+, E^+)$, i.e., $V^* = V \cup V^+$ and $E^* = E \cup E^+$. Object graphs corresponding to $S^+(V^+, E^+)$ and $S^*(V^*, E^*)$ are denoted by $O^+(v^+, e^+)$ and $O^*(v^*, e^*)$, respectively. Class C^+ is called a materialized derived class.

Let P_S be a path of classes, $C^+ \lhd P_S$ be a materialized derived class, $S^*(V^*, E^*)$ be a class schema obtained by adding C^+ to S where $S^*(V^*, E^*) = S(V, E) \cup S^+(V^+, E^+)$. $A^+ = V \cap V^+$ is the set of all the classes that belong to both S and S^+. Let $\{P_1, P_2, \ldots, P_n\}$ be the set of all the paths in S^+. $R(S^+) = R(P_1) \bowtie R(P_2) \bowtie \cdots \bowtie P(P_n)$. $R(S^+)[A^+]$ is a relation on attributes A^+ which is obtained from class schema S^+. $R(P_S)[A^+]$ is a relation on attributes A^+ which is obtained from class schema S.

Definition 5. $S^*(V^*, E^*)$ is consistent iff $R(S^+)[A^+] = R(P_S)[A^+]$. ☐

Example 6. In Fig.4(a), Presence is a materialized class derived from path (Person, Persons, Scene, Location), denoted by Presence ⊲ (Person, Persons, Scene, Location).

Objects in **Presence** are derived from paths in the undirected graph that corresponds to the object graph in Fig.4(b) as follows:

$$o_{11} \lhd (o_3, o_4, o_6, o_9) \quad o_{11} \lhd (o_3, o_4, o_7, o_9)$$
$$o_{12} \lhd (o_1, o_4, o_6, o_9) \quad o_{12} \lhd (o_1, o_4, o_7, o_9)$$
$$o_{13} \lhd (o_3, o_5, o_8, o_{10})$$
$$o_{14} \lhd (o_2, o_5, o_8, o_{10})$$

Let $S^*(V^*, E^*)$ denote the class schema. $S^*(V^*, E^*) = S(V, E) \cup S^+(V^+, E^+)$ where $V = \{$ Person, Persons, Scene, Location $\}$, $E = \{$ Persons $\twoheadrightarrow$ Person, Scene $\rightsquigarrow$ Persons, Scene $\rightsquigarrow$ Location$\}$, $V^+ = \{$Person, Presence, Location$\}$, and $E^+ = \{$ Presence $\rightsquigarrow$ Person, Presence $\rightsquigarrow$ Location$\}$. □

4   Maintaining Consistencies after Updates

When an object is inserted, deleted or modified in class schema S^* containing materialized derived classes, propagation of updates may occur to keep S^* consistent after the insertion, deletion or modification of objects. Let C^+ be a materialized derived class derived from a path of classes P. C^+ is updated based on preceding updates of P.

Processes required to update C^+ can be performed in three steps, i.e., *candidate retrieval*, *derivation test*, and *update*. Path p inserted into $inst(P)$ requires derivation of object $o \lhd p$ *(candidate retrieval)*. Also, if o is not in $inst(C^+)$ previously *(derivation test)*, o must be inserted into $inst(C^+)$ *(update)*. To check if o is in $inst(C^+)$, traversal of entire $inst(C^+)$ may be required. Path p deleted from $inst(P)$ requires derivation of object $o \lhd p$ *(candidate retrieval)*. Also, if p is the only path such that $o \lhd p$ in $inst(P)$ *(derivation test)*, o must be deleted from $inst(C^+)$ *(update)*. Finding such a path except for p that $o \lhd p$ normally requires much cost since entire $inst(P)$ are retrieved and object $o \lhd p$ are derived for every path $p \in inst(P)$ in the worst cases. In the following part of the paper, we reduce the costs of processes required to maintain consistencies after a deletion of an object.

Suppose $C^+ \lhd P$ is updated. Followings are candidate retrieval and derivation test that are represented as relational expressions. Let object o of class C_u in P be inserted, deleted or modified.

Candidate retrieval: Obtain $R^c = (R(P)[C_u = o] \bowtie R(S^+))[C^+]$.
Derivation test: Obtain $R^c - (R(P)[C_u \neq o] \bowtie R(S^+))[C^+]$

Following part of this section gives a procedure that is sufficient to keep S^* consistent after a deletion of an object in P. First, P' is defined to trim P for C^+.

Definition 6. Let $C^+ \lhd P$ be a materialized derived class. If P' is the minimal subgraph of P such that satisfies $C^+ \lhd P'$, P' is a *corresponding path* of C^+, denoted by $P' \unrhd C^+$. □

Only the updates of subgraph P' of P affect objects in C^+.

Lemma 7. *Let* $P' \unrhd C^+$ *be a subgraph of* P. $R(S^+)[A^+] = R(P)[A^+]$ *iff* $R(S^+)[A^+] = R(P')[A^+]$.

Proof. Since P' is a subgraph of P, $R(P') = R(P)[P']$. Thus, $R(P')[A^+] = R(P)[P'][A^+] = R(P)[A^+]$. If $R(S^+)[A^+] = R(P')[A^+]$, $R(S^+)[A^+] = R(P)[A^+]$. Also, if $R(S^+)[A^+] = R(P)[A^+]$, $R(S^+)[A^+] = R(P')[A^+]$. $\quad\square$

The following procedure updates materialized derived class C^+ after a deletion of an object in P' such that $P' \unrhd C^+$. If V^+ contains more than one materialized derived classes, apply the procedure to each of the materialized derived class. After applying the procedure, S^* is consistent.

Procedure 8. *Let* $C^+ \lhd P$ *be a materialized derived class and* $P' \unrhd C^+$ *be a subgraph of* P. *Given class schema* S^* *and deleted object* o *of class* C_u *in* P'.

(1) **Candidate Retrieval:** *Navigate in* P' *to find a path* $p \in inst(P')$ *that contains* o *and then navigate from* p *to obtain a set of objects in* C^+ *that are connected to* p. *The obtained objects are the candidate objects, denoted by* o^c.
(2) **Derivation Test:** *For each* $o^c \in o^c$, *navigate in* P' *to find all the paths in* $inst(P')$ *that do not contain* o *and* $o^c \lhd p$.
(3) **Deletion:** *If no path is found for* $o^c \in o^c$ *in the preceding derivation test, o and o^c are deleted. Otherwise, o is deleted.* $\quad\square$

Since navigations in Step 1 is performed with only the paths in $inst(P')$ that contains o, there is no need to traverse entire $inst(P')$. However, Step 2 may require to traverse entire $inst(P')$ in the worst cases.

Lemma 9. *Let* $S^*(V^*, E^*)$ *be a consistent class schema,* C *and* C^+ *be classes in* S^+, *and* P *and* P' *be paths of classes where* $C^+ \lhd P$ *and* $P' \unrhd C^+$. *Suppose* $o \in inst(C)$ *is to be deleted.* S^* *is consistent if Procedure 8 is applied to* S^*.

Proof. Let $R_1(X)$ and $R_2(X)$ be relational schemas and Y be a subset of attributes X. Since $R_1[Y] \supseteq (R_1 - R_2)[Y] \supseteq (R_1[Y] - R_2[Y])$, $(R_1 - R_2)[Y] = R_1[Y] - R_2[Y] + (R_1 - R_2)[Y]$.

Let $\Delta R(P') = R(P')[C = o]$ be tuples to be deleted in $R(P')$. After deleting o in $R(P')$, $R(P')$ becomes $R(P') - \Delta R(P')$. Since $(R_1 - R_2)[Y] = R_1[Y] - R_2[Y] + (R_1 - R_2)[Y]$, $(R(P') - \Delta R(P'))[A^+] = R(P')[A^+] - \Delta R(P')[A^+] + (R(P') - \Delta R(P'))[A^+]$.

In Procedure 8, followings are performed:

(1) $\Delta R(P')[A^+]$ is obtained in Step 1 of Procedure 8.
(2) $(R(P') - \Delta R(P'))[A^+]$ is obtained in Step 2 of Procedure 8.
(3) $R(S^+)[A^+]$ is changed to $R_{new}(S^+)[A^+]$ where $R_{new}(S^+)[A^+] = R(S^+)[A^+] - (\Delta R(P')[A^+] - (R(P') - \Delta R(P'))[A^+])$

Since S^* is consistent before the deletion, $R(S^+)[A^+] = R(P')[A^+]$. Then, $R_{new}(S^+)[A^+] = R(S^+)[A^+] - (\Delta R(P')[A^+] - (R(P') - \Delta R(P'))[A^+]) = (R(P') - \Delta R(P'))[A^+]$. Let $R(P') - \Delta R(P')$ be $R_{new}(P')$ and $R(P) - \Delta R(P)$ be $R_{new}(P)$. The above equation is equivalent to $R_{new}(S^+)[A^+] = R_{new}(P')[A^+]$. $R_{new}(S^+)[A^+] = R_{new}(P)[A^+]$ follows from Lemma 7. Thus, S^* is consistent after the deletion if Procedure 8 is applied to S^*. □

5 Efficient Deletions of Objects

In some cases, derivation test can be omitted in Procedure 8. This section includes a condition satisfied by class schemas which allow to omit derivation test or to perform derivation test with only navigations on a single relationship.

First, an example of a class schema which does not require derivation test is shown.

Example 7. Materialized derived objects are deleted when the objects they point to are deleted. Suppose object o_9 is deleted in Fig.4. Objects o_{11} and o_{12} which point to o_9 are deleted without derivation test.

In the class schema presented in Fig.5, derivation test for derived class Person'sScene can be always omitted in applying Procedure 8. Suppose object o_5 is deleted. Navigations from o_5 gives (o_2, o_5, o_8) and (o_3, o_5, o_8) and candidate objects o_{17} and o_{20} are obtained. Since paths in the instances of path (Person, Persons, Scene) and objects in class Person'sScene have one-to-one relationship, there is no such a path p in the instances of path (Person, Persons, Scene) such that $o_{17} \lhd p$ or $o_{20} \lhd p$ if o_5 is deleted. Therefore, derivation test is not required to know o_{17} and o_{20} must be deleted. □

The following procedure is the same as Procedure 8 except that it does not include derivation test.

Procedure 10.

(1) *Step 1 of Procedure 8*
(2) *o and every object $o^c \in o^c$ obtained in the candidate retrieval are deleted.*

□

The next two lemmas show the condition of class schemas for always omitting derivation test.

Lemma 11. *Let $S^*(V^*, E^*) = S(V, E) \cup S^+(V^+, E^+)$ be a consistent class schema, P and its subgraph P' be such paths of classes that $C^+ \lhd P$ and $P' \unrhd C^+$, and C be a class in P'. Suppose object $o \in inst(C)$ is deleted and Procedure 10 is applied to S^*. If functional dependency $A^+ \to C$ holds, S^* is consistent.*

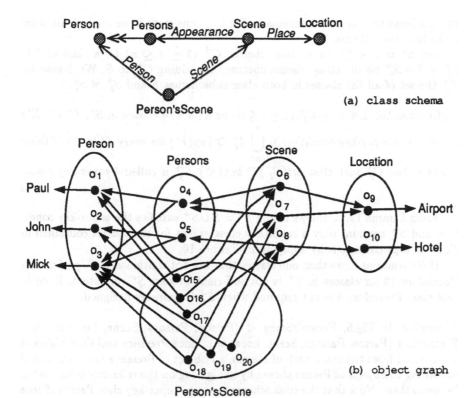

(a) class schema

(b) object graph

Fig. 5. Class schema containing super-key class

Proof. If there exists such a pair (o_1, o_2) of objects in $inst(C)$ that satisfies $R(P')[C = o_1][A^+] = R(P')[C = o_2][A^+]$, $A^+ \rightarrow C$ does not hold. Thus, if $A^+ \rightarrow C$, no path is found in derivation test of Procedure 8. Since Procedure 10 is the same as Procedure 8 except that it does not contain a step corresponding to Step 2 of Procedure 8, applying Procedure 10 is identical to applying Procedure 8. From Lemma 9, it follows that S^* is consistent. □

Lemma 12. *Let* $S^*(V^*, E^*) = S(V, E) \cup S^+(V^+, E^+)$ *be a consistent class schema, and* P *and* P' *be such paths of classes that* $C^+ \lhd P$ *and* $P' \unrhd C^+$. *Suppose object o in P' is deleted and Procedure 10 is applied to* S^*. *If* $A^+ \supseteq key(P')$, S^* *is consistent.*

Proof. Let P' be $(C_1, C_2, \ldots, C_n)$. From the definition of $key(P')$, $key(P') \rightarrow \{C_1, C_2, \ldots, C_n\}$. Since $\{C_1, C_2, \ldots, C_n\} \supseteq \{C_i\}$ $(1 \leq i \leq n)$, $\{C_1, C_2, \ldots, C_n\} \rightarrow C_i$. Thus, $A^+ \rightarrow C_i$ $(1 \leq i \leq n)$. From Lemma 11, it follows that as for a deletion of $o \in inst(C_i)$ $(1 \leq i \leq n)$, S^* is consistent if we apply Procedure 10 to S^*. □

In Fig.5, $A^+ = \{Scene, Person\}$ and $key(P') = \{Scene, Person\}$. From Lemma

12, it follows that the class schema in Fig.5 is consistent if we apply Procedure 10 to the class schema.

Let $S^* = S + S^+$ be a class schema, C_i^+ $(1 \leq i \leq n)$ be a class in S^+, $S_i^* = S + S_i^+$ be the class schema obtained by adding C_i^+ to S. We denote by A_i^+ the set of all the classes in both class subschemas S and S_i^+ of S_i^*.

Definition 13. Let $P' \trianglerighteq C_i^+$ $(1 \leq i \leq n)$ be a path of classes in S^*. $S^*(V^*, E^*)$ satisfies the super-key condition iff $\bigcup_{i=1}^{n} A_i^+ \supseteq key(P')$ for every P' in S^*. If there exists a class C_i^+ such that $Att(C_i^+) \supseteq key(P')$, C_i^+ is called a super-key class. □

From Lemma 12, it follows that if $S^* = S \cup S^+$ satisfies the super-key condition and S^+ contains only a super-key class except for the classes contained in S, S^* is kept consistent by applying Procedure 10.

If S^+ contains more than one classes that are not contained in S, performing Procedure 10 for classes in S^+ is not sufficient to keep S^* consistent. Even in this case, Procedure 8 is not required when S^+ is properly designed.

Example 8. In Fig.6, Person'sScene ◁ (Person, Persons, Scene, Location) and Presence ◁ (Person, Persons, Scene, Location). Since Presence and Person'sScene are derived from the same path of classes, an object of Presence can be updated according to objects of Person'sScene by navigating on the reference relationship between them. Note that the class schema contains super-key class Person'sScene and satisfies the super-key condition.

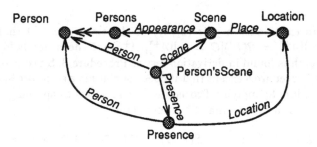

Fig. 6. Class schema allowing efficient deletions

□

Let $\{C_1^+, C_2^+, \ldots, C_n^+\}$ be a set of classes in $S^+(V^+, E^+)$, and C_1^+ be a super-key class. If there exist reference relationships $C_1^+ \leadsto C_i^+$ $(2 \leq i \leq n)$, they can be utilized in candidate retrievals and derivation test. Reference connections of reference relationships $C_1^+ \leadsto C_i^+$ must be double-linked and satisfy relational expression $(R(P) \bowtie R(S^+))[C_1^+, C_i^+] = R(C_1^+, C_i^+)$.

Procedure 14. *Let $\{C_1^+, C_2^+, \ldots, C_n^+\}$ be a set of classes in $S^+(V^+, E^+)$, C_1^+ be a super-key class in $\{C_1^+, C_2^+, \ldots, C_n^+\}$, and $C_1^+\leadsto C_i^+$ $(1 \leq i \leq n)$ be reference relationships in S^+.*

(1) **Candidate Retrieval:** *Apply the Step 1 of Procedure 8 to C_1^+, and let o_1^c be the set of candidate objects of C_1^+. Navigate the links of $C_1^+\leadsto C_i^+$ $(2 \leq i \leq n)$ to find objects linked to an object in o_1^c and let the resulting objects be o_i^c $(2 \leq i \leq n)$.*

(2) **Derivation Test:** *Navigate the links of $C_1^+\leadsto C_i^+$ $(2 \leq i \leq n)$ from o_i^c $(2 \leq i \leq n)$. Note that the connections of $C_1^+\leadsto C_i^+$ must be double-linked and satisfy $(R(P) \bowtie R(S^+))[C_1^+, C_i^+] = R(C_1^+, C_i^+)$.*

(3) **Deletion:** *Delete $o^c \in o_i^c$ if only one object of C_1^+ is connected to o^c. Delete all the object in o_i^c from C_1^+. Delete o from C_u.* □

Lemma 15. *Let $S^*(V^*, E^*) = S(V, E) \cup S^+(V^+, E^+)$ be a consistent class schema where $V^+ = \{C_1^+, C_2^+, \ldots, C_n^+\}$, $C_1^+ \in V^+$ be a super-key class, $C_1^+\leadsto C_i^+$ $(2 \leq i \leq n)$ be reference relationships, and reference connections of $C_1^+\leadsto C_i^+$ $(2 \leq i \leq n)$ be double-linked and satisfy $(R(P_S) \bowtie R(S^+))[C_1^+, C_i^+] = R(C_1^+, C_i^+)$. If object o is deleted in S^* and Procedure 14 is applied to S^*, S^* is consistent.*

Proof. Let $S_i^* = S \cup S_i^+$ $(1 \leq i \leq n)$ be the class schema obtained by adding class C_i^+ to S. We prove that every S_i^* $(1 \leq i \leq n)$ is consistent.

S_1^* is consistent since applying Procedure 14 to C_i^+ is equivalent to applying Procedure 10 to C_1^+. Applying Step 3 in Procedure 14 to S_i^* $(2 \leq i \leq n)$ is the same as applying Step 3 in Procedure 8 to S_i^* $(2 \leq i \leq n)$.

In Step 1 of Procedure 14, o_1^c corresponds to tuples obtained by evaluating $R_1^c = (R(P')[C = o] \bowtie R(S^+))[C_1^+]$. To obtain o_i^c $(2 \leq i \leq n)$ that corresponds to $R_i^c = (R(P')[C = o] \bowtie R(S^+))[C_i^+]$, navigations on $C_1^+\leadsto C_i^+$ $(2 \leq i \leq n)$ from o_i^c is performed producing pairs of objects corresponding to $(R_1^c \bowtie R(C_1^+, C_i^+))[C_i^+]$. Since $R(C_1^+, C_i^+) = (R(P') \bowtie R(S^+))[C_1^+, C_i^+]$, $(R_1^c \bowtie R(C_1^+, C_i^+))[C_i^+] = (R_1^c \bowtie (R(P') \bowtie R(S^+))[C_1^+, C_i^+])[C_i^+] = ((R_1^c \bowtie R(P') \bowtie R(S^+))[C_1^+, C_i^+])[C_i^+] = ((R(P')[C = o] \bowtie R(S^+))[C_1^+, C_i^+])[C_i^+] = (R(P')[C = o] \bowtie R(S^+))[C_i^+] = R_i^c$.

In Step 2 of Procedure 14, $R_i^{\bar{c}} = (R(P')[C \neq o] \bowtie R(S^+))[C_i^+]$ $(2 \leq i \leq n)$ need to be obtained. $R_1^{\bar{c}} = R(P')[C \neq o] \bowtie R(S^+)[C_1^+] = R(C_1^+) - R_1^c$. In this step, processes corresponding to evaluating $(R_1^{\bar{c}} \bowtie R(C_1^+, C_i^+))[C_i^+]$ are performed. Since $(R(P) \bowtie R(S^+))[C_1^+, C_i^+] = R(C_1^+, C_i^+)$, $(R_1^{\bar{c}} \bowtie R(C_1^+, C_i^+))[C_i^+] = (R_1^{\bar{c}} \bowtie (R(P') \bowtie R(S^+))[C_1^+, C_i^+])[C_i^+] = (R_1^{\bar{c}} \bowtie R(P') \bowtie R(S^+))[C_1^+, C_i^+][C_i^+] = (R(P')[C \neq o] \bowtie R(S^+))[C_1^+, C_i^+][C_i^+] = (R(P')[C \neq o] \bowtie R(S^+))[C_i^+] = R_i^{\bar{c}}$.

Thus, applying Procedure 14 to S^* is equivalent to applying Procedure 10 to C_1^+ and Procedure 1 to each of C_i^+ $(2 \leq i \leq n)$. □

In Procedure 8, Steps 1 and 2 require navigations on entire P'. However in Procedure 14, Steps 1 and 2 require navigations on only a subgraph of P'. Navigations on class schemas can be classified as follows:

(1) **Single-step navigation** A navigation on a single relationship.
(2) **Multi-step navigation** A navigation on multiple relationships.

Theorem 16. *Let $S^*(V^*, E^*)$ be a consistent class schema where $S^* = S \cup S^+$, $\{C_1^+, C_2^+, \ldots, C_n^+\}$ be the set of all the classes in S^+, C_1^+ be a super-key class in S^+, $C_1^+ \rightsquigarrow C_i^+ (2 \leq i \leq n)$ be reference relationships and reference connections of $C_1^+ \rightsquigarrow C_i^+ (2 \leq i \leq n)$ be double-linked and satisfy $(R(P) \bowtie R(S^+))[C_1^+, C_i^+] = R(C_1^+, C_i^+)$. Suppose object o is deleted in S^*. No multi-step navigation is required in the derivation test to keep S^* consistent.*

Proof. From Lemma 15, it follows that S^* is consistent if Procedure 14 is applied to S^*. Clearly, Procedure 14 requires no multi-step navigation in the derivation test. □

Although candidate retrieval requires multi-step navigations, only objects connected to o need to be retrieved.

Since the class schema in Fig.6 contains a super-key class Person'sScene and Presence is referenced by class Person'sScene, no multi-step navigation is required to keep the class schema consistent if the reference connections between Person'sScene and Presence are double-linked.

6 Design of Object Bases Allowing Efficient Updates

This section gives a procedure to design object bases that allow efficient retrievals and updates. Generally, objects in object bases are retrieved quickly by introducing redundancies into object bases. On the other hand, to reduce overheads to update redundant objects, redundancies should be reduced.

We introduce more redundancies into object bases to reduce overheads to update redundant objects. Let $S^* = S \cup S^+$ be a class schema that contains materialized derived classes. When S^* does not satisfy the super-key condition, multi-step navigations are required for each materialized derived class in S^+. The next procedure transforms class schemas to satisfy the super-key condition and thus allow single-step navigations in keeping S^* consistent after a deletion of an object.

Procedure 17. *Given a class schema $S^*(V^*, E^*)$,*

(1) *Let $C_1^+, C_2^+, \ldots, C_n^+$ be classes in S^+ that have tuple-values and S_i^* be a object schema obtained by adding C_i^+ to S. Obtain path $P_i' \trianglerighteq C_i^+$ for $1 \leq i \leq n$. Let the set of all path P_i' be $\{P_{k_1}', P_{k_2}', \ldots, P_{k_m}'\}$.*

(2) *Let $C_{k_1}^K, C_{k_2}^K, \ldots, C_{k_m}^K$ be super-key classes of $P_{k_1}', P_{k_2}', \ldots, P_{k_m}'$, i.e., $Att(C_{k_i}^K) \supseteq key(P_{k_i}')$. Construct an class schema from S^* and $C_{k_1}^K, C_{k_2}^K, \ldots, C_{k_m}^K$.*

(3) *Add reference relationship $C_{k_i}^K \rightsquigarrow C_{k_j}^+$ if $P_{k_i}' \trianglerighteq C_{k_j}^+$. Note that reference connection of $C_{k_i}^K \rightsquigarrow C_{k_j}^+$ must be double-linked and satisfy $(R(P) \bowtie R(S^+))[C_1^+, C_i^+] = R(C_1^+, C_i^+)$.*

(4) *Let the resulting class schema be $S'(V', E')$.* □

Theorem 18. *Let S' be a consistent class schema transformed by Procedure 17. No multi-step navigation is required to keep S' consistent after a deletion of object o in P_i'.*

Proof. Let $S_{k_i}^* = S \cup S_{k_i}^+$ $(1 \le i \le m)$, $\{C_1^+, C_2^+, \ldots, C_s^+\}$ be the set of all the classes in $S_{k_i}^+$ where $C_j^+ \lhd P_{k_i}'$ for $(1 \le j \le s)$, and $C_{k_i}^K$ be super-key class in $S_{k_i}^+$. Procedure 17 add $C_{k_i}^K$ if it does not exist in $\{C_1^+, C_2^+, \ldots, C_s^+\}$ and adds reference relationships $C_{k_i}^K \rightsquigarrow C_j$ $(1 \le j \le s,\ C_j \ne C_{k_i}^K)$, whose connection are double-linked. From Theorem 16, it follows that $S_{k_i}^*$ $(1 \le i \le m)$ is consistent after the deletion if Procedure 17 is applied to S^*. □

Procedure 17 may increase the costs in keeping S^* consistent after an insertion of an object. However, in general, the increase of the costs of an insertion can be ignored compared to the decrease of the costs of a deletion.

Costs of retrievals in S^* is not increased by Procedure 17.

Theorem 19. *Let S' be a class schema transformed by Procedure 17, $O^*(v^*, e^*)$ and $O'(v', e')$ be object graphs of class schema $S^*(V^*, E^*)$ and $S'(V', E')$, respectively. If $O(v, e)$ is an object subgraph of O^* that is accessed to perform retrieval query Q in S^*, $O(v, e)$ is also an object subgraph of $O'(v', e')$.*

Proof. Since Procedure 17 either adds classes or reference relationships to S^* to obtain S', S' subsumes S^*. Thus, an object subgraph of S^* is also an object subgraph of S'. □

Theorem 19 implies that retrieval query Q can be performed in the same object subgraph of both S^* and S'.

Example 9. The class schema in Fig.6 is transformed from the class schema in Fig.4 by Procedure 17. Connection of objects between classes **Person'sScene** and **Presence** is shown in Fig.7. **Person'sScene** is a super-key class of the class schema in Fig.6.

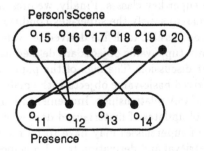

Fig. 7. Reference connection for efficient candidate retrieval and derivation test

Suppose object o_7 is deleted. Navigations from o_7 gives $\{o_7, o_4, o_3\}$ and $\{o_7, o_4, o_1\}$. o_{16} and o_{19} are candidate objects in Person'sScene since they refer $\{o_7, o_1\}$ and $\{o_7, o_3\}$, respectively. Also, o_{12} and o_{11} are candidate objects in Presence since they refer o_{16} and o_{19}, candidate objects in the super-key class Person'sScene. o_{16} and o_{19} is deleted without derivation test. o_{12} and o_{11} are not deleted from Presence since navigations from o_{12} and o_{11} in Presence give o_{15} and o_{18}, respectively.

Suppose object o_{21} referencing o_4 and o_9 is inserted in class Scene. Navigations from o_{21} gives $\{o_{21}, o_4, o_3, o_9\}$ and $\{o_{21}, o_4, o_1, o_9\}$. First, o_{22} referencing o_{21} and o_3 and o_{23} referencing o_{21} and o_1 are inserted in class Person'sScene. Since there exist object o_{11} referencing o_3 and o_9 and object o_{12} referencing o_1 and o_9, no object is inserted in class Presence .

Retrievals of corresponding persons and locations in Fig.6 is performed in the same manner as in Fig.4 using class Presence. □

7 Conclusion

If objects derived from several paths of objects are materialized in object bases, elimination of duplicates is required in performing incremental updates of materialized derived classes as is required in incremental updates of materialized views produced by relational expressions that include projections. The elimination of duplicates complicates incremental updates. Roussopoulos[10] decided not to discuss projections in incremental maintenance of ViewCache. Also, Qian and Wiederhold[9] pointed out the difficulty of the project operators for incremental recomputation of views. In this paper, we have described the super-key condition that allows efficient maintenance of materialized derived classes. Duplicates can be efficiently eliminated in performing incremental updates if object bases satisfy the super-key condition. We began by defining our model of object bases introducing class schemas, object graphs and functional dependencies defined on relations of connected objects. Class schemas always keep the condition of consistencies if we perform Procedure 8 that incrementally updates materialized derived classes after every update. Derivation test in Procedure 8, which requires to obtain $inst(P')$ for every candidate object in some cases, is omitted or performed as single-step retrievals if class schemas satisfy the super-key condition and contain super-key classes. Finally, we presented a procedure that transforms class schemas to satisfy the super-key condition.

Although it might be possible to define derived set-value objects and derived basic-value objects, only tuple-value objects are defined as materialized derived objects to simplify our discussion. The idea of the paper can be applied to derived set-value and derived basic-value objects with small modifications. It calls for further discussion of ISA relationships. Implementations of ISA relationships may affect efficiencies of updates of materialized derived classes in object bases. For example, objects of superclasses may have to be retrieved from their subclasses in candidate retrieval and derivation test. Implementation related issues include directions of reference relationships, available access paths, e.g., pointers, indices, and hashings. Object migrations in ISA hierarchies influence consistencies of object bases. Object migrations can be treated as insertions and deletions of objects if we leave the problem of object identifiers.

References

1. S. Abiteboul and A. Bonner, *Objects and Views*, Proc. ACM SIGMOD Int. Conf. Management of Data, pp.238–247, 1991.
2. J. A. Blakeley, N. Coburn and P. Larson, *Updating Derived Relations: Detecting Irrelevant and Autonomously Computable Updates*, ACM Trans. Database Syst., Vol.14, No.3, pp.369–400, 1989.
3. F. Bancilhon and N. Spyratos, *Update Semantics of Relational Views*, ACM Trans. Database Syst., Vol.6, No.4, pp.557–575, Dec. 1981.
4. T. Barsalou and N. Siambela, *Updating Relational Databases through Object-Based Views*, Proc. ACM SIGMOD Int. Conf. Management of Data, pp.248–257, 1991.
5. A. Kemper, C. Kilger and G. Moerkotte, *Function Materialization in Object Bases*, Proc. ACM SIGMOD Int. Conf. Management of Data, pp.258–267, 1991.
6. S. Konomi and T. Furukawa, *Updating Duplicate Values in Distributed Multi-database Systems*, Proc. IEEE 1st Int. Workshop on Interoperability in Multi-database Syst., pp.243–246, Apr. 1991.
7. R. Langerak, *View Updates in Relational Databases with an Independent Scheme*, ACM Trans. Database Syst., Vol.15, No.1, pp.40–66, Mar. 1990.
8. C. Lecluse, P. Richard and F. Velez, O_2, *an Object-Oriented Data Model*, Proc. ACM SIGMOD Int. Conf. Management of Data, pp.424–433, 1988.
9. X. Qian and G. Wiederhold, *Incremental Recomputation of Active Relational Expressions*, IEEE Trans. Knowledge and Data Eng., Vol.3, No.3, pp.337–341, 1991.
10. N. Roussopoulos, *An Incremental Access Method for ViewCache: Concept, Algorithms and Cost Analysis*, ACM Trans. Database Syst., Vol.16, No.3, pp.535–563, 1991.
11. P. Shoval, *One-to-One Dependencies in Database Design*, IEEE Trans. Knowledge and Data Eng., Vol.3, No.3, pp.371–379, 1991.
12. J. Srivastava and D. Rotem, *Analytical Modeling of Materialized View Maintenance*, Proc. ACM Symp. on Principles of Database Syst., pp. 126–134, 1988.
13. G. E. Weddell, *Reasoning about Functional Dependencies Generalized for Semantic Data Models*, ACM Trans. Database Syst., Vol.17, No.1, pp.32–64, Mar. 1992.

Applications of Deductive and Object-Oriented Databases

Moderator: Suzanne W. Dietrich

Department of Computer Science and Engineering
Arizona State University
Tempe, AZ 85287-5406

1 Introduction

Database technology provides various data models to the user community. Each data model has its advantages and disadvantages. The network and hierarchical data models, introduced in the 1960's, provide a very performant data organization for well-defined, update-intensive transaction processing of large volumes of data at the cost of conceptual complexity and inflexibility. The relational data model, introduced in the early 1970's, has now been accepted as a commercial alternative for application domains where the conceptual simplicity of tables and the flexibility of issuing ad hoc queries (via the industry-standard query language SQL) outweighs the cost of performance. The 1980's has introduced the emerging technologies of deductive databases and object-oriented databases. Deductive databases extend relational databases with inherent support for powerful rules that provide for the declarative specification of deductive rules and integrity constraints. Object-oriented databases provide complex data structuring including class hierarchies and inheritance. This conference focuses on the integration of the deductive and object-oriented technologies, providing an alternative data model with the power and flexibility of declarative rules and the structural richness of objects.

The DOOD technology is approaching a maturity level in which we can expect initial commercial products for developing applications. The use of DOODs as a viable alternative data model depends on the ability of the database application to take advantage of the additional capabilities that they provide. The acceptance of DOODs by a wider audience ultimately relies on realizing the applications that can take advantage of the technology and marketing the advantages realized by these nontrivial applications.

This panel focuses on applications of DOOD technology. Specifically,

— What are the characteristics of applications that can take advantage of the power and flexibility offered by DOODs?
— Is such an application better suited for DOOD rather than a relational system that offers both the industry standard query language SQL and performance resulting from years of implementation experience?
— What are the application domains that are currently being explored?
— For such applications, what language and architectural features are important for the effectiveness of DOOD systems?
— What applications are DOOD benchmark candidates, where the goal of a benchmark is to be a relevant application that is also simple, portable and scaleable?
— What knowledge management tools should be provided for the effective design and use of DOODs?

Beyond Data Dictionaries: Towards a Reflective Architecture of Intelligent Database Systems *

Rainer Manthey

Department of Computer Science III
University of Bonn
Römerstraße 164, D-53117 Bonn, Germany
e-mail: manthey@informatik.uni-bonn.de

Abstract. The main conjecture of this contribution is that forthcoming intelligent database systems - in particular future DOOD systems - should be designed in such a way that a major part of the services they provide are implemented using these same services in a bootstrapping-like manner. We call such an approach "reflective", as is often done by researchers in AI and programming languages. Data dictionaries, being part of any reasonable database system today, exhibit the reflective principle in a nutshell, if they are implemented by means of the same data structures that hold application data. However, even for data dictionaries the reflective implementation is often abandoned for performance reasons. Applying reflection for more advanced and ambitious purposes, up to integrity control or query optimization, is viewed even more skeptically by many, despite the conceptual elegance of the approach. On the other hand, there are a few successful approaches around today that can be interpreted as exhibiting a reflective nature. It is the purpose of this paper to identify such examples and to encourage research to invest more in the reflective style and to look for new solutions to the obstacles still ahead.

1 Introduction

The notion of an "intelligent database" is currently gaining increasing popularity within the database research community. There are two new international journals referring to intelligent databases in their name. A new series of international conferences on intelligent and cooperative databases has been launched. Workshops and courses, talks and articles on this topic can be encountered more and more frequently, and - last not least - a call for project proposals on intelligent databases was issued by the Commission of the European Community as part of their 1992 ESPRIT workprogramme. Like many other notions discussed in research these days, the term "intelligent database" is open to a wide range of interpretation. Rather than having been introduced on purpose by an individual person along with a fixed definition (as was the case for the relational or the ER model, e.g.), intelligent databases have been emerging gradually and unsystematically, thus reflecting the joint intuition of a group of researchers that certain aspects of DB technology are approaching a kind of new quality.

---

* This work was supported in part by the Commission of the European Community under ESPRIT project number 6333 (IDEA); however, this paper does not constitute a statement of the IDEA consortium, but represents the author's opinions only

Numerous proponents of this notion have been interpreting the qualification "intelligent" in terms of the kind of functionality offered at the user interface of a database system. Both, the way how knowledge can be represented and retrieved as well as the means of its manipulation can thus be qualified as (more or less) intelligent. It is not surprising that DOOD functionality - rules, objects, constraints and the like - has been rather frequently proposed as candidate features of such intelligent DB interfaces. However, there is another, complementary way how the term "intelligent database" can be interpreted, namely as a qualification of the internal organization of the respective DBMS. Although intuitively everybody will agree that a high degree of intelligence has to be incorporated into the sophisticated software modules from which a DBMS is composed (such as compilers, optimizers, storage managers etc.), it is by no means clear that the way how this system software itself is organized corresponds to the criteria defining "intelligence" at the interface of the very system.

It is the intention of this contribution to plead for an elegant and conceptually attractive way of designing future database systems in a more intelligent way. We believe that a wide range of knowledge built into DBMS components can be very adequately represented in terms of those features that an intelligent DB interface offers itself: facts, rules (both active and passive), objects, constraints, class hierarchies, attributes and so on. For sure such a representation is a nice device for formal studies and tutorial purposes. However, it is a possible paradigm of implementation as well, and it is this style of system implementation that we would like to suggest as a serious alternative here. We call this principle "architectural reflection": using the functionality realized at the interface of a system for implementing major parts of the system itself.

Of course, such a reflective architecture is feasible only if there remains a core of "irreducible" procedures from which more complex systems can be systematically bootstrapped. These core procedures would be applied to a basic collection of predefined knowledge available in the internal knowledge base of a reflective system. Identifying what exactly constitutes a core procedure, and how to represent the knowledge required for system bootstrapping in the most appropriate form is an exiting open problem, which is far from even a preliminary solution to date.

The idea of a reflective architecture, or reflective software in general, is absolutely not new in computer science. There are reflective paradigms such as compile-time reflection in programming languages, or meta-classes in object-oriented programming. AI systems organized in terms of extensive internal knowledge bases have been investigated since long. However, in the database community a conscious use of a reflective organization is still the exception rather than the rule.

At the very core of every attempt to realize database system software by means of database concepts is the old idea of organizing a database schema as a meta-database, more precisely: as an instance of a meta-schema expressing the concepts of a particular data model. This kind of primitive internal database of a DBMS is nowadays mostly called data dictionary. Already in the earliest specifications of SQL, the intention to manipulate and query schema data in terms of SQL itself are clearly stated, based on an implementation of the data dictionary of a relational system in terms of special system relations. In many systems even this very early step towards a reflective architecture has not been realized, mostly because of performance reasons.

In contrast to this reaction, there is a recent trend in object-oriented database systems to extend the data dictionary into a full-fledged meta-database, treating not only classes and attributes, but also rules and constraints, or even events as meta-objects [DPG91, DBM88, AMC93]. It is our purpose to encourage researchers and developers to revive the very idea prototypically represented by the data dictionary device and to extend it by making use of the enormously improved range of functionality of modern DBMSs.

We believe that time for a new and much more ambitious attempt in this direction has come, particularly because active DOOD systems offer such a high potential for expressing much more than just schema data or statistics in a data dictionary. Indeed there are quite a few indications suggesting that rules, constraints and objects together provide a "critical mass" for successful investigation into the idea of an extended data dictionary realizing a reflective architecture that goes far beyond the capabilities of today's data dictionaries:

- Queries, rules, constraints themselves can be modelized, stored and manipulated as objects in a DOOD model.
- Model-inherent constraints governing correct schema evolution can be enforced by means of efficient integrity checking methods originally developed for ensuring semantic integrity of application data rather than system data.
- Query optimization methods - such as e.g. magic sets - are based on a representation of optimized evaluation plans in form of deductive (magically rewritten) rules driven by a primitive (core) fixpoint engine.
- Services such as integrity checking or view materialization can be interpreted as being driven by event-reaction patterns, and are thus implementable by means of system-internal active rules.

These are just a few hints indicating what kind of solutions that are already around today can be regarded as manifestations of the reflective architecture paradigm. There are many more opportunities waiting for being explored in theory and practice. Once starting to identify all those aspects of data management that might be implemented by means of existing database services in a reflective manner, search for new examples can become a kind of obsession! Such investigations will, of course, not always lead to feasible solutions, but those solutions that appear to be realistic today definitely suggest that there is more behind the reflective ideal than maybe expected in the past.

The author is certainly aware that there are a lot of reasons why instances of this attractive theoretical perspective for system design have been heavily criticized by practitioners based on actual experience with their systems in the past. Statements like "implementing query answering by means of active rules will never work efficiently", or "implementing a data dictionary as metaclasses is simply too slow" have been stated again and again by people who cannot simply be disqualified as pessimistic ultra-conservatives not ready to accept new ideas anyway. However, we would like to implant new hope into the camp of those researchers who still didn't give up to believe in the power and elegance of the "reflective approach".

We believe that too often the argument "if it's too slow, then forget it" is applied prematurely, and without having identified the real culprit responsible for the failure of an ambitious idea. If the implementation of a data dictionary as a set of relations, e.g., is too slow for dynamic type-checking purposes, why do we give up this idea as such, rather than reconsidering the choice of data structures supported by our database systems for small or medium data sets. Maybe one uniform physical implementation of the logical device of a relation is not enough. One could imagine relational systems offering very different realizations of the concept "relation" depending on the size, the stability with respect to updates, or the frequency of querying of the respective data set.

In such a context, a data dictionary - constituting a comparatively small, rather stable, but frequently accessed set of relations - might be permanently cached in main memory, for performance reasons, making use of appropriate data structures of the programming language in which the DBMS is implemented without loosing the ability to access these data structures by means of the DBMS interface. There is no a priori reason why data sets physically realized in different ways (according to their particular size and access properties) should not be uniformly manipulated by the same set of query and update operators, controlled by one and the same kind of integrity constraints, intensionally defined by the same kind of deductive rules, and so on. There are many such cases where reconsideration of "classical" properties of database systems are a valid alternative for discarding the nice, but presumably slow reflective solution to a problem.

In the remainder of this paper we will try to substantiate some of the claims and ideas outlined in this introduction by means of more concrete evidence and arguments, thus hopefully provoking fruitful, though probably controversial discussions among system designers and implementors within the DOOD community. Of course, a short article like this cannot do full justice to the subject: many open questions have to be left unanswered, and many doubts will remain, simply because experience in consequently realizing a reflective architecture of a DBMS is missing.

Rather than outlining a potential DBMS architecture based on reflective principles, we will therefore discuss selected aspects of the issue, from which we try to derive arguments for our "vision" of an intelligent DBMS design methodology. This paper will not be a technical one in the sense of a formal elaboration of a well-defined, narrow topic, but an informal "ideas and arguments" paper, aiming at highlighting an emerging research direction. We do not aim at "selling" new, original results, but try to synthesize a unifying view out of known results, which might look unfamiliar to some if presented in the light of the reflective architecture ideal.

Whereas such kind of paper is not well-suited as a regular submission to a conference or journal, the particular role of an invited contribution as well as the (relative) freedom of its author in choosing topic and style might be a welcome (but rare) opportunity for thinking a little bit ahead, up to the risk of appearing idealistic at times. We go this risk consciously, but ask readers to bear in mind, that papers like this ought to be digested with a different perception than the technical ones we are used to read.

In the following three sections we will discuss the "reflective ideal" by prototypically looking at two central aspects in the design of active DOOD systems: inference methods for deductive rules, and the realization of deductive inference by trigger processes.

2 Meta-rule specifications of deductive inference processes

In this section we would like to concentrate on the two key functionalities of any system supporting deductive rules: the activation of these rules in response to a retrieval or an update request. We will point out how existing rule activation (inference) methods can be interpreted as first steps towards a reflective implementation of a deductive DBMS. Although the techniques we refer to have been developed for deductive relational systems, they are directly relevant for DOOD systems as well.

2.1 Query-driven inference

For sure, answering queries is the most important and most frequently called service a database system can offer. Therefore the organization of inferences over deductive rules in response to a retrieval request has been by far the most active area of research in deductive databases in the past. A multitude of different methods and optimizations have been proposed up till now (see, e.g., [CGT90] for an overview). Perhaps the most prominent of these approaches is the "magic sets" method [BMSU86] and its variations and extensions. Apart from its most frequently mentioned advantage of closely integrating deductive rule activation with the set-oriented, algebra-based data manipulation technology of conventional relational databases, the magic sets approach represents a particularly important example of what we call a reflective implementation.

There are three central implementation decisions characterizing the magic sets approach:

1. To represent answers to a given query and intermediate results required for their derivation as facts stored in temporary, internal relations.
2. To represent queries and subqueries arising during a top-down, left-to-right expansion of a query over some rule-defined relation as temporary, internal facts (the "magic" facts), too.
3. To represent a major aspect of the organization of the inference process itself in terms of internal deductive rules (the magic and magically rewritten rules) automatically derived from the source-level rules of the respective application.

All three decisions are remarkable indeed, as none of them (perhaps except the first) is really obvious, but all three together open up a very attractive perspective for implementation of inferencing in general.

The main advantage of the first two decisions is that system-generated data, (such as subqueries or intermediate results) are treated as "first-class citizens" of the database and thus are entitled to make use of the system's own services, e.g., to being manipulated by the query and update primitives of the database. There is no need to escape to data structures and operators of the host language or the implementation language of the DBMS any more, but one and the same set of data structures and manipulation primitives can be uniformly applied to external, application-specific data and to internal, system-generated meta-data. The benefit of being able to implement, e.g., a crucial step of top-down reasoning by simply joining a relation containing magic facts (i.e., representations of subqueries) with another relation containing extensional facts from the application-specific database, cannot be appreciated highly enough.

The third decision - expressing characteristics of the inference process in terms of meta-rules - is a consequence of the first two decisions (though again by no means an obvious one): once the data generated during inference have been represented (and implemented) as relational facts, they may benefit from all services a deductive relational system offers, in particular from being defined intentionally by declarative rules. This is what the magic and the magically rewritten rules do: define the internal relations for queries and answers intentionally and declaratively.

Doing so is no substitute for a proper inference procedure, of course, which actually drives the computation of a concrete set of answers to a concrete query. The magic sets method employs an iterative materialization procedure for this purpose, called bottom-up fixpoint procedure (or "naive" evaluation). The internal rules defining the data required for query answering are repeatedly applied bottom-up until all of these data have been materialized. Materialization by fixpoint iteration is a simple process, at least a much simpler one than a full set-oriented, top-down evaluation of a query over rules.

It is important to understand the essential difference between the way how the magic (and the magically rewritten) rules are explicitly processed, and the way how application rules are implicitly applied as a result. Whereas the internal rules are driven by the simple bottom-up procedure, the resulting complex computation realized that way is a set-oriented, top-down expansion over the application rules. This rather sophisticated relationship between the two modes of rule application (bottom-up and top-down) and the two levels of rules (external and internal) has been causing a lot of problems for nearly everybody who tried to understand the true nature of this approach. The magic sets computations emulate an abstract top-down machine by applying a concrete bottom-up machine to a set of declarative, internal rules.

The principle of two machines (or interpreters), the one being implemented by a simple procedure, the other specified by meta-rules driven by the first, has been analyzed and clearly presented in a paper first published at DOOD'89 [Bry90]. In this paper, bottom-up meta-rules are introduced which specify how set-oriented, top-down reasoning a la magic sets works in general - independent of a particular set of application rules. The magic rewriting process can then be obtained from this framework by systematic partial evaluation of the meta-rules (specifying the inference principle) over a particular set of application rules. Thus, top-down control is compiled into the application rules.

The technique introduced in this paper also shows very clearly the close relationship between methods like magic sets that are traditionally qualified as bottom-up methods and methods like QSQ [Vie86] that are regarded as top-down. Both qualifications are equally right or wrong. Only when distinguishing clearly which of the two levels of execution is qualified (that of the rewritten meta-rules, or that of the original application rules) it makes sense to speak of bottom-up or top-down. Magic sets is bottom-up on the meta-rule level and most presentations emphasize this aspect, while neglecting the top-down process thus implemented on the application rule level. Presentations of QSQ (and its variants) emphasize the top-down nature on the application rule level, but do not make sufficiently clear that implementations of this approach end up with techniques that are in essence performing fixpoint computations over internal rules as well [LV89].

The simple inference procedure driving the meta-rules (bottom-up fixpoint iteration) is a core procedure in the sense of the reflective principle outlined in the introduction. There is no way around such a procedure, even though an important part of the entire inference process has been specified declaratively. Apart from the advantage of arriving at a core procedure which is simpler than the original top-down inference method, there is another important benefit to be gained from the reduction of the top-down to a bottom-up procedure. Fixpoint iteration is a generic procedure that doesn't know (and doesn't need to know) about the meaning of the data it materializes. it is irrelevant whether rules define subqueries, intermediate results, answers, or anything else. By concentrating on the very problem of materialization, the aspects that are specific to this task can be optimized in isolation without being "diluted by problems specific to a particular kind of reasoning.

The most popular such optimization is the differential computation of rule-defined data, also called "semi-naive" fixpoint iteration [Bay85, BR86]. Recently, the reflective principle we try to trace in this paper, has been applied to differential optimization as well. In [SZ88] a rewriting approach to differential computation has been proposed that introduces "stage parameters" making explicit in which round of iteration a particular fact has been materialized. By doing so, differential control of the fixpoint computation can be expressed declaratively as well. The device of stage parameter can be used to express other aspects of control as well. Originally it had been introduced in the context of the counting method [SZ87]. In a new paper, to be presented at DOOD'93 as well [ZAO93], XY-stratification is proposed. For this class of rules, stage parameters can be used for making stratification layers explicit, thus enabling an "ordinary" fixpoint procedure to even handle certain locally stratified rule sets the processing of which normally requires the use of an iterated fixpoint procedure (which is much more expensive than the pure version). Again we have an example of a complex procedure implemented by a simple one which is applied to a declarative representation of control aspects in form of internal rules.

We believe that in fact many more optimization techniques can be expressed in rule form (and thus reflectively), particularly if working directly with the problem-independent meta-rule specification of an inference method as proposed in [Bry90]. Many parameters of optimization (such as statistical values, optimization criteria, thresholds, restrictions, heuristics) could be expressed declaratively as meta-facts, -rules, or -constraints and merged with declarative, rule-based specifications of various inference modes.

2.2 Update-driven inference

When thinking of deductive databases, people tend to identify the notion of inference with the problem of answering queries. However, there is a quite considerable amount of research concentrating on inference processes activated in response to updates, too. Most of this work is devoted to a particular application of update-driven inference, namely integrity checking over rule-defined data. It is well-known that there are other important problems similarly requiring computation of the consequences that an update on explicitly stored (base) data has on rule-defined data. In particular, incremental view materialization and condition monitoring for maintaining triggers, alerters or condition-action rules in general belong to this category of problems. The term "update propagation" is frequently used for the process of "pushing" base data updates bottom-up through rules in order to determine those updates that are implicitly induced on rule-defined data. One of the earliest fully implemented deductive database systems, BDGEN [NY83], was entirely based on update propagation, as all derived relations in this system were kept permanently materialized and were incrementally refreshed at update time.

Update propagation can be very conveniently implemented in a reflective manner too, based on a meta-rule representation of the particularities of this form of rule activation. Again the key to the reflective solution is the representation and implementation of the data generated by the DBMS during inference by means of the data structures, that the DBMS supports anyway. In case of update-driven inference, the individual updates to be propagated and/or computed are represented as internal facts. A device like this - called delta relations - is around in various forms since long, particularly in connection with recovery and (non-deductive) view refreshment techniques. In presence of deductive rules, the task of update propagation is to compute deltas for rule-defined relations, containing the individual induced updates arising from a particular base update.

Derived delta relations can be declaratively specified by meta-rules, too, that can be systematically generated from the rules defining an application. The corresponding rewriting process resembles the magic set transformation in many respects, although this time a particular form of bottom-up reasoning is specified by means of meta-rules. The "magic update rules", as we would like to call them due to the analogy with magic sets, are driven by bottom-up fixpoint iteration, too. For query-driven inference the representation of the respective query as a magic fact constitutes the "seed" from which subqueries, intermediate results and answers "grow" during fixpoint computation. In the "magic update" approach the update to be propagated can be regarded as the "seed" from which the derived deltas "grow" during propagation.

By formulating update propagation in terms of meta-rules and fixpoint computations, we do not introduce any new method for integrity checking or view refreshment, but just propose a particularly convenient implementation framework for such methods. Indeed we believe that most (if not all) of the approaches for instance to integrity checking in deductive databases can be formulated in terms of variations of the magic update rule device. It is surprising, however, that up till now none of the authors concerned with deductive update propagation seems to have noticed that the process of successively computing induced updates from base updates can be viewed (and more importantly: implemented) as a fixpoint computation as well.

In contrast to the well-documented magic sets approach, proper publications on the meta-rule approach to update propagation are still missing, though the approach has been presented on various occasions in the context of tutorials and invited talks by this author. A technical publication on "magic updates" is underway, however [BM]. Despite this apparent drawback, we would like to anticipate the results to be presented in that paper already, because of their direct and important relevance for our discussion of a reflective architecture. A method influenced by these ideas in an earlier phase and already exhibiting several of the characteristics of a reflective solution has been developed two years ago at ECRC and incorporated into the EKS-V1 deductive DBMS prototype [VBK91].

There are three advantages that we can identify as resulting from a meta-rule/fixpoint implementation of update propagation. First, by implementing update-driven inference on top of a fixpoint procedure, it is possible to reuse the same core procedure that has already been applied for query answering. Doing so results in a rather remarkable simplification of the overall architecture of a deductive DBMS. Instead of having to provide two separate inference engines, one for query-driven and one for update-driven inference, a single, well-optimized fixpoint computation procedure can be applied for both purposes. Depending on the kind of inference to be performed, this procedure will activate either the one, or the other set of meta-rules thus achieving the intended behaviour in each case.

A second advantage can be observed when implementing update propagation methods like those of [Dec86] or [DW89], where bottom-up propagation of updates is interleaved with top-down evaluation of queries in view of interrupting the propagation process as early as possible. Realizing such methods in a conventional framework, where two different inference components are used, results in constantly switching back and forth between the two engines. If both inference modes are uniformly expressed by meta-rules, however, and are driven by one and the same fixpoint procedure, the two inference processes are perfectly blended into one single fixpoint computation process. They can thus be optimized coherently and without any overhead resulting from repeated initialization of new subprocesses.

Finally, by basing update propagation on fixpoint computation, optimization techniques developed for improving the efficiency of fixpoint iteration in general (such as the differential optimization, but also including more sophisticated methods like the ones reported in [RSS90, SSRN91]), can be exploited for update-driven inference as well, not only in the query answering context they have been developed for.

3   Active rules for implementing deductive inference

The main advantage of a deductive system (at least for this author's taste) is its ability to hide from users and rule designers the details of how the DBMS reacts to queries and updates. Deductive rules can thus be regarded as declarative, high-level specifications of a whole bunch of reactions a deductive system will automatically perform due to the mere existence of the rules. In a database system that does not support deductive rules, but offers active rules instead, all these reactions would have to be explicitly and individually specified in terms of ECA-rules by the application designer. One could thus reasonably claim that deductive specifications are superior to active ones, at least as far as data derivation is concerned (including integrity checking, which is a special case of data derivation at update time).

Unfortunately, the high-level specification of system reactions achievable by deductive means is limited to particular ECA-patterns involving queries and updates only. Active databases as investigated by many research projects today have a much more ambitious scope and aim at providing a much more powerful set of features. Events can be any observable method or procedure call in the respective programming environment, or even input from external sources, such as clocks, sensors, buttons and the like. Actions can be arbitrary procedure calls as well, not just database operations, or even signals issued to agents in the outside world. In such systems, the role of the database during rule activation might be reduced to that of a rule repository and to serving as a source of background knowledge during condition evaluation.

In consequence more and more research projects are currently being launched that try to provide a common framework for both rule paradigms, resulting in active DOOD systems. Supporting both, active and deductive rules, within a single system bears the risk of a considerable increase in system complexity again. A deductive engine sits aside an active engine, both highly optimized and likely to consume considerable resources. Whenever an active rule is triggered, the deductive engine is likely to be activated as well, either during condition evaluation, or due to an update or a query issued as a reaction. Whenever a deductive rules is activated, the triggering of active rules is likely to occur due to query- or update-driven ECA-rules. In both cases we are back to the undesirable situation already encountered when looking at query- and update-driven inference: two independent engines mutually activating each other with high frequency and consequently producing considerable overhead and performance decline, not to speak of the resulting complexity of the overall architecture and maintenance.

It is not surprising that we recommend the same remedy that has already cured the multiple engines problem in the previous section: try to implement both engines by means of a common core procedure and express the differences between the two by means of appropriate system-internal (meta-)rules. In the present case, looking for a common core procedure for active and deductive rule processing, the solution seems to be more obvious, although the two paradigms are much more different from each other than query- and update-driven inference are. As active rules are the more expressive feature, and as all the reaction patterns to be provided by a deductive engine can be specified by suitable active rules, it looks like common sense to choose the engine driving event-action sequences as the core procedure and to express deductive inference by means of internal active meta-rules.

Several proposals for deriving triggers from deductive specifications have already been published (most prominently a series of papers in the context of the Starburst project [CW90, CW91, Wid91]). Most of these proposals did not yet have too much of an impact in the deductive community, possibly because they use SQL and do not clearly relate to standard methods in deductive database research. We believe, however, that a rather straightforward migration path from fixpoint-based approaches to equivalent methods based on active rules can be obtained that carry over all the optimizations and particularities of the pure deductive method into an active rule context.

The clue to such a transformation will probably be a formulation of (differential) fixpoint iteration by means of active meta-rules in a way that is analogous to Bry's formulation of top-down inference by means of bottom-up meta-rules. Most likely such a formulation will also be used as an intermediate step only, from which a direct rewriting of deductive rules into triggers can be derived systematically and automatically (probably by partial evaluation again). However, the existence of the application-independent meta-rule specification opens up the choice between a compiled and an interpreted approach. Moreover, the incorporation of new optimization parameters into the rewriting approach is considerably facilitated, if the respective optimization is first introduced into the general meta-rules before being compiled into the individual application rules.

Whether such an approach is going to be viable for the rewriting of deductive rules into active ones as nicely and unproblematically as it does for the magic rewriting remains to be proved and is an open problem. The perspective of a compact and simple system architecture of an active DOOD system based on just a single engine, namely an active rule driver, is definitely a very promising one. Again the generic task, organizing sequences of activities triggering each other in an efficient and well-organized manner, is factored out and can be optimized separately and independent from its various applications. As soon as a new optimization for active rule activation has been developed, it automatically is available for (possibly) improving efficiency of fixpoint computations as well. If the approach of implementing deductive functionality by means of active rules really turned out to be a "winner", this would mean an invaluable support for the reflective architecture ideal we have tried to put forward in this paper. Unfortunately it is far too early to seriously judge about this matter based on the current state-of-the-art.

4 Conclusion

When proposing the use of, e.g., a DOOD system as an advanced tool for solving knowledge-intensive software problems, we in fact ask our users to represent a major part of their software in terms of individual, comparatively small pieces of knowledge (facts, rules, constraints organized in class hierarchies), rather than as huge, often unintelligible chunks of procedural code. We believe in the benefit of this style of extracting knowledge out of programs and representing it in a high-level, declarative form mainly because of two reasons: on the one hand, the "intelligence" incorporated into our software becomes more clearly identifiable and understandable, thus making software more reliable and manageable. On the other hand, a centralized repository of individual items of knowledge can be much easier manipulated and changed, enabling us to flexibly modify and extend a system without being forced to rewrite major portions of procedural code each time we are upgrading it. If all these benefits for the organization of large software systems can really be obtained by means of an intelligent interface, then one should expect that we - the DBMS developers - would love to apply exactly this kind of functionality ourselves when solving the main software development task we are faced with, namely the implementation of DBMS components.

However, curiously enough, we don't! Most database management systems are nowadays still coded entirely procedurally, most of the time not even according to some object-oriented programming discipline, and definitely not making use of deductive or active functionality for internal purposes. Thus each implementation of a system module represents a high effort in manpower and development time, hard coding all design decisions and characteristics of the respective system in an often unpenetrable jungle of ten thousands of lines of code. The undesirable consequences of this style of system design and implementation have been pointed out again and again, and many new trends in database technology such as extensible systems or rule-based query optimizers can be regarded as attempts to cure symptoms of the observed shortcomings.

In this paper we have been arguing that various emerging trends in the implementation of intelligent DBMSs in fact should be interpreted as instances of a common general scheme, which is characterized by the systematic use of the key features of an intelligent DBMSs interface - such as objects, rules and constraints - for implementing such a system itself. Sometimes this is done consciously, e.g., when metaclasses are used, or when triggers and events are treated as objects, but often enough there is no awareness of having applied a general principle when arriving at a particular solution that can be interpreted in a reflective sense. The main message of this paper thus is: do consciously look for methods and models that make use of typical database functionality for the realization of database technology in a reflective manner. The resulting gain in economy and clarity of code, in flexibility in case of modification and thus in maintenance effort in general might be considerable.

Some might respond that they are doing so anyway since long: well-so, but then speak about it, point out the reflective nature of your results, report about positive and negative experience with this approach. Others will call reflection a dream, and continue to rely on their own craftsmanship as a systems programmer in tuning system code to highest performance. Maybe it is possible to persuade a few of them to try a reflective approach at least during an early design phase, and to switch to handcoding only in those well-analyzed cases where limits of a purely reflective solution become obvious and insurmountable. Those resisting even this temptation are requested to at least identify explicitly those obstacles that they regard as crucial, and to report about unsuccessful attempts to apply elegant solutions. A reflective architecture is not to be regarded as a dogma, but as a goal, from which to deviate is not a crime, but might be perfectly reasonable if done consciously. To improve the necessary consciousness is what this paper has been written for.

References

[AMC93]   E. Anwar, L. Maugis, and S. Chakravarthy: "A New Perspective on Rule Support for Object-Oriented Databases", in: Proc. SIGMOD 1993

[BMSU86]   F. Bancilhon, D. Maier, Y. Sagiv, and J. Ullman: "Magic sets and other strange ways to implement logic programs", in: Proc. PODS 1986

[BR86]   F. Bancilhon and R. Ramakrishnan: "An amateur's introduction to recursive query processing strategies", in: Proc. SIGMOD 1986

[Bay85]   R. Bayer: "Query Evaluation and Recursion in Deductive Database Systems", Techn. Report TUM-18503, Techn. Univ. Muenchen, Inst. f. Informatik, 1985

[Bry90]   F. Bry: "Query evaluation in recursive databases: bottom-up and top-down reconciled", Data and Knowledge Engineering, Vol. 5, 1990, (earlier version in Proc. DOOD 1989)

[BM]   F. Bry and R. Manthey: "On the magic of updates: a fixpoint approach to updatepropagation in deductive databases", in preparation

[CGT90]   S. Ceri, G. Gottlob, and L. Tanca: "Logic Programming and Databases", Springer Verlag, Berlin-Heidelberg-New York, 1990

[CW90]   S. Ceri and J. Widom: "Deriving Production Rules for Constraint Maintenance", in: Proc. VLDB 1990

[CW91]   S. Ceri and J. Widom: "Deriving Production Rules for Incremental View Maintenance", in: Proc. VLDB 1991

[DW89]   S. Das and M.H. Williams: "A path finding method for constraint checking in deductive databases", in: Data and Knowledge Engineering, Vol. 4, 1989

[DBM88]   U. Dayal, A. Buchmann, and D. McCarthy: "Rules Are Objects Too: A Knowledge Model for an Active, Object-Oriented Database System", in: Proc. 2nd Intern. Workshop on Object-Oriented Database Systems, LNCS 334, 1988

[Dec86]   H. Decker: "Integrity Enforcement on Deductive Databases", in: 1st Intern. Conf. on Expert Database Systems (EDS), 1986

[LV89]   A. Lefebvre and L. Vieille: "On Deductive Query Evaluation in the Dedgin* System", in: Proc. DOOD 1989

[NY83]   J.M. Nicolas and K. Yazdanian: "An Outline of BDGEN: A Deductive DBMS", in: Proc. IFIP 1983

[DPG91]   O. Diaz, N.W. Paton, and P.M.D. Gray: "Rule management in object-oriented database systems", in: Proc. VLDB 1991

[RSS90]   R. Ramakrishnan, S. Sudarshan, and D. Srivasta: "Rule ordering in the bottom-up fixpoint evaluation of logic programs", in: Proc. VLDB 1990

[SZ87]   D. Sacca and C. Zaniolo: "Magic Counting Methods", in: Proc. SIGMOD 1987

[SZ88]   D. Sacca and C. Zaniolo: "Differential Fixpoint Methods and Stratification of Logic Programs", in: Proc. 3rd Intern. Conference on Data and Knowledge Bases, Jerusalem, 1988

[SSRN91]   S. Sudarshan, D. Srivasta, R. Ramakrishnan, and J. Naughton: "Space Optimization in the Bottom-Up Evaluation of Logic Programs", in: Proc. SIGMOD 1991

[Vie86]   L. Vieille: "Recursive axioms in deductive databases: The Query-Subquery approach", in: Proc. 1st Intern. Conf. on Expert Database Systems (EDS), 1986

[VBK91]   L. Vieille, P. Bayer and V. Küchenhoff: "Integrity Checking and Materialized Views Handling by Update Propagation in the EKS-V1 System", ECRC Technical Report TR-KB-35, June 1991

[Wid91]   J. Widom: "Deduction in the Starburst Production Rule System", Research Report RJ 8135, IBM Almaden Research Center, 1991

[ZAO93]   C. Zaniolo, N. Arni, and K. Ong: "Negation and Aggregates in Recursive Rules: the LDL++ Approach", in: Proc. DOOD93

A deductive and typed object-oriented language

René Bal and Herman Balsters*

Computer Science Department, University of Twente,
P.O. Box 217, 7500 AE Enschede,
The Netherlands

Abstract. In this paper we introduce a logical query language extended with object-oriented typing facilities. This language, called DTL (from DataTypeLog), can be seen as an extension of Datalog equipped with complex objects, object identities, and multiple inheritance based on Cardelli type theory. The language also incorporates a very general notion of sets as first-class objects. The paper offers a formal description of DTL, as well as a denotational semantics for DTL programs.

Keywords: Query languages, object-oriented databases, inheritance, type theory, resolution, denotational semantics.

1 Introduction and results

In the last decade, the merge of object-oriented programming with object-oriented data structuring principles has lead to a rapid increasement of new developments in the field of databases and logical languages. Object-oriented databases have the advantages of a clean conceptual design as well as the possibility of enforcing better software engineering. Systems equipped with subtyping facilities, such as the Cardelli object-oriented type system (cf. [Card88]), offer a concise and clear way to deal with (multiple) inheritance. Inheritance is a very powerful modelling tool and forms the backbone of many object-oriented data models. Also the availability of complex objects, such as records, lists, variants, and sets offer a wide range of expressiveness. Examples of data models with facilities as mentioned above are O_2 ([LéRi89]), Iris ([LyVi87]) and Machiavelli ([OhBB89]).

Object-orientation has also not left the field of logical languages untouched. Languages like LIFE ([Aït-K91]), F-Logic ([KiLW90]), and [BrLM90,IbCu90, McCa92,MoPo90] are examples of such languages that make extensive use of object-oriented principles to enhance the field of logic programming with the expressiveness and concise modelling possibilities, typical for the object-oriented paradigm. Especially the use of subtyping makes logic programs more structured and easier to understand. In short, the combination of logic programming and object orientation is very promising.

Relational databases and logic programming have been combined resulting in so-called deductive databases. Deductive databases highlight the ability to use a

---

* Our E-mail addresses are, resp.: `rene@cs.utwente.nl`, `balsters@cs.utwente.nl`

logic programming style for expressing deductions concerning the contents of the database. Examples of such languages are Datalog [CeGT90] and LDL [NaTs89]. These languages have gained considerable popularity due to the ease in which it is possible to specify very complex queries.

Recently, research interest has started to arise in the combination of object orientation, databases and logical languages. For example, research initiatives have been started aimed at extending Datalog with object-oriented concepts. In such extensions, the logical component is used to specify the schema of the database, and a distinction is made between base relations and derived relations. Examples of such systems are LOGRES [CCCT90], and Complex Datalog [GrLR92]. Other examples are object-oriented logical languages primarily used for the querying of object-oriented databases, such as [AbKa89,Abit90,AbGr88] and LLO [LoOz91].

The language described in this paper is called DTL, which stands for DataType-Log. DTL is designed as a query language for a database specified in a language called TM. TM ([BaBZ93]) is a high-level specification language for object-oriented database schemas, and has all the facilities that one would expect from a state-of-the-art object-oriented data model. The main novelties of the TM language are the incorporation of predicative sets as first-class objects, and the possibility of defining static constraints of different granularity (i.e. at the object level, class level, and database level), and this in the context of multiple inheritance and full static typecheckability.

In DTL we have taken an approach which sometimes differs considerably from existing object-oriented query languages. For example, answers to DTL queries result in a set of homogeneous elements, in the sense that these elements all have the same so-called minimal type w.r.t. subtyping. This means that if a query asks for **persons**, then the answer should consist of **persons** and not, for example, also specializations of **persons**, say **employees**. This approach differs from the one followed by F-logic and LIFE, where basically there is no distinction made between types and instantiations of types. Our approach is also different from the one followed by IQL, ILOG ([HuYo90]), LOGRES and LLO, where the answer results in a collection of object identifiers. The object identifiers in these cases are related to o-values by means of an o-value assignment (to employ terminology taken from IQL), and in this way the answers actually include specializations of the requested original type.

As mentioned before, DTL incorporates general set constructions, including predicatively defined sets, as first-class objects; i.e. such sets are actual terms in the language. Languages like LOGRES, IQL and LLO also support sets, be it that these sets are restricted to enumerated sets as actual terms in the language. A distinct feature of DTL is its powerful usage of combining predicates and (multiple) inheritance; languages like LLO, LIFE and F-logic also offer a notion of inheritance, but in combination with predicates the version in DTL is less restricted. Yet another feature of DTL is the possibility to navigate freely through the terms by successive projection on attribute components. In other systems like LOGRES, Complex Datalog, IQL and LLO such a navigation is also possible, be it that the process of navigation in these languages is more complicated than in DTL .

The rest of the paper is organized as follows. We first give an impression of the TM datamodel and offer an example of a TM database specification. After that we will offer an introduction to the DTL language. In section 3 we shall give a more thorough account of DTL including matters concerning typing and the combination of using types and predicates in programs. In section 4 we will give a denotational semantics for DTL programs, and we end with some conclusions and suggestions for future research.

2 The datamodel TM

DTL is meant as a well-founded query language for TM, and within this paper we will only discuss those aspects of TM which are relevant for DTL. For more details on TM the reader is referred to [BaBB92,BaBZ93,BaBV92].

The TM language is a high-level object-oriented datamodel that has been developed at the University of Twente in cooperation with the Politecnico di Milano. The TM language is designed for describing conceptual schemas of object-oriented databases. The TM language contains all of the elements that one would expect from a state-of-the-art object-oriented model, but with important new features, namely the incorporation of

1. predicative descriptions of sets (predicative sets as complex values)
2. static constraints of different granularity (object level, class level, database level)

The strength of TM stems from its richness as a specification language and its formal, type-theoretic background. The TM language is founded in FM, which is based on a typed lambda calculus extended with logic and sets. The subtyping is based on the ideas of the Cardelli type system [Card88], which has been given a set-theoretical semantics in [BaFo91,BaVr91]. TM has complex objects formed from arbitrarily nested records, variant records, sets, and lists. Furthermore, TM is equipped with object identity, multiple inheritance, methods and method inheritance, and this in the context of full static typecheckability. Classes in TM specifications have an extension in the database; the prefix with extension in a TM Class declaration is followed by the name of the class extension in the database. For more details on TM and its relation to other object-oriented database languages, we refer to [BaBZ93].

Example 1. An example of a database specification within TM.

```
Class Person with extension PERS
   attributes
        name   : string
        age    : integer
        spouse : Person
```

```
        gender : string
    object constraints
        c1 : gender="Male"  or gender="Female"
        c2 : spouse·spouse=self
    class constraints
    key name end  Person
```

Class Employee ISA Person with extension EMP
```
    attributes
        colleagues : ℙEmployee
        salary     : ⟨m_salary:real⟩
    object constraints
        c3 : salary·m_salary ≥ 3000 and salary·m_salary ≤ 10000
end  Employee
```

Class Manager ISA Employee with extension MAN
```
    attributes
        salary     : ⟨m_salary:real, r_expenses:real⟩
        department : string
end  Manager
```

Class Secretary ISA Employee with extension SEC
```
    attributes
        boss : Manager
end  Secretary
```

In the example above, a generalization hierarchy is defined for **Persons**, **Employees**, **Managers** and **Secretaries**. This generalization hierarchy is defined by means of the statement C **ISA** C', occurring in the head of a class definition. It means that for every object e occurring in the extension of C, there is an object e' occurring in C' such that e' is a generalization of e; hence, the extension of C is a specialized subset of the extension of C'. In our example this means that generalizations of **Managers** occurring in the extension MAN also occur as **Employee** in EMP; .i.e., the extension MAN contains specializations of a subset of EMP.

In TM, objects have an object identifier used for referential integrity, for sharing and for implementation of recursive data structures. They are, however, not directly visible in TM, although there are operations to inspect the value of the object identifiers. As already stated, TM is formally founded in FM. In FM the object identifier is just a label of a record expression. For example, the FM representation of a **Person** is ⟨id:oid, name:string, age:int, spouse:oid, gender:string⟩, along with certain additional constraints ensuring that the oid-values correctly refer to their corresponding objects. For example, to enforce that the spouse of a **Person** corresponds to some **Person**, we shall add at the database level the following referential integrity constraint

$$\forall y \in PERS\ \exists x \in PERS\ \ y \cdot spouse = x \cdot \text{id}$$

For more details on such a translation from TM specifications to its FM-counterpart, we refer to [BaBZ93].

DTL is a user language which can be considered as a sugared version the formal language FDTL. Before presenting the formal language we first give a few example queries specified in DTL. The examples throughout this paper are all related to the TM specification in example 1

Example 2. Give all Employees in the database, which have a spouse who is the Secretary of a Manager earning more than 8000, and this Manager is to be a colleague of the Employee in question.

This query could easily be translated to the following DTL specification, where we use the predicate symbol p for the specification of the required Employees

```
    p(X)  ←  EMP(X), Y isa X·spouse, SEC(Y),
             Y·boss·salary·m_salary ≥ 8000, Y·boss in X·colleagues.

    ? p(X(Employee)).
```

Here the predicates EMP and SEC are used to denote that the variables X and Y reside in the extensions EMP and SEC, respectively. Furthermore, since the types of these extensions are known, the types of the variables occurring within the definition of the predicate can be omitted. In the formal language FDTL, we will use a special predicate, the **db**-predicate, to express that an expression denotes an object residing in the database. By using the **db**-predicate, explicit usage of extension names will not be necessary in FDTL programs.

The dot notation, as usual, denotes record projection; hence, X·spouse denotes a Person object being a spouse of Employee X. Another interesting predicate used in example 2 is the **isa** -predicate; this predicate is used to compare specializations with corresponding generalizations. Hence, the predicate Y(Secretary) **isa** X(Employee)·spouse, informally, evaluates to true if Y is indeed a specialization of the spouse of Employee X.

The query of example 2 could also be defined by making use of more than one predicate. First we introduce a predicate which defines a relation between Secretaries and Managers earning over 8000, after which we could use the predicate in the body of a rule instantiated by arguments of a super- or subtype. In the example below, the predicate is instantiated by a Person and an Employee, both of which have types that are supertypes of the original types Secretary and Manager.

```
    secr_wp_man(X(Secretary), Y(Manager))  ←  SEC(X), X·boss = Y,
                                               Y·salary·m_salary ≥ 8000.

    p(X)  ←  secr_wp_man(X·spouse, Y(Employee)), Y in X·colleagues,
             EMP(X).

    ? p(X(Employee)).
```

Analogously, we can use this kind of predicate inheritance to ask for all **Secretaries** which fulfill the requirement p. The query then becomes

   ? p(X), SEC(X).

If we want all **Persons** satisfying the predicate p, the query becomes

   ? p(X(Person)).

The instantiation of a predicate employing specialization or generalization is treated in more detail below.

3   The language FDTL

DTL is meant as a typed logical query language for TM which is able to deal with subtyping and inheritance. In the previous section a few example DTL queries were presented. These queries could easily be translated to the formal language FDTL treated below. The object identifiers which are invisible within DTL are used explicitly within FDTL. Furthermore, we have no classes in FDTL, but only types; hence, FDTL is defined on the FM representation of the database. After the definition of the language FDTL is given, we will discuss its semantics informally.

3.1   The definition of FDTL

FDTL supports arbitrarily nested records, variant records, sets and lists. Within this paper, however, we will only deal with records and sets for reasons of a clean exposition. Formal definitions of the full language can be found in [Bal92].

The Types. We assume that the basic types are in a postulated set B. This set contains, among others, the standard types **bool,int,real,string,char** and **oid**. The subtype relation defined on $B \times B$ is the identity, i.e. we have no subtype relation between different basic types, since this will lead to problems related to resolution in FDTL programs. We furthermore assume that we have a set of labels L, totally ordered and with lower bound **id** (such an ordering of labels enforces a canonical form for records and record types). We let a vary over L.

Definition 1. The set T (of *types*) is defined as follows

1. $\tau \in T$, whenever $\tau \in B$
2. $\langle a_1 : \tau_1, \ldots, a_m : \tau_m \rangle \in T$, whenever $a_i \in L$, $\tau_i \in T$ $(1 \leq i \leq m)$, $a_1 < a_2 < \ldots < a_m$ and $m \geq 0$.
3. $\mathbb{P}\tau \in T$, whenever $\tau \in T$

We let ρ, σ and τ over T.

We distinguish two subsets of the set of types. These are the *object types* and the *ordinary types*. The object types T_{obj} are all record types for which the first label is **id : oid**. The ordinary, or non-object, types T_{nor} are all expressions which do not contain any component of type **oid**.

Subtyping. The subtyping relation is defined, conform the well-known Cardelli type theory [CaWe85,Card84,Card88], on the set of object types and on the set of ordinary types, and is extended to the set of all types. The reason for this approach is that we do not want an object type to be a subtype of an ordinary type.

Definition 2. The relation $\leq$ on $T \times T$ is defined by induction as follows

1. $\beta \leq \beta$, whenever $\beta \in B$
2. $\langle a_1 : \sigma_1, \ldots, a_m : \sigma_m \rangle \leq \langle a_{j_1} : \tau_{j_1}, \ldots, a_{j_n} : \tau_{j_n} \rangle$, whenever $j_1, \ldots, j_n$ is a (not necessarily contiguous) sub-sequence of $1, \ldots, m$, $\sigma_{j_i} \leq \tau_{j_i}$ $(1 \leq i \leq n)$ and $a_1 = \text{id}$ iff $a_{j_1} = \text{id}$
3. $\mathbb{P}\sigma \leq \mathbb{P}\tau$, whenever $\sigma \leq \tau$

Example 3. We have $\langle \text{age:int, name:string, address:string} \rangle \leq \langle \text{age:int, name:string} \rangle$ since the former type has all properties of the latter type, but also an extra property, namely the additional address field. However $\langle \text{id:oid, name:string, address:string} \rangle \not\leq \langle \text{age:int, name:string} \rangle$ since the former type is an object type, while the latter is an ordinary type.

The Terms. The terms of FDTL are very similar to the expressions defined in TM and FM. We have constants, variables, records, variants, lists and sets. As explained earlier, we will not deal with lists and variant records within this paper, and furthermore, we will also not deal with aggregate operations defined on sets. The operations which we will discuss in this paper are the projection operation defined on records and the usual operations defined on sets.

For each $\tau \in T$ let C_τ be a (possibly empty) set (of constants), mutually disjoint. We let c_τ vary over C_τ. $C_{\text{bool}} = \{\text{true}, \text{false}\}$. Furthermore, for each $\tau \in T$ let X_τ be a set (of variables), mutually disjoint, countably infinite and disjoint from the sets C_σ $(\sigma \in T)$. We let $\mathtt{X}(\tau)$ vary over X_τ.

Definition 3. The set E (of *terms*) is defined inductively as follows

1. $c_\tau \in E$, whenever $\tau \in T$, $c_\tau \in C_\tau$
2. $\mathtt{X}(\tau) \in E$, whenever $\tau \in T$, $\mathtt{X}(\tau) \in X_\tau$
3. $\langle a_1 = t_1, \ldots, a_m = t_m \rangle \in E$, whenever $a_i \in L$, $t_i \in E$ $(1 \leq i \leq m)$ and $a_1 < a_2 < \ldots < a_m$ and $m \geq 0$
4. $t \cdot a \in E$, whenever $t \in E$, $a \in L$
5. $\{t_1, \ldots, t_m\} \in E$, whenever $t_i \in E$ $(1 \leq i \leq m)$ and $m \geq 0$
6. $t_1 \, set\_op \, t_2 \in E$, whenever $t_1, t_2 \in E$ and $set\_op \in \{ \text{union}, \text{intersect}, \text{minus} \}$

We let t vary over E.

The typing rules are often defined by means of minimal typing, since expressions, i.e. terms, can have more than one type, due to the subtyping environment[2].

---

[2] This kind of type polymorphism is obtained by the following rule

$$t : \sigma, \quad \sigma \leq \tau \Rightarrow t : \tau$$

Fortunately, every term also has a unique minimal type denoted by "::". Our definition of minimal typing [BaFo91] is basically the same as the one given in [Reyn85], and satisfies the following important properties: soundness ($t :: \sigma \Rightarrow t : \sigma$), completeness ($t : \tau \Rightarrow t :: \sigma$, for some $\sigma \in T$), and minimality ($t : \tau$, $t :: \sigma \Rightarrow \sigma \leq \tau$)

Definition 4. The typing rules for terms

1. $\dfrac{c_\tau \in C_\tau}{c_\tau :: \tau}$
$\qquad\qquad\qquad\qquad$ 2. $\dfrac{\mathbf{x}(\tau) \in X_\tau}{\mathbf{x}(\tau) :: \tau}$

3. $\dfrac{t_i :: \tau_i \ (1 \leq i \leq m)}{\langle a_1 = t_1, \ldots, a_m = t_m \rangle :: \langle a_1 : \tau_1, \ldots, a_m : \tau_m \rangle}$

4. $\dfrac{t :: \langle a_1 : \tau_1, \ldots, t_m : \tau_m \rangle}{(t \cdot a_j) :: \tau_j}(1 \leq j \leq m)$
$\qquad$ 5. $\dfrac{t_i :: \tau \ (1 \leq i \leq m)}{\{t_1, \ldots, t_m\} :: \mathbb{P}\tau}$

6. $\dfrac{t_1 :: \mathbb{P}\tau \quad t_2 :: \mathbb{P}\tau}{(t_1 \ set\_op \ t_2) :: \mathbb{P}\tau} set\_op \in \{\ \text{union}\ ,\ \text{intersect}\ ,\ \text{minus}\ \}$

Let E^* denote the set of all well-typed terms. $E^* \subseteq E$

If σ is a type then $\mathbb{P}\sigma$ denotes the powertype of σ. Intuitively, a powertype $\mathbb{P}\sigma$ denotes the collection of all sets of terms t of type σ. Note that the semantics of a powertype as well as elements thereof can be infinite, depending on the specific underlying type. The powertype constructor resembles the construction of the powerset $\mathcal{P}(V)$ of a set V in ordinary set theory. A term t in our language is called a *set* if it has a powertype as its type; i.e., $t : \mathbb{P}\sigma$, for some type σ. We stress here that a set in our theory is a *term* and not a type; i.e. we add to the set of types special types called powertypes, and, in addition, we add to the set of terms special terms called sets.

The typing rules 5 and 6 concerning set expressions are a direct consequence of the typing rules for equality, discussed in subsection 3.1. Therefore, we will defer the treatment of these rules until the typing rule for equality is discussed.

A subset of the well-typed terms are the basic terms E_B. This subset consists of all terms not containing operations, i.e. such terms contain only constants, variables and enumerated sets.

The operation Var is defined on all terms and returns the set of variables occurring within a particular term.

The Atoms. For each $n \in N$ let $Pred_n$ be a set (of *n-ary predicate symbols*) mutually disjoint, countably infinite and disjoint from the sets of constants and the sets of variables. We let p and q vary over $Pred_n$.

Definition 5. The set Atm (of *atomic formulas*) is defined as follows

- If p is an n-ary predicate symbol and $t_1 \ldots t_n \in E^*$, then $p(t_1 \ldots t_n)$ is an *atomic formula*, or more simply, an *atom*.

We let A vary over *Atm*.

We distinguish two kinds of predicates, the *ordinary* predicates and the *built-in* predicates. In addition to the standard built-in predicates which are also used within Datalog [CeGT90], FDTL also has a database predicate, an **isa** -predicate, a membership predicate, and a subset predicate. The database predicate, **db**, is used to denote that objects are taken from the database. Furthermore, since the typing rules for the equality predicate are very severe , an **isa** -predicate is defined to allow for a more liberal comparison of specialized expressions with generalized ones. Similar rules are offered for the membership predicate and subset predicate defined for sets; i.e. we have a strict form, and a more liberal form dealing with specializations and generalizations.

The reasons for adopting strict typing rules for the equality predicate, as well as for typing of object-oriented sets in our theory, are rather technical and are explained in detail in [BaVr91]. Informally, however, one could say that if two terms are to be equal, then they should be equal in *all* aspects; i.e., they should also have exactly the same typing possibilities in the context of subtyping. This leads us to our typing rule for equality of two terms: the predicate $t_1 = t_2$ is correctly typed and of type **bool**, iff t_1, t_2 have exactly the same typing possibilities; i.e., t_1 and t_2 have the same *minimal* type.

For sets we also make a distinction between severe and more liberal typing rules, similar to the situation with the equality predicate. For example, we have a strict form of set membership (**in**) stating that a term is to be *exactly equal* to some element of a set, and we have a more liberal form (**sin**) stating that a term is to be equal to a *specialization* of some element of a set. Again, the reader is referred to [BaVr91] for more details.

Definition 6. The built-in predicates $Atm_B \subset Atm$ and their typing rules are defined as follows

1. $\dfrac{t :: \sigma \quad \sigma \in T_{obj}}{\mathbf{db}(t)}$
2. $\dfrac{t_1 :: \sigma \quad t_2 :: \sigma \quad \sigma \in \{\text{int}, \text{real}, \text{string}, \text{char}\}}{t_1 \; op \; t_2 \quad op \in \{<, \leq, >, \geq\}}$

3. $\dfrac{t_1 :: \sigma \quad t_2 :: \sigma}{t_1 \; op \; t_2} op \in \{=, \neq\}$
4. $\dfrac{t_1 :: \sigma \quad t_2 :: \tau \quad \sigma \leq \tau}{t_1 \; \mathbf{isa} \; t_2}$

5. $\dfrac{t_1 :: \sigma \quad t_2 :: \mathbb{P}\sigma}{t_1 \; \mathbf{in} \; t_2}$
6. $\dfrac{t_1 :: \sigma \quad t_2 :: \mathbb{P}\tau \quad \sigma \leq \tau}{t_1 \; \mathbf{sin} \; t_2}$

7. $\dfrac{t_1 :: \mathbb{P}\sigma \quad t_2 :: \mathbb{P}\sigma}{t_1 \; \mathbf{subset} \; t_2}$
8. $\dfrac{t_1 :: \mathbb{P}\sigma \quad t_2 :: \mathbb{P}\tau \quad \sigma \leq \tau}{t_1 \; \mathbf{ssubset} \; t_2}$

Let Atm^* denote the set of well-typed atoms. $Atm^* \subseteq Atm$.

Example 4. The **isa** -predicate has the possibility to compare specializations with generalizations. The atom ⟨name="Mary", age=18⟩ **isa** ⟨name="Mary"⟩ is *true*, because the first argument is a specialization of the second argument. Analogously, the **sin** -predicate could be used to check if there exists a generalization of the expression occurring on the left-hand side, which occurs in the set expression on the right-hand side, for instance ⟨name="Mary", age=18⟩ **sin** {⟨name="Mary"⟩, ⟨name="Jane"⟩}. Analogously, the **ssubset** -predicate could be used for sets; for example, EMP **ssubset** PERS, in example 1.

A FDTL Program. A FDTL program is a sequence of Horn clauses.

Definition 7. A Horn clause H is of the form $A_0 \leftarrow A_1, \ldots A_n.$, where $A_i \in Atm^*$ and $A_0 \notin Atm_B (0 \leq i \leq n)$. The variables appearing within a Horn clause are assumed to be universally quantified. There are two notions defined on H: $Head(H) = A_0$ and $Body(H) = A_1, \ldots A_n$.

As usual, the scope of a variable is the Horn clause in which it appears. We will assume that each occurrence of a variable within a Horn clause has the same type; the type of the variable is therefore only stated once. Allowing occurrences of the variables to have different types does not have any effect on the expressiveness of FDTL; it does, however, have a serious effect on the semantics and the resolution of FDTL-programs (and on the readability of programs).

A set of Horn clauses forms a program, albeit not necessarily a correct program. In the next subsection constraints are defined for correct programs, as well as the (albeit informal) meaning of a correct program. For this reason, some additional definitions are presented below.

Definition 8. A *program* P is a set of Horn clauses (sometimes Horn clauses are also called clauses or rules). We let r vary over the rules in a program P.

Definition 9. The set of Horn clauses in a program P with the same predicate symbol q in the head is called the *definition* of q.
$Def_P(q) = \{r \in P \,|\, \text{predicate symbol of } Head(r) \text{ is } q\}$

Definition 10. Let A be an atom, then the type of A is defined by

$-$ $Type(A) = (\tau_1, \ldots, \tau_n)$, whenever $A = p(t_1, \ldots, t_n)$ and $t_i :: \tau_i$ $(1 \leq i \leq n)$.

The subtyping relation is extended in a straightforward manner to this Cartesian product construct.

Definition 11. Let P be a program and r be a rule occurring in $Def_P(q)$, then we say predicate q is *associated* with $Type(Head(r))$.

3.2 The meaning and correctness of an FDTL program

Due to typing and subtyping, it turns out that not every set of Horn clauses forms a correct program. Within this section we work towards the definition of a correct program, and we shall also provide for an informal semantics of correct programs. We shall start with a simple example and from then on work towards more complex situations.

First consider a situation where the arguments of a predicate all just have a basic type. As already stated there is no subtype relationship between different basic types, which means that for predicates having only arguments of a basic type, there is no possibility to use *predicate inheritance*. By predicate inheritance we mean that a predicate originally associated with a specific type, can also be used in the body of a rule by instantiating that predicate with specialized or generalized expressions w.r.t. the original type. We assume that a predicate is associated with one unique Cartesian product type. Later on we shall also experiment with a more liberal rule; it will turn out, however, that this more liberal rule gives rise to unexpected query results. This means that predicates associated with basic types can only be used by instantiating arguments of the same type as those for which the predicate was originally defined.

A more complex situation occurs when the arguments of predicates are associated with object types. In contrast to the situation sketched above, where only basic types play a rôle, concepts like inheritance are a major issue.

There are several ways to integrate inheritance into FDTL. One way to try to model inheritance, is to also put all specializations of a particular atom in the Herbrand model; i.e. if $p(e)$ is true and e' is a specialization of e, then $p(e')$ is also true. Hence, if $p(e)$ is in the model of an FDTL-program and e' **isa** e, then $p(e')$ occurs also in the model of the FDTL-program. This seems a rather natural rule; if a predicate is valid for a specific relation it is also valid for a specialization of this relation. Such an incorporation of specializations into the model, however, can lead to technical problems as illustrated in the following example

```
paid_6000(X(employee)) ← X·salary = (m_salary=6000).
```

Here, it is not possible to instantiate the variable X(employee) by an expression e of type **manager**, because then the equality predicate becomes incorrectly typed, since **managers** are specialized on the salary attribute. Therefore this way to integrate inheritance is not suitable for FDTL.

Another attempt at modelling predicate inheritance in FDTL is to have a more elaborate type system for variables. Instead of defining exactly the minimal type of the expressions which could be used to instantiate the variable, only an upperbound is specified. For example, if $p(e)$ is a fact and e ::employee, then it is possible to query the predicate p by ? p(X(person)). The informal semantics of such a query is: Give all instances for X having type **person** and that satisfy condition p. Hence, the term e is a correct instantiation of the variable X having upperbound **person**. This technique is used in, for example Login, F-logic and LLO. In our theory, based on Cardelli subtyping extended with set constructs, such an approach will give rise to answers of queries consisting of a set of terms that are not necessary all equipped with the same minimal type. Such sets of heterogeneously typed elements, however, lead to inconsistencies (cf. [BaVr91]), which makes such a liberal approach using upperbounds unfit for our purposes.

We have therefore chosen for another approach, which is also more powerful than the approaches sketched above. First let us consider how we could specify predicate inheritance in an explicit manner. Assume that a predicate is defined for a specific record type, then this predicate could be used to define predicates or terms having a sub- or supertype by using the built-in **isa** -predicate, as shown below.

```
well_paid_emp(X(employee))  ←  ..., X·salary·m_salary ≥ 6000.

well_paid_man(Y(manager))  ←  Y isa X(employee),
                               well_paid_emp(X), ....

well_paid_pers(Z(person))  ←  X(employee) isa Z,
                               well_paid_emp(X), ....
```

It is clear that such situations may occur often and therefore we would like to integrate this kind of inheritance within FDTL without having to explicitly specify **isa** -predicate instantiations. We will now explain how this can be achieved.

Suppose that we have the following rule (pertaining to example 1)

```
well_paid(X(employee))  ←  db(X(employee)),
                            X·salary·m_salary > 6000.
```

Informally, the predicate well_paid defines a set of employees occurring in the database which also have a monthly salary greater than 6000. Analogous to a typed logical language without subtyping it is possible to query this simple program by means of a goal where the predicate is equipped with a variable which has the same type as for which the predicate was originally defined. However, by using predicate inheritance we would also like to ask for well_paid managers, for example:

```
? well_paid(X(manager)).
```

This query can now be seen as shorthand for the query below, where only substitutions for the variable X(manager) are taken into consideration.

```
? well_paid(Y(employee)), X(manager) isa Y(employee).
```

The substitutions for Y(employee) could be eliminated by employing some additional dummy predicate. In this case, the query ? well_paid(X(manager)) can be seen as shorthand for

```
dummy(X(manager))  ←  well_paid(Y(employee)),
                       X(manager) isa Y(employee).

? dummy(X(manager)).
```

It should be noted that the goal ? dummy(X(manager)) would result in infinitely many substitutions for the variable X(manager), since the only requirement stated is that the manager occurs as an employee in the database. This will give rise to infinitely many substitutions for the department attribute, since this attribute is not available for employees. In order to make this query safe, the variable X(manager) should be bound in some manner. This can be done by means of another predicate, for example a database predicate as in

```
? well_paid(X(manager)), db(X(manager)).
```

This query has the same meaning as

```
dummy(X(manager)) ← well_paid(Y(employee)),
                     X(manager) isa Y(employee).
```

```
? dummy(X(manager)), db(X(manager)).
```

The answer to this query results in the set of managers occurring in the database which, as an employee, earn more than 6000 (it is assumed that we have, conceptually, a fully replicated database, i.e. all managers also occur as an employee in the database).

The same strategy as described above could also be used to obtain generalizations, as in

```
? well_paid(X(person)).
```

This query is then shorthand for

```
dummy(X(person)) ← well_paid(Y(employee)),
                    Y(employee) isa X(person).
```

```
? dummy(X(person)).
```

Hence, analogous to specializations, this technique can be extended to generalizations. The meaning of such a query is defined by considering these queries as shorthand for a query invoking a dummy predicate. Predicates are not only used within queries, they could also be used within bodies of rules defining other predicates. In that case there is no need for an additional dummy predicate; instead the body of the defined predicate can be extended with an extra isa -predicate.

Consider the following example using the well_paid predicate (defined for employees

```
satisfied(X(person)) ← well_paid(X(person)), ....
```

Analogous to queries, this rule can be regarded as shorthand for

```
satisfied(X(person)) ← well_paid(Y(employee)),
                        Y(employee) isa X(person), ....
```

We assumed earlier on that predicates were only allowed to be defined by using one fixed type declaration; i.e. even if a predicate is defined by different rules in some programs, it is defined by using the same type declaration in all of those rules. We will now clarify in more detail why we have chosen for this assumption. Consider the situation where we have more than one rule defining a predicate, and that the predicate is defined for more than one Cartesian product type, as in

```
well_paid(X(employee)) ← db(X(employee)),
                          X·salary·m_salary > 6000.
```

```
well_paid(X(manager))  ←  db(X(manager)),
                           X·salary·m_salary > 9000.
```

In the case of the following query

```
? well_paid(X(manager)).
```

we unfortunately not only get managers which are well paid as a manager and earn more than 9000 as answer, but also all managers which are well paid as an employee and earn more than 6000! The reason for this is that the query is actually shorthand for

```
dummy(X(manager))  ←  well_paid(X(manager)).

dummy(X(manager))  ←  well_paid(Y(employee)),
                      X(manager) isa Y(employee).

? dummy(X(manager)).
```

which will result in an answer being against our intuition. What we would expect are all well paid managers; i.e. well paid as a manager, and not the managers which are well paid as an employee. It is, however, impossible to query the predicate associated with one particular type, i.e. it is not possible to ask for well paid managers, which are solely well paid as a manager. In particular, if a predicate is defined by multiple rules and having different types, then this will often lead to unexpected results. Furthermore, apart from this problem, there exists also another problem of a more formal nature. A query results in a set of answers, and in our object-oriented theory dealing with sets, each set will contain elements all of the same minimal type. If we now allow a predicate to be defined for more then one Cartesian product type, then by querying such a predicate we will obtain a set of answers with different minimal types. This is therefore yet another reason to not allow for predicates defined by multiple rules having different Cartesian product types associated to them.

Let us now consider predicates associated to ordinary types. The interesting thing is that the strategy developed above for the treatment of predicates associated to object types is equally applicable to predicates associated to ordinary (i.e. non-object) types. For example, consider the following program

```
p(⟨name="Paul", age=20⟩).

p(⟨name="Eric", age=20⟩).
```

and the query

```
? p(X(⟨age:int⟩)).
```

This query can be regarded as shorthand for

```
dummy(X(⟨age:int⟩))  ←  p(Y(⟨name:string, age:int⟩)), Y isa X.
? dummy(X(⟨age:int⟩)).
```

Hence, we have defined a simple, but powerful mechanism to use predicate inheritance within an object oriented logical query language. The constraints specified for correct programs can now be defined more formally.

Definition 12 Type correctness of predicate definitions. Let q be an ordinary predicate defined in an FDTL program P. Program P should then satisfy the following requirement

$$\forall r, r' \in Def_P(q) \ Type(Head(r)) = Type(Head(r'))$$

Definition 13 Type correctness for usage of predicates. Let q be an ordinary predicate defined in an FDTL program P, and let A be a literal with predicate symbol q. Program P should then satisfy the following requirement

$$\forall r \in P \ (A \in Body(r) \Rightarrow \exists r' \in Def_P(q)$$
$$(Type(A) \leq Type(Head(r')) \vee Type(Head(r')) \leq Type(A)))$$

Definition 14. Let P be a correct program, and let q be an ordinary predicate defined in P. The type of q in P, conform definition 3.15, is then defined by

$$Typ_P(q) = Type(Head(r)), \quad \text{where } r \in Def_P(q)$$

4 A semantics of FDTL

In the previous section it has been demonstrated how inheritance of predicates can be integrated within FDTL by employing the **isa** -predicate. Furthermore it has been discussed how, by using shorthand notation, the **isa** -predicate could be omitted in some cases. We shall define a transformation Tf_P which translates a correct program P into a program P' where all abbreviations are removed and inheritance is made explicit by means of **isa** -predicates. For such an explicit FDTL-program we shall provide proper semantics.

Definition 15. The transformation Tf_P, which transforms a correct program P into a program P', is defined as follows

$Tf_P = $**while** $\exists A_i \in Body(r), r \in P, A_i = q(t_1, \ldots, t_n)$, q is an ordinary predicate
symbol, $Typ_P(q) = (\tau_1, \ldots, \tau_n)$ **and** $\exists t_j \ (1 \leq j \leq n) \ t_j :: \sigma, \sigma \neq \tau_j$
do
　replace A_i by: $q(t_1, \ldots, t_{j-1}, X(\tau_j), t_{j+1}, \ldots, t_n)$ where $X(\tau_j) \notin Var(r)$;
　if $\tau_j \leq \sigma$
　then add: t_j **isa** $X(\tau_j)$ to the body of r
　else add: $X(\tau_j)$ **isa** t_j to the body of r

The semantics of an FDTL program should provide a link between FM and FDTL. In this way, in contrast to other logical languages, we define an actual denotational semantics for terms in FDTL. This denotational semantics is used to obtain a typed Herbrand model of an FDTL program. The definitions of the denotational semantics are derived from [BaFo91]

Postulation 16. For $\beta \in B$, let $[\![\beta]\!]$ be a non-empty set. Let $[\![\texttt{bool}]\!] = \{\texttt{true,}$ $\texttt{false}\}$

Definition 17. For each $\tau \in T$, a set $[\![\tau]\!]$ is defined by induction on the structure of τ as follows

1. $[\![\beta]\!]$ is postulated
2. $[\![\langle a_1 : \tau_1, \ldots, a_m : \tau_m \rangle]\!] = \{(a_i, d_i) \mid 1 \leq i \leq m \wedge d_i \in [\![\tau_i]\!]\}$
3. $[\![\mathbb{P}\tau]\!] = \mathcal{P}([\![\tau]\!])$, where $\mathcal{P}$ denotes the power set operator

We let d vary over any $[\![\tau]\!]$

Definition 18. $U = \bigcup_{\tau \in T} [\![\tau]\!]$, the universe in which the semantics of both types and expressions will find their place.

The subtyping relation and a conversion function on the semantics is now defined formally as follows.

Definition 19. For each pair $\sigma, \tau \in T$ with $\sigma \leq \tau$ we define a function $cv_{\sigma \leq \tau} \in [\![\sigma]\!] \rightarrow [\![\tau]\!]$ by induction as follows

1. For each $\beta \in B$:
   - $cv_{\beta \leq \beta} = identity_\beta \in [\![\beta]\!] \rightarrow [\![\beta]\!]$
2. Let $\sigma = \langle a_1 : \sigma_1, \ldots, a_m : \sigma_m \rangle$ and $\tau = \langle a_{j_1} : \tau_{j_1}, \ldots, a_{j_m} : \tau_{j_m} \rangle$; if $j_1, \ldots, j_n$ is a (not necessarily contiguous) sub-sequence of $1, \ldots, m$ and $\sigma_{j_i} \leq \tau_{j_i}$ ($1 \leq i \leq n$) then:
   - $cv_{\sigma \leq \tau}(\{(a_i, d_i) \mid (1 \leq i \leq m)\}) = \{(a_{j_i}, cv_{\sigma_{j_i} \leq \tau_{j_i}}(d_{j_i})) \mid 1 \leq i \leq n\}$
3. Let $\sigma = \mathbb{P}\sigma'$ and $\tau = \mathbb{P}\tau'$; if $\sigma' \leq \tau'$ then:
   - $cv_{\sigma \leq \tau}(S) = \{cv_{\sigma' \leq \tau'}(d) \mid d \in S\}$ for $S \in [\![\sigma]\!]$

Definition 20. A database state db is a record $\langle a_1 = \{t_{1_1}, \ldots, t_{1_{n_1}}\}, \ldots, a_m = \{t_{m_1}, \ldots, t_{m_{n_m}}\}\rangle$, where each label a_i ($1 \leq i \leq m$) corresponds to the extension name of a table, and each t_{i_j} ($1 \leq j \leq n_i$) ($1 \leq i \leq m$) denotes an object occurring in the extension a_i.

Example 5. The database of example 1 has minimal type $\langle \texttt{PERS:}\mathbb{P}\texttt{person,}$ $\texttt{EMP:}\mathbb{P}\texttt{employee, MAN:}\mathbb{P}\texttt{manager, SEC:}\mathbb{P}\texttt{secretary}\rangle$. For more details we refer to [BaBZ93].

The *typed Herbrand interpretation* I for an FDTL program P belonging to database state db is given by the following:

1. The domain of I is the universe U
2. An assignment of an element d of U, to each ground term g in P.
3. An assignment of an n-ary predicate p_I, to each n-ary relation $< t_1, \ldots, t_n >$ in P.

Definition 21. An *assignment* A is a family of functions $A_\tau \in X_\tau \rightarrow [\![\tau]\!]$, ($\tau \in T$). For assignment A, $\tau \in T$, $\texttt{X}(\tau) \in X_\tau$, $d \in [\![\tau]\!]$ we define the assignment $A[x \mapsto d]$ for all $\sigma \in T$, $\texttt{Y}(\sigma) \in X_\sigma$ by

$$(A[x \mapsto d])_\sigma(\Upsilon(\sigma)) = A_\sigma(\Upsilon(\sigma)) \text{ , if } \sigma \neq \tau \text{ or } \Upsilon(\sigma) \neq \mathbf{X}(\tau)$$
$$= d \quad \text{ , if } \sigma = \tau \text{ and } \Upsilon(\sigma) = \mathbf{X}(\tau)$$

Definition 22 Minimal semantics. Let A be an assignment. A partial function $[\![\,]\!]_A^* \in E \hookrightarrow U$ is defined as follows by induction on the derivation of the minimal type of its argument

1. $[\![c]\!]_A^* = [\![c]\!]$, whenever $c \in C_\tau$
2. $[\![\mathbf{X}(\tau)]\!]_A^* = A_\tau(\mathbf{X}(\tau))$, whenever $\mathbf{X}(\tau) \in X_\tau$
3. $[\![\langle a_1 = t_1, \ldots, a_m = t_m \rangle]\!]_A^* = \{(a_i, [\![t_i]\!]_A^*) \mid 1 \leq i \leq m\}$, whenever $t_i :: \tau_i$
4. $[\![t \cdot a]\!]_A^* = f(a)$, where $f = [\![t]\!]_A^*$, whenever $t :: \langle a_1 : \tau_1, \ldots, a_m : \tau_m \rangle$, $a = a_j$ for some j, $1 \leq j \leq m$
5. $[\![\{t_1, \ldots, t_m\}]\!]_A^* = \{[\![t_1]\!]_A^*, \ldots, [\![t_m]\!]_A^*\}$, whenever $t_i :: \tau$ $(1 \leq i \leq m)$
6. $[\![t_1 \text{ union } t_2]\!]_A^* = [\![t_1]\!]_A^* \cup [\![t_2]\!]_A^*$, whenever $t_1, t_2 :: \mathbb{P}\tau$
7. $[\![t_1 \text{ intersect } t_2]\!]_A^* = [\![t_1]\!]_A^* \cap [\![t_2]\!]_A^*$, whenever $t_1, t_2 :: \mathbb{P}\tau$
8. $[\![t_1 \text{ minus } t_2]\!]_A^* = [\![t_1]\!]_A^* \setminus [\![t_2]\!]_A^*$, whenever $t_1, t_2 :: \mathbb{P}\tau$

Definition 23. The semantics of a Cartesian product type (which is used for the typing of predicates) is defined as follows

$$[\![(\tau_1 \ldots, \tau_n)]\!]_A^* = \{(d_1, \ldots, d_n) \mid d_i \in [\![\tau_i]\!]_A^* \ (1 \leq i \leq n)\}$$

For a predicate $q \in P$, this yields (cf. definition 14):

$$[\![q]\!]_A^* \subseteq [\![Typ_P(q)]\!]_A^*$$

Definition 24. For a given formula F, its truth under assignment A with database state db for I, written as $I \models_{A,db} F$ is inductively defined by

- if $p(t_1, \ldots, t_n)$ is an atomic formula and p is an ordinary predicate symbol then

$$I \models_{A,db} p(t_1, \ldots, t_n) \Leftrightarrow ([\![t_1]\!]_A^*, \ldots, [\![t_n]\!]_A^*) \in [\![p]\!]_A^* \wedge t_i \in E_B \ (1 \leq i \leq n)$$

- $I \models_{A,db} \mathbf{db}(t)$ iff there exists a table a in the database db, such that $[\![t]\!]_A^* \in [\![db \cdot a]\!]_A^*$, whenever $t :: \tau$, $t \in E_B$ and $\tau \in T_{obj}$
- $I \models_{A,db} t_1 \otimes t_2$ iff $[\![t_1]\!]_A^* \otimes [\![t_2]\!]_A^*$, whenever $t_1, t_2 \in E_B$ and $\otimes \in \{\leq, <, \geq, >\}$ and $t_1, t_2 :: \text{int}$ or $t_1, t_2 :: \text{real}$ or $t_1, t_2 :: \text{string}$, or $t_1, t_2 :: \text{char}$
- $I \models_{A,db} t_1 = t_2$ iff $[\![t_1]\!]_A^* = [\![t_2]\!]_A^*$, whenever $t_1, t_2 :: \tau$ and $t_1, t_2 \in E_B$
- $I \models_{A,db} t_1 \neq t_2$ iff $[\![t_1]\!]_A^* \neq [\![t_2]\!]_A^*$, whenever $t_1, t_2 :: \tau$ and $t_1, t_2 \in E_B$
- $I \models_{A,db} t_1 \text{ isa } t_2$ iff $cv_{\sigma \leq \tau}([\![t_1]\!]_A^*) = [\![t_2]\!]_A^*$, whenever $t_1 :: \sigma$, $t_2 :: \tau$ and $\sigma \leq \tau$ and $t_1, t_2 \in E_B$
- $I \models_{A,db} t_1 \text{ in } t_2$ iff $[\![t_1]\!]_A^* \in [\![t_2]\!]_A^*$, whenever $t_1, t_2 :: \mathbb{P}\tau$ and $t_1, t_2 \in E_B$
- $I \models_{A,db} t_1 \text{ sin } t_2$ iff $cv_{\sigma \leq \tau}([\![t_1]\!]_A^*) \in [\![t_2]\!]_A^*$, whenever $t_1 :: \sigma$, $t_2 :: \mathbb{P}\tau$ and $\sigma \leq \tau$ and $t_1, t_2 \in E_B$
- $I \models_{A,db} t_1 \text{ subset } t_2$ iff $[\![t_1]\!]_A^* \subseteq [\![t_2]\!]_A^*$, whenever $t_1, t_2 :: \mathbb{P}\tau$ and $t_1, t_2 \in E_B$
- $I \models_{A,db} t_1 \text{ ssubset } t_2$ iff $cv_{\mathbb{P}\sigma \leq \mathbb{P}\tau}([\![t_1]\!]_A^*) \subseteq [\![t_2]\!]_A^*$, whenever $t_1 :: \mathbb{P}\sigma$, $t_2 :: \mathbb{P}\tau$ and $\sigma \leq \tau$ and $t_1, t_2 \in E_B$

- $I \models_{A,db}$ **true**, whenever **not** $I \models_{A,db}$ **false**,
- if F and G are formulas then
  $I \models_{A,db}$ **not** F iff not $I \models_{A,db} F$
  $I \models_{A,db} F \vee G$ iff $I \models_{A,db} F$ or $I \models_{A,db} G$
  $I \models_{A,db} \forall x F$ iff $I \models_{(A,db)[x/t]} F$ for all $t \in D$ where $x :: \sigma \Leftrightarrow t :: \sigma$.

This definition is straightforward (cf. Lloyd [Lloy87]).

5 Conclusions and future work

We have defined a logical language, called DTL which can be considered as a far reaching extension of Datalog equipped with complex objects, object identities, and multiple inheritance based on an extension of Cardelli type theory. The DTL language also incorporates a very general notion of sets as first-class objects. It has furthermore been explained how this language could be used to query an object-oriented database specified along the lines of a state-of-the-art data model called TM. In DTL we have defined a simple, yet powerful way of combining multiple inheritance with predicates in logic programs. Furthermore, we have offered a simple denotational semantics for DTL programs. Though we have not described our evaluation strategy for DTL programs in this paper, we do mention that this strategy has been proven to be sound and complete. For details concerning the resolution of DTL programs we refer to [Bal92,BaBa93]

As far as future research is concerned, we are presently interested in implementation issues related to DTL. We mention that a TM-based DBMS prototype has been realized in the logical language LIFE, and that we are currently investigating implementation possibilities of DTL along similar lines.

6 References

[AbKa89] S. Abiteboul & P. C. Kanellakis, "Object identity as a query language primitive," in *Proceedings of ACM-SIGMOD 1989 International Conference on Management of Data, Portland, OR, May 31–June 2, 1989*, J. Clifford, B. Lindsay & D. Maier, eds., ACM Press, New York, NY, 1989, 159–173, (also appeared as SIGMOD RECORD, 18, 2, June, 1989).

[Abit90] S. Abiteboul, "Towards a deductive object-oriented database language," *Data & Knowledge Engineering* 5 (1990), 263–287.

[AbGr88] S. Abiteboul & S. Grumbach, "COL: A Logic-based Language for Complex Objects," in *Advances in Database Technology—EDBT '88*, J. W. Schmidt, S. Ceri & M. Missikoff, eds., Springer-Verlag, New York–Heidelberg–Berlin, 1988, 271–293, Lecture Notes in Computer Science 303.

[Aït-K91] H. Aït-Kaci, "An overview of LIFE," in *Next Generation Information System Technology*, J. W. Schmidt & A. A. Stogny, eds., Proceedings of the First International East/West Data Base Workshop, Kiev, USSR, October 1990, Springer-Verlag, New York–Heidelberg–Berlin, 1991, 42–58, Lecture Notes in Computer Science # 504.

[Bal92] R. Bal, "DataTypeLog a deductive object-oriented query language," University of Twente, Technical Report INF92-79, Enschede, 1992.

[BaBa93] R. Bal & H. Balsters, "DTL: A deductive and typed object-oriented language," Universiteit Twente, INF93-41, Enschede, The Netherlands, 1993.

[BaBB92] R. Bal, H. Balsters & R. A. de By, "The TM typing rules," University of Twente, Technical Report INF92-80, Enschede, 1992.

[BaBZ93] H. Balsters, R. A. de By & R. Zicari, "Typed sets as a basis for object-oriented database schemas," in *ECOOP 1993 Kaiserslautern*, 1993.

[BaBV92] H. Balsters, R. A. de By & C. C. de Vreeze, "The TM Manual," University of Twente, technical report INF92-81, Enschede, 1992.

[BaFo91] H. Balsters & M. M. Fokkinga, "Subtyping can have a simple semantics," *Theoretical Computer Science* 87 (September, 1991), 81–96.

[BaVr91] H. Balsters & C. C. de Vreeze, "A semantics of object-oriented sets," in *The Third International Workshop on Database Programming Languages: Bulk Types & Persistent Data (DBPL-3), August 27–30, 1991, Nafplion, Greece*, P. Kanellakis & J. W. Schmidt, eds., Morgan Kaufmann Publishers, San Mateo, CA, 1991, 201–217.

[BrLM90] A. Brogi, E. Lamma & P. Mello, "Inheritance and hypothetical reasoning in logic programming," in *Ninth European Conference on Artificial Intelligence*, L. C. Aiello, ed., Stockholm, Sweden, 1990, 105–110.

[CCCT90] F. Cacace, S. Ceri, S. Crespi-Reghizzi, L. Tanca & R. Zicari, "Integrating object-oriented data modeling with a rule-based programming paradigm," in *Proceedings of ACM-SIGMOD 1990 International Conference on Management of Data, Atlantic City, NJ, May 23–25, 1990*, H. Garcia-Molina & H. V. Jagadish, eds., ACM Press, New York, NY, 1990, 225–236, (also appeared as SIGMOD RECORD, 19, 2, June, 1990).

[CaWe85] L. Cardelli & P. Wegner, "On understanding types, data abstraction, and polymorphism," *Computing Surveys* 17 (1985), 471–522.

[Card84] L. Cardelli, "A semantics of multiple inheritance," in *Semantics of Data Types*, G. Kahn, D. B. Macqueen & G. Plotkin, eds., Lecture Notes in Computer Science #173, Springer-Verlag, New York–Heidelberg–Berlin, 1984, 51–67.

[Card88] L. Cardelli, "Types for data-oriented languages," in *Advances in Database Technology—EDBT '88*, J. W. Schmidt, S. Ceri & M. Missikoff, eds., Springer-Verlag, New York–Heidelberg–Berlin, 1988, 1–15, Lecture Notes in Computer Science 303.

[CeGT90] S. Ceri, G. Gottlob & L. Tanca, *Logic Programming and Databases*, Surveys in Computer Science, Springer-Verlag, New York–Heidelberg–Berlin, 1990.

[GrLR92] S. Greco, N. Leone & P. Rullo, "COMPLEX: An Object-Oriented Logical Programming System," *IEEE Transactions on Knowledge and Data Engineering* 4 (august 1992), 344–359.

[HuYo90] R. Hull & M. Yoshikawa, "ILOG: Declaritive Creation and Manipulation of Object Identifiers," in *Proceedings Sixth International Conference on Data Engineering, Los Angeles, CA, February 5–9, 1990*, IEEE Computer Society Press, Washington, DC, 1990, 455–468.

[IbCu90] M. H. Ibrahim & F. A. Cummins, "Objects with logic," in *AMC 18th Annual Computer Science Conference*, Washington DC, 1990, 128–133.

[KiLW90] M. Kifer, G. Lausen & J. Wu, "Logical Foundations of Object-Oriented and Frame-Based Languages," Dept. Comp. Sc. State University of New York at Stony Brook, 90/14, Stony Brook, 1990.

[LéRi89] C. Lécluse & P. Richard, "Modeling Complex Structures in Object-Oriented Databases," in *ACM SIGACT-SIGMOD Symposium on Principles of Database Systems*, 1989, 360–368.

[Lloy87] J. W. Lloyd, *Foundations of Logic Programming*, Symbolic Computation, Springer-Verlag, New York–Heidelberg–Berlin, 1987.

[LoOz91] Y. Lou & M. Ozsoyoglu, "LLO: A Deductive Language with Methods and Method Inheritance," in *Proceedings of ACM-SIGMOD 1991 International Conference on Management of Data, Denver, CO, May 29–31, 1991*, J. Clifford & R. King, eds., ACM Press, New York, NY, 1991, 198–207, (also appeared as SIGMOD RECORD, 20, 2, June, 1991).

[LyVi87] P. Lyngbaek & V. Vianu, "Mapping a semantic database model to the relational model," in *Proceedings of ACM-SIGMOD 1987 International Conference on Management of Data, San Francisco, CA, May 27–29, 1987*, U. Dayal & I. Traiger, eds., ACM Press, New York, NY, 1987, 132–142, (also appeared as SIGMOD RECORD 16, 3, December, 1987).

[McCa92] F. G. McCabe, *Logic and Objects*, International Series in Computer Science, Prentice-Hall International, London, England, 1992.

[MoPo90] L. Monteiro & A. Porto, "A transformational view of inheritance in logic programming," in *Seventh International Conference on Logic Programming*, D. H. D. Warren & P. Szeredi, eds., MIT Press, Cambridge, MA, 1990, 481–494.

[NaTs89] S. Naqvi & S. Tsur, *A Logical Language for Data and Knowledge Bases*, Principles of Computer Science, Computer Science Press, Rockville, MD, 1989, 288 pp..

[OhBB89] A. Ohori, P. Buneman & V. Breazu-Tannen, "Database programming in Machiavelli-a polymorphic language with static type inference," in *Proceedings of ACM-SIGMOD 1989 International Conference on Management of Data, Portland, OR, May 31–June 2, 1989*, J. Clifford, B. Lindsay & D. Maier, eds., ACM Press, New York, NY, 1989, 46–57, (also appeared as SIGMOD RECORD, 18, 2, June, 1989).

[Reyn85] J. C. Reynolds, "Three Approaches to Type Structure," in *Mathematical Foundations of Software Development*, H. Ehrig et al., ed., Lecture Notes in Computer Science #185, Springer-Verlag, New York–Heidelberg–Berlin, 1985, 97–138.

Noodle: A Language for Declarative Querying in an Object-Oriented Database

Inderpal Singh Mumick
AT&T Bell Laboratories
mumick@research.att.com

Kenneth A. Ross*
Columbia University
kar@cs.columbia.edu

Abstract

We present a language Noodle in which to specify declarative queries in an object-oriented database system. The language models object-identity, classes, relations, views, inheritance, complex objects, and methods, in addition to logical rules, and permits powerful schema querying. Noodle is intended to be used as a query language in an object-oriented database system, with the benefits of declarativeness, namely increased efficiency and reduced programming time.

Our work bridges the gap between relational, deductive and object-oriented databases. Noodle is being implemented in the SWORD database system: a declarative object-oriented database being built at AT&T Bell Laboratories.

1 Introduction

Motivation

The advance to network database systems from hierarchical systems provided additional data modeling abilities. The advance to relational systems provided a declarative querying capability, and moved optimization of access from the user to the system. The attempted move from relational databases to deductive databases was motivated by the goal of providing a more expressive, potentially complete query language and additional data structuring abilities. Object-oriented databases developed in parallel, offering significantly increased data modeling capabilities, but *moved back* to a procedural query language, and shifted the access optimization problem back to the user [26].

*This research was supported in part by NSF grant IRI-9209029, and by a grant from the AT&T Foundation.

Writing queries in a declarative query language is easier and faster than writing queries in a procedural query language. When using a declarative query language, the amount of code and the time to write the code is significantly reduced. The user does not have to optimize the code for access to the database. As the database characteristics (data organization, indices, and schema) change, the system can re-optimize the query with little or no code rewrite. In a procedural language, the code has to be manually optimized in response to such changes. Applications such as marketing databases, scientific databases, data mining, chemical structure analysis, persistent queries, and adhoc queries need a declarative language support. Consequently, the lack of a declarative query language in object-oriented databases is a drawback. It is also clear, from experience with relational and deductive database systems, that a declarative language by itself is not sufficient for most applications — certain parts of an application are best coded in a procedural manner. Thus, there is a real need for combining declarative and procedural styles of programming in an object-oriented database system.

There has been a lot of work done on object-oriented databases, and several systems have reached the marketplace [4, 5, 9, 20, 22, 29]. Logics of objects have been proposed: O-Logic [18] and F-Logic [17]. Many of the object-oriented systems provide a declarative SQL like query language: OSQL in IRIS [29], CQL++ in ODE [12], Reloop [11] and the O_2 query language ([5],Chapter 11) in O_2, and XSQL in UniSQL [16]. Recursive query languages have also been developed: COL [2], IQL [3], Logres [8], and CDOL [15]. Though reservations about mixing object-orientedness with declarativeness continue [27], we feel that the bridge between the two styles of programming is getting stronger.

We further strengthen this bridge between declarative and object-oriented databases by developing a general declarative query language Noodle for object-oriented databases, and shifting the burden of optimizing access for queries expressed in Noodle[1] to the database system. We are building a declarative object-oriented database system called SWORD[2] at AT&T, integrating Noodle with the O++ procedural language of the ODE database system [4].

Outline

The language Noodle borrows from deductive and object-oriented technology. Noodle is rule based. Relations are supported as objects with object identifiers, but individual tuples of a relation do not have object identifiers. Complex objects (functional and set valued) are supported using HiLog-like constructs [10]. Attributes of objects are referenced by name rather than position. Recursion is permitted.

There are several novel features in our system: (1) Variables can range over all classes, relations, attributes, and objects, in a manner similar to Hilog [10].

---

[1]Noodle stands for "Nonprocedural Object-Oriented Database LanguagE."
[2]SWORD stands for "System With Objects, Relations and Declarativeness."

This permits queries that are not possible in SQL extensions and other object-oriented proposals. (2) Classes, relations, methods, and objects are referenced in a uniform manner. (3) Queries can do implicit schema querying. Queries such as "find all classes (or find all subclasses of *vehicle* class) whose objects have an attribute *engine_capacity*" can be expressed without reference to the catalog. Queries to find objects for which some attribute value is equal to the string "Stanford University" can also be expressed. (4) Noodle is being integrated with a procedural language in the SWORD system [21]. The integration permits some of the methods of a class to be defined declaratively in Noodle, while others can be defined using the procedural language.

2 The Noodle Language: An Introduction

In this section we introduce the language Noodle. We give a walkthrough, without attempting to give a complete description. The language should be thought of as a declarative *query* language. It is not intended to be an all-purpose database manipulation language; rather, it will be integrated with a procedural data manipulation language.

2.1 Atoms

Noodle has the flavor of Datalog and HiLog, but we name attributes rather than rely on argument positions in fixed-arity relations. For example, here is an atom in our language.

$$p\,[name = N, year = Y]$$

Here p is, in general, an object identifier. Specifically, p may be a symbolic or physical identifier for any object in the database. The meaning of the above atom is a multirelation containing the single tuple corresponding to the name and year of object referred by p. For instance, if one refers to one's car by the name "speedy", then speedy$[name = N, year = Y]$ is an atom defining a multirelation with a single tuple containing the name and the year of the car called "speedy". Relations, classes, and other collections are considered to be objects in Noodle. For instance, if "red_cars" is the name of a relation, then red_cars$[creator = C, version = V]$ is an atom defining a multirelation with the single tuple containing the creator and the version of the relation "red_cars".

A second type of atom is available to range over elements of a collection (sets, multisets, classes, relations). If p is an object identifier of a collection object, then the atom

$$p\,\{name = N, year = Y\}$$

defines a binary multirelation with attributes N and Y, containing the *name* and *year* attributes of each tuple in the collection referenced by p. For instance, the atom red_cars{$name = N, year = Y$} defines a multirelation containing the name and year attributes of each car in the relation "red_cars".

The distinction between the { } syntax and the [ ] syntax is important. Given a relation object "red_cars", the attributes in

$$red\_cars[creator = C, version = V]$$

refer to the attributes of collection object "red_cars", rather than to the attributes of tuples in the relation "red_cars". However, the attributes in

$$red\_cars\{name = N, year = Y\}$$

refer to the attributes of tuples in the relation "red_cars". Atoms using { } will be called *collection atoms*, while atoms using [ ] will be called *object atoms*. In either case, an object identifier p used as above will be called an object, or a predicate.

There is no notion of *arity* associated with any predicate. An object has a declared signature that indicates its attributes and their types. Irrespective of the signature of an object p,

$$p\,[name = X, age = Y]$$

is a *legal* atom. Further, if p is a collection object, then

$$p\,\{name = X, age = Y\}$$

is also legal atom. The object p (and, in the second case the tuples in p) may simply have two attributes, *name* and *age*. There may be additional attributes, in which case the interpretation of the atoms above is a projection onto *name* and *age*. (Note that the order in which attributes are mentioned is not important.) If the signature of object p does not include one (or both) of the attributes *name* and *age*, then the multirelation defined by the atoms above is always empty.

In the style of HiLog, we allow object identifiers (similar to relation names in relational systems) to be variables that may appear as predicates in atoms. For example,

$$X[name = N, year = Y]$$

is a valid (*object*) atom, defining a multirelation that contains one tuple for each object that has (at least the) attributes *name* and *year*. The tuple contains the identifier of the object, and the *name* and *year* attributes of the object. Similarly,

$$X\{name = N, year = Y\}$$

is a valid (*collection*) atom that matches with every tuple in every collection object whose tuples have (at least the) attributes *name* and *year*. The atom thus defines a multirelation that derives one tuple from each such matching tuple. The tuple in the multirelation contains the identifier of the collection object, and the *name* and *year* attributes of the matching tuple. We also allow X to be bound to sets or classes, for which the atom above is a shorthand for a compound expression that is defined in the next section.

2.2 Classes

A class definition consists of a class name, names and types of attributes, method declarations, and a declaration of the position of the class in the class hierarchy. We use the underlying type system of the procedural language. In this paper we shall use a C++-like type system, with object identifiers represented as pointers. However, an alternative data definition language could be used if desired. A class *vehicle*, containing attributes *name*, *year*, and *manufacturer* may be defined as:

class *vehicle*{ string *name*;
        date *year*;
        company* *manufacturer*; // *company* is another class in the system };

string and date are assumed to be primitive types in the database system, and *company* is another user defined class. The attribute *manufacturer* is thus the object identifier of a company object.

The collection of all objects in class *vehicle* (objects can be in class *vehicle* directly, or indirectly, by virtue of being in a subclass of *vehicle*) is called its *class extent*. In any database state, the class extent will have zero or more objects. For example, *auto_1*, *auto_4*, and *yacht_6* may be three objects in the class extent.

Within Noodle, we model a class object by a stored unary relation of the same name as the class, with one attribute *member*, that contains the object identifiers of the objects in the class. For example, the class *vehicle* is modeled by a unary relation of the same name, with its attribute *member* being of type *vehicle**. Thus, for the above database state, the class object *vehicle* has the extension:

vehicle{*member* = *auto_1*}, *vehicle*{*member* = *auto_4*}, *vehicle*{*member* = *yacht_6*}

We assumed here that all the vehicle objects are included in the relation *vehicle*. However, this default can be overridden. Vehicle objects are created and destroyed from within a procedural language, and we permit the user to omit any or all of the vehicle objects from the default collection of vehicles, say for reasons of security. Further, the user can also choose to maintain other collections of vehicles. These collection can be populated from within the procedural language, and referenced from within Noodle. For the purpose of examples in this paper, we will assume that all the objects of a class are included in the default extension maintained for it. Also note that we do not require that a class extent be stored in any particular fashion. We simply provide a mechanism to *refer* to a class as a relation. The **Noodle** compiler is responsible for mapping the reference to the implementation for the class.

Thus, the atom $vehicle\{member = X\}$ retrieves members of class $vehicle$, as well as members of all subclasses of $vehicle$. **Noodle** also provides the syntax

$$@vehicle\{member = X\}$$

to retrieve members of a class $vehicle$ that do not belong to any subclass of class $vehicle$. For any class object c, we provide

$$c\{attrib1 = A1, attrib2 = A2\}$$

as a shorthand for

$$c\{member = X\}\ \&\ X[attrib1 = A1, attrib2 = A2].$$

where " & " is the symbol for logical conjunction. Thus, we can use the shorthand atom $vehicle\{name = N, year = Y\}$ to refer to the name and year attributes of each object in the vehicle class.

2.3 Rules and Views

Noodle has if-then rules similar to the rules in Datalog extensions, except that the collection and object atoms introduced above replace atoms of first order predicate calculus. The rules are used to write queries, and to define view collections. A view collection is a relation or a multirelation defined in terms of other collections (including classes) and objects. The type of the view collection must be defined in the database's schema definition language. The extent of the view collection is defined using rules. For example, the rule

$(Q1):\quad vehicle\_name\{name = N\}\ :-\ vehicle\{name = N\}.$

defines a unary view collection $vehicle\_name$ that contains the names of all vehicle objects, including the names of vehicles in any subclass of $vehicle$. The expression to the left of the :– symbol is called the head of the rule, and the expression to the right of the :– symbol is called the body of the rule. The body can have one or more atoms, each of which defines a multirelation over the variables that appear in the atom. In rule $Q1$, the body atom defines a multirelation over the variable N, with one tuple for every vehicle object. Both collections and object atoms can appear in the body.

The atom $vehicle\_name\{name = N\}$ in the head of the rule defines how new *tuples* in the view collection $vehicle\_name$ are derived; the tuples are obtained by a projection from the multirelation derived by the rule body. The type of the projection (set or multiset projection) depends on the type declaration for $vehicle\_name$. Only collection objects can appear in the rule head.

Atoms in the body may list a subset of the object's attributes; for example object $vehicle$ has attributes besides $name$. However, atoms in the head must appear with all attributes in their respective object's signature explicitly mentioned.

The names of vehicles can be listed without assigning them to a view by writing a rule of the form:

(Q2): N : $vehicle\{name = N\}$.

The variable N written to the left of the : symbol indicates that values assigned to variable N by the rule body must be returned as the answer to the query.

Implicit Schema Querying An important feature in Noodle is the ease of expressing views and queries that would require schema querying in other systems. Consider the case where *motor_vehicles* is a subclass representing motorized *vehicles*, with an additional attribute *engine_capacity*. *vehicle* also has other subclasses, some of which have the attribute *engine_capacity*, and others do not. Let *ford_fast_vehicle* be the (view) collection of the vehicles that have an engine_capacity greater than 100, and are manufactured by Ford. The rule

(Q3): $ford\_fast\_vehicle\{vehicle = V\}$:-
        $vehicle\{member = V\}$ &
        $V[engine\_capacity = E, manufacturer = M]$ & $E > 100$ &
        $M[name = \text{“Ford”}]$.

succinctly, and correctly, computes the view regardless of how many subclasses of *vehicle* have the attribute *engine_capacity*. The atom $V[engine\_capacity = E, manufacturer = M]$ is false for all vehicle objects that do not have the attribute *engine_capacity*, and succeeds for those that have the attribute. Also note that the view definition $Q3$ does not have to change in response to changes in the class hierarchy.

We can also retrieve the most specific subclass to which each *ford_fast_vehicle* belongs:

(Q4): C : $ford\_fast\_vehicle\{vehicle = V\}$ & $@C\{member = V\}$.

Recursive Views Noodle allows recursive view definitions. As an example, consider a CAD application where each cell is made up from a set of cells.

```
class cell{ string name;
            set<cell*> components;
            int x, y; // x and y are location attributes };
```

A **set** is a special type of a relation that has one attribute, *element*. The *components* field is defined to be a set of cell object identifiers. We define a view relation *cell_explosion* to associate, with each cell C, all the subcells S that are contained in cell C, directly or indirectly.

relation<**struct**{ *cell* supercell; cell* subcell;*}> *cell_explosion;*

(*U*1):   *cell_explosion*{*supercell* = *C, subcell* = *S*} :–
        cell{*member* = *C*} & *C*[*components* = *Ss*] & *Ss*{*element* = *S*} .

(*U*2):   *cell_explosion*{*supercell* = *C, subcell* = *S*} :–
        cell_explosion{*supercell* = *C, subcell* = *I*} &
        I[*components* = *Ss*] & *Ss*{*element* = *S*} .

Rules $U1$ and $U2$ define a transitive closure of *cell* on its *components* attribute. The atom $Ss\{element = S\}$ is used to refer to elements of a set field.

Aggregation   Noodle includes a grouping primitive and several aggregation functions such as **MIN, MAX, SUM, AVG, CNT, VARIANCE, SDEV, MEDIAN,** . . .

Composition of Views   A view can be used to define other views. As an example, consider a class *employee* with attributes *name, salary, bonus,* and *spouse.*

Example 2.1: The income of an employee, given by the sum of his *salary* and *bonus*, is defined using the following view:

(*V*1):   *income_view*{*object* = *E, result* = *I*} :–
        employee{*salary* = *S, bonus* = *B*} & *I* = *S* + *B* .

The census bureau will need to compute a relation of family incomes – defined as the sum of incomes of spouses if both spouses are employees, else the income of the working spouse.

(*V*2):   *fam_inc*{*inc* = *I*2} :–
        employee{*member* = *E*} & *income_view*{*object* = *E, result* = *I*1} &
        E[*spouse* = *W*] & *employee*{*member* = *W*} &
        income_view{*object* = *W, result* = *I*2} & *I* = *I*1 + *I*2.

(*V*3):   *fam_inc*{*inc* = *I*1} :–
        employee{*member* = *E*} & *income_view*{*object* = *E, result* = *I*1} &
        E[*spouse* = *W*] & ¬*employee*{*member* = *W*}.

□

2.4   Class Hierarchy

Classes in Noodle are related by a subclass relationship. A class inherits attributes and methods from its superclasses. A class contains all objects contained in subclasses. The subclass relationship is finite and acyclic, so that the class hierarchy is a directed acyclic graph.

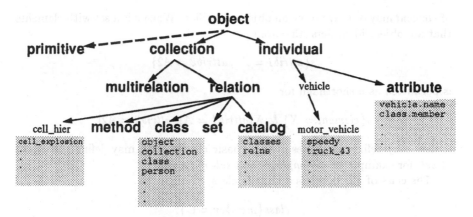

Figure 1: A Partial Class Hierarchy in Noodle.

Noodle has a number of built-in classes to facilitate declarative schema querying. Figure 1 shows the subclass relationship between some of the built-in classes (shown in bold font). Three user-defined classes, *dgraph*, *vehicle* and *motor_vehicle* are shown in regular font for comparison. Example member objects of some classes are listed in shaded rectangles.

The class of all objects is a built-in class (therefore, every object in the database is a member of at least this one class) and is available using

$$object\{member = C\}.$$

Objects belong to a subclass of one of three basic classes, *primitive*, *individual*, and *collection*. The *primitive* class consists of objects such as integers, characters, strings, dates, object identifiers, ..., which don't have a complex structure, and consist of a simple value. Since primitive objects are different from other objects in our language, we draw a dashed arc from *object* to *primitive*.

The class of individuals is the class whose members are individual objects. The *vehicle* class has vehicle objects as members, and is therefore a subclass of *individual*. The class *motor_vehicle* is a subclass of *vehicle*, and contains individual objects *speedy* and *truck_43*.

The class of collections has members that are collections of elements. Each collection of elements is a collection object with an object identifier.

The attributes of various classes are themselves objects, with attributes such as *name, defining_class, default_value*, etc. The attribute objects are members of the built-in class *attribute*.

Collections are of several types: *relations* and *multirelations* are listed, other types of collections (such as lists) are feasible. A *relation* is a set of tuples, and tuples do not have object identifiers. A *multirelation* is a multiset of tuples. Relations with a single attribute called *element* fall into the *set* class. The type of *element* may or may not be an object identifier. When s is a set with elements that are object identifiers, the atom

$$s\{attrib1 = A1, attrib2 = A2\}$$

is permitted as a shorthand for

$$s\{element = X\} \text{ \& } X[attrib1 = A1, attrib2 = A2].$$

A user may define subclasses of these basic classes. One may define subclasses of *set*, for example *set-of-employee* and *set-of-dgraph*.

The class of all classes is a built-in class, available as

$$class\{member = C\}.$$

In fact, all relations with a single attribute called *member* fall into the *class* class. The type of *member* is always an object identifier. Class objects such as *vehicle*, *person*, and *object* are members of class *class*. For the hierarchy of Figure 1, the extension of class *class* includes the class objects *object*, *primitive*, *collection*, *multirelation*, *relation*, *dgraph*, *method*, *class*, *multiset*, *set*, *catalog*, *individual*, *vehicle*, *motor_vehicle*, and *attribute*. Note that the class *class* is necessary in order to ask the query "Tell me all classes" since the alternative

$$C : C\{member = X\}.$$

lists only the *nonempty* classes.

The class *cell_hier* is a user-defined class containing relations representing hierarchies of cells. Members of this class must have the attributes *cell* and *subcell*. The *cell_explosion* relation of Section 2.3 is a member of this class.

Methods (or, more precisely, method implementations) are also modeled as relations (Section 3.3), and so they form a subclass of *relation*.

In order to facilitate querying of the schema, we include a class *catalog*. The elements of *catalog* are relations describing schema-level properties of some fragment of the system. In Figure 1 there are two catalog relations, namely *classes* (describing properties of each class) and *relns* (describing properties of each relation). The properties for *classes* would include *name*, *attribute_list*, *method_list*, *creator*, *stored_or_view*, *cardinality*, *version*, *security*, *triggerSet*, etc.

The subclass relation is built-in. If D is an immediate subclass of C then

$$@subclass\{super = C, sub = D\}$$

holds. We use *subclass* as the transitive closure of @*subclass*, which may be either built in or specified by standard transitive closure rules.

3 Advanced Features of Noodle

3.1 Complex Objects

Noodle models complex objects (sets and functional terms) in the spirit of object-oriented programming: by building an object X for the set or functional term, where X has its own unique object-identifier. For example, the set $\{stud\_1, stud\_2, stud\_3\}$ is modeled as

$$s\{element = stud\_1\},\ s\{element = stud\_2\},\ s\{element = stud\_3\}$$

The name and the object identifier of the set is s, and s will be a member of the class *set*. Unnesting of sets is done simply by referring to the elements of the set, as in

(r1): $students\_of\{prof = P, stud = S\}$:–
        $stud\_set\{prof = P, advisees = Ss\}$ & $Ss\{element = S\}$.

We allow a limited form of nesting in defining collection views, using *parametric collections* in a fashion similar to HiLog [10]. For example, suppose we had the opposite situation from rule $r1$, i.e., we have a stored relation *students_of* and want to derive a set of students for each teacher. We can use the following rules:

(r2): $stud\_of[[prof = P]]\{element = S\}$:– $students\_of\{prof = P, stud = S\}$.
(r3): $stud\_set\{prof = P, advisees = stud\_of[[prof = P]]\}$:– $profs\{member = P\}$.

For each *professor* object X, $stud\_of[[prof = X]]$ is the name of a new relation. This name can function as an object identifier, and can appear as an attribute of other relations. In order to avoid some semantic difficulties, such as implicit recursion through negation, and definition of infinitely many relations, we allow variables in parametric object identifiers to be *individual* objects only.

The functional term

$$address\_1[street = \text{``600 Mountain Ave''}, City = \text{``Murray Hill''}]$$

has the the object identifier $address\_1$. Components of the term can be accesed using object atoms, as in

(r4): $empCity\{name = N, city = C\}$:–
        $employee\{name = N, address = A\}$ & $A[city = C]$.

3.2 Attributes

Classes and relations have attributes. Each attribute has many properties that are of interest to the user (during schema querying) and to the system (during compilation and run-time). For instance, the name of an attribute, the class in which it was defined, the set of classes that inherit it, its default value, whether it is shared across all objects, its shared value, its offset position, its image size (number of distinct values), and whether it is indexed, are properties of interest. The syntax of an atom is extended to include variables in the positions where attribute names were used. Thus

$$vehicle\{A = b,\ engine\_capacity = E\}$$

is a valid atom, retrieving engine capacities of vehicles that have the object b as the value of at least one attribute. Variable A ranges over names of all attribute objects. Thus, the names (from the *name* field) of all the attributes that have value b are also retrieved.

3.3 Methods

Noodle allows methods to be defined declaratively (as views). However, not all methods can be expressed declaratively since methods, in general, have side-effects. A method can update the database, print results and in various ways change the state of the database. Hence, **Noodle** also permits methods to be defined imperatively within the procedural object-oriented language. Methods can be side-effect free, have benign side-effects (such as updating a system-maintained popularity count of all objects accessed by the method), or have real side-effects. **Noodle** models methods without side-effects, and methods with benign side-effects, as relations, and consequently the class *method* is a subclass of the class *relation* in Figure 1. (This is similar to the approach taken in the NAIL/Glue system [23].) Methods, viewed as a relation, must have an *object* attribute to specify the object to which the method applies, and a *result* attribute through which the method returns a value. Additional attributes may be present. For example, the view *income_view* defined by rule $V1$ in Section 2.3 meets the conditions for being a method. Note that not all views are methods, and not all methods are views. A view is a method if it has the *object* and *result* attributes. A method is a view if it is defined declaratively within **Noodle**.

Every class has a set of associated methods. A method definition consists of the method name and a pointer to the view definition or the procedural code implementing the method. The association between method names and method implementations is specified in the definition of the corresponding class. Consider the view *income_view* defined by rule $V1$ in Section 2.3 on employees. A method named *income* can be defined, and associated with the implementation *income_view* as follows:

```
class employee { string name;
                 int salary,bonus;
                 int income() = income_view; };
```

We can also replace references to *income_view* in the definition of *fam_inc* (in rules $V2$ and $V3$) with references to the method *income*.

Methods associated with superclasses may also be applied to objects in a subclass, unless the subclass has its own definition of a method with the same name. The method is then overridden by associating a different implementation for the same method name in the subclass. For instance, suppose *sales_employee* is a subclass of *employee* with additional attributes *sales* and *commission_percent*, declared as

```
class sales_employee : public employee {
    int sales;
    int commission_percent;
    int income() = sales_income_view; };
```

(The keyword **public** makes visible the attributes inherited from class *employee*.) The income of sales employees would be computed as:

$(V4)$: $sales\_income\_view\{object = E, result = I\}$:–
        $sales\_employee\{member = E\}$ &
        $E[salary = S, bonus = B, sales = X, commission\_percent = P]$ &
        $I = S + B + X \star P/100.$

If we now pose the query

$(Q5)$: $I : employee\{member = E\}$ & $income\{object = E, result = I\}.$

then the effect would be to apply *sales_income_view* to sales employees, and to apply *income_view* to the remaining employees. Also, the view *fam_inc* would automatically apply the correct income method to each employee. We can thus overload method names so that the method used for an object x is the one in the lowest class of the class hierarchy containing x.

3.4   Interchangeability of Attributes and Methods

Noodle provides a built-in method to access every attribute.

For example, since objects in class *employee* have a *salary* attribute, Noodle defines a *salary* method that can be accessed as

$$S : salary\{object = john, result = S\}$$

Conversely, every binary method (with the only attributes being *object* and *result*) can be referenced either as a method or as an attribute. Thus, the query $Q5$ above could be rewritten as:

$(Q5')$: $I : employee\{member = E\}$ & $E[income = I].$

In this way, the user does not have to know whether *salary* and *income* are attributes or methods in class *employee*.

373

4 Semantics

Noodle permits recursive view definitions, modularly stratified aggregation, and modularly stratified negation [24]. A model-theoretic semantics can be defined for queries and view definitions in Noodle, in a fashion similar to the semantics of HiLog. There are some differences since we must handle explicitly labeled attributes, multiset semantics for multirelations, and variables implicitly bound to *collections* or *objects*. Due to space limitations, we do not present the semantics here.

Given a database, the Noodle rules can be evaluated in a bottom-up fashion to compute the fixed-point semantics. The extent of all *collection* and *individual* objects is assumed available, and may be used to substitute for variables appearing in predicate positions. The schema information is used to prune the variable substitutions that are guaranteed to fail, say, due to the absence of an attribute that is mentioned in the query.

5 An Example

We illustrate several of the features of Noodle using an example of a composer database originally from [19]. The database has four classes, namely *person*, *composer*, *composition*, and *instrument*, related as shown in Figure 2.

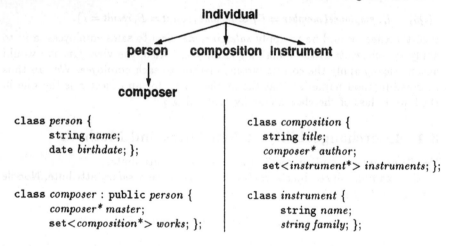

```
class person {
     string name;
     date birthdate; };

class composer : public person {
     composer* master;
     set<composition*> works; };
```

```
class composition {
     string title;
     composer* author;
     set<instrument*> instruments; };

class instrument {
     string name;
     string family; };
```

Figure 2: Composer Fragment of the Class Hierarchy

The notation "set<*composition**> *works*" means that the type of attribute *works* is a set of pointers to objects of class *composition*. The *master* attribute of a *composer* gives the identifier of the composer who acted as a mentor, while the *works* attribute gives an identifier for a set of *composition* objects created by the composer. The *instruments* attribute of a *composition* gives an identifier for a set of instruments used in the composition.

The query "Find the title of works by Bach that use a harpsichord and a flute" is expressed as:

(Q6): $T : composer\{name = $ "Bach", $works = Ws\}$ &
        $Ws\{title = T, instruments = Is\}$ &
        $Is\{name = $ "harpsichord"$\}$ & $Is\{name = $ "flute"$\}$.

Let *influencer* be a view such that $influencer\{master = M, disciple = D, gen = N\}$ holds if M is an Nth order ancestor of D in the master/disciple hierarchy.

(P1): $influencer\{master = M, disciple = D, gen = 1\}$:–
        $composer\{member = D\}$ & $D[master = M]$.

(P2): $influencer\{master = M, disciple = D, gen = N + 1\}$:–
        $influencer\{master = M, disciple = Y, gen = N\}$ &
        $composer\{member = D\}$ & $D[master = Y]$.

The query "Find names of all composers influenced by composers for harpsichord that lived at least six generations before" can then be expressed as

(Q7): $V : influencer\{master = M, disciple = D, gen = N\}$ & $N \geq 6$ &
        $X[name = V]$ & $Z[works = Ws]$ & $Ws\{instruments = Is\}$ &
        $Is\{family = $ "harpsichord"$\}$.

6   Related Work

Several efforts to integrate declarative querying in object-oriented database system have been made, and several others are in progress [1, 6], COL [2], Reloop [11], IQL [3], the O_2 query language ([5], Chapter 11), OSQL in the IRIS system [29], Logres [8], F-Logic [17], HiLog [10], Complex [13], XSQL [16], CQL++ [12], ZQL[C++] [7], Orlog [14], $QUIXOTE$ [30], CDOL [15], A DOOD Ranch [28], Coral++ [25], and our own SWORD [21] system based on Noodle. In this section, we compare the salient features of Noodle with several of the above systems.

Noodle supports relations with tuples that do not have object identifiers. Thus, every element of every collection is not forced to be an object with its own object identifier. The need for relations and tuples without object identifiers in an object oriented system has been realized by others ([1, 6], IQL, Logres, the O_2 query language, Orlog, Coral++), but is missing from some of the proposals (CQL++, CDOL, A DOOD Ranch, ZQL[C++]). The latter systems force new object identifiers to be created for each tuple generated in a query, leading to difficulties in duplicate elimination, view maintenance, and taking the difference of views.

Noodle is based on HiLog, a logic that provides a first order semantics to apparently second order logical formulae. Noodle extends HiLog to support inheritance and object identity. Noodle permits implicit schema querying, and permits variables to range over classes, relations, attributes, and methods. Built-in classes are also provided to do explicit schema querying. XSQL is the only other language with the above features; however XSQL is based on F-logic rather than HiLog. While Noodle has a clear distinction between subclasses and class objects, F-Logic does not distinguish between these two concepts. (We understand that, as a result of discussions with us, amongst others, F-logic has been modified to make the above distinction). Orlog has a higher order syntax, but cannot do schema querying. OSQL provides limited implicit schema querying, but queries such as $Q4$ (Page 7) cannot be expressed.

Noodle models sets as complex objects, with each set having its own object identifier. In contrast, Reloop, IQL, the O_2 query language, XSQL, Orlog, and Coral++ model set-valued attributes. In OSQL, the result of every query is a bag (that is, a multirelation), and bags are always treated as values, with references to bags leading to replication of the entire bag.

Noodle permits general recursion, and is more expressive than several SQL based proposals (Reloop, OSQL, CQL++, ZQL[C++]) that do not include recursion. CQL++ does not support taking the difference of the results of two queries (the EXCEPT clause of SQL). Several logic based query languages (COL, IQL, Logres, Complex, $\mathcal{QUIXOTE}$, CDOL, Orlog, Coral++) include recursion, but lack the expressive power of schema querying.

Noodle, as presented here, does not support general object creation. Parametric collection objects are however provided to mimic the behavior of certain types of object creation. COL, IQL, Logres, XSQL, and CDOL provide more powerful object creation primitives, with an associated overhead of maintaining complex object identifiers.

Noodle uses a uniform logic-based syntax to refer to relations, classes, and complex objects. Path traversal in complex structures is done through logical atoms that can be understood and optimized by the Noodle compiler. In contrast, Coral++ and ZQL[C++] use arbitrary C++ expressions to refer to complex structures in classes, and CQL++ uses the SQL dot notation. The user has to understand the path expressions as having a semantics distinct from other atoms in the language - for example, in Coral++ and CQL++, path expression can only serve as arguments to logical predicates, while in ZQL[C++] the path expressions can return a C++ boolean type. XSQL also uses the SQL dot notation for path expressions, but the expressions are in F-logic, and the system can interpret the expressions.

Ullman [27] presents two problems in adding declarativeness to an object-oriented database: (1) Duplicate elimination in presence of object identifiers is tricky. Duplicate elimination is often value-based, not object-based. If every derived object is given a new object identifier, duplicate elimination is not feasible. By explicitly introducing tuples without object identifiers, we resolve the incompatibility. (2) Lack of compositionality. Newly defined (derived) collection objects cannot be used to derive new collection objects, since no real operators are available on the newly derived collections. We address this criticism by modeling a *collection* class that contains all collection objects that are derived using rules. As a result, the relational operators, defined on the class of collections, are applicable to all newly defined collection objects. Consequently, **Noodle** is compositional.

7 Conclusions and Further Work

We have presented a declarative query language **Noodle** for an object-oriented database system. The language models object-identity, classes, relations, views, inheritance, complex objects, and methods, in addition to logical rules, and permits powerful schema querying.

A database system called SWORD, based on **Noodle**, is being implemented at AT&T. Designing an interface with a procedural language is an intricate task, with potential "impedance mismatch" problems. In the SWORD system, **Noodle** is being integrated with the $O++$ language of the ODE database system [4].

There are a number of implementation issues that would need to be addressed if this language is to be used in a real system. An obvious issue is optimization. As this language is implemented, we intend to study this question extensively.

Another issue involves schema querying. Some queries perform implicit schema queries. If these queries are *compiled*, then some of the schema information may be compiled into the code. If the schema changes, for example with the addition of a new class, then the query would have to be recompiled. If queries are *interpreted*, then the schema can be queried at run-time.

One might like to define classes using rules; let us call these "view classes." One would need to specify how the object identifiers of each derived object is obtained. In simple cases, derived classes can utilize existing object identifiers; however, in general new object identifiers must be created. Further, the object identifiers must be retained across different computations. The details on how we handle view classes are beyond the scope of this paper, and will be presented separately.

Additionally, we would like to provide support for other collection data types such as sequences and lists. It is not clear, though, what the semantics of lists should be under logical operations such as conjunction.

Acknowledgements

We thank S. Sudarshan for several suggestions and comments that influenced the design of **Noodle**, and its subsequent implementation in SWORD. We also thank

Narain Gehani, Richard Greer, Michael Kifer, Dan Lieuwen, H. V. Jagadish, Nandit Soparkar, Avi Silberschatz, and Jeff Ullman for comments on earlier drafts of this paper.

References

[1] S. Abiteboul. Towards a deductive object-oriented database language. In *Proceedings of the First International Conference on Deductive and Object-Oriented Databases*, pages 419–438, 1989.

[2] S. Abiteboul and S. Grumbach. Col: a logic-based language for complex objects. In *Proceedings of the International Conference on Extending Data Base Technology*, pages 271–293, March 1988.

[3] S. Abiteboul and P. C. Kanellakis. Object identity as a query language primitive. In *Proceedings of ACM SIGMOD 1989 International Conference on Management of Data*, pages 159–173, Portland, OR, May 1989.

[4] R. Agrawal and N. Gehani. Ode (object database and environment): the language and the data model. In *Proceedings of ACM SIGMOD 1989 International Conference on Management of Data*, pages 36–45, Portland, OR, May 1989.

[5] F. Bancilhon, C. Delobel, and P. Kanellakis. *Building an Object-Oriented Database System: The Story of O_2*. Morgan Kaufmann, Washington D.C., 1992.

[6] C. Beeri. Formal models for object-oriented databases. In *Proceedings of the DOOD89*, pages 370–395, Kyoto, Japan, December 1989.

[7] J. A. Blakeley. ZQL[C++]: Integrating the C++ language and an object query capability. In I. S. Mumick, editor, *Proceedings of the Workshop on Combining Declarative and Object-Oriented Databases*, pages 138–144, Washington, DC, May 29 1993.

[8] F. Cacace, S. Ceri, S. Crespi-Reghizi, L. Tanca, and R. Zicari. Integrating object-oriented data modeling with a rule-based programming paradigm. In *Proceedings of ACM SIGMOD 1990 International Conference on Management of Data*, pages 225–236, Atlantic City, NJ, May 23-25 1990.

[9] R. C. G. Cattell. *Object Data Management*. Addison-Wesley, 1991.

[10] W. Chen, M. Kifer, and D. S. Warren. HiLog: A foundation for higher order logic programming. *Journal of Logic Programming*, 1992.

[11] S. Cluet, C. Delobel, C. Lécluse, and P. Richard. Reloop, an algebra-based query language for O_2. In *Proceedings of the DOOD89*, Kyoto, Japan, December 1989.

[12] S. Dar, N. Gehani, and H. V. Jagadish. CQL++: A SQL for the Ode object-oriented DBMS. In *Proceedings of the Third International Conference on Extending Data Base Technology*, pages 201–216, Vienna, Austria, March 1992.

[13] S. Greco, N. Leone, and P. Rullo. Complex: An object-oriented logic programming system. *ACM Transactions on Knowledge and Data Engineering*, 4(4):344–359, Aug. 1992.

[14] M. H. Jamil and L. V. S. Lakshmanan. Realizing Orlog in $\mathcal{LDL}$. In I. S. Mumick, editor, *Proceedings of the Workshop on Combining Declarative and Object-Oriented Databases*, pages 45–59, Washington, DC, May 29 1993.

[15] A. Karadimce and S. Urban. CDOL: A declarative platform for developing OODB applications. In *Proceedings of the International Phoenix Conference on Computers and Communications*, pages 224–230, Tempe, AZ, Mar. 1993.

[16] M. Kifer, W. Kim, and Y. Sagiv. Querying object-oriented databases. In *Proceedings of the Eleventh Symposium on Principles of Database Systems (PODS)*, pages 393–402, San Diego, CA, June 2-4 1992.

[17] M. Kifer., G. Lausen, and J. Wu. Logical foundations of object-oriented and frame-based languages. Technical Report 90/14 (second revision), SUNY at Stony Brook, 1990. to appear in Journal of the ACM.

[18] M. Kifer and J. Wu. A logic for object-oriented logic programming (Maier's O-logic revisited). In *Proceedings of the Eighth Symposium on Principles of Database Systems (PODS)*, Philadelphia, PA, 1989.

[19] R. S. G. Lanzelotte, P. Valduriez, and M. Zaït. Optimization of object-oriented recursive queries using cost-controlled strategies. In *Proceedings of ACM SIGMOD 1992 International Conference on Management of Data*, pages 256–265, San Diego, CA, June 2-5 1992.

[20] D. Maier, J. Stein, A. Otis, and A. Purdy. Development of an object-oriented DBMS. In *OOPSLA 1986 Proceedings*, pages 472–482, 1986.

[21] I. S. Mumick, K. A. Ross, and S. Sudarshan. Design and implementation of the SWORD declarative object-oriented database system, 1993. Unpublished Manuscript.

[22] J. Orenstein, S. Haradhvala, B. Margulies, and D. Sakahara. Query processing in the objectstore database system. In *Proceedings of ACM SIGMOD 1992 International Conference on Management of Data*, pages 403–412, San Diego, CA, June 2-5 1992.

[23] G. Phipps, M. Derr, and K. A. Ross. Glue-Nail: A deductive database system. In *Proceedings of ACM SIGMOD 1991 International Conference on Management of Data*, pages 308–317, Denver, CO, May 29-31 1991.

[24] K. A. Ross. Modular stratification and magic sets for datalog programs with negation. In *Proceedings of the Ninth Symposium on Principles of Database Systems (PODS)*, pages 161–171, Nashville, TN, April 2-4 1990.

[25] D. Srivastava, R. Ramakrishnan, P. Seshadri, and S. Sudarshan. Coral++: Adding object-orientation to a logic database language. In *Proceedings of the Nineteenth International Conference on Very Large Databases (VLDB)*, Dublin, Ireland, August 24-27 1993.

[26] J. D. Ullman. *Principles of Database and Knowledge-Base Systems, Volume 1*. Computer Science Press, 1988.

[27] J. D. Ullman. A comparison between deductive and object-oriented database systems. In *Proceedings of the DOOD91*, pages 263–277, Germany, December 1991.

[28] S. D. Urban and S. W. Dietrich. A deductive, object-oriented model as a formal framework for active database environments. In I. S. Mumick, editor, *Proceedings of the Workshop on Combining Declarative and Object-Oriented Databases*, pages 101–110, Washington, DC, May 29 1993.

[29] K. Wilkinson, P. Lyngbaek, and W. Hasan. The Iris architecture and implementation. *ACM Transactions on Knowledge and Data Engineering*, 2(1):63–75, Mar. 1990.

[30] K. Yokota, H. Tsuda, and Y. Morita. Specific features of a deductive object-oriented database language $\mathcal{QUIXOTE}$. In I. S. Mumick, editor, *Proceedings of the Workshop on Combining Declarative and Object-Oriented Databases*, pages 89–99, Washington, DC, May 29 1993.

Tracking Causal Dependencies in an Active Object-Oriented Database

David Mattox, Ken Smith and Stephen C. Y. Lu

Knowledge-Based Engineering Systems Research Laboratory, University of Illinois, Urbana IL, 61801

Abstract. As active and deductive databases are applied to more complex domains (e.g. engineering design), the need to track the causality of data which has been derived by rules in the database becomes vital. Truth maintenance systems have been used in the area of artificial intelligence to track the causal dependencies of data derived from rules in knowledge-based systems. These same techniques can be applied to active object-oriented databases to provide the users with the means to track the relationships between data and rules. This paper describes the relevant features of a simple truth maintenance systems and puts forth a model of how truth maintenance systems can be integrated with an active object-oriented database, including the definition of new query operators to interpret the causal information for the end user.

1 Introduction

As the number of rules in a deductive or active object-oriented database grows, the complexity of the actions that take place within the database grows also. In order for active databases to be more readily accepted in complex domains such as engineering design, the database must have the capability to explain the actions of its active components. This capability is especially needed in the area of concurrent engineering. When groups of engineers are involved, then it is especially vital to be able to differentiate between data asserted directly by a user from data derived automatically from rules resident in the database and to determine the causal dependencies between asserted and derived data.

As an example, consider an active, object-oriented database used by a group of engineers collaborating to design an engine. One engineer adds rules to the database to check various aspects of the design for compliance with emission standards. Later another engineer makes changes to the design and receives a warning from the rules that the changes he or she made adversely effected emission. At this point there are several possibilities for what could have caused this.

1. The values the engineer added did indeed cause the problem.
2. Values another engineer added earlier, which were used by the rule system, are partially or wholly responsible.
3. The rules are wrong.
4. Some combination of the previous three possibilities.

In order to determine the cause of the problem the engineer must be able to query the database to determine what rules were used and what values were they used on. To support these types of questions, the query system in an active database needs to be able to answer queries of the following types:

- What chain of reasoning was used to derive some value v?
- What other values are derived from some value v?
- What rules fired when some value v was asserted?
- What values have been derived using some rule r?

The answers to these questions are an important means for providing justification for decisions made by the database. Without the ability to explain the reasoning behind derived data, active databases will not be readily accepted in the commercial arena. In most areas knowing *where* a value came from is as important as correctly deriving the value. In the example above, the engineer could use these types of queries to examine the relationships between the rules and values in the database in order to determine which of the four possibilities listed above are at the root of the problem.

For these types of queries to be possible, additional information about the dependencies between values and rules needs to be captured and managed within the DBMS. In the field of artificial intelligence, Truth Maintenance Systems (TMS) have been performing this task since the beginning of the last decade. A TMS works in conjunction with a reasoning system (such as an expert system) to record dependencies between different data and also to answer questions about those dependencies. It does so by building directed acyclic graphs (DAGs) of the dependencies and managing the truth or falsity of the values in the DAG. By maintaining this information in a database an active OODBMS will be able to dynamically access it in order to provide an accurate accounting of how values have been derived.

Section 2 gives a brief introduction to the relevant aspects of truth maintenance systems and is followed by section 3 which puts forth a model for integration of a TMS with an active object oriented database. Section 4 describes the new query operators that are used to answer the types of queries listed above. The closing sections describe current work in integrating a TMS with the ITASCA object-oriented database and discusses additional benefits of using a TMS in conjunction with an OODB and future work in this direction.

2 Justification-based Truth Maintenance Systems

Truth Maintenance systems have been used extensively in the area of Artificial Intelligence (AI) for the last decade [3, 4, 5, 13]. The main purpose of a TMS is to separate the task of maintaining dependency information from the task of applying domain knowledge to solve a problem. In the case of rule-based systems this technique provides an independent way of tracking the results of rule firings. By tracking these results, the rule-based system can use the TMS to identify responsibility for conclusions, maintain the consistency of its conclusions and maintain a cache of previous inferences.

There are many different types of truth maintenance systems but this paper discusses the most common type of truth maintenance system, the Justification-based TMS (JTMS). There are other types such as the Logic-based TMS (LTMS) and the Assumption-based TMS (ATMS) which add additional functionality to what the JTMS can do. However, the JTMS is the simplest and most commonly used type of TMS. For that reason this paper initially concentrates on the JTMS and explain how it can be integrated with and active OODB. A good explanation of truth maintenance systems and how they can be implemented is found in [6].

A JTMS provides all the basic facilities to generate and track dependencies between data. It is built separately from the inferencing mechanism and is accessed through a set of function calls. There are two basic data structures used by the JTMS. These are *nodes* and *justifications*. A node in a JTMS corresponds to a datum in the inference engine (or an object in a database as is described later) and can optionally be labeled as one of three types, a *premise*, *contradiction*, or *assumption*, or left as a simple node. There is a one to one correspondence between nodes in a JTMS and data in the inferencing mechanism. The nodes may be maintained separately from the data or combined with the data, depending on the implementation.

Each node exists in one of two states, **in** or **out**, depending on whether the node is believed or not. A node is marked **in** if it is believed and **out** if it is not believed. "Belief" in this case is defined by the semantics of the problem. A premise is a datum that is always believed (e.g. the earth is round). A contradiction is a datum that is never believed (e.g. Congress will balance the budget). An assumption is something that a user or the inference engine asserts to be true but its belief is subject to change (e.g. a Cray XMP is faster than all other computers).

Justifications are used to define the causal relationships between the different data. The JTMS doesn't decide how the justifications are used to connect data together, that is the domain of the inference engine. When the inference engine makes a deduction, it instructs the JTMS to connect the various nodes (premise, assumption, contradiction or simple) involved in the deduction with a justification. A justification has one or more JTMS nodes as its antecedents and a single node as its consequent. Assumptions do not have justifications. They form the base set of "beliefs" that justify the simple nodes. Premises are a special case of assumptions in that they are not allowed to be marked **out**. Contradictions are a special case of the simple nodes which indicate when impossible situations occur.

The rule system works with the JTMS, linking together nodes to create a network of nodes and justifications. As the inference engine fires each rule, it instructs the JTMS to create a justification for each consequent of the rule that connects it to the antecedents of the rule. For example, if the rule $a \wedge b \Rightarrow c$ is triggered, the inference engine, in addition to asserting c, also tells the JTMS to create a justification that has c as its consequent and a and b as it's antecedents. In this and all the following examples the nodes that form the leaves of the tree (in this case a and b) are assumptions. In addition, the rule itself may be added as an antecedent to the justification for c. This is illustrated in Figure 1.

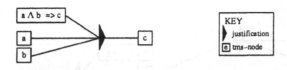

Fig. 1. Node c is justified by a rule and two other nodes

A JTMS can be explained in terms of propositional calculus in the following way. Each node in the JTMS is a symbol and each justification is a clause of the form:

$$\neg x_1 \vee \cdots \vee \neg x_m \vee n,$$

where $x_1, \ldots, x_m$ are nodes that justify n. This, of course, is equivalent to the implication

$$x_1 \wedge \cdots \wedge x_m \Rightarrow n,$$

As the rule system operates the nodes and justifications created by the JTMS creates a directed graph. This graph can be used to generate explanations for each JTMS node. One simply has to recursively traverse backwards from a node through the antecedents of its justification to gather a set of assumptions and premises which justify a value. *Well-founded support* [6] for a node consists of a sequence of nodes $n_1, \ldots, n_j$ which can be either simple nodes, assumptions or premises, and justifications $J_1, \ldots, J_k$. A node n has well-founded support if the following holds; n is justified by a some justification J_k, all the antecedents to J_k are assumptions or are justified earlier in $J_1, \ldots, J_k$, and there is at most one justification for any node in $n_1, \ldots, n_j$. A well-founded explanation is the enumeration of this support. A node can potentially have many well-founded explanations since each node can have multiple justifications. This is shown in Figure 2 where node g has two independent means of support. One well-founded explanation for node g in Figure 2 would be a sequence containing the rules $\{a \wedge b \Rightarrow c, d \wedge e \Rightarrow f, c \wedge f \Rightarrow g\}$ and the nodes $\{$a, b, d, e$\}$ the other would be the rule $x \Rightarrow g$ and the node x.

In addition to providing mechanisms for tracking data dependencies a TMS also provides a way to cache values. This feature is particularly useful if the cost of generating these values is high. Rules might be used to run a simulation on some elements of the working memory. If it is run once it would be better to save the results and refer to it again rather than re-running it every time the same conditions arise. Nodes in a JTMS can be marked as being **in** or **out**. A node is **in** when the set of assumptions that justify it are all **in**. It is marked as **out** otherwise. **in** and **out** are not the same as **true** and **false** however. **in** simply means that the node is believed. For example, the node $\neg a$ can be **in**

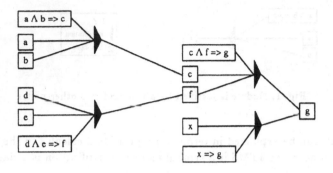

Fig. 2. Node g has multiple support

meaning that it is believed that *a* is false. ¬*a* being **in** is different from *a* being **out** because the latter means that either *a* is false **or** it cannot be derived from the current set of propositions.

The inference engine tells the JTMS which assumptions are to be believed (**in**) or not believed (**out**) and the JTMS propagates the "in-ness" and "outness" through the nodes in networks of justifications. A justification is an implicit **and** so if any of the antecedents of a justification are marked as being **out** then the consequent is no longer justified by that justification. *Or's* are accomplished through providing multiple justifications for a single node. Any node that has a single valid justification is **in**.

Nodes are not removed from the inference engine working memory when their well-founded support disappears. Instead they are marked **out**. This means that if the assumptions contributing to the node's support become valid again then it can be marked **in** without firing all of the rules again. In Figure 3 node *a* has been marked **out**. This causes the value it justifies, c, to be marked **out** also. Node *g* stays **in** because it still has well founded support in the form of *x* and *x* ⇒ *g*.

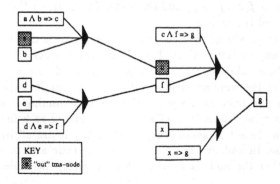

Fig. 3. Node A is marked out

3 Integrating a JTMS With An Active OODB

This section discusses how a JTMS can be integrated with an active object-oriented database. Integrating the functionality of a JTMS with an active object-oriented database requires the database designer to make design decisions affecting how both objects and rules are represented as well as how basic database functionality, such as the query language and some primitive operations, are implemented.

3.1 Persistent Object-Oriented JTMS Model

Not only must the database be modified to take advantage of the JTMS but the JTMS must also be modified to fit with an object-oriented database. There are issues which must be addressed concerning the integration of the JTMS with both the persistent and object-oriented aspects of the OODB. TMSs were originally designed to operate in a LISP based environment with non-persistent data and supported by garbage collection algorithms. Some of the features of a JTMS can become problems in a persistent environment. First, when using a JTMS, neither data nor justifications are deleted. When a datum becomes inconsistent with assumptions in the environment it is marked **out** rather than being deleted. The justification structure is maintained so that if the assumptions that support the datum are re-enabled it can be marked **in** again rather than having to be re-derived by the inferencing mechanism. What this means is that the amount of data and justifications being managed increases monotonically over time. In a non-persistent LISP environment, the life-time of the data and justifications generated is as long as the life-time of the application that generated them. In a persistent environment such as an OODB, the life-time of the data and justifications stretches beyond that of the application, and this can cause problems as the amount of data and justifications grows over time.

In addition, there are issues that need to be addressed for integrating the JTMS with an object model. Again, because the JTMS marks a value out rather than deleting or replacing it, storing values in object attributes can become complicated. In a standard AI production rule system, each datum is stored separately from the others. However, in an object-oriented system, values are associated with the attribute of an object. When the JTMS is merged with an object-oriented system this conceptually requires having attributes with multiple values, only one of which can be marked in at a time. While this is possible, it adds complexity to the object model that may affect performance in a database.

The problems described above in adapting the JTMS to persistence and the object-oriented paradigm stem from the fact that the JTMS is designed to save all the old values of attributes as they are replaced rather than deleting them. The purpose of this (as was explained earlier in Section 2) was to save the inference engine work by caching all the inferences that were made. This capability is not necessary to achieve the goals of this paper which is to extend the capabilities of the query language to encompass dependencies among derived data. The solution to the problems described above is to only allow single-valued attributes and delete justifications that are no longer needed. This is done at the cost of losing some of the caching ability of the JTMS. The justifications are removed via a garbage collection process that can be run in off peak hours.

Another problem that could arise from the use of a TMS is the loss of some concurrency while the JTMS propagates the belief states between dependent nodes. This can be reduced somewhat by employing a graph-based locking protocol for the propagation such as the one described by [15] or its variations such as [1]. These protocols work on directed, acyclic graphs like those used by the JTMS and allow for a higher degree of concurrency than two-phase locking.

3.2 Object Model

A JTMS is normally designed to track single datums like those found in the working memory of an inference engine. In the environment of an object-oriented database, the JTMS is used to track the values of object attributes. This requires that the two critical data structures of a JTMS, the justification and the node, conform to the object-oriented data model. The justification structure consists of a pointer to the JTMS node that is the consequent of the justification, a list of pointers to the JTMS nodes which are antecedents of the justification and optionally a text string which can be used in constructing explanations.

The node data structure is composed of a label (**in** or **out**), a pointer to the current justification, pointers to justifications of which this node is an antecedent and flags to indicate if this node is a contradiction or premise. In a "classic" JTMS the node structure also contains a pointer to an inference engine datum. The datum also contains a reverse pointer which indicates which JTMS node it is associated with. In this model, the JTMS node structure is combined with the objects, attributes and values in the OODB. This allows the justification structures to point to and be pointed at by objects, attributes and values as well as being able to be labeled as assumptions, premises and contradictions. This provides for more flexibility in constructing the graph of justifications that is used by the query language extensions described later in Section 4.

The addition of the extra information of the JTMS node to the OODB structures forces the database implementer to make some choices in how the object is represented on disk. By merging the node structure with the values, attributes and objects, the size of all these structures become variable. This is due the list of pointers to antecedent justifications in the node structure. This requires that the database support variable size objects and values.

3.3 Rule Model

In order to build the graph of justifications and values, the JTMS must be integrated with the active components of the database. The initial model for the rule system is based on the HiPAC model [2, 14] although it could also be applied to other active object-oriented database systems such as CACTIS [9]. However, this technology would be less appropriate for systems such as Starburst [16] which use a set-oriented approach to rules because the JTMS operates on instances of objects. HiPAC treats rules as first class objects (which is important since they are to be used to justify values) and uses the Event-Condition-Action

(ECA) model of rule operation. We modify the ECA model in two ways in order for it to work with the JTMS in recording causal dependencies. The syntax of the rules has been modified to provide control over how the dependencies are generated and the execution model has been changed to incorporate calls to the JTMS .

The rule designer will need to specify how the rules will create the dependency structures. To this end, two new optional clauses have been added to the syntax of the standard ECA-type rule, **Antecedents** and **Consequents**. As each rule fires it connects together the values queried in the **Condition** part of the rule with any attribute values updated or added to the database in the **Action** part of the rule. The **Antecedents** part of the rule specifies which of the values specified in **Event** and **Condition** will be used to justify the values specified in the **Consequents** part of the rule. For example, given the rule shown in Figure 3.3 and an update the **valvesize** of the **engine** object to 20, justifications are built with value of the **emission** attribute of **engine** being dependent on the object **rule1** and the value of the **valvesize** attribute of **engine**[1].

```
Name:           rule1
Event:          Update engine.valvesize
Antecedents:    engine.valvesize
Condition:      Where engine.valvesize > 10
Action:         update engine.emission to result of
                calc-emission(engine)
Consequents:    engine.emission
```

Fig. 4. Rule to calculate emissions

The rule manager must also be able to maintain the network of justifications and values as values are updated and deleted. This raises the question of what to do when the well-founded support for a value goes away as a result of an update or delete action. What should happen depends on the semantics of the rule that create the justifications. In the rule defined in Figure 3.3 the emission attribute of the engine is calculated from the valve size of the engine. If the valve size changes to a value above 10 the emission attribute is updated to a new value and the justification is still be correct. If the value for valve size falls to 10 or below, then the value for the engine's emission attribute is semantically incorrect for the current state of the database. In this case, it makes sense in the context of the problem for the JTMS to mark the value for **emission** as being **out**. However, it may not always be the case that dependent values should be marked **out** in this manner. For example, consider the similar rule shown in Figure 3.3. In this case, **rule2** is used to keep a count of the number of updates to the **b** attribute of **foo** where b was given a value greater than 10. If b changes to a value below 10 at some time then the **count** attribute of **foo** is still valid <u>and it should</u> not be marked **out**.

---

[1] The rule system uses the general functions provided by the JTMS. These functions can also be used to create dependencies in a manual update as well but that is beyond the scope of this paper.

```
Name:          rule2
Event:         update foo.b
Antecedents:   attribute(foo.b)
Condition:     where foo.b > 10
Action:        update foo.count to foo.count + 1
Consequents:   foo.count
```

Fig. 5. Counting rule

As can be seen from the above examples, the need for building justification structures is dependent on the semantics of the rules themselves. There are three types of dependencies which need to be covered by the rule system, value-value dependencies, attribute-value dependencies and no dependencies. The value-value dependency is used when the values generated by the rules need to be causally linked to other values. Figure 3.3 is an example of this. The value for **engine.emmision** is causally dependent on the *specific* value for valve.size. The attribute-value dependency is more general than the value-value type. This type of dependency is used when the values generated by a rule should not be causally linked to other values but it is still desirable to maintain *some* sort of dependency structure to understand the process by which the value was derived. The rule in **Figure 3.3** is an example of this. It is still valuable to know that the **count** attribute of object **foo** is related to attribute **b** of object **foo** and **rule2** even if the last value of **b** which caused the update to **count** no longer exists. The user is at least be able to find out what rules and what object attributes affect a particular value. The third situation is when dependency information is not needed. This is the case if a rule was used as a trigger to perform some action which doesn't effect values in the database (e.g. write to a log file or send some data to a line printer).

Our rule system uses the syntax of the rules to determine what type of dependencies to create. The value-value dependencies are specified by using the optional *antecedents* and *consequents* clauses in the rule. This is what happens if the rule shown in Figure 3.3 were to fire. The attribute-value dependencies are created by the addition of an **attribute** modifier to the **Antecedent** clause as shown in Figure 3.3. This indicates to the rule system that it should build a attribute-value dependency rather than a value-value dependency. Leaving the **Attribute** and **Consequent** clauses off the rule will mean that no dependencies will be recorded.

4 Queries

Once the network of justifications is in place the query system for the OODB can be used to inquire about dependencies that exist between various pieces of data. This section describes four new query operators which provide answers to the types of questions outlined in Section 1. These additional operators require that the query language be able to traverse the graph structure created by the values and justifications. Figure 6 is used to illustrate the examples of how the query operators work.

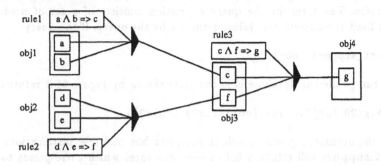

Fig. 6. An example set of justifications

As a notational convenience, objects attributes and values are be represented in the form, **object[.attribute[.value]]**. Using this notation, **engine.valvesize** means the valvesize attribute of the engine object, **engine.valvesize.10** means the value 10 which is stored in the valvesize attribute of engine and **engine** which refers to the engine object. In the examples below, the results of the queries actually return pointers to objects attributes or values. The pointers are returned in the form of list or tree structures. The general form for a tree returned in the examples is $(node(sub - tree)(sub - tree)...)$ where *node* is the root and each *sub-tree* is either a child of *node* which is a leaf of the tree or a sub tree which is rooted at a child of *node*. In addition, the term *node* refers to anything that can be justified or justify something (i.e. an object, attribute or value).

4.1 select_support

```
(select_support  instance [attribute]
 [Query Expression])
```

```
(select_support* instance [attribute]
 [Query Expression])
```

select_support returns a set of expressions which constitute the immediate support for the node (where immediate support corresponds to the antecedents of the justification that supports then node) indicated by the arguments. **select_support** takes an object instance as a required argument and an optional argument indicating an attribute. If just the object is specified **select_support** returns the immediate support for the object and all of its attribute values. If the attribute argument is specified, it returns support for only the value of that attribute. Additionally, the scope of the search may be limited using the *query expression*. The form for the query expression consists of a set of predicates which limit the objects and values returned by the query. If the query:

```
(select_support 'obj4 'g)
```

is run (while the database is in the state shown by Figure 6) it returns

```
(obj4.g.20 (obj3.c.10) (obj3.f.30) (rule3))
```

If the argument given to **select_support** has multiple justifications then **select_support** will return a list of tree structures which corresponds to each of the nodes justifications

select_support* performs the same operations as **select_support** except that it is recursively applied to all the objects and attributes that it finds. This corresponds to providing the well-founded explanation described in Section 2. **select_support*** returns a tree structure for the node given as an argument which represents the well-founded support for the node. Using the example in Figure 6 the query

```
(select_support* 'obj4 'g)
```

returns

```
(obj4.g.20 (obj3.c.10 (obj1.a.5) (obj1.b.5) (rule1))
           (obj3.f.30 (obj2.d.4) (obj2.e.4) (rule2))
           (rule3))
```

If a node has multiple justifications, **select_support*** will return a list containing each well-founded explanation.

4.2 select_derivation

```
(select_derivation  instance [attribute]
    [Query Expression])
```

```
(select_derivation* instance [attribute]
    [Query Expression])
```

select_derivation takes an attribute value of an instance and return all the other values that were directly derived from it. Using the objects shown in Figure 6 the query

```
(select_derivation 'obj1 'a)
```

produces (assuming that c has a value of 10) the results

```
(obj3.c.10)
```

since this result was derived from the values of obj1.a and obj1.b in conjunction with rule1.

select_derivation* recursively applies **select_derivation** resulting in all nodes derived from the node given as the argument, whether directly or indirectly. So

```
(select_derivation* 'obj1 'a)
```

produces

```
((obj3.c.10) (obj4.g.20))
```

4.3 Interaction with standard query functions

The standard query functions (e.g. select, select-any) are argumented by two additional functions, (**derived_from?** v1 v2) and (**type** v1) which provide access to the JTMS functionality. The first function, **derived_from**, is a predicate which provides a test to determine if two values are causally dependent on one another. The second, **type**, returns the type of JTMS node (i.e. assumption, premise, etc) that a value is associated with.

It is important to note that the general query language will not have access to all the information available from the JTMS. Specifically, it will not be able to retrieve values that have been marked out. It is unclear what the semantics of a value that has been labeled out are and, as well, out values conflict with the expected modality of a database (i.e. that values returned by a standard query are "believed"). Because of this the query language only operates on in values.

5 Execution of standard operations

Because the JTMS maintains the consistency of its dependency graph, standard database update operations on objects have JTMS-generated side effects. When a user inserts a new object into the database it is by default an assumption and labeled in. If rules fire due to the insertion, the JTMS builds the appropriate justifications into the dependency graph. These assumption nodes form the leaves of the dependency tree returned by **select_support***.

Object updates may generate three JTMS actions. The JTMS first removes the object from its previous justification context, which involves two parts. First, the object's own justification(s) are removed. Second, all objects justified by it are marked out, then this is propagated along the dependency graph. The JTMS also responds to the actions of rules which may be triggered by the update to place the object in a new justification context. If this happens, the third JTMS action is to rebuild the dependency graph from the updated object forward. When a value is deleted from the database a similar three part process occurs.

As an example, consider the objects and rule in Figure 5 once again. If **engine.emission** is updated, it is no longer justified by the current value of **valvesize** and by **rule1**. This justification is removed. If **engine.emission** were related to a value **comply** (determining whether the vehicle was in compliance with EPA emission standards) via another rule **rule1b**, and **comply** had a single justification, then **comply** would be marked out by the JTMS. The update to **engine.emission** may cause **rule1b** to fire again, generating a new value for **comply**. The JTMS would then add a justification for this new value to its dependency graph. Note that **engine.emission** has no justification in the database at this point, since it was preemptively asserted instead of being derived from values in the database. This kind of knowledge illustrates the utility of the JTMS, clearly it is important to be able to determine how **comply** is justified.

Since JTMS actions are logically connected to the actions which trigger them, and since their ordering affects their semantics, they execute atomically and serializably within database transactions. Immediately after updates and deletions occur, nodes are removed from their justification context in the graph: the justification of the node is removed, and out is propagated forward in the graph. These actions occur before the next update/delete/insert action. Any rules triggered by the action can be executed within the transaction according to the immediate or deferred modes described in [14]. Once a rule action is executed (in either mode), generating a new value in the database, its justification is immediately placed in the execution graph. As further rules fire in the rule execution algorithm, the ensuing justifications are also added immediately after the corresponding action. At the end of the transaction, TMS actions, just like direct database operations and rule actions, are either committed or rolled back.

The query operators defined in Section 4 also involve a traversal of the TMS dependency graph. In this case, the query system must acquire read locks (assuming a standard locking protocol is used) on all the nodes and justifications components that are traversed during the query. This prevents changes from being made to the objects during the course of the query that would affect the validity of the answer. If the query cannot acquire the locks it should abort and be re-tried.

6 Status and Future Work

This paper describes research which is part of an on-going effort at the Knowledge-based Engineering Systems Research Laboratory in providing computer tools to support concurrent engineering [12]. This section will describe the status of the work described in this paper as well as plans for integrating additionally TMS functionality into active object-oriented databases.

6.1 Current Implementation

The ideas outlined above are being implemented as part of a larger project in concurrent engineering called CIDEEA (for Collaborative, Intelligent Design

Environment for Engineering Applications). This environment is a persistent and distributed version of the IDEEA environment [7]. The object model described in the preceding section is based in part on the one used in the IDEEA system. The Itasca object-oriented database is being used as means to simulate an active database and the query language extensions described above. Itasca is a lisp-based object-oriented database based on the Orion database from MCC [10, 11].

Currently, several parts of the model outlined in the preceding sections has been implemented in LISP and integrated with Itasca. The object model has been partially implemented. Both objects and values have been integrated with JTMS nodes but not attributes. The JTMS is fully implemented and is able to track the objects and the attribute values. The justification structures have been implemented as first class objects and are persistent. This means that all the dependency relationships between values (and objects) created by the JTMS are persistent in nature.

A standard pattern-matching rule system exists in the current CIDEEA environment but it requires some extension in order to make it match the rule model put forth in Section 3.3. In its current state of implementation, the rule system is able to pattern match against objects in the database in order to fire the rules. This is equivalent to firing only on updates to the database. The rules also have the capability to create dependencies between values but currently does not do so automatically due to some of the problems discussed in Section 3.3. The rule manager will be extended in two areas to make it conform to the model presented earlier. First it will be modified to accept a wider range of database events in the style of HiPac. Second, the rules will be changed to allow a more detailed method for the specifying justifications.

The query language currently in use is the native Itasca query language. The proposed extensions to the query language are not yet implemented. These extensions will be added after the rule base is complete.

6.2 Future Work

Truth maintenance systems provide a broad range of functionality that can be applied to many other areas of active object-oriented databases. In addition to finishing the implementation described in the previous section, research is currently underway at the Knowledge-based Engineering Research Laboratory at the University of Illinois in two additional areas. The first is a flexible transaction manager which uses the dependency information to create "causal" transactions. The second area is in using an Assumption-based TMS for version management.

Causal Transactions Causal transactions are an extension of the ideas put forth in this paper. A JTMS will be used to build a flexible transaction manager for engineering applications that will allow the user to group atomic actions (write/update) by causal links and manipulate them through out the database session. This will provide several benefits. The database system will now keep track of data dependencies automatically. The user will be able to trace exactly how values were generated and what the consequences of changing values will be. If a user wants to abort a causal transaction, all of the data that is generated from an update will be returned to its original state. The dependencies recorded can be used to generate compensating transactions to restore the database to the state before the transaction was committed. This will allow causal transactions to be "aborted" after they are committed

ATMS Versioning The tracking and management of versions in design databases is an important problem. Work is currently under way to adapt an Assumption Based Truth Maintenance System (ATMS) for use in managing versions [8]. An ATMS is labels data nodes according to the context in which they are believed. By considering a version to be a context and a design object to be a TMS-node, an ATMS-like algorithm can be used to maintain version information about objects and answer questions about where objects belong.

7 Conclusions

In this paper we have shown that it is desirable for active object-oriented databases to be able to explain their actions to the user. We have also put forth a model for how this can be accomplished using technology borrowed from the field of artificial intelligence. Truth maintenance systems are tools that have been used by AI to build and manage networks of dependencies between objects. This model merges the functionality of a justification-based truth maintenance system with and active object-oriented database to provide the user with a richer query language which can answer questions about how values were derived.

The extensions to the query language defined in the previous sections will now allow a user to answer the type of queries described in Section 1. To continue the example from that section, suppose the engineer needed to know more about how the value for the emission attribute for the instance of the engine object called **engine1** was derived. Using the query language extensions described in Section 4 the engineer could:

1. Find the chain of reasoning which derived this value:

```
(select_support* 'engine1 'emission)
```

2. Find the other values which were derived from engine.emission

```
(select_derivation* 'engine1 'emission)
```

3. Find the all the other rules which fired as a result of the value for emission being changed. (This can not be accomplished with a single query but requires a combination.)

```
(dolist (item (select_derivation* 'engine1 'emission) return-val)
    (push (select_support (car item) (cdr item) (instance-of 'rule))
return-val))
```

4. Find all the values affected by the rule named **calc-emission**. (There may be more than one type of engine under consideration which is effected by this rule).

```
(select_derivation 'calc-emission)
```

The ability of the database to answer these types of questions will give the users tools help understand the reasoning behind the actions of the database and to assist them in evaluating the correctness of derived data. If an active database lacks the ability to explain its actions the level of confidence the users will have in the data will most likely be low. Tracking the dependencies of the derived data with a JTMS provides an active means of explaining where the data came from and why it exists.

Acknowledgments The authors would like to thank Allen Herman for many hours of fruitful discussion and critical comments on this paper.

References

1. V Chaudhri, V. Hadzilacos, and J. Mylopoulos. Concurrency control for knowledge bases. In B Nebel, C. Rich, and Swartout W., editors, *Proceedings of the Third Intl. Conf. on Principals of Knowledge Representation and Reasoning.* Morgan Kaufmann, October 1992.
2. U. Dayal, M. Hsu, and R. Ladin. Organizing long-running activities with triggers and transactions. In H. Garcia-Molina and H. V. Jagadish, editors, *Proceedings of the 1990 ACM SIGMOD*, volume 19, pages 204–214. ACM, ACM Press, 1990.
3. J. de Kleer. An assumption-based tms. *Artificial Intelligence*, (28):127–162, 1986.
4. J. de Kleer. Extending the atms. *Artificial Intelligence*, (28):163–196, 1986.
5. J. Doyle. A truth maintenance system. *Artificial Intelligence*, (12):231–272, 1979.
6. K. Forbus and J. de Kleer. *Building Problem Solvers.* MIT Press, Cambridge Mass., 1993.
7. A. Herman. An artificial intelligence based modeling environment for engineering problem solving. Master's thesis, University of Illinois, 1990.
8. A. Herman. Reasoning within collaborative activities. Technical Report KESRL-93-004, Knowledge-based Engineering Systems Research Laboratory, 1993.
9. S. Hudson and R. King. Cactis: A database system for specifying functionally-defined data. In *Readings in Object-Oriented Databases.* Morgan Kauffman, 1989.
10. ITASCA Systems, Inc. *ITASCA Users Guide.*
11. W. Kim. *Object-Oriented Databases.* MIT Press, Cambridge, Mass, 1990.
12. S. C-Y Lu and K. Smith. Swift: System workbench for facilitating and integrating teams. In *Proceedings of the 2nd IEEE Workshop on Enabling Technologies and Infrastructure for Collaborative Enterprises.* IEEE, April 1993.
13. J. P. Martins and M. Reinfrank. *Truth Maintenance Systems.* Number 515 in Lecture Notes in Artificial Intelligence. Springer-Verlag, Berlin, 1991.
14. D. McCarthy and U. Dayal. The architecture of an active data base management system. In J. Clifford, B. Lindsay, and D. Maier, editors, *Proceedings of the 1989 ACM SIGMOD*, volume 18, pages 215–224. ACM, ACM Press, 1989.
15. A Silberschatz and Z Kedem. Consistency in hierarchical database systems. *Journal of the Association of Computing Machinery*, 27(1):72–80, 1980.
16. J. Widom, R. Cochrane, and B. Lindsay. Implementing set-oriented production rules as an extension to starburst. Technical report, IBM, 1991.

Automatic Class and Method Generation for Object-Oriented Databases

Ramez Elmasri*   Suresh James**   Vram Kouramajian***

Abstract. Several approaches have been taken to incorporate integrity constraints into the class definitions of an object-oriented (OO) database. In this work, we generate constraint checks automatically in the basic methods of a class definition. The constraints are derived from the Extended Entity-Relationship (EER) model, and incorporated into the object-oriented classes. Our work investigates the issues in designing an OO database by mapping an EER[1] schema into an Object model[2]. We define a number of basic methods for each class, and automatically generate default class definitions including both attributes and basic methods. In our approach, the constraints are incorporated into the code of the basic methods for each object class.

1 Introduction

This paper investigates some of the issues involved in designing a database for object-oriented database systems. Both structural (attributes) and behavioral (methods) aspects of a class definition are considered. Object-oriented databases were developed to meet the needs of newer database applications in engineering design and manufacturing (CAD/CAM), image processing and scientific applications. They were also developed to provide persistent storage for objects used in object-oriented programming languages such as C++. In general, OO design methodologies and graphical Object models [3, 4, 5] are more developed in the software engineering field, for the purpose of analysis and design of software applications. However, database engineering requires more modeling power in terms of inherent and explicit constraint specification. In this paper, we address these and other design issues for object-oriented databases.

It has become common to use a high level conceptual data model during the database design process. One such model is the Entity-Relationship or in

* Computer Science Engineering Department,The University of Texas at Arlington, Arlington, TX 76019, Fax: (817) 273-3784, Telephone: (817) 273-3785, Email: elmasri@cse.uta.edu.

** Ingres, 1201 Marina Village Pkwy, Alameda, CA 94501, Fax: (510) 748-3617, Telephone: (510) 814-6748, Email: sjames@ingres.com. This work was done while the author was associated with The University of Texas at Arlington.

*** Office of the Vice President for Research & Information Technology, Rice University, P.O. Box 1892, Houston, TX 77251, Fax: (713) 523-0259, Telephone: (713) 523-0080, Email: vram@rice.edu. This work was done while the author was associated with The University of Texas at Arlington.

short, the ER model[6]. It is used widely to model data due to its flexibility and accuracy in representing the structure of information in applications[7]. Several extensions to the ER model have been proposed, such as the Entity-Category[8], the ERC+[9] and the EER models[1]. Many CASE tools convert EER schemas to relational, network or hierarchical schemas. This work will investigate the issues involved in mapping an EER schema into an object-oriented data model[2].

The ER is a semantic model that is used to model the structural aspects of database applications. Most OO models have been based on some OO programming language[7] and are used to model both the structural and behavioral aspects of applications. However, they have their limitations in offering formal syntax and semantics to express relationships as abstract notions and lack the capability to represent and manage constraints explicitly[10]. Zahir Tari[10] and Mokrane Bouzeghoub et al.[11] propose the addition of integrity constraints in class definitions as constraint methods. [10] uses *semantic* and *rule* models to represent the structural and behavior aspects of an application respectively and proposes a language that can represent both aspects. [11] proposes a specification language that is built over a *semantic network* to define integrity constraints and rules. Both of them ultimately map their models to O_2[12] class definitions.

The objective of an object-oriented database design methodology is to create a collection of class definitions for an object-oriented model. Our goal is to include all of the constraints defined in an EER schema into the object-oriented schema of class definitions by incorporating constraint checking into the basic methods of each class. This includes the implicit and explicit constraints of the EER model. Our target object-oriented model uses C++ as its basis. The methods generated can be considered as default basic methods for each class, which can be modified by database designers or programmers as needed.

We propose to incorporate the integrity constraints of the Object model into the basic methods of a class, namely, the *constructor* (creates an object), *destructor* (deletes an object), *modifier* (updates attributes of an object), *relater* (relates objects in a relationship) and *unrelater* (unrelates two objects in a relationship) methods. Relationships are represented by reference attributes to relate objects between classes.

Section 2 presents an overview of the ER, EER and Object models and defines the five basic methods that our algorithm will generate. Section 3 classifies the different types of classes and the different types of interactions between classes. It also discusses the semantics of the integrity constraints in the Object model. Section 4 presents the algorithm that maps an EER schema definition to class definitions containing attribute definitions and methods, and Section 5 is the conclusion.

2 Overview of the EER and Object Models

In this section, we give an overview of the EER[1] and the Object Models[2]. We then demonstrate the mapping rules by mapping an EER diagram of a COMPANY schema to the Object Model.

2.1   The Enhanced Entity-Relationship (EER) Model

The ER model [1, 6] models entity types, attributes, keys, relationships and
structural constraints. A key is an attribute or group of attributes whose values
are guaranteed to be unique across objects in a given entity type. Structural constraints include the relationship cardinality ratios and participation constraints.
Cardinality ratios are specified for each relationship type across any two entity
types participating in the relationship as 1:1, 1:N or M:N. Cardinality constraints
of relationships may also be specified more concisely using the (min, max) parameters. In this case, the number of relationship instances that each entity
participates in is constrained to be between *min* and *max*. For example (1,1),
(1,*), (0,1), (1,4) and so on. Participation constraints specify the dependency of
an entity on being related to another entity via a relationship type. Participation
can be *total* or *partial*.

The EER model [1] includes all the modeling concepts of the ER model and
incorporates the concepts of superclass, subclasses and the related concepts of
specialization/generalization. It also includes the concept of category. A specialization is the process of defining a set of subclasses of an entity type and is
defined on the basis of some distinguishing characteristic of the entities in the
superclass. A specialization has related inherent structural constraints, namely,
the *completeness constraint* in which each entity of the superclass has to (total) or need not (partial) participate in any of its subclasses. The *disjointness
constraint* specifies whether an entity of the superclass may participate in at
most one of its subclasses (disjoint) or could participate in more than one of
them (overlap). A specialization can be *predicate/attribute defined* or *user defined*. Predicate/attribute defined specializations use a condition on the value
of certain attributes to dictate membership of an object of the superclass in
one or more of its subclasses. Specializations that do not have such automatic
methods for evaluating membership in its subclasses are called user-defined. Another concept included is that of the shared-subclass and category. A *shared
subclass* inherits the properties and relationship types of *all* of its superclasses
and hence specifies *multiple inheritance*. A *category* is a subclass of a single super-
class/subclass relationship with more than one superclass where the superclasses
represents different entity types. A category inherits properties selectively from
one of its superclasses since an instance of the entity type is related to only one
of its superclasses. Figure 1 shows the EER schema for a company application.

2.2   Constraint Propagation Options

The EER model includes rules that specify the desired behavior in case a constraint is violated. These rules are necessary to generate the correct code for
constraint checking and enforcement in the basic methods of the Object model.
They apply to the (min, max) and participation constraints of relationships, specializations and categories. The options include *prohibit delete*, *propagate delete*
and *set to null*. Figure 2 shows where the options are specified in the EER
schema. Based on the constraint option chosen by the database designer, the

appropriate code to check the constraint is generated in the object methods. We discuss these further in Section 2.4.

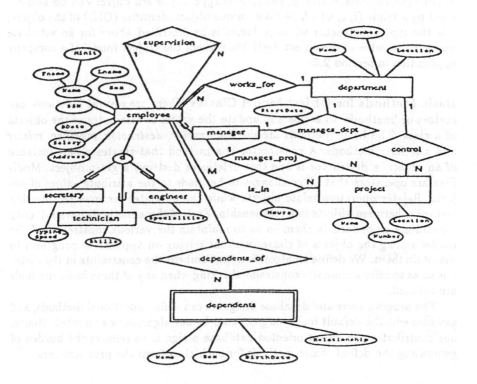

Fig. 1. EER Diagram of the Company Application

2.3 The Object Model

The object-oriented model specifies both the structure of arbitrarily complex objects and the operations that are applied to these objects.

Object Model Constructs In the OO model, complex objects are constructed from other objects by using certain type constructors. The basic constructors are the *atom, tuple, set* and *list* constructors. All values in non-atomic objects refer to other objects by their identifiers. Thus the only case where an actual value appears is in atomic objects. Each attribute in a class can be defined as a triple (n, c, t) where *n* is the attribute name, *c* is the type constructor whose valueset is one of {atom, set, list, tuple, reference, reference set, reference list, reference tuple} and *t*, is the type of the attribute whose valueset is {*integer, character, string, float, OID_type*...}. Each object can be also defined by a triple (i, c, v) where *i* is a unique object identifier (OID) of the object, *c* is the type constructor whose valueset is as described above for an attribute and *v* is the value of the object itself. We present the Object model of a company application in section 2.6.

Basic Methods for Object Model Classes There are several functions, operators or 'methods' to access and update the values of attributes of the objects of a class. The basic methods are the *constructor, destructor, modifier, relater* and *unrelater* methods. A constructor is a method that creates a new instance of an object, a destructor is one that deletes or destroys a given object. Modifiers are operators that allow changes to be made to the attribute values of objects. Relater operators relate objects while the unrelater removes relationship instances between objects in a relationship. Each of these methods have integrity constraints embedded in them so as to maintain the various constraints of the model among the objects of classes without relying on application programs to maintain them. We define an algorithm that embeds the constraints in the methods so as to offer automatic constraint checking when any of these basic methods are invoked.

The programmers and database designers can define additional methods, and can also edit the default methods generated by our algorithms as needed. Hence, our contribution to object-oriented database design is to remove the burden of generating the default basic methods for each class from the programmers.

2.4 EER diagram depicting the concepts of the Object model

Figures 2 and 3 describe the Object model concepts using EER notation. Figure 2 shows how a class may be classified and how relationships may be defined. A class can participate in 0 or more relationships and a relationship may relate 2 or more classes. Each relationship may have several implicit constraints defined. They are the relationship cardinality: (min,max), participation: {*total | partial*} and the deletion_option: {*prohibit_delete | propogate_delete | set_to_null*}. A class may be of one or more types. The possible class types in our Object model are entity type, superclass of a specialization, superclass of a category, subclass, shared subclass, category subclass, assembly class and component class.

Each specialization has a name associated with it and a number of constraints. The constraints are the completeness constraint: {*total | partial*}, the disjointness constraint: {*disjoint | overlap*} and the basis_of_specialization: {predicate_defined | user_defined}.

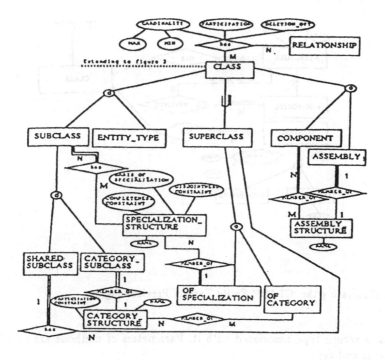

Fig. 2. EER Diagram of the Object Model

A shared subclass must be related to two or more superclasses. Each category structure consists of several superclasses and a category subclass class. Category structures are identified by a name and have a participation constraint: {*total* | *partial*} that may be defined. A category superclass may participate in one or more category structures. A category subclass must be related to two or more superclasses.

An assembly structure consists of a assembly class and several component classes. Each assembly structure is identified by a name. Component classes may participate in more than one assembly structure.

A class can have several attributes and methods, as shown in Figure 3. Attributes have a name and a type, and can be single or multivalued; atomic or composite. A method has a name and is either a procedure or function. A func-

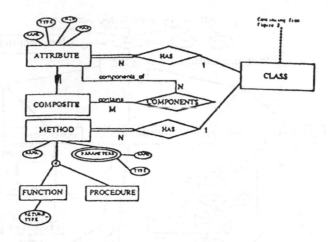

Fig. 3. Elaborating the 'CLASS' Entity Type of Previous Figure

tion has a return type associated with it. Parameters of methods are specified by a name and type.

2.5 Mapping the EER Model Data Structures to the Object Model

It is not our objective to discuss the different options for mapping an ER schema into an Object model. We use the mapping developed below as an example to show how basic methods can be automatically generated for the classes, as discussed in sections 3 and 4. Given below are the structural mapping rules we use for EER to the Object model.

- Attribute Mapping:
  Attributes of an EER model entity type may be atomic or composite and single-valued or multi-valued. Hence, four combinations of types are possible for an attribute. If an attribute is atomic and single-valued then it is atomic in the Object Model. If the attribute is atomic and multi-valued, then it is represented as a set, list or bag in the Object Model. If it is composite and single-valued, then it is represented as a tuple and if it is composite and multi-valued, then it can be represented as a set, list or bag of tuples.
- Relationship Mapping:
  Two or more entity-types may participate in a relationship. The EER model can express both binary and n-ary relationships while the Object model

cannot express *n*-ary relationships directly. There is no need to do so, since any *n*-ary relationship can be expressed as a set of *n* binary relationships, one between each participating class and a special *relationship* object[13]. Thus in this paper we shall deal with binary relationships only.

Relationships between entity types of the EER diagram are represented as reference attributes of the related classes in the Object model. These reference attributes may be single-valued or multi-valued depending upon the cardinality ratio of the relationship. The former are mapped to atomic reference attributes and the latter to set reference attributes in the Object model. In a 1:1 relationship, an *atomic* reference attribute is added to both the classes of the relationship. In a 1:N relationship, an *set* reference attribute is added to the class on the '1' side of the relationship while the class on the 'N' side receives an *atomic* reference attribute. In the case of a M:N relationship, both classes receive a *set* reference attribute, each referencing objects of the other class.

– Mapping other structures:
Structures such as specializations, shared subclasses and categories that are represented in an EER diagram are modeled by reference attributes between the related classes of the Object model. Given below is a description of the type and structure of the reference attributes that we use to model these structures. Other structural mappings are possible[1], but are not discussed here.

  • Specialization:
  For a given specialization, the superclass receives an atomic reference attribute for each subclass that participates in the specialization while an atomic reference attribute is added to each of the subclasses that refers back to the superclass. The reference attributes of the superclass that refer to the subclasses may be optimized if the disjointness constraint of the specializations is *disjoint*. The disjointness option of a specialization may be *disjoint* or *overlap*.

    * Disjoint :
    When a specialization is disjoint, the subclass reference attributes may be grouped into a union structure, since only one subclass will be referred to from each object. Given below is an example of the specialization EMPLOYEE that is depicted in Figure 1.
    union {
    subcl_secretary_ref : secretary;
    subcl_technician_ref : technician;
    subcl_engineer_ref : engineer;
    } spec_jobspec_ref;
    The notation used in the above definitions are found in the next section.

    * overlap :
    In this case, a tuple reference attribute is added whose constituent attributes are atomic references to each of its subclasses.

- Shared Subclass:
  A Shared Subclass structure has more than one superclass and is a subset of the *intersection* of its superclasses. The shared subclass has a tuple reference attribute that consists of atomic reference attributes, each referring to one of its superclasses while each of its superclasses receive an atomic reference attribute referring to the shared subclass.
- Category:
  A category is a structure that consists of a category class and its superclasses. A category is a subset of the *union* of its superclasses. A union structure containing references to each of the superclasses is added to the category class because an object in a category class exists in only one of its superclasses.

2.6 The Object Model of the COMPANY database

The EER diagram of Figure 1 shows a graphical representation of a COMPANY database schema. Given below is the Object model that has been mapped from the EER diagram. The notation used in the mapping distinguishes between the different types of reference attributes as being a reference to a superclass, subclass or to another class participating in a common relationship. Shown below is the notation used : All reference attributes are appended with a trailing '*_ref*'. A reference attribute to implement a relationship is prefixed with a '*reL*' and an optional '*_rolename*' is added in the case of a recursive relationship. A reference attribute to a superclass is prefixed with a '*supcL*'. A reference attribute of a superclass of a overlapping specialization to each of its subclasses is prefixed with a '*subcL*' followed by the subclass that it references.

For of a disjoint specialization a union structure is named '*supcL*' followed by the name of the specialization. The union attribute includes the reference attributes that refer to the subclasses. A reference attribute of a superclass of a category to the category class is prefixed with a '*categ_*'. The inverse reference from the category to its superclasses is a union structure named '*categ_*' followed by the name of the category structure and contains the reference attributes prefixed with a '*supcL*' followed by the superclass that it references. A reference attribute to a component class is prefixed with a '*compo_*'. A reference attribute to an assembly class is prefixed with a '*assem_*'. This EER diagram in Figure 1 can be represented in the Object model as shown in Figure 4.

3 Integrity Constraints on the Object Model

In this chapter, we present the EER integrity constraints that will be enforced on the Object model and discuss when they may be violated. In section 3.1 we summarize the various constraints. Section 3.2 lists the common constraints that can be violated for any type of object class. In section 3.3, we discuss the constraints that are specific to each type of class. The checks for these constraints are automatically generated into the code of the basic methods.

```
class employee
attributes
    (Sex, atomic, c9)
    (Name, tuple,
        < FName c15, Minit c1, LName c15 >)
    (Sex, atomic, c1)
    (BDate, atomic, c6)
    (Salary, atomic, float)
    (Address, atomic, c45)
    (spec_jobspec_ref, atomic reference, jobspec)
    where jobspec is a union type defined as
    union(
        (subcl_secretary_ref, atomic reference, secretary)
        (subcl_tecnician_ref, atomic reference, technician)
        (subcl_engineer_ref, atomic reference, engineer)
    )
    (subcl_manager_ref, atomic reference, manager)
    (rel_supervision_supervisor_ref,
        atomic reference, employee)
    (rel_supervision_supervisee_ref,
        set reference, employee)
    (rel_works_for_ref, atomic reference, department)
    (rel_is_in_ref, set reference, project)
    (rel_dependents_of_ref, set reference, dependents)

class secretary
attributes
    (Typing_Speed, atomic, integer)
    (supcl_employee_ref, atomic reference, employee)

class technician
attributes
    (Skills, set, c20)
    (supcl_employee_ref, atomic reference, employee)

class engineer
attributes
    (Specialties, set, c30)
    (supcl_employee_ref, atomic reference, employee)
```

```
class department
attributes
    (Name, atomic, c25)
    (Number, atomic, c2)
    (Location, atomic, c14)
    (rel_works_for_ref, set reference, employee)
    (rel_manages_dept_ref, atomic reference, manager)
    (rel_controls_ref, set reference, project)

class project
attributes
    (Name, atomic, c15)
    (Number, atomic, integer)
    (Location, atomic, c40)
    (rel_controls_ref, atomic reference, department)
    (rel_is_in_ref, set reference, employee_project)
    (rel_manages_proj_ref, atomic reference, manager)

class employee_project
attributes
    (Hours, atomic, float)
    (rel_employee_ref, atomic reference, employee)
    (rel_project_ref, atomic reference, project)

class manager
attributes
    (StartDate, atomic, c6)
    (rel_manages_dept_ref, atomic reference, department)
    (rel_manages_project_ref, set reference, project)

class dependents
attributes
    (Name, atomic, c15)
    (Sex, atomic, c1)
    (BirthDate, atomic, c6)
    (Relationship, atomic, c15)
    (rel_dependents_of_ref, atomic reference, employee)
```

Fig. 4. Object Model for the EER Schema in Figure 1

3.1 Summary of Object Model Constraints

There are several integrity constraints that are declared implicitly and explicitly in an EER schema, and must be enforced on the the Object model. The **Unique Key Constraint** specifies that the values of all keys of objects in a class are unique. A key is an attribute or a group of attributes that has the above property. **Structural Constraints** are defined using the (min,max) format, for each participation of a class in a relationship. **Attribute Cardinality** constraint for multivalued attributes specify the minimum and maximum number of values for the attribute that each entity can have.

Next, we discuss the specialization constraints. The totality constraint *[total | partial]* specifies the participation of objects of the superclass in its subclasses. A *total* specialization specifies that every entity in the the superclass must be a member of some subclass in the specialization. A *partial* specialization allows an object in the superclass not to participate in any of its subclasses. The **basis of specialization** *[Predicate | User defined]* defines some distinguishing characteristic of the superclass that expresses some distinction among objects of the class. Membership to a subclass in a predicate defined specialization is based on a condition on some attribute of the superclass. Specializations that do not have such membership rules are *user-defined*. Membership to a subclass is explicitly specified by the user and not by any condition that may be evaluated automatically. Defaults may be specified to base membership in the event that it is not specified in the application. The class in an EER schema are specified to be of one or more types, as discussed in Section 2.4. These are entity type, superclass of specialization, superclass of category, subclass, category, shared subclass, assembly, component or a legal combination of them. In the next two sections, we present the types of constraints relevant to each type of class. These are used by the constraint generating algorithm.

3.2 Constraints Common to all Types of Classes

Any type of class may participate in one or more relationships. The relationship participation and cardinality constraints, specified via (min, max), may be violated in the *insert, relating* and *deletion* methods. The *insert* may violate a $min \geq 1$ constraint on relationship if the object does not have the minimum number of references required. In the *relating* operation, a class may violate the max cardinality constraint of participation in a relationship. In the *deletion* operation, a class could violate the min cardinality constraint if the number of objects fell below the minimum value specified. *Unrelating* an object could violate the *min* cardinality constraint. We assume that all attribute values must be checked for being of the corresponding domain.

3.3 Constraints Specific to Each Type of Class

This section is organized on the *type* of the class. For each type of class, we discuss the constraints that may be violated, and that were not included in Section 3.1.

An *entity type* is a class that does not participate as a subclass in any specialization and is neither a category nor a shared subclass. In Figure 1, the classes 'project', 'department' and 'dependents' are entity types. Insertion of an object could violate the *unique key* and *attribute cardinality* constraints. Updating the attributes of an object could violate the *unique key* and *attribute cardinality* constraint.

If the class is a *superclass of a specialization*, then it has one or more subclass(es). A specialization has the following three inherent constraints : totality constraint *[total|partial]*, disjointness constraint : *[disjoint|overlap]* and basis of specialization : [User|Predicate] Depending on the combination of the above constraints, integrity checks have to be built into the methods. When the specialization is *user-defined*, then insertion of an object into the superclass will not invoke automatic insertion in any of its subclasses except for *total* participation, in which case a default subclass in the specialization must be specified. Given below are the remaining combination of the constraints.

When the specialization is predicate-defined, insertion of an object in the superclass must trigger automatic insertion of the object in all subclasses for which the object satisfies their defining predicate. If the specialization is user-defined and partial, insertion of an object in the superclass does not cause automatic insertion in any of its subclasses. If the specialization is user-defined and total, insertion of an object into the superclass must be followed by insertion into one (disjoint) or more (overlap) subclasses. A default can be specified. Deleting any object of a superclass deletes all related instances in all of its subclasses. This is done by checking if the reference attributes to the subclasses are null or not. When updating an object of a *predicate-defined specialization*, if a predicate attribute is modified, two violations are possible, the first checks that the new value is in the valueset (domain) and the second being that if the object has been linked to one or more of its subclasses, due to the possible change in the outcome of the predicate, the predicate must be re-evaluated to ensure consistent membership. Thus the object in the subclass is moved to its new subclass if necessary. If the class is a *superclass of a category* that has 'total' participation with the category subclass, then insertion of an object into any of the superclasses causes automatic insertion into the category subclass as well. When the participation is 'partial', insertion inserts an object into the superclass only. Deleting an object from the superclass will automatically delete the linked object in the category if any. Update has the same constraints for the respective operation as for the entity type.

If the class is a *subclass of specialization* and is 'total', insertion can be done only by its superclass directly when an object is inserted into the superclass. If the specialization is 'partial', then insertion is done directly to its subclasses and linked by references to an existing unlinked object in its superclass. When the specialization is *partial*, an object may be deleted from the superclass after setting the reference attribute of the linked object in its superclass to *null*. When *total*, the object can be deleted by propagation through the superclass only. Update has the same constraints for the respective operation as for the entity type.

A *category subclass* is a subclass of more than one superclass that is linked to all of them through a union (or an OR) relationship. Thus an object in a category exists in precisely one of its superclasses. If the category has *total* participation with its superclasses, insertion is invoked automatically by any of its superclasses when an object is inserted into any of them. In the case where there is *partial* participation, objects may be inserted into the category directly and be connected to an existing unlinked object in any of its superclasses. If the category has *total* participation with its superclasses, deletion is invoked automatically by any of its superclasses when an object is to be deleted from any of them. In the case where there is *partial* participation, objects may be deleted from the category after setting the relevant reference attribute of the linked object in the superclass to null. Update, relate and unrelate have the same constraints for the operation as for the entity type.

A *shared subclass* is a class that has more than one superclass. It is also called a *join class* [5] and specifies multiple inheritance. Insertion of an object in a shared subclass requires an existing unlinked object in *each* of its superclasses. Delete and update have the same constraints for the respective operation as for the entity type.

An *assembly* is a class related in a special type of relationship, called *aggregation* [5] with certain other classes called *component* classes. It is also called a *'part-of'* relationship [1]. Insert, delete and update have the same constraints for the respective operation as for the entity type. A *component* class is one that is related to an assembly class through an aggregation. The semantics of this relationship is that objects of the component class are tightly bound to those of an assembly class (i.e. they have *total* participation in the relationship). Insertion of an object into a component class causes the object to be automatically linked to an assembly object. Deletion may violate the MIN relationship cardinality constraint with the assembly class. Update has the same constraints for the respective operation as for the entity type.

4 Algorithms for Generating Class Definitions

We have defined algorithms for generating the basic methods of each class. We informally describe the algorithms here. Appendices A, B and C give a more detailed description of some of the algorithms. A complete specification is presented in [14].

The scope of the algorithms is to produce complete class definitions in the C++ language given an EER schema. A class definition is made up of a list of normal and reference attributes followed by methods.

A class definition is made up of a list of attributes followed by methods that update and access the objects of the class. The attribute list may be divided to three parts, the list of normal attributes, the list of reference attributes that implement the subclass and category concepts of an EER schema and the list of reference attributes that implement relationships in the EER schema. The basic methods generated are the *Constructor, Destructor, Updater, Relater* and *Unrelater*. They are described in section 2.3.

First, the list of *normal attributes* are generated in the class definition. This can be done quite simply by declaring the attributes represented explicitly in the EER diagram. The algorithm then needs to generate a list of reference attributes that implement *specializations and category structures*. If the class is a superclass of specialization, for each specialization the class participates as superclass, a reference attribute is added as a reference to each subclass participating in the

specialization. If the class is a superclass of a category, for each category structure the class participates as superclass, a reference attribute is added to the
superclass that references the category subclass. If the class is a subclass, for
each specialization the class is a subclass of, a reference attribute that references
the superclass is added. If the class is a category, for each of its superclasses, a
reference attribute that references the superclass is added to a union structure,
since only one of them would be used at a time. If the class is a shared subclass,
for each of its superclasses, a reference attribute that references the superclass
is added. If the class is an assembly, for each component class of the assembly, a
reference attribute that references the component class is added. The reference
attribute may be atomic or of set type depending upon the cardinality of the
relationship between assembly class and the component class.

Next, the list of *relationship reference* attributes for each relationship the
class participates in are generated. The cardinality of the relationship affects the
type of the attribute. In a 1:N relationship, if the class is at the '1' side of the
relationship, a *set* type is used while if it is on the 'N' side an *atomic* reference
type is used. The cardinality is of the relationship is found using the (min, max)
cardinality constraints defined for the relationship.

At this point in the algorithm, all the required attributes have been generated
for the class definition. Next, we begin generating the five basic methods. The
Constructor method whose name is identical to the class name is generated first.
It is made up of a parameter list followed by the body of the method. The
parameter list is made up of a list of normal parameters and a list of reference
parameters which correspond to the normal and reference attributes of the class.
If the class has total participation in a relationship, checks are incorporated in
the body of the method to check that the corresponding reference parameter
contains a valid reference to an existing object. Checks to enforce the unique key
constraint are added. Checks are inserted in the body of the method that test if
a reference attribute is null or not. These checks are necessary when an object
is created in a subclass of specialization, category subclass or shared subclass
because the created object must have the reference(es) to its superclass(es) to be
linked. Also when a class is a superclass of a predicate defined specialization, the
parameters corresponding to the attributes in the predicate cannot be null. If all
the checks for integrity constraints are successful, the constructor code creates
an object and assigns the value of its parameter variables to the corresponding
attributes of the object.

The *Destructor* method has no parameters. The algorithm for generating this
method first creates a check on the min cardinality constraint. It then generates
type-based constraints and the logic to delete the object if all the checks are
satisfied. It can also generate code to propagate the deletion to other objects if
specified in the schema.

Next, we generate the *Updater method*. The parameter list is first generated.
Checks to determine if the class is a superclass of a predicate-defined specialization are added to the method body, since updating a predicate attribute of
an object of a superclass of a predicate-defined specialization could lead to re-

evaluation of the defining predicate. This could cause the object to change its membership from one subclass to another. If all checks are satisfied, the attributes of the object are updated.

A *Relater method* is generated for every relationship the class participates in. The name of the method is 'relate_' followed by the relationship name. Its parameters are references to objects from the participating classes. The algorithm first generates a check in the relater method for the max cardinality constraint and then generates the code to relate the objects.

An *Unrelater method* is also generated for every relationship the class participates in. The name of the method is 'unrelate_' followed by the relationship name. Its parameters are references to objects from the participating classes. The algorithm first generates a check in the unrelate method for the min cardinality constraint and then generates the code to unrelate the objects.

Appendix A presents the top level for the mapping algorithm, Appendix B describes the generation of type-based reference attributes and Appendix C, the algorithm that generates the basic *Updater* method. The full algorithms for generating the Constructor, Destructor, Relater, Modifier, relater and Unrelater are presented in [14], and are not included here due to space limitations.

5 Conclusion

Currently available OODBMSs do not directly implement many of the implicit and explicit constraints that can be specified in semantic data models, such as the EER model. There are several ways by which constraints may be implemented in OODBMSs. The option we have proposed in this paper is to encapsulate constraints within the basic methods defined for each class in the OO schema. The constraints are inferred from the EER schema and automatically incorporated into the code of the basic methods. The EER schema is first mapped to the Object model[2] where additional reference attributes are added to implement superclass/subclass, category structures and relationships. Using the information represented in the EER schema, each class is classified by its types. Constraints related to each type are then encapsulated into the basic methods that are generated, namely, the *constructor, destructor, updater, relater* and *unrelater*. This allows constraints to be checked automatically when any of the basic methods are invoked. We consider the code generated for the basic methods as default methods. Database designers may edit these methods, and define additional ones as needed. The algorithms can be adapted to generate code in languages other than C++, for example CO_2 for the O_2 system.

References

1. Ramez Elmasri and Shamkanth Navathe. *Fundamentals of Database Systems*. Benjamin/Cummings, 1989.
2. Ramez Elmasri and Shamkanth Navathe. *Fundamentals of Database Systems*, 2nd *Edition*. Benjamin/Cummings, 1993.

410

3. Sally Shlaer and Steve Mellor. *Object-Oriented Systems Analysis*. Prentice Hall, 1988.
4. Grady Booch. *Object-Oriented Design with Applications*. Benjamin/Cummings, 1991.
5. James Rumbaugh et al. *Object-Oriented Modeling and Design*. Prentice Hall, 1991.
6. Peter Pin-Shan Chen. The Entity-Relationship Model - Towards a Unified View of Data. In *ACM Transactions on Database Systems*, March 1976.
7. Micheal F. Kilian. Bridging the Gap Between O-O and E-R. In *Proceedings of the 10th International Conference on the Entity-Relationship approach*, San Mateo, California, October 1991.
8. R. Elmasri, J. Weeldreyer, and A. Hevner. The Category Concept: An Extension to the Entity-Relationship Model. In *Data and Knowledge Engineering*, 1985.
9. S. Spaccapietra and C. Parent. ERC+: An Object based Entity-Relationship Approach. In P. Loucopoulos and R. Zacari, editors, *Conceptual Modeling, Databases and CASE: An Integrated View of Information Systems Development*. John Wiley, 1992.
10. Zahir Tari. On the Design of Object-Oriented Databases. In *Proceedings of the 11th International Conference on the Entity-Relationship approach*, Karlsruhe, Germany, October 1992.
11. Mokrane Bouzeghoub and Elisabeth Métais. Semantic Modeling of Object Oriented Databases. In *Proceedings of the 17th International Conference on Very Large Data Bases*, Barcelona, Spain, September 1991.
12. O.Deux et al. The O_2 System. In *Communications of the ACM*, volume 34, October 1991.
13. H.V.Jagadish and Xiaolei Qian. Integrity Maintenance in a Object Oriented Database. In *Proceedings of the 18th VLDB Conference*, Vancouver, British Columbia, Canada, 1992.
14. Suresh James. Methodology to Generate Integrity Constraints for Object Oriented Databases. Master's thesis, University of Texas at Arlington, December 1992.

Appendices

In the appendix, we present some of sections of the algorithm. Pseudo-ADA has been used as a specification language to specify the algorithm. The complete algorithm may be found in [14].

Appendix-A

This section presents the driver routine of the algorithm that generates the class definitions.

```
procedure Algorithm_Driver is
  THISclass := get_first_class;
  loop
    -- Generate the list of normal attributes
    generate_normal_attributes(THISclass);
    -- Generate the list of reference attributes depending on the
    -- types of the class. These attributes implement subclass
```

```
    -- and category constructs in the EER schema
    generate_type_based_reference_attributes(THISclass);
    -- Generate reference attributes that implement relationship
    -- constructs in the EER schema
    generate_relationship_reference_attributes(THISclass);
    -- Generate the methods for the class.
    write_attribute_buffer(THISclass);
    generate_constructor(THISclass);
    write_method_buffer(THISclass);
    generate_destructor(THISclass);
    write_method_buffer(THISclass);
    generate_relater(THISclass);
    write_method_buffer(THISclass);
    generate_unrelater(THISclass);
    write_method_buffer(THISclass);
    generate_modifier(THISclass);
    write_method_buffer(THISclass);
    THISclass := get_next_class;
    exit when THISclass = NULL;
  end loop;
end Algorithm_Driver;
```

Appendix-B

This procedure generates the type based reference attributes in a class definition.

```
procedure generate_type_based_reference_attributes(THISclass) is
  -- Since a class may be of more than one type, we implement
  -- the next functionality in a loop, including the necessary
  -- reference attributes, once during each loop.
  class_type := get_first_class_type(THISclass);
  loop
    if class_type = 'superclass_of_specialization' then
      specialization := get_first_specialization(THISclass);
      loop
        subclass := get_first_subclass(THISclass, specialization);
        loop
          add_to_attribute(SUBCL_:subclass:_ref, subclass);
          subclass := get_next_subclass(THISclass, specialization);
          exit when subclass = NULL;
        end loop;
        specialization := get_next_specialization(THISclass);
      end loop;
    elsif class_type = 'superclass_of_category' then
      category_struct := get_first_category_structure(THISclass);
      loop
        category := get_category_class(category_struct);
        add_to_attribute(CATEG_:category:_ref, category);
        category_struct := get_next_category_structure(THISclass);
        exit when category = NULL;
```

412

```
    end loop;
  elsif class_type = 'subclass_of_specialization' then
    specialization := get_first_specialization (THISclass);
    loop
      superclass := get_superclass (THISclass, specialization);
      add_to_attribute(SUPCL_:superclass:_ref, superclass);
      specialization := get_next_specialization (THISclass);
      exit when specialization = NULL;
    end loop;
  elsif class_type = 'category' then
    category_struct := get_category_structure(THISclass);
    superclass := get_first_superclass (THISclass);
    add_to_attribute("union {");
    loop
      -- Actually union structure of all superclasses in the category
      add_to_attribute(SUPCL_:superclass:_ref, superclass);
      superclass := get_next_superclass (THISclass);
      exit when superclass = NULL;
    end loop;
    add_to_attribute("}");
    add_to_attribute(CATEG_:category_struct:_ref);
  elsif class_type = 'shared_subclass' then
    superclass := get_first_superclass (THISclass);
    loop
      add_to_attribute(SUPCL_:superclass:_ref, superclass);
      superclass := get_next_superclass (THISclass);
      exit when superclass = NULL;
    end loop;
  elsif class_type = 'assembly' then
    assembly_structure := get_first_assem_struct(THISclass);
    loop
      component := get_first_component (THISclass,assembly_structure);
      loop
        max := get_max_compo_cardinality(assembly_structure,THISclass);
        if max = 1 then
          add_to_attribute (COMPO_:component:_ref, component);
        else
          add_to_attribute (COMPO_:component:_ref, set, component);
        end if;
        component := get_next_component (THISclass,assembly_structure);
        exit when component = NULL;
      end loop;
      assembly_structure := get_next_assem_struct(THISclass);
      exit when assembly_structure = NULL;
    end loop;
  elsif class_type = 'component' then
    assembly_structure := get_first_assem_struct(THISclass);
    loop
      assembly := get_first_assembly (THISclass, assembly_structure);
      loop
```

```
          add_to_attribute (ASSEM_:assembly:_ref, assembly);
          assembly := get_next_assembly (THISclass, assembly_structure);
          exit when assembly = NULL;
        end loop;
        assembly_structure := get_next_assem_struct(THISclass);
        exit when assembly_structure = NULL;
      end loop;
    end if;
    class_type := get_next_class_type(THISclass);
    exit when class_type = NULL;
  end loop;
end generate_type_based_reference_attributes;
```

Appendix-C

This is the procedure that generates checks in the *updater method* if the class is
a superclass of a predicate-defined specialization.

If the class is a superclass of a specialization that is *predicate-defined*, checks
have to be included if any of the attributes that have been specified in the
predicate are updated. This is due to the fact that the subclass(es) to which th
e object is a member of may change on re-evaluation of the predicate with the
updated attribute values.

```
procedure generate_check_if_superclass (THISclass) is
  if class_type = 'superclass_of_specialization' then
    add_to_body ("RECALC_FLAG == FALSE;");
    specialization := get_first_specialization (THISclass);
    loop
      -- for each specialization, class is superclass loop
      basis := get_basis_of_specialization(specialization, THISclass);
      if basis = predicate then
        attribute := get_first_predicate_attribute(THISclass,
                                                 specialization);
        loop
          -- for each attribute in the predicate loop
          add_to_body ("
            if :predicate: /= NULL then
              -- check if corresponding parameter is not NULL
              set RECALL_FLAG := TRUE;
            end if;
          ");
          attribute := get_next_predicate_attribute(THISclass,
                                                 specialization);
          exit when RECALL_FLAG = TRUE OR attribute = NULL;
        end loop;

        add_to_body ("
          if RECALC_FLAG = TRUE AND
            :predicate: /= parameter.:predicate: then
```

414

```
        for each reference to a subclass of that specialization loop
          reference->delete();
        end loop;
        Recalculate membership based on new values in predicate;
        if number of subclass that qualify = 0 AND
          specialization is TOTAL then
          put ("Zero subclass qualify in predicate");
          abort;
        end if;
      end if;
    ");
  end if;

  specialization := get_next_specialization (THISclass);
  exit when specialization = NULL;
end loop;
end if;
end generate_check_if_superclass;
```

Modeling Multilevel Entities Using Single Level Objects

Elisa Bertino[1,*] and Sushil Jajodia[2,†]

[1]Dipartimento di Scienze dell'Informazione
Università di Milano - Milano (Italy)
[2]Department of Information and Software Systems Engineering
George Mason University - Fairfax, VA (USA)

Abstract

An earlier paper by Jajodia and Kogan [5] introduced an approach for building multilevel secure object-oriented database systems based on a secure message
filtering mechanism. Under this approach each object has a unique security level
and, therefore, multilevel objects are not supported. In the present paper, we
discuss an approach, based on composite objects, that allows multilevel entities
to be represented in terms of single level objects. The main qualifying aspect of
our approach is that the object interfaces can be provided to users as if multilevel
objects were directly supported.

1   Introduction

Object-oriented database management systems (OODBMSs) today represent
one of the most active areas in both academic and industrial worlds. OODBMSs
combine object-oriented programming technology with database technology, thus
providing the strengths of both. The need for those systems has been driven by
several advanced applications, such as CAD/CAM, cartography, and multimedia, for which relational systems have been proven inadequate. However, at
the current state of the art, those systems do not provide mandatory security.
Actually, in most cases, they do not even provide adequate discretionary authorization facilities (a notable exception is presented by the ORION/ITASCA
system [7]). We can expect, however, that the broadening of application scope
of those systems will require them to enforce both mandatory and discretionary
security requirements.

A basic model of security is represented by the Bell-LaPadula paradigm [1].
This paradigm is based on the notions of *subject* and *object*. An object is data
item and is assigned a classification. A subject is an active entity requiring

---

*The work reported in this paper was carried out by E.Bertino when visiting the Department
of Information and Software Systems Engineering, George Mason University, during summer
1992.

†The work of S. Jajodia was partially supported by a grant from the National Science
Foundation under IRI-9303416.

access to objects and is assigned a clearance. Classifications and clearances are collectively referred to as *security levels*. Security levels are partially ordered. A subject can read an object only if the level of the latter is lower or equal than the level of the former ("no read up"). A subject can write an object only if the level of the latter is higher or equal than the level of the former ("no write down").

Applying Bell-LaPadula paradigm to object-oriented data models is not straightforward because of the increased complexity of these data models. An object-oriented data model for example includes notions such as complex objects and inheritance hierarchies, that must be accounted for when designing a secure object-oriented database model [5,6,8]. However, despite this complexity, the use of an object-oriented approach offers several advantages from the security perspective. The notion of encapsulation, which was originally introduced in object-oriented systems to facilitate modular design, can be used to express security requirements in a way that is comprehensible to the users. Moreover, the notion of information flow in security has a direct and natural representation in terms of message exchanges. In object-oriented systems all information exchanges among objects within the system are executed via messages. In [5], Jajodia and Kogan thus proposed a filtering mechanism that checks all message exchanges among objects so that no security violations arise. In this model all objects are single level, in the sense that a unique classification is associated with the entire object. This constraint is essential in order to make the security monitor small enough so that it can be easily verified. However, entities in real world are often multilevel, in that one entity may have attributes of different levels of security. A preliminary approach, based on using inheritance hierarchies, that maps multilevel entities in terms of single level objects was also discussed by Jajodia and Kogan. However, this approach has several problems that are discussed in Section 2.2. In this paper, we propose an alternative approach based on the notion of composite objects.

The problem of security in object-oriented databases has been previously addressed by Millen and Lunt [6] and by Thuraisingham [8]. The approach of Millen and Lunt [6] is based on single level objects. The strategy proposed by Millen and Lunt [6] for handling multilevel entities is based on using references to relate objects corresponding to the same entity. Our approach is similar since composite objects are obtained by imposing the part-of semantics on normal references [4]. However, our approach differs in several aspects. First, we make full use of the features of object-oriented data models by showing how, through the use of methods, it is possible to define objects which, even though they are single levels, are able to provide the same interfaces[1] as if multilevel objects were directly supported. Moreover, we introduce some extensions to the composite object model to better model the notion of exclusive references, so that no security flaws are introduced. The approach proposed by Thuraisingham [8] mainly discusses rules stating the security policy that must hold among the various objects in an object-oriented database (e.g., the security level of a subclass must dominate the security levels of its superclasses). However, no discussion is presented on the additional complexity of the security monitor due to the enforcement of the security policy rules. Moreover, [8] does not discuss the problem

---

[1]An interface of an object is the set of messages that are defined for the object.

of handling multilevel entities.

The remainder of this paper is organized as follows. Section 2 presents some preliminary definitions and recalls some notions from [3] and from [5]. Section 3 presents an approach to model multilevel entities in terms composite objects and discusses the mapping of multilevel entities that organized in specialization hierarchies in specialization hierarchies of composite objects. Section 4 presents two new types of composite object references. Finally, Section 5 concludes the paper.

2 Preliminary Concepts

In this section, we first summarize the main features of object-oriented data models by describing the reference model introduced in [3]. We next give a brief description of the message filter model [5], followed by a description of the approach proposed in [5] to model multilevel entities in terms of single level objects.

2.1 Reference object-oriented data model

The main concepts of an object-oriented model can be summarized as follows:

- *Objects* Each real-world entity is modeled by an object. Each object is associated with a unique identifier (called object-identifier, abbreviated as OID).

- *Complex objects* Each object has a set of instance attributes (also called instance variables); the value of an attribute can be an object or a set of objects.

- *Encapsulation* The attribute values represent the object's state. This state is accessed or modified by sending messages to the object to invoke the corresponding methods.

- *Classes* Objects sharing the same structure and behavior are grouped into classes. A class represents a template for a set of similar objects. Each object is an instance of some class.

In the reference model a class is defined by specifying its name, its attributes, its methods, and the names of its superclass(es). Multiple inheritance and the existence of a default class, called TOP_CLASS, root of an inheritance hierarchy encompassing the entire database, are assumed. An attribute is defined by specifying its name and its domain. Attributes can be single valued or multivalued. In defining multivalued attributes, the various object-oriented data models use different constructors such as set, list, tree, or array. We assume that multivalued attributes are defined by using a constructor denoted as set-of. The following definitions specify the notation for the reference model.

If a_i is an attribute name and C_i is a class name then:

- $A_i = a_i : C_i$ is the definition of a single valued attribute;

- $A_i = a_i :$ **set-of** C_i is the definition of a multivalued attribute.

A method definition consists of a signature and a body. The signature specifies the method name and the classes of the objects that are input and output parameters for the method. The body provides the implementation of the method

418

and consists of a sequence of statements written in some programming language. If M is a method name, In_i ($1 \leq i \leq n$) is an input parameter specification and Out is an output parameter specification, $M(In_1, In_2, ..., In_n) \rightarrow Out$ is a method signature definition. An input parameter specification consists of the parameter name and the parameter domain. The parameter domain is either a class name or can be defined as a collection of instances of a class, in the same manner as attributes are specified. An output parameter is either a class name or a collection of instances of a class. The invocation of a method M on an object O has the form $O.M(O_1, O_2, ..., O_n)$ where $O_1, O_2, ..., O_n$ are objects that are passed as input parameters.

Classes are recursively defined as follows:

- Integers, floats, strings, text, and Boolean are classes (called primitive classes)

- There is a special class, called TOP_CLASS, which has no superclass; it is default for superclass if no superclasses are specified

- If $A_1, A_2, ..., A_n$ ($n \geq 1$) are attribute definitions, with distinct names; if $M_1, M_2, ..., M_k$ ($k \geq 0$) are method definitions, with distinct names; and $C_1, C_2, ..., C_h$ ($h \geq 0$) are distinct class names;

  then   **Class** C
  Attributes $A_1; A_2; ....; A_n$;
  Methods $M_1; M_2; .....; M_k$;
  Superclasses $C_1, C_2, ..., C_h$
  End

  is a class definition.

In the present discussion, we make the assumption that classes have both the intensional and extensional meaning and an object can be instance of only one class. An object, however, can be *member* of several classes through the inheritance hierarchy. Note, however, that in several object-oriented data models the class does not have the extensional meaning. In this case, the set of instances of a class must be explicitly managed by users using collections, or other set constructors provided by the data definition language of the model at hand.

We use throughout the graphical notation for OODB schema's from [2]. A box represent a class. Each box has two regions for entities and three for classes. The first region contains the class name, the second the attribute definitions, the third the methods. For entities the regions have the same meaning, except that there are no methods. There is a dotted arc from a class C to a class C' if C' is the domain of a composite attribute of C. Moreover, there is a directed bold arc from a class C to a class C' if C is a subclass of C'. See Figure 1.

2.2 Message filter model

The basic idea of the message filter model [5] is that information flow control can be achieved by mediating the flow of messages among objects and, therefore, the security is achieved by checking message exchanges among objects. This approach is very simple, in that it requires us to deal only with two elements: objects and messages. It is based on two basic principles governing message exchanges among objects in the system

1. if the sender of the message is at a strictly higher level than the receiver's level, the method is executed by the receiver in restricted mode (that is no updates can be performed)

2. if the sender of the message is at a strictly lower level than the receiver's level, the method is executed by the receiver is executed in normal mode, but the returned value is *nil*.

The first principle ensures that a subject does not write down, while the second one ensures that a subject does not read up. Further details can be found in [5].

Moreover, the model introduces two constraints concerning security relationships among instances and classes, and among superclasses and subclasses. It is important to stress, however, that those constraints were not introduced for security reasons, rather to ensure that the class hierarchy design and the object creation are correct so that no errors due to security would arise. In the remainder, given an instance o (class C), $L(o)$ ($L(C)$) denotes the security level of o (C).

Instance Constraint

  If o_j is an instance of class C_j, then $L(C_j) \leq L(o_j)$.

Subclass Constraint

  Given classes C_i and C_j such that C_j is a subclass of C_i in the class inheritance hierarchy, then $L(C_i) \leq L(C_j)$.

The motivation for the first constraint is based on the observation that an instance inherits from its class. Since inheritance can be seen as a read operation, for the inheritance to be secure the instance must have a higher or equal security level than its class. The same motivation justifies the second constraint.

Jajodia and Kogan [5] also propose an approach to model multilevel entities in terms of single level objects. The approach is based on the use of inheritance. Given an entity type E with attributes of n_l different levels of security, this approach consists of defining a class for each level l_i ($i \in n_l$). A class C_{l_i} contains all attributes having security level l_i. Moreover, subclass relationships are established so that C_{l_i} is a direct superclass of C_{l_j} if $l_i <_s l_j$, where $l_i <_s l_j$ holds if $l_i < l_j$ in the security lattice and there is no level l_k, $k \in n_l$, such that $l_i < l_k$ and $l_k < l_j$. Figure 1 shows how multilevel entity types are represented using this approach. In the figure, a multilevel entity type **EMPLOYEE** and a typical multilevel instance of **EMPLOYEE** are shown on the left. **EMPLOYEE** can be realized as the inheritance hierarchy shown on the top right corner. The multilevel instance of **EMPLOYEE** can be realized as two separate instances o_1 and o_2, shown on the right.

This approach suffers from several problems. First, it leads to a replication of information. Since a multilevel entity is modeled as several single level objects in a class hierarchy, some attributes of high level objects are replicas of attributes of low level objects (because of inheritance). Second, if not carefully monitored, updates may lead to mutual inconsistency of replicated data. For example, both objects o_1 and o_2 in Figure 1 have the attributes 'name' and 'age' and the values of those attributes should be mutually consistent. Suppose that an update is performed on an attribute of the high level object, say on attribute 'name' of o_1. This update cannot be propagated to the corresponding attribute of the low level object, since this writing down is not allowed under the Ball-LaPadula model. Finally, the notion of inheritance hierarchy tends to be overloaded under this

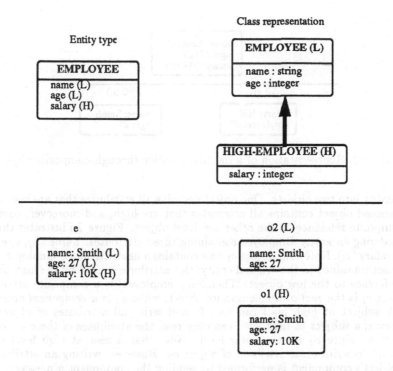

Figure 1: Representation of multilevel entities types through inheritance hierarchies

approach since it is used both for conceptual specialization and for supporting multilevel entities.

3 A Design based on Composite Objects

This section describes how to model multilevel entities on top of single level objects through the use of composite objects. We first provide an overview of the approach. Next we show how our design also accommodates the case of entities with multivalued attributes that have values at different security levels.

3.1 Approach overview

The approach proposed in this paper is based on the use of *composite objects*. The notion of composite object is a modeling construct that allows to consider an object and a set of component objects as a single object [4].

Given an entity type E with attributes of n_l different levels of security, this approach consists of defining a class for each level l_i ($i \in l_i$). A class C_{l_i} contains all attributes having security level l_i. Moreover a class C_{l_i} contains a composite attribute whose domain is a class C_{l_j} if $l_j <_s l_i$.

For example, given an entity with a number of attributes of level low (L) and a number of attributes of level high (H), the approach is based on decomposing

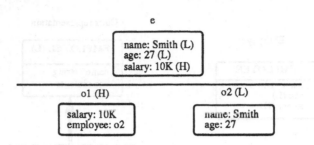

Figure 2: Representation of a multilevel entity through composite objects

the entity into two objects. One object contains all attributes that are low, while the second object contains all attributes that are high, and moreover, contains a composite reference to the other low level object. Figure 2 illustrates this by considering an entity Employee containing three attributes: name (L), age (L), and salary (H). Note that object o_1 now contains a new attribute, 'employee' that was not contained in the original entity; this attribute is used by the high object to reference to the low object. Therefore, 'employee' is a composite attribute. Object o_1 is the *root* of the composite object, while o_2 is a *component* object.

A subject at high level can modify and write all attributes of object o_1. However, a subject at high level can only read the attributes of the component object o_2, since o_2 is at a lower level. Note that a user at high level could attempt to write some attribute of object o_2. However, writing an attribute of an object's component is performed by sending the component a message. This message can then be checked by the message filter.

3.2 Multivalued attributes

An important characteristic of object-oriented data model is that it supports multivalued attributes. Unlike the relational model in which multivalued attributes are simply handled by normalizing them, object-oriented data models provide a direct representation of entities with multivalued attributes. In this section, we address how we can model an entity having a multivalued attribute with values that have different security levels. The approach in this case is to partition the multivalued attribute into several attributes; the first storing the low values, the second storing the high values, and so on. The first attribute will be an attribute of the low object, the second one will be an attribute of the high object, and so forth

As an example, we extend the example of Figure 2 by adding a multivalued attribute, named 'skills'. Suppose that entity e of Figure 2 has the following skills: {database (L), cryptography (H)}. By using the above approach, the entity e will be modeled as represented in Figure 3.

3.3 Class design

The approach previously sketched has a main disadvantage that a high user in order to see all attributes an employee must access two different objects. This problem can be eased by adding the appropriate methods. For example, in the case of objects o_1 and o_2 the methods that would be added are the following.

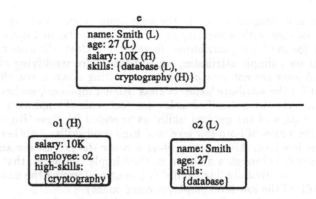

Figure 3: Representation of a multilevel entities with multivalued attributes

(In the example, the invocation of a method m on an object o, is denoted as $o.m$; cascaded method invocations are also used.)

o_1:name ( )→ string
        { return(self.employee.name) }
  age ( )→ integer
        { return(self.employee.age) }
  skills ( )→ set-of(string)
        { return({self.high-skills} $\bigcup$ {self.employee.skills})}

o_2:name ( ) → string
        { return(self.name)}
  age ( ) → integer
        { return(self.age) }
  skills ( ) → set-of(string)
        { return(self.skills) }

The methods in o_2 simply return the values of attributes 'name' , 'age', and 'skills'. The first two methods in o_1 return the values of the nested attributes 'name' and 'age'. The implementation of method 'name' of object o_1 consists of sending a message to the component object o_2, whose OID is stored in the attribute 'employee' of o_1, to invoke the method 'name' of o_2. The method 'skills' of object o_1 simply performs a union. Note that all methods of object o_1 invoke methods from the object o_2 which are read-only methods. Therefore, the methods of object o_1 will pass the message filtering algorithm when invoked from high subjects. Note that the language we used to define the method's bodies can be easily translated in the language of any of the currently available OODBMSs. Methods like those for object o_2 are often called *accessor methods*, since their purpose is to simply return attribute values. By the same token, the methods of o_1 whose purpose is the retrieve the values of the nested attributes of o_1 are called *nested accessor method*. Finally, methods that return values of both direct and nested attributes of an object are called *combined accessor methods*; an example is represented by the method 'skills' of object o_1 that returns the values of both the attribute 'high-skills' and the nested attribute 'skills'.

Figure 4.a presents the overall schema for classes, including the methods. In the figure, the key-word **composite** following an attribute name indicates that the attribute is a composite one. In the definitions reported in Figure 4.b each class is also labeled with a security level. For simplicity, in Figure 4 we omit the methods for modifying attributes. In general, a class will have methods for modifying its own simple attributes, while methods for modifying attributes of component objects are not provided, because writing down is not allowed.

Note that for the attribute 'skills' of class 'High-Employee', we have made the hypothesis that the skills classified as low are real skills of employees. Therefore, the implementation of the method 'skills' as provided for class 'High-Employee' is to return the union of both low level and high level skills. Another possibility would be that low level skills just represent a *cover story*. This semantics can be also easily modeled through a different method implementation, that would just return the value of attribute 'high-skills' (without performing the union with the attribute 'skill' of the low level employee component).

Using the composite object approach together with the generation of the appropriate nested accessor methods, the resulting objects are able to provide the same interface as if multilevel objects were directly supported. For example, consider an instance of a class 'High-Employee', such an instance will be able to respond to the following messages: 'name', 'age', 'salary', 'skills'. In addition, other messages that the instance will be able to respond are 'set-salary' (to modify the salary of an employee) and 'add-skills' and 'remove-skills' (to add a skill and to remove a skill). Note, however, that all skills added to an instance of class 'High-Employee' will be inserted in the attribute 'high-skills'. Therefore, the method for modifying the high skills has to be designed with the appropriate semantics in order to do appropriate integrity checking. The above messages are exactly those that would have been provided to a high subject if multilevel objects were directly supported.

This approach can be generalized to the case of more then two levels. Suppose that entity *e* has an additional attribute 'proposed-salary-increase' which is very high (VH). Then *e* would be modeled by three objects, where the first contains the very high attributes, the second object the high ones, and the third object the low one. The overall design is illustrated in Figure 5.

4 Composite Objects and Semantic Integrity

In this section we investigate the impact of security considerations on semantic integrity of composite objects. There are several types of composite references that can be categorized as follows [4]:

1. exclusive dependent reference
   if an object O is component of an object O', it cannot be component of another object; moreover if O' is removed, O is also removed

2. exclusive independent reference
   if an object O is component of an object O', it cannot be component of another object; the deletion of O' does not imply the deletion of O

3. shared dependent reference
   an object O can be component of several objects; O is removed when all parents objects, on which O depends for existence, are removed

424

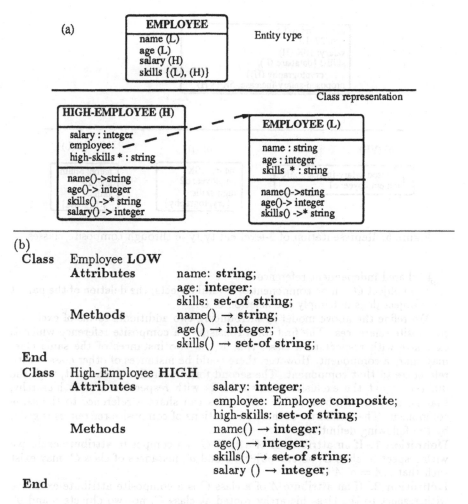

(b)

Class   Employee **LOW**
    Attributes   name: **string**;
                             age: **integer**;
                             skills: **set-of string**;
    Methods   name() → **string**;
                             age() → **integer**;
                             skills() → **set-of string**;
End
Class   High-Employee **HIGH**
    Attributes   salary: **integer**;
                             employee: Employee **composite**;
                             high-skills: **set-of string**;
    Methods   name() → **integer**;
                             age() → **integer**;
                             skills() → **set-of string**;
                             salary () → **integer**;
End

Figure 4: Representation of a multilevel entity type through composite classes

e

```
name: Smith (L)
age: 27 (L)
salary: 10K (H)
skills: {database (L),
        cryptography (H)}
proposed-salary-increase: 5K (VH)
```

o3 (VH)

```
proposed-salary-increase :5K
high-employee: o1
```

o1 (H)

```
salary: 10K
employee: o2
high-skills:
      {cryptography}
```

o2 (L)

```
name: Smith
age: 27
skills:
    {database}
```

Figure 5: Representation of 3-level entity type through composite classes

4. shared independent reference

an object O can be component of several objects; the deletion of the parent object does not imply the deletion of O.

We refine the above model by introducing two additional forms of exclusive composite references. The first form consists of a composite reference which is exclusive with respect to a class, that is, no two instances of the same class may share a component. However, there could be instances of other classes with references to that component. The second form is similar to the first, with the difference that the exclusivity constraint is with respect to a class hierarchy, that is, no two members of the same class can share a reference to the same component. The semantics of these new notions of composite references is given by the following definitions.

Definition 1. If an attribute A of a class C is a composite attribute exclusive with respect to class C, no two objects o and o', instances of class C, may exist such that $o.A = o'.A$ □

Definition 2. If an attribute A of a class C is a composite attribute exclusive with respect to the class hierarchy rooted at class C, no two objects o and o', members of class C, may exist such that $o.A = o'.A$ □

The reason why we introduce those additional form of exclusivity constraints is to be able to support some form of semantic integrity of composite objects. The exclusivity constraint as originally formulated for the Orion model would allow a low user to infer that some high objects exist.

Composite objects in our model must satisfy the following constraint.

Composite Object Constraint-1

Let $\mathcal{C}(o)$ be the set of direct and indirect components of an object o,

then $\forall o' \in \mathcal{C}(o), L(o) \geq L(o')$.

The previous constraint states that the security level of the root of a composite object must be greater or equal to the security level of the component objects (both direct and indirect). This constraint, however, does not need to be implemented as part of the security monitor, since we make the assumption that the operations of reading the attributes of a component object pass through the message filter.

```
Class    High-Employee    HIGH
         Attributes       salary: integer;
                          employee: Employee composite exclusive(self-class)
                          high-skills: set-of string;
         Methods          name() → integer;
                          age() → integer;
                          skills() → set-of string;
                          salary() → integer;
End
```

Figure 6: Definition of classes using a revised model of composite objects

To see why the additional constraints are necessary, suppose we wish to enforce the requirement that a component object is referenced only by one instance of another class. (For example, we may require that an instance of the low class Employee should be referenced only by one instance of the high class High-Employee.) In absence of security concerns, this can be easily accomplished using exclusive composite references. However, exclusive composite references cannot always be used in a secure environment since they may allow a low user to infer the existence of high objects. For example, suppose that a additional entity type, called Project, with low level must be stored into the database where Project has a list of employees working in the project. An attempt to add an employee to the list of employees working in a project would be rejected, if composite references from the class 'High-Employee' to the class 'Employee' were exclusive.

We solve this problem by using the refined form of exclusivity constraint that we have introduced. The modification consists of using composite references that are exclusive with respect to the class 'C', that is, instances of class 'C' cannot share an instance of the component class. However, instances of classes, other than 'C', can have references to instances of the component class.

Using this approach the definition of class 'High-Employee' would be modified by declaring the composite attribute 'employee' to be exclusive with respect to 'High-Employee' itself (denoted in the definition by the pseudo-variable 'self-class'). Note, however, that this approach is correct only if all instances of class 'High-Employee' have level high. If there are instances at level higher than high (for example very high) this approach cannot be used because high users may infer the existence of very high instances. This is summarized by the following rule.

Composite Object Constraint-2

Given two classes C and C', C' can be an exclusive component of class C with respect to C itself if for each instance o of C, $L(o) = L(C)$.

Using the revised definition of composite objects, the definition of class 'High-Employee' presented in Figure 4.b is modified as shown in Figure 6. In the definition the key-word **exclusive** is followed by the name of the class 'High-Employee' itself to express the fact that no two instances of class 'High-Employee' may share a reference to the same instance of class 'Employee'.

When dealing with inheritance hierarchies, the exclusivity constraint must be stated with respect to a class hierarchy. Consider the class design represented in Figure 7 and consider the exclusivity constraint 'employee: Employee

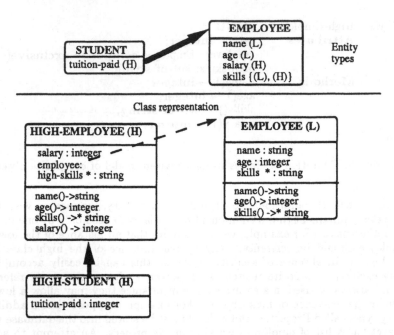

Figure 7: Representation of entity type hierarchies through composite class hierarchies

composite exclusive(self-class)' (reported from the definition of class 'High-Employee' from Figure 4.a). That constraint prevents two instances of class 'High-Employee' from sharing a reference to the same instance of class 'Employee'. However, it does not prevent an instance of class 'High-Employee' from sharing a reference with an instance of class 'High-Student'. Therefore, we need to use the exclusivity constraint with respect to an entire class hierarchy that we introduced earlier.

From the syntactical point of view such a constraint is declared by associating a '*' character to the pseudo-variable 'self-class'. Therefore, the previous exclusivity constraint from Figure 4.a would be declared as follows: 'employee: Employee **composite exclusive**(self-class*)'.

This extension requires us to introduce a constraint stronger than Composite Object Constraint-2 to enforce the exclusivity constraint with respect to a class inheritance hierarchy. In the following constraint, $\mathcal{H}(C)$ denotes the set of classes in the class inheritance hierarchy rooted at C (including C itself).

Composite Object Constraint-3

> Given two classes C and C', C' can be an exclusive component of class C with respect to $\mathcal{H}(C)$ if for each instance o of C'', $C'' \in \mathcal{H}(C)$, $L(o) = L(C)$.

The above constraint states that if the constraint must be enforced that no two members of a class can share a reference to a component object, then all members of the class must have the same security level[2].

---

[2]We recall that an object is instance of a class C if is the most specific class of the object. An object is member of a class C if the object is an instance of C or of any subclass of C

5 Conclusions and Future Work

In this paper, we have addressed the problem of modeling multilevel entities in terms of single level objects. This problem is quite important since it seems likely that secure object systems will be based on single level objects. As discussed by various authors [5,6] directly supporting multilevel objects may be quite difficult and leads to increased complexity in the design of the security monitor.

In this paper, we have shown that it is indeed possible to have single level objects and at the same time support multilevel entities. The approach we have used is based on composite objects. We have refined the composite model defined by Kim, Bertino, and Garza [4] by allowing exclusivity constraint to hold only with respect to a class or a class inheritance hierarchy. Note, however, that our approach could be implemented even on OODBMSs not supporting composite objects. In those systems, our approach could be implemented using aggregation. Of course, the constraint on exclusivity may not be supported on those systems.

Future work to be carried out includes the development of a specification language to state security requirements for application entities and of tools to automatically generate object schemas from these specifications. The problem of secure object delete operations and secure garbage collection will also be investigated.

References

[1] D. E. Bell and L. J. LaPadula, *Secure computer systems: Unified exposition and multics interpretation.* The Mitre Corp., March, 1976.

[2] E. Bertino and L. Martino. *Object-Oriented Database Systems: Concepts and Architectures.* Addison-Wesley, 1993.

[3] E. Bertino, M. Negri, G. Pelagatti, and L. Sbattella, "Object-Oriented Query Languages: the Notion and the Issues," *IEEE Trans. on Knowledge and Data Engineering*, Vol. 4, No. 3, 1992, pp. 223-237.

[4] W. Kim, E. Bertino, J. Garza, "Composite Objects Revisited", *Proc. of ACM-SIGMOD Conference on Management of Data*, Portland (Oregon), May 29-June 3, 1989.

[5] S. Jajodia, and B. Kogan, "Integrating an Object-Oriented Data Model with Multilevel Security", *Proc. of the 1990 IEEE Symposium on Research in Security and Privacy*, Oakland (Calif.), May 7-9, 1990.

[6] J. Millen, and T. Lunt, "Security for Object-Oriented Database Systems", *Proc. of the 1992 IEEE Symposium on Research in Security and privacy*, Oakland (Calif.), May 4-6, 1992.

[7] F. Rabitti, E. Bertino, W. Kim, and D. Woelk, "A Model of Authorization for Next-Generation Database Systems", *ACM Trans. on Database Systems*, Vol. 16, No.1, 1991, pp.88-131.

[8] B.Thuraisingham, "Mandatory Security in Object-Oriented Database Systems", *Proc. of the Object-Oriented Programming Systems, Languages, and Applications*, New Orleans (Louisiana), Oct 1-6, 1989.

A Model Using Classes as a Basic Organization Tool*

Thong Wei Koh   *Beng Chin Ooi*   *Yin Seong Ho*

Department of Information Systems and Computer Science
National University of Singapore
Kent Ridge, Singapore 0511
{kohthon1, ooibc, hoys}@iscs.nus.sg

Abstract. In this paper, we present a framework based on the notion of classes as an organizational tool to model some common concepts in Database. The creation of a simple and representational model helps to reconcile the seemingly different organization in traditional relational databases in the form of relations and classes in the newer object oriented database. The paper also discusses the various issues of complex type structures faced in such a theoretical model including the idea of composite objects. The main contribution of the paper is the introduction of the concept of α abstraction and approximations of databases. This development of the mathematical model accommodates the idea of schemas, creation of views and retrieval.

1 Introduction

The notion of classes appeared very early in database technology. It has been used as a conceptual modelling tool in Semantic Data Model, and the E-R Model[Che76] and more recently in a more focused form in Object Oriented Data Model[Kim90,ABD89,Bee89].

Object Oriented Data model emerged as an amalgamation of techniques from Object Oriented Programming Languages and evolving database technology. In particular it gained considerable interests in the field of Spatial Database systems, CAD/CAM and other dedicated systems. The main principle behind the Object Oriented paradigm lies in the recognition of real world objects and modelling them and their activities in a representational system in which classes serve primarily as an organizational tool.

In Object Oriented Programming languages like Simula67, smalltalk and C++, classes are treated as templates for object instantiation. For example, in C++, classes are almost synonymous with types with the exception of the inclusion of methods and inheritance. Because of the nature of the application, which is to model an often static world problem, classes are used more as a 'factory' of objects than a repository for them. In the database context, however, we are dealing with a dynamic world with the need for a class hierarchy to act as a natural index to classes which are repository for these objects. In a truly extensible system, objects which may be captured by the database may not necessarily be limited to types predefined upon the conception of the schema. As

---

* This work was partly supported by a National University of Singapore Research Grant. RP910694

such, it would be advantageous if the class hierarchy could maintain a consistent index naturally and correctly rather than be a template for objects.

In database, the naturalness of using the concept of classes to organize data conceptually or concretely by a hierarchy of classification is intuitively appealing. However, much of the terminology are not compatible across the different models. In addition, the concept of classes are defined quite distinctly by the different models even within the area of the Object Oriented Data Model. It would seem that classes do not enjoy the same well-definedness of relations in the Relational Data Model [Cod79]. This is a major source of problems in terminology as we have difficulty then, in identifying the exact relationships between classes and objects, relations and classes, objects and attributes. Lacking this foundation, or 'common ground', it is particularly difficult for researchers to develop general techniques across the different models.

In this paper, we identify the various concepts like relations (in relational data model), and classes as mathematical ideas within the same framework with well defined properties. By doing so, it will then be possible to define the relationships between the different concepts precisely. In the context of the same framework, we demonstrate some constructions that correspond closely to the ideas of schemas, creation of views and retrieval common in database systems. In particular, all the abovementioned activities may be modelled easily by a new notion of approximation. This theoretical framework will aid further understanding of these common concepts in database and form a basis for future applications and extensions of the model. An example is the extension of the notion of superclasses to a new concept of a generalization operator which generalizes arbitrarily defined sets [KHO93]. In addition, we have utilized this same framework to define and study a particular class of dependency rules which have application in Knowledge Mining[KOH93].

The interpretation of databases as representations characterized by a concept lattice is not new. In fact it is used in indexing applications as way back as in 1982 [Ho82]. The main contribution in this paper is the introduction of the new concept of α abstraction which 'approximates' instances of databases. It is the combination of these two concepts that allows many of the database concepts to be modelled adequately. The concept lattice allows only classification but approximations allow aggregations.

The paper is organized into 5 sections. The next section contains the necessary mathematics of the model. It defines the various terms and introduces the notion of approximation. Section 3 discusses how the common concept of schemas, retrievals and views may be modelled in the framework. Section 4 describes how complex and composite objects can be modelled easily using classes and approximations. We end with a conclusion in section 5.

2 Representation

As with all forms of abstraction, and modelling, we have to make certain assumptions and decide on what to ignore as irrelevant to the conception of the model. This section actually rephrases the well known concept of a Galois Correspondence in the language of categories. This was done intentionally so as to streamline the proof of certain claims in section 2.3 and to preserve consistency when we extend the ideas of the paper to speak of a category of databases (not discussed in this paper).

The main aim of the model is to study the concept of classes as an organizational tool in relation to the other common concept of relations, schemas, view creation and retrieval. To achieve a simple and manageable model, we have ignored issues such as methods in classes and dependency relations. These issues are important in their own right though not necessary for our purpose

To begin, we shall have to abstract the idea of a database into a more manageable form stripping away various model dependent features and implementation detail. We note that the basic idea of a database is to store facts, or in a another perspective, data objects (entities) which are identified by one or more attributes. The description of entities may be structured [LeS90] or complex or both. These structures are arbitrary and to a certain extent subjective. However, the underlying assumption is that we can associate a (finite) list of attributes to an object. This leads us to the first definition of a representation.

Definition 1. A *representation*, REP, is a 3-tuple $(r_{REP}, A_{REP}, E_{REP})$ where
(i) A_{REP} is a finite set of attributes.
(ii) E_{REP} is a finite set of objects (entities).
(iii) $A_{REP} \cap E_{REP} = \emptyset$.
(iv) $r_{REP} \subseteq A_{REP} \times E_{REP}$.
(v) The inverse relation of r_{REP} is defined as
$r_{REP}^{-1} \subseteq E_{REP} \times A_{REP}$, and $\forall a \in A_{REP}, e \in E_{REP}, (e,a) \in r_{REP}^{-1} \Leftrightarrow (a,e) \in r_{REP}$
and the relation r_{REP} are total.

Definition 1 is a very simple requirement for a representation (database). It simply suffice to have a relation between two finite sets. For convenience, we shall use the same notation to denote functions
$r_{REP} : A_{REP} \longrightarrow \wp(E_{REP})$ where $r_{REP}(a) = \{x | (a,x) \in r_{REP}\}$ and
$r_{REP}^{-1} : E_{REP} \longrightarrow \wp(A_{REP})$ where $r_{REP}^{-1}(e) = \{x | (x,e) \in r_{REP}\}$

2.1 Galois correspondence

Next, we construct composite functions $g = r_{REP}'^{-1} r_{REP}'$ and $h = r_{REP}' r_{REP}'^{-1}$.
where $r_{REP}' : \wp(A_{REP}) \longrightarrow \wp(E_{REP})$ is defined as $r_{REP}'(x) = \bigcap_{a \in x} r_{REP}(a)$ and
$r_{REP}'^{-1} : \wp(E_{REP}) \longrightarrow \wp(A_{REP})$ as $r_{REP}'^{-1}(x) = \bigcap_{e \in x} r_{REP}^{-1}(e)$.
These two composite functions form a Galois correspondence[Mac71] between sets $\wp(A_{REP})$ and $\wp(E_{REP})$.
Function g has properties of:

- Increasing : $a \subseteq g(a)$
- Monotonic : $a \subseteq a' \Rightarrow g(a) \subseteq g(a')$
- Idempotent : $g(a) = gg(a)$

Function h has also similar properties of being increasing, monotonic and idempotent.
There are certain subsets of A_{REP} which are stable sets invariant under the application of function g. The same can be observed in some subsets in E_{REP} which are invariant under the application of function h. There is an isomorphism[Ho82,Mac71] between the stable subsets in A_{REP}, related by the simple set inclusion relation, and the stable subsets in E_{REP}.
We call these subsets classes. Intuitively, *'a class is a collection of entities with some common attributes'*. Function r_{REP}' takes a subset X of attributes and

maps it to a subset Y of entities each of which possesses at least the attributes in X. Likewise, function r'^{-1}_{REP} maps a subset Y of entities to a subset X of attributes which are common to entities in Y. Function $g : \wp(A) \longrightarrow \wp(A)$ is increasing in the sense that it takes a subset of attributes X and maps it to a larger set of attributes which are common to the set of entities in $r'_{REP}(X)$. Idempotence of g guarantees that this maximizing process terminates in two steps.

We shall drop the subscripts denoting the particular representation when it is clear from the context.

2.2 Galois correspondence as adjuncts

Alternatively, this Galois correspondence between the two sets, $\wp(A)$ and $\wp(E)$ may take another familiar form of an adjunction. To see this, we construct a pair of categories, $(\mathcal{A}, \mathcal{E})$ where $obj(\mathcal{A}) = \{S | S \subseteq A\}$ and the simple set inclusion as (mono)morphisms and likewise for the category $\mathcal{E}$. The left adjoint functor $R : \mathcal{A} \longrightarrow \mathcal{E}^{op}$ is defined as $R(A') = \bigcap_{a \in A'} r(a)$ with $R(\emptyset) = E$ on objects and $\forall A', A'' \in Obj(\mathcal{A}), \forall f \in Hom_{\mathcal{A}}(A', A''), R(f) : R(A') \longrightarrow R(A'')$ on arrows. The right adjoint functor $R' : \mathcal{E}^{op} \longrightarrow \mathcal{A}$, where $R'(E') = \bigcap_{e \in E'} r^{-1}(e)$ with $R'(\emptyset) = A$ on objects and $\forall E', E'' \in Obj(\mathcal{E}^{op}), \forall f \in Hom_{\mathcal{E}^{op}}(E', E''), R'(f) : R'(E') \longrightarrow R'(E')$ on arrows.

A representation r may then also be written as a four-tuple $(R_r, R'_r, \eta_r, \varepsilon_r)$ where R_r and R'_r are functors as described in the previous paragraph and natural transformations $\eta_r : 1_{\mathcal{A}} \longrightarrow R'R$ and $\varepsilon_r : RR' \longrightarrow 1_{\mathcal{E}^{op}}$.

The properties of

- *Increasing*: $\exists \eta : 1_{\mathcal{A}} \longrightarrow R'R$.
- *Monotonic*: $\forall A, B \in \mathcal{A}, \forall f : A \longrightarrow B, R'R(f) : R'R(A) \longrightarrow R'R(B)$
- *Idempotent*: $R'R \cong (R'R)(R'R)$

are observed as in the previous subsection 2.1.

Proposition 2. *The quadruple* $(R_r, R'_r, \eta_r, \varepsilon_r)$ *characterizing a representation* r, *with natural transformations*, $\eta_r : 1_{\mathcal{A}_r} \longrightarrow R'_r R_r$ *and* $\varepsilon_r : R_r R'_r \longrightarrow 1_{\mathcal{E}^{op}_r}$ *is an adjunction.*

In this way, the stable sets (classes) described in the previous subsection(2.1) can be identified as the objects in the full subcategories ($\mathcal{A}_0$ of $\mathcal{A}$ (dropping the subscripts) and $\mathcal{E}_0$ of $\mathcal{E}$) of the adjunction with adjoint functors R and R' whose objects $obj(\mathcal{A}_0) = \{a \in obj(\mathcal{A}) | R'R(a) = a\}$ and $obj(\mathcal{E}_0) = \{e \in obj(\mathcal{E}) | RR'(e) = a\}$[Mac71].

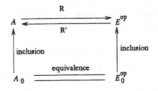

Definition 3. **A class** is an object in the full subcategory $\mathcal{E}_{r,0}$ of $\mathcal{E}_r$ in a representation r.

To give a better intuition about the constructions in this section, figure 1 gives a graphical representation of an example of a database of two entities, $\{Ship, Cars\}$ described by a set of attributes, $\{Speed, Wheels\}$ [2].

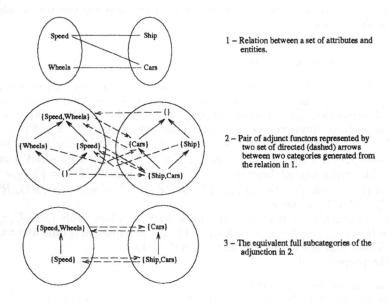

1 – Relation between a set of attributes and entities.

2 – Pair of adjunct functors represented by two set of directed (dashed) arrows between two categories generated from the relation in 1.

3 – The equivalent full subcategories of the adjunction in 2.

Fig. 1. Graphical example of discussion in section 2.2.

By no means are the result in this section new, it is an application of a well known mathematical theory to a database concept. The advantages of using such a structure include a natural and optimized indexing structure which has been utilized in many indexing applications. The following section will develop on this idea.

2.3 Approximation and aggregation

Here, we introduce the concept of approximation of a representation. Intuitively, this notion is a generalization of relations in relational data model. Relations, in this context are an approximation of its objects as tuples. We note that the objects, or tuples, in this case belong to a relation because they have the same 'structure' of attribute types but may be differentiated by different attribute values. If there is a function that maps a set of attribute values to another set

---

[2] The language of categories allows one then to speak of a category of representations (database) with α abstraction (defined later on in section 2.3) as morphisms. This would require more work of the notion of representation which will not be elaborated here. The (over)use of categories here is unfortunate but necessary to keep a uniform and consistent style.

of attribute types, the entities that are described by the set of attribute values are 'forced' into equivalence classes (relations in relational data model). We give a graphic depiction of such a process in figure 2.

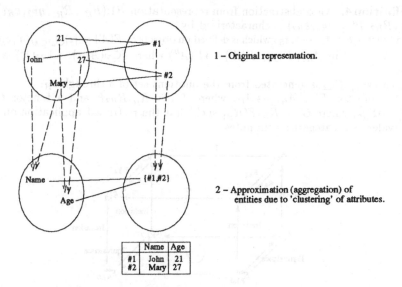

1 – Original representation.

2 – Approximation (aggregation) of entities due to 'clustering' of attributes.

	Name	Age
#1	John	21
#2	Mary	27

Fig. 2. Figure showing the aggregation of entities during an approximation.

Before we give a proper definition for an approximation in definition 4, we have to define some useful terminologies.

Given two sets E, $\wp(A)$ and a total function, $p : E \longrightarrow \wp(A)$,
(i) The quotient set $[E]$ induced by p has elements $[e] = \{e' | e' \in E, p(e) = p(e')\}$.
(ii) There exists a unique function $h : [E] \longrightarrow \wp(A)$ where $h([e]) = p(e)$.

Recall that a representation R1, may be characterised by a 3-tuple $(r_{R1}, A_{R1}, E_R$
We define a total relation $\delta \subseteq \wp(A_{R1}) \times (A_{R2} \cup \emptyset)$ where A_{R2} is a disjoint set from A_{R1}. This relation may be defined as a function $f : \wp(A_{R1}) \longrightarrow \wp(A_{R2})$ such that $f(a) = \{c | \bigcup_{a' \subseteq a}(a', c) \in \delta\}$. Let function $p : E_{R1} \longrightarrow \wp(A_{R2})$ be $p = f r_{R1}^{-1}$. Let the quotient set induced by p be E_{R2}. The unique function, $h : E_{R2} \longrightarrow \wp(A_{R2})$ may be defined as a relation $r_{R2}^{-1} \subseteq E_{R2} \times A_{R2}$ and $r_{R2} \subseteq A_{R2} \times E_{R2}$ as its inverse.

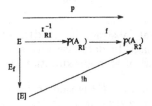

It is clear that the 3-tuple (r_{R2}, A_{R2}, E_{R2}) satisfies the definition of a representation. This requires that relations δ and its inverse are total. The construction of this new representation, (r_{R2}, A_{R2}, E_{R2}) from the representation, (r_{R1}, A_{R1}, E_{R1}) is said to be *based* on δ. Alternatively, we call δ the *basis* of the construction. We call the set E_{R2} the quotient set of δ through r_{R1}.

Definition 4. An α abstraction from representation $R1:(R_{R1}, R'_{R1}, \eta_{R1}, \varepsilon_{R1})$ to $R2:(R_{R2}, R'_{R2}, \eta_{R2}, \varepsilon_{R2})$ is characterized by

(i) a functor $F : \mathcal{A}_{R1} \longrightarrow \mathcal{A}_{R2}$ which is defined on objects as $F(A') = \{c | \bigcup_{a' \subseteq A'}(a', c) \in \delta\}$. $\forall f : A' \longrightarrow A''$ in $\mathcal{A}_{R1}$, $F(f) : F(A') \longrightarrow F(A'')$ where $\delta \subseteq \wp(A_{R1}) \times (A_{R2} \cup \emptyset)$ is the *basis*.

(ii) category $\mathcal{E}_{R2}$ is generated from the quotient set of δ through r_{R1}.

(iii) a functor $F' : \mathcal{A}_{R1} \longrightarrow \mathcal{A}_{R2}$ where $F' = R'_{R2} R_{R2} F$ and a functor $G' : \mathcal{E}^{op}_{R1} \longrightarrow \mathcal{E}^{op}_{R2}$, where $G' = R_{R2} F' R'_{R1}$ such that the restricted application on the equivalent subcategories commutes.

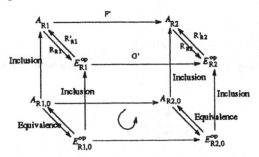

Actually, the condition of commutativity is superfluous in the presence of the equivalence between the full-subcategories of the abjunctions. This is stated to emphasize the connection between the two representations.

Proposition 5. *There exists a natural transformation* $t : F \longrightarrow F'$.

Proof. This is an immediate result from the existence of natural transformation, $\eta_{R2} : 1_{A_{R2}} \longrightarrow R'_{R2} R_{R2}$ enabling the natural transformation, $\eta_{R2} F : 1_{A_{R2}} F \longrightarrow R'_{R2} R_{R2} F$ where $F' = R'_{R2} R_{R2} F$. $\square$

Proposition 5 says that 'abstraction' of attributes may cause a class to be larger in the approximation. In database terms, a reorganization of the class hierarchy may be necessary if an approximation is performed.

Definition 6. A representation $R2$ is said to be an *approximation* (view) of a representation $R1$ iff there exists an α abstraction from $R1$ to $R2$. We write $R1 \prec R2$

Proposition 7. *An approximation of a representation preserves class hierarchy.*

Proposition 7 is obvious from the definition of a functor (in particular F') and proposition 8 assure us that successive approximations are homomorphic images of the initial representation. This makes sense intuitively as we wish to preserve the structure of a representation through any constructions.

Proposition 8. *Sucessive approximation from a representation preserves class hierarchy;* $R1 \prec R2 \prec R3 \Rightarrow R1 \prec R3$.

Proof. The same homomorphic property is inherited by the composition of the functors $F_1' : \mathcal{A}_{R1,0} \longrightarrow \mathcal{A}_{R2,0}$ and $F_2' : \mathcal{A}_{R2,0} \longrightarrow \mathcal{A}_{R3,0}$. □

3 Schemas, Views and Retrievals

The approximation process may be interpreted as providing an external view of the database which abstracts unnecessary details and to provide a specialized view of the specified objects.

This idea of approximation is also applicable in the organization of data. The approximation of objects into sets of objects helps to organize objects in collections with similar structure. This is a common organization in many data models (eg. relations). Such an approximation process using the α abstraction also ensures that the class hierarchy is preserved.

The notion of the α abstraction unifies the idea of organization, retrieval and views. In this way, the retrieval mechanism may be viewed conceptually and defined very consistently with the other major operations on the database. In addition, we note that all retrievals are performed such that the set of desired objects retrieved are shown to be a class in some approximation. This corresponds to relations as first class types in the Relational Data Model where views and retrievals are performed and results returned as relation tables.

3.1 Schemas

In general, a database comprises of a data schema and an instantiation in the data domain. Usually, there are also considerations of functional dependencies[LeS90]. However, we note that as we treat tuples in a relation as objects, the structuring of the objects would have taken functional dependencies into consideration. Structurally, we have a consistency criteria based on the preservation of of classes.

Definition 9. A database representation $R1$ with a data schema representation $R2$ is *Class-Type* consistent iff $R1 \prec R2$.

The data schema may be viewed as an approximation of its instantiation. The approximation of the objects of a representation into a single object in the approximated representation models the collection of objects with similar structures(relations in Relational Data Model). Classification of these instances into classes in the original representation is also preserved into the classification of its abstraction in the approximation.

This perspective of schemas helps to reconcile the seemingly different organization used in relational databases and databases using classes. Relations are nothing but equivalence classes of objects with similar structures. This is differentiated from classes as classes serve as repositories for objects with some similar value of attributes. The equivalence classes, or relations are further subject to generalization. This is obvious as the relations are nothing more than objects in the newly approximated representation. This perspective helps to clear up some confusion with regards to certain sets of objects being classes and 'relations' at the same time.

This view of the form of organization in relational databases as an approximation of the original representation leads to the proposition that a valid schema for a database is a valid approximation for any instantiation of the database. It further points to the possibility of the extension of current relational databases to have a 'meta-level' class hierarchy.

The abstraction of the schemas as homomorphisms of the original or instantiation of the database leads naturally to the idea of 'schemas of schemas'. which will then describe a hierarchy of schemas related by homomorphisms.

3.2 Retrieval

Like conventional relational databases, creation of views and retrievals are closely related. In relational databases, the result of a retrieval is a relation, in our model, the result is a valid class in an approximation of the original representation.

We have to differentiate the difference between queries as commonly known and retrievals. Retrievals within our context is to be interpreted narrowly as the retrieval of entities by the description of attributes using only a positive non-implicative fragment of propositional calculus. This notion of retrieval is meant to mirror the low level retrieval activity of a database management system. Whereas the concept of query allows more expressive power in manipulating the results of a series of retrievals.

In [KHO93] we demonstrated theoretically that with just a concept of classes and approximation, we are able to perform some form of retrieval. This is consistent with our motive for a simple model with a minimal set of operations representative of the common activities in database. However, with the extension of the notion of abstraction in this paper, we are able to streamline the retrieval mechanism in [KHO93] by considering a series of approximations than one large expensive one.

Intuitively, the idea is to find an approximation such that the desired set exists as a valid class in the approximation. To do that, we have to construct a series of approximations from the description of the retrieval.

Example 1. To give an idea of how the retrieval process works, consider a retrieval term, $t = (g \vee (a \wedge e))$ in the context of description (representation) with the class hierarchy in figure 3(i). Figure 3(ii) and 3(iii) shows the successive approximations to reach the desired representation such that the desired retrieval set exists as a class.

3.3 Views

Creation of views are important for security reasons and aids user's comprehension of a large database system. Similar to views in relational databases, views are treated very much the same way retrievals are handled. However, in this

438

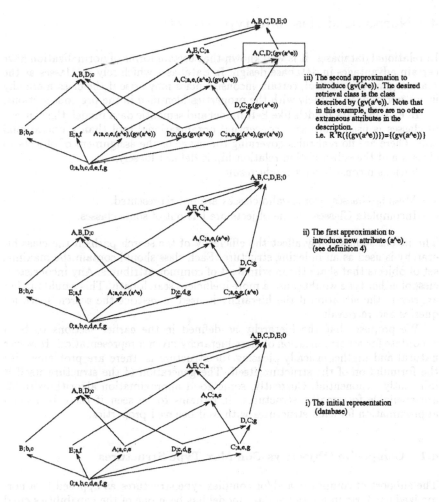

Fig. 3. Sample retrieval using approximations

case, instead of just creating one relation, we produce an approximate class hierarchy with the attributes involved. It is not difficult to see how the concept of
approximation may be immediately extended to the creation of views. Relevant
attributes are preserved in the map and aggregation of other attributes may be
performed. Restricted attributes may be aggregated into a specially designated
attribute. This attribute which is the image of the restricted attributes will be
transparent to the user or simply appear as a null attribute. The view will then
contain the coherent class hierarchy with the desired attributes instead of an
incomplete partial hierarchy.

This is advantageous as it forms a consistent hierarchy of the classes visible
to the user, making it consistent with the rest of the underlying application. It
is interesting to note that a view is a particular case of a valid user-restricted
schema.

4   Normalized class and type structures

In relational databases, it is well known that certain forms of normalization have certain advantages in database design. In databases which rely on classes as the main organizational tool, certain inconsistencies may arise if the class hierarchy is not normalized, namely with the properties identified in the previous sections.

In existing data models like E-R model and semantic data model, the concept of classes is used more as a conceptual organizational tool than a operational one. There are no real rules governing the usage or the assignment of objects to classes and the subsumption relationship is defined loosely.

Various inconsistencies might result:

- Missing Classes - some valid classes are not represented.
- Incomplete Classes - some objects are left out of some classes.

The inconsistencies may affect the efficiency of the search paths if the class hierarchy is used as an indexing structure. Each class should contain the maximal set of objects that share the maximal set of common attributes. Any inconsistencies, of either type would cause a more inefficient search path. This would further aggravate the situation if the hierarchy is used to restrict the search space for queries and retrievals.

We propose that the hierarchy as defined in the earlier sections to be a candidate for a normalization of class hierarchy given a representation. However natural and mathematically pleasing the structure is, there are problems with the formulation of the structure itself. The generation of the structure itself is inherently exponential. Currently, some good approximation algorithms[Ho82] are available for smaller structures. It remains to be seen if there is a good approximation for such structures with well behaved properties.

4.1   Composite Objects vs Complex Type Structures

The support of composite and/or complex type structures as opposed to a normalized flat form in relational data model has been one of the capabilities cited by some as desirable for an object oriented data model[ABD89].

Composite objects In certain literature [Kim90], attributes are perceived as objects and the hierarchical composition of complex objects as composition of less complex objects. This however confused the line between objects and attributes. In the extreme case, a representation of this idea would entail a reflexive composition relation in a set of objects. We can however 'flatten' this relation by designating an attribute for each object. The relation between this attribute set and the object set can be found by a transitive closure of the composition relation.

Example 2. Consider a description of a car and that of a boat which are made up of other composed objects. We assign an attribute θ' for each object θ. For the composition in figure 4, we have the associated relation r which is constructed by the transitive closure of the composition relation.

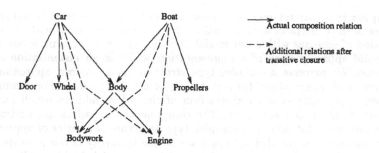

Fig. 4. The composition relation for sample objects

r	Car'	Door'	Wheel'	Body'	Bodywork'	Engine'	Boat'	Propellers'
Car	1	1	1	1	1	1	0	0
Door	0	1	0	0	0	0	0	0
Wheel	0	0	1	0	0	0	0	0
Body	0	0	0	1	1	1	0	0
Bodywork	0	0	0	0	1	0	0	0
Engine	0	0	0	0	0	1	0	0
Boat	0	0	0	1	1	1	1	1
Propellers	0	0	0	0	0	0	0	1

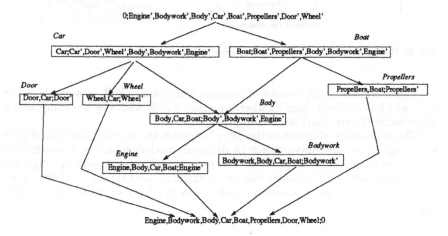

Fig. 5. Class hierarchy as derived from relation r drawn upside down.

As we can see, the class hierarchy in figure 5 derived from the representation r accurately mirrors the component hierarchy in figure 4. Thus, a consistent class hierarchy not only maintains a correct relation of subsumption of classes but also reflects the composition of complex objects (inverted). This points immediately to the automatic preservation of this composition structure when one constructs views from the representation.

Complex type structures To represent a complex structure we would require the use of the concept of approximation which is more consistent with the representation of schemas within our model. Recall that a valid schema is one which is a valid approximation of a representation which is an instantiation of the database. We perceive a complex type structure as a 'coarser' approximation as a result of 'aggregation' through typing of attribute values. For example, a complex type, address is an abstraction of the actual address which includes city, street name and area code. The components themselves are abstraction of the instances. Intuitively, a complex type structure is a series of approximation whose consecutive abstractions describe the hierarchy of components. This view is consistent with the usage of abstraction to model the idea of 'typing' in databases. This is illustrated in figure 6.

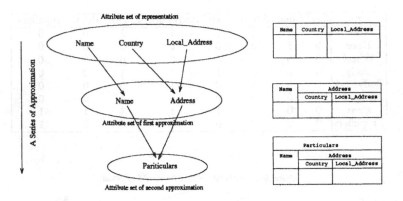

Fig. 6. Nested relations modelled as successive approximations

This is similar to the concept of complex attributes in E-R data model(figure 7(i)) which is different from another construct which describes the composition of an entity (figure 7(ii)) as in example 2.

This separation of intent in the use of complex types and composite objects lends significant expressive power to database modellers. As we move further away from the conceptual notion of 'classes as types' in programming languages towards the notion of 'classification as organization and typing as abstraction', this separation of the two notion as modelled in this framework becomes increasingly attractive.

5 Conclusion

This paper seeks to find a simple and minimal theoretical model which can represent some of the more common concepts in database. Such a description helps to abstract the ideas into precise mathematical objects and constructions free from implementation details. Although much of current object oriented database techniques emerged as a natural evolution of database technology, it is important to review and form a precise understanding of the various phenomena and investigate their inter-relationships. It is our opinion that there are several important underlying ideas which are common or applicable in nearly all the data

442

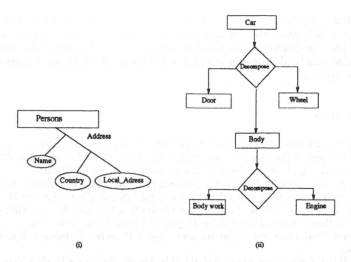

Fig. 7. Complex attribute (i), Composition of objects (ii)

models. The abstraction of these ideas help to give a guide to possible new data models and applications. For example we introduced a new notion of generalization in [KHO93] which may have application in expert systems or advanced query systems. A new class of dependency relations was also introduced which is of interest in Knowledge Mining[KOH93].

The main contribution of the paper was the introduction of the concept of approximation through α abstractions. This concept of approximation can be understood as a special relationship between two galois correspondence. An approximation 'aggregates' data items of a database into sets of data items in its approximation. This form of storage organization 'abstracts' objects (entities) into sets of objects (entity sets) by 'abstracting' attribtute values into their respective types. Complex attributes may be modelled as a series of such approximatios. This was contrasted with the use of classes as an organizational tool to generalize objects with similar attributes in a database. The notion of classes was also shown to mirror the composition hierarchy of objects. In our opinion, the collection of objects by classification and aggregation by approximation is different and is reflected as two very different mathematical constructions in our framework.

We are in the process of designing a new object-oriented data model based on some of the observations in this theoretical model. The aim of the new data model is to provide the minimal set of constructs which may be combined or used in various ways to achieve the common activities in database management. The mathematical framework as presented in this paper will lay the foundation for subsequent work in this area.

By providing a common framework whereby diverse concepts may be interpreted, and their inter-relationships studied, we hope to apply much of the matured techniques in relational data model in some ways to new data models like the object oriented data model. It may be possible ultimately to built a prototype of a data model with the characteristics of an object oriented data model on top of a conventional relational database system.

We have currently a working prototype of a system which include a class generator which generates an approximation of the structures and automating some of the constructions described in the paper. Studies have also been made on possible practical indexing structures (H-Trees) [LOL92] for a class oriented database system.

References

[ABD89] M. Atkinson, F. Bancilhon, D. DeWitt, K. Dittrich, D. Maier, S. Zdonik: The Object-Oriented Database System Manifesto, *Proc. of 1st International Conference on Deductive and Object Oriented Databases*, Kyoto, Japan (1989).

[AbH87] S. Abiteboul, R. Hull: IFO: A Formal Semantic Database Model, *ACM Transactions on Database Systems*, Vol 12, No.4, pg 525-565 (December 1987).

[BaW90] M. Barr, C. Wells: *Category for Computing Science*. Prentice Hall (1990).

[Bee89] C. Beeri: Formal Models for Object Oriented Databases, *Proc. of 1st International Conference on Deductive and Object Oriented Databases*, Kyoto, Japan (1989).

[Che76] P.P.S. Chen: The Entity-Relationship Model: Toward a Unified View of Data, *ACM Transactions on Database Systems*, Vol 1, No. 1 pg 9-336 (March 1976).

[Cod79] E.F. Codd: Extending the Database Relational Model to Capture More Meaning, *ACM Transactions on Database Systems*, Vol 4, No. 4, pg 397-434 (December 1979).

[Ho82a] Y.S. Ho: The planning process: structure of verbal description. *Environment and Planning B*, 1982, vol 9, pg 297-420.

[Kim90] Won Kim: *Introduction to Object Oriented Databases* MIT Press (1990).

[KHO93] T.W. Koh, Y.S. Ho, B. C. Ooi: *Generalization in an Object Oriented Data Model* Tech. Rep TRB8/93 DISCS National University of Singapore (1993).

[KOH93] T.W. Koh, B.C. Ooi, J.W. Han: *A Semantic Interpretation of extractable rules in Knowledge Mining* Unpublished paper (1993).

[LaS86] J. Lambek, P.J. Scott: *Introduction to higher order categorical logic*. Cambridge University Press (1986).

[LeS90] S. K. Lellahi, N. Spyratos: Towards a Categorical Data Model Supporting Structured Objects and Inheritance. *Proc. First International East/West Data Base Workshop*, Kiev, USSR, (October 1990).

[LOL92] C. C. Low, B. C. Ooi, H. J. Lu: H-trees: A Dynamic Associative Search Index for OODB. *Proc. ACM SIGMOD*, (June 1992).

[Mac71] S. Maclane: *Categories for the working Mathematician*, Springer-Verlag.

[Myl91] J. Mylopoulos: Object-Orientation and Knowledge Representation, *Proc. of the IFIP TC2/WG 2.6 Working Conference on Object-Oriented Databases: Analysis, Design & Construction*, (July 1990).

[NQZ91] R. Nassif, Y. Qiu, J. Zhu: Extending The Object-Oriented Paradigm To Support Relationships and Constraints, *Proc. of the IFIP TC2/WG 2.6 Working Conference on Object-Oriented Databases: Analysis, Design & Construction*, (July 1990).

Knowledge Base Revision Using Circumscription [*]

Li Yan Yuan and Jia-Huai You
Department of Computing Science
University of Alberta
Edmonton, Canada T6G 2H1
{yuan, you}@cs.ualberta.ca

Abstract

In this paper we present a framework of *retrospective reasoning* to deal with the belief revision problem in knowledge systems. First, a first-order knowledge base is represented by a set of formulas in a first order epistemic belief language that contains objective formulas as well as belief formulas. Secondly, we define the revision operation by applying a form of prioritized circumscription to this representation of the knowledge base.

The retrospective ability is achieved by maintaining the evolutional information of a knowledge system. We compare our approach with previously proposed methods and show this ability is important to belief revision. In particular, we show that the revision semantics defined in this way satisfies the AGM postulates that are reformulated in our belief language.

1 Introduction

A knowledge base should be updated as our perception of the world described by it changes. Revision is the most common type of updates: it adds newly acquired knowledge to the system. If the new knowledge is consistent with current beliefs, the revision is simple – just add it to the system. However, if the new knowledge is inconsistent with current beliefs, the conflict must be resolved somehow, usually by derogating some old beliefs. The question is how to choose a subset of the old beliefs as victims, and decide on a set of criteria for doing so.

Alchourron, Gardenfors, and Makinson have proposed a set of postulates, called the AGM postulates, which are based on well justified philosophical ground and provide a foundation for knowledge base revision [1]. Most proposals treat belief revision as a change operation over a set of propositional sentences (see, for example, [13, 7]), where both the representation and the semantics of knowledge systems are defined by the same set of logic sentences. It

---

[*]This research is partially supported by the NSERC grants OGP42193 and OGP9225.

has been noticed that this approach, though provides a unified point of view on knowledge systems, lacks retrospective power[1], the main reason for its not being able to satisfy the AGM postulates.

Alchourron et al. proposed the *partial meet* revision semantics which satisfies the AGM postulates. The idea is to take the intersection of all possible candidate theories that reflect minimal changes. This semantics is not considered very realistic since by taking the intersection of all such theories, useful information may be lost and in many cases the resulting theory is simply the empty one. A more realistic semantics has been suggested by Fagin, Ullman, and Vardi [3] (henceforth the FUV semantics), which takes the disjunction of all such candidate theories. As indicated in [7], the FUV semantics is syntax dependent and therefore fails to satisfy the AGM postulates.

The revision problem over a theory in its syntactic form other than its closure is discussed by Nebel [13], where it is called *base revision*. Nebel discovered that base revision with epistemic relevance does not satisfy all of the AGM postulates and identified the cases where they are satisfied.

Belief revision in its essence is a meta level concept and operation. Therefore, it is natural to use some type of meta language to describe change operations. Recently, semantics for belief revision have been formulated in terms of some type of modal systems [2, 4]. In these approaches, reasoning about changes in ones beliefs reduces to model checking of certain meta level sentences. Both approaches in [2, 4] have been proved to satisfy all of the AGM postulates.

In this paper, we propose a new framework to deal with the belief revision problem in knowledge bases. In this framework, a knowledge base is represented by a set of formulas in a belief language that contains objective as well as belief propositions. The revision operation is defined by applying a form of circumscription to the representation of the knowledge base. Since circumscription formulas do not eliminate any sentences from knowledge bases, our approach possesses full retrospective power, that is, all previous revisions are kept in the system. It is this retrospective ability that enables us to demonstrate that all of the AGM postulates, if reformulated in our framework, can be satisfied.

There are two basic premises on which our approach is based. First, like Nebel [13], revision in our framework is carried out over theories in their syntactic form other than their closure, i.e., deductively closed set. We argue that the notion of deductively closed set does not provide an appropriate framework for knowledge base revision.

Secondly, we will consider knowledge bases with an *arbitrary* binary relation, augmented by transitivity, over the set of all sentences in the underlying language. Such a binary relation will be called a *priority relation* in this paper; this is due to the common realization by the researchers in the field that knowledge revision must respect the epistemic importance in a knowledge base. As shown in [5, 13, 3], the AGM postulates can be satisfied by some revision semantics if the priority relation representing the epistemic importance satisfies certain

---

[1] By retrospective power we mean the capability of revising one's beliefs according to the evolution process of the concerned knowledge system.

conditions. These conditions actually express special cases of partial ordering. Thus the assumption of priority relation makes our approach more general.

Although our approach also relies on the concept of meta level objects, which we have called belief propositions, it is quite different from the work in [2, 4] in that our formulation of revision semantics is not semantically based on or dependent upon any modal logic. As a matter of fact, our approach can be formulated entirely in a conventional first order language. This is because a belief proposition $\mathcal{L}\phi$ in our epistemic belief language is treated as a *named* object, not as applying some modal operator $\mathcal{L}$ to ϕ, and thus can be viewed as, or simply replaced by, a *distinct* objective proposition. Thus, the problem of belief revision in our approach reduces to the problem of reasoning with minimal models. An advantage of this is that revision operations can be realized directly on top of a circumscription algorithm (see, for example, [14]).[2] That our approach does not depend on any modal logic, plus the fact that our approach is based on circumscription of first order theories, permits us to define our revision operation for first order theories rather than propositional theories. This is another significant difference with all the other revision semantics in the literature.

The paper is organized as follows. In the next section we will carefully define and explain the belief language used in this paper; we will use an example to illustrate this language as well as the main idea in our approach. Since the original definition of prioritized circumscription is defined only for complete preordering, in Section 3 we present an extension of prioritized circumscription that can perform minimization according to a partial ordering. In Section 4 we introduce our new framework for knowledge base revision. A revision operation is defined in Section 5. Section 6 shows that our approach satisfies the reformulated AGM postulates. The last section uses examples to demonstrate relationships between our proposal and other approaches.

2 The Belief Language

In this paper we assume a first order *belief* language L, which is a usual first order language that contains a set of objective predicate symbols and a set of belief predicate symbols. A usual first order formula is referred to as an *objective formula*. In the language of autoepistemic logic [11], belief formulas are of the form $\mathcal{L}\phi$ where ϕ is a formula and $\mathcal{L}$ is a special symbol in the alphabet of the language. For the purpose of this paper, we only need belief predicates. The name of an n-nary belief predicate consists of two parts: a normal predicate symbol and a prefix $\mathcal{L}$, such as $\mathcal{L}p(x_1, ..., x_n)$, where $\mathcal{L}p$ stands for a single predicate name. A belief predicate name, such as $\mathcal{L}p$, can technically be replaced by a *distinct* (or *reserved*) predicate symbol, and as such, whether the language contains the special symbol $\mathcal{L}$ or not is technically insignificant. The language can be equally defined as a purely first order language with some distinct predicate symbols. For this reason, in the rest of paper we will not use

---

[2]However, this is by no means to imply that circumscription is an easy problem.

the usual belief symbol $\mathcal{L}$ but Greek letters such as α, β, and γ to denote belief predicates or belief propositions (i.e., 0-ary belief predicates). We will consider in this paper first order theories that consist of sentences with universally quantified variables. We often omit these quantifiers in sentences with the understanding that all free variables therein are universally quantified.

To illustrate the main idea in our approach, let us consider the following example.

Example 2.1 Consider a knowledge base expressed by the following set of formulas

$$K = \{bird,\ fly \leftarrow bird\}.$$

Should we later observe $\neg fly$, we need to revise our knowledge base K by the newly acquired knowledge $\neg fly$. Simply adding $\neg fly$ to K would result in an inconsistent set K':

$$K' = \{bird,\ fly \leftarrow bird,\ \neg fly\}.$$

To resolve inconsistency, one can remove a minimal amount of sentences so that the remaining sentences are consistent. These type of subsets have been called *maximum consistent subsets* in the literature. For K' above we obtain two maximum consistent subsets that contain $\neg fly$:

$$\Delta_1 = \{bird,\ \neg fly\}$$
$$\Delta_2 = \{fly \leftarrow bird,\ \neg fly\}.$$

By the FVU method, the revision semantics is then defined by taking the disjunction of all such candidate theories.

In our approach, each sentence ϕ in a knowledge base is represented by a formula $\phi \leftarrow \alpha(x_1, ..., x_{\hat{n}})$ where x_i occurs in ϕ and α is a distinct belief predicate intuitively meaning ϕ is believed. As usual, all the variables in the formula are universally quantified. Further, if no variables occur in ϕ then α is simply a belief proposition. The revised system of the above is then represented by the following set of sentences:

$$T_{K'} = \{bird \leftarrow \alpha,\ (fly \leftarrow bird) \leftarrow \beta,\ \neg fly \leftarrow \gamma\}.$$

Note that although K' is inconsistent its belief representation $T_{K'}$ is consistent.

Then the semantics of the system can be defined by applying circumscription to *maximize* the belief propositions (i.e., minimize the negations of the belief propositions) with γ having higher priority to be maximized, which yields

$$T_{K'} \wedge \gamma \wedge (\alpha \vee \beta) \wedge (\neg \alpha \vee \neg \beta).$$

Note that this expression implies $\neg fly$ and either $bird$ or $(fly \leftarrow bird)$ but not both at the same time. $\square$

For the above example, the method defined in terms of maximizing beliefs is essentially the same as that of taking the disjunction of all candidate theories

[3], as far as logical consequences of objective formulas are concerned. However, there is a key difference. Note, for the above example, that in our approach the semantics of a knowledge base and its revised version are determined the result of circumscription. The fact that circumscription *does not eliminate* any sentences from the belief representation of a theory gives us an opportunity to maintain the entire evolutional process of such a knowledge base. We will show it is this retrospective ability that differentiates our approach with all the others, and it is this ability that makes our approach a semantically faithful one to the AGM postulates.

3 Priority Circumscription Based on Partial Ordering

McCarthy introduced *circumscription* to express the idea that the extension of abnormal predicates should be minimized [9, 10]. Let $A(P, Z)$ be a first order theory, where P and Z are disjoint sets of predicates in A, and M and N be two models of A. Then we say N is (P, Z)-smaller than M if both models have the same extension over all predicates other than P and Z, but the extension of the predicates from P in N is a proper subset of that in M; and we say N is (P, Z)-minimal if no model of A is (P, Z)-smaller than N. Then $CIR(A; P; Z)$, the circumscription of A on P with variable Z, denotes a second order formula whose models are all (P, Z)-minimal models of A. Furthermore, prioritized circumscription $CIR(A; P^1 \succ \cdots \succ P^n; Z)$, where the P^i's form a partition of P, is used to represent the idea that the extension of predicates from P^1 should have higher priority to be minimized than that of P^2 and the extension of predicates from P^2 have higher priority than that of P^3, etc.

As we mentioned earlier, our approach is based on maximizing belief propositions. The mechanism is called *maximizing circumscription*. This notion can be precisely defined.

Let $A(P)$ be a theory in a belief language, where P is the set of belief predicates whose extension is to be maximized. Then the *maximizing circumscription* of A on P, denoted as $MCIR(A; P)$, is defined as

$$MCIR(A; P) \equiv A(P) \wedge \neg \exists \mathcal{P}(A(\mathcal{P}) \wedge (\mathcal{P} > P))$$

where $\mathcal{P} > P$ means the extension of P is a proper subset of that of P. Maximizing circumscription can also be formalized in terms of circumscription on the negations of those predicates. For convenience, we may use $CIR(A; \neg P)$ to denote $MCIR(A; P)$, and $MCIR(A; \neg P)$ to denote $CIR(A; P)$. The priority version of maximizing circumscription $MCIR(A; P_1 \succ \cdots \succ P_n; Z)$ is similarly defined.

Lifschitz has shown that prioritized circumscription can be represented by parallel circumscription [8], that is, given a first order theory A and disjoint sets

$P^1, ..., P^n, Z$ of predicate symbols,

$$CIR(A; P^1 \succ ... \succ P^n; Z) = \bigwedge_{i=1}^{n} CIR(A; P^i; P^{i+1}, ..., P^n, Z).$$

The priority relation in the priority circumscription above is a linear, total relation amongst all predicate blocks of P^i's. In real applications, however, many priority relations are partial ordering, not total ordering, and prioritized circumscription cannot directly be used to express such minimization based on partial ordering. An extension of prioritized circumscription into partial ordering is given below.

Let P be a set of predicates, and $\preceq$ be a binary relation amongst P, augmented by obvious transitive closure. The binary relation is used to represent the priority relation amongst P, that is, $a \preceq b$ implies that b has at least as high priority as a to be minimized, and when $a \preceq b$ and $b \not\preceq a$ then b is considered having higher priority than a to be minimized. A partition $\{P^1, ..., P^n\}$ of P is $\preceq$-compatible if it is defined by the equivalence relation that $a \equiv b$ if and only if $a \preceq b$ and $b \preceq a$, that is, $\{a, b\} \subseteq P^i$, for some i, if and only if $a \preceq b$ and $b \preceq a$. Obviously, for any given relation $\preceq$, its $\preceq$-compatible partition is unique. Furthermore, for each P^i, we define $LOW(P^i)$ as the set of all predicates in P that have lower priority than any predicate in P^i to be minimized according to $\preceq$; that is, $LOW(P^i) = \{p \mid p \prec a \text{ for some } a \in P^i\}$. Now, we define

Definition 3.1 Let $A(P, Z)$ be a theory, where P and Z are disjoint sets of predicates in A, $\preceq$ be a priority relation defined over P, and $\{P^1, ..., P^n\}$ be a $\preceq$-compatible partition. Then the $\preceq$-based prioritized circumscription is defined as

$$CIR(A(P, Z); P|\preceq; Z) = \bigwedge_{i=1}^{n} CIR(A(P, Z); P^i; (LOW(P^i) \cup Z)).$$

$MCIR(A(P, Z); P|\preceq; Z)$ is defined similarly. □

Priority circumscription $CIR(A; P^1 \succ ... \succ P^n; Z)$ is just a special case of $\preceq$-based circumscription when $\preceq$ is a linear order on $\{P^1, ..., P^n\}$.

4 Representation and Semantics of Knowledge Systems

In this section, we present a new framework to represent knowledge systems and define their semantics.

In most proposals, a knowledge system is represented by a logically closed set which is also the set of all theorems in the system. Thus if the logically closed set is inconsistent, to avoid inconsistency of the system, some sentences in the set must be eliminated, which inevitably throw out some useful information.

In our proposal, we use a finite set of sentences to represent a knowledge system and we never eliminate any sentences from the set.

A *knowledge set* is a finite set of first order sentences which may or may not be consistent, together with a priority relation (i.e., an arbitrary binary relation, closed under transitivity) over all sentences of the underlying language.[3]

Let $K(P)$ be a knowledge set with priority relation $\preceq$, where P is the set of all objective predicates in language L. Then K can be represented as follows: For each sentence t in K, a belief predicate $\pi_t(x_1, ..., x_n)$ is introduced, where π_t is a distinct *new* predicate symbol not in P, and $x_1, ..., x_n$ are universally quantified variables occurring in t. Let B be the set of all such belief predicates. Then $T_K(P, B)$, called the *belief theory* of $K(P)$, is defined as

$$T_K(P, B) = \{t \leftarrow \pi_t(x_1, ..., x_n) \mid t \in K \text{ and } x_i \text{ occurs in } t, 1 \leq i \leq n\},$$

with the priority relation $\preceq$ carried over to B, i.e., $\alpha_1 \preceq \alpha_2$ iff t_1 and t_2 are in K such that $t_1 \preceq t_2$, and $t_1 \leftarrow \alpha_1$ and $t_2 \leftarrow \alpha_2$ are in T_K. For simplicity, we will denote $T_K(P, B)$ simply by $\{t \leftarrow \pi_t \mid t \in K\}$. Thus, π_t may represent, depending on the context, a belief predicate symbol in B, or a belief predicate with variables in a sentence.

Example 4.1 Consider

$$K = \{a, \ b \leftarrow a, \ \neg b\}$$

with the priority relation

$$\preceq = \{\{a\} \preceq \{b \leftarrow a\}, \{b \leftarrow a\} \preceq \{\neg b\}\}.$$

Then

$$T_K(P, B) = \{a \leftarrow \alpha, \ b \leftarrow a \wedge \beta, \ \neg b \leftarrow \gamma\},$$

where $B = \{\alpha, \beta, \gamma\}$ and $\preceq = \{\alpha \preceq \beta \preceq \gamma\}$. Note that $b \leftarrow a \wedge \beta \equiv (b \leftarrow a) \leftarrow \beta$.
□

Example 4.2 Let

$$K = \{bird(penguin), \ fly(x) \leftarrow bird(x), \ \neg fly(x) \leftarrow x = penguin\}$$

be a knowledge set with the following priority relation:

$$bird(penguin) \preceq (\neg fly(x) \leftarrow x = penguin)$$
$$(fly(x) \leftarrow bird(x)) \preceq (\neg fly(x) \leftarrow x = penguin)$$

Then $T_K(P, B)$ contains

$$bird(penguin) \leftarrow \alpha$$
$$(fly(x) \leftarrow bird(x)) \leftarrow \beta(x)$$
$$(\neg fly(x) \leftarrow x = penguin) \leftarrow \gamma(x)$$

where $B = \{\alpha, \beta(x), \gamma(x)\}$ and $\preceq = \{\alpha \preceq \gamma(x), \ \beta(x) \preceq \gamma(x)\}$.   □

---

[3]Note that the question of what priority relations are useful, or even meaningful, is not the focus of this paper (but see [5]).

Definition 4.1 Let K be a knowledge set with priority relation $\preceq$, and $T_K(P, B)$ be the corresponding belief theory. Then the semantic closure of K, denoted as $F_{sem}(K, \preceq)$, or $F_{sem}(K)$ if $\preceq$ is understood, is defined by

$$MCIR(T_K(P, B); B| \preceq; P).$$

An objective formula ϕ is true in a knowledge system K if and only if $F_{sem}(K)$ logically implies ϕ. □

Example 4.3 Consider, for example, the K and $T_K(P, B)$ in Example 4.1. We then have

$$F_{sem}(K) = MCIR(T(P, B); B| \preceq; P) \equiv T_K \wedge \gamma \wedge \beta,$$

which implies $\neg b$ and $(a \leftarrow b)$. Note that to maintain consistency, either a or $(a \leftarrow b)$ may be removed. However, according to the priority relation a should be removed since it has lower priority to survive.

For the K and $T_K(P, B)$ in Example 4.2, we have

$$F_{sem}(K) = MCIR(T(P, B); B| \preceq; P) \equiv$$

$$T_K \wedge \forall x \gamma(x) \wedge \forall x(x \neq penguin \rightarrow \beta(x)) \wedge (\alpha \leftrightarrow \neg \beta(penguin))$$

The formula $\forall x \gamma(x)$ holds because the belief predicate γ is maximized with the highest priority. The belief predicates β and α are unrelated in the priority relation. Conflict arises only when both $\beta(penguin)$ and α attempt to hold true. That is, the maximal extension of $\beta(x)$ includes any $\beta(t)$ where t is not $penguin$. This results in $\forall x(x \neq penguin \rightarrow \beta(x))$. When x is $penguin$, either $\beta(penguin)$ or α, but not both, holds true. This is expressed by $(\alpha \vee \beta(penguin)) \wedge (\neg \alpha \vee \neg \beta(penguin))$. □

We thus have established a framework for knowledge revision, a knowledge system is represented by its belief theory, and the semantics of the system is determined by its "belief semantics" of maximizing the belief predicates. Therefore, all query evaluations toward the knowledge system should be directed to the belief semantics. However, there are two possible ways to view revision operations.

Suppose K is the given knowledge base with a priority relation $\preceq$. Consider the revision requests $\phi_1, ..., \phi_n$ in that order. With each revision request, the priority relation is enhanced so that the most current one always has the highest priority to survive. For the above revision sequence, let us denote the corresponding priority relations as $\preceq_1, ..., \preceq_n$.

In the first view, F_{sem} is taken purely as an operator, repeatedly applying to a knowledge set. In this view, a knowledge system's evolution with the above revision requests, given K and $\preceq$, can be described as the following sequence of the knowledge systems:

$$K_0 = F_{sem}(K, \preceq)$$
$$K_1 = F_{sem}(K_0 \cup \{\phi_1\}, \preceq_1)$$
$$K_2 = F_{sem}(K_1 \cup \{\phi_2\}, \preceq_2)$$
$$......$$
$$K_n = F_{sem}(K_{n-1} \cup \{\phi_n\}, \preceq_n)$$

Note that in this view, the knowledge system and its semantics are uniformly presented to the user of the system.

In the second view, F_{sem} is treated as a mapping from an underlying physical system to a semantically meaningful knowledge system on which user's queries are evaluated against. More precisely, for each revision request ϕ_i, we simply add ϕ_i to the previous knowledge set. The underlying system contains a set of sentences, which may or may not be consistent; it is the mapping F_{sem} that interprets the system and provides the semantics. This can be described as the sequence:

$$K_0 = F_{sem}(K, \preceq)$$
$$K_1 = F_{sem}(K \cup \{\phi_1\}, \preceq_1)$$
$$K_2 = F_{sem}(K \cup \{\phi_1, \phi_2\}, \preceq_2)$$
$$......$$
$$K_n = F_{sem}(K \cup \{\phi_1, ..., \phi_n\}, \preceq_n)$$

The second view is not only simpler but more intuitive. More importantly, a revision in this framework is simply an addition. We will adopt the second view in describing our revision semantics in the rest of this paper.

5 Revision Semantics

In this section, we define our revision semantics for knowledge sets.

Definition 5.1 Let K be a knowledge set with priority relation $\preceq$, and μ be a new sentence. Then the new knowledge set by revising K with μ is represented by $K \hat{+} \mu = K \cup \{\mu\}$, together with a revised priority relation $\preceq' = \preceq \cup \{\mu \succeq t \mid t \in K\}$. Furthermore, the semantics of K revised by μ is defined as $F_{sem}(K \hat{+} \mu, \preceq')$. □

The revision of a knowledge set, now, is as simple as an addition, as shown below.

Lemma 5.1 Let K be a knowledge set with priority relation $\preceq$, T_K be the belief theory for K, and μ be a sentence. Then we have

$$F_{sem}(K \hat{+} \mu) \equiv F_{sem}(K \cup \{\mu\}, \preceq) \wedge \mu \equiv MCIR(T_K \wedge \mu; B| \preceq; P). \quad □$$

The proof of the lemma can be found in [16]

Note that, in Definition 5.1, the new priority relation $\preceq'$ means the new sentence μ has the highest priority amongst all sentences in K in the revised knowledge system. This treatment is not necessary at all, and the status of a new sentence can be determined on per application.

6 Relationships with the AGM postulates

First, we present the AGM postulates. In the framework of AGM, revision is an operation over deductively closed sets in the language of propositional logic [1]. Given a theory Γ, the deductively closed set of Γ is defined as the closure $\{\phi \mid \Gamma \vdash \phi\}$.

Let K be a deductively closed set, μ and ν be consistent sentences. The revision of K by μ, denoted as $K\hat{+}\mu$, represents a new knowledge system obtained from K by adding new knowledge represented in μ. Then the AGM postulates for revision are as follows:

(P1) $K\hat{+}\mu$ is a deductively closed set;

(P2) $K\hat{+}\mu \models \mu$;

(P3) $K \wedge \mu \models K\hat{+}\mu$;

(P4) $K\hat{+}\mu \models K \wedge \mu$ if $K \wedge \mu$ is consistent;

(P5) $K\hat{+}\mu$ is consistent;

(P6) $\models (K\hat{+}\mu \equiv K\hat{+}\nu)$ if $\models (\mu \equiv \nu)$;

(P7) $(K\hat{+}\mu) \wedge \nu \models K\hat{+}(\mu \wedge \nu)$;

(P8) $K\hat{+}(\mu \wedge \nu) \models (K\hat{+}\mu) \wedge \nu$ if $(K\hat{+}\mu) \wedge \nu$ is consistent.

The first postulate states that the revision of a deductively closed set must result in a deductively closed set. The second states that the new knowledge must be contained in the revision. P3 implies that the revision must be contained in the range of the simple union of old and new knowledge. The fourth together with the third gives the idea that the revision is done by simply adding μ to K if K is consistent with μ. P5 requires that the revision be consistent. The sixth specifies the principle of irrelevance of syntax. The seventh, similar to P3, states that the revision of K by $\mu \wedge \nu$ must be subsumed by $K\hat{+}\mu$ augmented by ν. The last one, together with P7, states that if $K\hat{+}\mu$ is consistent with ν, then $(K\hat{+}\mu) \wedge \nu$ is equivalent to $K\hat{+}(\mu \wedge \nu)$.

Because of different frameworks used in the AGM and our approach, we need to reformulate the AGM postulates to suit our new framework. We will denote the revision of K by μ under the F_{sem} semantics as $F_{sem}(K\hat{+}\mu)$, i.e., $F_{sem}(K\hat{+}\mu) = F_{sem}(K \cup \{\mu\})$.

Definition 6.1 Let K be a knowledge set, μ and ν be consistent sentences, and $K\hat{+}\mu$ represent K revised by μ. Then

(R1) $K\hat{+}\mu$ is a knowledge set;

(R2) $F_{sem}(K\hat{+}\mu) \models \mu$;

(R3) $F_{sem}(K) \wedge \mu \models F_{sem}(K\hat{+}\mu)$;

(R4) $F_{sem}(K\hat{+}\mu) \models F_{sem}(K) \wedge \mu$ if $K \wedge \mu$ is consistent;

(R5) $F_{sem}(K\hat{+}\mu)$ is consistent;

(R6) $F_{sem}(K\hat{+}\mu) \equiv F_{sem}(K\hat{+}\nu)$ if $\mu \equiv \nu$;

(R7) $F_{sem}(K\hat{+}\mu) \wedge \nu \models F_{sem}(K\hat{+}(\mu \wedge \nu))$;

(R8) $F_{sem}(K\hat{+}(\mu \wedge \nu)) \equiv F_{sem}((K\hat{+}\mu)\hat{+}\nu)$ if $\mu \wedge \nu$ is consistent.   □

The modification to the AGM postulates is minimum, possibly except R8, in that the postulates are revised only to suit our new framework, and the underlying meanings are not affected. This can be seen from the fact that the revised postulates are exactly the same as the original AGM postulates if both K and $F_{sem}(K)$ are defined as the same deductively closed set of sentences.

In the ideal situations, independence of revision orders is required. That is, K revised with μ first and then ν should be the same as K revised with ν first and then μ, i.e.,

$$(K\hat{+}\mu)\hat{+}\nu \equiv (K\hat{+}\nu)\hat{+}\mu,$$

as long as μ and ν can peacefully live together. The eighth AGM postulate expresses a weaker desire for such independence. Despite the fact that it is weaker than desired, P8 is the main obstacle for many revision semantics to satisfy the AGM postulates [7, 15]. On the other hand, the revised, i.e. R8, implies that

$$F_{sem}((K\hat{+}\mu)\hat{+}\nu) \equiv F_{sem}((K\hat{+}\nu)\hat{+}\mu)$$

that is, a total independence of revision orders. From such a point of view, R8 is stronger than P8.

However, there may be different interpretations of the AGM postulates. If P8 is interpreted as

(P8′) $F_{sem}(K\hat{+}(\mu \wedge \nu)) \models F_{sem}(K\hat{+}\mu) \wedge \nu$ if $F_{sem}(K\hat{+}\mu) \wedge \nu$ is consistent,

then R8 is weaker than P8 since P8′ implies R8 but not vice versa. We doubt the legitimacy of such an interpretation. Otherwise, it is not difficult to show that no reasonable revision semantics satisfies the postulate, other than either throwing out all old conflicting beliefs or imposing a linear ordering on all beliefs [3, 1].

The following theorem shows that our revision semantics satisfies the revised AGM postulates. The proof is rather straightforward and thus is omitted here.

Theorem 6.1 The revision semantics defined in Definition 5.2 satisfies the revised AGM postulates.

Example 6.1 The following example how our approach satisfies the revised postulates.

$$K = \{a, \ a \leftarrow b \wedge c, \ b, \ c, \ c \leftarrow d, \ d\},$$

with the priority relation $\preceq$:

$$(b) \preceq (a \leftarrow b \wedge c)$$
$$(c) \preceq (a \leftarrow b \wedge c)$$
$$(d) \preceq (c \leftarrow d) \preceq (a \leftarrow b \wedge c)$$

Let $\mu = \{\neg a\}$ and $\nu = \{\neg d\}$ be the new sentences to be added.

Then K is represented by its belief theory

$$T_K(P, B) = \{a \leftarrow \alpha_1, \ a \leftarrow b \wedge c \wedge \alpha_2, \ b \leftarrow \alpha_3, \ c \leftarrow \alpha_4, \ c \leftarrow d \wedge \alpha_5, \ d \leftarrow \alpha_6\}$$

where

$$P = \{a, b, c, d\}$$
$$B = \{\alpha_1, \alpha_2, \alpha_3, \alpha_4, \alpha_5, \alpha_6, \alpha_7, \alpha_8, \alpha_9\}$$
$$\preceq = \{\alpha_2 \preceq \alpha_3, \ \alpha_2 \preceq \alpha_4, \ \alpha_2 \preceq \alpha_5, \ \alpha_5 \preceq \alpha_6\}.$$

Now let

$$T_{K_\mu} = T_K \cup \{\mu \leftarrow \alpha_7\}$$
$$T_{K_{\mu+\nu}} = T_K \cup \{\mu \leftarrow \alpha_7, \ \nu \leftarrow \alpha_8\}$$
$$T_{K_{(\mu \wedge \nu)}} = T_K \cup \{(\mu \wedge \nu) \leftarrow \alpha_9\}$$
$$\preceq' = \preceq \cup \{\alpha_i \preceq \alpha_j \mid (1 \le i \le 6) \wedge (j = 7, 8, 9)\} \cup \{\alpha_7 \preceq \alpha_8\}.$$

Then we have

$$F_{sem}(K \hat{+} \mu) = MCIR(T_{K_\mu}(P, B); B| \preceq'; P)$$
$$F_{sem}((K \hat{+} \mu) \hat{+} \nu) = MCIR(T_{K_{\mu+\nu}}(P, B); B| \preceq'; P)$$
$$F_{sem}(K \hat{+} (\mu \wedge \nu)) = MCIR(T_{K_{(\mu \wedge \nu)}}(P, B); B| \preceq'; P)$$

It is easy to show that

$$F_{sem}((K \hat{+} \mu) \hat{+} \nu) \equiv F_{sem}(K \hat{+} (\mu \wedge \nu))$$
$$F_{sem}(K \hat{+} \mu) \models \{\neg a, \ a \leftarrow b \wedge c, \ c \leftarrow d, \ b \vee c, \ b \vee d\}, \text{ and}$$
$$F_{sem}((K \hat{+} \mu) \hat{+} \nu) \models \{\neg a, \ \neg d, \ a \leftarrow b \wedge c, \ c \leftarrow d, \ b \vee c\}$$

□

7 Comparisons

In this section, we briefly compare our approach with some other proposals.

First and foremost, to the best of our knowledge, our approach is the only one that keeps all sentences in the knowledge base, and therefore provides a capacity of reversing previous revisions if necessary.

Example 7.1 Consider a knowledge system K_0 represented by a base set $B = \{a, b\}$. Suppose we first revised the system with $\neg(a \vee b)$ and obtained a new system K_1. Further assume that later we found out that the previous revision was based on a misleading observation. This appears to be a very difficult task, and sometimes impossible. For example, if we had chosen a selected group of maximum consistent sets, by taking the disjunction we simple cannot recover the original knowledge base[4].

---

[4] The problem becomes even more troublesome in the situation where the discovery of the wrong observation happened at the time after a long sequence of revisions had been performed already.

In our approach, the correction can be done simply by adding $a \lor b$ into K_1 to obtain K_2, which will contain both a and b. This approach cannot be adopted for almost all the other proposals, including those in [3, 5, 12], since it would give $K_2 = Cn(a \lor b)$, in which both a and b are lost. □

The following example, which have been used in Example 6.1, shows the difference between our approach and the FUV method [3] and the like, which are based on taking the disjunction of all or selected maximum consistent theories. Note that the FUV method does not satisfy the AGM postulates.

Example 7.2 Consider the following knowledge set:

$$K = \{a,\ a \leftarrow b \land c,\ b,\ c,\ c \leftarrow d,\ d\}.$$

Assume the following priority relation $\preceq$:

$$(b) \preceq (a \leftarrow b \land c)$$
$$(c) \preceq (a \leftarrow b \land c)$$
$$(d) \preceq (c \leftarrow d) \preceq (a \leftarrow b \land c)$$

and $\mu = \{\neg a\}$ and $\nu = \{\neg d\}$ are new sentences to be added.

Suppose we revise K by μ. Since $K \cup \{\neg a\}$ is inconsistent, we need to obtain maximum consistent subsets of $K \cup \{\neg a\}$; i.e., the consistent subsets of $K \cup \{\neg a\}$ with a minimal number of sentences removed and with less important sentence(s) removed first. Since $\{\neg a\}$ is the most recent knowledge, it should be included in any maximum consistent subset. Now $(a \leftarrow b \land c)$ has the next highest priority to be retained. Then, retaining both b and c would result in inconsistency, and thus, because b and c are not related by $\preceq$, either b or c but not both can be retained. This gives two ways of removing minimal amount of sentences. Should b be retained, either d or $(c \leftarrow d)$ should be removed to maintain consistency. This results in d being removed since $(c \leftarrow d)$ has the higher priority to be retained. We thus get two maximal consistent subsets under the priority relation given above:

$$\Gamma_1 = \{\neg a,\ a \leftarrow b \land c,\ b,\ c \leftarrow d\}$$
$$\Gamma_2 = \{\neg a,\ a \leftarrow b \land c,\ c,\ c \leftarrow d,\ d\}$$

By the FUV method, we get the disjunction of the above two subsets, i.e.,

$$K \hat{+} \mu = \{\neg a,\ a \leftarrow b \land c,\ c \leftarrow d,\ b \lor c,\ b \lor d\}.$$

Thus

$$(K \hat{+} \mu) \land \nu = \{\neg a,\ \neg d,\ a \leftarrow b \land c,\ c \leftarrow d,\ b\}.$$

On the other hand, by a similar process, K revised by $(\mu \land \nu)$ also has two maximum consistent subsets:

$$\Delta_1 = \{\neg a,\ \neg d,\ a \leftarrow b \land c,\ b,\ c \leftarrow d\}$$
$$\Delta_2 = \{\neg a,\ \neg d,\ a \leftarrow b \land c,\ c,\ c \leftarrow d\}.$$

Taking the disjunction, we get

$$K \hat{+} (\mu \wedge \nu) = \{\neg a, \neg d, a \leftarrow b \wedge c, c \leftarrow d, b \vee c\}.$$

Now we have $K\hat{+}(\mu \wedge \nu) \not\models (K\hat{+}\mu) \wedge \nu$, violating postulate P8. $\square$

8 Final Remarks

The main goal that this paper has achieved is to define a framework for first order belief revision systems that gives an agent retrospective power to monitor knowledge evolution. The semantics we propose in this paper is based on a form of circumscription, which we have called *maximizing circumscription*. The most important features of this semantics we believe are that (1) the evolution process of knowledge systems can be utilized in belief revision, (2) a revision operation under this semantics is a simple addition of the new knowledge to the underlying knowledge system, and (3) it deals with belief revision of first order knowledge systems.

References

[1] C. Alchourron, A. Gardenfors, and D. Makinson. On the logic of theory change: Partial meet contradiction and revision functions. *The Journal of Symbolic Logic*, 50:510–531, 1985.

[2] C. Boutilier A logic for revision and subjunctive queries. In *Proc. AAAI-92*, 609-615, 1992.

[3] R. Fagin, J. Ullman, and M. Vardi. On the semantics of updates in databases. In *Proceedings of the 2nd ACM PODS*, pages 352–365, 1983.

[4] G. Grahne, A. Mendelzon, and R. Reiter On the semantics of belief revision systems. In *Proceedings of TARK'92*, pages 132–142, 1992.

[5] A. Gardenfors and D. Makinson. Revision of knowledge systems using epistemic entrenchment. In *Proceedings of the 2nd Workshop on Theoretical Aspects of Reasoning about Knowledge*. Morgan Kaufmann, 1988.

[6] Hadley, Fagin, and Halpern. On logical omniscience: A critique with an alternative. In *Proceedings of the 6th Canadian Conf. on AI*, pages 49–56, 1986.

[7] H. Katsuno and A.O. Mendelzon. Propositional knowledge base revision and minimal change. *Artificial Intelligence*, 52:263 – 294, 1991.

[8] V. Lifschitz. Computing circumscription. In *Proceedings of the 9th Int. Joint Conference on AI*, 1986.

[9] J. McCarthy. Circumscription – a form of non-monotonic reasoning. *AI*, 13:27–39, 1980.

[10] J. McCarthy. Applications of circumscription to formalizing common sense knowledge. *AI*, 28:89–116, 1986.

[11] R.C. Moore. Semantic considerations on non-monotonic logic. *AI*, 25:75–94, 1985.

[12] B. Nebel. A knowledge level analysis of belief revision. *KR'89*, pages 301–311, 1989.

[13] B. Nebel. Belief revision and default reasoning: Syntax-based approaches. *KR'91*, pages 417–428, 1991.

[14] T. Przymusinski. An Algorithm to Compute Circumscription. In *Artificial Intelligence*, vol 38, pages 47-73, 1989.

[15] L. Willard and L. Yuan. The revised gardenfors postulates and update semantics. In *Proceedings of 1990 International Conference on Database Theory*, pages 409 – 421, 1990.

[16] L.Y. Yuan and J.H. You. Semantics of First Order Belief Revision Based on Circumscription. Technical Report TR92-17, Department of Computing Science, University of Alberta, 1992.

Versioning of Objects in Deductive Databases

F. Nihan Kesim   Marek Sergot

Department of Computing, Imperial College
London, SW7 2BZ

Abstract. The object-based event calculus is a modified version of the event calculus which is a general approach to the treatment of time and change in a logic programming framework. We present here the use of the object-based event calculus in describing versioning of objects. We begin by describing the maintenance of a historical object database by the use of event descriptions. We then present the extensions that are necessary to support different kinds of versioning. The aim is to provide a framework where complex changes to objects can be performed in a descriptive way.

1   Introduction

A great number of attempts have been made to combine the deductive approach and the object-oriented approach in databases. Existing work can be largely divided into three categories, depending on whether the semantics of complex objects is viewed as a single tuple in a higher-order relation [1, 11, 23, 25], as a collection of simple atomic formulas [10, 14, 24] or some element in a partially ordered domain [4, 6, 19, 18]. There are several advantages and disadvantages of choosing one or the other approach, but the important thing is that these approaches have paid little or no attention to the dynamic aspects of objects. On the other hand database applications require an ability to model a changing world and therefore need update operations frequently.

In [16] we presented an object-based variant of the event calculus [22] to describe changes to the states of object in a logic programming framework. The change is formulated in the context of a historical database which stores all past states of objects. A snapshot of the historical database at any given time is an object-oriented database in the sense that it supports an object-oriented data model. The state of the database can only be changed by the addition of new events. The events correspond to natural occurrences in the real world being modeled. The object-based event calculus (OEC) constructs the state history of objects using a given set of event descriptions. It is then possible to determine which objects "exist" at which times and query any past state of an object.

The ability to keep all past states of objects makes it possible to describe versions of objects. There is a general consensus that version control is an important function in various data-intensive applications such as computer-aided design and office information systems dealing with compound documents. In this paper we present a logic-based framework to define and manipulate object versions. We show how the object-based formulation of the event calculus can be used to describe versions of objects over time, and how these versions can be manipulated in a logic programming framework. Our aim is to show that different versioning models adapted to different kinds of applications can be described using the object-based event calculus. In this way we propose a deductive analogue of version environments supported in object-oriented databases.

In the following section the basic data model that is supported by the historical database is presented. Section 3 gives a brief summary of the object-based event calculus. Section 4 discusses basic notions of versioning. Section 5 introduces the formulation of the event calculus to support different kinds of versioning. In section 6 the operations that can be performed on the versions of objects are discussed. We conclude the paper by summarizing and making some remarks about other applications of the object-based event calculus.

2 The Data Model

The basic building block of the model is the concept of an object. An object corresponds to a real world entity. We view an object as a named collection of *object-attribute-value* triplets. Every object is abstracted by a unique identity which distinguishes it from other objects. Following [19] we use individual terms to denote object identities. A term representing the object identity is composed of function symbols, constants and variables in the usual way. For example *john*, X, $path(X,a)$ can be terms denoting object identities.

The objects have attributes whose values can be other objects (or more precisely their identities). We assume that all attributes are single-valued. As we will see in the following section, the functionality constraint of such attributes is satisfied within the formulation of the object-based event calculus.

Objects are organized into class hierarchies. A class hierarchy is defined explicitly by *is_a* relationships among classes. Each class has a unique name to distinguish it from other classes. A class denotes a set of object identities. The class-subclass relation (*is_a*) is the subset relation. The relation between a class and its instances is represented by the *instance_of* relation. The notion of inheritance is limited to only the subset relation between classes and monotonic inheritance of attribute names.

The data model is based on the relational semantics of complex objects given in the transformation of C-logic into first-order logic [10]. In this approach, the semantics of complex objects is first-order and can be understood within predicate calculus. The information about an entity can be specified and accumulated piecewise which facilities the update of subparts of an object independently of others. This basic data model has been extended to include more object-oriented features like multi-valued attributes, methods and inheritance [17]; but for the purposes of this paper we take this simple data model.

3   Object-Based Event Calculus

The object-based event calculus is a modified version of the event calculus which is a general approach to the treatment of time and change within a logic programming framework. It is based on the notion of an event as primitive. Given a description of events (changes in the world), OEC constructs the state of a historical object-oriented database. We regard the database as object-oriented in the sense that it supports the simple object-based data model presented in the previous section.

OEC is based on a special, simplified, asymmetric case of the event calculus, where periods of time are assumed to persist only into the future. In this case, the assimilation of events into the database is assumed to keep step with the occurrence of changes in the world, and the times of all event occurrences are known. This special case of the event calculus corresponds closely to the updates in conventional databases. Updates in conventional databases are performed by adding or deleting tuples of relations and the relationships are interpreted as persisting from the time they are recorded until the time they are deleted.

The state of an object is determined by the values assigned to its attributes and a state change corresponds to changing the value of any of the attributes. We deal with the evolution of the object over time by parameterizing its attributes with times at which these attributes have various values. Formulation of this idea within the spirit of the event calculus is straightforward. Events initiate and terminate periods of time for which a given attribute of a given object takes a particular value. The effects of the events are described by the predicates *initiates* and *terminates*. For example an event of type 'promote employee X to new rank R', initiates a period of time for which employee X holds rank R and terminates whatever rank X held at the time of the promotion:

$initiates(promote(X, R), X, rank, R)$

The occurrence of events is specified by the predicate *happens* in the extensional database. Given a fragment of data :

happens(promote(jim, assistant), 1986).
happens(promote(jim, lecturer), 1988).
happens(promote(jim, professor), 1991).

the object-based event calculus computes answers to queries such as :

?- holds_at(jim, rank, R, 1989).
?- holds_at(jim, Attr, Val, 1989).

The following is the basic formulation of the object-based event calculus used to reason about the changing state of objects :

$holds\_at(Obj, Attr, Val, T) \leftarrow \quad happens(Ev, Ts), Ts \leq T,$
$\qquad\qquad\qquad\qquad\qquad\qquad initiates(Ev, Obj, Attr, Val),$
$\qquad\qquad\qquad\qquad\qquad\qquad not\ broken(Obj, Attr, Val, Ts, T).$

$$broken(Obj,\ Attr,\ Val,\ Ts,\ T)\ \leftarrow happens(Ev^*,\ T^*),$$
$$Ts < T^* \leq T,$$
$$terminates(Ev^*,\ Obj,\ Attr,\ Val).$$

$$terminates(Ev^*,\ Obj,\ Attr,\ \_)\ \leftarrow initiates(Ev^*,\ Obj,\ Attr,\ \_).$$

Informally, to find the value of an attribute of an object at time T, we find an event which happened before time T, and initiated the value of that attribute; and then we check that no other event which terminates that value has happened in the meantime. The last clause for *terminates* is to satisfy the functionality constraint of the attributes. Since we are considering only single-valued attributes we can simply state that the value of an attribute is terminated if an event initiates it to another value. The interpretation of *not* as negation by failure in the last condition for *holds_at* gives a form of default persistence.

Object creation and deletion are also described in terms of event descriptions. For creation, we need to say what the class of an object is and specify its initial state. Assigning the new identity to the class initiates a period of time for which the new object is a member of that class. This makes it necessary to treat class membership (i.e. *instance_of*) as a time-dependent relationship. The predicate *assigns* is used to assign the identity of the new object to its class; the *initiates* statements are used to initialize the object's state. Creating a new object of class C, creates a new instance of the superclasses of C as well. The simplest way to formulate this is to write:

$$assigns(Ev,\ Obj,\ Class)\ \leftarrow is\_a(Sub,\ Class),\ assigns(Ev,\ Obj,\ Sub).$$

When an object is deleted it is removed from the set of instances of its class and the superclasses, and all its attribute values are terminated. The predicate *destroys* is used to specify the effects of the events that delete objects:

$$terminates(Ev,\ Obj,\ Attr,\ \_)\ \leftarrow destroys(Ev,\ Obj).$$

This rule has the effect that all attributes of the object are terminated by any event which destroys the object. Deletion of an object can lead to dangling references. Such references are eliminated by the following rule:

$$terminates(Ev,\ Obj,\ Attr,\ Val)\ \leftarrow destroys(Ev,\ Val).$$

We obtain the effect that the value Val of the attribute $Attr$ is terminated by any event which destroys the object Val.

The time dependent behaviour of class membership is modeled by parameterizing the *instance_of* relation with times. This relation is affected when a new object is assigned to a class or when an object is destroyed (assuming that objects do not change class). By analogy with *holds_at*, the following computes the instances of a class at a specific time :

$$instance\_of(Obj,\ Class,\ T)\ \leftarrow\ happens(Ev,\ Ts),\ Ts \leq T,$$
$$assigns(Ev,\ Obj,\ Class),$$
$$not\ removed(Obj,\ Class,\ Ts,\ T).$$

$$removed(Obj,\ Class,\ Ts,\ T) \leftarrow happens(Ev^*,\ T^*),$$
$$Ts < T^* \leq T,$$
$$destroys(Ev^*,\ Obj).$$

With this time varying class membership we can ask queries to find the instances of a class at a specific time.

4 Basic Notions of Versioning

There have been many proposals to incorporate versioning in object-oriented databases. This problem has not received a complete and satisfactory solution yet mainly because several distinct models have been proposed for complex objects, but also because it is not clear what are the main concepts which concern object evolution. Usually the proposed version models are specific to the application domain and show different characterizations according to the needs of the application. Broadly speaking there are three kinds of versioning that the existing work can be classified under [8]: 1) object state history, 2) checkpoint versions and 3) complex versions.

Keeping the state history of objects is the simplest kind of versioning where any update to an object will generate a new version of only those parts of the object which have been modified [2, 8, 13]. However retaining information about all past states of objects does not provide true version management, since it does not provide identifiable versions to applications.

Checkpoint versioning adds facilities for managing a sequence of identifiable points in time of the state history. Versions are like snapshots of the object in certain states and they are immutable. [3, 8]. We call this kind of versioning *linear versioning*, because the object shows a linear history with some identifiable points.

In some applications linear version structures are not adequate. In a typical design environment, several valid representations of an object can coexist at any one time. This scenario necessitates the creation of a hierarchy or a graph to capture the evolution history of versions from the initial design. After the initial creation of a design object, new versions of the object can be derived from it and new versions can in turn be derived from them, forming a *version-derivation hierarchy* (or *graph* if merging the versions is possible) for the object [7, 8, 9, 12, 21].

In the following sections we discuss how these different kinds of versioning can be described within the spirit of OEC.

5 Version Handling in OEC

The formulation of the object-based event calculus already provides us with the state history of objects. Therefore the first and simplest kind of versioning is supported in the event calculus. At the application level we can always query the state of an object at a specific time point in the past by using *holds_at* predicate. The state of the object can be determined by querying all the attributes at that time point. This state of the object can be viewed as a version of the object.

However as stated earlier manipulating the state histories of objects does not correspond to true versioning. The user should be able to access and manipulate identifiable versions. We need some modifications to the formulation of *holds_at* to describe linear and complex versions.

First of all we devise a naming convention in order to uniquely identify the versions. Suppose we have an object with the identity o and we create versions of this object. One way of distinguishing these versions is to number them. The first version of o will be $v(o,1)$, the second $v(o,2)$, the nth $v(o,n)$ and so on. When versions of versions are created, the same naming convention can be used to uniquely identify the new versions. The first version of the object $v(o,1)$ for example, will be named as $v(v(o,1),1)$, the second will be $v(v(o,1),2)$ and so on. This naming makes it possible to identify all ancestors of a version, since the first argument of the functional term denotes the identity of the parent object from which the version is created.

5.1 Version Creation

Versions are created by events. In keeping the state history of objects, every event which cause a change in the value of the object's attribute creates a new state of the object. In linear versioning however, not every event is considered as a version creating event. Only certain events can cause the creation of identifiable versions. Some attributes can be classified as version significant attributes, whose update would force the creation of a new version. Events that are specified as having effects on these attributes can be defined to be version-creating events. These special events will mark the state of the object (as of the time of their occurrences) as being a version. Linear versioning is described pictorially in Fig. 1. e_1, e_2, ... denote the occurrences of events affecting an object. The time of the special events are marked by **x**'s. The boxes denote the states of the object which are checkpointed as versions of the object.

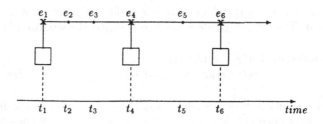

Fig. 1. Linear Versioning

We now consider the case of creating complex (parallel) versions, where an object can have several versions at one time and these versions can also be modified to create versions of versions. The evolution history of an object with several versions is shown in Fig. 2. Each branch of this tree structured history corresponds to a different version. The root object is considered as the initial version. There are parallel histories for the initial object. Each version has its own history starting from its creation time. Once a version is created it is treated as other objects in the database. It can be updated, deleted or versioned. Meanwhile its parent object can be directly updated, even after one or more versions have been derived from it. The events which cause branching on the tree are version-creating events.

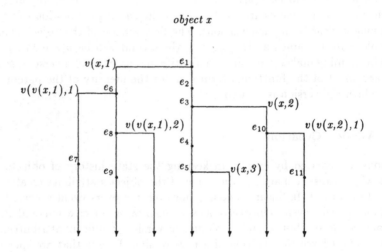

Fig. 2. Parallel Versioning

In order to specify the effects of version-creating events, we introduce the predicate *creates_version* which will be used to mark the occurrences of such events in the object's history and also to generate a unique identity for the version. For example consider the design of a VLSI chip. Different versions of the chip may be derived, say to reduce the chip size or reduce the power consumption etc. Every time a "reconfigure" operation is performed, a new version is assumed to be created. The following rule is used to describe the situation [1]:

$$creates\_version(Ev, v(C, N)) \leftarrow$$
$$event: Ev[act \Rightarrow reconfigure, chip \Rightarrow C, number \Rightarrow N].$$

---

[1] In general it is difficult to devise a fixed arity representation for events. Here we use a syntax similar to that of C-logic [10] as a convenient shorthand for describing events. In this representation labels are interpreted as binary predicates and a structured complex term is considered as conjunctions of atomic formulas.

The functional term $v(C, N)$ is the identity of the new version where N is an integer value denoting the version number. The variable C denotes the object whose version is being created. In linear versioning it is the checkpointed object, in complex (parallel) versioning it can be a version identifier allowing the generation of identities for versions of versions.

An important point to consider in creating versions is to assign the new versions to classes. The existing object-oriented systems which support versioning usually define a special class and assign all the versionable objects and their versions to this class [7, 8, 12, 21]. In some systems [12] different types of versions are distinguished on the basis of their capabilities: transient (temporary), working (stable), and released versions. Intuitively, a transient version is an intermediate design that has been actively worked on and may be subject to extensive modifications. When the design reaches a stable stage, the designer may promote the version of the design to a working version, ready to be shared by other users. Finally as the design matures it is promoted to being a released version. This kind of classification among the versions is possible in the event calculus. Every event creating the version can specify the class of the version and by the use of *assigns* predicate, the version can be assigned to the corresponding class. Promoting a version from one class to another is also possible in our framework as it corresponds to changing the class of the object. Mutation of objects within OEC was discussed in [16] and it can be directly applied to version objects. Here we take a simple approach by assuming that versions are also instances of the class to which their parent version belongs. Continuing with our example, the event of reconfiguring a chip assigns the new version to the class VLSI-chip:

$$assigns(Ev, \; v(C,N), \; VLSI\text{-}chip) \leftarrow$$
$$event : Ev[act \Rightarrow reconfigure, \; chip \Rightarrow C, \; number \Rightarrow N].$$

5.2 Reasoning with Versions

The current formulation of *holds_at* needs to be modified in order to handle reasoning with linear and parallel versions.

Formulation of Linear Versions. Linear versioning does not add much complexity to the formulation of *holds_at*. Consider Figure 3 which shows a pictorial view of the document d's history. The document has three versions. When a version is created, it is assigned to the state that the original object has at the checkpoint time. However the event causing the creation of a new version may specify some new values for some of the attributes. This additional change is valid only for the version and it is kept immutable while the parent object can be changed independently.

The formulation of *holds_at* as in section 3, can be used to reason about the state of d without any modifications. Querying the state of a version at a specific time, however, needs some other considerations. We know that once a version is created it is not subject to change. Therefore it is sufficient to find the creation

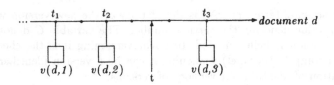

Fig. 3. Checkpoint versions

time of the version to retrieve its state. We introduce another clause for *holds_at* to reason about the state of versions:

$$holds\_at(Vid,\ Attr,\ Val,\ T) \leftarrow$$
$$happens(Ev,\ Tc),\ Tc \leq T,$$
$$creates\_version(Ev,\ Vid),$$
$$(\ initiates(Ev,\ Vid,\ Attr,\ Val)\ )$$
$$or$$
$$(\ Vid = v(Oid,\ \_);$$
$$holds\_at(Oid,\ Attr,\ Val,\ Tc)\ ).$$

The effect of copying the state of the parent object as the state of the new version is obtained by finding out the identity of the original object, *Oid*, and querying its state at the creation time *Tc* of the version *Vid*. If the version-creating event is defined also to affect the values of attributes, then the new values are taken into account with the first condition of the disjunction.

In our example we can ask the following queries about different states of the document:

$$?\text{-}\ holds\_at(d,\ Attr,\ Val,\ t).$$
$$?\text{-}\ holds\_at(v(d,1),\ Attr,\ Val,\ t).$$

These two queries will most likely return different answers as there might be changes in the state of the object according to the effects of the events happening between times t_1 and t where t_1 is the time at which the version $v(d,1)$ was created (see Fig. 3).

Parallel Versions. In parallel versioning, the versions have their own history. They can be updated after the time of their creation. In finding out the state of a version we have to take into account the events affecting the version as well. Consider Fig. 4 which shows a section of an object's version derivation history. Here *Vid* is a version identifier and *Oid* is the object from which it is derived. *Oid* can be another version or the initial object. T_c denotes the creation time of the version *Vid*, *T* denotes the time at which we query its state. The history of *Vid* starts at T_c and at that time *Vid* as its initial state has the same state as *Oid*

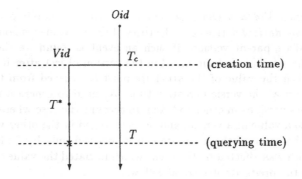

Fig. 4. A section of an object derivation hierarchy

has as of time T_c except the values of the attributes which might be affected by the version-creating event. At any time after its creation, say at T^*, the version's state can be changed by an event. If no such event happens between T_c and T, the state of the version at time T is the same as its state at time T_c. However if there are some events that have happened after T_c and have changed the values of one or more attributes of the version, then we have to consider the effects of these events as well. The formulation of *holds_at* to reason with the state of parallel versions is as follows:

$$
\begin{aligned}
&holds\_at(Vid,\ Attr,\ Val,\ T) \leftarrow \\
&\quad happens(E,\ Tc), \\
&\quad creates\_version(E,\ Vid), \\
&\quad happens(Ev,\ T^*),\ T^* \leq T, \\
&\quad (\ Tc \leq T^*, \\
&\quad\quad initiates(Ev,\ Vid,\ Attr,\ Val), \\
&\quad\quad not\ broken(Vid,\ Attr,\ Val,\ T^*,\ T) \\
&\quad) \\
&\quad or \\
&\quad (T^* \leq Tc,\ Vid = v(Oid, \_), \\
&\quad\quad derived(Vid,\ Pid), \\
&\quad\quad initiates(Ev,\ Pid,\ Attr,\ Val), \\
&\quad\quad not\ broken(Vid,\ Attr,\ Val,\ T^*,\ T), \\
&\quad\quad holds\_at(Oid,\ Attr,\ Val,\ Tc) \\
&\quad).
\end{aligned}
$$

We first find the version creation time (Tc). We then find an event Ev which happened before time T (querying time). If the event happened after time Tc and initiated the value of the attribute in the version object then we check that the value has not been terminated by another event. If the event happened before time Tc then we check if it initiated the attribute in one of the previous versions.

The condition $Vid = v(Oid,\_)$ is used to find the immediate parent object and the predicate *derived* derives the identities of the previous versions starting from the immediate parent version. If such an event is found we then check if the value of the attribute is terminated in the version object after it was created. If it is not then the value of the attribute must be derived from the state of the parent object at the version creation time. We need to generate the identities of the previous versions in order to take into account the case where an attribute is initiated to a value in a version and never changed in the other versions derived from it. The value of the attribute can be derived only by finding the version object which was affected by the event which initiated the value of the attribute. We define the predicate *derived* as follows:

$$derived(v(Oid,\_),\ Oid).$$
$$derived(v(Oid,\_),\ Pid) \leftarrow derived(Oid,\ Pid).$$

The recursive definition of *holds_at* given above, is used to navigate through the versions. It stops when the recursion reaches the root object. This modified *holds_at* can also be used to reason with the state of objects without any versions, provided that the event creating the object is defined to be a version-creating event as well.

6 Operations on Versions

Depending on the application domain, several operations can be required on versions. One may be interested in finding the existing versions of an object at a specific time. A new predicate is defined for this operation:

$$version\_of(Oid,\ Vid,\ T) \leftarrow$$
$$happens(Ev,\ Tc),\ Tc \leq T,$$
$$creates\_version(Ev,\ Vid),$$
$$derived(Vid,\ Oid),$$
$$not\ deleted(Vid,\ Tc,\ T).$$

The condition *not deleted* basically checks whether the version still exists since its creation time. As we pointed out earlier, versions are like other objects in the database. They can be deleted as any other object. Deletion of a version can be described by events. However there is one point to notice in deleting versions. If an object (or a version) becomes invalid during a design process and needs to be deleted, then it does not make sense to keep the versions of the object in the database. We need to have a mechanism to delete all versions of an object in case of deleting the object itself. We can achieve this by adding another clause for the predicate *destroys*:

$$destroys(Ev,\ v(Oid,\_)) \leftarrow destroys(Ev,\ Oid).$$

The proposed formulation of OEC may be further extended to describe more complex operations. For instance, an important operation on versions is the "merge" operator. In our framework it corresponds to joining two parallel histories into a single one. In this case there will be two parent versions for the newly generated version. The state of the new version can be derived by navigating through the histories of both of the parents. The naming convention can be extended to specify the merged version. For instance, a version generated from versions $V1$ and $V2$ can be described by the identity $v(V1+V2, 1)$. The initial state of the new version can be determined by the specification of the merge event, which is provided by the user. The specification should provide the information for each attribute which parent should be considered in determining the value of that attribute. We have omitted the formulation here.

When a new version is generated from an old version, it may be necessary to update other objects that directly or indirectly reference the old version of the object. In the current framework, the propagation of the effects of version-creating events must be described explicitly by the user. This mechanism may be improved by giving support to generic objects proposed in other systems [7, 12]. When an event creates a versionable object A, a generic object $gen(A)$ can be created along with the first version object. The generic object can point to different versions of the object at different points in time. The referent can be initiated or terminated by events and it can be derived in a similar manner like the values of the attributes of objects. The version pointed by the generic object will be used as the default version by other objects referencing the generic object.

The versioning model proposed in this paper can not stand alone. It should be integrated into broader contexts. Most design applications require capability to define and manipulate composite objects. The creation of object versions in composite objects requires some other considerations [5, 9, 20]. Adding a new version of a component of a larger object might cause a new version of the larger object. This can be done through the use of the *part-of* relationship which permits reading a composite object bottom-up. In order to support composite objects, the data model must be extended to include the *part-of* relation with some integrity constraints. The versioning of composite objects can then be achieved by propagating the effects of the events which modify subobjects, to the parent objects via the *part-of* links.

A comprehensive treatment of the issues raised in this section should be studied further.

7 Conclusions

In this paper we have presented a general approach for modeling versions of objects in a logical framework. We have shown how a theory of time such as the event calculus may be used to represent and manipulate complex objects and their versions in a natural and descriptive way. We distinguish three kinds of versioning. The first type which is simply keeping the state history of objects comes freely from the properties of the event calculus. The second type is linear versioning in which created versions are immutable. The third one is parallel versioning where one can have several current versions of an object. This case requires keeping several parallel histories which can be accessed and modified independently of each other.

OEC has been developed and extended in various different ways to model different temporal aspects of objects. One important change was identified as mutation of objects [16]. Events can be naturally used to describe evolution of objects and it is still possible to retain their identity. Another application of OEC is to extend versioning to schema level. It is possible to derive the history of class definitions using event descriptions. The theory can be implemented in different programming languages in different ways. It can be translated more or less directly into a Prolog program or a suitable algorithm can be constructed to perform the same task in a procedural language. An efficient implementation based on lemma generation is described in [17]. The idea is to store all derivable facts about objects in a separate database and solve the queries using the information in this database only.

The problems in integrating deductive and object-oriented approaches cannot be realized and solved if the dynamic aspects of objects are ignored. We believe that objects and events combined under a single framework provide a higher-level modeling methodology for structural semantics and dynamic aspects of objects. This can provide a foundation for a temporal deductive and object-oriented database system.

References

1. S. Abiteboul and S. Grumbach. COL : A logic-based language for complex objects. In *International Conference on Extending Database Technology- EDBT'88*, pages 271–293, Venice, Italy, March 1988.
2. M. Adiba and N.B. Quang. Historical multi-media databases. In *Proceedings of the 12th International Conference on VLDB*, pages 63–70, Kyoto, Japan, August 1986.
3. Michel E. Adiba. Histories and versions for multimedia complex objects. *IEEE Database Engineering*, 7(4):181–188, 1988.
4. H. Ait-Kaci and R. Nasr. Login: A logic programming language with built-in inheritance. *The Journal of Logic Programming*, 1986.
5. T.M. Atwood. An object-oriented DBMS for design support applications. In Proceedings IEEE COMPPINT 85, pages 299-307, 1985.
6. F. Bancilhon and S. Khoshafian. A calculus for complex objects. In *Proceedings of the 5th ACM-SIGACT-SIGMOD Symposium on Principles of Database Systems*, pages 53–59, Cambridge, Massachusetts, March 1986.
7. D. Beech and B. Mahbod. Generalized version control in an object-oriented database. In *Proceedings of the 4th International Conference on Data Engineering*, pages 14–22, Los Angeles, CA, February 1988.
8. A. Bjornerstedt and C. Hulten. Version control in an object-oriented architecture. In Won Kim and F.H. Lochovsky, editors, *Object-Oriented Concepts, Databases and Applications*, pages 451–485. ACM Press, 1989.

9. W. Cellary and G. Jomier. Consistency of versions in object-oriented databases. In *Proceedings of the 16th International Conference on VLDB*, pages 432–441, Brisbane, Australia, 1990.

10. W. Chen and D. Warren. C-logic of complex objects. In *Proceedings of the 8th ACM SIGACT-SIGMOD-SIGART Symposium on the Principles of Database Systems*, 1989.

11. D. Chimenti et al. The LDL system prototype. *IEEE Transactions on Knowledge and Data Engineering*, 2(1):78–90, March 1990.

12. Hong-Tai Chou and Won Kim. A unifying framework for version control in a CAD environment. In *Proceedings of the 12th International Conference on VLDB*, pages 336–344, Kyoto, Japan, August 1986.

13. J. Clifford and A. Croker. Objects in time. *IEEE Database Engineering*, 7(4):189–196, 1988.

14. M. Dalal and D. Gangopadhyay. OOLP: A translation approach to object-oriented logic programming. In *Proceedings of the First International Conference on Deductive and Object-Oriented Databases*, pages 555–568, Kyoto, Japan, December 4-6 1989.

15. M. Jarke, M. Jeusfeld, and T. Rose. Software process modeling as a strategy for KBMS implementation. In *Proceedings of the First International Conference on Deductive and Object-Oriented Databases*, pages 531–550, Kyoto, Japan, December 4-6 1989.

16. F. N. Kesim and M. Sergot. On the evolution of objects in a logic programming framework. In *Proceedings of the International Conference on Fifth Generation Computer Systems*, volume 2, June 1992.

17. F. Nihan Kesim. *Temporal Objects in Deductive Databases*. PhD thesis, Department of Computing, Imperial College, 1993.

18. M. Kifer and G. Lausen. F-logic: A higher-order language for reasoning about objects, inheritance, and scheme. In *Proceedings of the 8th ACM SIGACT-SIGMOD-SIGART Symposium on Principles of Database Systems*, pages 134–146, 1989.

19. M. Kifer and J. Wu. A logic for object-oriented logic programming (Maier's O-logic revisited). In *Proceedings of the 8th ACM SIGACT-SIGMOD-SIGART Symposium on Principles of Database Systems*, 1989.

20. W. Kim. *Introduction to Object-Oriented Databases*. The MIT Press, 1990.

21. P. Klahold, G. Schlageter, and W. Wilken. A general model for version management in databases. In *Proceedings of the 12th International Conference on VLDB*, pages 319–327, Kyoto, Japan, August 1986.

22. R.A. Kowalski and M. Sergot. A logic-based calculus of events. *New Generation Computing*, 4:67–95, 1986.

23. G.M. Kuper. Logic programming with sets. In *Proceedings of the 6th ACM-SIGACT-SIGMOD-SIGART Symposium on Principles of Database Systems*, San Diego, CA, 1987.

24. D. Maier. A logic for objects. In *Proceedings of the Workshop on Foundations of Deductive Databases and Logic Programming*, pages 6–26, Washington D.C., August 1986.

25. C. Zaniolo. The representation and deductive retrieval of complex objects. In *Proceedings of Very Large Databases*, page 458, Stockholm, 1985.

A Model for Sets and Multiple Inheritance in Deductive Object-Oriented Systems

Gillian Dobbie[1] and Rodney Topor[2]

[1] Department of Computer Science, The University of Melbourne,
Parkville, Vic. 3052, Australia. Email: gill@cs.mu.oz.au
[2] School of Computing and Information Technology, Griffith University,
Nathan, Qld 4111, Australia. Email: rwt@cit.gu.edu.au

Abstract. We consider the addition of set-valued methods and multiple inheritance to a simple deductive object-oriented language we defined and studied previously. We show how the previously defined declarative semantics can be extended to provide a natural semantics for inheritance and overriding in this more general setting, and similarly extend our previously defined evaluation procedures.

1 Introduction

There have now been many proposals for a simple mathematical foundation for object-oriented systems with deduction [1, 2, 3, 4, 7, 9, 14, 15, 17]. Most of these proposals do not address the issue of method overriding or dynamic binding. Three proposals that do seriously consider this issue are Kifer et. al.'s F-logic [14], McCabe's $L\&O$ [17] and Abiteboul et. al.'s $datalog^{meth}$ [4]. F-logic describes the declarative semantics of a deductive object-oriented language with overriding and also presents a proof theory. However, the semantics of overriding in F-logic is complex, and not addressed in the proof theory. $L\&O$ is also a deductive object-oriented language with overriding. The semantics of $L\&O$ programs is given by translating $L\&O$ programs to logic programs and thus provides little direct insight into the relationship between inheritance, overriding and deduction. Query processing is also described using a translation to Prolog. McCabe does state that Gurr has provided an independent semantics for $L\&O$. This semantics is based on the fact that an $L\&O$ program comprises independent programs which interact. This approach is similar to that described by Brass and Lipeck [8] where the global semantics of a program is defined in terms of the local semantics of each object in the program. $Datalog^{meth}$ is also a deductive object-oriented language with overriding. The semantics of $datalog^{meth}$ and query evaluation are again described using a translation to datalog with negation. There is no notion of set-valued methods or multiple inheritance in $datalog^{meth}$.

In [11], we defined and studied a simple deductive object-oriented language called Gulog to investigate the interaction of deduction, inheritance, and overriding in the simplest possible context. In particular, we only considered single-valued methods, definite clauses, and simple inheritance in [11]. Distinguishing features of our language are that it separates schema declarations from data definitions, and that it allows methods to be overridden on specific instances of a subclass, thus generalizing other deductive object-oriented languages. We presented a declarative semantics for Gulog based on Przymusinski's perfect model semantics for logic programs [18]. This semantics required the definition of a priority relation between atoms (and between models) that characterizes overriding in a natural way and the definition of preferred models based on this priority relation. We also defined bottom-up and top-down query evaluation procedures. The bottom-up method requires the program to be stratified according to the priority relation and generalizes Apt et. al.'s construction of the standard model of a stratified logic program [6]. The stratification ensures that clauses defining overriding methods are in lower strata than clauses defining possibly overridden methods. In the top-down procedure, the set of possible answers to each atom in a goal is computed, the subset of minimal answers according to the priority relation is selected, and the subsets for each atom combined to yield the computed answers for the goal. Both procedures are sound with respect to the declarative semantics.

With the restriction to single-valued methods, our semantics for inheritance and overriding is equivalent to that of F-logic and the dynamic inheritance described in [4]. However, we provided a new characterization of the semantics by showing its relationship to similar methods used in the semantics of logic programs. The approach to overriding in Gulog (and F-logic) is more general than that of $L\&O$, as we allow a method in a superclass to be overridden by a method in a subclass for some instances of the subclass but not others, depending on whether the body of the method definition in the subclass succeeds or not. This generalization appears to be necessary for reasoning about inheritance hierarchies in artificial intelligence [20].

In this paper we consider the addition of set-valued methods and multiple inheritance to Gulog. These additions make the language more expressive and provide more powerful modelling facilities. Our main contributions are the definition of a declarative semantics for this richer language and generalizations of our bottom-up and top-down query evaluation procedures.

Our syntax for set-valued methods is the same as that in F-logic. Our semantics is different from the definition in the original version of F-logic, but close to that in the revised version of F-logic. In the original version of F-logic, a set-valued method defined on a class does not override a set-valued method defined on a superclass if the value defined on the subclass is a subset of the value defined on the superclass. For example, if the value of method m defined in class c is $\{a\}$, and the value of method m defined in class c' is $\{a, b\}$, where c is a subclass of c', then overriding does not occur. The value of method m in class c is $\{a, b\}$. In Gulog, overriding does occur in this case. In the revised-version of F-logic, one of several possible models corresponds to our semantics. We argue that our semantics is more natural, and can be implemented more efficiently [16]. Like F-logic, Gulog remains first order with set-valued methods, as we do not allow variables to range over sets of objects.

The biggest change in extending Gulog to include set-valued methods is to the bottom-up query evaluation procedure. Previously it relied on the functionality of methods and the fact that there is only one clause defining the value of a method for an object. With set-valued methods, we need to redefine the immediate consequence operator to be a mapping from typed interpretations to typed interpretations.

The problem with multiple inheritance is that, if a method is defined in more than one superclass of a class and not redefined in the subclass, it is not clear which method definition should be inherited by the subclass. Different programming languages and database systems solve this problem in different ways. In F-logic the credulous approach is used. This means that if there is a conflict then either inherited method may be used. Przymusinski also takes the credulous approach [19], following his work on disjunctive databases. Other systems such as LOGIN [5] do not distinguish between classes and objects and handle inheritance in the unification procedure. For multiple inheritance the greatest lower bound of two definitions is taken, and there may be no defined greatest lower bound. In L&O [17] multiple inheritance is described before overriding is included, so all definitions are inherited.

Because we wish to retain our similarities with logic programming we consider only two-valued interpretations and programs similar to definite logic programs. We define a condition which restricts programs to those in which there are no method definition conflicts. In so doing very few changes to the procedures are necessary. In comparison with the approaches described above our approach is more restrictive, but a program can easily be checked for conflicts and the user warned if any exist.

This paper is organised as follows. Section 2 describes the syntax, semantics and query evalaution procedures for Gulog, including set-valued methods. Section 3 discusses multiple inheritance and describes how to extend the language and procedures to incorporate it. The final section discusses the significance of this work and suggests further problems to study.

2 Set-Valued Methods

In this section we describe the syntax and semantics of Gulog when extended with set-valued methods. We also present bottom-up and top-down query evaluation procedures.

For a comparison of Gulog with other languages, see [11]. Our approach to set-valued methods is similar to that in F-logic, namely the syntax is second order but the semantics is first order. The syntax we use is also similar to that of F-logic, but our semantics with respect to overriding is more natural the description of overriding in the original version of F-logic, and can be implemented more efficiently [16]. The latest version of F-logic deals with inheritance in the same way that we do.

2.1 Syntax and Informal Semantics

In this section we describe the syntax of declarations, and of programs with respect to a set of declarations. We describe typed substitutions and a class of programs which we are particularly interested in, namely simple programs. Note that we separate schema declarations from data definitions.

A *schema declaration* is defined as follows:

- If c and c' are type symbols then $c < c'$ is a type hierarchy declaration. We say c is a subtype of c', and c' is a supertype of c. For any type c'' such that $c' < c''$, c is also a subtype of c'' and c'' is a supertype of c. If $c < c''$ or $c = c''$ we write $c \leq c''$.
- If a is an object symbol and c is a type symbol then $a : c$ is an object declaration. We say a is an object of type c. For any type c' such that c' is a supertype of c, a is also of type c'.
- If p is an n-ary predicate symbol and $c_1, \ldots, c_n$ are type symbols then $p(c_1, \ldots, c_n)$ is a predicate declaration. We say the signature of predicate p is $c_1 \times \cdots \times c_n$.
- If m is an n-ary single-valued method symbol and $c, c_1, \ldots, c_n, c'$ are type symbols then $c[m@c_1, \ldots, c_n \Rightarrow c']$ is a single-valued method declaration. We say the signature of single-valued method m is $c \times c_1 \times \cdots \times c_n \to c'$.
- If m is an n-ary set-valued method symbol and $c, c_1, \ldots, c_n, c'$ are type symbols then $c[m@c_1, \ldots, c_n \Rightarrow c']$ is a set-valued method declaration. We say the signature of set-valued method m is $c \times c_1 \times \cdots \times c_n \twoheadrightarrow c'$.

We now define data definitions. Data is defined by a program with respect to a set of declarations. As described above, the declarations define a set of types arranged in a hierarchy, a set of typed object symbols, a set of single-valued method symbols each with a given signature, a set of set-valued method symbols each with a given signature, and a set of predicate symbols each with a given signature. It is possible for the same symbol to be used for both single-valued and set-valued methods.

In Gulog, variables are typed. If x is a variable and c is a type then $x : c$ is a *type assignment* declaring that variable x is of type c. A *variable typing* is a set of type assignments and will be denoted by Γ.

The definitions of terms, atoms, and clauses are similar to those in logic programming except that in Gulog we include type information.

A *term* is defined as follows:

- $\Gamma \vdash x : c$ is a term if x is a variable and $x : c \in \Gamma$. We usually write $\Gamma \vdash x$ when the type of x is obvious. The variable x can be assigned to an object o if and only if o is of type c.
- $\Gamma \vdash a : c$ is a term if a is an object of type c. We write the term simply as a when the type of a is clear.

The term $\Gamma \vdash t : c$ is called a *ground term* if t is not a variable.

An *atom* is defined as follows:

- If p is an n-ary predicate symbol with signature $c_1 \times \cdots \times c_n$ and there exists a variable typing Γ that contains type assignments for all the variables in t_i, and $\Gamma \vdash t_i : d_i$ is a term with $d_i \leq c_i$ $(1 \leq i \leq n)$, then $\Gamma \vdash p(t_1, \ldots, t_n)$ is a *predicate atom*.

- If m is an single-valued n-ary method symbol with signature $c \times c_1 \times \cdots \times c_n \rightarrow c'$ and there exists a variable typing Γ that contains type assignments for all the variables in t, t_i and t', and $\Gamma \vdash t : d$, $\Gamma \vdash t_i : d_i$ $(1 \leq i \leq n)$, and $\Gamma \vdash t' : d'$ are terms with $d \leq c$, $d_i \leq c_i$ and $d' \leq c'$, then $\Gamma \vdash t[m@t_1, \ldots, t_n \rightarrow t']$ is a *single-valued method atom*.

- If m is an n-ary set-valued method symbol with signature $c \times c_1 \times \cdots \times c_n \twoheadrightarrow c'$ and there exists a variable typing Γ that contains type assignments for all the variables in t, t_i and t', and $\Gamma \vdash t : d$, $\Gamma \vdash t_i : d_i$ $(1 \leq i \leq n)$, and $\Gamma \vdash t' : d'$ are terms with $d \leq c$, $d_i \leq c_i$ and $d' \leq c'$, then $\Gamma \vdash t[m@t_1, \ldots, t_n \twoheadrightarrow t']$ is a *set-valued method atom*.

An atom is a *method atom* if it is a single-valued method atom or a set-valued method atom. The atom $\Gamma \vdash A$ is called a *ground atom* if it contains no variables.

A clause also has type information. If $\Gamma_A \vdash A, \Gamma_{B_1} \vdash B_1, \ldots, \Gamma_{B_n} \vdash B_n$ are atoms where the variables common to $\Gamma_A, \Gamma_{B_1}, \ldots, \Gamma_{B_n}$ have the same types then $\Gamma_A \cup \Gamma_{B_1} \cup \cdots \cup \Gamma_{B_n} \vdash (A \leftarrow B_1 \wedge \cdots \wedge B_n)$ is a *clause*.

If $\Gamma \vdash t[m \rightarrow y]$ (resp. $\Gamma \vdash t[m \twoheadrightarrow y]$) is an atom, where t is of type d then this atom is of type d. The type of a predicate atom is undefined. If the head of a clause is an atom of type d, then the clause is of type d.

In [11] we described how some conjunctions of atoms could be written more concisely as compound atoms (called "molecules" in [14]). We now define the term $\Gamma \vdash (t[m@t_1, \ldots, t_n \rightarrow \{t'_1, \ldots, t'_p\}]$ to be a shorthand for the conjunction $\Gamma \vdash t[m@t_1, \ldots, t_n \rightarrow t'_1] \wedge \cdots \wedge t[m@t_1, \ldots, t_n \rightarrow t'_p]$. As the head of a clause cannot be a conjunction of atoms we further define

$$\Gamma \vdash t[m@t_1, \ldots, t_n \twoheadrightarrow \{a_1, \ldots, a_p\}] \leftarrow B_1 \wedge \cdots \wedge B_m$$

to be a shorthand for the p clauses

$$\Gamma \vdash t[m@t_1, \ldots, t_n \twoheadrightarrow a_1] \leftarrow B_1 \wedge \cdots \wedge B_m$$

$$\vdots$$

$$\Gamma \vdash t[m@t_1, \ldots, t_n \twoheadrightarrow a_p] \leftarrow B_1 \wedge \cdots \wedge B_m,$$

where $a_1, \ldots, a_p$ are object symbols.

A *goal* is a clause of the form $\Gamma \vdash \leftarrow B_1 \wedge \cdots \wedge B_n$, i.e., a clause with an empty head. If Γ is empty we write $\leftarrow B_1 \wedge \cdots \wedge B_n$.

A *program* with respect to a set of declarations is a finite set of clauses.

Example 1. Assume the following set of declarations D:

$$node[edges \Rightarrow node] \qquad node[paths \Rightarrow node]$$
$$a : node \qquad b : node$$
$$c : node.$$

The following is a program P with respect to D:

$a[edges \twoheadrightarrow b]$
$b[edges \twoheadrightarrow c]$
$\{x : node, y : node\} \vdash x[path \twoheadrightarrow y] \leftarrow x[edges \twoheadrightarrow y]$
$\{x : node, y : node, z : node\} \vdash x[path \twoheadrightarrow z] \leftarrow x[edges \twoheadrightarrow y] \wedge y[path \twoheadrightarrow z]$.

Informally the meaning of program P can be described as follows. There is an *edge* between nodes a and b, and an edge between b and c. There is a *path* between two nodes if there is an *edge* between those nodes, or if there is an *edge* from the first to another node and there is a *path* from the other node to the second node.

In [11] we define substitutions which are similar to those in logic programming except that they are typed and hence satisfy additional restrictions.

To ensure that programs have well-defined semantics, we impose restrictions that ensure they are "stratified" and that single-valued methods really are single-valued. Programs that satisfy these restrictions are called "simple". Before defining the classes of stratified and simple programs, we must define a relationship "possibly overrides" between clauses.

Let P be a program, C be $\Gamma \vdash x[m@y_1, \ldots, y_k \rightarrow z] \leftarrow B$ (resp. $\Gamma \vdash x[m@y_1, \ldots, y_k \rightarrow z] \leftarrow B$) and C' be $\Gamma' \vdash x'[m@y'_1, \ldots, y'_k \rightarrow z'] \leftarrow B'$ (resp. $\Gamma' \vdash x'[m@y'_1, \ldots, y'_k \rightarrow z'] \leftarrow B'$), where $C, C' \in P$, $\Gamma \vdash x : \sigma$ is a term, $\Gamma' \vdash x' : \tau$ is a term and $\sigma < \tau$. If there are ground instances $C\theta$ of C and $C'\theta'$ of C' such that $x\theta = x'\theta'$, $y_i\theta = y'_i\theta'$ for all i, $1 \le i \le k$, and $z\theta \ne z'\theta'$ then clause $C\theta$ *possibly overrides* clause $C'\theta'$ with respect to P.

A program P is *inheritance-stratified* (or i-stratified) if there exists a mapping μ from the set of ground atoms to the set of non-negative integers such that, for every ground instance $C\theta$ of every clause C in P,

- $\mu(A') \le \mu(A)$, where A' is an atom in the body of the clause instance $C\theta$, and A is the head of the clause instance $C\theta$, and
- $\mu(A') < \mu(A)$ for every ground instance $C'\theta'$ which possibly overrides $C\theta$, where A' is the head of $C'\theta'$, and A is the head of $C\theta$.

We illustrate i-stratification in the following example.

Example 2. Assume a set of declarations including $export\_lada < lada$ and $el5 : export\_lada$. Consider the program P :

$\{x : lada\} \vdash x[forms \rightarrow green] \qquad \{x : lada\} \vdash x[forms \rightarrow red]$
$\{x : export\_lada\} \vdash x[forms \twoheadrightarrow blue] \; \{x : export\_lada\} \vdash x[forms \twoheadrightarrow red]$.

The relationship of the ground atoms of P is:

$\mu(el5[forms \twoheadrightarrow blue]) < \mu(el5[forms \twoheadrightarrow red])$
$\mu(el5[forms \twoheadrightarrow red]) < \mu(el5[forms \twoheadrightarrow green])$
$\mu(el5[forms \twoheadrightarrow blue]) < \mu(el5[forms \twoheadrightarrow green])$.

P is i-stratified.

Now, to ensure that single-valued methods really are single-valued, we impose the following range-restriction condition on programs. A variable z is *restricted* wrt the terms $t, t_1, \ldots, t_n$ in the conjunction C if C contains a method atom $t'[m'@t'_1, \ldots, t'_k \rightarrow z]$ and any variable in $t', t'_1, \ldots, t'_k$ either occurs in $t, t_1, \ldots, t_n$ or is itself restricted wrt $t, t_1, \ldots, t_n$ in the remainder of C. For example, the variable z is restricted wrt u and x in the conjunction $u[m'@x \rightarrow y] \wedge u[m''@y \rightarrow z]$.

A program P is *well-defined* if the following two conditions hold:

- For each clause $\Gamma \vdash t[m@t_1, \ldots, t_n \rightarrow u] \leftarrow C$ in P, u is either an object symbol or is a variable that is restricted wrt $t, t_1, \ldots, t_n$ in C. This is the usual "safety" condition.
- For each single-valued method m of signature $\tau \times \tau_1 \times \cdots \times \tau_n \rightarrow \tau'$, and for each type $\sigma \leq \tau$, program P does *not* contain two clauses

$$\Gamma \vdash t[m@t_1, \ldots, t_n \rightarrow u] \leftarrow C$$
$$\Gamma \vdash t'[m@t'_1, \ldots, t'_n \rightarrow u'] \leftarrow C'$$

such that $\Gamma \vdash t : \sigma$, $\Gamma \vdash t' : \sigma$, and atoms $t[m@t_1, \ldots, t_n \rightarrow x]$ and $t'[m@t'_1, \ldots,$
$t'_n \rightarrow x']$ (where x and x' are new variables) are unifiable. This together with the first condition ensures that single-valued methods really are single-valued.

We can now define "simple programs".

A program P is *simple* if the following two conditions hold:

- P is i-stratified, and
- P is well-defined.

2.2 Semantics

In this section we describe the declarative semantics of simple programs. We use typed Herbrand interpretations and models. A simple program may have more than one minimal model, so we also use a priority relation between ground atoms that is used to identify preferred models of a program.

The semantics of sets in our language is different from that in F-logic. In F-logic if the declared value of a set-valued method in a subclass is a subset of the value of the same method inherited from a superclass then overriding does not occur whereas in our language it does. In our language if a set-valued method is redefined in a subtype then the value in the subtype overrides the value defined in the supertype.

Due to space limitations we do not include a full description of the declarative semantics. Briefly, an *interpretation* for a program P is a set of ground atoms that are consistent with the program's schema declaration D. A ground clause C *overrides* a ground clause C' with respect to program P and interpretation I if C possibly overrides C' with respect to P and the bodies of C and C' are both true in I.

An interpretation I for a program P is a *model* of P if, for every ground instance C' of a clause in P, either C' is true in I or there exists another ground instance C of a clause in P such that C overrides C' with respect to I. Note that a program may have more than one model and that not every clause need be true in a model.

As in [18], we can define a priority relationship between ground atoms (but using possible overriding instead of negation), and use this to define a preference relationship between models. As in [18], we prefer models in which there are fewer occurrences of higher priority atoms. We say a model of a program P is *preferred* if no models of P are preferable to it.

We refer the reader to [11] for the details.

We illustrate the declarative semantics of programs with set-valued methods with two examples.

Example 3. Assume a set of declarations including $export\_lada < lada$ and $ell : export\_lada$. Consider the program P:

$$\{x : lada\} \vdash x[forms \longrightarrow red]$$
$$\{x : lada\} \vdash x[forms \longrightarrow green]$$
$$\{x : export\_lada\} \vdash x[forms \twoheadrightarrow blue] \leftarrow x[destination \rightarrow france]$$
$$\{x : export\_lada\} \vdash x[forms \twoheadrightarrow red] \leftarrow x[destination \rightarrow australia],$$

and the interpretations:

$$I_1 = \{ell[destination \rightarrow australia], ell[forms \twoheadrightarrow red]\},$$
$$I_2 = \{ell[destination \rightarrow france], ell[forms \twoheadrightarrow blue]\},$$
$$I_3 = \{ell[forms \twoheadrightarrow red], ell[forms \twoheadrightarrow green]\}.$$

Since all the ground clauses of P are true or overridden in each of these interpretations, I_1, I_2, and I_3 are all models of P. The priority relationship gives the following relationships between the ground atoms of P:

$$ell[forms \twoheadrightarrow blue] \leq ell[destination \rightarrow france]$$
$$ell[forms \twoheadrightarrow red] \leq ell[destination \rightarrow australia]$$
$$ell[forms \twoheadrightarrow red] < ell[forms \twoheadrightarrow blue]$$
$$ell[forms \twoheadrightarrow green] < ell[forms \twoheadrightarrow red]$$
$$ell[forms \twoheadrightarrow green] < ell[forms \twoheadrightarrow blue].$$

Model I_3 is preferable to I_1 because $ell[forms \twoheadrightarrow green] < ell[destination \rightarrow australia]$. Model I_3 is preferable to I_2 because $ell[forms \twoheadrightarrow red] < ell[forms \twoheadrightarrow blue]$ and $ell[forms \twoheadrightarrow green] < ell[forms \twoheadrightarrow blue]$. As there are no other models preferable to I_3, I_3 is a preferred model of P.

Example 4. This example illustrates that subsets in subclasses do override sets in superclasses. Assume a set of declarations including $a : t$ and $t < t'$. Consider the program:

$$\{x : t'\} \vdash x[m \twoheadrightarrow \{c, d\}]$$
$$\{x : t\} \vdash x[m \twoheadrightarrow \{c\}]$$

This program has two models, $I_1 = \{a[m \twoheadrightarrow c], a[m \twoheadrightarrow d]\}$ and $I_2 = \{a[m \twoheadrightarrow c]\}$. Because there are no atoms in $I_2 - I_1$, model I_2 is preferable to I_1, as expected.

The following result motivates our definition of simple programs.

Theorem 1. *Let P be a simple program. Then P has a unique preferred model.*

We denote the unique preferred model of a simple program P by M_P.

This preferred model semantics agrees with our intuition about the interaction between inheritance, overriding and deduction. The corresponding definitions of answers and correct answers to programs and goals are standard and are omitted for brevity.

2.3 Bottom-Up Evaluation

In [6], Apt et al. defined a bottom-up procedure to compute the standard model of a stratified logic program. In this section we describe a similar bottom-up procedure to evaluate the preferred model of a simple program. This procedure differs from the one defined in [6] as it is based on the possibility of overriding, rather than the presence of negation. It differs from that defined in [11] as the immediate consequence operator is a mapping between typed interpretations rather than interpretations. In the restricted language with only single-valued methods the typing was dealt with in the stratification but this is not the case for set-valued methods. We first define "conflicts" and "clause, type pairs".

Let A' be the ground method atom $a[m@a_1, \ldots, a_k \to b']$ and A the ground method atom $a[m@a_1, \ldots, a_k \to b]$ (resp. let A' be $(a[m@a_1, \ldots, a_k \twoheadrightarrow b']$ and A be $(a[m@a_1, \ldots, a_k \twoheadrightarrow b])$. We say A *conflicts* with A' if $b \neq b'$.

Let P be a simple program. The set of ground *clause, type pairs* of P are $\{(p, \tau) \mid p$ is a ground clause of P and τ is the type of the clause from which p is derived$\}$.

A *typed interpretation* (or t-interpretation) is an extension to an interpretation where each atom is replaced by a pair (A, τ) where A is a ground atom and τ is a type attached to A. The immediate consequence operator is a mapping from typed interpretations to typed interpretations. With only single-valued methods the typing is implicit in the stratification. This occurs because there can only be one clause defining each method for an object and it will be in a lower stratum than any clause it possibly overrides. With set-valued methods, the same method may be defined on an object in more than one clause and these clauses can be in different strata so we need to consider both typing and i-stratification.

The immediate consequence operator is defined as follows: Let P be a set of ground clause, type pairs, I a t-interpretation and τ a type. Then $T_P(I) = \{(A, \tau) \mid (C, \tau)$ is a clause, type pair of P, $C = A \leftarrow B_1 \wedge \cdots \wedge B_k$ for each B_i and type τ_i, $(B_i, \tau_i) \in I$, and, if A is a method atom and A' is another method atom with $(A', \tau') \in I$, and $\tau \neq \tau'$, then A and A' do not conflict $\}$.

The powers of T_P are then defined:

$$T_P \uparrow 0(I) = I$$
$$T_P \uparrow (n+1)(I) = T_P(T_P \uparrow n(I))$$
$$T_P \uparrow \omega(I) = \bigcup_{n=0}^{\infty} T_P \uparrow n(I).$$

Every ground atom of an i-stratified program can be assigned a stratum. P_i is the set of ground clause, type pairs where the head of the ground clause has stratum i.

Then M_P^* is computed using the immediate consequence operator to find a fixpoint of P_1, $P_1 \cup P_2$ and so on.

$$M_1' = T_{P_1} \uparrow \omega(\emptyset),$$
$$M_i' = T_{P_i} \uparrow \omega(M_{i-1}') \cup M_{i-1}', \text{ for } 1 < i \le n$$
$$M_n = \{A \mid (A, \tau) \in M_n'\}$$
$$M_P^* = M_n.$$

Example 5. Consider program P in Example 3. One of the possible i-stratifications of P gives the following ordering on ground clause, type pairs:

$$P_1 = \{(ell[forms \twoheadrightarrow b] \leftarrow ell[destination \rightarrow france], export\_lada)\}$$
$$P_2 = \{(ell[forms \twoheadrightarrow r] \leftarrow ell[destination \rightarrow australia], export\_lada),$$
$$\qquad (ell[forms \twoheadrightarrow r], lada)\}$$
$$P_3 = \{(ell[forms \twoheadrightarrow g], lada)\}$$

M_P^* is computed as follows:

$$T_{P_1} \uparrow 0(\emptyset) = \emptyset, M_1' = \emptyset$$
$$T_{P_2} \uparrow 0(M_1') = \emptyset, T_{P_2} \uparrow 1(M_1') = \{(ell[forms \twoheadrightarrow r], lada)\},$$
$$M_2' = \{(ell[forms \twoheadrightarrow r], lada)\}$$
$$T_{P_3} \uparrow 0(M_2') = \{(ell[forms \twoheadrightarrow r], lada)\}$$
$$T_{P_3} \uparrow 1(M_2') = \{(ell[forms \twoheadrightarrow r], lada), (ell[forms \twoheadrightarrow g], lada)\}$$
$$M_3' = \{(ell[forms \twoheadrightarrow r], lada), (ell[forms \twoheadrightarrow g], lada)\}$$
$$M_P^* = \{ell[forms \twoheadrightarrow r], ell[forms \twoheadrightarrow g]\}$$

Note that each M_j is a model for $\bigcup_{i \le j} P_i$ and that M_P^* is a model of P, indeed the preferred model of P, in this example. In fact, these properties hold for all simple programs, and the following key result holds.

Theorem 2. *Let P be a simple program. Then M_P^* does not depend on the particular i-stratification chosen for P, and M_P^* is equal to the preferred model M_P of P.*

A problem with this procedure is the difficulty of assigning strata to the ground facts before starting the computation, and we are investigating means of avoiding this task. Another problem is that, like other naive bottom-up evaluation procedures, this one is not goal directed, indicating the need for optimizations perhaps based on program transformation, and suggesting the investigation of goal-directed top-down procedures such as those considered in the next subsection.

2.4   Top-Down Evaluation

In this section we outline an alternative evaluation procedure which might be
more efficient in practice than the bottom-up method just described. This top-
down procedure is based on typed unification and a variant of SLD-resolution.
The typed unification procedure is described in [11]. The resolution procedure
differs from SLD-resolution as answers for each subgoal are computed independently. For each atom of the goal a set of possible answers is computed, and a
minimisation operation is applied to find which of the possible answers has not
been overridden. The sets of minimal answers for each atom are combined to
give the set of computed answers for the goal.

If an atom in a query has the form $\leftarrow a[m \rightarrow b]$, where a and b are object
symbols, this atom may unify with the head of a clause that is overridden by
another clause and hence return an incorrect answer. To ensure our procedure
computes the expected answer, the value of each method atom in the query must
be a variable. We say such atoms are in *standard form*. In [11] we described how
single-valued method atoms in a goal or clause body can be transformed into
standard form by adding equality atoms. This technique can easily be extended
to goals and programs with set-valued methods.

We now describe a derivation step in our procedure, the derivation of a
possible computed answer for a program and an atom, and the ground instances
of a possible computed answer.

Let $\Gamma \vdash A$ be an atom and C a clause $\Gamma' \vdash A' \leftarrow B_1 \wedge \cdots \wedge B_q$. Suppose that
the variables of A and C are standardised apart. Then the goal G and type τ
are *derived* from $\Gamma \vdash \leftarrow A$ and C using substitution θ if the following conditions
hold:

- θ is the mgu of $\Gamma \vdash A$ and $\Gamma' \vdash A'$,
- G is the goal $(\Gamma' \vdash \leftarrow B_1 \wedge \cdots \wedge B_q)\theta$, and
- τ is the type of $\Gamma' \vdash A'^3$.

Suppose θ is $\Gamma \vdash \theta'$ and τ is a type. The *ground instances* of (θ, τ) are
$\{(\sigma, \tau) \mid \sigma \in [\theta]\}$, where $[\Gamma \vdash \theta']$ is the set of all ground instances of θ' consistent
with Γ. We write $[\theta, \tau]$ for the set of ground instances of (θ, τ).

Let P be a standard program and $\Gamma_A \vdash A$ a standard atom. If the empty
goal and type τ are derived from $\Gamma_A \vdash \leftarrow A$ and clause $\Gamma_{A'} \vdash A' \leftarrow$ in P using
substitution θ, then $[\theta, \tau]$ is a set of *possible computed answers* of $P \cup \{\Gamma_A \vdash \leftarrow A\}$.

Otherwise, suppose the non-empty goal G and type τ are derived from
$\Gamma_A \vdash \leftarrow A$ and clause $\Gamma \vdash A_1 \leftarrow B_1 \wedge \cdots \wedge B_n$ in P using substitution θ.
Let $\Theta = \{\theta_1, \ldots, \theta_m\}$ be the set of computed answers for $P \cup \{G\}$. Then
$\{[\theta\theta_1, \tau], \ldots, [\theta\theta_m, \tau]\}$ is the set of *possible computed answers* for $P \cup \{\Gamma_A \vdash \leftarrow A\}$.

Note that if the derivation of $P \cup \{\Gamma \vdash \leftarrow A\}$ fails, the set of possible
computed answer for $P \cup \{\Gamma \vdash \leftarrow A\}$ is empty. If a derivation of $P \cup \{\Gamma \vdash \leftarrow A\}$

---

[3] Recall that the type of a method atom $\Gamma \vdash t[m \rightarrow t']$ is the type of the term $\Gamma \vdash t$,
the type of a predicate atom is undefined.

succeeds with an empty substitution, then one of the possible computed answers for $P \cup \{\Gamma \vdash \leftarrow A\}$ is (ε, τ), where ε is an empty substitution and τ is the type of the clause with which the atom A unified.

We have defined the set of possible computed answers for $P \cup \{\Gamma \vdash \leftarrow A\}$. We now define the set of computed answers for $P \cup \{\Gamma \vdash \leftarrow A\}$.

Let P be a standard program, $\Gamma \vdash A$ a standard method atom, and Ψ the set of possible computed answers for $P \cup \{\Gamma \vdash \leftarrow A\}$. A possible computed answer $\psi_1 = (\theta_1, \tau_1) \in \Psi$ is *smaller* than another possible computed answer $\psi_2 = (\theta_2, \tau_2) \in \Psi$ if $A\theta_1$ conflicts with $A\theta_2$, and $\tau_1 < \tau_2$. In this case we write $\psi_1 < \psi_2$. We say that ψ_k is *minimal* with respect to Ψ if there is no $\psi_j \in \Psi$ such that $\psi_j < \psi_k$.

If $\Gamma \vdash A$ is a predicate atom, then every possible computed answer for $P \cup \{\Gamma \vdash \leftarrow A\}$ is minimal.

Let P be a standard program and $\Gamma \vdash A$ a standard atom. The *computed answers* of $P \cup \{\Gamma \vdash \leftarrow A\}$ are the minimal possible computed answers for $P \cup \{\Gamma \vdash \leftarrow A\}$ whose variables are restricted to the variables in $\Gamma \vdash A$. The empty substitution $\{\varepsilon\}$ is the computed answer for $P \cup \{\Gamma \vdash \leftarrow A\}$, if there are no variables in A and the set of possible computed answers of $P \cup \{\Gamma \vdash \leftarrow A\}$ is not empty.

Obviously if $\Gamma \vdash A$ is a predicate atom all possible computed answers for $P \cup \{\Gamma \vdash \leftarrow A\}$ are computed answers for $P \cup \{\Gamma \vdash \leftarrow A\}$.

Note that we have not yet defined the set of computed answers for $P \cup \{G\}$, where G is $\Gamma \vdash \leftarrow A_1 \wedge \cdots \wedge A_n$ and $n > 1$. We now describe two operations $+$ and $\times$ used to combine the sets of computed answers for the atoms of a goal to give the set of computed answers for the complete goal.

Let θ_1 and θ_2 be ground substitutions $\Gamma_1 \vdash \theta_1'$ and $\Gamma_2 \vdash \theta_2'$ respectively. Suppose that, if $x \in dom(\theta_1') \cap dom(\theta_2')$, then there is some type c such that $x : c \in \Gamma_1 \cap \Gamma_2$. If there is some variable x such that $x/t \in \theta_1'$, $x/t' \in \theta_2'$, and $t \neq t'$, then $\theta_1 + \theta_2 = \emptyset$. Otherwise $\theta_1 + \theta_2 = \Gamma \vdash \theta_1' \cup \theta_2'$, where $\Gamma = \{x : c \mid x/t \in \theta_1' \cup \theta_2' \text{ and } x : c \in \Gamma_1 \cup \Gamma_2\}$.

Let Θ_1 and Θ_2 be sets of ground substitutions. Then $\Theta_1 \times \Theta_2$ is $\{\theta_1 + \theta_2 \mid \theta_1 \in \Theta_1 \text{ and } \theta_2 \in \Theta_2\}$.

Let P be a standard program, G a standard goal $\Gamma \vdash \leftarrow A_1 \wedge \cdots \wedge A_n$, where $n > 1$. Let the set of computed answers of $P \cup \{\Gamma \vdash \leftarrow A_i\}$ be $\Theta_i = \{\theta_{i1}, \ldots, \theta_{ik_i}\}$, for $1 \leq i \leq n$. Then the set of *computed answers* of $P \cup \{G\}$ is $\Theta_1 \times \cdots \times \Theta_n$.

Example 6. Let program P' be program P in Example 3 with the additional clause $ell[destination \rightarrow australia]$. Consider the goal

$$G = \{x : form\_type, y : country\} \vdash \leftarrow ell[forms \rightarrow x] \wedge ell[destination \rightarrow y].$$

The possible computed answers for $P' \cup \{\{x : form\_type\} \vdash \leftarrow ell[forms \rightarrow x]\}$ are $\{(\{x:form\_type\} \vdash \{x/red\}, export\_lada), (\{x:form\_type\} \vdash \{x/red\}, lada \, (\{x : form\_type\} \vdash \{x/green\}, lada)\}$. The computed answers are the minimal possible computed answers, $\Theta_1 = \{\{x : form\_type\} \vdash \{x/red\}\}$.

The computed answers for $P' \cup \{\{y : country\} \vdash \leftarrow ell[destination \rightarrow y]\}$ are $\Theta_2 = \{\{y : country\} \vdash \{y/australia\}\}$. The computed answer for $P' \cup \{G\}$ is $\Theta_1 \times \Theta_2 = \{\{x : form\_type, y : country\} \vdash \{x/red, y/australia\}\}$.

The following soundness result holds.

Theorem 3. *Let P be a simple program, and G a goal. Then every computed answer of $P \cup \{G\}$ is a correct answer for $P \cup \{G\}$.*

3 Multiple Inheritance

In the previous sections we assumed single inheritance, that is, each type had only one parent in the type hierarchy. In this section we relax this restriction by allowing types to have more than one parent in the type hierarchy. This is called multiple inheritance. We discuss possible ways of dealing with multiple inheritance, and describe the method we use with respect to the semantics and procedures given in the previous section. An interesting result of our approach is that the same bottom-up and top-down procedures work in this more general setting.

The following example illustrates alternatives when types of methods are inherited from more than one parent.

Example 7. Consider the following declarations:

$employee < person$ $student < person$
$assistant < employee$ $assistant < student$
$bargain\_vehicle < bargain$ $bargain\_vehicle < vehicle$
$person[name \Rightarrow string]$
$employee[drives \Rightarrow vehicle]$ $student[drives \Rightarrow bargain]$
$lada : bargain\_vehicle$ $holden : bargain\_vehicle$

Here, the possible type of method *drives* in *assistant* could be *bargain* inherited from *student*, *vehicle* inherited from *employee*, or *bargain* and *vehicle* inherited from *student* and *employee*. In Gulog the type of method *drives* in type *assistant* is $\{bargain, vehicle\}$, i.e., *bargain* and *vehicle*. The type of the value is then compatible with both types *student* and *employee*. The inheritance of signatures is monotonic as in F-logic.

The following example illustrates alternatives when values of methods are inherited from more than one parent.

Example 8. Consider the program P wrt the declarations in Example 7:

$\{x : student\} \vdash x[drives \rightarrow lada]$
$\{x : employee\} \vdash x[drives \rightarrow holden]$.

Here, an object of type *assistant* could inherit the value *lada* for method *drives* from *student* or inherit the value *holden* for method *drives* from *employee* or inherit both values.

There are three main approaches in the literature for dealing with such conflicts.

- Prohibit them.
- Provide a static ordering on supertypes that determines which subtype should be inherited from first, next, and so on.
- Allow the user to write programs that determine which supertype to inherit from depending on the particular concept.

For simplicity, we simply disallow programs with such conflicts in this paper. (We are currently investigating the semantics and evaluation of programs in which a static ordering is used to determine the inheritance order.) Suppose that τ is a direct subtype of σ_1 and σ_2, and that $\sigma_1 < \sigma$ and $\sigma_2 < \sigma$. We say that program P is *unambiguous* (wrt multiple inheritance) if every method m (of arity n) that can be applied to objects of type τ is either (a) defined on type τ, or (b) defined on type σ and not defined on any type σ' with $\sigma_i \leq \sigma' < \sigma$, for $i = 1, 2$.

We then change the definition of a well-defined program given in Section 2 to also require the program be unambiguous with respect to multiple inheritance.

Because we do not allow programs that inherit methods from two distinct supertypes, no changes are necessary in the bottom-up procedure. The top-down procedure changes only in the definitions of typed substitution, typed composition, and computation of the most general unifier. In these definitions, instead of checking whether one type is a subtype of another type, we now check whether the two types have a common subtype (or whether they have a greatest lower bound in the type hierarchy). We describe these changes in [12] and illustrate them in the following example.

Example 9. Assume the declarations given in Example 7. Let S be a set of expressions $\{\{x : employee, z : vehicle\} \vdash x[drives \rightarrow z], \{x' : student\} \vdash x'[drives \rightarrow holden]\}$ to be unified. Then the disagreement set D_0 is $\{x : employee, x' : student\} \vdash \{x, x'\}$, and the unifier σ_1 is $\{x : employee, x' : student, y : assistant\} \vdash \{x/y, x'/y\}$. Note that a new variable y is introduced. The type of y is a common subtype of the types of x and x'. The next disagreement set D_1 is $\{z : vehicle\} \vdash \{z, holden\}$, and the next (and most general) unifier σ_2 is $\{x : employee, x' : student, y : assistant, z : vehicle\} \vdash \{x/y, x'/y, z/holden\}$. Thus, $S\sigma_2 = \{\{y : assistant\} \vdash y[drives \rightarrow holden]\}$.

With these changes, the obvious generalizations of Theorems 2 and 3 still hold.

4 Discussion

We have extended our simple deductive object-oriented language, Gulog, with set-valued methods and multiple inheritance. We described a declarative semantics, and bottom-up and top-down query evaluation procedures for this extended language. Based on previous results [11] the bottom-up and top-down procedures described in Section 2 and 3 are sound with respect to the declarative semantics. The bottom-up procedure is complete and the top-down procedure would be complete if some tabling mechanism [10] were added to eliminate infinite branches from which no answers are currently computed.

We have shown that the restricted logic language described in [11] can easily be extended and that these extensions have little effect on the interaction between inheritance, overriding and deduction. We have also shown that many of the object-oriented features can be captured in a natural way in a first order language which has many analogies with datalog. An advantage of these analogies is that work which has been carried out in the area of logic programming can be adapted to this language.

This approach provides a more direct explanation of the semantics of inheritance and overriding than that taken by Abiteboul et al. in [4] and us in [13], where the semantics of $datalog^{meth}$ and Gulog (respectively) were described by translation into datalog.

In the future we intend to extend Gulog further, and to investigate the expressiveness and complexity of its sublanguages. Possible extensions include negation and monotonic inheritance of methods, as in $L\&O$. These will obviously make the language more expressive, for example adding negation will allow queries on set equality and set inclusion as well as on set membership. We have already commenced an implementation of Gulog, and intend to complete this implementation in order to evaluate the efficiency of the procedures, and to compare the complexity of implementations of F-logic and Gulog.

Acknowledgement

We are grateful to Michael Lawley, Alexandre Lefebvre and Christopher Higgins for discussions and helpful suggestions.

References

1. S. Abiteboul. Towards a deductive object oriented database language. *Data and Knowledge Engineering*, 5:263–287, 1990.
2. S. Abiteboul and S. Grumbach. COL: A logic-based language for complex objects. In F. Bancilhon and P. Buneman, editors, *Advances in Database Programming Languages*, pages 347–374. ACM Press/Addison-Wesley (Frontier Series), New York, 1990.
3. S. Abiteboul and P. C. Kanellakis. Object identity as a query language primitive. In *Proc. of the ACM SIGMOD International Conference on the Management of Data*, pages 159–173, 1989.
4. S. Abiteboul, G. Lausen, H. Uphoff, and E. Waller. Methods and rules. In *Proc. of the ACM SIGMOD International Conference on the Management of Data*, pages 32–41, 1993.
5. H. Ait-Kaci and R. Nasr. LOGIN: A logic programming language with built-in inheritance. *Journal of Logic Programming*, 3:185–215, 1986.

6. K. Apt, H. Blair, and A. Walker. Towards a theory of declarative knowledge. In J. Minker, editor, *Foundations of Deductive Databases and Logic Programming*, pages 89–148. Morgan Kaufmann, 1988.

7. C. Beeri. A formal approach to object-oriented databases. *Data and Knowledge Engineering*, 5:353–382, 1990.

8. S. Brass and U. Lipeck. Semantics of inheritance in logical object specifications. *Proceedings of the Second International Conference on Deductive and Object-Oriented Databases*, pages 411–430, 1991.

9. C. Delobel, M. Kifer, and Y. Masunaga, editors. *Proceedings of the Second International Conference on Deductive and Object-Oriented Databases*, Munich, Germany, 1991. Springer-Verlag. Published as Lecture Notes in Computer Science 566 by Springer-Verlag.

10. S. W. Dietrich. Extension Tables: Memo Relations in Logic Programming. In *Proc. 3rd Symposium on Logic Programming*, pages 264–272, San Francisco, California, 1987.

11. G. Dobbie and R. W. Topor. A model for inheritance and overriding in deductive object-oriented systems. In *Proc. 16th Australian Computer Science Conference*, pages 625–634, Brisbane, Australia, 1993.

12. G. Dobbie and R. W. Topor. A model for sets and multiple inheritance in deductive object-oriented systems. Technical report, Collaborative Information Technology Research Institute, University of Melbourne, 1993.

13. G. Dobbie and R. W. Topor. Representing inheritance and overriding in Datalog. In *Proc. of the Deductive Database Workshop in conjunction with ICLP'93*, Budapest, Hungary, 1993.

14. M. Kifer, G. Lausen, and J. Wu. Logical foundations of object-oriented and frame-based languages. Technical Report 90/14 (revised), Department of Computer Science, State University of New York at Stony Brook, 1990. Further revised as Technical Report 93/06, April 1993.

15. W. Kim, J.-M. Nicolas, and S. Nishio, editors. *Proceedings of the First International Conference on Deductive and Object-Oriented Databases*, Kyoto, Japan, 1989.

16. M. J. Lawley. A Prolog interpreter for F-logic. Unpublished report, Griffith University, 1993.

17. F. G. McCabe. *Logic and Objects*. Prentice Hall, 1992.

18. T. Przymusinski. On the declarative semantics of deductive databases and logic programs. In J. Minker, editor, *Foundations of Deductive Databases and Logic Programming*, pages 193–216. Morgan Kaufmann, 1988.

19. T. C. Przymusinski. Semantics of disjunctive logic programs and deductive databases. *Proceedings of the Second International Conference on Deductive and Object-Oriented Databases*, pages 85–107, 1991.

20. D. S. Touretzky. *The Mathematics of Inheritance Systems*. Morgan Kaufmann, Los Altos, CA, 1986.

Springer-Verlag
and the Environment

We at Springer-Verlag firmly believe that an international science publisher has a special obligation to the environment, and our corporate policies consistently reflect this conviction.

We also expect our business partners – paper mills, printers, packaging manufacturers, etc. – to commit themselves to using environmentally friendly materials and production processes.

The paper in this book is made from low- or no-chlorine pulp and is acid free, in conformance with international standards for paper permanency.

Lecture Notes in Computer Science

For information about Vols. 1–680
please contact your bookseller or Springer-Verlag

Vol. 717: I. Sommerville, M. Paul (Eds.), Software Engineering – ESEC '93. Proceedings, 1993. XII, 516 pages. 1993.

Vol. 718: J. Seberry, Y. Zheng (Eds.), Advances in Cryptology – AUSCRYPT '92. Proceedings, 1992. XIII, 543 pages. 1993.

Vol. 719: D. Chetverikov, W.G. Kropatsch (Eds.), Computer Analysis of Images and Patterns. Proceedings, 1993. XVI, 857 pages. 1993.

Vol. 720: V.Mařík, J. Lažanský, R.R. Wagner (Eds.), Database and Expert Systems Applications. Proceedings, 1993. XV, 768 pages. 1993.

Vol. 721: J. Fitch (Ed.), Design and Implementation of Symbolic Computation Systems. Proceedings, 1992. VIII, 215 pages. 1993.

Vol. 722: A. Miola (Ed.), Design and Implementation of Symbolic Computation Systems. Proceedings, 1993. XII, 384 pages. 1993.

Vol. 723: N. Aussenac, G. Boy, B. Gaines, M. Linster, J.-G. Ganascia, Y. Kodratoff (Eds.), Knowledge Acquisition for Knowledge-Based Systems. Proceedings, 1993. XIII, 446 pages. 1993. (Subseries LNAI).

Vol. 724: P. Cousot, M. Falaschi, G. Filè, A. Rauzy (Eds.), Static Analysis. Proceedings, 1993. IX, 283 pages. 1993.

Vol. 725: A. Schiper (Ed.), Distributed Algorithms. Proceedings, 1993. VIII, 325 pages. 1993.

Vol. 726: T. Lengauer (Ed.), Algorithms – ESA '93. Proceedings, 1993. IX, 419 pages. 1993

Vol. 727: M. Filgueiras, L. Damas (Eds.), Progress in Artificial Intelligence. Proceedings, 1993. X, 362 pages. 1993. (Subseries LNAI).

Vol. 728: P. Torasso (Ed.), Advances in Artificial Intelligence. Proceedings, 1993. XI, 336 pages. 1993. (Subseries LNAI).

Vol. 729: L. Donatiello, R. Nelson (Eds.), Performance Evaluation of Computer and Communication Systems. Proceedings, 1993. VIII, 675 pages. 1993.

Vol. 730: D. B. Lomet (Ed.), Foundations of Data Organization and Algorithms. Proceedings, 1993. XII, 412 pages. 1993.

Vol. 731: A. Schill (Ed.), DCE – The OSF Distributed Computing Environment. Proceedings, 1993. VIII, 285 pages. 1993.

Vol. 732: A. Bode, M. Dal Cin (Eds.), Parallel Computer Architectures. IX, 311 pages. 1993.

Vol. 733: Th. Grechenig, M. Tscheligi (Eds.), Human Computer Interaction. Proceedings, 1993. XIV, 450 pages. 1993.

Vol. 734: J. Volkert (Ed.), Parallel Computation. Proceedings, 1993. VIII, 248 pages. 1993.

Vol. 735: D. Bjørner, M. Broy, I. V. Pottosin (Eds.), Formal Methods in Programming and Their Applications. Proceedings, 1993. IX, 434 pages. 1993.

Vol. 736: R. L. Grossman, A. Nerode, A. P. Ravn, H. Rischel (Eds.), Hybrid Systems. VIII, 474 pages. 1993.

Vol. 737: J. Calmet, J. A. Campbell (Eds.), Artificial Intelligence and Symbolic Mathematical Computing. Proceedings, 1992. VIII, 305 pages. 1993.

Vol. 738: M. Weber, M. Simons, Ch. Lafontaine, The Generic Development Language Deva. XI, 246 pages. 1993.

Vol. 739: H. Imai, R. L. Rivest, T. Matsumoto (Eds.), Advances in Cryptology – ASIACRYPT '91. X, 499 pages. 1993.

Vol. 740: E. F. Brickell (Ed.), Advances in Cryptology – CRYPTO '92. Proceedings, 1992. X, 593 pages. 1993.

Vol. 741: B. Preneel, R. Govaerts, J. Vandewalle (Eds.), Computer Security and Industrial Cryptography. Proceedings, 1991. VIII, 275 pages. 1993.

Vol. 742: S. Nishio, A. Yonezawa (Eds.), Object Technologies for Advanced Software. Proceedings, 1993. X, 543 pages. 1993.

Vol. 743: S. Doshita, K. Furukawa, K. P. Jantke, T. Nishida (Eds.), Algorithmic Learning Theory. Proceedings, 1992. X, 260 pages. 1993. (Subseries LNAI)

Vol. 744: K. P. Jantke, T. Yokomori, S. Kobayashi, E. Tomita (Eds.), Algorithmic Learning Theory. Proceedings, 1993. XI, 423 pages. 1993. (Subseries LNAI)

Vol. 745: V. Roberto (Ed.), Intelligent Perceptual Systems. VIII, 378 pages. 1993. (Subseries LNAI)

Vol. 746: A. S. Tanguiane, Artificial Perception and Music Recognition. XV, 210 pages. 1993. (Subseries LNAI).

Vol. 747: M. Clarke, R. Kruse, S. Moral (Eds.), Symbolic and Quantitative Approaches to Reasoning and Uncertainty. Proceedings, 1993. X, 390 pages. 1993.

Vol. 748: R. H. Halstead Jr., T. Ito (Eds.), Parallel Symbolic Computing: Languages, Systems, and Applications. Proceedings, 1992. X, 419 pages. 1993.

Vol. 749: P. A. Fritzson (Ed.), Automated and Algorithmic Debugging. Proceedings, 1993. VIII, 369 pages. 1993.

Vol. 750: J. L. Díaz-Herrera (Ed.), Software Engineering Education. Proceedings, 1994. XII, 601 pages. 1994.

Vol. 751: B. Jähne, Spatio-Temporal Image Processing. XII, 208 pages. 1993.

Vol. 752: T. W. Finin, C. K. Nicholas, Y. Yesha (Eds.), Information and Knowledge Management. Proceedings, 1992. VII, 142 pages. 1993.

Vol. 753: L. J. Bass, J. Gornostaev, C. Unger (Eds.), Human-Computer Interaction. Proceedings, 1993. X, 388 pages. 1993.

Vol. 754: H. D. Pfeiffer, T. E. Nagle (Eds.), Conceptual Structures: Theory and Implementation. Proceedings, 1992. IX, 327 pages. 1993. (Subseries LNAI).

Vol. 755: B. Möller, H. Partsch, S. Schuman (Eds.), Formal Program Development. Proceedings. VII, 371 pages. 1993.

Vol. 756: J. Pieprzyk, B. Sadeghiyan, Design of Hashing Algorithms. XV, 194 pages. 1993.

Vol. 758: M. Teillaud, Towards Dynamic Randomized Algorithms in Computational Geometry. IX, 157 pages. 1993.

Vol. 760: S. Ceri, K. Tanaka, S. Tsur (Eds.), Deductive and Object-Oriented Databases. Proceedings, 1993. XII, 488 pages. 1993.

Vol. 761: R. Shyamasundar (Ed.), Foundations of Software Technology and Theoretical Computer Science. Proceedings, 1993. XIV, 456 pages. 1993.